CULTURAL DIVERSITY:
CURRICULUM, CLASSROOM, & CLIMATE ISSUES

W9-CJS-768

Edited by
J. Q. Adams
Janice R. Welsch

Prepared with Higher Education Cooperation Act Funds
Awarded by the Illinois Board of Higher Education

to

Board of Trustees of
Western Illinois University

for a project entitled

Expanding Cultural Diversity
in the Curriculum and in the Classroom

HECA GRANT
COOPERATING INSTITUTIONS
1998-1999

DEDICATION

To the Survivors
  of the Middle Passage
  of the Trail of Tears
  of U.S. Exclusionary Immigration Practices

  of apartheid and ethnic cleansing
  of sexism and homophobia

To the Survivors
  of our inhumanity to one another

To the Survivors
  who continue the struggle
  for Equality
  among all of Humankind.

ACKNOWLEDGEMENTS

We want to thank the Illinois Board of Higher Education for funding this publication and for supporting all aspects of the Expanding Cultural Diversity Project.

We also want to thank our contributors whose experience, knowledge, and understanding of cultural diversity complement their commitment to their students and to justice and equity, making them exceptionally well qualified multicultural educators.

We have received expert assistance from many behind-the-scenes Western Illinois University colleagues, most notably John Maguire, Paul Stubblefield, Dave Gravino, Katherine Dahl, Jean Kipling, and Nita Burg. Nita Burg must be singled out for particular recognition because we have depended on her professional skills, good will, and generosity throughout every phase of this project and she has not disappointed us. We are very grateful for her remarkable ability and commitment.

J.Q.A.
J.R.W.
August 1999

TABLE OF CONTENTS

Part II.   Curriculum and Instruction

Part III. Climate, Co-Curricular Activities, and Assessment

PREFACE

This book is part of the Expanding Cultural Diversity project, an initiative supported by the Illinois Board of Higher Education through Higher Education Cooperation Act grants. When the project began a decade ago, some educators were deeply involved in multicultural education. They were exploring and defining the issues around which multicultural education revolves, integrating multicultural scholarship and insight into their courses, and creating supportive and inclusive campus climates for students, faculty and staff. Over the past ten years many more faculty, staff, and administrators have joined this group, advancing the understanding and appreciation of the cultural diversity that has always characterized the United States and to which we are heirs. We are pleased to make available in this volume the work of pioneers of multicultural education as well as that of educators who are expanding and applying this earlier scholarship.

Most of the essays here appeared in the earlier anthologies published through the Expanding Cultural Diversity project; many have been revised. All offer insight into one or more aspects of multicultural education and continue to be relevant in our increasingly diverse and challenging world. Generally, they fit into three categories, with several bridging the categories and with some ideas, nuanced to provide different perspectives, appearing and reappearing from one essay to another. Part One covers broad issues and overviews, setting the contexts for the analyses of curriculum and instructional methods that follow in Part Two and the co-curricular and assessment activities explored in Part Three.

The authors represented in Part One discuss the scope and goals of multicultural education and examine myths and misinformation that have at times diverted attention from its value and importance. They explore issues of race, gender, sexual orientation, and disability; analyze the role media can play in strengthening or undermining respect for cultural diversity; and respond to some of the questions linked to specific traditionally marginalized ethnic groups within the United States. The section ends with an essay reminding readers of an immensely valuable quality for multicultural educators: humor.

In Part Two, contributors focus more directly on the classroom, often intertwining curriculum and course content issues with discussions of student learning styles and instructional methods. They specifically cover cultural diversity, teacher education, composition, women's studies, mathematics, and literature courses but go beyond these in their explorations of the principles underlying their text choices and the educational philosophy determining their interaction with students.

The first four essays in Part Three are on assessment: the impact of multiculturalism and diversity programs on students and the methods colleges and universities are adopting to evaluate this impact. The remaining articles explore admission and retention, counseling, and faculty development initiatives and suggest how important these and other co-curricular programs are in creating and sustaining a culturally diverse student population.

Reflected through the chapters of this volume is the recognition that diversity is an essential and defining characteristic of our nation—of the world—and the conviction that this diversity can enrich all of us if we respect, value, and cultivate it. Multicultural education can help us and our students do this. The essays here offer an assist.

INTRODUCTION

by
J. Q. Adams

One of the many challenges our nation will face in the 21st century will be the question of our collective and individual identities. In many ways the 19th and 20th centuries were dominated by the European immigrants who transitioned in their identities from ethnicity to race. While the "melting pot theory" did not entirely capture the experiences of all groups in the U.S., it certainly cemented our social conventions on the significance of race and clearly situated the "white race" as the dominant race of the continent. However, understanding this process of shedding one's ethnic identity and establishing a racial identity can be an incredibly difficult process. While some groups are able to do it within the native-born children of the first generation, others may take several generations or may never accomplish this phenomenon. But for most people living in this country, whether we like it or not, our public appearance in the civil state has been identified with our racial identity first and with our ethnicity of far less consequence.

I would be naive to argue that class and gender have diminished in respect to social identity but their effect in the 21st century may be somewhat blurred by incremental distinctions that are less indelible. For example, within a move towards greater gender equity within the home and in the business world, the once sharp distinctions of maleness and femaleness have given way to a kind of socially ambiguous androgyny that requires almost carnal proof to determine who a he or she is. Social class identification, with the exception of the extremes of wealth and poverty, gets lost in a myriad of labels, utterances, and material things that distinguish us from each other. Still, a good majority of us have been sucked into the vast "black hole" called the middle class. However, race is quick, and it is sharp and has been made necessary in the U.S.A. because it modifies privilege in ways gender and class cannot. It is the genetic trap that racial supremacists hold as their global trump card. Race marks the lines of social distance in a way that betrays our beliefs of equity, equality, and justice.

Our continued belief in the social construct of race as a means of determining hierarchical solidarity, superiority, and destiny holds the greatest threat to our mutual peaceful existence nationally and internationally, more so than any weapon of mass destruction because race is the ultimate weapon. What other force, save organized religion, has stirred such passion and obsession in believers? When one observes racial centrists, regardless of their distinctions, their rhetoric becomes strangely similar. Their attitudes, beliefs, values, and behaviors become remarkably singular in their exclusiveness, with the "final solution" being, for some, an ultimate solution to the inevitable conflict of racial differences that arises from a belief that, alas, "this town is not big enough for the two of us."

During the spring of 1999 I spent my sabbatical crisscrossing the nation interviewing scholars, politicians, authors, and students. I asked them a variety of questions dealing with the issues of race, class, and gender in the U.S.A. I had an opportunity to interview David Duke, shortly before his unsuccessful run for the vacated congressional seat of Rep. Robert Livingston of Louisiana. During this interview Duke shared some of his own views on "race" which mirror the sentiments I expressed above about the dangers of centrism. Duke inferred that it was never God's intention for races to intermingle; the proof he claims is inescapable: it resides in the geographic differences of thousands of years of genetic isolation that has created our phenotypical distinctiveness. Duke clearly believes "Birds of a feather flock together" and that muddying the races is the greatest threat to the "white" race, which he describes as a relative minority to the "other" races on the planet. And according to Duke the "white" race has been and continues to be the greatest contributor to world civilization. In fact, Duke would have us believe that almost all of the great discoveries of humans have been made by "whites."

Interestingly enough, in my interviews, African American scholars Molefi Kete Asante. author of the book *Afrocentricity*, and Maulana Karenga, originator of Kwanzaa, both made similar claims of the greatness that should be attributed to the "black" race. It is crucial that we realize they do so to raise the self-esteem and historical consciousness of Diaspora Africans and to counter the results of hundreds of years of racist subordination suffered in the Americas. And they certainly do not share the "final solution" offered up by Duke. They do, however, use the "we" versus "they" imagery that centrism invites.

Not so amazingly, in this post-civil-rights era, the "white right" has adopted backlash strategies that at once echo and distort sentiments of the social activists of the civil rights era. The right preaches that "minorities" have more privileges than "whites," that "whites" have become second-class citizens and now suffer from a loss of self esteem and opportunity. These strategies have proven to be effective in many states, especially in those regions of the country that are experiencing the greatest flow of "non-white" immigration. English-only legislation, the defeat of affirmative action policies, and the suspension of services to illegal aliens represent examples of this backlash.

The knowledge of the changing demographics of this country has also perhaps driven the greatest surge of white supremacist groups since the beginning of the 20th century. While these groups may not be numerically significant, their ability to disrupt our civil society appears to be unprecedented. One only has to examine the impact of the Oklahoma City bombing, the Columbine High School massacre, and the Benjamin Smith shooting spree to see the difficulties our nation now faces.

During an interview with Marcelo Suarez-Orosco, a Professor at Harvard who studies the impact of immigration groups in the U.S.A., I learned that by the mid-21st century the United States will be the only "post-industrial" nation in the world that will have a "non-white" majority population. It is both exciting and frightening to think about what our nation will be like under these conditions. Will this signal the end of "race" as it has been practiced? Or will Michael Omi's vision materialize? In an interview, Omi, a Professor at the University of California at Berkeley, offered the possibility that "whites" will enfranchise certain Asian and Latino groups as "pseudo-whites" in order to offset their dwindling numerical advantage in the body politic.

It would seem that "white privilege" is still the question with which this nation must struggle. Close examination of the vital social statistics of this nation leave no question that "race" continues to dominate the lives of the "haves and have nots" of our country. But as Peggy McIntosh, Co-Director of the Wellesley College Center for Research on Women, asserted in an interview, "unearned privilege" is difficult for most "white" people to acknowledge because it is so taken for granted that it becomes almost invisible to detect.

This nation is at a crossroads. It cannot survive the 21st century with a "race based" social construct as its source of individual and collective identity. Individuals' cultural identity is important, but that identity, if tied to an exclusionary ethnocentrism, can be detrimental to our pluralist society. Identity with our nation must be the unifying force for both the diverse ethnic groups coming to this country as well as those groups already here. "Race" as a means of sustaining the hierarchical solidarity and superiority of one group denies the other "races" access to privilege which can result in only one outcome: unearned disadvantage. If democracy, a noble and enabling goal, is to be realized our nation must reeducate itself about the meaning of race. This means that our society must develop a serious ongoing dialogue that leads to meaningful changes in our nation's social conventions around the construct of "race." Our nation's educational institutions, its teachers and administrators, must lead the way in order for this evolution to take place. We must change our policies, curriculum, and standards but most importantly, we must change ourselves.

CONTEXTS AND CONTENT

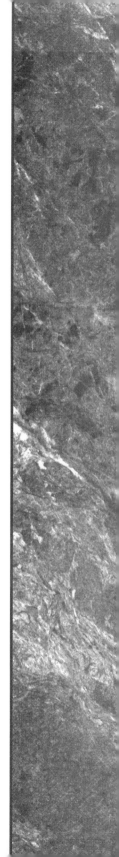

MULTICULTURAL EDUCATION:
DEVELOPMENT, DIMENSIONS, AND CHALLENGES

by
James A. Banks

The bitter debate over the literary and historical canon that has been carried on in the popular press and in several widely reviewed books has overshadowed the progress that has been made in multicultural education during the last two decades. The debate has also perpetuated harmful misconceptions about theory and practice in multicultural education. Consequently, it has heightened racial and ethnic tension and trivialized the field's remarkable accomplishments in theory, research, and curriculum development. The truth about the development and attainments of multicultural education needs to be told for the sake of balance, scholarly integrity, and accuracy. But if I am to reveal the truth about multicultural education, I must first identify and debunk some of the widespread myths and misconceptions about it.

Myths About Multicultural Education

Multicultural Education Is for the Others

One misconception about multicultural education is that it is an entitlement program and curriculum movement for African Americans, Hispanics, the poor, women, and other victimized groups.[1] The major theorists and researchers in multicultural education agree that the movement is designed to restructure educational institutions so all students, including middle-class white males, will acquire the knowledge, skills, and attitudes needed to function effectively in a culturally and ethnically diverse nation and world.[2] Multicultural education, as its major architects have conceived it during the last decade, is not an ethnic- or gender-specific movement. It is a movement designed to empower all students to become knowledgeable, caring, and active citizens in a deeply troubled and ethnically polarized nation and world.

The claim that multicultural education is only for people of color and for the disenfranchised is one of the pernicious and damaging misconceptions with which the movement has had to cope. It has caused intractable problems and has haunted multicultural education since its inception. Despite all that has been written and spoken about multicultural education being for all students, the image of multicultural education as an entitlement program for the "others" remains strong and vivid in the public imagination, as well as in the hearts and minds of many teachers and administrators. Teachers who teach in predominantly white schools and districts often state that they don't have a program or plan for multicultural education because they have few African American, Hispanic, or Asian American students.

When educators view multicultural education as the study of the "others," it is marginalized and held apart from mainstream education reform. Several critics of multicultural education, such as Arthur Schlesinger, John Leo, and Paul Gray, have perpetuated the idea that multicultural education is the study of the "other" by defining it as synonymous with Afrocentric education.[3] The history of intergroup education teaches us that only when education reform related to diversity is viewed as essential for all students—and as promoting

3

the broad public interest—will it have a reasonable chance of becoming institutionalized in the nation's schools, colleges, and universities.[4] The intergroup education movement of the 1940s and 1950s failed in large part because intergroup educators were never able to persuade mainstream educators to believe that the approach was needed by and designed for all students. To its bitter but quiet end, mainstream educators viewed intergroup education as something for schools with racial problems and as something for "them" and not for "us."

Multicultural Education Is Opposed to the Western Tradition

Another harmful misconception about multicultural education has been repeated so often by its critics that many people take it as self-evident. This is the claim that multicultural education is a movement that is opposed to the West and to Western civilization. Multicultural education is not anti-West, because most writers of color—such as Rudolfo Anaya, Paula Gunn Allen, Maxine Hong Kingston, Maya Angelou, and Toni Morrison—are Western writers. Multicultural education itself is a thoroughly Western movement. It grew out of a civil rights movement grounded in such democratic ideals of the West as freedom, justice, and equality. Multicultural education seeks to extend to all people the ideals that were meant only for an elite few at the nation's birth.

Although multicultural education is not opposed to the West, its advocates do demand that the truth about the West be told, that its debt to people of color and women be recognized and included in the curriculum, and that the discrepancies between the ideals of freedom and equality and the realities of racism and sexism be taught to students. Reflective action by citizens is also an integral part of multicultural theory. Multicultural education views citizen action to improve society as an integral part of education in a democracy; it links knowledge, values, empowerment, and action. Multicultural education is also postmodern in its assumptions about knowledge and knowledge construction; it challenges positivist assumptions about the relationships between human values, knowledge, and action.

Positivists, who are the intellectual heirs of the Enlightenment, believe that it is possible to structure knowledge that is objective and beyond the influence of human values and interests. Multicultural theorists maintain that knowledge is positional, that it relates to the knower's values and experiences, and that knowledge implies action. Consequently, different concepts, theories, and paradigms imply different kinds of actions. Multiculturalists believe that, in order to have valid knowledge, information about the social condition and experiences of the knower are essential.

A few critics of multicultural education, such as John Leo and Dinesh D'Souza, claim that multicultural education has reduced or displaced the study of Western civilization in the nation's schools and colleges. However, as Gerald Graff points out in his welcome book, *Beyond the Culture Wars*, this claim is simply not true. Graff cites his own research at the college level and that of Arthur Applebee at the high school level to substantiate his conclusion that European and American male authors—such as Shakespeare, Dante, Chaucer, Twain, and Hemingway—still dominate the required reading lists in the nation's high schools and colleges.[5] Graff found that, in the cases he examined, most of the books by authors of color were optional rather than required reading. Applebee found that, of the ten book-length works most frequently required in the high school grades, only one title was by a female author (Harper Lee's *To Kill a Mockingbird*), and not a single work was by a writer of color. Works by Shakespeare, Steinbeck, and Dickens headed the list.

Multicultural Education Will Divide the Nation

Many of its critics claim that multicultural education will divide the nation and undercut its unity. Schlesinger underscores this view in the title of his book, *The Disuniting of America: Reflections on a Multicultural Society*. This misconception is based partly on questionable assumptions about the nature of U.S. society and partly on a mistaken understanding of multicultural education. The claim that multicultural education will divide the nation assumes that the nation is already united. While we are one nation politically, sociologically our nation is deeply divided along lines of race, gender, and class. The current debate about admitting gays into the military underscores another deep division in our society.

Multicultural education is designed to help unify a deeply divided nation rather than to divide a highly cohesive one. Multicultural education supports the notion of *e pluribus unum*—out of many, one. The multiculturalists and the Western traditionalists, however, often differ about how the *unum* can best be attained. Traditionally, the larger U.S. society and the schools tried to create unity by assimilating students from diverse racial and ethnic groups into a mythical Anglo American culture that required them to experience a process of self-alienation. However, even when students of color became culturally assimilated, they were often structurally excluded from mainstream institutions.

The multiculturalists view *e pluribus unum* as an appropriate national goal, but they believe that the *unum* must be negotiated, discussed, and restructured to reflect the nation's ethnic and cultural diversity. The reformulation of what it means to be united must be a process that involves the participation of diverse groups within the nation, such as people of color, women, straights, gays, the powerful, the powerless, the young, and the old. The reformulation must also involve power sharing and participation by people from many different cultures who must reach beyond their cultural and ethnic borders in order to create a common civic culture that reflects and contributes to the well-being of all. This common civic culture will extend beyond the cultural borders of any single group and constitute a civic "borderland" culture.

In *Borderlands*, Gloria Anzaldúa contrasts cultural borders and borderlands and calls for a weakening of the former in order to create a shared borderland culture in which people from many different cultures can interact, relate, and engage in civic talk and action. Anzaldúa states that "borders are set up to define the places that are safe and unsafe, to distinguish us from them. A border is a dividing line, a narrow strip along a steep edge. A borderland is a vague and undetermined place created by the residue of an unnatural boundary. It is in a constant state of transition."[6]

Multicultural Education Has Made Progress

While it is still on the margins rather than in the center of the curriculum in most schools and colleges, multicultural content has made significant inroads into both the school and the college curricula within the last two decades. The truth lies somewhere between the claim that no progress has been made in infusing the school and college curricula with multiethnic content and the claim that such content has replaced the European and American classics.

In the elementary and high schools, much more ethnic content appears in social studies and language arts textbooks today than was the case 20 years ago. In addition, some teachers assign works written by authors of color along with the more standard American classics. In his study of book-length works used in the high schools, Applebee concluded that his most striking finding was how similar present reading lists are to past ones and how little change has occurred. However, he did note that many teachers use anthologies as a mainstay of their literature programs and that 21% of the anthology selections were written by women and 14% by authors of color.[7]

More classroom teachers today have studied the concepts of multicultural education than at any previous point in our history. A significant percentage of today's classroom teachers took a required teacher education course in multicultural education when they were in college. The multicultural education standard adopted by the National Council for Accreditation of Teacher Education in 1977, which became effective in 1979, was a major factor that stimulated the growth of multicultural education in teacher education programs. The standard stated: "The institution gives evidence of planning for multicultural education in its teacher education curricula including both the general and professional studies components."[8]

The market for teacher education textbooks dealing with multicultural education is now a substantial one. Most major publishers now have at least one text in the field. Textbooks in other required courses, such as educational psychology and the foundations of education, frequently have separate chapters or a significant number of pages devoted to examining concepts and developments in multicultural education.

Some of the nation's leading colleges and universities, such as the University of California at Berkeley, the University of Minnesota, and Stanford University, have either revised their general core curriculum to include ethnic content or have established an ethnic studies course requirement. The list of universities with similar kinds of requirements grows longer each year. However, the transformation of the traditional canon on college and university campuses has often been bitter and divisive. All changes in curriculum come slowly and painfully to university campuses, but curriculum changes that are linked with issues related to race evoke primordial feelings and reflect the racial crisis in American society. For example, at the University of Washington a bitter struggle ended with the defeat of the ethnic studies requirement.

Changes are also coming to elementary and high school textbooks. I believe that the demographic imperative is the major factor driving the changes in school textbooks. The color of the nation's student body is changing rapidly. Nearly half (about 45.5%) of the nation's school-age youths will be young people of color by 2020.[9] Black parents and brown parents are demanding that their leaders, their images, their pain, and their dreams be mirrored in the textbooks that their children study in school.

Textbooks have always reflected the myths, hopes, and dreams of people with money and power. As African Americans, Hispanics, Asians, and women become more influential, textbooks will increasingly reflect their hopes, dreams, and disappointments. Textbooks will have to survive in the marketplace of a browner America. Because textbooks still carry the curriculum in the nation's public schools, they will remain an important focus for multicultural curriculum reformers.

6

The Dimensions of Multicultural Education

One of the problems that continues to plague the multicultural education movement, both from within and without, is the tendency of teachers, administrators, policy makers, and the public to oversimplify the concept. Multicultural education is a complex and multi-dimensional concept, yet media commentators and educators alike often focus on only one of its many dimensions. Some teachers view it only as the inclusion of content about ethnic groups into the curriculum; others view it as an effort to reduce prejudice; still others view it as the celebration of ethnic holidays and events. After I made a presentation in which I described the major goals of multicultural education, a math teacher told me that what I said was fine and appropriate for language arts and social studies teachers, but it had nothing to do with him. After all, he said, math was math, regardless of the color of the kids.

This reaction on the part of a respected teacher caused me to think more deeply about the images of multicultural education that had been created by the key actors in the field. I wondered whether we were partly responsible for this teacher's narrow conception of multicultural education as merely content integration. It was in response to such statements by classroom teachers that I conceptualized the dimensions of multicultural education. I will use the following five dimensions to describe the field's major components and to highlight important developments within the last two decades: 1) content integration, 2) the knowledge construction process, 3) prejudice reduction, 4) an equity pedagogy, and 5) an empowering school culture and social structure.[10] I will devote most of the rest of this article to the second of these dimensions.

Content Integration

Content integration deals with the extent to which teachers use examples, data, and information from a variety of cultures and groups to illustrate the key concepts, principles, generalizations, and theories in their subject area or discipline. In many school districts as well as in popular writing, multicultural education is viewed almost solely as content integration. This narrow conception of multicultural education is a major reason why many teachers in such subjects as biology, physics, and mathematics reject multicultural education as irrelevant to them and their students.

In fact, this dimension of multicultural education probably has more relevance to social studies and language arts teachers than it does to physics and math teachers. Physics and math teachers can insert multicultural content into their subjects—e.g., by using biographies of physicists and mathematicians of color and examples from different cultural groups. However, these kinds of activities are probably not the most important multicultural tasks that can be undertaken by science and math teachers. Activities related to the other dimensions of multicultural education, such as the knowledge construction process, prejudice reduction, and an equity pedagogy, are probably the most fruitful areas for the multicultural involvement of science and math teachers.

Knowledge Construction

The **knowledge construction process** encompasses the procedures by which social, behavioral, and natural scientists create knowledge in their disciplines. A multicultural focus on knowledge construction includes discussion of the ways in which the implicit cultural assumptions, frames of reference, perspectives, and biases within a discipline influence the construction of knowledge. An examination of the knowledge construction process is an important part of multicultural teaching. Teachers help students to understand how knowledge is created and how it is influenced by factors of race, ethnicity, gender, and social class.

Within the last decade, landmark work related to the construction of knowledge has been done by feminist social scientists and epistemologists, as well as by scholars in ethnic studies. Working in philosophy and sociology, Sandra Harding, Lorraine Code, and Patricia Hill Collins have done some of the most important work related to knowledge construction.[11] This ground-breaking work, although influential among scholars and curriculum developers, has been overshadowed in the popular media by the heated debates about the canon. These writers and researchers have seriously challenged the claims made by the positivists that knowledge can be value-free and have described the ways in which knowledge claims are influenced by the gender and ethnic characteristics of the knower. These scholars argue that the human interests and value assumptions of those who create knowledge should be identified, discussed, and examined.

Code states that the sex of the knower is epistemologically significant because knowledge is both subjective and objective. She maintains that both aspects should be recognized and discussed. Collins, an African American sociologist, extends and enriches the work of writers such as Code and Harding by describing the ways in which race and gender interact to influence knowledge construction. Collins calls the perspective of African American women the perspective of "the outsider within." She writes, "As outsiders within, Black women have a distinct view of the contradictions between the dominant group's actions and ideologies."[12]

Curriculum theorists and developers in multicultural education are applying to the classroom the work being done by the feminist and ethnic studies epistemologists. In *Transforming Knowledge*, Elizabeth Minnich, a professor of philosophy and women's studies, has analyzed the nature of knowledge and described how the dominant tradition, through such logical errors as faulty generalization and circular reasoning, has contributed to the marginalization of women.[13]

I have identified five types of knowledge and described their implications for multicultural teaching.[14] Teachers need to be aware of the various types of knowledge so they can structure a curriculum that helps students to understand each type. Teachers also need to use their own cultural knowledge and that of their students to enrich teaching and learning. The types of knowledge I have identified and described are: 1) personal/cultural, 2) popular, 3) mainstream academic, 4) transformative, and 5) school. (I will not discuss school knowledge in this article.)

Personal/cultural knowledge consists of the concepts, explanations, and interpretations that students derive from personal experiences in their homes, families, and community cultures. Cultural conflict occurs in the classroom because much of the personal/cultural knowledge that students from diverse cultural groups bring to the classroom is inconsistent with school knowledge and with the teacher's personal and cultural knowledge. For example, research indicates that many African American and Mexican American students are more likely to experience academic success in cooperative rather than in competitive learning environments.[15] Yet the typical school culture is highly competitive, and children of color may experience failure if they do not figure out the implicit rules of the school culture.[16]

The popular knowledge that is institutionalized by the mass media and other forces that shape the popular culture has a strong influence on the values, perceptions, and behavior of children and young people. The messages and images carried by the media, which Carlos Cortés calls the societal curriculum,[17] often reinforce the stereotypes and misconceptions about racial and ethnic groups that are institutionalized within the larger society.

Of course, some films and other popular media forms do make positive contributions to racial understanding. *Dances with Wolves, Glory,* and *Malcolm X* are examples. However, there are many ways to view such films, and both positive and negative examples of popular culture need to become a part of classroom discourse and analysis. Like all human creations, even these positive films are imperfect. The multiculturally informed and sensitive teacher needs to help students view these films, as well as other media productions, from diverse cultural, ethnic, and gender perspectives.

The concepts, theories, and explanations that constitute traditional Westerncentric knowledge in history and in the social and behavioral sciences constitute mainstream academic knowledge. Traditional interpretations of U.S. history—embodied in such headings as "The European Discovery of America" and "The Westward Movement"—are central concepts in mainstream academic knowledge. Mainstream academic knowledge is established within mainstream professional associations, such as the American Historical Association and the American Psychological Association. It provides the interpretations that are taught in U.S. colleges and universities.

The literary legacy of mainstream academic knowledge includes such writers as Shakespeare, Dante, Chaucer, and Aristotle. Critics of multicultural education, such as Schlesinger, D'Souza, and Leo, believe that mainstream academic knowledge in the curriculum is being displaced by the new knowledge and interpretations that have been created by scholars working in women's studies and in ethnic studies. However, mainstream academic knowledge is not only threatened from without but also from within. Postmodern scholars in organizations such as the American Historical Association, the American Sociological Association, and the American Political Science Association are challenging the dominant positivist interpretations and paradigms within their disciplines and creating alternative explanations and perspectives.

Transformative academic knowledge challenges the facts, concepts, paradigms, themes, and explanations routinely accepted in mainstream academic knowledge. Those who pursue transformative academic knowledge seek to expand and substantially revise established canons, theories, explanations, and research methods. The transformative research methods and theory that have been developed in women's studies and in ethnic studies since the 1970s constitute, in my view, the most important developments in social science theory and research in the last 20 years.

It is important for teachers and students to realize, however, that transformative academic scholarship has a long history in the United States and that the current ethnic studies movement is directly linked to an earlier ethnic studies movement that emerged in the late 1800s.[18] George Washington Williams published Volume 1 of the first history of African Americans in 1882 and the second volume in 1883. Other important works published by African American transformative scholars in times past included works by W. E. B. Du Bois, Carter Woodson, Horace Mann Bond, and Charles Wesley.[19]

The works of these early scholars in African American studies, which formed the academic roots of the current multicultural education movement when it emerged in the 1960s and 1970s, were linked by several important characteristics. Their works were transformative because they created data, interpretations, and perspectives that challenged those that were established by white, mainstream scholarship. The work of the transformative scholars presented positive images of African Americans and refuted stereotypes that were pervasive within the established scholarship of their time.

Although they strove for objectivity in their works and wanted to be considered scientific researchers, these transformative scholars viewed knowledge and action as tightly linked and became involved in social action and administration themselves. Du Bois was active in social protest and for many years was the editor of *Crisis*, an official publication of the National Association for the Advancement of Colored People. Woodson co-founded the Association for the Study of Negro (now Afro-American) Life and History, founded and edited the *Journal of Negro History*, edited the *Negro History Bulletin* for classroom teachers, wrote school and college textbooks on Negro history, and founded Negro History Week (now Afro-American History Month).

Transformative academic knowledge has experienced a renaissance since the 1970s. Only a few of the most important works can be mentioned here because of space. Martin Bernal, in an important two-volume work, *Black Athena*, has created new interpretations about the debt that Greece owes to Egypt and Phoenicia. Before Bernal, Ivan Van Sertima and Cheikh Anta Diop also created novel interpretations of the debt that Europe owes to Africa. In two books, *Indian Givers* and *Native Roots*, Jack Weatherford describes Native American contributions that have enriched the world.

Ronald Takaki, in several influential books, such as *Iron Cages: Race and Culture in 19th-Century America* and *Strangers from a Different Shore: A History of Asian Americans*, has given us new ways to think about the ethnic experience in America. The literary contribution to transformative scholarship has also been rich, as shown by *The Signifying Monkey: A Theory of African-American Literary Criticism*, by Henry Louis Gates, Jr.; *Long Black Song: Essays in Black American Literature and Culture*, by Houston Baker, Jr.; and *Breaking Ice: An Anthology of Contemporary African-American Fiction*, edited by Terry McMillan.

A number of important works in the transformative tradition that interrelate race and gender have also been published since the 1970s. Important works in this genre include *Unequal Sisters: A Multicultural Reader in U.S. Women's History*, edited by Carol Ellen DuBois and Vicki Ruiz; *Race, Gender, and Work: A Multicultural Economic History of Women in the United States*, by Teresa Amott and Julie Matthaei; *Labor of Love, Labor of Sorrow: Black Women, Work, and the Family from Slavery to the Present*, by Jacqueline Jones; and *The Forbidden Stitch: An Asian American Women's Anthology*, edited by Shirley Geok-lin Lim, Mayumi Tsutakawa, and Margarita Donnelly.

The Other Dimensions

The **prejudice reduction** dimension of multicultural education focuses on the characteristics of children's racial attitudes and on strategies that can be used to help students develop more positive racial and ethnic attitudes. Since the 1960s, social scientists have learned a great deal about how racial attitudes in children develop and about ways in which educators can design interventions to help children acquire more positive feelings toward other racial groups. I have reviewed that research in two recent publications and refer readers to them for a comprehensive discussion of this topic.[20]

This research tells us that by age four African American, white, and Mexican American children are aware of racial differences and show racial preferences favoring whites. Students can be helped to develop more positive racial attitudes if realistic images of ethnic and racial groups are included in teaching materials in a consistent, natural, and integrated fashion. Involving students in vicarious experiences and in cooperative learning activities with students of other racial groups will also help them to develop more positive racial attitudes and behaviors.

An **equity pedagogy** exists when teachers use techniques and teaching methods that facilitate the academic achievement of students from diverse racial and ethnic groups and from all social classes. Using teaching techniques that cater to the learning and cultural styles of diverse groups and using the techniques of cooperative learning are some of the ways that teachers have found effective with students from diverse racial, ethnic, and language groups.[21]

An **empowering school culture and social structure** will require the restructuring of the culture and organization of the school so that students from diverse racial, ethnic, and social-class groups will experience educational equality and a sense of empowerment. This dimension of multicultural education involves conceptualizing the school as the unit of change and making structural changes within the school environment. Adopting assessment techniques that are fair to all groups, doing away with tracking, and creating the belief among the staff members that all students can learn are important goals for schools that wish to create a school culture and social structure that are empowering and enhancing for a diverse student body.

Multicultural Education and the Future

The achievements of multicultural education since the late sixties and early seventies are noteworthy and should be acknowledged. Those who have shaped the movement during the intervening decades have been able to obtain wide agreement on the goals of and approaches to multicultural education. Most multiculturalists agree that the major goal of multicultural education is to restructure schools so all students will acquire the knowledge, attitudes, and skills needed to function in an ethnically and racially diverse nation and world. As is the case with other interdisciplinary areas of study, debates within the field continue. These debates are consistent with the philosophy of a field that values democracy and diversity. They are also a source of strength.

Multicultural education is being implemented widely in the nation's schools, colleges, and universities. The large number of national conferences, school district workshops, and teacher education courses in multicultural education is evidence of its success and perceived importance. Although the process of integration of content is slow and often contentious, multicultural content is increasingly becoming a part of core courses in schools and colleges. Textbook publishers are also integrating ethnic and cultural content into their books, and the pace of such integration is increasing.

Despite its impressive successes, however, multicultural education faces serious challenges as we move toward the next century. One of the most serious of these challenges is the highly organized, well-financed attack by the Western traditionalists who fear that multicultural education will transform America in ways that will result in their own disem-powerment. Ironically, the successes that multicultural education has experienced during the last decade have played a major role in provoking the attacks.

The debate over the canon and the well-orchestrated attack on multicultural education reflect an identity crisis in American society. The American identity is being reshaped as groups on the margins of society begin to participate in the mainstream and to demand that their visions be reflected in a transformed America. In the future, the sharing of power and the transformation of identity required to achieve lasting racial peace in America may be valued rather than feared, for only in this way will we achieve national salvation.

Endnotes

[1]Glazer, N. (1991, Sept. 2). In defense of multiculturalism. *New Republic*, 18-22; and D'Souza, D. (1991, March). Illiberal education. *Atlantic*, 51-79.

[2]Banks, J. A. (1994). *Multiethnic education: Theory and practice* (3rd ed.). Boston: Allyn and Bacon; Banks, J. A., & McGee, C. A. (Eds.). (1993). *Multicultural education: Issues and perspectives* (2nd ed.). Boston: Allyn and Bacon; and Sleeter, C. E., & Grant, C. A. (1988). *Making choices for multicultural education: Five approaches to race, class, and gender*. Columbus, OH: Merrill.

[3]Schlesinger, Jr., A. M. (1991). *The disuniting of America: Reflections on a multicultural society*. Knoxville, TN: Whittle Direct Books; Leo, J. (1990, Nov. 12). A fringe history of the world. *U. S. News & World Report*, 25-26; and Gray, P. (1991, July 8). Whose America? *Time*, 13-17.

[4]Taba, H. et al. (1952). *Intergroup education in public schools*. Washington, DC: American Council on Education.

[5]Graff, G. (1992). *Beyond the culture wars: How teaching the conflicts can revitalize American education*. New York: Norton; and Applebee, A. N. (1992, Sept.). Stability and change in the high school canon. *English Journal*, 27-32.

[6]Anzaldúa, G. (1987). *Borderlands: La Frontera: The new mestiza*. San Francisco: Spinsters/Aunt Lute, 3.

[7]Applebee, p. 30.

[8]*Standards for the accreditation of teacher education*. (1977). Washington, DC: National Council for Accreditation of Teacher Education, 4.

[9]Pallas, A. M., Natriello, G., & McDill, E. L. (1989, June/July). The changing nature of the disadvantaged population: Current dimensions and future trends. *Educational Researcher*, 16-22.

[10]Banks, J. A. (1993). Multicultural education: Historical development, dimensions, and practice. In L. Darling-Hammond (Ed.), *Review of research in education*, (Vol. 19, pp. 3-49). Washington, DC: American Educational Research Association.

[11]Harding, S. (1991). *Whose science, whose knowledge? Thinking from women's lives*. Ithaca, NY: Cornell University Press; Code, L. (1991). *What can she know? Feminist theory and the construction of knowledge*. Ithaca, NY: Cornell University Press; and Collins, P. H. (1990). *Black feminist thought: Knowledge, consciousness, and the politics of empowerment*. New York: Routledge.

[12]Collins, p. 11.

[13]Minnich, E. K. (1990). *Transforming knowledge*. Philadelphia: Temple University Press.

[14]Banks, J. A. (1993, June/July). The canon debate, knowledge construction and multicultural education. *Educational Researcher,* 4-14.

[15]Slavin, R. E. (1983). *Cooperative learning*. New York: Longman.

[16]Delpit, L. D. (1988). The silenced dialogue: Power and pedagogy in educating other people's children. *Harvard Educational Review, 58,* 280-98.

[17]Cortés, C. E. (1981). The societal curriculum: Implications for multiethnic education. In J. A. Banks (Ed.), *Education in the 80s: Multiethnic education* (pp. 24-32). Washington, DC: National Education Association.

[18]Banks, J. A. (1992, Summer). African American scholarship and the evolution of multicultural education. *Journal of Negro Education*, 273-86.

[19]A bibliography that lists these and other more recent works of transformative scholarship appears at the end of this article.

[20]Banks, J. A. (1991). Multicultural education: Its effects on students' racial and gender role attitudes. In James P. Shaver (Ed.), *Handbook of research on social studies teaching and learning* (pp. 459-69). New York: Macmillan; and Banks, J. A., (1993). Multicultural education for young children: Racial and ethnic attitudes and their modification. In Bernard Spodek (Ed.), *Handbook of research on the education of young children* (pp. 236-50). New York: Macmillan.

[21]Shade, B. J. R. (Ed.). (1989). *Culture, style, and the educative process*. Springfield, IL: Charles C. Thomas.

Bibliography

Amott, T. L., & Matthaei, J. A. (1991). *Race, gender, and work: A multicultural economic history of women in the United States*. Boston: South End Press.

Baker, H. A., Jr. (1990). *Long black song: Essays in black American literature and culture*. Charlottesville: University Press of Virginia.

Bernal, M. (1987, 1991). *Black Athena: The Afroasiatic roots of classical civilization*, 2 vols. New Brunswick, NJ: Rutgers University Press.

Bond, H. M. (1939). *Negro education in Alabama: A study in cotton and steel*. Washington, DC: Associate Publishers.

DuBois, C. E., & Ruiz, V. L. (Eds.). (1990). *Unequal sisters: A multicultural reader in U.S. women's history*. New York: Routledge.

Du Bois, W. E. B. (1896). *The suppression of the African slave trade to the United States of America, 1638-1870*. Millwood, NY: Kraus-Thomas.

Gates, H. L., Jr. (1988). *The signifying monkey: A theory of African-American literary criticism*. New York: Oxford University Press.

Geok-lin Lim, S., Mayumi, T., & Donnelly, M. (Eds.). (1989). *The forbidden stitch: An Asian American women's anthology*. Corvallis, OR: Calyx Books.

Jones, J. (1985). *Labor of love, labor of sorrow: Black women, work, and the family from slavery to the present*. New York: Vintage Books.

McMilllan, T. (Ed.). (1990). *Breaking ice: An anthology of contemporary African-American fiction*. New York: Penguin Books.

Takaki, R. T. (Ed). (1979). *Iron cages: Race and culture in 19th century America*. Seattle: University of Washington Press.

Takaki, R. T. (1989). *Strangers from a different shore: A history of Asian Americans*. Boston: Little, Brown.

Van Sertima, I. (Ed.). (1988). *Great black leaders: Ancient and modern*. New Brunswick, NJ: African Studies Department, Rutgers University.

Van Sertima, I. (Ed.). (1989). *Great African thinkers, Vol. 1: Cheikh Anta Diop*. New Brunswick, NJ: Transaction Books.

Weatherford, J. (1988). *Indian givers: How the Indians of the Americas transformed the world*. New York: Fawcett Columbine.

Weatherford, J. (1992). *Native roots: How the Indians enriched America*. New York: Fawcett Columbine.

Wesley, C. H. (1935). *Richard Allen: Apostle of freedom*. Washington, DC: Associated Publishers.

Williams, G. W. (1989). *History of the negro race in America from 1619 to 1880: Negroes as slaves, as soldiers, and as citizens, 2 vols*. Salem, NH: Ayer. (Original works published 1882-1883)

Woodson, C. G. (1921). *The history of the Negro church*. Washington, DC: Associated Publishers.

CREATING CONDITIONS FOR A CONSTRUCTIVE DIALOGUE ON "RACE": TAKING INDIVIDUAL AND INSTITUTIONAL RESPONSIBILITY

Invited Presentation to President Clinton's Race Advisory Board
September 30, 1997, Washington, D.C.

by
Derald Wing Sue

Introduction

Good afternoon everyone.

First of all, let me quickly acknowledge how pleased and honored I am to have this opportunity to share some of my research and work in the area of race relations and diversity training with such a distinguished panel. I believe that if we are to become a fair, just, and equitable society, we must heed President Clinton's call for a constructive dialogue on "race."

It will succeed, however, only if we are able to acknowledge our biases and preconceived notions; to be open and honest with one another; to hear the hopes, fears, and concerns of all groups in this society; to recognize how prejudice and discrimination hurt everyone; and to seek common solutions that allow for equal access and opportunities.

Achieving the Cultural Mosaic of One America

Achieving what I call "the cultural mosaic of one America" is a monumental task because it requires (a) an honest examination of unpleasant racial realities like racial prejudice, racial stereotyping and racial discrimination, and (b) accepting responsibility for changing ourselves, our institutions, and our society. My two other learned colleagues have already established the fact that bias, prejudice and discrimination are deeply embedded in individuals, institutions, and our society; that they are often expressed not only overtly, but unintentionally and at an unconscious level. One of the greatest difficulties White Americans have in understanding racism is that they perceive and experience themselves as moral, decent, and fair people. Thus, they often do not realize that their beliefs and actions may be discriminatory in nature. What, however, can we do as individuals?

Personal Responsibility for Change

We need to realize that the concept of racism, prejudice, and discrimination is not just an intellectual concept for objective study and "for the other person." It has very personal consequences for those who are the victims. For example, not only have I been stereotyped throughout my life as an Asian American and seen as an outsider, but I have had the sanctity of my home violated by our community police. At some point you realize that no matter what your station in life may be, there are some in our society who continue to believe that racial/ethnic minorities are undesirable, "less than," and a threat to their existence.

I believe the responsibility for change resides strongly in two major domains: individual and institutional. Let me elaborate on the first of these levels.

While many of us are willing to acknowledge that racism must be addressed at an institutional and societal level, we often avoid addressing this on a personal level and fail to identify personal growth as a necessary element. I would argue that it is difficult, if not impossible, for any of us to be race-sensitive without understanding and working through our own personal biases and prejudices. It must entail a willingness to address internal issues related to personal belief systems, behaviors, and emotions when interacting with other racial groups.

There must be a personal awakening and a willingness to "root out" biases and unwarranted assumptions related to race, culture, ethnicity, etc. When confronting racism on a personal level, several psychological assumptions can guide us in facilitating difficult dialogues on race.

- No one was born wanting to be "racist" or bigoted. No one was born with racist attitudes and beliefs. Misinformation related to culturally different groups is not acquired by our free choice. These are imposed through a painful process of social conditioning; one is taught to hate and fear others who are different in some way. In a strange sort of way, White Americans are as much victims as persons of color in this respect. For example, for me to believe that after being born and raised in the U.S. for some 55 years, that somehow I have been immune from inheriting the racial biases of my forebears may be the height of naiveté or arrogance.

- Having racist attitudes and beliefs is harmful not only to persons of color, but to White EuroAmericans as well. It serves as a clamp on one's mind, distorting the perception of reality. It allows some White Americans to misperceive themselves as superior and all other groups as inferior. It allows for the systematic mistreatment of large groups of people based upon misinformation.

- People of color also grow up in an environment in which they, too, acquire misinformation about themselves and about Whites and other minority groups. They may come to believe in the inferiority of their group and themselves, or they may become unable to separate their oppressive experiences from accurate information about White Americans.

The 1947 doll identification study of Kenneth and Mamie Clark is a prime example of this process. Kenneth Clark, by the way, was the first person of color to become President of the American Psychological Association. He and Mamie Clark gave Black and White Children a Black doll and a White one. Through a series of questions they determined that societal forces had deeply infected the self-esteem of Black children. Many of the Black youngsters attached negative descriptors to the Black doll and positive ones to the White doll. What was surprising, however, was that some of the African American children chose the White doll as most like them!

- Overcoming our biased cultural conditioning means that we must overcome the feeling of inertia and powerlessness on a personal level. People can grow and change if they are personally willing to confront and unlearn their racist conditioning. To accomplish this task, we must unlearn racist misinformation not only on a cognitive level (factual), but the misinformation which has been glued together by painful emotions. We must begin to accept the responsibility for the pain and suffering we may have personally caused others.

Unlearning our biases means acquiring accurate information and experiences. Much of how we come to know about other cultures is through the media, what our family and friends convey to us, and through public education texts. These sources cannot be counted upon to give an accurate picture because they can be filled with stereotypes, misinformation and deficit portrayals. Thus, I propose four principles (many supported from psychological studies) to guide us in obtaining an accurate picture of culturally different groups.

Principle 1

- First, we must experience and learn from as many sources as possible (not just the media or what our neighbor may say) in order to check out the validity of our assumptions and understanding.
  a. Read literature written by or for persons of the culture. This applies to both fiction and nonfiction. While the professional and nonprofessional literature often portrays minorities in stereotypic ways, writings from individuals of that group may provide a richness based upon experiential reality. For example, books like *The House on Mango Street, Now I Know Why the Caged Bird Sings, The Joy Luck Club, The Trail of Tears,* and *Unpacking the Invisible Knapsack of White Privilege* make it possible to enter the culture in a safe, nonthreatening way. Other sources of information include minority-run or minority-edited radio and T.V. stations or publications.

Principle 2

- Second, a balanced picture of racial/ethnic minority groups requires that we spend time with healthy and strong people of that culture.
  a. The mass media and our educational texts (written from the perspectives of EuroAmericans) frequently portray minority groups as uncivilized, pathological, criminal or delinquent. No wonder the images we have are primarily negative. We must individually make an effort to fight such negative conditioning and ask ourselves what the desirable aspects of the culture, the history, and the people are. This can only come about if we have contact with representatives of that group.

Principle 3

- Third, we must supplement our factual understanding with the experiential reality of the groups we hope to understand.
  a. It may be helpful to identify a cultural guide: someone from the culture who is willing to help us understand his/her group; someone willing to introduce us to new experiences; someone willing to help us process our thoughts, feelings and behaviors. This allows us to more easily obtain valid information on race and racism issues.
  b. Attend cultural events, meetings and activities of the group. This allows us to view the people interacting in their community and observe their values in action. Hearing from church leaders, attending open community forums, and attending community celebrations allow us to sense the strengths of the community, observe leadership in action, personalize our understanding, and identify potential guides and advisors.

- Last, our lives must become a "have to" in being constantly vigilant to manifestations of bias in both ourselves and in the people around us.
  a. Learn how to ask sensitive racial questions from our minority friends, associates and acquaintances. Persons subjected to racism seldom get a chance to talk about it with an undefensive and non-guilty person from the majority group. White Americans, for example, often avoid mentioning race even with close minority friends. Most minority individuals are more than willing to respond, to enlighten, and to share, **if they sense that our questions and concerns are sincere and motivated by a desire to learn and serve the group.** When a White person listens undefensively to an African American speak about racism, for example, both gain.
  b. When around people of color or when race-related issues or racial situations present themselves where are the feelings of uneasiness, differentness, or outright fear coming from? They may reveal or say something about our biases and prejudices. Why do we cross the street when we see Black youngsters approaching us? Do we do it when whites approach us? Why do we tense up and clutch our purses more securely when a minority person enters? Don't make excuses for these thoughts and feelings, dismiss them, or avoid attaching some meaning to them. Only if we confront them directly, can they be unlearned or dealt with in a realistic manner.
  c. Dealing with racism means a personal commitment to action. It means interrupting other White Americans when they make racist remarks, jokes or engage in racist actions even if this is embarrassing or frightening. It means noticing the possibility for direct action against bias and discrimination in our everyday life—in the family, at work, and in the community. For persons of color, dealing with bias and prejudice is a day to day occurrence. If White Americans are to be helpful, their lives must also be a constant "have to be" in dealing with racism.

Additional Thoughts

Many of these suggestions are applicable to persons of color as well. In addition, racial minorities also need to do several things: (a) realize that many White Americans are eager to help and represent powerful allies; (b) recognize that we also need to reach out to each other to form multicultural alliances and to realize that race, culture, ethnicity are functions of each and every one of us—they are not just an "Asian American or African American" thing; (c) we must avoid the "who's more oppressed" trap because all oppression is damaging and serves to separate rather than unify; and (d) realize that we all need an opportunity to learn and grow (i.e., making insensitive remarks or racial blunders cannot be the sole determinant of dismissing a person's value).

Organizational Responsibility for Change

Earlier, we heard facts and statistics regarding the changing demographics which I refer to literally as the "changing complexion of our society" or the "diversification of the United States." Already, some 75% of those now entering the labor force are minorities and women. All organizations whether business or industry, government, mental health agency or educational institution have an organizational culture. In my work as a diversity consultant, I have begun to realize that our institutions are structured in such a way as to put a large segment of our working population at a disadvantage. Racial minorities encounter barriers to being hired, retained, or promoted. The existence of a "glass ceiling," while invisible, is very real.

To allow for equal access and opportunity, we must attempt to change, refine, instill or create new policies, programs, practices, and structures which are fair, just, and equitable. In my work with organizations, I have found that a number of conditions will facilitate equal access and opportunity in the work force.

Facilitative Conditions for Implementing Diversity in Organizations

• Commitment must come from the top.

Diversity implementation is most effective when strong leadership is exerted on its behalf. Workers are most likely to watch the actions (not just the words) of their leaders. For business, the Board of Directors, CEO, and management team are the principals; for government agencies, it is often the Head of the service or unit (Secretary of Labor, Housing, etc.); for education, it is the School Board, Superintendent, Principal, etc.; and for our nation it is the President of the United States, Congress, the Judiciary, and local, state, and federal leaders.

Commitment must be manifested in action. It is more than a written policy statement. What specific steps has the leadership taken to implement diversity goals and what are the results?

• Organizations should have a written policy, mission or vision statement which frames the concepts of diversity, equal access and opportunities into a meaningful operational definition.

• A diversity action plan should be developed complete with clear objectives.

These goals should directly outline specific time frames for implementation of diversity goals. For example, both short-term and long-term plans should describe a time line of readiness (preparatory forces which must be put in play) and infusion (actual change).

• A superordinate mechanism or oversight team/group should be empowered to monitor the organization's development with respect to the goals of diversity.

This group must have the power to operate rather independently and share an equal status with other central divisions and units. It cannot be ancillary, but central to the governance of the organization. Some of its goals may revolve around program development, assessing the corporate culture, and monitoring the goals of diversity.

• Fostering employee advocacy, focus, and advisory groups to identify work climate issues, corporate policies and practices, etc. as to how they enhance or negate diversity goals is important.

Feedback from employee groups related to issues of race, culture, and ethnicity represents a rich source of information which organizations may find useful in their movement toward valuing diversity.

• Related to accountability is the need to redefine promotion criteria.

If an organization values diversity competencies, it should be built into performance appraisal systems. For example, in the world of business, a definition of good management may entail knowledge, sensitivities, and skills related to cross-cultural competence. Those individuals would be hired and promoted because they possess multicultural skills. By incorporating diversity competence into performance evaluations, the issue of race (reverse racism) would be minimized because a White male with multicultural competence would also be valued.

- Organizations with mentoring and support networks for nontraditional employees are likely to move toward diversity goals much more quickly.
- Education of the entire work force concerning diversity issues, concepts and goals is central to successful implementation of multiculturalism. In-service diversity training should be an intimate part of the organization's activities. This includes not only employees at the lower levels of employment, but . . . the entire work force up through the management team, to the senior executives and the CEO or President.
- Coalition building and networking for minorities and women are very important for support and nourishment.

It is important for them to identify allies and resources. Being a culturally different individual in a primarily monocultural work situation can deplete energy, alienate, and discourage the minority employee, thereby reducing work productivity. Remember, very few of us can do it alone.

- No organization exists apart from the wider community or society.

Community linkages are very important to aid in the recruitment, retention and promotion of minority employees.

Concluding Thoughts

While engaging in an honest and open dialogue on race is a necessary condition for equality and justice, commitment on an individual and institutional level may produce conflict, intense emotions, or resistance. However, people who have taken this journey often remark that they have personally benefited. They have:

- experienced a broadening of their horizons,
- experienced an increased appreciation of people (all colors and cultures),
- become less afraid and intimidated by differences, and
- have been able to communicate more openly and clearly with their family, friends, and co-workers.

Thus, their effectiveness in relating to others has improved their own personal lives and their functioning in a pluralistic society as well.

Likewise, a society which values racial equality is one which makes use of all its resources and maximizes the contributions of all groups. A harmonious and inclusive society allows our children to acquire the knowledge and skills necessary for them to function and contribute as productive citizens in a pluralistic society and global world.

In closing, let me again reiterate the three imperatives we must undertake: first, we must acknowledge that we all have biases, stereotypes, and preconceived notions based on race; second, we must take personal responsibility for combating prejudice and discrimination; and finally, we must fight for social justice to insure equal access and opportunities in our society and institutions.

Thank you for your patience in listening to my perspective.

MULTICULTURAL TRANSFORMATION
OF THE ACADEMY

by
James B. Boyer

In the United States, all post-secondary education seems to have borrowed its format and substance from the 1636 Harvard University model. We in the United States still think of that model as providing the classic definition of higher education despite the major changes in our demographic mosaic, in the way information is produced, stored, and transmitted, and in the emphasis and power of information in our **information society**. I want to make a case for the total multicultural transformation of the academy that includes the state university, the liberal arts college, the technical college, the community college, graduate schools, and the full array of adult post-secondary efforts to educate the United States' populace. We must all raise new questions about the appropriateness of the substantive content we consider essential in higher education.

The multicultural transformation of the academy is necessary because graduates of post-secondary education participate not only in shaping the future, but in also **executing** the future, and in the United States, that future will be characterized by diversity in all its forms. While there are those who are in denial of this reality and others who are in opposition to it, the academy has a responsibility to foster the new competencies for full participation in the diverse life of our nation. To succeed, the traditional academy must be transformed.

Leadership for Curriculum Transformation

Persons whose careers place them in curriculum leadership roles in the academy must become culturally competent in curriculum design, instructional services, program policy making, assessment measures, and the capacity to envision schools of the future. We must seek to make connections across cultures in ways that enhance the academic experience for all collegiate learners. As we communicate across cultures, we must humanize the experience while working to accommodate psychologically all the clients and potential clients of the academy.

Since our work is pivotal in determining and communicating the substance of the academic curriculum, the multicultural transformation of the academy must begin with us. What is our multicultural literacy level? What is our level of multicultural comfort in the academy? How do we see curriculum and instructional power? How do we engage our diverse students in the academic enterprise?

The transformation of the academy means the transformation of our perspectives, practices, programs, and provisions whether we work in collegiate classrooms, counseling offices, administrative offices, libraries, cultural centers, or residence facilities. Given the rapid ethnic and linguistic transformation of our society, our own levels of ethnic awareness and competency in cross-ethnic teaching and learning will be tested in the future. Self-assessment of our lives, our careers, and the essence of our services in the academy becomes a necessity. Are we ready for this level of change in the academy? Are we committed to serving clients of all descriptions? Can we survive? Can they?

The work involved in transformation must deal with curriculum content, instructional delivery systems, and structures and strategies for pluralizing the postsecondary curriculum in quest of greater ethnic diversity. It goes without saying that gender equity is also a major component of such transformation and that multicultural, multilingual understandings are essential as we embrace nontraditional populations of collegiate students. Nontraditional undergraduate populations include persons who are not in the age category of 19 to 26 years, while graduate students range in age from the early 20s to over 80; collegiate services, particularly instructional services, can no longer assume that clients will represent young minds that are presently unfolding.

Explorations of degree programs, ideas for program overlays, and analyses of essential content in all disciplines are part of the multicultural transformation of which we speak. We must be aware that the transformation of the post-secondary academy in the United States is a new idea since, historically, many persons have felt all transformation must be done by the clients-students since they chose to come to the institution to be, supposedly, changed. It may be true that clients have come to be changed but the process of change is now under social, political, economic, and technological scrutiny. As Leon Botstein (1991) points out: The relative homogeneity . . . of the professoriate and student body in America and the undisturbed allegiance to nineteenth century epistemological foundations are connected historically. Complementary relationships existed among (1) stable intellectual ideology of knowledge and inquiry; (2) the structure of the university; and (3) the elite population the university served. The symmetry and symbiosis among these three elements has gone down since the early 1960s (p. 93).

The changes in the population, the advances in the use of the academy, and the expanding sources of post-secondary learning in our information society all demand a multicultural transformation. The social and economic democratization of access to the academy now demands that programmatic diversity become the norm rather than the exception in what is learned as well as what is taught. Since what is learned is often shaped in emphasis by who is doing the teaching, transformation involves personnel as well as personal decisions.

Why a Multicultural Transformation?

What are the goals of a multicultural education? Why should the academy embrace multicultural programming for college learners who are not ethnically or linguistically different from the masses who have benefitted from college in earlier times? In other words, why multicultural education? A multicultural perspective and overview characterizing collegiate curriculum programs as well as human service delivery are intended to result in a society that is nonviolent, open, and diverse in its framework and supportive of all humanity, especially participants in the academic marketplace.

Multicultural, multiethnic curriculum can only be effective when it is accompanied by culturally sensitive instruction, appropriately diverse curriculum materials, and an understanding of culturally influenced learning styles. The ultimate outcomes of a multicultural transformation of college learning should include a **celebration** of ethnic identity, a **recognition** of gender adequacy, and an **understanding** of the necessity for economic sufficiency. Gender adequacy involves understanding that neither gender is better than the other and that equality does not mean sameness. No one should ever have to apologize for his or her gender, personal ethnic, linguistic, or economic profile as a college participant. As college professionals we are human service providers and function in a profession devoted to the enhancement of the **quality of life** for all learners who come for our services. As such, the professoriate must now undergo serious analysis, with due respect for academic freedom, but with clear understanding that clients also have freedoms. As college professionals we never have the right to embarrass, exclude, psychologically assault, or intellectually downgrade a student who comes for our services. The transformation of the academy, then, involves a friendly confrontation with professional perspectives that fail to embrace such responsibility.

The following five factors are critical to college training in an information-based society.

College Learning in the Age of Information

Today five times the quantity of information is available for college learning as was available just 40 years ago. Information selectivity is, therefore, a new competence needed within the academy, whether one is primarily engaged in research or in direct instruction. Secondly, in an age of information, a new consciousness of **who is included** in such information is critical since information is power. New analyses of power and power brokering are needed. What is truth? How is it determined? How is it transmitted? Why are certain truths emphasized more than others?

College Learning in the Age of the Consumer

After the academy's position on access changed, the clientele also changed, with the academy the center of an academic marketplace where ideas are created, refined, stored, retrieved, and **sold**. Because the consumers have changed and they insist on the production and utilization of knowledge deemed most functional, their **rights** must be addressed. Who are our consumers? What do we know about them? What is our cultural competence regarding these students who come for collegiate curriculum services? What do they respect? How do they feel? How do they vote on our courses, classes, internships, assignments, and instructional performances?

College Learning in the Age of Intelligence Redefined

Never before has the issue of intelligence been such a matter of interest and discussion in the academy as now. Intelligence is being more broadly defined and channels of learning are no longer limited to the impact of an information society. Who knows what? How do they know? What knowledge is worth knowing—as determined by whom? Howard Gardner's work in *Frames of Mind* (1983) has alerted us that diversity extends to more than telephone companies. No longer is it appropriate to ask if a college applicant or student is intelligent. Rather, one must ask in what ways he or she is intelligent. Cultural differences in how information, knowledge, and skills are acquired need to be studied by more college professionals than ever before.

College Learning in the Age of Self-Definition

Historically, in collegiate learning instructional perspective defined learners both intellectually and sociologically. Generally, those definitions attempted to be ethnically neutral, but diverse learners viewed them as disturbing. College populations now define themselves, and professionals in the academy have the responsibility of discovering these new definitions even though they are not static or conveniently announced in all instances. Ruth Burgoss-Sasscer (1987) suggests the task of empowering Hispanic students poses a special challenge, with many academics studying Hispanics as if they were one ethnic group and failing to take into account that Puerto Ricans in New York are quite different from Cubans in Miami or Mexican Americans in California. Collegiate services need to explore the more intricate details of culturally diverse populations. Almost all professionally conscious college teachers know the impact of labeling in instances of gender concern; they also need to understand the impact of ethnically related definitions.

College Learning in the Age of Options and Alternatives

Post-secondary learning centers need to become centers for options and alternatives for both learners and professors where present concepts of college learning can be significantly changed and upgraded. In more than 75% of U.S. homes today, cable television is a reality. Most people acquired cable because they wanted more options than those provided by the three traditional television networks. At one time the networks commanded some 90% of television viewership, but today they command less than 60% of that total viewership. In our age of information and diversity, providing options in completing tasks for collegiate credit must become part of the normal operations of colleges and universities. Even the definition of degree programs and the processes through which degrees are earned must be critically examined.

The multicultural transformation of the post-secondary institution must begin to address numerous environmental and procedural areas of its structure. Even *Time* (1990) referred to the inadequacies of a monocultural curriculum that failed to address diversity when stating, "If you create a curriculum that lauds the achievements of one group and omits and distorts the achievements of another, it has its effect" (p. 89).

What Is Multicultural Education?

Multicultural education is a comprehensive curriculum program that embraces cultural differences as basic foundational components of collegiate learning. It enhances the presence of ethnic, linguistic, gender, age, ability, and economic variations through curriculum content, especially in the social sciences, natural sciences, and humanities, in collegiate curricular policies, procedures, and practices, including practices of recognition, reward, and endorsement. The curriculum reflects the experiences, perspectives, cultural orientation, and mannerisms of culturally different populations. Instruction, counseling, administration, coaching, mentoring, and communication all reflect diversity in implementation and assessment.

Collegiate multicultural education encompasses the six Cs: consciousness, commitment, cohesiveness, collaboration, cultural competence, and courage.

- Consciousness of diversity by all parties engaged in higher education.
- Commitment to equity by those responsible for designing collegiate experiences for learners.
- Cohesiveness of collegiate curriculum through carefully planned programs, including ethnic and women's studies programs, and the integration of ethnic and women's studies scholarship into traditional disciplines to enrich the learning experiences of all students.
- Collaboration of persons from different academic programs to insure the full transformation of the academy.
- Cultural Competence of collegiate curriculum workers to include our understanding of the differences in the way members of different cultural groups **prefer** to learn.
- Courage to confront tradition that is deeply entrenched institutionally and personally. **Leaders** of the transformation must be personally **strong**. Leadership is essential to any transformation of any institution. The academy is a powerful institution in society, transforming raw intelligence into sophisticated thinking and organized direction. It impacts the quality of life, the quality of institutional practice, and the destiny of citizens. Strong leadership for the multicultural transformation must include all those whose work provides direction for learning whether as instructors, administrators, or support service workers.

Institutional Commitment to Diversity

James Montford, Jr. (1990), writing in *Black Issues in Higher Education*, asserts that institutions must make a commitment to diversity at every level, particularly at the support programs level. He writes, "The mission of cultural diversity means the institutionalization of a cross-cultural perspective into curriculum, programs and services at any institution" (p. 64). Further, he insists "It is incumbent upon all institutions of higher education to move forward with deliberate speed to develop draft proposals designed to address infusion of cross-cultural education into the very fabric of higher learning" (p. 64).

Once commitment is made for all areas of the academy to recognize and institutionalize diversity, the following dimensions need specific study and reorganization.

Cultural Diversity in Student Affairs

This would involve a service orientation for all staff and a constant review by leadership teams to monitor the program's focus, the students' involvement level, and the extent the programming meets the needs of all clients. For example, does the lyceum program include speakers and resource persons from diverse populations? Is there planned, active inclusion of all the cultural profiles enrolled in the academy? Is anyone being left out? Have efforts been made to attract all groups to the full resources of the student services programs? Is the academy perceived as providing diverse cultural experiences for the campus community?

Race Relations

Because of the seeming deterioration of healthy race relations in the United States over the past decade, colleges and all post-secondary programs must become deliberate and comprehensive in their efforts to upgrade race and ethnic relations. The post-secondary institution is a public academic marketplace, and all cultural and ethnic groups are to be comfortably included at a meaningful level. Improved race relations will involve intellectual interaction within the social context of higher education. Respect for differences and respect for differences of opinion must be developed so leadership can emerge and enhance healthy exchanges between ethnic groups. The institution is a nonprofit workplace, an academic corporation, and the ideas, the concepts, the perspectives developed there should have a substantive support stance for a **better United States**, not a more divisive one.

Cultural Competence

Cultural competence involves the ability of an individual or agency to give assistance to clients in ways acceptable and useful to the clients; it must make sense in terms of clients' backgrounds and expectations. All members of the academy's work force must seek to understand not only the power of ethnic identity but also what it means to diffuse hostility and resentment even when they are not directly caused by the service provider him- or herself. A professional commitment to all, whatever their cultural framework, is needed without regard for differences. Workers must understand ethnic values and the extent of significance placed on non-harmful behavior by those whose cultural comfort zones differ from traditional behavior within the academy.

Diversity, Mental Health, and Human Relationships

All human relationships are affected by the biographical frameworks, the life experiences, of the individuals involved. If someone does not have multicultural experiences during the first 18 years of life, some training will likely need to occur to develop strong levels of psychological comfort in such relationships, whether they are student-teacher relationships, worker-to-worker relationships, supervisor to supervisee relationships, or others. In all of these, the academy must embrace a commitment to the preservation of the mental health of individuals, to the urgency of diversity, and to comfortable multicultural working environments.

To insure healthy human relationships, we must analyze whether we are essentially isolated or essentially connected to others in the academy. We must constantly appraise whether we display negative interactors or positive interactors across culture. Our decisions must be balanced between traditional concepts of objectivity and compassion for the reality of our clients' worlds. We must, within the context of the diverse academy, remind ourselves we are competent and comfortable in the delivery of human services, that we are committed to growing on the job and to becoming better activists in an academy that is better because of its diversity.

Areas and Stages of the Multicultural Transformation

To effect the multicultural transformation of collegiate curriculum and instruction we must develop the following:
• Insight into the disciplines, into ourselves, into others;

26

- Perceptions about change, about people, about systems, about programs, practices, and policies;
- Knowledge about scores of topics and events as the United States becomes increasingly a society of information and the academy accepts more responsibility in brokering that information;
- Skills of all kinds, including verbal, social, political, writing, analytical, and practical skills, from traditional agricultural skills to computer skills, but perhaps most significantly, cross-cultural skills;
- Concepts that go beyond definitions, beyond limited, perhaps isolated notions about phenomena, to include understanding of contextual frameworks—among the more urgent being the concept of multicultural, rather than monocultural, comprehension;
- Theories that embrace the diversity in the academy and that can be tested and researched effectively; and
- A more open system of reviewing and analyzing relationships and cause-effect outcomes: how, for instance, can an institution that functions on the intellectual level of existence ignore the causes of violence within our society?

Curriculum Realities in Higher Education

Three dimensions of higher education curriculum are critical to understanding the totality of the multicultural transformations of the academy: the psychological, the cognitive, and the political.

The **psychological dimension** of collegiate curriculum involves the way both clients and service providers **feel** about their presence in the academy, their assigned responsibilities, and the ongoing assessment of their participation. Obviously, this involves perspectives on **who** should enjoy access and who should be privileged to pursue successfully goals in this arena. For many years, the academy did not embrace the culturally different, including women, in our society. Today, that is changed and the psychological inclusion must be reflected in textbooks, assignments, staff, resources, lyceum programs, residential considerations, and celebrations. This can only occur with deliberate training and attention to this dimension.

The **cognitive dimension** of curriculum involves the art and science of **knowing** and the decisions surrounding **what** is to be known and **how** that knowing is to occur. We now recognize that there are many ways of knowing. In an information society, major selections must be made about what is to be known. What knowledge is of most worth? And of most worth to whom? Over the last 40 or 50 years, Benjamin Bloom's taxonomy of the cognitive domain has been the basis for analyzing much about cognition and has served a useful purpose. Our concern today, however, is the patterns of **selection** of the information to be known and how **inclusive** that information is for all clients in the academy.

The **political dimension** of curriculum involves the forces driving program emphasis, degree requirements, course syllabi, textbook selection, library acquisitions, and the scores of other factors that impact the academy. The U.S. has done a relatively decent job in keeping up with technological advancements but we have failed in our progress with multicultural, multiethnic, multilingual competencies in the academy. This is partially because legislators, administrators, and citizens at large, as well as faculty and students, have not been informed that such transformation **should** occur. Multicultural issues grew out of our effort to desegregate our major institutions and, for many, desegregation has always been viewed negatively. To transform the academy multiculturally is still a bitter pill for many practitioners and citizens. Our political agenda, however, suggests it will occur despite the efforts of those who would like to ignore its meaning and its evolving power. A multicultural transformation brings reality and the Constitution of the United States into closer alignment: we are a nation committed to democracy for **all the people**. The curriculum of the academy must embrace this dimension and implement it in all programming.

The politics of the curriculum involves collegiate learning priorities, academic language adoption, collegiate program requirements, and much more. However, one must remember **learner vulnerability** as well as **professional prerogative**. Herein lies the political agenda. If the academy is not committed to diversity, it will fight to save the monocultural curriculum and perspective. Only when it commits to an **inclusive** way of programming and serving will it truly upgrade itself for the year 2000 and beyond.

The Two-Year Academy and Diversity

Perhaps more than the four-year institutions, the two-year academy tends to attract clients who are **more** interested in immediate workplace competency than in the liberal education traditions. Consequently, the clients in such programs have even more urgent need for environments that embrace diversity than some others. Given this, the two-year academy must seek to create policies, programs, and procedures for every unit within its purview that deliberately respect the dynamics of diversity in the schooling process. Not only will clients hold us responsible for such provisions once they are alumni, but the corporate agencies, whose work force participants come primarily from these programs, will charge the academy with inadequacy unless their graduates bring pluralistic perspectives to the entry-level work force.

Diversity Issues in the Research Paradigm of the Academy

Perhaps no area of the academy's function is more complex than research, its agenda, scope, and implications. In the United States we depend on the academic research community for information about national policy and priorities in addition to academic policy and priorities. **Diversity** must become part of the foundational base on which research endeavors and discussions are built.

Expanding the Definition of Academy Research

What constitutes research? How will it be used? Which research functions and projects are worthy of the academy's seal and image? Who shall make these decisions? On what basis? Despite a tendency to favor research parameters of the past, a stronger level of **inclusion** must be part of our research definitions. What is the prevailing definition and who created or offered it? Should research be designed to improve the quality of life for the people? If so, which people? All the people—including those who are culturally different from the masses? This will involve greater comprehensiveness in definition and scope.

Choice of Research Topics

As research topics are chosen by students and faculty, what types of topics are encouraged? Which are discouraged? To what extent are candidates encouraged to engage in research on issues of race, gender, ethnicity, bilingualism, and economic exploitation? In the natural sciences, to what extent are concerns about ethical issues investigated? How, for example, are decisions made about where toxic waste dumps are placed? Or which patients shall get organ replacements in medical facilities? Academic research must be deliberate in its concern for the diversity such questions imply. How are research topics chosen? With which populations in mind? Much technical research is conducted to enhance the life of all human beings, regardless of ethnic-racial-gender profiles, but much research in the academy is related specifically to culturally identified groups. This research must become more responsive to the differences that help define us.

Research Production and Consumption

Research production is both a science and an art. To what extent do researchers feel that all clients and potential researchers must **duplicate** the patterns and techniques of past research? Why must research in one area be acceptable to academicians who are engaged in other categories of research activity? Researchers must expand the range of research topics, methods, and outcomes to reflect their own cultural diversity. The academy's research specialists need not be threatened or alarmed by this. Diversity implies that some traditions and customs will be challenged within the research community.

Research consumption is an ever expanding endeavor. Since the invention of the printing press, the academy has assumed that the only way to expand consumption was through the printed word. While that is still the most common form of dissemination, it is certainly not the **only** way to share. The electronic media, with its advances in educational technology and other forms of publishing and communication, are equally valid and valuable. Transformation demands respect for these additional channels of communication.

Summary

Much of the academic research activity, particularly educational and social science research, has assumed a monocultural audience and a monolingual readership. Such a limited western civilization, English-speaking, middle-class Eurocentric perspective is no longer adequate for our comprehensive definition of academic research or of the academy itself. The quest for diversity within the community of scholars and educators who comprise the academy cannot be overemphasized. Whatever way one defines diversity, the bottom line is its expansion of tradition and its **inclusiveness**. To insure progress toward greater expansion and inclusiveness in the curriculum, in staff and students, in instructional styles, in research, in every aspect of the academy, we must continuously ask the hard questions of what, why, who, and how. What is the academy? Why does it exist now? Who is it to serve now? How is it to do so effectively? Given the demographic profile of our nation and the information explosion of our era, a transformation of the academy must respect our diversity, our multicultural reality.

References

Botstein, L. (1991). The undergraduate curriculum and the issue of race? Opportunities and obligations. In P. G. Altbach & K. Lomotey (Eds.), *The racial crisis in American higher education*. Albany, NY: Suny Press.

Boyer, J. (1989). *Collegiate instructional discrimination index*. (Multiethnic, multilingual, cross-racial, non-sexist). Manhattan, KS: College of Education, Kansas State University.

Boyer, J. (1992, Spring). Multicultural concerns in educational research, *Midwestern Educational Researcher, 9*(2), 7-8.

Burgos-Sasscer, R. (1987, Spring). Empowering Hispanic students: A prerequisite is adequate data. *Journal of Education Equity and Leadership, 7*(1).

Cox, Jr., T. (1993). *Cultural diversity in organizations: Theory, research and practice*. San Francisco: Berrett-Moehler Publishers.

Gardner, H. (1983). *Frames of Mind: The theory of multiple intelligences*. New York: Basic Books.

Montford, Jr., J. W. (1990, May 10). Institutions must make commitment to diversity at every level. *Black Issues in Higher Education*, p. 64.

Time (1990, September 24), p. 89.

MULTICULTURALISM IN U.S. SOCIETY AND EDUCATION: WHY AN IRRITANT AND A PARADOX?

by
Carlos J. Ovando and Luise Prior McCarty

Society in the United States is becoming increasingly diverse ethnically, racially, linguistically, and economically. With this growing diversity, there is a renewed public debate regarding the best way to induct minority groups into the sociocultural fabric. Some argue that unless diversity is harnessed into some sort of common culture and language, the country will become divided into myriad ethnic enclaves with very particular agendas that could threaten the unity and future of the nation. The influential American historian, Arthur Schlesinger, Jr., in his controversial book entitled *The Disuniting of America: Reflections on a Multicultural Society* (1992), echoes this concern:

> Instead of a transformative nation with an identity all its own, America increasingly sees itself in this new light as preservative of diverse alien identities. Instead of a nation composed of individuals making their own unhampered choices, America increasingly sees itself as composed of groups more or less ineradicable in their ethnic character. . . . (p. 16) Will the center hold? or will the melting pot give way to the Tower of Babel?" (p. 18)

Others, however, suggest that it is not only possible but essential to maintain cultural and linguistic roots while concurrently sharing a set of pluralistic democratic principles, especially through the school curriculum. The latter hold that the inclusion of diversity in the content and process of democratic schooling gives society its vibrancy and sociocultural coherence (Banks & Banks, 1989; Nieto, 1992). Such a view, however, has the potential for creating irritation and a strong backlash. This is so because multicultural education

> . . . entails a direct challenge to the societal power structure that has historically subordinated certain groups and rationalized the educational failure of children from these groups as being the result of their inherent deficiencies. Multicultural education . . . challenges all educators to make the schools a force for social justice in our society. (Cummins, 1992, p. xviii)

The above debate, however, does not help teachers address the pressing cultural and linguistic issues in today's classrooms. Frequently missing from the political debate on diversity and multicultural education are resolutions to the following more immediate concerns:

> Will diversity polarize our school constituents or unite us?; Will academic standards be sacrificed?; If the school takes a strong stand on diversity, will these values and lessons find support at home?; If a multicultural curriculum demands more time and energy, where will it fit in an already over-extended teaching load? (Carter, 1991, p. 1)

In this paper we contend that the idea of multiculturalism is an irritant because it challenges us to rethink not only our conception of a just society (cf. Cummins, 1992) but our conceptions of identity—of who we are and what gives us our particularity. We also

31

contend that multicultural education is a difficult task because it challenges us to rethink our ideas of what constitutes teaching: Is a teacher a transmitter of consensual values or by default a cultural change agent? We suggest that a focus on cultural dialogue—as opposed to a focus on mainstream versus "other" cultures—will help teachers put a more constructive vision of multiculturalism to work in their classrooms.

As a way of affirming the importance of cultural dialogue, we propose to examine the above issues through a conversation between two educators from different disciplines and also from very different cultural backgrounds. Initially, Luise McCarty, in her preparatory remarks for a potential dialogue about the political debate on multiculturalism, sets forth her thesis that much of the source of irritancy and paradox associated with multiculturalism stems from two flawed images of culture. Two of these incorrect images are that culture is an isolation chamber with no connecting points to other cultures, and that cultural knowledge, as packaged in textbooks, is subject to manipulation and is teachable. Drawing from hermeneutic philosophy, she suggests a more complex, multidimensional and interconnected paradigm as a more promising approach to understanding multiculturalism in U.S. society. Ovando then responds to and builds on the points raised by McCarty's philosophical perspective on culture after each one of her sections. We conclude the paper with two caveats we hope can provide alternatives for global interdependence and survival as a multicultural society.

A Philosophical Perspective on Conceptions of Culture: McCarty

A goodly part of what we call "the problem of multiculturalism" is not a problem with the demographic or the pedagogical facts of multiculturalism. It is a problem in our ways of viewing those facts. I believe that unfortunate conceptions of culture, ways of picturing culture, give rise to the emotional and intellectual irritation that often accompanies discussions of multiculturalism. My hope is that, by leaving faulty images of culture behind or by putting them into perspective, some of the irritation can be left behind as well. I find two images particular obstacles to a clear understanding. The first I call "culture as isolation chamber"; the second "culture as a disposable." I want to look at them one at a time and, in each case, I hope to suggest other, less irritating, images of culture to put in their place. My alternative images are drawn from hermeneutic philosophy. The first comes from Hegel's (1977) discussion of "the alien" within objective spirit and the second from Hans-Georg Gadamer's (1990) reconstruction of the old notion of **Takt**.

Out of Isolation: How to Picture Cultural Diversity

There is the temptation, when comparing non-European with European cultures—say, the culture of the Hopi with that of Manhattan stockbrokers—to think of the two cultures as thoroughly isolated, almost as if they were quarantined within medical isolation chambers. Each culture is conceived of as an enclosed bubble, a region in space separated from the other by a constant cultural distance, completely enclosed within a wall-like cultural barrier. We think of the thoughts, feelings, plans, and desires—the entire mental lives—of the members from each group as wholly surrounded by the barrier-like culture and incapable of extending outside it. When we think of culture in this way, the actions and reactions of one group are thought to make sense and work effectively only within its own cultural enclosure and as either partially or wholly ineffective within the confines of the other isolated culture. Here we are imagining cultural differences between two groups as if they were bounded regions in a space, regions separated by sizeable linear distances. In this way, the separation of cultures turns unnoticed into total disjointedness, a cultural isolation enforced by circumferential cultural walls.

Certainly, there are felt difficulties in intellection and acclimation to be faced when we enter into alternative cultures. It is natural to respond to these feelings by speaking of a "distance between cultures" and "cultural barriers." But these forms of speech—and the forms of imaging that go with them—are not the products merely of untutored imagination or of popular turns of phrase. They begin much higher and run much deeper than that. They may be born and raised in the speaking and writing of professional anthropologists. Well known anthropologist Edward T. Hall (1989) writes as follows of his experiences on the Atoll of Truk: "In addition, I felt it my duty to do what I could to *bridge the gap between my own culture and that of the Trukese*" [emphasis added] (p. 37). In its extreme form, the language of isolation likens cultural difference not simply to separated portions of a single ambient space but to wholly separate **worlds**, as if the cultures with which we share the one Earth had their origins on the planet Uranus. I quote again from Hall (1989):

> In sharp contrast, high context peoples like the Pueblo, many of Africa's indigenous cultures, the Japanese, and apparently the Russians . . . inhabit a "sea of information" that is widely shared. . . . The "sea of information" group lives in a unified, very high context *world* [emphasis added] in which all or most of the parts interrelate. (p. 39)

Communication—or meaningful interaction of any kind—between cultures conceived as isolation chambers looks, at best, like a serious problem. At worst, it becomes a near impossibility. If **everything** I do gets real meaning only within the strict, isolated confines of my own culture, then the prospect for true communication, which requires shared meanings, becomes nil. Just think of us trapped within actual isolation chambers. If our cultural prisons stand only small distances apart, we can signal, mutely, out of the window of one bubble and toward another. Perhaps select and attenuated messages, devoid of any rich meaning, can be passed between, as if telegraph wires had been strung from our isolation bubble. (But in which language are we to send the telegrams?) Or perhaps we can construct *ex nihilo* means of communication or interfaces between cultures. Hall (1989) again speaks of cultural interfaces to be built at the boundary walls of cultures (p. 41).

If images such as these reflect our thinking, the prospects for multiculturalism are grim indeed. We face a series of unnecessary questions: "How are we to break out of our little bubble so as to find a common understanding with the inhabitants of another?" "Are we even able to do so?" "If we do break out of our bubble, haven't we left our own cherished culture behind?" "Would we not have to break down the barriers that guarantee our culture its integrity?" I often wonder whether it might not be such worries, ones tied to the "isolation chamber" model of culture, that do most to aid and abet a deadening uniculturalism. The kind of uniculturalism I have in mind demands that there be, for each group, only a single culture and that any accommodation of "alien culture" can only affect the dissipation of the "home culture." The spatial isolation picture of culture lends to these untoward ideas an unfortunate integrity. If alternative cultures are properly understood by comparison with relatively isolated places, then we must grant credence to this uniculturalism. It is true that we can only occupy one of two or more distinct spots at a time and that, if we leave one place and move to another, we must leave our original place behind, possibly for good.

I am not so naive as to think that spatial metaphors, so deeply hewn into the ground of thought, can be left behind when we think about cultural difference. It is natural, even inevitable, to draw difference as a map of quasi-spatial distance. But there is no necessity to think always in terms of everyday distance, of inflexible linear displacement. The picture of our intercultural geometry is not a landscape of thoroughly closed regions isolated within a single flat space. Its real geometry is open and nonEuclidean. First, cultures are not walled-in regions in space cut off by fixed distances. Think of them not as enclosed but as open. Not as finite but as endless, as reaching over a horizon. Heidegger (n.d.) thought of the culture of philosophy as a pathway and so should we think of our culture as a whole. Imagine cultures as pathways running with variable distances in between. As I move along a pathway, some other paths I see draw closer while others diverge. In this way, I can move toward rapprochement with another culture, another path, without leaving the confines of my own. Think of the way paths intersect in the woods.

Second, if paths can intersect, they may even share segments relatively often—traveling together for a time and then moving apart. It is natural to think of any path as containing elements from other paths. In fact, there are geometric models for paths on which no two paths are ever completely disjoint but share a number of intersections. I will describe one in a moment. Anyone who has been lost in the woods can tell you that it is, at times, difficult to locate an intersection or common segment in paths, but they are there all the same.

Third, we can picture each culture as a path identified among all paths only by perspective, that is, only in relation to the other paths. Indeed, it may be that, in isolation from others, I can't even see my own path very well. Perhaps I can only learn to study my path's course by watching others moving along paths of their own.

By drawing a geometrical comparison, you can see why and how all this can be so. I think of the paths that are cultures as marked out by lines drawn on the surface of a huge sphere. The sphere is, in certain respects, like the surface of the earth, except that I am thinking of it as featureless. (It is featureless apart from the lines forming the edges of the paths.) To be definite, think of the sphere as uniformly white and paths as black. Imagine now that the black paths run along the great circle lines of the sphere, lines similar to the equator or to any of the meridians on the earth. As navigators will tell you, the great circles always represent the shortest distance between any two places on the earth; transatlantic flights follow the great circle routes. A little spherical geometry will show that any two distinct great circles will intersect in at least two places—think of the equator and Greenwich meridian. Moreover, there is no fixed distance between any two of these curved lines; as I move along any one path or great circle, my distance to another changes in tandem. If the cultures are these paths, cultures are open not closed; in fact, they are "too big" to fit into any delimited barrier. Moreover, each culture contains elements of every other.

The converse is also true. As with more familiar "linear" forms of line, our paths on the sphere are made-up of many points and, given any point, it is the common intersection of an indefinite number of other paths. Every segment of a path becomes a place-in-common between two or more distinct paths. Therefore, every culture, in the analogy, becomes a patchwork of similarities and borrowings from many others. Lastly, since the surface of the sphere is itself featureless—other than the paths—there are no absolute landmarks—other than alternate paths—against which to measure position or motion. In fact, I can only distinguish one path from another by reference to the course of yet further paths. If I draw the analogy to culture, this will mean that cultures are not isolated but are necessarily inter-active, so much so that, for one culture to have a self-conscious identity, a direction as a path, it must fix that direction with respect to other cultures.

Now it is my contention that this is a way of addressing cultural alternatives less open to a stultifying uniculturalism and to allied irritations of thought. No culture stands in total conceptual isolation from others; no culture is an ideological region that is self-enclosed. Each culture today is an accumulation of the cultural remains from the alternative cultures that form its own past. As the philosopher Bachelard (1984) has emphasized, each of our contemporary concepts is a quilt-like patchwork of conceptual artifacts from earlier eras. He wrote, "Science is like a half-renovated city, wherein the new . . . stands side by side with the old" (p. 7). No culture is devoid of the tradings and borrowings from others ubiquitous in European cultures. Think of the vast lexical borrowings that compose the "English" language. And words rarely travel from one language to another without a conceptual, technical, and administrative entourage.

Just as the spherical paths can draw near and come to intersect, alternative cultures are located, at times, within the clear view of one another. I may have to travel intellectually and morally to find places of intersection with another, but I am sure they do exist. In fact, if Hegel were right about culture, then they must exist. And this way of conceiving culture seems not just casually more attractive than the other, but absolutely required by the very idea of self-conscious culture. Hegel (1977) had this to say, as paraphrased by Gadamer (1990):

> To recognize one's own in the alien, to become at home in it, is the basic movement of spirit, whose being consists only in returning to itself from what is other. Hence all theoretical edification, even acquiring foreign languages and conceptual worlds, is merely the continuation of a process of edification that begins much earlier. (p. 14)

I must emphasize that, in the last line, the words "much earlier" mark not mere temporal but full metaphysical priority. The process which Gadamer, and Hegel, thought to begin "much earlier" is not so much a psychological as a philosophical prerequisite for the "basic movement of the spirit."

Hegel draws a number of conclusions simultaneously, ones to make us turn from the isolationist and toward our path-like model of culture. First, Hegel claims that one only comes to recognize and to appreciate a culture—even a "home culture"—by reflection in and upon other cultures. Nowadays, this may count as an anthropological truism, yet it is a truism often forgotten in heated debates over multiculturalism. But, in Hegel, the meetings between cultures that are required for the self-consciousness of culture are not **any** movements of the spirit, say, one from a wholly familiar sphere into one wholly alien, the kind of movement we would think of on the isolationist model. In Hegel, as on the path model, one moves and yet never leaves the place which is "one's own." Hegel wrote that, rather than moving into a completely separate sphere, one must, in grasping a new culture, "recognize one's own in the alien" and "become at home in it." Hegel is here adverting to what I called "intersections of paths" in the picture I just sketched. We are to enter alter-native cultures by finding homes **there**—in **that new culture**—and by returning to ourselves **in those alternative homes**.

Second, and importantly, the possibility for self-recognition within the home of another is not something incidental for Hegel, a matter that "it would be nice to have but we can do without." In Hegel, our being "consists only in returning to itself from what is other." In each of the world's cultures, there is a home for us; I believe that Hegel understands this fact as critical for a common, thoughtful humanity. As in the path picture, there are no other landmarks by which to locate the course of our own path except by reflection upon other converging and diverging paths.

Finally, there is the matter of the last line of the quotation and the issue of the "edification that begins much earlier." Hegelian cultural self-consciousness is not a process into which I enter when I first learn foreign languages or art in school. It is a process I am always in, from the time at which I learned my first word. For, as we have seen, to wield a word is already to wield a cultural history, one that picks out intersections and contains common elements from a great number of other paths.

Ovando's Response to McCarty's Perspective on Culture[2]

McCarty has made a strong case for the need to affirm the web-like, complex, and intertwined characteristics of cultural processes. I am especially intrigued by the role that she ascribes to dialogues as necessary means for creating cultural meaning through intersecting pathways. Equally cogent is her proposition, as reflected in Hegel and Gadamer, that we can all find a home in each of the world's cultures if we accept the notion of "the alien" within objective spirit.

Yet, in order to understand why multiculturalism is an irritant, we must also understand how different conceptions of culture are translated, ultimately, into different conceptions of ourselves, of our identities as individuals, affiliated with or disengaged from a variety of cultural groups. For example, wanting to communicate with members of another culture may stem from a desire to transmit one's values to the other side but not to make oneself vulnerable to their values. The fear or desire to connect with other cultures may likewise be linked to apprehensions of having to give up something from one's culture in order to obtain something else from the other one: a zero-sum game in which one robs Peter to pay Paul culturally and metaphorically speaking. In my own case, what price have I had to pay for becoming a bilingual-bicultural individual affiliated concurrently with the Hispanic cultural ethos and with the Anglo-Saxon cultural ethos? How do I deal with the psychological ambivalence that often surrounds individuals straddling two cultures?

Another way to understand the dynamics of multiculturalism is to examine the acculturation and/or assimilation ideology of students who are newcomers to U.S. society. Depending on the level of sociocultural approval of the student's heritage by the larger and more powerful mainstream society, students will tend to make their adjustments in one of three directions: (1) the student will undergo an ethnocultural revitalization phenomenon that manifests itself in a strong affirmation or reaffirmation of her or his heritage; (2) the student will reject his or her cultural and linguistic heritage and try to blend in as inconspicuously as possible with the mainstream culture; or (3) the student will develop a creative and eclectic synthesis of both the mainstream and the home culture (Ovando, 1990, p. 295).

If multiculturalism is viewed as a political idea, as a "we" and "they" contest, the zero-sum game metaphor is appropriate. Irritancy then becomes a natural outcome of attempts to communicate cross-culturally. This is so, of course, because in a zero-sum game there is always a winner and a loser. In this framework, the third option for our hypothetical student above, the "eclectic synthesis" is not possible. If, however, we see many cultures as being potential nesting grounds for each one of us, then it is possible to strike a creative cross-cultural balance in our lives.

McCarty does not ascribe much importance to changing demographics or to multicultural education as a source of the negative image of multiculturalism. Her view that, "it is a problem in our ways of viewing those facts," while powerful, does not explain fully why this topic has become so vitriolic. I believe the identity crisis felt by many in the United States today is exacerbated because of specific demographic and political events that have taken place during the last few decades. Until recently we have not had to rethink our isolationist chamber model of culture. However, the demographic shift that has taken place in the United States since the 1970s has raised pointed questions about the nation's cultural and educational agenda. Such diaspora is revealed in the following data.

Between 1970 and 1980, U.S. society became increasingly multiracial, multicultural, and multilingual. The demographic trend shows that in these ten years the total population of the United States grew by 11.6%. But when separated ethnically and racially, there emerges a demographic picture of minority groups galloping ahead of the rest of the European American and non-Hispanic population. During that decade, Hispanics increased by 61%, Native Americans by 71% (Cortés, 1986, pp. 8-9) and Asian Americans by 141% (Banks, 1987, p. 412).

Between 1980 and 1990, the total U.S. population grew by 9.8%, Whites only grew by 6.0%, while African Americans grew by 13.2%, American Indians (including Eskimo and Aleut) by 37.9%, Asian and Pacific Islanders by 107.8%, Hispanic Americans by 53% and "Others" by 45. 1% (NABE, n.d., p. 1). Increased immigration from both Latin America and Asia as well as high fertility rates within these populations are the major factors contributing to this recent demographic shift.

California, with its large language minority population, has become the Ellis Island of the 1980s. By the year 2000, the state is projected to have a minority population between 40% and 50% (Cortés, 1986, p. 9). If these figures are examined in relation to school-age populations, it is projected that in the year 2000, 52% of students in California will be ethnic minorities. This is not surprising, considering that as recently as 1985 California's minorities represented "47 percent of the 4.15 million students, including more than one-half million limited English proficient students" (Cortés, 1986, p. 10).

The 1990 Census indicated a total resident U.S. population of 248.7 million. Broken down ethnically, there were 30 million African Americans (12%), 9.7 million Asian Americans (3%), 2.0 million American Indians (0.8%), 22.4 million Hispanic Americans (9%), and 9.8 million "Others" (3.9%) (Barringer, 1991, p. 1). Moreover, according to Banks, Cones, Gay, Garcia, and Ochoa (1991),

> . . . the 1990 Census revealed that one out of every four people who live in the United States is a person of color and that one out of every three will be a person of color by the turn of the century. Likewise, the ethnic and racial make-up of the nation's classrooms is changing significantly. Students of color constitute a majority in twenty-five of the nation's largest school districts. They . . . will make up nearly half (46%) of the nation's school-age youth by 2020, and about 27% of those students will be victims of poverty. (p. 1)

Again, the educational challenge of this demographic shift is captured in the following statement by Banks, et al. (1991):

One important implication of these demographic trends is that education in the 21st century must help low-income students and students of color to develop the knowledge, attitudes, and skills necessary to participate in the workforce and in society. This goal is not possible without restructuring schools, colleges, and universities and institutionalizing new goals and ideals within them. As currently conceptualized and organized, schools today are unable to help most low-income students and students of color attain these goals.

Another important implication of the demographic imperative is that students from all social groups, i.e., class, racial, ethnic, cultural, and gender groups, must attain the knowledge, skills, and competencies necessary to participate in public discourse and civic action with people who differ from them in significant ways. People are socialized within families and in communities where they learn the values, perspectives, attitudes, and behaviors of their primordial cultures. Community culture enables people to survive. It also, however, restricts their freedom and ability to make critical choices and to reform their society. (p. 1)

Suggestions such as those proposed by Banks and others to conceptualize and implement more culturally compatible classroom practices have often drawn swift and strong reactions from individuals who interpret such goals as being politically motivated and divisive. Short (1988), for example, in his article . . . Diversity' and 'Breaking the Disciplines': Two New Assaults on the Curriculum," suggests that

> . . . there is the familiar charge that the traditional curriculum unjustly neglects the contributions of women, black Americans, and other ethnic groups. This charge is much weakened by the current celebration of inferior works chosen simply on the basis of the race or sex of their authors. Better works by women and blacks have long been included in the traditional curriculum. However, the real error lies in the inference that is drawn. The alleged neglect of the contributions of women and blacks does not entail charges that the traditional curriculum represents a culture peculiar to white men. (p. 10)

Educators who, based on research findings in cognitive psychology and linguistics, have advocated bilingual education for limited English proficient students have likewise drawn very negative reactions to their proposals. Again, Schlesinger (1992) echoes in a strident tone his feelings toward the role that bilingual education, as part of multicultural schooling, plays in the potential decomposition of the United States:

> Alas, bilingualism has not worked out as planned: rather the contrary. Testimony is mixed, but indications are that bilingual education retards rather than expedites the movement of Hispanic children into the English-speaking world and that it promotes segregation more than it does integration. Bilingualism shuts doors. It nourishes self-ghettoization, and ghettoization nourishes racial antagonism. Bilingualism "encourages concentrations of Hispanics to stay together and not be integrated," says Alfredo Mathew, Jr., a Hispanic civic leader, and it may well foster "a type of apartheid that will generate animosities with others, such as Blacks in the competition for scarce resources, and further alienate the Hispanic from the larger society."
>
> Using some language other than English dooms people to second-class citizenship in American society. (p. 108)

Unlike McCarty's holistic and intertwined view of culture, Short's and Schlesinger's critiques of multiculturalism as being politically motivated and divisive, reveal in bold relief a paradox associated with the "we" and "they" notion of multiculturalism. That is, they proclaim that national unity can be achieved only if history and culture are not used by minorities for political, therapeutic, and cheerleading aims. For all their good intentions the "we" and "they" view of culture *ipso facto* creates tension and irritancy among both sides— something that neither Short nor Schlesinger wants. Conversely, McCarty's web-like notion of culture, in which the many (*pluribus*) and the one (*unum*) are mutually dependent entities, is much more inclusive.

Disposable Culture and a Paradox of Disposability: McCarty

I am also concerned that a good deal of our musings about culture are made more difficult by conceiving of culture as itself a form of information or as something fully encodable in such a form. I am thinking of forms of information so as to include words, sentences, theories, pictures, anything fully transmittable from a source to a receiver. I am afraid that, in our desire to encourage multicultural education, we are tempted to think that what is called "cultural knowledge" can be fully represented in textbooks or as museum displays or as videotapes or, perhaps, as all of these together. This is natural since it is through information-bearing media that we first strive to acquaint our children with other cultures. Once again, anthropologist E. T. Hall affords a good example of the tendency to an "informational" reading of culture. He wrote, "The principal point to remember concerning high and low context communication is that a considerable part of the [cultural] message is already encoded in the receiver" (Hall, 1989, p. 38).

1 am worried by this because a notion of culture to which informational ideas are attached, an idea I call "culture as disposable" is, at best faulty and, at worst, inconsistent or paradoxical. By "disposable" in this sentence, I do not necessarily mean "treatable as refuse." Rather, when culture is conceived as disposable, it is seen as subject to our **dispositions**, subject to manipulation, shaping, and displacement under individual or bureaucratic control. This is the way the word "disposable" works in the expression "disposable income." The Latin root of the word, the verb "disponere" already points in the right semantic direction: "disponere" means "to arrange or to alter in place." It speaks already about a thing of limited permanence, open to transmission, bearing no intrinsic relation to a particular location. (The story of "disponere" is, by the way, a fine example of one of Hegel's cultural intersections. With this word, I find myself "a home within the alien.") So, if culture is completely representable as information—as messages to be sent or stored—then it is obvious that culture is disposable, is subject to group or to individual whim, to the enhancements, reinterpretations, corruptions to which all information, all messaging, is subject.

But, as the spatial metaphors surrounding culture rightly reflect, something is badly amiss in the mere suggestion that culture be disposable. Again, there is a cross-cultural clue to what I mean waiting in the word "culture" itself and in its historical relation to "agriculture" and "horticulture." "Culture," in the Latin "cultura" and "cultus," names what comes from the care of the soil in a place. Culture is, therefore, connected intrinsically with place. But here I do not mean simple physical or geographic place. I refer as well to linguistic, techno-logical, and ideological mastery of place; as in Gadamer's paraphrase of Hegel, culture is the means of getting around in a place, of making it one's very own. To make a home in the alien is to exercise a mastery there. And this mastery, these techniques for "getting around" in a place, are not wholly representable in textbook accounts, in travelogues, or in museum displays. They are not information for me to dispose.

It may not be obvious that "ways of making a place one's own" are not translatable completely into forms of information. You may be tempted to object that one can always draw maps of new places. One can even take pictures. In response, I remind you that maps and drawings and accounts and pictures are not culturally neutral entities. They are themselves cultural artifacts. We must know how to read them and how to apply them and that, too, is part of "getting around in a place." You should notice, also, that the ability to read a picture is not just an ability to see the picture. One has to **see the important things** in the picture. Think, in this case, of meteorological charts or medieval maps, wherein—to our eyes—decoration and geography are thoroughly mixed. Can we always see what is important in these? You cannot respond, now, by saying, "Well, I will just include instructions on reading the maps and pictures and charts." These are themselves more items to be read, themselves no more transparent or self-intimating than the original maps and drawings and the means to read these; to "find our way around in them," is no more informational than they are. To every culture there is, therefore, something noninformational, something to be conceived as an intrinsic, nontransmittable orientation to a place.

This insight, if unheeded, has the effect of making certain approaches to multiculturalism seem paradoxical. I might even say that, if we think of culture completely on the disposable model, as something available transparently through textbooks, through schools as institutions of discursive learning, through pieces of information transmitted to students, then the more we succeed in putting cultures across to our students, the more we falsify and obscure those cultures. The more we succeed in encoding cultures, even European cultures, as forms of information, as sets of beliefs to be inculcated, the more we prove unfaithful to the very cultures we hope to convey. This is because of the essentially non-informational, orientative aspect of every culture. I am afraid, then, that the effort made to squeeze a culture into a textbook is in effect, sending this metamessage to the student: "This is all there is to culture, what you see in this book. Multiculturalism is a course like mathematics or accounting. It is another batch of information to be "taken in" and "processed." But culture is, in itself, not disposable and to treat it in this way is to corrupt it.

This raises our final questions, "If I am not to reduce a knowledge of culture to texts, to artifacts, to images to be put before my students, then what am I to do in the classroom? How are alternative cultures to be taught?" In answer, I refer to an idea of Helmholtz, one also taken up by Gadamer, the idea of **Takt**. In its original form, the idea of Takt in Helmholtz was applied to the understanding of historical periods relatively distant in time from our own, but its extension to contemporary alternative cultures is immediate. I must caution you not to conflate Takt with its English cognate, tact. Tact, in the latter sense, is that by which we navigate the waters of privileged conversation and matters diplomatic. Takt in Gadamer is the development of that non-subjective potential in all of us by which we can obey Hegel's command, find our own homes in the alien and return to ourselves in those homes. Takt, then, is a geographic facility, a way of looking around. It is not uninformed looking or openmouthed gaping. It draws aid from information, from maps and guides, but cannot be replaced by them. Gadamer (1990) writes of Takt "as keeping oneself open to what is other— to other, more universal points of view. It embraces a sense of proportion and distance in relation to itself, and hence consists in rising above itself to universality" (p. 17).

The architectural coloring of Gadamer's remark is no accident. The education of Takt is the construction in oneself of an aesthetic discernment. And a technical knowledge (of art) is surely relevant to the learning of discernment. But that is not all. For Takt, one's eyes must be fully open and one must also be, as Gadamer wrote, "open to what is other."

But this openness is as much a moral virtue as a cognitive attainment. To repeat, I have compared a culture to a particular mastery of a place and, to attain that mastery, I must develop a sense of local direction. That is, I have to be able to learn the **right** way to travel thereabouts. And, for Gadamer as for Hegel, Takt is not just a way to get around in strange places. I quote from Gadamer (1990) again:

> For the Takt which functions in the human sciences is not simply a feeling and unconscious, but is at the same time a mode of knowing and mode of being.... What Helmholtz calls Takt includes edification and is a function of both aesthetic and historical learning. (pp. 16-17)

Thus, Gadamer's Takt will **include** proper edification and, so, will take formal education as a proper part. This is to say that, if we understand education in the right way—as a looking across to other paths and a turning around to see what lies behind on our own path—then all education will be multicultural.

Ovando's Response to McCarty's Discussion of Disposable Culture and Takt

McCarty's discussion of the flawed concept of disposable culture embodies for me a similar zero-sum notion as the isolation chamber metaphor. The disposable image of culture prompts teachers to ask questions such as "What should I leave out of the existing curriculum in order to teach multiculturalism?" When such questions are asked, they suggest a view of culture as being transmitted piecemeal and that transmitting one thing means leaving something else out. What McCarty suggests to me is that teaching students about cultures—and about different cultures—does not mean that at all. It means cultivating in students a certain meta-awareness of the complexities of cultural differences. By "meta-awareness" I mean giving students a chance to experience the deeper meanings of cultural practices—to be able to stand back and reflect not only on what culture is but how cultural tendencies fit into the larger web or webs. It is giving the students a mountain-top view of their culture but also of the surrounding valleys, mountains, rivers, streams, clouds, and trees. As such the learning of cultural details (such as festivities, eating habits, and discourse patterns) becomes incidental to the fundamental goal of giving students a chance to experience the deeper meanings of cultural processes. Such a deep and complex view of culture is captured by Geertz (1973) when he says:

> Believing, with Max Weber, that man is an animal suspended in webs of significance he himself has spun, I take culture to be those webs, and the analysis of it to be therefore not an experimental science in search of law but an interpretive one in search of meaning.
>
> Cultural analysis is intrinsically incomplete. And, worse than that, the more deeply it goes the less complete it is. It is a strange science whose most telling assertions are its most tremulously based, in which to get somewhere with the matter at hand is to intensify suspicion, both your own and that of others, that you are not quite getting it right.... Anthropology, or at least interpretive anthropology, is a science whose progress

is marked less by a perfection of consensus than by a refinement of debate. What gets better is the precision with which we vex each other. (pp. 5, 29)

Viewing culture this way also means that making students aware of differences is tantamount to teaching them about themselves. Exposing a student from a small rural community in the American Midwest to information about the subsistence lifestyles of Athapaskan Indians in Nulato, Alaska is also enabling the student to learn about herself and her place in the human web of paths. Seen in this way it is difficult to see what is being "sacrificed"— what of ourselves is being lost—when we learn about others. From a teacher's point of view, this non-disposable, the Takt, view of culture would mean emphasizing the interactions of humans with their environment. The folklorist, Henry Glassie (1992), captures the opposite of our view of culture. He believes that culture is constructed completely from experience, whereas we believe that we are born into a culture. (For instance, a person could not construct a language alone even if she or he wanted to do so).

A person is not born into a culture, a person is born into a room and in that room that person begins to assemble little hints, bright lights, warm touches and out of those hints, out of those experiences, this little person becomes a big person and that big person has accumulated more of those experiences and out of those experiences that person has accumulated a thing we can call culture, because that person will share it with other persons who have gone through a similar series of experiences. (p. 12)

Sharing common experiences with kindred spirits, however, is only part of the cultural iceberg. Meaningful and creative cultural dialogue also requires a certain amount of existential dissonance. I believe that it is when similarities and dissimilarities are shared in the spirit of transmitting and receiving that cross-cultural communication is at its best. In essence, then, cultural transmission, analysis, and acceptance are complex processes that entail being culture-bearers and culture-makers. In U.S. society this means identifying and understanding how fundamental core values serve as the nuclei around which a galaxy of contested micro values shape the macro culture.

Contested Core Values in U.S. Society

Dialogue is possible because we have shared and nonshared experiences and values that make the conversation potentially interesting, rich, and desirable. Dialogue, moreover, requires openness and vulnerability to other cultures and lives. Dialogues at their best are not instruments of colonization or domestication. This, for me is what McCarty means by the ubiquitous nature of intersecting paths. It is possible through dialogue to find niches, if not homes, in other cultures. On the point of needing shared and dissimilar points of view in order to create dialogue, the Spindlers (1990) have identified a set of contested core values in U.S. society around which a good portion of cultural dialogue in this country can take place. George and Louise Spindler, educational anthropologists, have spent a lifetime examining the complex role that formal schooling plays in the transmission of cultural values in multicultural contexts. The Spindlers describe the dynamic process of contested core values as follows:

The cultural mainstream is defined by the American cultural dialogue. This dialogue pivots around independence, freedom, conformity, success, community, optimism,

42

idealism, materialism, technology, nature, work, and other value orientations and their permutations and oppositions. This dialogue goes on and has gone on since the Revolution. Immigrants and those rising from lower socioeconomic ranks assimilate, appropriate, and acquire this dialogue as they become mainstream. This assimilative process will go on, for it is the American ethos, the central process of American culture and society. Ethnicity is not lost but participation is gained. However, ethnicity is reshaped. (pp. x-xii)

. . . The balancing of assimilation and preservation of identity is constant and full of conflict. This is part of the American dialogue and it has always been a part of this dialogue. It is the nature of cultural dialogues that they rationalize, deny, defend, protest, and exhibit. (p. xii)

In 1963 George Spindler wrote an article titled "Education in a Transforming America." There he examined the challenges to the core values by "several hundred students enrolled in professional education courses representing lower-middle-class to upper-middle-class socioeconomic status in the early 1960s" (Pai, 1990, p. 27). Based on the findings of this study, Spindler concluded that the traditional core values were in fact being questioned and modified to reflect the changing nature of U.S. society (Pai, 1990, p. 27). According to Pai's interpretation of the study by Spindler,

. . . the core values of college students had shifted considerably from those of their parents. Unlike their parents, the subjects held as their core values (1) sociability, (2) a relativistic moral attitude, (3) consideration for others, (4) a hedonistic present-time orientation, and (5) conformity to the group. (p. 27)

The fluid and shifting-sand characterization of U.S. cultural values that George Spindler documented in the 1960s has been further documented by other social scientists. Such research covering the periods from the mid-1960s to early 1980s is summarized by Pai (1990, pp. 28-32). The gist of these studies is that change in cultural values is a constant in U.S. society and that schools do play an important role in the transmission of such values. This change, in turn, is catalyzed by such variables as social stratification, politics, religious values, technology, demographics, economics, and ideology. For example, as noted earlier, demographic trends continue to change dramatically the character of the society. As the United States becomes more pluralistic, the debate as to what it means to be an American intensifies. Nunis (1981), for instance, states that

For the first time in American experience, some concerned observers have pointed out, a large immigrant group may be electing to bypass the processes of acculturation and assimilation that turned previous immigrant groups into English-speaking Americans. (p. 24)

Likewise, Glazer (1981) points out that

. . . most American parents liked what the public schools were offering. Most had come to this country not to maintain a foreign language and culture but with the intention, in the days when the trip to the United States was long and expensive, to become Americans as fast as possible, and this meant English language and American culture. They sought the induction to new language and culture that the public schools provided—as do many present-day immigrants, too—and while they often found, as time went on, that they regretted what they and their children had lost, this was **their** choice, rather than an imposed choice. And every choice involves regret for the path not taken. (pp. 61-62)

This tension between those who wish to assimilate and those who wish to acculturate into the mainstream culture is further illustrated by the changing use of metaphors. Thus, for example, the melting pot metaphor, so valued rhetorically in the past, is in disrepute because of its highly discriminatory track record toward racially and linguistically stigmatized groups. As Jessie Jackson, one of the leading African American political figures in the United States, has said, "Blacks were stuck on the side of the pot and never melted." Today, instead, many ethnic and racial minorities feel that it is possible and desirable to maintain contact with one's ancestral cultural and linguistic roots while adhering to shared democratic practices in the society. Havighurst (1978) refers to this process as "constructive pluralism" and defines it as follows:

a. Mutual appreciation and understanding of every subculture by the other ones;
b. Freedom for each subculture to practice its culture and socialize its children;
c. Sharing by each group in the economic and civic life of the society;
d. Peaceful coexistence of diverse life styles, folkways, manners, language patterns, religious beliefs and practices, and family structures. (p. 13)

Today the "American mosaic" and the "salad bowl" metaphors have emerged as contenders for the subtractive and zero-sum game notion associated with the "melting pot" metaphor. To date, the contest between these opposing metaphors has produced much ideological irritancy in the society. Yet, a basic point remains as documented by the Spindlers: schools continue to be paramount instruments of cultural transmission regardless of what the cultural mix is.

My own position is that schooling processes that allow **all** children (minority and non-minority) to become successful participants in the educational process can help mend social and economic tears in the national fabric. For a democratic, pluralistic, and complex society to function true to its underlying premises, its members need an awareness of their responsibilities as citizens, and they need skills to carry out these responsibilities. Learning to get along in a multicultural society should be an imperative of the schooling process, not a neglected option. Of course, carrying out the above is not easy even when there is the desire for cultural dialogue. For example, an existing paradox of multicultural education centers around the desire to produce cultural knowledge that can be transmitted to others. The assumption is that through provision of cultural information, cross-cultural communication can be enhanced. But when cultural knowledge is transmitted it can become a source of stereotypical frameworks that discredit the truly fluid, complex, and three-dimensional nature of culture. Still, I believe it is possible for non-mainstream students to achieve integrative acculturation—a creative and eclectic synthesis of both the mainstream and the home culture—if we accept conceptually the path-like view of culture proposed by McCarty.

In all this, I believe that teachers play a key role in contextualizing children's identity formation. The role of multicultural teachers then becomes one in which they are creators of situations in which students can have meaningful experiences and conversations with others representing different cultures: between students and students; students and teachers; students and texts or authors; and students and people in the community. However, because most of us are used to associating predominantly with culturally kindred spirits, moving away from this cultural comfort zone will not be easy. There will often be more than just ethnic, linguistic, or racial barriers—there are, for example, potential social, political, gender, regional, and age barriers. Such barriers do tend to inhibit the desire for participation in culturally mediated negotiations. Yet, as the following examples will help illustrate, this type of instruction is possible and pedagogically defensible.

Let us say that a teacher is developing a set of lessons on the 500th anniversary of Christopher Columbus's voyage to America. If the teacher is interested in enabling students to visualize cultures in a more dynamic, complex, and path-like manner, just what could she do? In the culture-as-isolation-chamber/culture-as-disposable-model, a teacher in the 1990s might teach students that white Anglo-Saxon Protestants have one interpretation of what happened; indigenous groups, another; the Spaniards, another; the British, another, and so on. The learning objective might be that students know how these different groups have viewed that event.

But in culture-as-intersecting paths/culture-as-Takt, the teacher would have a slightly different agenda. The teacher would want the students to learn and think about the ways these groups communicated with each other (or didn't) and how this dialogue continues today. Nearly 500 years later, in 1990, what has led 300 American Indians from North, South, and Central America to gather in Ecuador to participate in the First Continental Conference of Indigenous Peoples? What did these indigenous persons have to say about the impact that Columbus' legacy had on their cultures, their human rights, and their environment? Why have the Lakotas of South Dakota decided to celebrate October 12 as "Indian Day" instead of "Columbus Day"? The video, *Columbus Didn't Discover Us*, could provide students with some American Indian perspectives on the above questions. There are many questions here, but questions are crucial to dialogue, and with such related questions about the past and the present, for example, teachers can reduce the breakdown of cross-cultural communication among contemporary groups.

Having suggested the above pedagogical strategy as a way to start a meaningful cultural conversation, a caveat is in order. A truly multicultural education about Columbus is not achieved by one or another rearrangement of supposed "information." A truly multicultural education requires that the student gain an appreciation of cultural details. This kind of appreciation, however, is not engendered by books and lesson plans alone. Both teachers and students must be authentic culture-bearers and culture-makers of a specific kind. As such, teachers and students can be seen as gift-giving embodiments to each other of cultural processes.

McCarty and I would like to end with another caveat taken from Mexican author Carlos Fuentes' article, "The mirror of the other." In it he captures for us beautifully the life-giving and interdependent characteristics of cultural processes when he writes: "People and their cultures perish in isolation, but they are born or reborn in contact with other men and women" (1992, p. 410). Multiculturalism in U.S. society and in its schools can become a source of life and vibrancy rather than a nagging irritant or paradox. To ignore such a possibility is not only to miss a life-giving opportunity but to court disaster.

Endnotes

[1]This paper was first presented at the World Council for Curriculum and Instruction, Seventh Triennial World Conference, held at Mena House Oberoi, Cairo, Egypt, from July 25 to August 2, 1992.

[2]I wish to credit the useful suggestions and insightful comments of Amy Andrews, a graduate student in the School of Education at Indiana University, Bloomington.

References

Bachelard, G. (1984). *The new scientific spirit.* (A. Goldhammer, Trans.). Boston: Beacon Press. (Original work published in 1934)

Banks, J. A. (1987). *Teaching strategies for ethnic studies* (4th ed.). Boston: Allyn and Bacon.

Banks, J. A., & Banks, C. A. M. (Eds.). (1989). *Multicultural education: Issues and perspectives.* Boston: Allyn and Bacon.

Banks, J., Cones, C. E., Gay, G., Garcia, R. L., & Ochoa, A. S. (1991). *The NCSS task force on ethnic studies curriculum guidelines* (rev. ed.). A National Council for the Social Studies Position Statement. Washington, DC.

Barringer, F. (1991, March 11). Census shows profound change in racial makeup of the nation. *The New York Times,* pp. 1, A-12.

Carter, R. (1991, Fall). The diversity debate and independent schools. *Multicultural Update.*

Cortés, C. E. (1986). The education of language minority students: A contextual interaction model. In California State Department of Education. *Beyond language: Social and cultural factors in schooling language minority students.* Los Angeles: Evaluation, Dissemination, and Assessment Center, California State University.

Cummins, J. (1992). Foreword. In S. Nieto, *Affirming diversity: The sociocultural context of multicultural education.* New York: Longman.

Fuentes, C. (1992, March). The mirror of the other. *The Nation,* p. 410.

Gadamer, H. G. (1990). *Truth and method* (2nd, rev. ed.). (J. Weinsheimer & D. G. Marshall, Trans.). New York: Crossroad Publishing. (Original work published 1960)

Geertz, C. (1973). *The interpretation of cultures.* New York: Basic Books.

Glassie, H. (1992, June). First thoughts. In I. G. Carpenter & C. Nelson (Co-chairs), *Cultural basics: Educating with the grain.* Bloomington: Indiana University Folklore Institute.

Glazer, N. (1981). Pluralism and ethnicity. In M. Ridge (Ed.), *The new bilingualism: An American dilemma* (pp. 55-70). Los Angeles: University of Southern California Press.

Hall, E. T. (1989). Unstated features of the cultural context of learning. *The Educational Forum, 54,* 21-34.

Havighurst, R. J. (1978). Structural aspects of education and cultural pluralism. *Educational Research Quarterly, 2*(4), 5-19.

Hegel, G. (1977). *Phenomenology of spirit.* (A. Miller, Trans.). New York: Oxford University Press. (Original work published 1807)

Heidegger, M. (n.d.). *What is philosophy?* (W. Kluback & J. Wilde, Trans.). Albany, NY: New College and University Press. (Original work published 1956)

Kincheloe, J. L., & Pinar, W. F. (1991). *Curriculum as social psychoanalysis: The significance of place.* Albany: State University of New York Press.

National Association for Bilingual Education. (n.d.). Fact sheet: Need for additional funding for the federal bilingual education act. Washington, DC. Author.

Nieto, S. (1992). *Affirming diversity: The sociocultural context of multicultural education.* New York: Longman.

Nunis, D. B., Jr. (1981). Bilingualism and biculturalism: A time for assessment. In M. Ridge (Ed.), *The new bilingualism: An American dilemma* (pp. 23-27). Los Angeles: University of Southern California Press.

Ovando, C. J. (1990). Intermediate and secondary school curricula: A multicultural and multilingual framework. *The Clearing House, 63*(7), 294-298.

Pai, Y. (1990). *Cultural foundations of education.* Columbus, OH: Merrill.

Schlesinger, A.M., Jr. (1992). *The disuniting of America: Reflections on a multicultural society.* New York: Norton.

Short, T. (1988). Diversity and breaking the disciplines: Two new assaults on the curriculum. *Academic Questions, 1*(3).

Spindler, G., Spindler, L, Trueba, H., & Williams, M. C. (1990). *The American cultural dialogue and its transmission.* New York: The Falmer Press.

Spindler, G. D. (1963). Education in a transforming America. In G. D. Spindler, (Ed.), *Education and culture* (2nd ed.) (pp. 132-147). New York: Holt Rinehart & Winston.

Theobald, P. (1992). The concept of place in the new sociology of education. *Educational Foundations, 6*(1), 5-19.

CREATING INCLUSIVE AND MULTICULTURAL COMMUNITIES: WORKING THROUGH ASSUMPTIONS OF CULTURE, POWER, DIVERSITY, AND EQUITY

by
Brenda M. Rodriguez

What does it mean to create inclusive, multicultural communities, especially in our classrooms and institutions? For multicultural and inclusive education to move beyond its current rudimentary stage, we must examine our institutional and personal assumptions about culture, power, diversity, equity, and community. Without further reflection and understanding of these concepts, we will not be able to understand the strength multicultural, inclusive education brings to our pluralistic nation and world, nor will we be able to avoid the pitfalls of implementing multiculturalism in education and creating more inclusive school communities.

Culture

I like to define culture as the framework that guides and bounds life practices: it shapes everything we do. All of us are cultural beings, with culture influencing the development of our beliefs, perspectives, and behavior. According to Anderson and Fenichel (1989), our "cultural framework must be viewed as a set of tendencies or possibilities from which to choose (p. 8), not a rigidly prescribed set of assumptions. Cultural frameworks are constantly evolving and being reworked, and we are continuously observing and participating in events that shape our individual experience within those frameworks. Thus, although persons of the same cultural background share a readiness to act or think similarly, not all members of the group will behave in the same manner. Individuals may differ in the degree to which they choose to adhere to a set of cultural patterns. For instance, some individuals identify strongly with one particular group; others combine practices from several cultural groups. Either way, the multiple dimensions of culture help form an individual's identity. Because of variations within cultures and the multiple cultural groups within society, as well as individuals' different experiences of cultural events and responses to cultural influences, an appreciation and respect for both individual and cultural diversity is crucial for educators.

Self-Awareness

Everyone has a culture and belongs to multiple communities, but often individuals are not aware of the behaviors, habits, and customs that are culturally based (Athen, 1988). Becoming aware of our own cultures facilitates our capacity to:
- explore, understand, appreciate, and assess the many aspects of culture that make up our social background, including our ethnicity, social class, gender, geographic region, sexual orientation, exceptionality, age, and religion or mode of spirituality;
- increase our awareness and insight into our own learning processes, strengths, weaknesses, successes, failures, biases, values, goals, and emotions;
- experience our own cultures in relation to others as they are illuminated through cross-cultural interactions;

- understand and confront areas of conflict and tension when we encounter individuals from unfamiliar cultures and learn to become more comfortable with being uncomfortable;
- explore and appreciate thought processes that occur across cultures but may also take on different shapes and meanings for different cultural groups and for individual group members; and
- understand more deeply the cultural values and beliefs of those with whom we come in contact.

According to Hall (1976):

There is not one aspect of human life that is not touched and altered by culture. This means personality, how people express themselves (including shows of emotion), the way they think, how they move, how problems are solved, how their cities are planned and laid out, how transportation systems function and are organized, as well as how economic and government systems are put together and function. (pp. 16-17)

Although this is true for all people, Anglo-Europeans and some other European Americans who are part of the dominant or mainstream United States culture may have the least awareness of the ways their culture influences their behavior and interactions. They have predominated in this country, and their culture, customs, and habits have shaped and been acknowledged by themselves, as well as other ethnic groups, as shaping the society more than any other single group. In addition, the "melting pot" to which the United States aspired during the early waves of immigration took its toll on the diversity among European American groups, diminishing the distinctiveness of early immigrants' roots as they became mainstream members of the United States and deemphasizing their separate ethnic cultural heritages without noting that the process of joining the mainstream involved adopting or adapting to a new culture. This process results in an ethnocentrism and a notion of monoculturalism that is often not even recognized because it has been identified as the norm.

To understand and appreciate fully the diversity that exists among us, we must first understand and appreciate our own culture. Self-awareness (Tiedt & Tiedt, 1990) is the first step toward cross-cultural competence or capacity.[1] But how does cultural self-awareness begin? What are the steps we can take to achieve it? How does cultural self-awareness lead to improved understanding of other cultures? And what does this understanding have to do with multicultural education?

Cultural self-awareness begins with an exploration of our own heritage, encounters, and experiences. Place of origin, language(s) spoken, time and reasons for immigration, relocation, or colonization, and the place of the family's first settlement, as well as geographic relocations and movement within the United States, all help to define one's cultural heritage. The political leanings, jobs, status, beliefs, religions, and values of one's first peoples, as well as whether they were voluntary or involuntary immigrants, help portray a cultural picture of one's family. Also contributing to this portrait are the economic, ethnic, political, religious, social, and vocational changes that subsequent generations have undergone. Another important factor is a recognition of how one's cultural group relates to the mainstream culture of the United States and how it is or has been reflected through history.

Perhaps the most enriching way to gather this information is through the recollections of the oldest family members as they tell stories of their early lives and the lives of their grandparents and great grandparents. When it is possible, oral history provides a wonderful bridge between generations and can be supplemented by photographs, journals, family albums, or notes and letters about important events.

Learning about one's own roots is the first step in determining how one's values, beliefs, group or collective consciousness, customs, and behaviors have been shaped by culture. Frequently, we learn the shaping reflects not one culture but multiple cultures since we belong to multiple communities, communities identified by, for example, our ethnicity, religion, region, socioeconomic status, or gender. This knowledge helps us realize the ways of thinking, believing, and behaving we may have assumed to be universal, rigid, and static are actually based upon cultural beliefs and biases. When one has explored one's own cultural heritage, the second step of discovery can begin.

The second step is to examine in depth some of the values, behaviors, beliefs, and customs that are identified with one's own cultural heritage (in its broadest sense). Educators and students will be better prepared to learn about diverse cultures if they are first certain of the significance of their own identity. It is also important, particularly for educators, to understand how their own cultural assumptions about education and educational institutions, and about teaching and learning influence what they teach, how they teach it, and how they relate to students. Cultural self-awareness is the bridge to other cultures. To be truly sensitive to someone else's culture, we must be sensitive to our own and to the impact cultural frameworks, customs, values, beliefs, and behaviors have on education.

Cross-Cultural Sensitivity/Awareness

Because the reality of a pluralistic society and world is confronting us so much more quickly and tangibly than previously, many individuals are converging to classes, in-services, and special programs to learn all there is to know about other cultures. We approach cultural learning and related issues in the tradition of our U.S./Western educational culture and history: with the notion that we can attend a class or seminar and digest all we need to know in a few sessions to achieve cross-cultural knowledge. In the workshops and training I conduct, I am continually reminding and cautioning participants against overgeneralizing or characterizing cultural groups in a rigid, unidimensional, and static way.

Earlier, we discussed what culture is, but it is equally important to understand what it is not. Culture **is not**:

- mere artifacts or materials used by people;
- a laundry list of behaviors, values, and facts;
- the pseudo-biological or pseudo-scientific trait of "race";
- the ideal and romantic heritage or experience of a people as seen through music, myths, dance, holidays, and folklore;
- stereotypic depictions of groups as seen in television, movies, newspapers, and other media;
- objects to be bought, sold, and distributed;
- generalized explanations about the behavior, emotions, or values of groups of people applied to individuals; or
- higher class status derived from a knowledge of arts, manners, literature.

Consequently, cultural capacity or awareness **is not** becoming a member of another culture by a superficial, wholesale adoption of elements, such as customs, language, dress, or behavior, of that group's culture. Such shallow identification could "be manipulative and patronizing" (Green, 1982, p. 52) and could suggest that changing one's own cultural identity is easy. Culture encompasses values, attitudes, and beliefs as well as customs and behaviors. While the latter can be readily adopted, the former requires deeper and more fundamental awareness and changes. Additionally, cultural capacity recognizes that individuals cannot be categorized into totally discrete groups and that much variability within cultural groups exists. Cultural identification is a complex network of intertwining cultural influences that frames individuals' identities and values and influences their choices and behavior in continually evolving and dynamic ways.

Being culturally competent or aware does not mean knowing everything about every culture. It is, instead, respect for difference, eagerness to learn, and a willingness to accept that there are many ways of viewing the world. As Anderson and Fenichel (1989) relate:

> Cultural sensitivity cannot mean knowing everything there is to know about every culture that is represented in a population to be served. At its most basic level, cultural sensitivity implies, rather, knowledge that cultural differences as well as similarities exist. . . . Cultural sensitivity further means being aware of the cultures represented in one's state or region and learning about some of the general parameters of those cultures. . . . Cultural knowledge helps a professional to be aware of possibilities and to be ready to respond appropriately. (pp. 8-9)

Culture is akin to being the observer through a one-way mirror; everything we see is from our own perspective. It is only when we join the observed on the other side that it is possible to see ourselves and others clearly, but getting to the other side of the glass presents many challenges. As Storti (1989) so aptly stated in *The Art of Crossing Cultures*: "The old proverb notwithstanding, we cannot put ourselves in someone else's shoes; or, rather, we can, but it's still our own feet we will feel" (p. 51). Although it may be impossible to feel or experience what someone else is feeling, becoming more culturally sensitive can help us as educators understand, appreciate, and support our students and colleagues more effectively.

Achieving cultural sensitivity or cross-cultural capacity requires that we lower our defenses, take risks, and practice behaviors that may feel unfamiliar and uncomfortable. It requires a flexible mind, an open heart, and a willingness to accept alternative perspectives. It may mean setting aside some cherished beliefs to make room for others whose value is unknown. It may mean changing what we think, what we say, and how we behave, even acknowledging that we have learned and taught untruths, myths, and misinformation about ourselves and others that affect our own and their beliefs and identities. The rewards, however, are significant: bridging disparate cultures, knowing more about ourselves, and becoming more effective interpersonally.

Power, Privilege, and Diversity

Diversity is about difference. But how does difference impact our daily lives as educators and members of communities? Audre Lorde (1984) poignantly describes difference as something that is feared in our society.

> Institutionalized rejection of **difference** is an absolute necessity in a profit economy which needs outsiders as surplus people. As members of such an economy, we have **all** been programmed to respond to human differences between us with fear and loathing

and to handle that difference in one of three ways: ignore it, and if that is not possible, copy it if we think it is dominant, or destroy it if we think it is subordinate. But we have no patterns for relating across our human differences as equals. As a result, those differences have been misnamed and misused in the service of separation and confusion. (p. 115)

Frequently, educators have taken a safer and simpler approach to diversity than Lorde's call to relate "across our human differences as equals." We have chosen instead to celebrate discrete aspects of different cultures, i.e. holidays and individuals who excel in some way. Although this is not wrong, it is inadequate in a society that is stratified on the basis of conceptions of race, ethnicity, gender, and socioeconomic class. We need to look at diversity issues as they relate to issues of power and oppression. In the classroom with young people and in workshops among adults, differences exist—differences in gender, ethnic heritage, age, physical ability, economic class, and sexual orientation, among others. Some differences are visible, some we look for automatically, some we may pretend not to see. But all of them are used to separate us along lines of power. This power takes the form of access to resources, work, housing, education, physical security, protection by law, and representation in government. This power is institutionalized discrimination. And while some groups are socially sanctioned to be powerful, they are permitted to have their power at the expense of other groups whose access to resources is correspondingly limited or denied. Examples of such unequal power relationships are evident between landowners and migrant workers, males and females, and students in well-financed suburban school districts and those in underfunded inner city schools.

The social perspective from which I conduct my training and teaching is that the primary root of violence in the United States is the systematic, institutionalized day-to-day imbalance of power. This means that social groups—most recognizably women, children, people of color, workers, and others who do not have power equal to that enjoyed by those wielding the greatest amount of power in our society—have less control over their lives and are often targets of physical and sexual violence, discrimination, harassment, and poverty at home, in the workplace, and in the wider community.

The reason issues of power have to be addressed by educators is that patterns of power imbalances are continually renewed through the socialization of each generation of young people. When children in this country learn about the groups of people different from themselves through misinformation, distortions, jokes, stereotypes, history, and biased research and textbooks, they are being taught to justify, enforce, and continue the power differences. Frequently, they are learning to hate. This is how our society, including our educational institutions, creates "-isms" such as, racism, classism, sexism, heterosexism, ethnocentrism, and ableism. These -isms refer to prejudice, stereotypes, and discriminatory actions that are systematically perpetuated or enforced by those with more power, authority, and resources to their advantage. Supported by institutions, cultural attitudes, and values, these -isms have far-reaching effects on people's lives.

Systemic power is one critical element that makes -isms much different and more complex than prejudice, stereotypes, and discrimination alone. Because the institutions of family, education, work, business, religion, housing, law, and government in which we are raised sustain these -isms, the inequality they sanction is accepted as normal, goes unnoticed, or is easily denied. But it is precisely because inequality is institutionalized that the mistreatment of nonpower groups is so complete. And since the institutional imbalance is in one direction—power over nonpower—it is counterproductive to use concepts like "reverse racism" or "reverse sexism." Individuals in a nonpower group can stereotype or have prejudices about people in a power group. They can act aggressively toward them, but the power imbalance between them nonetheless targets nonpower groups. Nonpower groups do not have the social power and command of resources to limit the powerful or protect themselves from system-wide violence and discrimination.

We cannot expect to support each other and young people in unlearning the myths of inequality unless we are prepared to assist them and ourselves in unlearning all the -isms while modeling other examples of behavior and value. We must understand that our differences do not cause the institutional power imbalances; they are used to **justify** already existing imbalances. People do not earn mistreatment because they are darker-skinned, Latino, women, or have disabilities. Nothing natural or biological about these differences causes oppression.

Once we begin addressing the issues of power and social inequities, the concomitant aspect of privilege must also be explored. Privilege is an unearned right or resource that one group has access to that other groups are denied. Because it is unearned, we are often unaware of the privileges that we might have. And since we apparently have always had them, they seem normal (See McIntosh, 1988). Consider the privileges we exercise as adults, as educators, as able-bodied persons, as men, as persons with light skin, as gentiles, or as heterosexuals. How are these privileges connected to our fears of loss of control or our notions of power? These questions have no set answers; they are contested as people in our society struggle to decide how to treat each other.

Equity

What is equity? How should it be defined within a democratic, pluralistic society? Issues of power and privilege impact our construction of equity and compel us to question how they are related to multicultural education and inclusive schools. Secada characterizes equity in the following way:

> The heart of equity lies in our ability to acknowledge that, even though our actions might be in accord with a set of rules, their **results** may be unjust. Equity goes beyond following the rules, even if we have agreed that they are intended to achieve justice. . . . Educational equity . . . should be construed as a check on the justice of specific actions that are carried out within the educational arena and the arrangements that result from those actions. (quoted in Pignatelli and Pflaum, 1992, p. ix)

To struggle for equity sometimes means to struggle against the rules or the common assumptions of a community. When these struggles focus on multicultural issues, they raise community as well as individual passions and often prompt advocates and opponents alike to claim the moral high ground and mobilize the rhetoric of democracy. Such moves demand we be particularly sensitive to the personal and sometimes religious and moral values that drive persons to action. We must also be ready to assume a position of opposition, particularly to the negative and destructive practices within our own cultures. Logic, reason, theoretical commitments are not enough. Equity is a passionate issue and it must engage the passions of people who struggle for it, just as it releases the passions and fears of those who resist it. Struggles for equity often entail conflict and pain as power and privilege are rethought and redistributed, but the resistance and discomfort should lead to the greater recognition of basic human rights and to empowerment of individuals and the growth of community.

Envisioning Educational Communities

Theories of power and equity are implicitly theories of community. Acknowledging this encourages us to begin envisioning a new definition of power, one that focuses on empowerment and embraces the concept of power as energy, capacity, and potential rather than as domination. This is an image of power as the glue holding a community together, giving the people the opportunity "to act, to move, to change conditions, for the benefit of the whole population" (Lane, 1983). Under traditional conceptions of power as domination, justice requires that limits be placed on power and that a balance of power be achieved to mitigate the results of domination. Under conceptions of power as capacity, the goal is not to limit the power of some but to increase the power of all actors. To do this we need to develop strategies to counteract unequal power arrangements, strategies that recognize the potentiality for creating equal relations.

This conception of power as creative community energy recognizes that people need power, both as a way to maintain a strong and positive sense of self and as a way to accomplish ends (Janeway, 1980). Power can be used to enhance both autonomy and mutuality. To be empowered is to be able to "claim an education" as Adrienne Rich (1979) urges us. To be empowered is to act to create a more humane social order. To be empowered is to engage in significant learning. To be empowered is to connect with others in mutually productive ways.

A walk through a garden reveals a panoply of lovely plants—all varied in form, blossoms, and size. All share such basic needs as soil, water, and sunlight; yet each plant may have different needs as to the type of soil, amount of water, and the degree of sunlight required for life and growth. Each type of plant is of interest to the observer and offers its own beauty and special characteristics. However, seen together, as a whole, the plants form a wondrous garden to behold. (Hanson, 1992, p. 3)

Like the garden, communities are made up of individuals—all of whom contribute their own unique characteristics to the sense of place in which they live. However, communities are also highly interactive, dynamic settings where individuals are constantly interacting and responding to one another and where the characteristics of those individuals are being modified through those interactions.

Although communities are not static and generally are not planned, societies do have cultural mores and practices that guide human behavior and provide a socialization framework that shapes and directs interactions. In an educational community this framework is often described in the mission statement, a statement of purpose that should be driving the institution's decisions. That the mission statement address issues of diversity and equity is critical. Evidence suggests schools act as systems that continue to perpetuate patterns of hierarchy and an oppressive "power over" approach with their implicit valuing of certain groups of people over others. As educators and members of multiple communities, we need to dismantle these notions of **up/down**, **them/us**, and **power over** and to transform our relationships into partnerships where **power with** is the norm for our interactions.

Conclusion

Creating inclusive schools is an evolutionary process. What we are undoing did not happen overnight. These systems and ways of thinking have been deeply embedded in our societal psyche for a long time. Our society faces many legitimate concerns and profound challenges, challenges reminding us that schools exist and need to be understood within their sociopolitical contexts. Our schools exist in a society in which societal and economic stratification are facts of life, where competition is taught over caring, and where the early sorting (tracking) that takes place in our educational settings often lasts a lifetime. Supporting multicultural education and inclusive communities requires a very active process and a commitment to change that incorporates social justice as a major consideration of this process.

Single courses or step-by-step checklists to create this change do not exist. Understanding this can free us from frustration when we do not see a quick fix for the imbalances of power and privilege, the inequities we observe and experience as members of a less-than-perfect world. As educators, we have to prepare ourselves for the long haul. Creating inclusive schools and fostering multiculturalism in education involves an awareness that the very process of relating to one another is moving us toward more inclusive institutions, ones that encourage all members to succeed. We do not have to embark on this great mission by ourselves, but we must take individual responsibility in learning to teach in new ways and with new perspectives. We must enter other worlds of imagination, culture, and justice, of literacy, history, and communication, of science, psychology, and art to enrich ourselves and our teaching and to serve as models for others. This enrichment is at the heart of pluralism and excellence and at the core of equity and social justice. To further equity and social justice is our only responsible choice.

The challenge for the years ahead is to conquer our fear of change and difference and imagine how we might create and realize the exciting possibilities of equity for ourselves, our students, and our communities—one by one, step by step, voice by voice.

Endnote

[1] I prefer cultural capacity to cultural competence since competence suggests to me something that can be measured or evaluated.

References

Anderson, P. P., & Fenichel, E. S. (1989). *Serving culturally diverse families of infants and toddlers with disabilities.* Washington, DC: National Center for Clinical Infant Programs.

Athen, G. (1988). *American ways—A guide for foreigners in the United States.* Yarmouth, ME: Intercultural Press.

Green, J. W. (1982). *Cultural awareness in the human services.* Englewood Cliffs, NJ: Prentice-Hall.

Hall, E. T. (1976). *Beyond culture.* Garden City, NY: Anchor Books.

Hanson, M. (1992). Ethnic, cultural and language diversity in intervention settings. In Lynch, E., & Hanson, M. (Eds.), *Developing cross-cultural competence: A guide for working with young children and their families* (pp. 3-18). Baltimore, MD: Brookes Publishing.

Janeway, E. (1980). *Powers of the weak*. New York: Knopf.

Lane, A. M. (1983). The feminism of Hannah Arendt. *Democracy 3*, 107-17.

Lorde, A. (1984). *Sister outsider: Essays and speeches by Audre Lorde*. Trumansburg, NY: The Crossing Press.

McIntosh, P. (1988). White privilege and male privilege: A personal account of coming to see correspondences through work in women studies. Wellesley, MA: Wellesley College Center for Research on Women.

Pignatelli, F., & Pflaum, S. (Eds.). (1992). *Celebrating diverse voices: Progressive education and equity*. Newbury Park, CA: Corwin.

Rich, A. (1979). *On lies, secrets, and silence*. New York: W. W. Norton.

Storti, C. (1989). *The art of crossing cultures*. Yarmouth, ME: Intercultural Press.

Tiedt, P. L., & Tiedt, I. M. (1990). *Multicultural teaching—A handbook of activities, information, and resources* (3rd Ed.). Boston: Allyn & Bacon.

INTERACTIVE PHASES OF CURRICULAR RE-VISION:
A FEMINIST PERSPECTIVE

by
Peggy McIntosh

I want to speculate here[1] about a theory of five interactive phases of personal and curriculum change which occur when new perspectives and new materials from Women's Studies are brought into a traditional curriculum or a traditional consciousness. After a number of years of work in curriculum revision involving Women's Studies, I found that my colleagues and I were frequently making judgments without having made the grounds of our judgments explicit. That is, we were seeing some efforts of curriculum revision as better than others, more advanced along a spectrum of curricular possibilities which had not yet been described. My theory is an attempt to describe the spectrum.

Such theories have their dangers. Typologies scare me because abstract schema have so often left out most people, including me. Stage theories in particular are dangerous because they can so easily reinforce present hierarchies of power and value. Nevertheless, I want to speak in terms of curricular phases here, partly because colleagues in Women's Studies on many campuses are making similar analyses, speaking and writing about the process of curriculum change as if we could see in it identifiable varieties and types of change. "Such and such a course still has a long way to go," we say. A long way toward what? This is what I will try to spell out here. I like the tentativeness with which others interested in stage or phase theories in this field have drawn their pictures. D'Ann Campbell, Gerda Lerner, Catherine Stimpson, Marcia Westkott and the faculty development team of Arch, Tetrault, and Kirschner at Lewis and Clark College have developed theories that do not entail ranking and labeling of a sort which perpetuates oppression and exclusion. I take them as models.

For my own analysis, I have adopted, instead of the word "stages," the phrase suggested by Prof. Joan Gunderson of St. Olaf College: "interactive phases." Initial phases of perception do not disappear, but can be felt continually in the mind or the discipline, as one moves toward or away from a more inclusive body of knowledge, a more active process of learning, and a greater ability to see the dominant modes of thought and behavior which we wish to challenge or change.

I begin also with a sense of indebtedness to many other colleagues, including especially the women and men who have taken part over the last four years in the Mellon Seminars at the Wellesley College Center for Research on Women. These seminars are focused on liberal arts curriculum re-vision in two senses: **re-seeing** and **re-making** of the liberal arts curriculum. Each year, the Mellon Seminar participants meet together once a month for five hours to consider each of their academic areas or disciplines in turn. The questions we ask in that seminar for each discipline are the same: "What is the present content and scope and methodology of the discipline?" (Or, to use a phrase of Elizabeth Minnich's: "What are the **shaping dimensions** of the discipline at present?") And then, "How would the discipline need to change to reflect the fact that women are half the world's population and have had, in one sense, half the world's experience?"

The phases in curricular revision which I will describe owe their conceptualization in part to the work of the seminar. Sometimes after a presentation, a member of this group will say, "We really can't get any further in my field on this question." Or "I think you can get further ahead in Religion than we can in Philosophy; we can't make most women's experience visible, given the self-definition of the field." There is a sense among the seminar members that degrees of change do exist in the process of curriculum transformation. I will trace here what I think are the types of curriculum corresponding to five phases of perception.

In naming the five phases I will use history as the first example. I call Phase 1 Womanless History; Phase 2 Women in History; Phase 3 Women as a Problem, Anomaly, or Absence in History; Phase 4 Women **As** History; and Phase 5 History Redefined or Reconstructed to Include us All.

Analogously, we can have Womanless Political Science, then Women in Politics, then Women as an Absence, Anomaly or Problem for Political Science (or in Politics); next, Women **As** Political, (the study of women's lives in all their political dimensions, or, to use a phrase from Elizabeth Janeway's, *The Powers of the Weak*, the politics of the family, the school, the neighborhood, and the curriculum, the politics of culture, class, race and sex); and finally, Politics Redefined or Reconstructed to include multiple spheres of power, inner and outer.

Or we can have Womanless Biology, followed by (great) Women in Biology. Here, Phase 2 tends to be about a few of the few who had access to lab equipment, a handful of women still remembered for their work. In Phase 3 we have Women as Problems or Absences or Anomalies in Biology, for example as analyzed in the collection of essays called *Women Look at Biology Looking at Women*. In Phase 4 we have women taking the initiative to do science in a new way, on a differing base of assumptions and finally, we can imagine Biology Reconstructed to Include us All.

The Phase 1 syllabus is very exclusive; Phase 4 and 5 syllabi are very inclusive. Individuals and courses do not, as I have said, exist in fixity in given phases, but will show points of dynamic interaction among several of the phases, if the teacher or researcher is conscious of the magnitude of the problem of women's invisibility, and of the many forms of the problem. I think that superficial curriculum change gets arrested in what I have called Phases 2 and 3.

In proposing these phases of curriculum change, I may seem to be creating yet another ladder of values and arranging things so that Phase 1 is the bottom and Phase 5 is the top. This is not quite so; in one respect it is the reverse of what I intend, and what I see in my mind's eye. For Phase 1 thinking reinforces what we have been taught is the "top" and Phase 4 corresponds to what we have been taught is the "bottom" according to present hierarchies of knowledge, power and validity. Phase 5 puts what we were taught to devalue and to value into a new revolutionary relation to each other.

For me, the varieties of curriculum change in order to be accurately understood need to be set against models of the larger society and should be overlaid on an image of a broken pyramid. This image has come for me to stand for our culture as a whole. In my imagination it represents our institutions and also our individual psyches. I want to spend some time now developing this image of the broken pyramid and setting what I see as phases or types of curriculum development against the background of that image.

The upper part of the broken pyramid consists of peaks and pinnacles, peaks and pinnacles particularly in the public institutional life of nations, of governments, of militia, universities, churches, and corporations. Survival in this world is presented to us as a matter of winning lest you lose. We are taught to see both our institutions and ourselves within this framework: either you are a winner or you are among the losers. The winners are few, and high up on narrow bits of land which are the peaks; the losers are many and are low down, closer to the bottom. Institutions, groups, and individuals are seen as being on their way to the bottom if they are not on their way to the top.

The mountainous and pyramidal form of our society and of our psyches is a social construct invented by us. The shape of the pyramid was not necessarily inherent in the human materials but developed in our minds, and has now become reified, not only in our minds but in our institutions and in our behavior. We are taught that civilization has a clear top and a clear bottom. The liberal arts curriculum has been particularly concerned with passing on to students the image of what the "top" has been.

Both our public institutions and collective as well as innermost psyches have taken on the hierarchical structure of this winning-versus-losing kind of paradigm. Those who climb up get power; we are taught that there is not power for the many but there is power at the top for those few who can reach the peaks and pinnacles. College liberal arts catalogues, which package liberal arts education for sale to incoming students and to parents of students, make the claim that colleges help students to realize themselves, to discover their individual uniquenesses and to develop confidence which will lead to achievement, accomplishment, and success in the world outside the university. Most of this language masks, I think, the actual liberal arts function which is, at present, to train a few students to climb up to pinnacles and to seize them so as to have a position from which power can be felt, enjoyed, exercised and imposed on others. Images of upward mobility for the individual pervade the admissions literature of most of our colleges and universities today. We are taught that the purpose of education is to assist us in climbing up those peaks and pinnacles to enjoy the "fulfillment of our potential," which I take to mean the increased ability to have and use power for our individual selves.

As I have said, we are taught that only a few will be able to wield power from the summits. Behind the talk about scholarly excellence and teaching is hidden a voice that says: "The territory of excellence is very small. Only a few will be allowed to gain the peaks, having had access to excellent teaching and having earned excellent grades." A few will be "winners," perhaps featured in the subject matter of future courses, as winners in the history of the world—those worthy of the limelight. A few will be tenured and promoted in the pyramid of the college or the university or in the pyramids of legal, medical, financial, and governmental institutions, but the rest in some sense or other are made to be or feel like losers. The words "success," "achievement," and "accomplishment" have been defined in such a way as to leave most people and most types of life out of the picture.

Now, Womanless History is characteristic of thinking which reflects the society's pyramidal winning-vs-losing mentality. Phase 1 curriculum in the United States reflects only the highest levels of the existing pyramids of power and value. Womanless History specializes in telling about those who had most public power and whose lives were involved with laws, wars, acquisition of territory, and management of power. History is usually construed, in other words, to exclude those who didn't possess a good deal of public power. This kind of history perfectly reinforces the dominant political and social systems in that nonwhite males and women, the vast majority of the world's population, are construed as not worth studying in a serious and sustained way, and not worth including in the version of reality passed on to students.

Womanless History, in other words, is about "winning" and has been written by the "winners." Feminist analysts of that version of reality have come to realize that a privileged class of men in western culture have defined what is power and what constitutes knowledge. Excluded from these definitions and hence from consideration in the traditional History curriculum are types of power and versions of knowledge which this privileged class of men does not share. Hence a corrective is called for if the definitions of power and knowledge are to become more complete.

At first glance, the Phase 2 corrective, Women in History, appears to be an improvement over Phase 1, but Phase 2 History is very problematical for me and for many of my colleagues. I have come to think that it is worse than the traditional curriculum, worse than Womanless History in that it pretends to show us "women" but really shows us only a famous few, or makes a place for a newly-declared or a newly-resurrected famous few. It is problematical to argue **against** Phase 2 history at a time when many are concerned that young women have something up there on the pinnacles for them to look at and when many others want to restore to women of the past a historical record which has been taken from them. But Phase 2 is all too often like an affirmative action program which implies that institutions are model places which need only to help a few of the "inferior" Others to have the opportunity to climb onto these pinnacles with their "superiors." Affirmative action programs rarely acknowledge that the dominant group can and should learn from the Other. Phase 2 curricular policies, like most affirmative action programs, assume that our disciplines are basically functioning well, and that all that women or Blacks or Chicanos could need or want is to be put into higher slots on the reading list. In other words, the World Civilization course just needs a little attention to Africa, as a disadvantaged culture, giving Africa the time of day but from a position of "noblesse oblige."

In Phase 2 History the historians' spotlight is simply trained a little lower than usual on the pinnacles, so that we see people like Susan B. Anthony trying to scramble up the rocks. Anthony is featured as a hero in that she tried to make it into men's territory and succeeded. And she gets on the silver dollar. But there were all the other women on behalf of whom she was speaking whose lives remain completely invisible to us. That's the trouble with Phase 2 History. It conveys to the student the impression that women don't really exist unless they are exceptional by men's standards. Women don't really exist unless we "make something of ourselves" in the public world. Phase 2 History or Literature or Science or Economics repeatedly features the famous or "notable" or salaried women. In the American Literature course on 19th Century America, Emerson's friend Margaret Fuller may get added to the syllabus but all the women of Emerson's family, as representative of the women whose unseen labor made possible that transcendental obliviousness to daily life, get left out. You never see in English courses anything about all the women who were preparing Emerson's meals while he wrote "Self Reliance." In Phase 2 History we particularly see consorts featured. Sometimes they are neutered consorts like Betsy Ross who is seen as a sort of asexual "forefather." Sometimes you see a woman who is both a public figure and a consort, like Cleopatra, or a consort manqué, like Queen Elizabeth. But very rarely do you get a sense of all that substructure of the culture composed of women who didn't "make it" into the spheres of power, and who did not furnish material for myths. And almost always (or quite often) the women who did "make it" are devalued in the historical record by being portrayed chiefly in terms of sexual relationships. Phase 2 thinking never recognizes "ordinary" life, unpaid labor, or "unproductive" phenomena like human friendship.

Phase 3 takes us further down from the pinnacles of power toward the valleys. It brings us in touch with most women, and makes us realize that curriculum change which addresses only discrimination against women or "barriers" to women hardly begins to get at the major problems we have faced and the major experiences we have had. Phase 3 introduces us to the politics of the curriculum. We can't simply "include" those who were left out, who were "denied opportunity" to be studied. It's not an accident we were left out. And as Marilyn Schuster, a Dean at Smith College, has said: "First you study women to fill in the gaps, but then it becomes more complicated because you see that the gaps were there for a reason."

Phase 3 curriculum work involves getting angry at the fact that we have been seen only as an absence, an anomaly or a problem for History, for English, for Biology, rather than as part of the world, part of whatever people have chosen to value. There is anger at the way women have been treated throughout history. We are angry that instead of being seen as part of the norm, we have been seen, if at all, as a "problem" for the scholar, the society, or the world of the powerful. People doing scholarship in Women's Studies get particularly angry at the fact that the terms of academic discourse and of research are loaded in such a way that we are likely to come out looking like "losers" or looking like pathological cases. A teacher at one of the Claremont Colleges has eloquently asked, "How can we alter the making and the finding of knowledge in such a way that difference needn't be perceived as deprivation?" Phase 3 work makes us angry that women are seen either as deprived or as exceptional. I think that the anger in Phase 3 work is absolutely vital to us. Disillusionment is also a feature of Phase 3 realizations, for many teachers. It is traumatically shocking to white women teachers in particular to realize that we were not only trained but were as teachers unwittingly training others to overlook, reject, exploit, disregard, or be at war with most people in the world. One feels hoodwinked and also sick at heart at having been such a vehicle for racism, misogyny, upper class power and militarism.

Phase 3 challenges the literary canon. We ask who defined greatness in literature, and who is best served by the definitions? We ask the same in Religion—who defined "major" theology, and "important" church history? In Music and Art, who defined greatness and whom do the definitions best serve? Both the definers and those best served by the definitions were Western white men who had positions of cultural power or who fared fairly well within cultural systems.

In Phase 3, scholars rankle against statements like this which as freshmen they might have taken for granted: "The quest for knowledge is a universal human undertaking." "Economic behavior is a matter of choice." "Man has mastered the environment and harnessed the resources of the planet." We may laugh today, but as freshmen, we didn't laugh. We just absorbed these ideas.

Once when I was a Freshman, the present personality in me, then a hidden part of the psyche, below the winning and losing part, spoke up—just once, six weeks into a freshman social science course on the History of the Church in Western Civilization. I suddenly blurted out something I hadn't meant to say at all. It was that voice which is now speaking to you directly today, briefly speaking then, 26 years ago. I was in a small discussion section which accompanied one of the Harvard lecture courses. The "section man," who was a graduate student, was running a discussion on fine points of theology, and on the governance of bishops and kings. Joined with him in this conversation were two dazzling freshmen; one was Reinhold Niebuhr's son, who knew all the fine points of theology; the other was from Pasadena, a tall, godlike man, with a tan and a tennis racket; I remember him as wearing a cream-colored cable sweater with the two blue and red stripes, and knowing all the fine points of theology, too. I couldn't understand what was going on in any of this course. I had not even begun to learn about the medieval feudal system until I took this course. Then suddenly one day, in the middle of a discussion, I blurted out: "I don't see why the serfs stood for it."

We hadn't even been talking about the serfs. You can imagine the dilemma of the teacher, hearing this utterly irrelevant freshman comment coming from someone who hadn't said anything for six weeks. He said gently, but in a very somber voice, "I think you had better see me in office hours." I was of course too scared to go see him in office hours; as one who had not yet noticed how the pyramids of power work, I was afraid of those in authority, and I always hoped that the professors wouldn't notice me. I was humiliated by my comment. I assumed that the others in the class understood how the feudal system worked, and that I was the only one who didn't understand "why the serfs stood for it."

I went through four years at Harvard thinking that everyone else had understood medieval social systems, but then in later years, after I had done some teaching, I began to see further dimensions in that uncontrolled comment. It was coming from a "serf," a freshman girl who was asking not only "Where are the serfs, and where are the women?" but also "Where am I in this picture, and why am I standing for this picture that leaves me out, and this discussion which leaves me out?" Years later I began to see that, uncontrolled though that comment was, it was based on very important material which hadn't been covered in that course about the pinnacles. We never studied the peasant woman on her knees in Chartres; we only studied Abelard in the streets of Paris and discussed what various intellectual geniuses or power-holders were saying. And the discussion itself was only among the power-holders.

It seems to me now, in retrospect, that if my teacher had really been able to do the kind of systemic teaching which Women's Studies encourages and enables one to do, he could have quickly filled me in on a number of points which would have shed light on the stability of the pyramidal feudal system. He could have mentioned the psychological theory of identification with authority; there was more in it for the serfs to identify upward with the apparent protector than to identify laterally with people who couldn't help them. He could have reminded me that before the Industrial Revolution serfs didn't have telephones, newsletters or political movements to allow them to work for revolution. He could have mentioned the serfs' identification with the Kingdom of Heaven. Years later, I began to realize that all teachers are trained to isolate bits of knowledge and that this very training keeps their students in turn oblivious of the larger systems which hold pyramids of power in place. I was obediently oblivious; having been raised on the American myth of individuality, I thought that there were no social systems anywhere, and then couldn't imagine why a serf wouldn't assert that God-given gift of individuality and make his way out of what I considered to be "the bottom," in the first social system I had ever noticed.

This autobiographical vignette is important to me now, though it shamed me and gnawed at me for years at Harvard. For a long time I thought it was "the stupidist thing I ever said in college," but now that I have flip-flopped the pyramid, I think it was one of the smarter things I said in college. This inchoate and uncontrolled outburst of the serf against a Harvard education came from a voice which spoke for people and functions of personality which we are trained to disregard.

Phase 3 gives way to Phase 4 at the moment when all of those who were assigned to specialize in the functions of life below the fault line refuse to see ourselves only as a problem and begin to think of ourselves as valid human beings. Phase 4 vision construes the life below the break in the pyramid as the real though unacknowledged base of life and civilization. In the 4th phase we women say: "On our own ground, we are not losers; we have had half the human experience. The fact that we are different from men and diverse within our own group doesn't necessarily mean we are deprived." Those who embark on Phase 4 thinking find the accepted pyramidal modes of seeing and evaluating are inappropriate to our sense of worth. For within the pyramidal images we can be seen only as being "at the bottom." All of the first three phases of curricular revision which I have described omit that positive look at us which is the crucial healing ingredient of the 4th phase and the chief revolutionary ingredient of the 5th phase. In other words, I see Phases 1, 2 and 3 in varying degrees as misogynist. In Phase 1, we weren't in history; Phase 2 allows that only a few exceptional women were in history, and Phase 3 says we were in history problematically, messing up the purity of the historical model, or making demands and being victimized. Women or men who say only these things have internalized the view of women as problems, or as deviant people with "issues." Such people can demonstrate persistent internalized misogyny in the midst of their righteous and legitimate anger on behalf of wronged women.

Phase 4 is the development in which we see Women As History, and explore all the life existing below the public world of winning and losing. Now I want to go back to the image of the broken pyramid and say that in the top part of the pyramid I drew, the only two alternatives are to win or to lose. But there is another whole domain of the psyche and of the public and private life that works on a different value system or ethical perception altogether. These are a value system and an ethical system which operate laterally on the principle that you work for the decent survival of all, and that this effort conduces to your own survival and your humanity as well. This value system is approved in the spheres we have called private, invisible, and domestic. I cannot claim that families actually work on a lateral model. But mothers are not specifically trained to do with their children something that would involve, for example, marking the children and grading them to see which will win and which will lose. The publicly sanctioned behavior of mothers, though it is partly to make the children adjust to the pyramids in the public spheres, is partly to work for the decent survival of all the children at once. Moreover, the idea of decent survival of all lies behind our friendships and our conversations and much of our daily life as we go about our ordinary business. Most of what we do is on this lateral plane of working for our own decent survival rather than "getting ahead."

Now, the assigned work of women in every culture has chiefly been in this unacknowledged, lateral network of life below the fault line, supporting the rest of the pyramid but really opposed to it, because lateral consciousness is at odds with the value system of winning versus losing. The two systems have been pitted against each other through projection onto two "opposite" sexes. The value system of winning and losing has particularly been projected onto white Western man, and men in power in all cultures, and the value system and the work of the part below the break involving decent survival of all has been particularly projected onto women and other lower caste people. However, in the pyramidal configuration, one system is subordinated to the other. The contest is not equal. In Phase 4 thinking, whether in daily life or in curriculum revision, you call into question whether all that work behind the scenes is the work of losers. You ask if it isn't the real work of civilization. And you may also ask whether it isn't the work of the "haves" rather than the "have-nots." That's the moment at which the pyramid in a social construct begins to be seen as the creation of a special interest group. The work of taking care of ourselves and other people can be seen as a role assignment in our society, carrying many rewards and gratifications as well as punishments. If it is seen only as the work of victims, then it is still seen, I believe, in a misogynist way. We who were assigned the work of domestic upkeep and maintenance for the human race and the making of ties and relationships have done in many ways a reasonably good job of it. The race hasn't blown itself up yet. We most need continued work for decent survival of all in a nuclear age. The collaborative values coming out of the base of the pyramid are the ones we desperately need in public policymakers.

We cannot, by wishing, dismantle the upper parts of the pyramid, or bring the unseen base into compatibility with the upper part. The two types of existence are presently in enmity with each other, as two differing value systems of "mastery" and "decency" (or compliance) projected onto powerful men and onto lower caste people respectively. But we desperately need for the future to try to carry the values from the undervalued sphere into the public spheres, in order to change the behavior and the sense of reality of all of our public institutions and the people who control them. The study of women, like women themselves, can help to supply the vision, the information, and the courage needed for this task, and can thus increase our chances of global and personal survival. I hope you realize that I am not claiming that women are morally superior to men by birth, and hence able to save the world. It is just that we were assigned the task which Jean Baker Miller calls "developing ourselves through the development of others." And that has meant that we have developed skills in keeping the human race alive which are the basic indispensable skills in an age of nuclear weapons.

Curriculum work in Phase 4, when you have begun to construe women as the world majority and see women in some respect as the "haves," not simply the "have nots," breaks all the rules of ordinary research or teaching. One studies American literature of the 19th century not by asking, "Did the women write anything good?" but by asking "What did the women write?" One asks not "What great work by a woman can I include in my reading list?" but "How have women used the written word?" In Phase 4 one asks, "How have women of color in many cultures told their stories?" not "Is there any good third world literature?" Phase 4 looks not at Abelard but at that peasant woman who didn't have any "pure" theology or even understand the heresies, but who rather had an overlay of platitudes and "Old Wives' Tales" and riddles and superstitions and theological scraps from here and there and kitchen wisdom in her mind. In Phase 4, one looks at the mix of life, and instead of being scared by the impurity of the mix, notices that the impurities reflect the fact that we have been terribly diverse in our lives. Biology taught from a Phase 4 perspective does not define life in terms of the smallest possible units that may be isolated and then examined in isolation. When you are doing Phase 4 Biology, it seems to me you particularly teach reverence for the organism, identification with it, and you see in terms of large, interlocking and relational systems which need to be acknowledged and preserved or whose balance needs to be observed and appreciated.

Many of civilization's present emergencies suggest that we need wider constructions of knowledge in all fields than our present investigators have developed, with their exclusive methods of study, whether empirical or otherwise. All of Phase 4 work is highly speculative and experimental in its epistemology, for we have not yet learned to name unnamed experiences of the plural, the common, the lateral and the "ordinary" life. In Phase 4 curriculum development, it feels as though we are all making it up together. Teachers can look at each other's bibliographies, but this work is so new that we need people to invent their own ways of describing what they are finding, to invent new categories for experience, new ways of doing research, and new ways of teaching.

In Phase 4, most of the teaching materials are non-traditional. Moreover, the boundaries between disciplines start to break down, for scholars doing feminist work come to realize that boundaries between disciplines serve to keep our present political, economic and social arrangements in place. There are a number of other boundaries that break down also. The relationship between the teacher and the material changes in Phase 4 because the material is so nontraditional and includes so much that we have never studied before that the teacher becomes less of an expert. The relationship between the teacher and the student changes because the teacher now seems less "high" and the student less "low" in knowledge about the areas of life being studied. Then, in addition, there is less of a distinction between the "observer" and the "observed," and often the "subject" of study is treated, in Phase 4 work, as a primary authority on her own experience. That is, economists doing really good work on women will listen very seriously to what a housewife wants to say about spending and then borrow from Psychology and Religion and Sociology to analyze her spending patterns and perceptions, rather than trying to fit her into an intricate economic model already built, which could account for her behavior in terms of a number of variables which have already been identified but not by her.

The pinnacles of fragmented and isolated knowledge seem more and more abstract and irrelevant as you try to learn from within women's experience what women's experience has been like. Phase 1 reinforces vertical value systems; Phase 4 reveals systems of lateral values and relationships. One key hallmark of Phase 4 consciousness and curriculum is that the Other stops being considered something lesser to be dissected, deplored, devalued or corrected. The Other becomes, as it were, organically connected to one's self. Realities, like people, seem plural but unified. That fragmentation of knowledge which characterizes our disciplines at present begins to end if you descend to the valleys of civilization in Phase 4 and you start to study commonality, plural experience and the work of daily survival. You also come to realize that the valleys are in fact more suitable places to locate civilization than are the deoxygenated summits of the mountains. The heights of specialization, like the concentration of economic power in the hands of a few are seen to have questionable usefulness to our continued survival.

One danger of Phases 3 and 4 work is that scholars trying to alter the structures of knowledge or society make the mistake of thinking that all women are alike, so that the study of a few will suffice to fill in the picture. Minority women in particular have often stated that Women's Studies tends to fall into some of the same traps as the traditional curriculum in describing chiefly the elites and the worlds they control, or in polarizing the elites and non-elites along bipolar lines.

When well done, Phase 4 work honors particularity at the same time it identifies common denominators of experience. It stresses diversity and plurality, and for many people doing work on women in Phase 4, William James's *Varieties of Religious Experience* seems like a model book. It takes the pluralistic view that there are many varieties of religious life, and that one needn't rank and judge them. It shows a cast of mind which also accompanies serious work on women.

Now, Phase 5 curriculum revision is the hardest to conceive. I said it was the phase in which History (or Knowledge) gets redefined, reconstructed to include us all. But how can this be done? At a conference in 1981 for college deans and presidents held at the Johnson Foundation's Wingspread Center in Wisconsin, Gerda Lerner gave the keynote address on "Liberal Education and the New Scholarship on Women." After her talk, I asked, "On the basis of all the work you have now done on American women's history and on the experience of Black Americans, how would you organize a basic text called *American History?*" She answered, "I couldn't begin to do that; it is too early. It would take a team of us, fully funded, two years just to get the table of contents organized—just to imagine how we would categorize it." And then she said, "But don't worry, we were 6,000 years carefully building a patriarchal structure of knowledge, and we've had only 12 years to try to correct it, and 12 years is nothing."

As Elizabeth Minnich has pointed out, there have been important movements, to do and to institutionalize women's scholarship in earlier decades, so this isn't only a 12-year effort. But Lerner's larger point is important. We have had only a little time to correct major paradigms. We don't know yet what reconstructed History would look like. In my view, the reconstructed curriculum not only draws a line around the vertical and lateral functions, examining all of human life and perception. It also puts these horizontal and vertical elements in a revolutionary new relation to one another, so that the pyramidal shapes of the psyche, the society, the world are discarded, seen as inaccurate and also incompatible with the decent, balanced survival of human psyches, institutions, and nations. Global shapes replace the pyramids. Human collaborative potential is explored and competitive potential subjected to a sustained critique. A genuinely inclusive curriculum, based on global imagery of self and society, would reflect and reinforce the common human abilities and inclinations to cultivate the soil of the valleys and to collaborate for survival.

A teacher doing work in Phase 5 develops inclusive rather than exclusive vision and realizes that many things hang together. A Phase 5 curriculum would help us to produce students who can see patterns of life in terms of systems of race, culture, caste, class, gender, religion, national origin, geographical location and other influences on life which we haven't begun to name. At the same time, Phase 5 curriculum promises to produce students who can carry with them into public life the values of the private sphere, because inclusive learning allows them to value lateral functions rather than discredit them in the context of paid or public life. Right now, Phase 2 thinking tends to work only for the promotion of individual values; it tends to advance a few women who can "make it in the public world." But I think that putting women's bodies into high places does little for people in the aggregate and little or nothing for women in the aggregate. It makes life nice for, or brings power to, a few women but it doesn't necessarily bring about social change. At present our so-called "leaders," women included, are mostly working from that misguided world view that says either you win or you lose. It's not true, and women in the aggregate know it's not true. And the conviction that you either win or lose is, as I have said, a very dangerous ethic and prescription to carry into public life and into leadership positions at a time when nuclear weapons are what you have to test the idea with.

We can't afford to have leaders who think only in terms of winning or losing. And so it seems to me critically important for us to develop a Phase 5 curriculum. But lest you think

I am forgetting the educational world in my interest in world peace, let me say that the development of Phase 5 curriculum is also important to colleges and universities because of their own educational claims. The university claims to develop and to pass on to students and to the wider society an accurate and comprehensive body of knowledge. And in the words of Ruth Schmidt, the Provost of Wheaton College, and now President of Agnes Scott College, "If you claim to teach about the human race, and you don't know anything about half the human race, you really can't claim to know or teach much about the human race." The main argument for curriculum change is that it will help universities to fulfill their acknowledged primary responsibility: to develop and pass on to the society and to students accurate bodies of knowledge. Since women are now left out, those bodies of knowledge are grossly inaccurate.

I want now to illustrate these five interactive phases of curriculum development in five specific disciplines. While I was writing this part of my talk, discipline by discipline, abstractly analyzing Psychology, English, and so on, I heard the voice of Florence Howe asking her familiar question, "Where are the women?" So I stopped organizing my ideas according to those fragmented peaks and pinnacles called "disciplines," and began mentally to follow a group of women like ourselves studying in a variety of curricula from the most exclusive to the most inclusive I could imagine, and then I watched the effects on their minds and their lives. These women are named Meg, Amy, and Jo, and Jo's children: Maya and Angela and Adrienne.

Meg feels extremely privileged to go to college and to sit at the feet of her professors. Her Phase One freshman English class is called "Man's Quest for Knowledge." She studies *Huckleberry Finn*, *Moby Dick*, Walt Whitman's poetry, Emerson on "Self Reliance," Thoreau's *Walden*, a Hemingway novel and Norman Mailer. Meg thinks it really is amazing when you think about it, how man has quested for knowledge; it's a universal trait! The expository essays are very difficult for Meg to write, and she cannot remember after she's handed them in what any of them were about. She gets middling grades; her professors find her indecisive. In Medieval History she studies bishops and kings. She wonders once or twice, but doesn't ask, why the serfs stood for the feudal system. Mostly she hopes that she will marry a strong man who will take care of her just as a bishop or a king must have taken care of the serfs.

In Psychology, Meg learns of a number of interesting complexes, and she feels particularly glad that she has studied the Oedipus complex because it will help her as a parent, some day, to understand her sons. In Freud's model of the personality she identifies strongly with the superego. She is very relieved that there is a part of the personality with which she can identify as a beautiful soul, one who has transcended the moiling, toiling world and the need to compete. She overlooks the fact that Freud did not think women had highly developed superegos. She is vulnerable, deluded, and ignorant about what Freud really said, since she has received no training in looking for herself in the curriculum.

In Biology, having been told that man has mastered nature and that knowledge is mastery, Meg dissects a frog. She finds this repulsive, but necessary for Science. After all, Scientists would have to take life apart in order to understand it, wouldn't they? Mostly she dreams of security, and will succeed in marrying, at the end of her junior year, her lab partner. In Art History, which is Meg's favorite course, she moves away from that bewildering world which really hasn't made much sense to her and looks at beautiful things. She really respects her art professor, a kindly man who is teaching her what to admire in the great masters' work. She hopes that when she and her husband have raised their children and have some extra money, they can themselves collect some beautiful works of art for the walls of their house. She would, however, not want to collect second-rate art, so that may be a problem.

Amy goes to college a few years after Meg. Amy talks a lot about role models. Amy intends to Make It. She says things like "My mother never did anything." Amy's freshman English course is called "The Individual versus Society." She studies *Huckleberry Finn*, *Moby Dick*, Walt Whitman's poetry, Emerson's "Self Reliance," Thoreau's *Walden*, *The Autobiography of Frederick Douglass*, Hemingway, Kerouac and Sylvia Plath. This is a Phase 2 course; there is a black writer and a woman on the reading list. The curriculum has started to change to include a few "exceptional" members of minority groups who are considered capable of "making it" in the syllabus. Amy gets a lot of "ammunition" for her life from Sylvia Plath's character in *The Bell Jar* who says, "I didn't want to be the platform that the man shoots off from; I wanted to be the rocket myself and shoot off in all directions." Amy is fueled by Esther Greenwood's words to drive herself to exceptional heights. She doesn't notice that the speaker, like Plath herself, was suicidal. She is identifying upward, and she likes the Medieval/Renaissance course best when it moves from that static feudal system into the development of guilds, and the middle class, and upward mobility. She is psychologically tuned into the theme of individual autonomy that is running through that part of the course.

In her Women in Psychology course, Phase 2, she learns about women who "made it" in Psychology. She learns nothing of their struggles nor of the many who have remained invisible to us. "They did it, I can too," Amy believes. "Women can do whatever they want; if they want anything enough to really work for it. Of **course** Biology isn't destiny." Amy is, however, very little interested in the psychology of women, and her courses don't give her anything to make her interested in her own psychology, or make her ask why she has switched from pre-law to art or wonder about any inner life in women which psychological research hasn't named.

In her Biology course, she is interested in Darwin's theories about competition and the "survival of the fittest." She thinks of herself as one of the "fittest." The losers will lose, but she, Amy, is going to make it in a man's world. She thinks of herself as a Frederick Douglass, "smart enough to get away," and as an organism ready to adapt to a particular niche in the environment, her niche; she intends to fight for her niche.

Amy's Art History work further demonstrates to her that women have now "arrived," because her Impressionists course includes Mary Cassatt and Berthe Morisot. Amy does not notice that they are called "Mary" and "Berthe" throughout the course, whereas the men are "Monet" and "Degas." All of Amy's eloquent papers in her freshman year in every course are variations on the theme of "The Individual vs Society." She never sees herself as "Society." Amy has been given the Phase 2 vision of herself as the unique woman rising up in history and leaving her mother behind where mothers really always were.

Jo comes to college later than Amy, tired and rather battered by certain personal episodes in her life. She comes reluctantly to college for further training; she is a "re-entry" woman. She finds to her surprise that college speaks to her condition. She comes alive in class. Other students like to be with Jo and Jo likes to be with them. She is somewhat older than most around her. In her freshman English course she reads Dale Spender's *Man Made Language* and she reads Nancy Henley and Barrie Thorne, and then she reads Emily Dickinson and is invited to take an interdisciplinary look at Emily Dickinson after having read five other feminist critics. She writes a paper she will never forget, on Emily Dickinson as a person working on many rebellions at the same time—against the social mores and axioms of her community, against patriarchal, public "authorities," against intellectual certainty, against the theology of her church, and against conventions of the sentence and of language itself. She will never forget this paper; it actually possesses her while she writes it. Somewhere in the curriculum she is finding something that speaks to her personally and directly about her own life.

In Medieval History, Jo's teacher introduces her to the essay by Joan Kelly-Gadol: "Did Women Have a Renaissance?" She gets mad, particularly when learning the answer is "No, not in the Renaissance," and she determines to mistrust periodization of history from then on. She has found something that fits with her sense of not having fitted in. She is being given the "doubled vision" which Joan Kelly refers to in one of her last works, of both fitting in and being alien and apart from a dominant culture. She is being given the enabling doubled vision that explains her life to her.

Then in Psychology Jo reads Naomi Weisstein on "How Psychology Constructs the Female," and Carol Gilligan. In a time warp, Jo has just received Gilligan's latest book, *In a Different Voice*. She reads that women don't fit the existing models of moral development and that they really seem to test out differently. She learns that Lawrence Kohlberg's "Six Universal Phases" are not after all universal but were based on a small white male sample. But because Jo is in a Phase 3 curriculum, she is also told that Gilligan's sample has its limits too. She learns that women are probably more diverse than most of the existing research shows. She reads Berger and Luckmann's *The Social Construction of Reality* and learns that the world of "knowledge" was constructed by cultural authority figures. She finds herself almost insouciant in starting to write a paper now.

In Biology, she reads Ruth Hubbard's essay, "Have Only Men Evolved?" She is shocked to learn that scientific knowledge is permeated with politics. She learns that accounts of evolution and of human propensities which she had taken as objective are completely andro-centric. She learns that all forms of female life have been seen as defective or incapacitated versions of male life. She can hardly bear to think that even Science is not objective, but as her distress grows she finds herself grateful to Ruth Hubbard for a metaphor which explains her distress to her: she looks out the back window of a bus and sees that she is herself pushing the bus in which she is riding.

And then in her Art History course Jo, in another time warp, goes to New York City and sees Mary Beth Edelman's work, filled with anger and expressiveness and female nudity. Jo is shaken but not revolted. She invites Amy who lives in New York, to join her at the show. Amy is patronizing; Jo has nothing much to say but is moved by the show in ways she cannot express.

Some time later, Jo's children come to college. They are twins. She has named them Maya and Angela, not by accident. Their freshman English course isn't in English at all. It is in Spanish. They need Spanish for an oral history project they are doing. In my fantasy they are at college at Humboldt State. They are spending a great deal of time becoming proficient in Spanish, and moreover, their final exams in the Spanish Language and Compo-sition course are not only on the way they read and write the language but also on their ability to elicit information from others in Spanish, their ability to understand what they have heard, and their ability to carry on a conversation in Spanish, linking on to previous things said rather than directing the talk or making statements.

In the History component of their curriculum, these twins have a project on which they are doing oral history research with six Spanish-speaking women. It started to be the history of migrant labor in a certain part of northern California but the students persuaded the professor not to label it a history of migrant labor before they had interviewed these women, lest they narrow the canvas too much. The students have decided that right now it will be an open-ended series of interviews and the topic will not be named. They will ask the women about their lives rather than asking them about migrant labor history; then they'll see where the women start.

In Psychology, Maya and Angela read Jean Baker Miller's *Toward a New Psychology of Women* and they feel they have been invited on an exploration with her, to try to name all of that women's experience in us that doesn't come under the public spotlight and hasn't yet been focused on or seen to exist. They also read Caroll Smith-Rosenberg's essay, "The Female World of Love and Ritual: Relations Between Women in Nineteenth Century America," and see what a rich world is revealed when you look at women's lives starting from women's own ground. They begin to care about their mother's letters and their mother's past in a new way, and begin to understand why their mother named their sister Adrienne.

In Biology, Maya and Angela take a course called "A Feeling for the Organism: Science Without Mastery," read Evelyn Fox Keller's book of this title and Barbara McClintock's work on genetics in a field of corn. The course syllabus opens with a remark of McClintock's on receiving the Nobel Prize: "It might seem unfair to reward a person for having so much pleasure over the years, asking the maize plant to solve specific problems and then watching its responses."

Last of all, in Art, Maya and Angela have a terrific project and they are having a lot of fun doing it. They have two assignments in Art. Humboldt State, in my fantasy, has a big art building whose front hall is decorated by a long mural made by art students. Every year a student replaces a part of the mural. Maya and Angela each have to replace a previous year's painting with a tempera painting of their own. But what are they to replace? This is where their teaching assignment comes in. In this Phase 4 curriculum every student is also a teacher. Therefore Maya and Angela have to spend part of every day teaching some young children in a subject which they are themselves "taking." Maya and Angela have a group of ten children working with them to decide whose work from the previous year's mural will be taken down and whose work will be replaced by Maya's and Angela's new work. How will the judgments be made? The children are doing a number of things, both talking and writing about the paintings that are to be replaced and also copying them with their own paints. Maya and Angela are teaching art at the same time they are studying art because this revised Phase 4 curriculum not only lowers the usual wall between the teacher and the taught but also alters the relationship radically. Moreover, art is construed in my fantastic Humboldt State as including decoration of all of the environment beyond walls and canvases and pieces of paper. Therefore the second art assignment which Maya and Angela and their students have is to take care of one of 30 gardens assigned to their art class and they are allowed to plant it as they like but they must then maintain it throughout the year. The children dislike this assignment very much. Maya and Angela have chosen succulents and shrubs which need pruning and cleaning up; those plants thrive in the climate of the campus. The children wish there were flowers. Maya and Angela explain why this isn't a flower garden. The children watch the flowers wilting in other people's beds and gradually learn that there is a reason to plant shrubs which strike them nevertheless as unpromising, unpretty, and unromantic.

Maya and Angela have an ambition for the years after college. Their father lives in New Hampshire. Whenever they visit him in the summers they are galled by the New Hampshire license plate. It has a slogan which reads "Live Free or Die." The more they read it, the more it annoys them. So they are going to spend their time after college working for a few years in New Hampshire. They'll earn a living, but their aim is to change that slogan. They have a slogan they are going to try to get put in its place: "Share Life or Perish." They'll learn the political ropes, work through the legislature or lobby, or work through the state's committee system or campaign, or run for office; this is partly a lark but they're in dead earnest, and they'll give it a good try for ten years or so, as they make a living in New Hampshire. They imagine they'll have several public and professional and perhaps several private lives as well, before they're through.

Now these phases of curriculum have socialized each woman differently. Meg has been socialized to "fit in," oblivious to and therefore very vulnerable to the forces at work on and around her. Amy has been socialized to kill herself trying to be, and dreaming that she is, exceptional, different from other women, and dreaming that she will be seen as different from other women. Jo has been socialized to understand the interlocking systems that work to produce Meg's illusions, Amy's internalized misogyny, and the dangers to all of learning systems that exclude them. Maya and Angela have been educated to be quite happy with the diversity of life and canny about systems; they are able to use their anger in a way that gives them pleasure. They are real to themselves and may well become real to larger groups: a legislature, or drivers on the roads of New Hampshire. Well, what of Adrienne? Phase 5 remains for her. I dream we invent for her a circular, multicultural, inclusive curriculum which socializes people to be whole, balanced, and undamaged, which includes rather than excludes most parts of life, and which both fosters a pluralistic understanding and fulfills the dream of a common language. This is the Phase 5 curriculum.

Ten years after graduation Meg, deserted, divorced, and still not knowing what hit her reenters college as a Continuing Education student and now again reads the Masterworks of Western Civilization. She finds them not so great. She has learned that the bishops and kings do not take care of the serfs. She is bewildered, amazed by Jo's girls, Maya and Angela. She is in one course with them. They say things she couldn't have imagined at their age. She admires them, she likes them, and to her amazement, she is learning from them.

Amy does all right in New York as an artist; she is tough as nails, lonely, and scornful of the women's groups. She hasn't joined any collective. She's furious that she hasn't had her own show yet. She thinks if you're good enough you'll get recognized and that if women would only pull "their" act together and stop bitching, her chances for recognition would improve. Jo feels more and more whole and effective as her life goes on. She is past her first self-directed anger and her years from 40 onward are her best; she has herself learned to see systemically and become a force for personal and for aggregate change.

Maya and Angela—will they change the New Hampshire license plate? But wait—they haven't yet gone to college. We haven't yet got the Phase 4 curriculum. And the Phase 5 curriculum has not yet been invented for Adrienne. So the answer about what Maya and Angela and Adrienne will be able to do lies in us, and in the work we do now for their future and for ours.

Endnote

[1]This talk was originally prepared for the Claremont College Conference "Traditions & Transitions: Women's Studies and the Balanced Curriculum," in February 1983. Altered or expanded versions have been given at conferences or workshops at St. Olaf College, Mills College, University of California at Hayward, Wheaton College, Sarah Lawrence College, University of Idaho, Old Dominion University, Haverford College, the University of Maine at Farmington, Wellesley College and the National Women's Studies Association. Sections of the talk have been included in presentations at secondary schools, the Headmistresses' Association of the East and the National Association of Independent Schools.

INTERACTIVE PHASES OF CURRICULAR AND PERSONAL RE-VISION WITH REGARD TO RACE

by
Peggy McIntosh

This paper expands on the author's 1983 paper on interactive phases of personal and curricular re-vision (WP #124 in the Wellesley College Center for Research on Women series). The curricula of several hypothetical students—Meg, Amy, Jo, Maya, and Angela— are described in terms of the teaching they receive about Native Americans.

Nearly 20 years ago, one afternoon in 1972, a friend on the faculty of the University of Denver was standing in the door of my office. We were talking about some aspect of race relations. My colleague said, with gentle offhandedness, "I wouldn't want to be white if you paid me five million dollars." I was startled to hear that she would not want to trade her racial identity for mine. In the previous three years, I had seen this friend survive many problems caused by systemic and personal racism. My dim awareness of, and paltry education in, just about everything pertaining to our lives made me think that hers was a racial identity[1] not to be desired. Now I learned that I had a racial identity that she wouldn't think of wanting.

My friend's candor was a gift. Her comment opened doors into areas whose distinctness I had been taught not to see: her culture and my culture. Like many people of my race and economic class, I had been taught that there was only one culture, and that we were both in it. Looking toward hers for the first time, I began to see what I had missed. I learned that my colleague would want to change her circumstances in a racist society, but not her cultural identity. I had been led to assume that her circumstances relative to mine **were** her cultural identity, which I thought must consist mostly of burdens. Her strong words made things more complicated, pluralized the picture, and started me doing what felt and still feels like essential Ethnic Studies homework on the elements of my friend's culture that sustained her and the elements in mine which made the idea of being "white" anathema to her.

I tell this story as a description of an awakening from what I now see as a generic state of mind trained into middle-class "white" Americans: monoculturalism, or single-system seeing. Racial or ethnic monoculturalism is the assumption that we are all in the same cultural system together, and that its outlines are those which have been recognized by people who have the most ethnic and racial power.

Single-system seeing with regard to gender takes a related form. I see it especially when men, and many women, assume that we who work in feminist movements toward alternative ways of organizing life and using power must want to do what men have done. I know a number of men who think that when we women get together, we must talk about them, or plot against them. But if one listens plurally instead of monoculturally, one will hear that women want to survive with dignity, and agency, but in general do not want to do what white Western men have done, or been asked to do.

Monoculturalism, like all forms of single-system seeing, is blind to its own cultural specificity. It cannot see itself. It mistakes its "givens" for neutral, preconceptual ground rather than for distinctive cultural grounding. People who have been granted the most public or economic power, when thinking monoculturally about "others," often imagine that these others' lives must be constituted of "issues," "problems," and deficits relative to themselves. But in fact, the politically "lesser" are, or can be, culturally central to themselves. Most will see much that is positive about their lives, through strength inherited with their traditions. Most will have learned despite and through the conditions of their lives how to behave in ways that sustain and stabilize themselves and the cultural fabrics of the world.

I write about monoculturalism and single-system seeing both as a financially secure white person in the United States who has been, within those dimensions of my identity, seen as fitting a monocultural norm, and as a woman who has been, in my gender identity, seen as culturally lesser, in Anglo-European male terms. I now know that with regard to my sex I do not simply have a deficit identity, i.e., a defective variant of male identity. Moreover, though my chosen place of work is located at the very edge of a College, we who work here call this marginal place devoted to research on women the Center. So it is with people in all cultures, I now think; we can be culturally real or central to ourselves, knowing that no one center is entitled to arbitrary dominance. And if we do not challenge the single-system seeing which projects deficit identities onto us, we will continue to be seen only as defective variants of ideal types within ruling but unacknowledged monoculture.

One great gift of my colleague's comment nearly 20 years ago was that she located herself in a position of strength and made it clear that she saw my racial group as something she would under no circumstances want to join. Within white monoculture, her position was unfamiliar; she was locating herself outside what I imagined was her status within the "one system." Her words made me begin to see my own culture as ethno-particular, ethno-specific, and in fact ethno-peculiar.

It took me some years to revise my understanding to the point at which my colleague's words came to bear very directly on the ways I taught. For like most traditionally trained "white" teachers, I needed a long time to reconceive myself before I could ground teaching in cultural pluralism. While coming around to seeing both my culture and hers in their distinctness and their interrelations, I experienced with regard to race the same slow inter-active processes of re-vision which I have traced with regard to teaching about women. It is the process I described in my 1983 paper "Interactive Phases of Curricular Re-Vision: A Feminist Perspective."[2] [See this volume, pp. 59-74]

I review here that typology of Interactive Phases of Curricular Re-Vision, this time with a focus on race, and on processes of making curricula and personal perception more multi-cultural. Once again, a group of hypothetical 17-year-old students appears at the end of the paper, and in this case, I write about the various kinds of understanding the "Little Women" are given with regard to Native American women and men.

In working on this account, I was reminded again that typologies are rather blunt instru-ments, which can be misused and misunderstood. It is important in the case of this typology of Interactive Phases to keep in mind the key adjective "interactive." Interactive ways of seeing coexist in dynamic interrelation. Varieties of awareness are within us; we are not fixed within them. For this reason, it is a mistake to use the typology of Interactive Phases to label, type, or critique individual persons, as though they were fixed forever in one or another form of awareness, or as though we could pass from one to another form of awareness forever. Plural ways of seeing contextualize but do not simply erase single-system under-standings. When we widen our ways of knowing, we cannot simply leave previous ways of knowing behind, nor the understandings they gave us. We can become aware of the cultural particularity and the societal consequences of various ways of knowing, seeing, or being.

At their best, typologies create frameworks within which we can understand frequently observed phenomena which at first were not seen to be in coherent relation to each other. The theory of Interactive Phases of Curricular and Personal Re-Vision has spoken to some readers about their own and others' efforts to put academic understandings on a broader and more humane base. For some readers, the phase theory illuminates the evolution of a disci-pline, a department, an idea, or an institution. For some it has been a tool for evaluation or assessment of curriculum in general, individual course syllabi, or assignments. For many it has been useful in describing, inspiring, and justifying shifts in teaching methods. It has been applied by me and others to analysis of patterns in management, leadership, government, science, social and economic policy, education and interpersonal behavior. It has illuminated for many individuals their own changing thoughts and practises in educa-tional settings and beyond.

At the outset of this discussion of interactive phase theory in terms of race, I want to mention three matters which often need to be clarified in faculty development discussions of curriculum change along lines of race. First, to repeat what I have already said, all people have racial and ethnic identities. Each "white" person has a racial and an ethnic background; there is no culturally unmarked person. Second, each person brings to his or her life the influences of a particular complex of circumstances. For example, my academic writing, including this piece, bears the marks of my own experience as a Caucasian woman who has worked in several private and wealthy sectors of American society, and who has both resisted some of their norms and at the same time internalized and benefitted from their powers. Third, as I have suggested, when "whites" look at "race" only under the rubric of "others" and "issues," this is a sign of monocultural and single-system seeing, which is culturally controlling. All people have racial identities, and people in all racial groups have more to their lives than their "issues" relative to dominant groups. Academic work in broadening racial or ethnic understanding is ineffectual if it doesn't result in shifts of sensibility such as my colleague's comment produced for me, shifts into pluralized awareness. Ethnic Studies reinforces white dominance and Women's Studies reinforces male dominance if they measure by previous norms rather than recognizing distinct being in people of all groups and all circumstances.

My discussion of phase theory and race needs one further prefatory comment: work in developing racial awareness ought to produce greater awareness of gender relations as well. As we begin to work on curricular and personal re-vision, however, "white" people often reflect previous miseducation by speaking as though race and sex are wholly separate factors of people's experience. In the monocultural, vertical worlds of either/or thinking one can't think of both **at once**. For in a white male monocultural frame of reference, whatever isn't the norm is cast as a separate and different form of anomaly. In discussing the first three interactive phases of curricular and personal re-vision here, I will keep sex and race "issues" separate as if it were indeed possible to focus on race without seeing intersecting conditions of experience which impinge on racial experience. But in Phase IV, one sees that sex and race are not separate "issues," and that the commonly used phrase "women and minorities" serves monocultural ends while having no more logic than the phrase "parents and men," or "Chinese and men," since "women" are comprised of people in every cultural group, and half of every racial and ethnic group is female. People of color and "white" women constitute a substantial majority in the U.S., while our present monoculture over entitles a "white" male minority. As long as monoculture's racial and gender outlines are unrecognized, it will be able to project separate problematical status by race and sex on those it does not entitle, and thus keep the actual majority conceptually divided against itself, not knowing in any politically usable way what is happening.

My 1983 typology of Interactive Phases of Curricular and Personal Re-vision derived from work with college faculty members to bring into the liberal arts curriculum new materials and perspectives from Women's Studies. I saw that in the early 1980s, traditionally trained white faculty members in History, for example, were likely to move from Phase One: Womanless History, to Phase Two: Women in History, on its terms. Both kinds of thinking are challenged by what I identified as Phase Three: Women as a Problem, Anomaly, or Absence in History. I meant "in History" in two senses: in the past, and in History's telling of the past. Phase Three involves and requires more anger and critique than either of the first two, but can get arrested in victim studies. It can also lead constructively to a potent wordlessness and to a daring plunge into the moving, grounded, humble, and plural inquiry of Phase Four: Women's Lives **As** History, looking toward Phase Five: History Reconstructed and Redefined to Include Us All, which I said would take us 100 years to conceive.

After observing traditionally trained faculty in all academic fields over the last eleven years, I think that the schema can be applied to the processes of faculty growth and development in all of them, even the so-called hard sciences. Teachers in any field are likely to begin teaching chiefly in what I termed Phase One: Womanless Scholarship or Science, with perhaps a little attention to Phase Two: Women in Scholarship or Science, but only on the existing terms. There may follow, if the faculty member has been keeping up with scholarship on women, and is not too defensive about what it reveals, some teaching along lines of Phase Three: Women as a Problem, Anomaly, Absence, or victim in and of the Scholarship or Science. Phase Four teaching and inquiry dares put what was neglected or marginal at the center, to see what new insight or theory can be developed from hitherto excluded or overlooked sources whose absence helped to determine the shape of each field. It can be called Experienced-based Scholarship and Science; it goes far beyond the exceptional achievements allowed in Phase Two and the discussion of "issues" allowed in Phase Three. Always the dynamic interactions among the phases suggest the making of new knowledge, the making of Phase Five: Scholarship and Science Redefined and Reconstructed to Include Us All.

As I have said, no one person or course exists in complete fixity in a given phase, and the phases I describe do not always occur in the chronological order given. Some of those who are born either within or outside of dominant groups may have been immersed since childhood in awareness of the "issues" of Phase Three, or in the relational alertness and the plural consciousness which I attribute to Phase Four. Most traditionally trained white faculty members, however, started teaching within the framework of Phase One monoculturalism, oblivious of the racial and gender elements they were immersed in. Some have moved on to think in rather predictable Phase Two ways about how to get more overlooked individuals (for at first it is seen only as a matter of overlooked individuals) into the essentially single-system version of reality which is handed on to students and is not, within monoculture, acknowledged as a version at all. One sees often in sequence the dawning realizations and syllabus changes which I identify as belonging to Phases Two, Three, and Four of consciousness.

When one considers Interactive Phase Theory with regard to race, an obvious curricular example to begin with is the U.S. History course required of all students in high school or college, or both. This course is not usually liked by students. Though it is required of all students at some point, it seems not to provide them with a sense that they are in History as voters-to-be or active makers of political policy. As it undergoes revision in the hands of teachers and textbook authors who hope to make it more representative and engaging, it usually follows predictable patterns with regard to race.

Phase One: All-White History is followed by Phase Two: Exceptional Minority Individuals in U.S. History, which leads to Phase Three: Minority Issues, or Minority Groups as Problems, Anomalies, Absences, or Victims in U.S. History. Then may come a rare and important conceptual shift to Phase Four: The Lives and Cultures of People of Color Everywhere **As** History. I think such courses, if they survive at all, will move toward an eventual Phase Five: History Redefined and Reconstructed to Include Us All.

A Phase One all-white course in U.S. History usually begins by describing the voyages of Europeans, and this entry point does not bring any challenges from students. A Phase Two course will encourage students of color to emulate the most "ambitious" of their forbears and overcome obstacles to advancement in American society. In the case of Native Americans, there may be an emphasis on those who are seen to have interacted well with the "settlers." Phase Three courses focus on, or at least give serious attention to, racism and other systemic oppressions. In the case of Native peoples, the late 19th century U.S. government policy of genocide is recognized. Phase Four is entirely different, imaginatively honoring a variety of cultures on their own terms, trying to see them through the testimony or actions of their people. For example, teaching in this mode goes far beyond Indian "issues" to Indian cultures; it suggests the wholeness and intricacy of Native cosmologies, and the Indians' particular relation to the land and consonance with the spirit in the land, before the Anglo-European ethos of land ownership was imposed. Phase Four recognizes Anglo-European ideas, actions, and standards as ethno-specific. Phase Five will require a vocabulary for perceiving, feeling, and analyzing which is both plural and coherent, and will put us in a new relation to ourselves and the world.

My original analysis of Interactive Phases of Curricular Re-Vision was placed in context of, and diagrammatically overlaid upon, my theoretical model of double structures within both psyche and society in the industrialized West: overvalued, overdeveloped, "vertical," competitive functions at odds with undervalued, under recognized, "lateral" collaborative functions. The shape of the whole is that of a faulted pyramid or mountain range with a vertical "grain" in the higher rocks and a horizontal "grain" in the rock of the substructure.

Phases One, Two, and Three, all on a vertical axis, focus respectively on the top, middle, and bottom of the pyramidally shaped competitive functions of psyche and society. Phase One: Exclusive History focuses on the functions of controlling, ordering, subduing, or prevailing. It tends to emphasize laws, wars, contests, or management of systems, and to tell the stories of winners, at the tops of the ladders of so-called success, accomplishment, achievement, and excellence. A little lower on the ladders comes the Phase Two: The Exceptions History of "ambitious" Others. Then at the bottom of the win-lose vertical territory comes the Issues-oriented History of the losers, and struggling but often defeated fighters.

79

Phase Four gives us the lateral valleys and plains below the geological fault line. This is the territory of the sustaining fields and the cyclical growing and harvesting of food. This is the territory of repetitive upkeep and maintenance, the daily making and mending of the social, material, intellectual, and spiritual fabrics, without which the climbing work within vertical structures of psyche and society is not possible. To observe the lateral world is to observe most of inner and outer life, quite beyond what the formal academy has sanctioned as worthy of study. I think the lateral world corresponds to what Paul Tillich has called "the ground of our being." Phase Four provides Experience-based History, which recognizes and strengthens fabrics and interconnections and knowledge of the multiplicities of self. Phase Five will give us Reconstructed Global and Biological History to Survive By. The present histories of conflict which implicitly underlie all of the disciplines are not histories we can survive by, in an age when we must learn to connect or reconnect, for our survival.

Phases One, Two and Three teach monocultural modes of dominance and defense, and educate the wary and controlling self; Phase Four fosters the making of what I have proposed we should call **the contingent self**, and the responsive society. Phases One, Two and Three can only see in terms of the "top" and the "bottom;" Phase Four looks to the far vaster and sustaining lateral habitat, and to the mystery of how connections, communities, and vulnerable growing things are best fostered. The hidden ethos hanging over Phases One, Two, and Three is competitive and has an either/or axis: "You win lest you lose; kill or be killed." The hidden ethos of Phase Four is collaborative and has a both/and feel: "You work for the decent survival of all, for therein lies your own best chance for survival."

Phase One consciousness involves identification with publicly powerful "white" Western males. In this phase, "whites" neither study people of color nor notice that they have not. The obliviousness of single-system seeing is a hallmark of this phase. The Phase Two remedy admits a few "minorities" to History, but only on History's terms, still without any reflectiveness on the racial history of those traditional terms and definitions. Phase Three takes us into "race issues." It identifies "race" monoculturally, ascribing race only to people of color, and sees people of color only in the category of Problem, identifying whole groups of people chiefly with losers' "issues" rather than with human life experienced fully. Doing work only in Phase Three can be inadvertently racist or sexist, for it is a cultural insult to any group to imply that its main feature is what I have called above a **deficit identity**. Phase Three never does a full analysis of the psyche or peculiarity of the "oppressor." The oppressed group is set up to look powerless and defective by contrast with the more powerful group, which is seen as the norm, and not examined for its cultural specificity, peculiarity, or pathology. Still, Phase Three at least encourages students to recognize the existence of invisible systems of power and disadvantage.

Phase Four comes out of and recognizes the lateral, connected and diverse functions of psyche and society; it is about creativity, integrity, wholeness, ordinariness, and multiple forms of power and talent unrecognized in vertical systems of appraisal. It honors both/and thinking about who exists and what counts. Without it, we will not be able to make sense of the world nor policy for our survival. Phase Four reveals us, in LeRoy Moore's language, as "bodies in the body of the world," and as distinctly different from each other, not measurable against one standard, and indeed not hewing to one, any more than the biological forms of life on the planet belong to one type.

Phase Four can be healing. But Phase Four unattached to the issues-awareness of Phase Three can be sentimental. It may be a celebration of diversity as if there were no politics which had prevented, and keeps working against, such celebration. If teachers lapse into Phase Four while forgetting about vertical power structures, they may become romantic, and not face the pain which systems of subjection inflict. For example, while honoring the strengths of African-American culture as Toni Morrison may describe them, I need to keep in mind the contexts that produced these strengths. My ancestors on one side were slave-owners. This fact bears on the conventions and particularities of many aspects of Morrison's culture and of mine. Only it bears differently on each.

Though Phase Four without Phase Three awareness can be naive, Phase Four has potential reconstitutive power for all students and teachers. For an enormous shift in the consciousness occurs when the ordinary lives of people, including people of color as the world's majority, are seen to constitute the main human story, and history is defined as all of those elements of the past in the multiplicities of our heritages which can make each of us feel **fully real** in the context of education or life. In Phase Four, the question of "How was it for people?" opens the study of History to every kind of humble detail. All voices count. Pedagogy shifts so that the professor's forms of knowing are not necessarily superior to the students' forms of knowing. The elements of Phase One are not obliterated, but take a new place in the picture. Someone has said that if you study the experience of an escaped slave woman in Boston in the 1850s you will find Lincoln, but if you start with Lincoln, you will not necessarily get to the experience of any slave. Phase Four stays very close to the ground of daily human experience, and asks many questions of people about their lives, listening for many human voices, and examining the cultural and political specificity of frameworks for collecting and evaluating information. All experience is seen as a source of knowledge.

My previous paper provided brief examples of Phase Four teaching with regard to both race and gender in the disciplines of Literature, Psychology, Biology, and Art. I concluded by saying that I saw the work toward Phase Five as taking one hundred years because it involves a reconstruction of consciousness, perception and behavior. It will very likely attempt to create, and then maintain, public awareness that we must, locally and globally, value life more than conflict, and attend to the processes of maintaining life. I think we cannot at this time even imagine the categories within which we will collect information for plural Phase Five understandings and reconstructions of education. Most "educated" minds seem terribly stuck in narrow frameworks leading to personal anxiety, and accepting of social repression, turmoil, and global danger. But if our descendants work at Phase Five, they will probably find many fugitive precedents for their work in the perplexed and tentative legacies we leave now.

With regard to race in the undergraduate curriculum, most of our universities still feature Phase One introductory courses in virtually all departments. These courses feature the thought and research of Anglo-European-American scholars, i.e. "white" forefathers in the making of knowledge. The courses feature winners in law, war, or trade; the getting and holding of literal or conceptual territory; the making of frameworks for understanding; the wresting of "order" from "chaos"; the development of cultural traditions from nothingness or from "primitive" originals. In such courses, one may study people of color like Egyptians under the impression that they are really "white." In monocultural, single-system courses, students of all races are asked to imagine that the essential insights into human thought, labor, imagination, and care can all be found in the study of Caucasian people.

My generalizations may bring objections from some who say that the introductory level college curriculum is now overstretched through inclusion of new materials on "race and class." This is an illusion. The fact is that no works by people of color are seen as **central** to understanding any of the traditional liberal arts disciplines, and people of color are presented chiefly as disadvantaged, or as primitive forbears of real civilization, or as recent immigrants with cultural traditions that create problems for "America." Moreover, there is very little material of any kind by and about non-Western majorities in most college and school students' courses.

If readers doubt this, they should examine the introductory-level course reading lists of their own institutions. "White" teachers should imagine themselves as students of color, for example as Asian-American students, trying to find their people reflected as valid in basic readings. Most courses are still monocultural, even Anthropology, in which teachers focus on the thinking of "white," mostly male, anthropologists. This gives "white" students the impression that there is one main piece of cultural turf and it is their turf. The students of color, like the "white" women, are implicitly shown they have not been necessary to knowledge, enterprise, and past culture-making, nor are they essential to future cultural invention or reclamation. In such courses, oral traditions are seen to count for nothing at all; argumentative written traditions, though very culture and gender specific in origin, inform most of the "objective" texts and all of the assignments. Historiography courses, much touted for their plural, comparative sophistication, focus on "white" men.

Phase Two courses bring in a few famous or notable people of color but do not challenge the traditional outlines and definitions of what is worth studying. Therefore the emphasis continues to be on "firsts," laws, wars, winners, talented individuals, fighters, and those who nearly matched what is taken to be "white" male achievement. People of color who succeeded in getting and holding onto some kinds of social, political, or artistic territory are seen as possibly worth studying. But often those who are noticed in Phase Two courses are represented as having gone far but not irrationally far in challenging existing "white," male, or colonial frameworks, and therefore are seen as being worth noticing: Sacajawea, Sequoyah, Black Elk, Douglass, Baldwin, King, Walker, Morrison. Usually, Latinos and Asian-Americans do not get into Phase Two courses at all; recent and rare exceptions are Maxine Hong Kingston, Yoko Ono, and Cesar Chavez. Those who most strongly rebelled against "white" dominance are usually annihilated in the telling of history as they were in life. Those who accommodated or assimilated somewhat may become cultural heroes, especially in retrospect; they may come to be seen as almost within the "mainstream."

In Phase Two, teaching about people of color as exceptional and therefore worthy of notice, can create psychological problems. Many teachers think that in holding up "exceptions," they are providing role models for students of color, and demonstrating to "white" students that people of color should be taken seriously. The impulse can be genuine, and a fairly wealthy "white" person like myself should take care not to dismiss models of "success" for students who may be feeling desperate and continually put down. It is easy to critique prevailing definitions of success from a position of economic security. Still, the Phase Two-Famous Few curriculum can be damaging, as it may deliver to students of color the message that most of their people are not worth studying, and that if they become **unlike** their people, they may be worthy of notice. It may serve as a bribe: leave your people and you may rise up the "real life" ladders from the bottom to become an American hero. Phase Two can put students at psychological risk, encouraging them to make their way not as members of their ethnic group but as soloists.

Elizabeth Minnich has pointed out that this loner status makes a person from a nondominant group vulnerable to every setback. Once the loner goes through the gates alone, refusing to identify with her or his stigmatized group, then every setback must seem like something which has been caused by personal behavior or is at some level merited.

A second psychological danger to students of Phase Two-Famous Few teaching is the implication that if you are "really good," you will not be seen as African-American, Latino, Asian-American, or Native-American, but only "as a person." We women are sometimes taught that we will be seen as persons, if we will just forget that we are women. No; we will be seen as having sex and race and ethnic identity, especially if we are female or dark-skinned, or have features identified with a cultural subgroup. It is mere illusion to imagine that American adults see anyone as "just a person"; our "educational" and media training in typecasting, hierarchical placing, and mistrust has been too strong. Phase Two success stories of "achievers" imply to students that all they need to do to get out of their debilitating circumstances is to work a little harder and "make it on their own," without complaint, and without ties to their (impaired) people.

One further problem with Phase Two teaching is that the singling out of cultural heroes misrepresents the values of cultures in which the making of the individual hero is not thought of as possible or desirable. Sojourner Truth and Harriet Tubman were working for and with their people, yet are featured as outstanding individuals. Often collaborative group work is not seen to exist. The chief poster for the UN Decade for Women 1985 conference in Nairobi features a single woman weaving a basket. Women weave baskets together in Kenya; it is a group activity. In order to create the poster the designer had to misrepresent the culture. Phase Two courses featuring a famous few who stand out "above the crowd" can grossly misrepresent Asian-American, Native American, and Latino cultures in which the star system is not the norm. American baseball players in Japan today have said, "The Japanese play for ties; no team and no player should get too far ahead." Asian-American youngsters who do very well in the American school system may be doing so not for stardom but as a reflection of other cultural values, for example, duty, obedience, or honor, a cultural ideal poorly understood by North Americans who do not have Asian ancestry.

The shift to Phase Three usually comes when teachers realize that Phase Two is politically naive: it features a few who survived in society but gives little attention to the structures of power in society. An important emotional shift occurs when teachers look past individual lives and experiences to invisible hierarchical systems which have very strong predictive power for the general outlines of any given life. Most teachers in the United States were not educated in school to see these systems at work, but were taught that the individual is the main unit of society and that the U.S. system is a meritocracy. It is a sign of personal growth when teachers begin to pass on to students systemic awareness of social inequities in resources, opportunities, and access to public power.

Phase Three, then, focuses on racism, classism, sexism, struggle, overt violence, persecution, persistence, protest, and work toward new policies and laws. Especially in the field of social history, the emphasis is on those who fought for change which would benefit oppressed people. Phase Three usefully focuses on interlocking oppressions, and at its best it links the study of power within the United States to power worldwide, so that students can see how patterns of colonialism, imperialism, and genocide outside of the U.S. match patterns of domination, militarism, and genocide at home. All teachers and students in the United States need this experience of asking who has the most power, and why, and how it is used, and what is going on.

But Phase III has its weaknesses. Many white social historians think they are studying multiculturally when in fact they are merely studying protest movements monoculturally. All the protestors look more or less the same. Phase Three scholarship never asks "ordinary" people about their lives, never takes children, women, or servants as authorities, never listens to voices which the academic world has not yet respected.

Phase Three, then, like Phase Two, opens some doors and keeps others shut. Its main conceptual fault is that it keeps the powers of definition and evaluation in the hands of the present "authorities," within a single system of meaning and value defined monoculturally. We will never make most people's experience seem either real or valid if our teaching and research still rest on the kinds of credentialling and vertical appraisal derived from the experience of those who have had the most power. Just as Phase Two analyses of "Black achievement" rarely encompass one chief achievement of African Americans, which is to have survived and endured with dignity, Phase Three tends to focus on visible political deficits without acknowledging any political dimension in focusing on "deficits" to begin with. The analysis of others' "issues" does not prepare Caucasian people to look at their own psyches, or to learn from "others."

I have noticed that many or most of us in the "white" academic world are more comfortable discussing issues of disempowerment than taking seriously those lives which do not center on, depend on, or resist "white" male governance, and which embody alternative forms of power. As I have said, Phase Three attributes to whole groups **deficit identities**, while denying their **cultural identities**, and in doing so it maintains control for the dominant group. It sets up a dominant paradigm in the mind of the student and then allows the underdog to be seen only as challenging it. It says to students of color, "You can be a fighter," not "You are a maker of culture and of life." It says to "white" students, "You are high; others are low." Such monocultural teaching about racism may ironically increase arrogance or ignorance in "white" students. It may teach them to sympathize with, or even admire the struggles of people of color but it will not teach that "winners" have anything to learn from "losers," except perhaps how to fight. Its lenses are useless for clarifying my colleague's comment that she would not want to be white.

Phase Four, on the other hand, illuminates her comment. For Phase Four makes a crucial shift to a lateral, plural frame of reference beyond winning and losing. It produces courses in which we are all seen to be in it together, all having ethnic and racial identity, all having culture, all placed by birth in particular social and political circumstances, all with some power to say no, and yes, and "This I create"; all with voices to be heard, all damaged, and all in need of healing, all real, very distinctively ourselves, potential makers of new theories and new understandings of life. When I say "all damaged," I am thinking of the fact that my slave-holding ancestors were damaged. They were not damaged in the same ways that their slaves were, but they were made cruel and sick by their roles. Phase Four, being a frame of mind that goes beyond monoculturalism to cultural pluralism, allows me to see this. It opens the doors that my friend opened for me, onto my own culture newly realized by me as a culture, and onto hers, formed on a different base of experience. Phase Four suggests multiple worlds, or in the words of the Pueblo Indian Gregory Cajete, it suggests **Multiversal Realities**, rather than a single **Universe**.

Phase Four reading lists in any discipline often contain multiple short works or kinds of material, including work by students, and provide multiple insights on any situation in several media, with a de-emphasis on "issues" of disempowerment and a more unusual emphasis on cultural detail, and voices from daily life. Phase Four classes can be wondrous in their energy, interest, and healing power. Students feel co-ownership of them, and sometimes experience such courses as life-lines. It is true that competitiveness, anxiety, and vertical stereotyping from the conventional types of teaching carry over into the work of Phase Four classes, but teachers creating laterally expanded and culturally explicit syllabi usually try to redistribute power more evenly than usual in a classroom, and to weaken privilege systems which interfere with listening to many voices, and respecting testimony from many sources.

Whereas Phase III emphasizes differences from an assumed but unexamined norm, Phase IV recognizes distinctiveness without accepting any norm; it recognizes in experience the equivalent of what Gerard Manley Hopkins named as the "inscape" of created things—particular and vivid internal distinctness.

Some time ago I wrote a paper which lists 46 ways in which I daily experience having "white" skin privilege relative to my African-American colleagues in the same building.[3] This is a Phase Four analysis. The paper rests on my sense of ethno-particularity, ethno-specificity, and ethno-peculiarity with regard to unearned advantage in my workplace. "White" skin privilege is invisible in the Phase Three monocultural focus on "others" issues and deficits. I could see the cultural circumstance of having unearned over-advantage and its attendant cultural deformities only within the multicultural framework of Phase Four, in which my racial group is not assumed to embody a neutral or desirable norm.

Phase Four understandings take some blame out of the description of dominant groups; all people are seen as born into circumstances they did not ask for and systems they did not invent. The processes at work in Phase IV include listening, observing, making connections, respecting many kinds of life, power, and thought, including one's own, and imagining how to institutionalize the protection of diverse forms of life including distinct forms of human community.

Phase Five is needed to help us to an as-yet-unthinkable reconciliation between our competitive, hierarchical propensities and our contingent and relational propensities. Phase Four education helps to develop and reward the capacity for being in relation to others; Phase Five will need to help us also to rethink organizational structures in complex worlds where distribution of resources, services, and basic supports requires balanced uses of vertical and lateral abilities.

For this reason, as I imagine Phase Five, my diagrammatic model of psychic and societal structures turns into a large, three-dimensional globe. The faulted pyramids, with their bedrock lateral functions underlying the vertical functions, become simply one element in the topology of each continent, in a world like our own in which mountain ranges are one of the forms of geography. Each continent, each group of cultures, has its ranges, its "peaks," its dynasties, but mountain climbing is understood to be one particular human activity, not the only human activity. Sending expeditions to climb very high mountains requires preparation, equipment, freeze-dried food, support systems, base camps, porters, sponsorship, and people who can bow out of other life-sustaining activities or responsibilities. Certain maps can be drawn from high summits only. Many useful maps can never be drawn from summits at all. In any case, high summits do not support most forms of life. They are deoxy genated, and it is well known that people on too little oxygen do not make very wise decisions about the welfare of themselves or others.

It is the foothills, valleys, and alluvial plains which support life best, with rainfall, fertile soil, and concentrations of human knowledge about growing and harvesting. And at the edge of the water we can learn to farm the sea as well. For the last 40 years, we in the U.S. have, figuratively speaking, taught that mountain climbing is the worthiest activity, the mark of ambition and of success. To shift to metaphors of making and mending the fabrics of culture and environment seems to me to make more sense now. We can also usefully teach metaphors of journeying. Many of our students in the U.S. are free to travel, metaphorically speaking, to many sites in the topology, to experience many varieties of life, on many figurative continents. Some will stay in single locations throughout a lifetime. But we will continue to suffer if educators keep teaching that mountain climbing and peak experience are the best activities, and that the resources of the society are well spent operating base camps which help a few people or nations to stand briefly on summits and feel they have prevailed over life or each other.

The metaphysical shift from a faulted pyramid to a globe in which peaks and valleys are parts of cultural topology is accompanied by a further conceptual shift. The multicultural globe is interior as well as exterior; the multicultural worlds are in us as well as around us. Early cultural conditioning trained each of us as children to shut off awareness of certain groups, voices, abilities, and inclinations, including the inclination to be with many kinds of children. Continents we might have known were closed off or subordinated within us. The domains of personality that remain can and do fill the conceptual space like colonizing powers. But a potential for pluralized understanding remains in us; the moves toward reflective consciousness come in part from almost silenced continents within ourselves. Greater diversity of curriculum reflects not just the exterior multicultural world but the interior self which in early childhood was aware of, and attuned to, many varieties of experience.

Readers of my 1983 paper on phase theory will know that I matched the phases with the sensibilities of hypothetical first-year college students called Meg, Amy, Jo, and Jo's twin daughters, Maya and Angela, and their younger sister Adrienne. I wished to indicate that what and how we teach in each of these frames of reference actually have life outcomes for students. This is true for the various ways we teach Ethnic Studies. I cannot guess about the effects on students of color of Phases One, Two, and Three, but I will sketch some portraits of the ways in which I have seen instruction in these phases affect the development of Anglo-European-American students, and then suggest the consonance between Maya and Angela's lives and Phase Four curriculum. My focus here is on the various kinds of understanding which the "Little Women" are given with regard to Native American culture.

Meg, who is a casualty of a Phase One curriculum, is a white girl who tries very hard to be good. she wants to be "sugar and spice," and also to be kind. When she is growing up, her brother plays Cowboys and Indians every afternoon with his friends in the neighborhood. She watches shows on cowboys and Indians. She learns in elementary school that the "settlers" had to contend with many "dangers of the wilderness," which included Indians and wild animals. She learns in high school that the settlers had to protect their families from Indians, who took scalps. In four years of college, she reads one chapter on "The North American Indian," which cites 12 white male anthropologists, refers to nearly 300 tribes and hundreds of language groups, yet does not make Indians seem the slightest bit real to her. This is Phase One Ethnic Studies in which "white" people neither study people of color nor notice that they haven't. Meg has studied "white" anthropologists. During her years in college, Meg will never start a conversation with a student of color. The way they "band together" makes her nervous. She seeks her friends, for safety. Meg will marry young, feeling a need of protection from many perceived dangers. She will marry a "white" man who turns out later to be neither a settler nor a protector. Many years later, as a Continuing Education student, Meg will find herself in another college course, reading for the very first time the words of a Native American. She reads *Black Elk Speaks*, and she is in tears. The sacred hoop is broken. Meg is devastated to discover the wholeness of Indian worlds just at the same time that she learns of their near destruction.

Amy, the ambitious art student schooled in Phase Two, appraises Indian work casually, as well as competitively. She knows it is only "craft," not Art, but feels the need to find grounds for putting it down. She finds it repetitive, primitive, inexpressive, and of course merely functional. Amy thinks some of the rugs and pots are handsome, and she is sure that she would recognize the work of a first-rate Indian artist, if only these people would put away their talk about broken treaties, and transcend their "cause." Amy cannot understand why they keep repeating old stories of their traditions, instead of joining what she thinks of as the cultural mainstream. She feels no curiosity about Indians, but gives a silent cheer when she hears that Wilma Mankiller has become Principal Chief of the Cherokee Nation. "That's the way it should be done," she thinks. "Just go for it and don't let anything get in your way." The idea that Wilma Mankiller was chosen because of her consonance with, rather than her competition against, others in her nation does not occur to Amy, who has been deeply dyed in the tradition of "the individual versus society." Amy takes a passing interest in Curtis's photographs of Indians, for their strong and striking faces. She feels, however, that if these people were "really good," they would have prevailed. She cannot imagine a culture in which the aim is not to prevail. As a gallery owner in middle age, Amy is criticized for her failure to show works by artists of color. She says that she would show some if she could find a truly outstanding artist. Her mind is as open as the "exceptions" curriculum of Phase Two can make it.

Jo, the older "white" woman who comes to college out of a failed marriage at the age of 40, is appalled by what she learns in her course on Gender, Race, and Class in American society. She had never understood why the Indians disappeared; she had known nothing of the slaughter of the buffalo, which took away the Plains Indians' means of existence, the Trail of Tears which killed tens of thousands of Cherokees and deprived most of the Nation of its native habitat, or the outlawing of Indian languages, laws and rituals. She sees in the silencing and crippling and betrayal of the Indians the same kinds of systemic oppression she has felt as a woman, silenced, dispossessed, beaten and battered in a marriage which now feels to her like a broken treaty. She is outraged that the books in which "white" anthropologists speak about Indian demographics do not make Indians' sufferings come alive. She writes a history paper on the way in which "whites" have named as "great" Indians only those who met Europeans halfway, but she does not know what to say about the corrective except that the American historians should recognize the fiercest fighters more honestly, and make the betrayals by European-Americans clearer. Jo is distressed by this paper as she hands it in; something is missing, but she does not know what.

After the class ends, Jo starts a correspondence with an Indian woman in prison whose name she has found in an anthology of writing by North American Indians. As this correspondence goes on, she begins a support group for imprisoned Indian women, in order to raise money for their legal expenses and their families, and to provide them with reading and writing materials. Jo feels that she is at the edge of a vast territory about which she is wholly ignorant, and is angered to see in retrospect that the book she read on United States Women's History in a Women's Studies course did not contain a single mention of Native American women. She wonders whether she shouldn't have majored in Ethnic Studies rather than having to find out about Indians in this roundabout way. She can't seem to get people in her field, Women's Studies, interested in Native Americans. She persuades the Student Union Committee to show the film *Broken Treaty at Battle Mountain*. She thinks of her work for Indians as being **for them**, but not for herself.

Maya and Angela, Jo's twin children, are attached both through schooling and through life outside of school to both their Anglo-American and their African-American cultural roots. Whereas the "white" feminists they meet often talk about inventing new forms beyond patriarchy, they think of their "black" culture as both prepatriarchal and nonpatriarchal, and assume that it is these cultural traditions which need to be reclaimed in order to make the world a saner place. They own a cassette of the television interview in which Bill Moyers asks Louise Erdrich how Indian values can survive in this world of individuality, competition, and technology. Erdrich asks how the world can possibly survive **without** Indian values, saying that it has come to the brink of ecological crisis without them. The twins also like Michael Dorris's account of the mailman who came to his door asking him how to run an all-Iroquois week for a group of Cub Scouts in the woods. Dorris laughs and says that the most important thing was to take these boys' mothers, because Iroquois boys wouldn't possibly know how to get along in the woods without their mothers to teach them.

Maya and Angela are of course aware of Indian persecution, but they share Beth Brant's feeling that they are not victims; they are "organizers, freedom fighters, feminists, healers, and . . . none of this is new; it has been true for centuries." They like their own laughter, their powers of spirit, **their identities**. They would not like to trade their identities for anyone else's. They feel affinities with Native Americans, with many other men and women of color, and with the few "white" feminist women and men who have made common cause with them. Their mother wants to talk about Indian Issues with the Cherokee friend whom they bring home for a meal. Maya and Angela have to explain why their friend did not make eye contact and did not respond warmly to this subject. They explain that her lack of eye contact is a mark of respect, and that her manner reflects Tsalagi cultural values of patience, respect for age, personal caution, listening and observing, making criticism indirectly, and keeping the emphasis on the whole group.

Maya and Angela see themselves as coming from different Nations than Indians, with heritages of different stories, but feel that they are similarly guided by spirits, and they have deep attachments to the "black" community. In their identification with darkness, they find nurturance. They do not study Indians so much as to derive strength from them: Carol Lee Sanchez, Joy Harjo, Beth Brant, Marilou Awiakta, Bea Medicine, Brenda Collins, Linda Hogan. They feel connected to their ancestors, to the invisible world, and to birds, trees, earth and sky. Maya and Angela write on Native American cultures in college term papers; Maya writes on Mother Earth and Grandmother Earth, describing the distinction between Mother Earth, who brings forth trees and corn, and Grandmother Earth, who appears in some Indian cosmologies as the growing principle itself. She contrasts Plato's view of the defects of the accidental or merely actual, as against the pureness of pure Form, with the

Indian view that Mother Earth's products are not defective reductions of any purer principle. Angela, in a Phase Four Education course, writes a primer for grade school children, explaining that the Indians were the settlers, and illustrating elements of the wholeness and integrity of their lives, before the European invaders arrived. It is no surprise when several years after their leaving college, these women are adopted into one of the clans of the Cherokee Nation and continue various forms of teaching and learning on the Cherokee theme that we are all part of the human circle.

Adrienne, their younger sister, is trying to help work on the curriculum toward survival. She dreams of balance between the creatures of the earth and their habitats, and she dreams of balance among nations and individuals so that all may survive with dignity. She is rather abstracted and preoccupied and is working toward metaphors for the new texts which might sustain us.

Maya, Angela, and Adrienne have refused to accept the projections onto them of deficit identity by the dominant culture. Though my description of them may sound simple and even halcyon, they are doing heroic work in refusing monocultural messages about what they are. Their affirmation of their wholeness and their will to connect rather than sever themselves from others is a hard-won sanity which could cost them very heavily. They may be seen as unnatural, neurotic, unambitious, devious, secretive, out of touch with the "realities" of modern civilization, non-professional, unable to "progress." They may be seen as enemies of the government and vilified both subtly and obviously by those who have the most cultural power. Ethnic Studies and Women's Studies can strengthen their hand if taught not only with a focus on aspiration (Phase Two) or understanding of systemic oppressions (Phase Three), but also with respect for and reinforcement for their personal and cultural integrity. Mending the sacred hoop is dangerous political work, but it is work toward survival. When Women's Studies makes common cause with the Ethnic Studies to put human dignity and integrity at the center, then both will be doing their most dangerous and healing work.

It is significant that Meg, Amy, and Jo never receive a version of curriculum that goes much beyond the boundaries of the United States. Maya and Angela, on the other hand, have been supported to think beyond national boundaries, recognizing people everywhere, and seeing the earth and the sky as more basic organizers of human life than local governments. They have cross-cultural curiosity and commitment, trusting their own daily experience to lead to questions about larger world patterns. It is as though they have mentally signed a treaty of peace with others across national boundaries, regardless of what national leaders allow or want. They think of people in cultures other than their own as having cultural complexity and integrity, and as being unknown to them, but potentially in conversation with them. They feel a strong need to find common bonds and make some common policy amidst the diversities. Differences in governing bodies and strategies are not to them any indicator of final separateness; instead, they feel they belong in contingent affiliation with life everywhere. To citizens like this, we could entrust policy making. Our choices about education will determine whether we will have such citizens.

Endnotes

[1]My colleague is Gwendolyn Thomas, who in 1972 was Assistant Professor of English at the University of Denver. She is now Assistant Vice President of Student Affairs at Metropolitan State College in Denver.

[2]McIntosh, Peggy. (1983). "Interactive Phases of Curricular Re-Vision: A Feminist Perspective." Working Paper #124, Wellesley, MA, Wellesley College Center for Research on Women.

[3]McIntosh, Peggy. (1988). "White Privilege and Male Privilege: A Personal Account of Coming to Understand Correspondences Through Work in Women's Studies." Working Paper #189, Wellesley, MA, Wellesley College Center for Research on Women.

PERSONALITY AND PREJUDICE

by
Bem P. Allen

There are three reasons why Allport's book *The Nature of Prejudice* (1954) is perhaps the single most important work ever done on the subject. First, it was the earliest comprehensive discussion of prejudice that was based on a significant body of scientific research. Second, it was extremely influential in shaping social scientists' thinking concerning prejudice. Third, because Allport has had so much influence on prejudice research done since 1954, it is relatively easy to fit some of today's findings regarding prejudice into his theoretical framework.

Prejudice Defined

According to Allport (1954), prejudice is felt or expressed antipathy based upon a faulty and inflexible generalization and may be directed toward a group as a whole, or toward an individual because of membership in the group. Thus, prejudice is negative feelings regarding members of some group that are sometimes just felt internally and sometimes expressed openly. It is based on the faulty generalization that most, or all, members of some group, such as Native Americans, possess certain negative traits, such as drunkenness. Such a generalization is always erroneous in the sense that no trait will apply to most, much less all, members of a large group—even skin color varies greatly among people who are called "black."

Discrimination usually has meant directing more negative behaviors toward a particular group, compared to others, but may include having more negative thoughts and feelings about some group relative to others. People can be discriminatory in regard to their feelings and thinking, just as they are in terms of their behavior: "I **hate** them (feelings) because they are **trash**" (thinking). Many measures of prejudice amount to asking people—usually via questionnaire—how much they discriminate so their level of prejudice can be inferred. For this reason, it is possible to offer a more empirical definition of prejudice consistent with Allport's theoretical definition. Prejudice measures typically ask about **self-perceptions** of discrimination. Therefore, **prejudice** may be seen as the degree to which people believe they discriminate against members of some group in terms of directing relatively more negative behaviors, as well as thoughts and feelings, toward group members. As prejudice is most often assessed with the use of questionnaires completed anonymously, people's pronouncements about their level of prejudice probably represent what they really believe.

Social Distance

Given this empirical definition, it is immediately obvious that what people believe about their level of discrimination may not be accurate. Because nobody has total insight, some people who honestly claim not to discriminate against others may do so anyway. To explore this logical conclusion, it is necessary to consider Social Distance (SD), a measure of discrimination that requires individuals to indicate how close to themselves they would allow members of some group to come. Allport (1954, p. 39) listed the items of the SD scale as follows:

I would admit (members of some group):
1. To close kin by marriage
2. To my club as personal chums
3. To my street as neighbors
4. To employment in my occupation
5. To citizenship in my country
6. As visitors only to my country
7. Would exclude from my country

Notice that the social relations to which the members of some group can be admitted vary from those involving a great deal of **intimacy** with group members, **commitment** to them, and **permanency** of relationships involving them (top of list) to those involving no intimacy, commitment, and permanency (bottom of list).

Not only do people who strongly claim not to discriminate against some often-disparaged group really believe themselves; these self-proclaimed "unprejudiced" people probably do not discriminate under most circumstances. Nevertheless, would they discriminate when asked to accept the same group's members for social relations that entail high intimacy, commitment, and permanency? An answer to the question may tell us whether what people believe about their level of discrimination tends to be accurate.

A number of years ago, I gave some European American college students a test to determine the degree to which they were prejudiced against African Americans (Allen, 1975). Based on their scores, some students were classified as "unprejudiced," some as "prejudiced" and some as "ambivalent" (gave mixed signals about their level of discrimination). All of these subjects were then asked to indicate the degree of closeness they would allow African Americans by use of an SD scale composed of items 1 and 3 (Triandis, Loh, & Levine, 1966). Results showed that all categories of these white subjects, even those who claimed they did not discriminate according to race, in fact did so. When it comes to relations involving intimacy, commitment, and permanency, even "unprejudiced" subjects show racial discrimination.

Although unprejudiced white subjects did discriminate on the SD scale, when it came to indicating whom they admire, another part of the same study showed they did not discriminate by race. In fact, they actually expressed more admiration for African Americans than for European Americans. (This so-called "reverse discrimination" effect reverted to no discrimination when subjects thought they were hooked up to a lie detector machine). But why do all categories of European Americans, even self-proclaimed non-discriminators, in fact discriminate when it comes to choices for intimate, committed, permanent social relations? European Americans show great individual differences in prejudice, but they do not display great individual differences in discrimination for intimate, committed, permanent relations. Perhaps some underlying dimension for which individual differences are not great explains why most such people sometimes discriminate by race.

In the case of discrimination against African Americans, such a dimension appears to exist. **Racism** is widespread negative sentiment directed toward African Americans and other people of color (Allen, 1975; 1990). It has been argued that racism is a part of the mainstream culture in this country (Gaines & Reed, 1995). When people incorporate their culture, largely through the process of identification, they swallow it whole. They ingest not only the good aspects of their culture, of which there are many; they also consume the bad— racism. Because most people fully adopt their culture, most European Americans incorporate racism within themselves. This may be the reason even unprejudiced European Americans show discrimination in some areas: racism rears it ugly head when it comes to making choices of others for intimate, committed, permanent relations, although it fails to show up in other realms, such as deciding whom to admire. It should be added that racism also may show up in subtle ways. By contrast, racism is reflected often in a wide spectrum of prejudiced people's expressions and behaviors. The top of Figure 1 shows the degree to which racism is **incorporated** by European Americans who range across the prejudice spectrum. You can see that racism is rather universally incorporated, even by the "unprejudiced." The bottom of Figure 1 shows the degree to which racism shows up in the **social choices and reactions** of European Americans who range across the prejudice spectrum. You can see that racism clearly and regularly shows up only in the social choices and reactions of high prejudiced people (bottom). It shows up in the choices/reactions of low prejudiced and especially "unprejudiced" people only in terms of permanent, intimate, and committed choices and in subtle ways. Also, note that, with this schema, only high prejudiced people are considered "racist."

Figure 1
The relationship between racism and prejudice

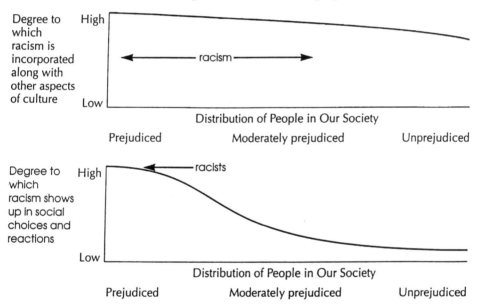

Consistent with this consideration of racism, Allport (1954) found that racial animosity is very widespread. After examining the polls, assessing antagonism toward various groups—most frequently African Americans—Allport concluded, "These . . . studies tempt us to estimate that four-fifths of the American population harbors enough antagonism toward minority groups to influence their daily conduct" (p. 78). Although his statement was based on polls taken many years ago, there is reason to believe it is still accurate today. While animosity was very open in the early fifties, today, in the case of most European Americans, it has become limited to a few social relations and it has evolved to be more underground and subtle. European Americans' reluctance to engage in intimate, committed, permanent relations with African Americans is reflected in the still very low, but growing, interracial marital rate (Allen, 1990). Also, many careful investigations of subtle behaviors done over the years have revealed definite traces of racial antipathy even in "unprejudiced" European Americans (Allen, 1978; Dovidio, Evans, & Tyler, 1986; Winterbrink, Judd, & Park, 1997).

"Race" Differences

Allport (1954) traces continued interest in alleged racial differences to arguments that subcategories of humans exist and can be arranged in a hierarchy from best to worst. It makes thinking and life itself simpler to believe that there are big differences between one "race" and the next and few differences among people of a given racial designation. It is also gratifying: one can declare one's own race "best" and view the members of other races as uniformly inferior.

Allport (1954) asserted that gender mirrors how we react to the races. "Only a small part of our human nature is differentiated by sex. . . .[T]he vast proportion of human physical, physiological, psychological traits are not sex linked" (p. 109). Yet, despite the evidence of no difference on critical traits such as IQ, "women are regarded as inferior, kept in the home . . . [and] denied many of the rights and privileges of men. The special roles assigned to them are far in excess of what sexual genetic difference would justify. So it is with race" (p. 109). That we may habitually exaggerate gender differences is the focus of much current research (Allen, 1995; but see Eagly, 1987). Allport (1954), a pioneer in questioning "race," makes two important points about the concept. First, most of the world's people are of "mixed stock"; thus most do not fit any racial category. Second, "Most human characteristics ascribed to race are . . . [actually] ethnic, not racial" (p. 113). Today, the validity of "race" is again being challenged (Cavalli-Sforza, Menozz, & Piazza, 1994; Katz, 1995; Weizmann, Wiener, Wiesenthal, & Ziegler, 1990; Yee, Fairchild, Weizmann, & Wyatt, 1993; Zuckerman, 1990). It now appears that three criteria must be met before "race" is applicable to humans: (1) consensually accepted criteria for differentiation among races must be developed and shown to actually erect clear boundaries between one "race" and the next; (2) variability within "races" must be adequately reconciled with assumptions of intraracial uniformity; and (3) overlap among races must be reconciled with the assumption that "races" are meaningfully distinct (Allen & Adams, 1992).

Stereotypes

According to Allport (1954), prejudice affects our thinking as well as our feelings. It is associated with the development of beliefs concerning the traits supposedly possessed by all or most members of a group. A belief of this sort is called a stereotype, an exaggerated belief that members of a group possess a certain trait; "Its function is to justify (rationalize) our conduct in relation to that [group]" (p. 191). Such beliefs may have a "kernel of truth" to them. In centuries past, Jews were "money handlers" in Europe, simply because they were allowed few alternatives for making a living. The problem is that this veridical observation evolved to become "most [or all] Jews are obsessed with making money." Though there may be a "kernel of truth" to a stereotype, it is almost always false to assume that most of any large group possess any trait one can conjure up (excepting those characteristics that define the group; e.g., all Catholics are Catholic).

Stereotypes do tend to change somewhat in content over time, and the overall valence of their emotional tone may show some change in response to major events over time. Before World War II, the tone of our stereotypes of the Japanese was negative, but not strongly so. As soon as Pearl Harbor was bombed, stereotypes of the Japanese became viciously negative. As the Japanese wrought their economic miracle following the war, stereotypes became more positive. Our current perception of them as economically too strong has swung the pendulum in a negative direction, but their economic recession of the late 1990s has moderated that perception somewhat.

What of the tone and content of stereotypes about African Americans? Allport lists the following stereotypes of African Americans held by European Americans at the time he was writing his 1954 book: unintelligent, morally primitive, emotionally unstable, overassertive, lazy, boisterous, fanatically religious, gamblers, flashy dressers, criminal, violent, reproductively prolific, occupationally unstable, superstitious, happy-go-lucky, ignorant, musical. To find out how these stereotypes might have changed 81 white undergraduate students were asked to each write down five words to describe African Americans (Allen, 1996). Sixty-three African American students were given the same instruction. Next the words most frequently used to describe African Americans were tallied. The results are presented in Table 1.

Table 1
African Americans described by themselves and by European Americans
(% of each sample using each word)

By Themselves	By European Americans
6 misunderstood	6 boastful
6 emotional	6 fast
6 poor	6 moody
6 funny	6 poor
6 humorous	6 strong
6 inventive	7 musical
6 powerful	7 obnoxious
8 corrupt	7 prejudiced
8 determined	9 black
8 educated	9 mean
10 independent	9 smart
10 friendly	10 arrogant
11 athletic	10 funny
13 intelligent	10 independent
14 beautiful	11 corrupt
14 oppressed	11 friendly
27 strong	21 humorous
27 smart	25 loud
40 athletic	

You can see that European Americans' stereotypes of African Americans are still negative. Though some content remains the same—"musical" and "loud" (boisterous)—there have been some changes. African Americans are now seen as "humorous" and "athletic." Notice also that African Americans agree with European Americans on "independent," but mention "athletic" much less often and include "intelligent," omitted by European Americans.

Unlike the vast majority of other stereotype studies, this one involved asking African Americans to indicate stereotypes of European Americans. (Usually African Americans are not asked, or stereotypes of various "white" ethnic groups are assessed, not "whites" in general). Table 2 displays the stereotypes of European Americans.

Table 2
European Americans described by themselves and by African Americans
(% of each sample using each word)

By Themselves	By African Americans
6 corrupt	6 inventive
6 free	6 competitive
6 happy	6 powerful
6 kind	6 wealthy
7 conceited	8 educated
7 educated	10 racist
7 egotistical	11 selfish
10 intelligent	11 greedy
10 prejudiced	13 rich
10 rich	16 mean
12 humorous	19 smart
12 independent	24 prejudiced
12 inventive	41 corrupt
12 lazy	
15 arrogant	
15 friendly	
19 competitive	
19 greedy	
32 smart	

Again, African Americans and European Americans show limited agreement. African Americans are more negative about European Americans than European Americans are about themselves. Both agree that European Americans are "greedy" and "smart," though European Americans are more extreme in this perception. In a switch over time, European Americans now see themselves as "lazy," but no longer see African Americans that way (African Americans rarely used the word "lazy"). They also see themselves as "intelligent," but African Americans do not.

Neither these results nor those reported by Allport (1954) were produced by large, representative samples of U.S. citizens. These results, however, were produced by procedures with certain advantages. One plus is that subjects produced the words from their own vocab-

96

ularies, rather than being forced to choose from some limited, possibly biased list. This fact probably accounts for results not predicted on the basis of previous research, such as European Americans being seen as "corrupt" "prejudiced," and "greedy" and African Americans as "friendly" "funny" and "humorous."

Painting the Picture of the Prejudiced Personality

The traits highly prejudiced people share can be summarized in the phrase "threat oriented." The reference is partly due to viewing the world as a threatening place. However, some of the threat comes from within. The prejudiced person "seems fearful of himself, of his own instincts, of his own consciousness, of change, and of his social environment" (Allport, 1954, p. 396). To put it another way, very prejudiced people suffer from "crippled egos." By promoting oppression of other groups, they can ensure their own status in society is not threatened.

Covered next are some specific traits that Allport believed prejudiced people tend to have in common. This consideration is relevant to the question "If most European Americans incorporate racism when they swallow their culture whole, why do only a relative few turn out to be racists?" (highly prejudiced). The answer may partially lie in the practices used to rear them and in their childhood experiences. These practices and experiences may act on racism, dragging it from the fringe to the core of some people's personalities, thereby pushing them into the "racist" category.

Ambivalence about Parents

As one kind of "ism" tends to resemble other kinds, Allport (1954) often used anti-Semitism as a model for the "isms." Research showed that anti-Semitic women students are ambivalent toward their parents. While they overtly praised their parents, on projective tests these women covertly showed hostility toward parents. Tolerant subjects were the opposite: they were overtly critical of their parents, but the projective tests revealed no underlying hostility toward parents. Prejudiced students' hostility toward their parents may stem from child rearing themes of obedience, punishment, and actual or threatened rejection.

Moralism

Allport (1954) reported that very prejudiced people tend to be highly moralistic as reflected in high attention to cleanliness and good manners. When the anti-Semitic students were asked what would embarrass them the most, they "responded in terms of violations of mores and conventions in public. Whereas [the] non-prejudiced spoke more often of inadequacy in personal relations" (p. 398). Again child rearing practices are implicated. The prejudiced had parents who punished them severely for any show of interest in their genitals and for aggression against the parents. The result is children who are guilt-ridden and full of self-hatred due to repeatedly being reminded of their wickedness. As adults their suppressed hostility explodes onto members of other groups and their rigid morality is the source of a rationale for rejecting those group members.

Dichotomization

Highly prejudiced people literally see in black and white. There is good and there is bad; there is right and there is wrong. This orientation was forced on them by parents who dished out approval and disapproval categorically: everything the child did was either right, or it was wrong; there was no middle ground. Little wonder that as adults they see only two classes of people: those who are acceptable and those who are not.

Need for Definiteness

Allport (1954) believed very prejudiced people are distinguished by their unique cognitive processes. Consistent with their tendency to classify everything into two categories, they show another critical characteristic. They have little tolerance for ambiguity; their cognitive orientation requires that everything be clearly distinguished from everything else, questions have definite answers, and problems have simple solutions. In short, prejudiced people want everything to be clear-cut, no gray areas. Shown an illusion involving a stationary point of light presented in darkness that **appears** to move, prejudiced people "reported the light as moving in a constant direction from trial to trial and to [move] a constant number of inches" (p. 401). By contrast, unprejudiced people saw movement in all directions and to a variable extent. Prejudiced people imposed clarity and order on an inherently ambiguous situation, while unprejudiced people tolerated the ambiguity. Inspired by Allport's belief that prejudiced people have a strong need for definiteness, Schaller, Boyd, Yohannes, & O'Brien (1995) found that forming erroneous stereotypes, a tendency of prejudiced people, was positively related to high Personal Need for Structure.

Externalization

Allport (1954) saw very prejudiced people as lacking in self-insight. They do not see their own faults; they project them onto other people. Further, "things seem to happen 'out there.'" (p. 404). In Horney's terms, they externalize. Rather than believing they control what happens to them by use of their own resources, they believe fate controls them. Rotter would class these people as externals. Allport explained, "It is better and safer for a person in inner conflict to avoid self-reference. It is better to think of things happening to him rather than as caused by him" (p. 404). Also, prejudiced people externalize punishment: "it is not I who hates and injures others; it is **they** who hate and injure me" (p. 404).

Institutionalization

Allport (1954) believed the highly prejudiced person prefers order, especially social order. He finds safety and definiteness in his institutional memberships. "Lodges, schools, churches, the nation, may serve as a defense against disquiet in his personal life. To lean on them saves him from leaning on himself" (p. 404). Also, the prejudiced are more devoted to institutions than the unprejudiced. The anti-Semitic college women were more wrapped up in their sororities and more patriotic. While patriotic people are not necessarily prejudiced, Allport referred to evidence that very prejudiced people are almost always super-patriots. He cites an investigation in which club members completed a lengthy belief-questionnaire in return for a monetary contribution to their clubs. The large number of variables examined were reduced to only one trait held in common: **nationalism**. Allport is quick to point out that "the nation" to these people is not what it is to most. When most people think of "the nation," what comes to mind is the people, the principles of the consti- tution, and the lands. Instead, prejudiced people view "the nation" as something that will protect them from people seen as unlike themselves and that will preserve the **status quo**.

Authoritarianism

Allport (1954) believed very prejudiced people are uncomfortable with democracy. "The consequences of personal freedom they find unpredictable." (p. 406). It is easier to live in a power hierarchy where everyone has a place and the top spot is occupied by an all-powerful person. In a word, prejudiced people are **authoritarian**, they show high deference for authority figures, submission to the power of authority, and a need to command those seen as lower in power than themselves. Allport cites a study in which prejudiced people listed dictators such as Napoleon when asked whom they admired most, while unprejudiced people listed figures such as Lincoln. Authoritarianism is seen in prejudiced people's mistrust of others. Authority embedded in a strong nation can save oneself from suspected others. "To the prejudiced person the best way to control these suspicions is have an orderly, authori- tative, powerful society. Strong nationalism is a good thing. Hitler [wasn't] so wrong . . . America needs . . . a strong leader" (p. 407). This crucial concept is still receiving attention from researchers (Peterson, Doty, & Winter, 1993; Wagner, Lavine, Christiansen, & Trudeau, 1997).

Allport and Du Bois on the African American Experience
and the Nature of Prejudice and Stereotyping

African American social psychologists Stanley Gaines and Edward Reed are among Allport's many admirers (Gaines & Reed, 1994; 1995). Nevertheless they think Allport's writings contain some serious shortcomings. They (1995) contrast Allport's view that "black" experience is simply a variant of "white" experience with the position of W.E.B. Du Bois, a famous African American historian and student of American Psychology's founder, William James. Du Bois believed that a certain duality, resulting from their unique experience, characterized the self-conceptions of African Americans. African Americans see themselves as American and not American, as citizens and not citizens, and as partici- pants in the American dream but excluded from that dream. African Americans are caused to think of themselves as "white" as well as "black": they are often enticed to "be white" by the media and by European American acquaintances, but are constantly reminded they are "black" and, thus, can never be accepted in the "white" world. The conflicting poles of this duality are seen in the condemnation by African Americans of African Americans who "act white." An African American is supposed to "act black." To put this predicament into perspective, consider the question, "Wouldn't it be odd if 'whites' were supposed to 'act white'?" Speaking of oddities, weird is the way wannabes are regarded: "white" people who "act black."

Another Du Boisian duality is collectivism, which is natural to people of African descent, and individualism which (mostly male) European Americans hold up to African Americans as the means to "making it" in the United States. African Americans must figure out how to fit both of these extremes. Gaines and Reed (1995) also point out that Allport had his own duality: extropunitive—blaming others—and intropunitive—blaming oneself. Allport saw some African Americans as extropunitive and some as intropunitive. Gaines and Reed viewed Booker T. Washington, known for his attempts to appease "whites," as intropunitive and Du Bois, founder of the National Association for the Advancement of Colored People (NAACP), as extropunitive. But they also feel that the dichotomy is false. Because of the oppressive circumstances of African Americans, each would reflect some mixture of extropunitive and intropunitive orientation.

Gaines and Reed also rejected the notion attributed to Allport that prejudice and stereotyping naturally flow from normal cognitive processes. To the contrary, prejudice/stereotyping stem from slavery and its legacy of oppression, as well as attempts to justify both that cruel institution and its horrific aftermath. Racism came to the United States with the culture European Americans brought from Europe. Slavery and oppression flowed directly from the arrival of that culture (see Allen, 1978, for a historical perspective consistent with this view). In turn, prejudice/stereotyping stems from slavery and oppression.

Although Allport showed extraordinary insight into the workings of racism and prejudice, he suffered from the myopia common to European Americans viewing African Americans. He failed to see what is all two clearly in focus for most African Americans: full participation in the American Dream is dangled in front of African Americans and then withdrawn when they attempt to grasp it. The only way European Americans are going to approximate an appreciation of African Americans' lives is to read and to hear the words of African Americans, such as W. E. B. Du Bois, who so ably articulate the essence of black existence.

Conclusion

Gordon Allport was among the first members of the white psychological community to recognize that racism is pervasive among European Americans. He also was in the forefront of efforts to show that notions of "race" are mythical rather than factual and, therefore, discussions of "race differences" are worse than a waste of breath. His ideas also suggest an answer to the crucial question "If most European Americans incorporate racism when they swallow their culture whole, why do only a relative few turn out to be racists?" Certain childhood experiences and child rearing practices may operate on some white people's psyches so that racism is transported from the periphery to the core of their personalities. These are among the profound lessons Gordon Allport could have taught European Americans had they been more attentive pupils. It is not too late to learn from him.

References

Allen, B. P. (1975). Social distance and admiration reactions of "unprejudiced" whites. *Journal of Personality, 43,* 709-726.

Allen, B. P. (1978). *Social behavior: Fact and falsehood.* Chicago: Nelson-Hall.

Allen, B. P. (1990). *Personality and adjustment.* Pacific Grove, CA: Brooks/Cole.

Allen, B. P. (1995). Gender stereotypes are not accurate: A replication of Martin (1987) using diagnostic, self-report, and behavioral criteria. *Sex Roles, 32,* 583-600.

Allen, B. P. (1996). African Americans' and European Americans' mutual attributions: Adjective Generation Technique (AGT) Stereotyping. *Journal of Applied Social Psychology, 26,* 884-912.

Allen, B. P. & Adams, J. Q. (1992). The concept "race": Let's go back to the beginning. *Journal of Social Behavior and Personality, 7,* 163-168.

Allport, G. W. (1954). *The nature of prejudice.* Reading, MA: Addison-Wesley.

Cavalli-Sforza, L. L., Menozzi, P., & Piazza, A. (1994). *The history and geography of human genes.* Princeton NJ: Princeton University Press.

Dovidio, J. F., Evans, N., & Tyler, R. B. (1986). Racial stereotypes: The contents of their cognitive representations. *Journal of Experimental Social Psychology, 22,* 22-37.

Dovidio, J. F., Gaertner, S. L., & Validzic, A. (1998). Intergroup bias: Status, differentiation, and a common in-group identity. *Journal of Personality and Social Psychology, 75,* 109-120.

Eagly, A. H. (1987). *Sex differences in social behavior: A social role interpretation.* Hillsdale, NJ: Erlbaum.

Gaines, S. O., & Reed, E. S. (1994). Two social psychologies of prejudice: Gordon W. Allport, W.E.B. Du Bois and the legacy of Booker T. Washington. *Journal of Black Psychology, 20,* 8-29.

Gaines, S. O., & Reed, E. S. (1995). Prejudice: From Allport to Du Bois. *American Psychologist, 50,* 96-103.

Katz, S. H. (1995). Is race a legitimate concept for science? *Unesco race statement.* Available from S. H. Katz, Anthropology, University of Pennsylvania, 3451 Walnut Street, Philadelphia, PA 19104.

Peterson, B. E., Doty, R. M., & Winter, D. G. (1993). Authoritarianism and attitudes toward contemporary social issues. *Personality and Social Psychology Bulletin, 19,* 174-184.

Schaller, M., Boyd, C., Yohannes, J., & O'Brien, M. (1995). The prejudiced personality revisited: Personal need for structure and formation of erroneous group stereotypes. *Journal of Personality and Social Psychology, 68,* 544-555.

Triandis, H., Loh, W., & Levine, L. (1966). Race status, quality of spoken English, and opinion about civil rights as determinants of interpersonal attitudes. *Journal of Personality and Social Psychology, 3,* 468-472.

Wagner, S. H., Lavine, H., Christiansen, N. & Trudeau, M. (1997). Re-evaluating the structure of right-wing authoritarianism. Paper presented at the Midwestern Psychological Association Convention, Chicago.

Weizmann, F., Wiener, N. I., Wiesenthal, D. L., & Ziegler, M. (1990). Differential K theory and racial hierarchies. *Canadian Psychology, 31,* 1-13.

Winterbrink, B., Judd, C. M., & Park, B. (1997). Evidence for racial prejudice at the implicit level and its relationship with questionnaire measures. *Journal of Personality and Social Psychology, 72,* 262-274.

Yee, A. H., Fairchild, H. H., Weizmann, F., & Wyatt, G. E. (1993). Addressing psychology's problems with race. *American Psychologist, 48,* 1132-1140.

Zuckerman, M. (1990). Some dubious premises in research and theory on racial differences: Scientific, social, and ethical issues. *American Psychologist, 12,* 1297-1303.

MOTIVATIONS THAT DRIVE PREJUDICE AND DISCRIMINATION: IS THE SCIENTIFIC COMMUNITY REALLY OBJECTIVE?

by
Duane M. Jackson

We are taught that science, unlike religion and philosophy, is based on empirical evidence, that science is a dynamic process and is self-correcting. Existing theories are constantly being modified or abandoned in the face of new evidence. But what truly sets science apart from other disciplines is **objectivity**. As an African American scientist and a student of history, I do not question the objectivity of science as a discipline, but science is done by individuals, and I question the objectivity of scientists and the scientific community. Prejudice (perceptions) and discrimination (actions based on prejudice) have prevented the scientific community from being objective. I will examine the historical roots of this discrimination in science—scientific racism and the eugenics movement, race, intelligence and the IQ controversy, the misuse of heritability, and the inability of the field of psychology to deal with the issue of race.

When we look for motives behind discrimination and prejudice in science, we see three types of individuals emerge: the don't-know, the don't-want-to-know, and the know-and-will-not-accept. The three types are driven by prejudice but the latter two are also driven by discrimination. Individuals who fall into the don't-know category are simply unaware of the accomplishments and contributions that African Americans have made in science. Don't-want-to-know individuals believe African Americans cannot make contributions in science, in part because such accomplishments undermine the don't-want-to-know type's belief in themselves. Individuals who know-but-will-not-accept are the most dangerous of the three, however, since they will attempt to discredit, block, or conceal the truth about the actual scientific contributions African Americans have made.

Three African American Scientists

When I gave a talk, titled "Carver, Just, and Turner: Scientists Against the Odds," at a predominantly European American institution during Black History Month several years ago, I began my paper by asking the audience if they knew who George Washington Carver, Ernest Everett Just, and Charles Turner were. The majority of the audience were aware of Carver, but only a few African Americans knew of Just, and no one in the audience had ever heard of Turner. These three men had several things in common. They were all African Americans born in the 19th century who spent part of their careers teaching and doing research in Historically Black Colleges (HBCs).

Just taught at Howard University in Washington D.C., Carver taught at Tuskegee Institute (now Tuskegee University) in Alabama; and Turner taught at Clark University (now Clark-Atlanta University) in Atlanta. Being 19th-century African Americans at HBCs worked against them since HBCs had far fewer resources than their European American counterparts. Further, being educated and intellectual African Americans in the 19th century presented a problem: they were not supposed to exist. That they did challenged the very foundation of the European American belief that African Americans were intellectually and socially inferior.

Just and Turner spent most of their lives in frustration. Both Just and Turner received their doctorates from the University of Chicago. As noted above, Just taught at Howard University; he spent twenty years during the summer doing research at Woods Hole Marine Biology Laboratory in Woods Hole, Massachusetts. Known worldwide, this laboratory has attracted scientists and students to pursue research in the areas of biology, chemistry, physics, and geology. Just's research on cell membrane activity demonstrated that the cell's cytoplasm and ectoplasm are equally important as the nucleus for heredity. Just was prolific: he wrote two books and over sixty articles. Though he was respected and honored in the scientific capitals of Europe, he received little recognition for his accomplishments in the United States. Because of racial prejudice and discrimination in the scientific community in the United States, he spent the last ten years of his life in voluntary exile in Europe.

Charles Turner, the first African American animal behaviorist, published over fifty papers. His first, "Psychological notes upon the gallery spider" (1892a) published in 1892, appears to be the first published paper in psychology written by an African American. It is believed, but difficult to document, that his paper, "A few characteristics of the avian brain," published in *Science* (1892b) was the first paper by an African American published in that highly respected scientific journal. Some of his work was published by T. C. Schneirla and E. L. Thorndike, two eminent scientists of the time who initiated detailed laboratory studies in insect (Schneirla) and animal learning (Thorndike).

Convinced that education was the key to overcoming prejudice, Turner developed an argument drawing from comparative psychology and a comparative study of history.

Among men . . . , dissimilarity of minds is a more potent factor in causing prejudice than unlikeness of physiognomy. . . . [T]he new Southerner is prejudiced against the new Negro because the new Negro is very unlike him. He does not know that a similar education and a like environment have made the new Negro and himself alike in every-thing except color and features. (1902, pp. 163-164)

He goes further to suggest the problem was that "the white trash and the vagrant Negro form a wedge separating the new Southerner from the new Negro so completely that they cannot know each other" (1902, p. 164). He later suggested that the only way to overcome this was to transform the white trash and the vagrant Negro into new Southerners and new Negroes through education. But we shall see that traditional education is not enough to cover some prejudice and discrimination; in fact, in some ways, traditional education has actually perpet-uated these problems.

This is evident when men of "science" such as Jensen (1969), Herrnstein (1973), Rushton, (1988), and Herrnstein and Murray (1994) in their recently published book, *The Bell Curve*, propose that genetic differences exist among the races and that these differences create inequalities among the races in regard to behaviors from intelligence to criminality. The educational system has either ignored or, in many cases, been inadequate in educating students about the role genes play in behavior and about the interaction between genes and the environment.

Turner's dream of eventually having a position at a major European American research institution never materialized. He spent his last years as a professor of biology and psychology at Sumner High School and Teacher College in St. Louis where his duties included collecting meal tickets at the school cafeteria.

Carver, Just, and Turner all made major contributions in science. Why then is Carver remembered and Just and Turner forgotten? How was Carver able to gain, to some degree, the respect and recognition of the scientific community for his accomplishments? Several factors could account for this. First, Carver was raised by European Americans. He never knew his father, and his mother disappeared when he was an infant. He was adopted by his former slave master. Additionally Carver, unlike Turner and Just, received the majority of his primary and secondary education from European Americans. Also, Carver taught at an HBC that was an industrial and agricultural school, while Turner and Just taught at HBCs that were liberal arts institutions. Teaching African Americans to be farmers and factory workers was more palatable to the European American community than teaching African Americans to be lawyers, doctors, and scientists.

Carver's research was applied, while Just's and Turner's work was for the most part theoretical. Carver's research on the peanut was far easier to grasp than Just's research on the internal workings of cells and Turner's research on the cognitive abilities of insects. It may have been far easier to accept an African American man doing applied rather than theoretical research.

Finally, however, I propose that the most important factor helping Carver gain some acceptance by the European American scientific community was his political activism. Carver had seen and experienced the brutality of racism, but he had been raised and taught by European Americans. This created a dilemma. He attempted to resolve this conflict by working for racial harmony. He was very active on the Commission on Interracial Cooperation and with the YMCA. Despite all of this, however, even Carver never received full recognition for his accomplishments.

The Eugenics Movement and the Roots of Scientific Racism

The eugenics movement attempted to legitimize racism under the guise of science and served as a foundation for scientific racism. Allen Chase defines scientific racism as "the creation and employment of a body of legitimately scientific, or patently pseudoscientific data as rationales for the preservation of poverty, inequality of opportunity for upward mobility and related regressive social arrangements" (1977, p. 72). According to Chase, during its conception, scientific racism was not concerned much with racial or cultural differences. Although it was anti-Semitic, anti-Catholic, and white supremacist, it was primarily concerned with profit. The founding father of scientific racism, Thomas Malthus, laid out the purpose of scientific racism in 1826: to maximize profits and to minimize taxes on those profits. Malthus also stated in *An Essay on the Principle of Population* (1826) that the state is not obligated to support the poor.

The eugenics movement, founded by Francis Galton, guaranteed a future for scientific racism. Galton (1869) coined the word *eugenics* from the Greek word *eugenes*, meaning well born. The primary purpose of the movement was to improve the races by boosting the birthrate of the "well born" and decreasing the birthrate of the less well born. The eugenics movement has a long history of racism and its doctrines have been used to justify racist ideologies. Galton, in 1869, stated that black people were inferior to the lowest of whites and he went further to state, without empirical evidence, ". . . that the average intellectual standard of the negro [sic] race is some two grades below our own" (p. 327).

The eugenics movement had an impact on immigration and sterilization laws in the United States during the early part of this century. President Theodore Roosevelt, who was greatly influenced by the eugenics movement, wrote a letter on January 14, 1913 to the Committee to Study and to Report on the Best Practical Means of Cutting Off the Defective Germ-Plasm in the American Population, a committee started by the American Breeders Association's Eugenics Section. Roosevelt stated:

It is obvious that if in the future racial qualities are to be improved, the improving must be wrought mainly by favoring the fecundity of the worthy types. . . . At present, we do just the reverse. There is no check to the fecundity of those who are subordinate. . . . (cited in Chase, 1977, p. 15)

The eugenics movement was most fully exploited by Nazi Germany. Its doctrine was perfect for a regime that sought to rule the world by breeding a "master race." The eugenics movement gave scientific justification for breeding programs, the creation of Nazi Eugenics Court, and the extermination of an entire "race." The German Sterilization Act of 1933, which was enforced by the Nazi Eugenics Court, was based on the Model Eugenical Sterilization Law written by Harry L. Laughlin (1922) at the Eugenics Record Office of Cold Spring Harbor in New York.

Dr. Lothrop Stoddard, an American eugenicist, who was widely read by Hitler's closest advisors, went to Germany, met with Hitler, and sat on the Eugenics Court. Stoddard stated in his book, *Into the darkness: Nazi Germany today*: ". . . once the jews [sic] and other inferior stocks were annihilated, the Nazi state would be able to concern itself with the improvements within racial stock that are recognized everywhere as constituting the modern science of eugenics, or racial betterment" (1940, p. 189). Eugenics was interwoven into the very fabric of the Nazi creed. Although the Nazi Third Reich fell almost fifty years ago, we have seen in the nineties in Eastern Europe similar atrocities committed in the name of "ethnic cleansing."

The Search for the Genetic Basis of Intelligence
The Race-Intelligence Controversy

The question as to whether African Americans as a group are genetically inferior to European Americans in regard to intelligence is like a vampire. This question keeps rising out of the grave, and no one seems to have the wooden stake to lay this question to an eternal rest. The notion that different ethnic groups were different in regard to intelligence has its roots in Galton's 1869 book, *Hereditary Genius*. As the title implies, Galton believed that intelligence was inherited, although he had no scientific basis for this conclusion: The test that Galton used to measure intelligence lacked reliability as well as validity, and genetics was not a science until the triple rediscovery of Mendel's work in 1900 (Hirsch, 1982, p. 1).

The first intelligence test to demonstrate reliability and validity (validity in regard to academic performance) was developed by Alfred Binet in 1905. The French government commissioned Binet to construct a test to identify students who had low academic aptitudes. Unfortunately, this test, which was designed to help educators identify students with learning disabilities, has over time become synonymous with intelligence testing. The Americanized version, the Stanford-Binet, was published by Lewis Terman (1916) in a book titled *The Measurement of Intelligence*.

Many of the early pioneers in the American testing movement—Lewis Terman, Henry Goddard, and Robert Yerkes—were members of the eugenics movement. These individuals concluded that the Stanford-Binet test measured an "innate intelligence," and this test could be used to identify genetically inferior individuals (Kamin, 1974, pp. 5-6). Terman in *The Measurement of Intelligence* states:

> . . . [I]n the near future intelligence tests will bring tens of thousands of these high-grade defectives under the surveillance and protection of society. This will ultimately result in curtailing the reproduction of feeble-mindedness and in the elimination of an enormous amount of crime, pauperism, and industrial inefficiency. (pp. 6-7)
>
> . . . [A]mong spanish-indian [sic] and Mexican families of the Southwest and also among negroes [sic] dullness seems to be racial, or at least inherent in the family stocks from which they come. . . . Children of this group should be segregated in special classes. . . . They cannot master abstractions, but they can often be made efficient workers. . . . There is no possibility at present of convincing society that they should not be allowed to reproduce, although from a eugenic point of view they constitute a grave problem because of their unusually prolific breeding. (pp. 91-92)

However, there was also strong resistance in the field of psychology to the notion that genetics had a role in individual differences in behavior. This resistance was led by the behaviorists who felt that all individual differences could be explained by environmental factors. Watson, in his 1930 book, *Behaviorism*, stated:

> Our conclusion, then, is that we have no real evidence of the inheritance of traits. I would feel perfectly confident in the ultimately favorable outcome of careful upbringing of a *healthy, well formed baby* born of a long line of crooks, murderers and thieves, and prostitutes. Who has evidence to the contrary? (p. 103)

He goes on to say:

> I should like to go one step further now and say, "Give me a dozen healthy infants, well-formed, and my own specified world to bring them up in and I'll guarantee to take any one at random and train him to become any type of specialist I might select—doctor, lawyer, artist, merchant-chief and, yes, even beggar-man and thief, regardless of his talents, penchants, tendencies, abilities, vocations, and race of his ancestors." I am going beyond my facts and I admit it but so have the advocates of the contrary and they have been doing it for thousands of years. (p. 104)

When we look at the race-intelligence controversy, we see that what Watson said over sixty years ago is still correct. Individuals on both sides have gone beyond their facts.

Problems to Resolve Before the Search Begins

I do not question the legitimacy nor the ethics in the search for the genetic basis of intelligence. In a survey of 134 psychology majors at Morehouse College, where I teach, when asked "what is your view of scientific investigators asking questions dealing with **race and intelligence**," the responses were enlightening. Twenty-two percent felt that it was a valid question, twenty-seven percent wanted to know the answer, and forty-six percent felt that the question has racist overtones and implications (Jackson, 1997). William Tucker (1994) in his book *The Science and Politics of Racial Research*, proposed that much of the work in this area has been motivated by the desire to promote some political, economic, or social policy agenda. I feel that looking for genetic correlates to intelligence is a legitimate line of scientific enquiry, but I strongly believe certain problems must be resolved before this can become a worthwhile scientific endeavor. These problems are: 1) the lack of clear definitions of race and intelligence; 2) the limitations of the investigators in the field; and 3) the misconception that the underlying genetic basis for intelligence consists of a few genes or genetic systems.

What does it mean to be intelligent? Some view the use of language and abstract reasoning as the hallmark of intelligence. Others think intelligence is uniquely associated with the mind and thinking, while still others see intelligence as the ability to learn or to adapt to changes in the environment. Unfortunately, no universally accepted operational definition of intelligence exists. One might think it would be far easier to define race, but this has also been a problem.

Yee, Fairchild, Weizmann, and Wyatt (1993), in a paper titled "Addressing Psychology's Problem with Race," deal with the difficulties science has had in clearly defining race. Yee and his co-writers state that not having a scientific definition for race results in investigators conceptualizing and using race in a variety of ways, causing confusion and controversy. Having no clear definitions of intelligence or race limits research design and theory building. It also calls into question "race difference" research: How does one claim a race difference if the researchers have not agreed upon a definition of race that allows them to say the races they are referring to are different races?

The second problem I see is that many investigators involved in searching for the genetic basis of intelligence have limited training. Many psychologists have limited training in genetics, so they go outside their field to geneticists for advice. Most geneticists, however, have little training in psychology.

Finally, there exists an oversimplification of the genetic basis for intelligence and a misuse of the concept of heritability. Heritability is a dynamic population measure that must be recalculated each generation and holds only for the single population investigated at the time it was investigated. Yet we see some investigators using it as a static individual measure.

Evidence tends to support strongly the notion that the genetic basis of intelligence is far from simple. For example, Tryon (1940) demonstrated genetic variation in maze learning in rats when he created a strain of "bright" rats and "dull" rats to run a maze. But in 1949 Searle ran these selectively bred strains through a variety of mazes and found that on some tasks the bright strain was superior to the dull strain and on some tasks the reverse was true. He concluded

> The finding . . . indicates that a "general intelligence" factor, if it exists at all, may be regarded as of little or no importance. . . . [F]rom this together with the intercorrelational evidence that brights and dulls are differently organized it may be assumed that the differences in the maze-learning ability represent differences in patterns of behavior traits rather than in degree of any single psychological capacity. (p. 320)

The importance of this work is that it demonstrates that "intelligence" even in the rat is complex and not governed by one gene. As a graduate student I was able to demonstrate through bidirectional selective breeding for high and low memory and average learning in blowflies in a classical conditioning test that learning and memory in blowflies was governed by **two different** genetic systems (1990). If there are different genetic systems for maze learning in rats, and for learning and memory in blowflies, the number of genes and genetic systems involved in human intelligence, which has still not been clearly defined, must be very large. Yet we see genetic models and the misuse of heritability reducing the genetic basis of intelligence to a simple system.

After we have clear, concise definitions of race and intelligence and individuals who have thorough training in genetics and psychology, then we may be able to deal with the complex search for the genetic correlates of behavior and to tackle the far more complex problem of the genetic X environment interaction. It is also hoped that line of research will be motivated to look for differences among groups rather than the superiority of some groups.

Prejudice and discrimination in science exist because science is done by scientists who are no different from other members of society. In a recent article by Schulman, et al (1999) it was shown in a controlled experiment that medical doctors, when presented with two patients that have identical problems, will prescribe different treatments based on race and sex. However, there is hope in science, for in science, old theories and concepts are modified or abandoned when new evidence is presented. Science can abandon old ideas based on prejudice and discrimination in the face of existing data, and scientists must do the same.

References

Chase, A. (1977). *The legacy of Malthus: The social costs of the new scientific racism.* New York: Alfred A. Knopf.

Galton, F. (1869). *Hereditary genius.* London: Macmillan.

Herrnstein, R. J. (1973). *IQ in the meritocracy.* Boston: Atlantic-Little Brown.

Herrnstein, R. J., & Murray, C. (1994). *The bell curve.* New York: The Free Press.

Hirsch, J. (1982). Introduction. In J. Hirsch & T. McGuire (Eds.), *Behavior-genetic analysis.* Stroudsburg, PA: Hutchinson Ross.

Jackson, D. (1990). *Behavior-genetic analysis of conditioning and retention in Phormia regina (blow flies): A search for relationships between learning and memory.* Unpublished doctoral dissertation, University of Illinois, Champaign-Urbana.

Jackson, D. (1997). Behavior genetic analysis and the African American community: Objective science or voodoo genetics. Paper presented at the European Behavioral and Neural Genetics Society, Orleans, France.

Jensen, A. (1969). How much can we boost IQ and scholastic achievement? *Harvard Educational Review, 39,* 1-123.

Kamin, L. (1974). *The science and politics of I.Q.* New York: John Wiley & Sons.

Laughlin, H. L. (1922). *Eugenical sterilization in the United States, Chicago: Psychopathic laboratory of the municipal court of Chicago* (rev. ed., 1926). New Haven, CT: American Eugenics Society.

Malthus, T. (1826). *An essay on the principle of population, it affects the future improvement of society* (6th ed.). London: Norton.

Rushton, J. P. (1988). Race differences in behaviour: A review and evolutionary analysis. *Personality and Individual Differences, 9,* 1009-1024.

Schulman, K. et al. (1999). The effect of race and sex on physicians' recommendations for cardiac catheterization. *The New England Journal of Medicine, 340,* 618-626.

Searle, L. V. (1949). The organization of hereditary maze-brightness and maze-dullness. *Psychology Monographs, 39,* 283-325.

Stoddard, L. (1940). *Into the darkness: Nazi Germany today.* New York: Duell, Sloan, & Pearce.

Terman, L. M. (1916). *The measurement of intelligence.* Boston: Houghton Mifflin.

Tryon, R. C. (1940). Genetic differences in maze-learning ability in rats. *Thirty-ninth yearbook of the national society for the study of education.* Bloomington, IL: Public School Publishing.

Tucker, W. (1994). *The science and politics of racial research.* Urbana, IL: University of Illinois Press.

Turner, C. H. (1892a). Psychological notes upon the gallery spider. Illustration of intelligent variations in the construction of the web. *Journal of Comparative Neurology, 2,* 95-110.

Turner, C. H. (1892b). A few characteristics of the avian brain. *Science, 19,* 16-17.

Turner, C. H. (1902). Will the education of the Negro solve the race problem? In D. W. Culp (Ed.). *Twentieth century Negro literature or cyclopedia of thought on the topics relating to the American Negro* (pp. 162-166). Naperville, IL: J. L. Nichols.

Watson, J. B. (1930). *Behaviorism.* Chicago: University of Chicago Press.

Yee, A., Fairchild, H. F., Weizmann, F., & Wyatt, G. (1993). Addressing psychology's problem with race. *American Psychologist, 48,* 1132-1140.

MASS MEDIA AS MULTICULTURAL CURRICULUM: PUBLIC COMPETITOR TO SCHOOL EDUCATION

by
Carlos E. Cortés

The spread of multicultural education has raised a number of critical questions concerning such issues as curricular content, classroom pedagogy, school climate, and student learning. This has led to a proliferation of books and articles on school multicultural education. Yet some of these publications treat schools as if they comprised the totality of multicultural education.

But schools do not **control** multicultural education (for that matter, education in general). They merely **participate** in the multicultural educational process. They sometimes compete with and sometimes (intentionally or unwittingly) reinforce the multicultural teaching of non-school educators.

Unfortunately school multicultural education scholars have devoted relatively little attention to non-school multicultural education, what I have referred to as the "societal curriculum"—that massive, ongoing, informal curriculum of families, peer groups, neighborhoods, churches, organizations, institutions, mass media, and other socializing forces that educate all of us throughout our lives (Cortés, 1981). In particular, multicultural education scholars and practitioners have tended to ignore—or avoid addressing—the pedagogical implications of that powerful public multicultural educator, the mass media.

Research for my book-in-progress, *Hollywood's Multicultural Curriculum: A History of the Treatment of Race and Ethnicity in American Motion Pictures,* has documented that gaping hole in the development of multicultural education research and practice. However, I became even more troubled with this gap when I wrote my essay, "Knowledge Construction and Popular Culture: The Media as Multicultural Educator," for the . . . *Handbook of Research on Multicultural Education,* edited by James and Cherry McGee Banks.

Despite a growing literature on multicultural education and on the mass media treatment of race and ethnicity, scholars in the two areas have tended to march down separate investigatory avenues (Woll & Miller, 1987). Media scholars analyze media multicultural content, while multicultural education scholars analyze textbooks and curricula for their treatment of different racial, ethnic, and cultural groups. Media scholars examine media decision making and actions concerning diversity, while education scholars dissect decision making and actions within the textbook industry, within school systems, and by teachers and administrators. Media scholars attempt to assess reader, viewer, and listener learning, while education scholars assess student learning. Yet seldom have these scholarly efforts intersected.

Given the evidence of lifelong multicultural learning from the mass media, it behooves multicultural educators to become more cognizant of and analytical about such media teaching (Cortés, 1991). But educators need to go beyond awareness . . . or, for that matter, merely moaning about media content or the amount of time that students spend with the media, particularly television. They need to become more adept at integrating media into their curriculum development efforts, particularly critical analysis of (not just criticism or complaints about) the media.

Multicultural education seeks to empower young people in a variety of ways: for example, to critically evaluate multicultural information and ideas as a basis for personal knowledge construction. Throughout their lives, much of that information and many of those ideas will come through the mass media. Therefore, schools need to help students learn to analyze media multicultural content, not just the multicultural content of books, articles, and printed documents. As Wilma Longstreet (1989) appropriately warned in her article, "Education for Citizenship: New Dimensions":

> We spend years teaching reading and remedial reading while we hardly glance at these newer, more powerful media. Our young are literally at the mercy of television, besieged by far greater amounts of information on each screen than was ever possible on the pages of a book, and we give them no help in sorting and analyzing that barrage of data or in defending themselves from the high level of stimuli that accompany the barrage. (p. 44)

And the media barrage comes from more than television. It emanates from all media—television and motion pictures, radio and recorded music, newspapers and magazines. Moreover, the barrage consists of more than data. The media send fictional as well as non-fictional images and messages, disseminated through programs, films, and publications presumably made just to entertain (and make money) as well as through those intended to provide information and analysis.

But whatever the stated or unstated goals of mediamakers, audiences learn from both fictional and non-fictional media sources, although they may not realize that such media-based learning is occurring. These learners include students (as well as teachers, administrators, and parents). We need to help prepare them for this lifetime process of engaging the media as multicultural teacher and becoming more empowered as conscious co-constructors of multicultural knowledge as they interact with the media.

Mass Media as Multicultural Message System

For more than two decades, I have been involved in media research and teaching, including efforts to integrate, expand, and strengthen multicultural analysis of the media as an integral element of K-12 and college education. On that basis I have concluded that the media, both fictional and non-fictional, teach in a variety of ways, including the following:

1. Media Provide Information—Nonfictional media seek to provide information. Entertainment media provide "stuff" that viewers may internalize as information. This raises the question of accuracy . . . but also much more. Beyond such issues as factual accuracy, all media presentations of information also involve interpretation. While presenting information, media also inevitably interpret—by selecting information for inclusion and exclusion, by structuring presentations of that information, by choosing or rejecting words and images, and by commenting upon that information.

2. Media Help Audiences Organize Information and Ideas—Through the repetition of selected themes, the reiteration of similar interpretations of those themes, and the continual use of certain words when identifying or describing specific subjects—for example, people of different racial and ethnic backgrounds—media influence how readers and viewers organize information and ideas. In short, they help create, reinforce, and modify reader and viewer mental schema, which in turn influence future reception of information and ideas.

3. Media Influence Values and Attitudes—All news stories implicitly support certain values (for example, the democratic process or the free-market economy) or condemn others (for example, certain kinds of perceived anti-social behavior). Think of the varying values underlying the myriad "news" stories about multiculturalism and diversity. Movies and television have always taught values, including values about race and ethnicity, although those value lessons have changed over time (Peterson & Thurstone, 1933; Matabane, 1988). Likening television to schools and television programs to school courses, sociologist Herbert J. Gans (1967) argued:

> almost all TV programs and magazine fiction teach something about American society. For example, *Batman* is, from this vantage point, a course in criminology that describes how a superhuman aristocrat does a better job eradicating crime than do public officials. Similarly, *The Beverly Hillbillies* offers a course in social stratification and applied economics, teaching that with money, uneducated and uncultured people can do pretty well in American society, and can easily outwit more sophisticated and more powerful middle-class types. . . . And even the innocuous family situation comedies such as *Ozzie and Harriet* deal occasionally with ethical problems encountered on a neighborhood level. . . . Although the schools argue that they are the major transmitter of society's moral values, the mass media offer a great deal more content on this topic. (pp. 21-22)

4. Media Provide Models for Behavior—Media have sometimes intentionally, sometimes unintentionally, provided models for action. During World War II, the American media used both fictional and non-fictional presentations to appeal to Americans of all backgrounds to sacrifice for their country. For example, by flooding theatres with feature films that included explicitly multiethnic military units, Hollywood spread the message that Americans of all racial and ethnic backgrounds should be willing to fight for their country, regardless of the discrimination they might have encountered in American society (Koppes & Black, 1987). And fight they did, with honor. Similarly, many post-World War II movies role-modeled opposition to anti-ethnic bigotry and discrimination. In these films, villains were often driven by racial, ethnic, and religious prejudice, while (usually white) heroes took direct action to confront such bigotry. In such a manner, movies encouraged people to take action to oppose individual acts of bigotry, but tended to avoid issues of institutional or systemic racism or sexism.

Implications for School Multicultural Education

In short, the mass media provide multicultural education. This raises at least two critical school-related questions. First, how has media teaching interacted with school teaching in contributing to the construction of multicultural knowledge (including beliefs and attitudes)? Second, how can schools build more effectively from the growing scholarship on the media-based construction of multicultural knowledge?

School multicultural educators need to become more aware of the research on media multicultural education. For example, some communications scholars have focused on the role of the media in fostering interracial, interethnic, and intercultural learning among those of school age (Berry & Asamen, 1993; Dates, 1980) and in socializing children of different racial and ethnic backgrounds (Berry & Mitchell-Kernan, 1982; Stroman, 1991).

We need to examine more thoroughly the relationships between media and school multi-cultural knowledge construction. Gerald Michael Greenfield and I (1991) explored one avenue of potential media/schools multicultural education research in our article, "Harmony and Conflict of Intercultural Images: The Treatment of Mexico in U.S. Feature Films and K-12 Textbooks." While the article addresses the treatment of a foreign nation rather than race and ethnicity within the United States, its methodology suggests one strategy for linking media and school multicultural education research and teaching. In that article, we compared and contrasted the ways in which U.S. social studies textbooks and feature films have treated both Mexico in general and a series of critical themes in Mexican history, such as Mexican immigration into the United States. On that basis we indicated places where textbooks and feature films have provided mutually reinforcing intercultural messages, where they have challenged each other, and where by omission each has left the other sector more dominant as an educational force.

Yet school educators need to move beyond an understanding of the role of the mass media in the social construction of knowledge about race and ethnicity. They also need to develop more effective ways to draw upon that understanding in order to improve school multicultural education. During the past two decades there has been a growing interest in the areas of media literacy and critical pedagogy, including scholarship and curriculum materials aimed at helping teachers draw upon media at various grade levels (Brown, 1991; Rapaczynski, Singer, & Singer, 1982; Schwoch, White, & Reilly, 1992). Although most of these media literacy materials deal only tangentially with race and ethnicity, some scholarship has dealt directly with the question of critically integrating media into multicultural education (Cortés, 1992).

Yet much more needs to be done to increase the effective use of media to strengthen school multicultural education. Following are suggestions for a few basic pedagogical strategies related to the four described dimensions of the media message system.

1. Help students become more aware that all non-fictional sources of information—be they newspapers, news magazines, newscasts, talk shows. or documentaries—also inevitably interpret. Teachers should use such media "informational" sources as primary documents for classroom or homework critical analysis. In this manner, students can identify patterns of news selection concerning different groups, become cognizant of different media interpretive techniques that shape the presentation of information about those groups, and develop hypotheses about potential multicultural teaching/learning implications of such treatment. Moreover, through interviews and surveys they can assess what others have actually learned from those "informational" presentations.

2. What multicultural themes do media tend to repeat and how do different media frame those themes, such as through headlines and illustrations? Let students discover the answers through content analysis of mass media—for example, community coverage by local newspapers and television news programs. . . . [O]ver time they can compare how different local news media cover and frame a specific diversity-related event or controversy or how different national news media treat and frame a national multicultural issue.

3. What values do current movies and television series teach (explicitly or implicitly) about multicultural topics? Have students examine such fictional sources and identify what values they believe are being taught, whether intentionally or unintentionally. Have them write about and discuss in class the media techniques used to teach those values and debate their hypotheses concerning the likelihood that some viewers might be influenced by these multicultural value lessons. They might then test these hypotheses by interviewing other viewers, such as fellow students.

4. What multiculturally related behaviors do movies and television model today? Students can assess media content and compare their observations. But they can also go further. In what respects are students (or adults) likely to model their behavior on such media teaching? Have students address this question by reporting on their assessments of themselves or observations of others in order to hypothesize the degree to which different people have adopted or rejected such behavior after viewing those shows.

Conclusion

These introductory strategies merely suggest the possibilities of using mass media in school multicultural education. In such ways teachers can enhance the effectiveness of their own multicultural education pedagogy by addressing the mass media message system. Through the thoughtful use of mass media, teachers can improve their students' multicultural learning, deepen student understanding of multicultural knowledge construction, and sharpen student analytical thinking about diversity.

For the full flourishing of school multicultural education, we need to develop more innovative and sophisticated ways to strengthen multicultural educational pedagogy and curriculum. The mass media provide both teaching competition and a fascinating pedagogical opportunity. By continuously involving students in the analysis of the media message system dealing with diversity, schools can play a greater role in preparing young people for a lifetime of multicultural learning, in which the analytical use of media will become increasingly vital.

References

Allen, R. L., & Hatchett, S. (1986). The media and social effects: Self and system orientations of Blacks. *Communication Research, 13*(1), 97-123.

Berry, G. L., & Asamen, J. K. (Eds.). (1993). *Children and television: Images in a changing socio-cultural world.* Beverly Hills, CA: Sage.

Berry, G. L., & Mitchell-Kernan, C. (Eds.) (1982). *Television and the socialization of the minority child.* New York: Academic Press.

Brown, J. A. (1991). *Television critical viewing skills education: Major media literacy projects in the United States and selected countries.* Hillsdale, NY: Lawrence Erlbaum.

Cortés, C. E. (1981). The societal curriculum: Implications for multiethnic education. In J. A. Banks (Ed.), *Education in the 80's: Multiethnic Education* (pp. 24-32). Washington, DC: National Education Association.

Cortés, C. E. (1991). Pride, prejudice, and power: The mass media as societal educator on diversity. In J. Lynch, C. Mogdil, & S. Mogdil (Eds.), *Prejudice, polemic or progress* (pp. 367- 381). London: Falmer Press.

Cortés, C. E. (1992). Media literacy: An educational basic for the information age. *Education and Urban Society, 14*(4), 489-497.

Dates, J. L. (1980). Race, racial attitudes and adolescent perceptions of Black television characters. *Journal of Broadcasting, 24*(4), 549-560.

Gans, H. J. (1967). The mass media as an educational institution. *Television Quarterly, 6,* 20-37.

Greenfield, G. M., & Cortés, C. E. (1991). Harmony and conflict of intercultural images: The treatment of Mexico in U.S. feature films and K-12 textbooks. *Mexican Studies/Estudios Mexicanos, 7,* 283-301.

Koppes, C. R., & Black, G. D. (1987). *Hollywood goes to war: How politics, profits, and propaganda shaped World War II movies.* New York: Free Press.

Longstreet, W. S. (1989). Education for citizenship: New dimensions. *Social Education, 53,* 41-45.

Matabane, P. (1988). Television and the Black audience: Cultivating moderate perspectives on racial integration. *Journal of Communication, 38,* 21-31.

Peterson, R. C., & Thurstone, L. L. (1933). *Motion pictures and the social attitudes of children.* New York: Macmillan.

Rapaczynski, W., Singer, D. G., & Singer, J. L. (1982). Teaching television: A curriculum for young children. *Journal of Communication, 32*(2), 46-55.

Schwoch, J., White, M., & Reilly, S. (1992). *Media knowledge: Readings in popular culture, pedagogy, and critical citizenship.* Albany, NY: State University of New York Press.

Stroman, C. A. (1991). Television's role in the socialization of African American children and adolescents. *Journal of Negro Education, 60*(3), 314-327.

Woll, A. L., & Miller, R. M. (1987). *Ethnic and racial images in American film and television: Historical essays and bibliography.* New York: Garland.

U.S. NEWS MEDIA: A CONTENT ANALYSIS
AND MEDIA CASE STUDY

by
Pearlie Strother-Adams

Introduction

Media representation can either promote attitudes of acceptance or encourage fear and/ or hostility. When possible, educators might consider incorporating content analysis of media into their classroom activities to give students an opportunity to see how both print and broadcast media work to create, shape, and promote cultural trends, thus influencing the formation and spreading of stereotypical cultural concepts and conclusions.

In the midst of such media images as Willie Horton (1988, George Bush presidential campaign) and Susan Smith's phantom kidnapper/car jacker (1994), I began to wonder how often such images are featured in the media and to what end. In essence, how effective are such representations and for what purpose? Hopefully, this study of media images of African American males, though not exhaustive, will provide students with some insight into conducting a media content analysis. I focus on coverage of crimes, allegedly committed by African American and European American male offenders, that involve race. I include an analysis of the media of the late 1800s to mid 1900s that reveals media's role in promoting and perpetuating racism and a spirit of mob violence that, I contend, echoes in the U.S. today.

George Simpson (1936), in a study of the Philadelphia press, discussed the invisibility of African Americans in the mainstream press except for their stereotypical portrayals as perpetrators of violent crimes, and, in a report of the National Advisory Commission on Civil Disorder (Kerner, 1968), the Kerner Commission criticized mainstream media's tendency to focus on negative images of African Americans as a contributing factor to racism.

Selected Literature Review

While many studies (see Ginzburg, 1988; Raper, 1969; Howard, 1995, for further examples) have examined the effects of mainstream media coverage of African Americans, few have touched upon the relationship between the stereotypical, provocative "lynch mob" style of language created and popularized by U.S. media and key political figures in the period from the late 1800s to the mid 1900s and that used today to describe African American males alleged to have committed crimes against whites, particularly white women. The negative descriptors or depictions used in today's media echo the earlier sentiments and language when such crimes are reported. Though little research draws a direct correlation between the language of the late 1800s to mid 1900s and that of today, a body of evidence supports this claim. More literature that better synthesizes, interprets, and explains this evidence, however, is needed. Further explanation of this continuing phenomenon of negative images and its evolution are also needed.

Corea (1990) examined media portrayals of African Americans in television news and their impact on white perceptions of African American offenders as well as on the African American community. Corea also studied the limited positions of power African Americans have in the media and how negative portrayals are in part due to this. Corea looked specifically at television coverage of two highly publicized cases of rape and violence and in one instance, murder. According to Corea, the television coverage of the 1989 attack (beating and rape) of a young white woman, known as the "Central Park Jogger," by African American males and a Hispanic male, assumed that all African American men are liable to be violent, cruel, and vicious. Unlike white males who commit similar crimes or worse, Corea pointed out, these male offenders were not afforded any extenuating circumstances to excuse their behavior. In essence, growing up in a deprived situation and coming from low socioeconomic backgrounds were used against them. They were assailed by the press, leading the white community to suggest they be castrated, locked up with no hope of parole, and eventually sentenced to death. This contrasted sharply with what the press deemed the "Preppie Murder," said Corea, where a young, wealthy, white male raped and murdered a young, white woman in Central Park in 1987. The white male was represented in the press as a "Preppie" behaving out of character. In short, society was asked to forgive him. His victim, the young white woman, was treated as a "quasi prostitute"; her fate, the media suggested, was her own fault as they hinted she was a bit wild.

Corea concluded media promote the belief that white males are not prone to violence and are coerced to commit such acts only under extenuating circumstances, while African Americans have an "inherent tendency to mug, rape, and otherwise disrupt the normal orderly processes characteristic of white society" (p. 261). Corea's findings are noteworthy; however, a larger sample of cases would prove more conclusive. Corea used two cases from the same area, using the same media, one of the strengths of her study. Though she provides no samples from other areas of the country, her research is a valuable, concise, analytical work comparing and contrasting the coverage of African American and white male offenders in situations involving crimes committed in the same location against white women and adds a great deal to media study. Ironically, as Corea put it, the white male offender, who raped and murdered his female, white victim, is shown compassion in the press, while the African American offenders, who raped and beat their female, white victim are demonized.

A more extensive scholarly study (Gomes & Williams, 1990) challenged the accuracy of media portrayals of the relationship between race and crime, primarily using *Boston Globe* and *Boston Herald* accounts of the 1989 Charles Stuart case. Stuart, a furrier earning over $100,000 a year, accused a phantom black man of shooting and wounding him severely and killing his pregnant, attorney wife. The press, according to the study, generated disgust for the accused man but also raised questions about a community that could produce such a "gruesome" murderer. Press accounts of a community "run wild," populated with "animalistic" people, became common. Once a suspect was arrested, he was described as uneducated, mentally deficient, and "monstrous," with the press usually identifying him as "the killer" rather than a suspect (Gomes & Williams, p. 58). Elected officials called for a reinstatement of the death penalty, and Mission Hill's black residents were subjected to indiscriminate police harassment such as "stop and search" procedures. Stuart himself was later accused of the crime by his brother who confessed to being an unwitting accomplice. Charles Stuart's understanding of the potency of blaming an African American man, Gomes and Williams assert, was grounded in a long history of media popularization of an existing relationship between crime and race. They concluded: "African American perpetrators of crime tend to receive exaggerated coverage, especially when the victim is white" (p. 59). This study is crucial in investigations of the 1994 Susan Smith case.

Susan Smith, a young white mother first claimed her two sons were kidnapped when a black man, waving a handgun and wearing a knit cap and a flannel shirt, car jacked her vehicle and ordered her to get out, while refusing to let the children go. Smith later admitted to strapping her two sons into her car and drowning them. The Gomes and Williams study pointed out the dynamics of such uses of negative perceptions of African American males: having a white woman yell "black man" can work today as it did in the 1800s and in 1923 in Rosewood, Florida, when African Americans were run out of their homes, and many of them killed, when a white woman accused a "Negro" of attacking her (see Tolnay & Beck, p. 211).

Stereotypical depictions of African American males in the late 1800s to mid 1900s are strikingly similar to those prevalent in media today. Brundage (1988) looked at lynching in Georgia and Virginia from 1880 to 1930. According to his study, one of the loudest political expressions of racist dogma came from a Governor Hoke Smith, editor of the *Atlanta Journal* when he referred to the "Negro" as "beast rapists" who needed to be held down by force as they "degenerated towards extinction" (p. 198). Character assassination was central in the media's early campaign against African American men (see Raper 1969; Smead, 1986; Howard, 1995), but Brundage's work is supremely valuable in that it examined lynch mob violence as communal. Through a comparison of lynching statistics in Virginia and Georgia, Brundage connected the systemic violence perpetrated upon African Americans between 1880 and 1930 in southern Georgia to the white man's need to control and suppress African Americans in the "cotton belt" (p. 108). He concluded that the seriousness with which Southern whites viewed the need to subordinate African American sharecroppers often resulted in a communal quality of lynching. Like Corea, Brundage provided evidence of the use of provocative, stereotypical language in the press from the early 1800s to the 1930s as well as evidence to support the media's effectiveness in promoting a lynch mob mentality.

In a historical study Tolnay and Beck (1995) analyzed Southern newspaper accounts of lynch mob violence perpetrated on African Americans between 1882 and 1930 and found that editorials in the mainstream Southern press supported a "Doctrine of Radical Racism," ascribing to black behavior urges and instincts more characteristic of lower animals than humans. This study substantiates Gomes and Williams' research and ties the term "animalistic," which was used to describe the phantom killer in the Stuart case, directly to the description of African American males dating back to the early 1800s.

Tolnay and Beck document a change from a view of the African American slave as a childlike creature in need of a paternal master to the more malignant image of a subhuman, animalistic creature (p. 89). African American males were described as "beastly and loathsome" while also being characterized as strangely attracted to the white woman. The rape of a white woman by a "Negro" was the most "malignant atrocity" having no "reflection" in the "whole extent of the natural history of the most bestial and ferocious criminals" (Tolnay & Beck, pp. 89-90). In short, rape by a black man was described as a crime more vicious than rape itself. This recalls Corea's (1990) conclusion that African American men suspected of raping a white woman are viewed more harshly than a white man who committed both rape and murder (Central Park jogger-rape and Preppie Murder).

Finally, Ginzburg (1988) provides scholars with a much needed reference to specific cases of lynch mob violence over a period of 100 years. Typical of the news accounts he assembled is a story of the lynching of Sam Holt in Georgia. The *Kissimee Valley Florida Gazette* picked the story up on April 28, 1899. Holt, burned at the stake for the alleged crimes of killing a white man and raping the victim's wife, is described as being as brave as a man could be in such a matter, only murmuring a sound when knives plunged into his flesh and his "life blood sizzled in the flames" (p. 11). His lynching, like many others, was attended by as many as 2000, a crowd of both townspeople and others who came from good distances to see the affair. Ginzburg reports that a placard placed on the hanging tree read: "We must protect Southern women at all costs." Another sign warned "darkies" to beware (pp. 13-21). Such a warning was common in the case of violence perpetrated against African Americans during the period. This is demonstrated in many of the articles featured in Ginzburg's collection. The events are depicted as the root of what Corea and Gomes and Williams discuss in their studies as the tendency of mobs, with encouragement from the media, to hold the whole African American community hostage when a crime is reportedly committed by one. Ginzburg's collection of articles extends into the 1960s and includes stories from a variety of newspapers, both liberal and conservative, both black and white. While not an analytical study, Ginzburg's selections make apparent the stereotypical, provocative language so often used and allow for an analysis of the coverage of events from different angles and perspectives.

Research Overview

My study examined several primary sources using textual analysis and led me to themes and patterns evident through linguistic and qualitative analysis.

Although I examined many news articles and editorials as well as broadcast transcripts in this study, I will feature only news coverage here. The particular news programs I used are CNN's "Larry King Live" and ABC's "20/20." The print media are newspapers: the *New York Times*, *Los Angeles Times*, *Boston Globe*, and *USA Today*. The cases were selected because they were high profile and received a great deal of media attention. All involve a racial element except one, the "Sam Manzie" case, which added a much needed element in that Manzie is a white male accused of a crime against a white child. A comparison of Manzie's treatment in the media to the treatment of African American males proved valuable in two ways: as an example of a white male being vindicated in the murder of a white child (a case that deserves study along class lines) and as an indication that white males are often protected in the system and are not harshly treated even if the victim is white. More study in this area is greatly needed. The cases I used are:
* Susan Smith's,
* Sam Manzie's,
* Charles Stuart's and
* the rape and murders of Sherrice Iverson and the Central Park Jogger.

Actual Excerpts from Broadcast Transcripts

Case 1: The Susan Smith alleged car jacking and kidnapping in South Carolina.

Larry King: . . . If you drive a car, listen up. You don't want to be the victim of a car jacking. Take it from Susan Smith. Her worst nightmare began 48 hours ago. . . .

Asking about the sketch of the phantom black man, the alleged kidnapper, car jacker:

120

Larry King: Can you put that up closer to—put it right on camera. Let's see what it looks like. . . Hold it up a little. Hold the paper up a little. [Shows picture of alleged assailant]. After a commercial: Welcome back to . . . . And joining us are two who know how to throw the book at car jackers. Representative Charles Schumer wrote the first federal car jacking law and co-sponsored a bill signed last month by President Clinton, making car jacking a death-penalty offense. . . .

Rep. Charles Schumer: . . . There are various degrees depending on the harm done to the person. The recent crime bill reintroduced capital punishment . . . in the most heinous of offenses.

"Larry King Live" CNN Report on October 27, 1994

Case 2: Sam Manzie, accused murderer of 11-year-old Eddie Werner

Hugh Downs: The parents of Sam Manzie tell their story. Sam Manzie, 15, killed an eleven-year-old boy who came to his home selling candy and gift wrapping paper. Prior to the murder, Manzie was seduced via the Internet by a white male pedophile. . . . You have seen the dark side of the new computer technology.

Barbara Walters: . . . What the country heard about was the murder of an 11-year-old boy, killed while selling candy door-to-door in the neighborhood. . . . Sam Manzie's parents . . . talk publicly about what went wrong when they were trying to do everything right. Their story is heartbreaking. It is also a powerful warning to all young people and the parents who love them. . . . A nightmare with terrifying images. The 43-year-old who lures a 14-year-old Internet buddy into unimaginable depravity. An innocent 11-year-old who becomes the victim of the other boy's torment. . . . When the secret came out, . . . Sam apparently snapped, and this 11-year-old, Eddie Werner, became the target of Sam's rage and shame. How could this tragedy happen in a family that seemed so filled with affection, where parenting was taken so seriously? . . . Manzie was the perfect target for the sexual predators who freely roam the Internet . . . confused about his sexual identity, tortured by it, and he was lonely . . . grades, mostly A's until then, plummeted . . . behavior . . . erratic. . . .

Hugh Downs: It's a story not only about the Internet . . . , but about how the system failed a family in need and the community. . . .

"Sam's Story," ABC's "20/20," October 31, 1997

Case 3: The murder of 7-year-old Sherrice Iverson in a casino

ABC's "20/20," with an introduction from Barbara Walters and a special ABC News report from Antonio Mora, September 12, 1997: "Where are Their Parents? Children Roam Casinos While Their Parents Gamble." A seven-year-old girl is molested and murdered in a casino. The focus of this story, however, is the neglect of children, in general, in casinos. The murdered child is mentioned once on page four of the twenty-eight-page transcript.

Barbara Walters: Antonio Mora has startling footage of a growing and outrageous trend. As you'll see, when the chips are down the children have the most to lose.

Antonio Mora (voice-over): It looks like every child's fantasy land—medieval castles, side by side with Egyptian pyramids, battling pirate ships next door to a lava-spewing volcano. And down the street, towering buildings that scrape the sky . . . the perfect place for baby boomers to bring their kids. . . . But what happens to the kids after the roller coaster and the pools shut down? "20/20" decided to investigate. . . .Young kids, . . . in the wee hours of the morning, loitering just off the casino floors, waiting for their parents to quit gambling . . . , a tired 14-year-old holding her more tired five-year-old brother. At 2:00 a.m. . . .

Philip Coltoff, Children's Aid Society: It's neglect. It's wrong. It's dangerous . . . something at some point very bad is going to happen to children. Very dangerous.

Antonio Mora (voice over): Something very bad did happen this spring to little Sherrice Iverson (photo) at a casino just outside Las Vegas. At about 3:45 a.m., casino security cameras show the seven-year-old running into a bathroom with a young man following. There, he allegedly sexually assaulted Sherrice and then snapped her head, breaking her neck. At the time of the murder Sherrice's father was gambling. . . . Months later, we still found dozens of parents like him, willing to play the slots, even if it meant playing roulette with their children's safety. . . . The law, as far as I can tell, is being violated right here, right now. . . . Some casinos are trying to address the problem of neglected children. . . .

ABC's "20/20," October 31, 1997

Excerpts from Newspaper Articles

Case 1: Susan Smith: Alleged kidnapping and car jacking

The majority of articles examined in print media were done with extreme caution and are discussed below.

Case 2: Sam Manzie, fifteen-year-old accused murderer of eleven-year-old Edward Werner

"Suspect in New Jersey Strangling was Reportedly Sex-Case Victim: Fifteen-year-old Sam Manzie murderer of eleven-year-old, Edward P. Werner, was seduced via the Internet by Stephen P. Simmons, 43, Holbrook, N.Y." " . . . Just as the slaying raised concerns about the safety of children venturing to the doors of strangers, the latest revelations raised new concerns about the safety of children roaming the Internet."

Robert McFadden, *New York Times* Oct. 3, 1997

"Days Before Slaying, Parents of Suspect Pleaded for Help." "Three days before . . . , a state judge refused to order that the 15-year-old be committed. . . ."

Robert Hanley, *New York Times*, Oct. 4, 1997, p. 5

Case 3: The murder of 7-year-old Sherrice Iverson in a casino

"Casino Surveillance Footage Tells Story of Girl's Killing; Crime: Man follows her into restroom, emerges later. Officials warn children shouldn't be left alone in arcades. . . . It was there, next to an arcade with pinball games and Homer Hippo and Ms. Pac-Man, that 7-year-old Sherrice Iverson was killed in the wee hours of Sunday morning. Her strangled body was found seated on a toilet in a restroom stall. The father then demanded that the casino give him a six-Pack of beer and $100, pay for the girl's funeral, fly the girl's mother to Las Vegas from Los Angeles and provide him and the mother a room for the night, the source said. At 1:33 a.m. hotel security officials had noticed that the little girl was unattended . . . left alone . . . she played in the arcade . . . her father in the upstairs casino.

Tom Gorman, *Los Angeles Times,* May 28, 1997, p.5

"Suspect told two classmates of the casino crime, and their parents called police. He is described as a smart but troubled youth . . . Jeremy Joseph Stromeyer, a once-promising 18-year-old high school senior . . . was behind bars . . . as the suspected killer of 7-year-old Sherrice Iverson, who was raped and slain this week at a Nevada state-line casino. . . .

Jeff Leeds & James Rainey, the *Los Angeles Times*, May 30, 1997, p.2

"Officials Call Girl's slaying a Tragic example of Neglect; Children: Authorities in O.C. say many parents leave kids unsupervised and in periling malls, theaters and parks."

Bonnie Hayes & Emily Otani, the *Los Angeles Times*, May 29, 1997

"Slaying Fuels Debate Over Children's Safety in Casinos; Crime: Unattended youngsters are major problem."

Tom Gorman & John Mitchell, the *Los Angeles Times*, May 29, 1997, p.1

"Supervision of children can't Be a Sometime Thing; slaying raises Questions About parental and casino oversight.

Editorial, the *Los Angeles Times*, May 29, 1997

"Suspect in girl's slaying at casino in custody." "Jeremy Joseph Stromeyer, . . . under suicide watch in a Long Beach, Calif., jail. Sherrice Iverson had been left alone in the casino's arcade while her father gambled, police said.

USA Today, May 30, 1997, p.6

"Children die just out of focus." In this commentary, Smith did refer to Sherrice Iverson's alleged assailant as a "monster" but later in the commentary she says of the father, "He gambles her away."

Patricia Smith, *Boston Globe*, June 2, 1997, p.1

Promotion of Gross Generalities

Historically, the mainstream press has perceived minorities as a people outside of the American system, thus representing them as a problem people (see Martindale, 1997; West, 1996). The Susan Smith case is perhaps the best example of the widely held view of African Americans as criminals. "Susan Smith knew what a kidnapper should look like," said Richard Lacayo in an article in *Time* (1994). "He should be a remorseless stranger with a gun." However, Lacayo added, "But the essential part of the picture—the touch she must have counted on to arouse the 'primal sympathies' of her neighbors and to cut short any doubts— was his race. The suspect had to be a black man." Better still, said Lacayo, he had to be a black man in a knit cap, "a bit of a hip-hop wardrobe" that can be "menacing" in [many] minds. Lacayo further asked, "Wasn't that everyone's most familiar image of the murderous criminal?" As was demonstrated by Gomes and Williams in their examination of the Stuart case of Boston, the African American male as "criminal" is deeply embedded in the U.S. psyche due in large part to the media. Further, the mainstream media reflect the racism prevalent in the United States and are themselves a racist institution (Martindale, p. 91).

Media's Tendency to Provoke Anger and Hostility Towards African Americans

Susan Smith's allegation resulted in an uproar in Union, South Carolina. Perhaps, the Charles Stuart case of Boston and "her [Susan Smith's] own not quite right account of the kidnaping" cautioned the press, the U.S. on the whole, and Union residents (p. 47). One Union resident said, "This whole idea of her labeling a black man as the criminal sends a message of the black male as savage and barbarian" (Lacayo, p. 48).

The CNN "Larry King Live" transcript (Case 1, broadcast) shows King and a guest discussing the death penalty for the alleged "car jacker/ kidnapper." Changes in the law are also discussed. Just as Southern lynch mobs justified mob violence as a "necessary response to black crime and an inefficient legal system for virtually any perceived transgression of the racial boundaries or threat to the system of white supremacy, King and his guest, Rep. Charles Schumer, concurred that something of a more drastic nature had to be done since car jackings had increased dramatically:

Schumer: " . . . The recent crime bill reintroduced capital punishment . . . in the most heinous of offenses. . . ."

Further, listeners were continually told in the report that the crime of car jacking was increasing. This gave the impression, since the African American male had been associated with car jacking and with the Susan Smith case, that African American males were dangerous and likely to commit such acts often. Larry King began his report announcing, urgently:

If you drive a car, listen up, you don't want to be the victim of a car jacking. Take it from Susan Smith. Her worst nightmare began 48 hours ago and she's living it right now. . . . An armed car jacker pushed his way into her car. . . . He's still on the loose (p. 1).

In both the Charles Stuart and the Central Park rape cases, media indicted the whole black community. In both instances, as Corea explained, the African American male was cast in a subhuman light as the media referred to him in harsh terms and language. Corea's examination of broadcast media revealed the use of such terms as "brutally beaten, gang raped, and left to die" by the "cruel" African Americans and Latino "thugs" who were referred to as "animals." Thus, the terms "beast and brute" used in early media became "animal or vicious animal and thug." Only one young man is singled out as having come from a "good family" and once having prospects of a promising future, now dashed. Corea concluded, information about these young men's community and living conditions flowed into the airwaves of broadcast news and onto the pages of newspapers, painting a picture of African American males, in general, as violent, cruel and vicious (p. 259).

The same trend was seen in the Susan Smith case. Both Larry King and his guest agreed the death penalty should be a consideration when it was thought the assailant was African American (p. 5). In the Central Park jogger case, Corea explained, viewer outrage and a "hang 'em high" response ranged from a call for castration to life imprisonment to the death penalty (p. 260). A study of *New York Times* coverage of the case substantiates Corea's findings. In one article, the boys, said to be ages 13 to 15, were out "wilding" and had attacked several people. They are described as "calculating and menacing attackers who were lying in wait for their next prey," part of a "loosely organized gang of 32 who . . . terrorized at least eight other people." In the same article readers are told the youths probably attacked the woman because she was at an economic level they could not hope to attain. In another article, the attack is described as being an "especially ferocious version of group delinquency" (*New York Times*, 1987). Despite these depictions the *New York Times* seems oblivious it might be responsible in part for the African American community's fear that the crime will "further fuel a misconception that African Americans, particularly, young males, will be subjects of fear and scorn."

In the case of Charles Stuart, Lacayo (1994) observed, the police, and other officials, with the assistance of the media, bought his story and placed Boston's Mission Hill residents under siege. Referring to the Stuarts as the "Camelot couple," both the *Boston Globe* and the *Boston Herald* played the role of instigator as police rounded up and interrogated scores of African American men and eventually arrested a suspect (pp. 46-47). Gomes and Williams (1990) point out the press even raised questions about a community that could "produce such a vicious animal." The suspect was labeled a monster (p. 57). Likewise, viewers are told that both Susan Smith and her husband were from good family backgrounds and had good upbringing. Both the Smith and Stuart cases provide further evidence of the African American man's crimes being viewed more harshly than similar acts committed by white offenders.

Framing to Excuse White Criminal Behavior

The murder of Edward Werner and the Casino murder, provide evidence white males are often handled with "kid gloves" when they commit crimes while African Americans are often vilified. Both the defendant and the victim in the Werner case are white.

Sam Manzie's parents, Delores and Nick Manzie, discussed their family in the "20/20"(1997) special report, with Barbara Walters telling listeners the Manzies were a "family filled with affection. . . . Parenting was taken seriously" (p. 3). Manzie is said to be a victim of a sex offender who seduced him through the Internet. The Internet is blamed: " . . . Manzie was the perfect target for the sexual predators who roam the Internet . . . confused about his sexual identity, tortured by it, and he was lonely" (p. 10). His mother discusses his "isolation" and describes his "violence" as his crying out in pain (p. 15). Eddie Werner becomes a metaphor and is described as the "innocent trip wire for all of his rage" (p. 24). He is mentioned for the first time on page 18 of the transcript. We are told that he was "brutally" murdered and raped, but Walters explains that Manzie was in therapy almost until that day (p. 18). We are told Werner's mother deserves sympathy but that we cannot bring Eddie back and Manzie really needs support now.

Downs refers to Manzie as a "child who is in desperate need of some kind of help" (p. 27). In the end we are told "It's a story not only of the dangers of the Internet but about how the system failed a family in need and a community" (p. 28) since the Manzie family reportedly tried to get their son committed. Such references to Sam Manzie as "a child" and an "innocent victim" are in direct contrast to the labeling of African Americans who are accused of similar crimes, i.e., the Stuart case and Central Park jogger cases. The offenders in the Central Park jogger case might be more applicable here since they and Manzie are in a similar age category. Corea asserts, such crimes, when committed by whites, are regarded as out of character and are treated as unreal while the media communicate the notion that African American males should know better and sidestep any discussion of their possible psychological needs (p. 260), thus no such calming devices of language or circumstance are used to garner sympathy.

In the Casino murder case, the African American father and the casino are blamed for the death of his daughter, Sherrice Iverson. The arcade within the casino where she is murdered is a monster, not the young, white man who killed her. Again, "20/20"(1997) reports on the case; however, the focus of the report is child neglect at casinos. The headline reads "Where Are Their Parents?" Several incidents of children found without their parents are discussed and described as a roving reporter scans casinos nationwide. Sherrice Iverson is briefly mentioned on page 4 of the transcript as simply one of many cases. Her father is blamed for her murder. Her killer is said to have "snapped her head, breaking her neck . . . while Sherrice's father was gambling" (p. 4). Antonio Mora, the commentator, asserts, " . . . dozens of parents like him, [are] willing to play the slots, even . . . playing roulette with their children's safety" (p. 4). The killer's name, Jeremy Joseph Stromeyer, is not even mentioned in the transcript. He is removed from blame altogether. The father is said to be the greatest culprit; casino security is mildly blamed; and the arcade pinball games, Homer Hippo and Ms. Pac-Man, are identified as the real dangers parents should look out for (p. 4). The print media provided similar coverage, showing very little sympathy for the family of the victim. Even though the father was surely careless and negligent, he did not commit murder, but he is tried and convicted in the media and treated as if he did, while the actual murderer is said to be a good student with a once promising future. The irony is that the media, in setting an agenda that concentrated on the dangers of leaving children unattended in casinos and arcades failed to alert the public to the potential dangers posed by strangers, even white strangers.

Implications for Today's Media

Mass media set the agenda for the public. News coverage is framed in such a way as to support the accepted societal order. Given this, it is crucial that mass media use their role responsibly—to bring the country together as a national community, taking into account its diverse audience and recognizing the damaging and divisive effects of its negative coverage of African Americans. Not only does such negative reporting damage the psyches of African Americans, but it also creates disturbing images in the minds of white citizens. Whites who commit heinous acts must not be given special treatment in the press and excused from their crimes. Media must see the importance of respecting victims' rights and their families' rights as well. To devalue the murder of an innocent, seven-year-old African American child or an innocent eleven-year-old white child because they are murdered by white males is not indicative of a press fighting for the good of the whole society and the humanity of all of its people.

While the research I've used here is not extensive, it does scratch the surface and can serve as a model and a catalyst for further research in this area. Media journalists and executives as well as scholars and students must explore the prejudices and stereotypes they have bought into as well as the dynamics of unbalanced reporting. They impact all Americans:

those who fall victim to the press as well as everyone else in society who buys into the biased accounts and, even if unwittingly, bases his or her judgments and actions on them. Content analysis provides us with an excellent tool for studying past and present media representations, a first step in understanding and countering the negative images that have been, as the Kerner Commission (Kerner, 1968) found, a contributing factor to racism.

References

Primary Sources:

Broadcasting

Car jacking and kidnaping in South Carolina. (1994, October 27). *Larry King live.* Special CNN Report.

Sam's story. (1997, October 31). *20/20.* ABC Special Report.

Where are their parents? Children roam casinos while their parents gamble. (1997, September 12). *20/20.* ABC Special Report.

Newspapers

Boston Globe. (1989, October 27).

Gibbs, N. (1994, November 14). Death and deceit. *Time, 144,* 43-45.

Gorman, T. (1997, May 28). Casino surveillance footage tells story of girl's killing. *Los Angeles Times,* p. 5.

Gorman, T., & Mitchell, J. (1997, May 29). Slaying fuels debate over children's safety in casinos. *Los Angeles Times,* p. 1.

Hayes, B., & Otani, E. (1997, May 29). Officials call girl's slaying a tragic example of neglect. *Los Angeles Times.*

Lacayo, R. (1994, November 14). Stranger in the shadow. *Time, 144,* 46-48.

Leeds, J., & Rainey, J. (1997, May 30). Suspect told two classmates of the casino crime. *Los Angeles Times,* p. 2.

Mariott, M. (1989, April 24). Harlem residents fear backlash. *New York Times,* p. B4.

McFadden, R. (1997, October 3). Suspect in New Jersey strangling was reportedly sex-case victim. *New York Times,* p. 5.

Police say youths were part of loosely organized gang. (1987, April 22). *New York Times,* p.2.

Smith, P. (1997, June 2). Children die just out of focus. *Boston Globe,* p. 1.

Suspect in girl's slaying at casino in custody. (1997, May 30). *USA Today,* p. 6.

Wolff, C. (1989, April 21). Group of youths rape and severely beat young woman jogger. *New York Times,* p. B1.

Secondary Sources:

Baker, J. F., Reid, C., & O'Brien, M. (1992, September 28). Willie Horton in print?: Big time politics. *Publisher's Weekly, 239,* 9.

Brundage, F. W. (1988). *Lynching in the new south: Georgia and Virginia, 1880-1930.* Chicago: University of Illinois Press.

Corea, A. (1990). Racism and the American way of media. In J. Downing, A. Mohammadi, & A. Sreberny-Mohammadi (Eds.), *Questioning the media* (pp. 345-361). Thousand Oaks, CA: Sage.

Duster, A. M. (Ed.). (1970). *Crusade for justice: The autobiography of Ida B. Wells.* Chicago: University of Chicago Press.

Ginzburg, R. (1988). *100 years of lynching.* Baltimore: Black Class Press.

Gomes, R., & Williams, L. F. (1990, Summer). Race and crime: The role of the media in perpetuating racism and classism in America. *Urban League Review, 14(1),* pp. 57-69.

Howard, W. (1995). *Lynching.* Cranbury, NJ: Associated University Press.

Kerner, O. (1968). Kerner report: The 1968 report of the National Advisory Commission on Civil Disorder. Washington, DC.

Martindale, C. (1986). *The white press and black America.* New York: Greenwood.

Peyser, M., & Carroll G. (1995, July 17). Southern Gothic on trial. *Newsweek, 126,* 29.

Raper, A. F. (1969). *The tragedy of lynching.* Montclair, NJ: Patterson Smith.

Simpson, G. (1936). *The Negro in the Philadelphia press.* Philadelphia: University of Philadelphia Press.

Smead, H. (1986). *Blood justice: The lynching of Mack Parker.* New York: Oxford.

Timbs, L. (1994, December 17). To print or not to print. *Editor and Publisher, 239,* 12-14.

Tolnay, E., & Beck, E. M. (1995, July 17). *A festival of violence: An analysis of southern lynching, 1882-1930.* Chicago: University of Illinois Press.

Wulf, S. (1995, July 31). Elegy of lost boys. *Time, 146,* 36.

IMAGE AND IDENTITY: SCREEN ARABS AND MUSLIMS

by
Jack G. Shaheen

"Arabs [and Muslims] have been the victims of ugly racial stereotypes in recent years . . . [and] the widespread casual violation of such standards threatens all potential victims of racial slurs. It ought to stop." (Editorial, *The New Republic*, March 1, 1980)

Regrettably, some Americans are still *"imprisoned because of their prejudices. I know that Arab Americans still feel the sting of being stereotyped in false ways. The saddest encounter of course [was] the heartbreaking experience of Oklahoma City."* (President Bill Clinton, Arab American Institute, Washington D.C., May 7, 1998)

"We are all diminished when a person is subject to discrimination." (Janet Reno, Attorney General, American-Arab Anti-Discrimination Conference, June 11, 1998)

Introduction

This essay presents an overview and analysis of selected media portraits, giving specific attention to television programs and motion pictures, and the impact the screen images have on America's Arabs and Muslims. For more than two decades I have been studying the manner in which purveyors of popular culture project Arabs and Muslims, and the effect their images have on individuals. Examples here are drawn from more than 800 feature films, and hundreds of television newscasts, documentaries, and entertainment shows, ranging from animated cartoons to soap operas to movies-of-the-week. Not included, although in themselves an extremely interesting study, are print and broadcast news stories, editorial and op-ed pages, editorial cartoons, children's books, comic books, textbooks, print advertisements, toys, and games. Explanations as to why these disenchanting images exist, and some possible ways of curtailing the stereotyping, will be considered. The underlying thesis is that stereotypes can lower self esteem, injure innocents, impact policies, and encourage divisiveness by accentuating our differences at the expense of those things that tie us together.

In 1982, I began soliciting information about stereotyping from a number of producers, writers, and network executives. I still recall the rationale for stereotyping offered by James Baerg, Director of Program Practices for CBS-TV in New York City: "I think," he remarked, "the Arab stereotype is attractive to a number of people. It is an easy thing to do. It is the thing that is going to be most readily accepted by a large number of the audience. It is the same thing as throwing in sex and violence when an episode is slow" (Shaheen, 1984, p. 122; Shaheen, 1980). Not much has changed since then. Research verifies that lurid and insidious depictions of Arab Muslims as alien, violent strangers, intent upon battling nonbelievers throughout the world, are staple fare. Such erroneous characterizations more accurately reflect the bias of Western reporters and image makers than they do the realities of the Arab and Muslim people in the modern world. Although the majority of Muslims are not Arabs, most Americans wrongly perceive Arabs and Muslims as one and the same people; the same attributes are almost always invariably linked to both peoples. Thus, in this essay, the terms "Muslim" and "Arab" are used interchangeably or substituted by the terms, "Arab Muslim" or "Muslim Arab."

On the silver screen, the Arab Muslim continues to surface as the threatening cultural "Other." Fear of this "strange" faith, Islam, keeps us huddled in emotional isolation. As Professor John Esposito (1992) says, "Fear of the Green Menace [green being the color of Islam] may well replace that of the Red Menace of world communism . . . Islam is often equated with holy war and hatred, fanaticism and violence, intolerance and the oppression of women" (p. 5). Esposito asserts that narratives about the Muslim world all too often assume that there is a monolithic Islam out there somewhere, as if all Muslims believe, think and feel alike. The stereotypical Muslim presented to Americans resembles Iran's Ayatollah Khomeini, Libya's Moammar Gadhafi, or Iraq's Saddam Hussein. Muslims and Arabs in this country, who overwhelmingly do not identify with these political leaders, feel that other Americans assume they do. As 30-year-old Shahed Abdullah, a native Californian, says, "You think Muslim, you think Saddam Hussein, you think Ayatollah" (Power, 1998, p. 35).

Through immigration, conversion, and birth Muslims are this nation's fastest growing religious group. Regrettably, the approximately five to eight million Muslims who live in the United States are confronted with a barrage of stereotypes which unfairly show them as a global menace, producers of biological weapons, zealots who issue *fatwas* or burn Uncle Sam in effigy. In reality, Muslims are an integral part of the American mainstream, individuals who respect traditions, who are committed to education, faith, family and free enterprise. Indeed, the community is generally a peace loving blend of cultures: 25% are of South Asian descent, Arabs represent another 12%, and nearly half are converts, mainly African Americans. They contribute to their respective communities as teachers, doctors, lawyers and artists.

This mix of ethnic, racial, and cultural backgrounds offers a broad range of Muslim viewpoints. As Professor Sulayman Nyang (1996) of Howard University explains, "Muslims can be compared to Catholics. They are as different from each other as Mexican American Catholics in Southern California are from Polish and Italian Catholics in Chicago or Philadelphia" (p. B10). Muslims are a diverse group: the "seen one, seen 'em all" cliche does not apply. According to Steven Barboza (1993) in *American Jihad*, "There are more than 200,000 Muslim businesses [in the U.S.], 165 Islamic schools, 425 Muslim associations, 85 Islamic publications, and 1,500 mosques" spread from Georgia to Alaska (p. 9). Many Muslims hold prominent positions in business and public service. They appreciate the religious freedom in America, freedom not always available in the lands they left. Nevertheless, although Muslim Americans are an integral part of the American landscape, enriching the communities in which they live, the United States is seldom referred to as a Judeo-Christian-Muslim nation.

In a recent national survey, cited by John Dart (1996) of the *Los Angeles Times*, the Americans polled viewed Christians in general, Jews, and on balance, Mormons, as good influences on U.S. society, but more than 30% regarded Muslims as having a "negative influence" (p. 19). Muslims maintain they are perceived as a "negative influence" because producers of entertainment are ignorant of Islam and as a result tend to focus on a violent and extreme minority. On television and in feature films, they argue, you only see Arabs as bearded fanatics out to seduce blond, western heroines. Chanting "Death to the great Satan," they appear as the enemy, as anti-Jewish, anti-Christian terrorists out to destroy the U.S. and Israel.

Motion Pictures

It seems that most people have difficulty distinguishing between a tiny minority of persons who may be objectionable and the ethnic strain from which they spring. "The popular caricature of the average Arab is as mythical as the old portrait of the Jew," writes columnist Sydney Harris (1986). "He is robed and turbaned, sinister and dangerous, engaged mainly in hijacking airlines and blowing up public buildings." "If the Italians have their Mafia, all Italians are suspect; if the Jews have financiers, all Jews are part of an international conspiracy; if the Arabs have fanatics, all Arabs are violent," says Harris. "In the world today, more than ever, barriers of this kind must be broken, for we are all more alike than we are different."

Virtually since its inception the Hollywood film industry has promoted prejudicial attitudes toward numerous groups: viewers have seen the Asian as "sneaky "; the black as "Sambo"; the Italian as the "Mafioso"; the Irishman as the "drunk"; the Jew as "greedy"; the Indian as the "savage"; and the Latino as "greasy." In the "enlightened 90s," however, such offensive labeling is no longer tolerated. Now, "it appears that we're down to one group, the Arabs," writes columnist Jay Stone (1996). "When was the last time you saw an Arab character in a movie who was anything but one of three Bs (billionaire, bomber, belly dancer)" (p. 1C)? "One group should not be singled out as enemies of all that is good and decent and American," adds Stone. "Where are the movies about Arabs and Muslims who are just ordinary people? It is time for Hollywood to end this undeclared war?" Sam Keen (1986), author of *Faces of the Enemy*, shows how Arabs are still vilified: "You can hit an Arab free; they're free enemies, free villains—where you couldn't do it to a Jew or you can't do it to a black anymore (pp. 29-30)."

As President John Kennedy (1962) said, "The great enemy of truth is very often not the lie, deliberate, contrived and dishonest, but the myth, persistent, persuasive and realistic." For more than a century movies have created myths. Ever since the camera began to crank, the unkempt Arab has appeared as an uncivilized character, the outsider in need of a shower and a shave, starkly contrasting in behavior and appearance with the white Western protagonist. Beginning with Universal's *The Rage of Paris* (1921), in which the heroine's husband "is killed in a sandstorm by an Arab," Hollywood's studios have needlessly maligned Arabs. Motion pictures such as *The Sheik* (1921) and *Son of the Sheik* (1926), which starred the popular Rudolph Valentino as Sheikh Ahmed, displayed Arab Muslims as brutal slavers and promiscuous desert sheikhs. Of course, Valentino, as the hero, cannot really be an Arab:

Purrs Diana, the heroine: "His [Ahmed's] hand is so large for an Arab."

Ahmed's French friend: "He is not an Arab. His father was an Englishman, his mother, a Spaniard."

Hollywood's romantic sheikh of the 1920s became the oily sheikh of the 1970s and 1980s; concurrently, the industry's bedouin bandit of the 1920s became the "fundamentalist" bomber who prays before killing innocents. The cinema's sheikhs are uncultured and ruthless, attempting to procure media conglomerates (*Network*, 1977), destroy the world's economy (*Rollover*, 1981), kidnap Western women (*Jewel of the Nile*, 1985), direct nuclear weapons at Israel and the United States (*Frantic*, 1988), and influence foreign policies (*American Ninja 4: The Annihilation*, 1991) (Shaheen, 1990b, p. C1-C2).

131

Then and now Arab characters are carefully crafted to alarm viewers. Films project the diverse Islamic world as populated with bearded mullahs, billionaire sheikhs, terrorist bombers, backward bedouin, and noisy bargainers. Women surface either as gun toters or as bumbling subservients, or as belly dancers bouncing voluptuously in palaces and erotically oscillating in slave markets. More recently image makers are offering other caricatures of Muslim women: covered in black from head to toe, they appear as uneducated, unattractive, and enslaved beings. Solely attending men, they follow several paces behind abusive sheikhs, their heads lowered.

Mindlessly adopted and casually adapted, these rigid and repetitive portraits narrow our vision and blur reality. The screen Arab Muslim lacks a humane face. He/She lives in a mythical kingdom of endless desert dotted with oil wells, tents, run-down mosques, palaces, goats, and camels. These caricatures and settings serve to belittle the hospitality of Arabs and Muslims, their rich culture, and their history. Functioning as visual lesson plans, movies, like books, last forever. No sooner do Hollywood's features leave the movie theaters than they are available in video stores and broadcast on TV. From 1986 to 1995, I tracked feature films telecast on cable and network channels in St. Louis, Missouri. Each week, 15 to 20 movies mocking or denigrating Arab Muslims were telecast. In numerous films such as *Navy Seals* (1990), *Killing Streets* (1991), *The Human Shield* (1992), *The Son of the Pink Panther* (1993), *Bloodfist V: Human Target* (1994) and *True Lies* (1994), viewers could see American adolescents, intelligence agents, military personnel, even Inspector Clouseau's son, massacring obnoxious Arab Muslims.

Since 1970, more than 300 major films have vilified Arabs. They have featured Arab curs drawing sabers (*Paradise*, 1982), abducting blondes (*Sahara*, 1983), buying America (*Network*, 1996), siding with the Nazis against Israel (*Exodus*, 1960), and tossing bombs—even nuclear ones—at the West (*True Lies*, 1994). Unsightly Arab Muslims and prejudicial dialogue about them also appear in more than 200 movies that otherwise have nothing at all to do with Arabs or the Middle East. In films such as *Reds* (1981), *Cloak and Dagger* (1984), *Power* (1986), *Puppet Master II* (1990), *The Bonfire of the Vanities* (1990), *American Samurai* (1992), and *Point of No Return* (1993), Muslim caricatures appear like phantoms. Libyans, especially, are a favorite target. In films like *Back to the Future* (1985), *Broadcast News* (1987), and *Patriot Games* (1992), Libyan "bastards" shelter Irish villains, bomb U.S. military installations in Italy, and shoot a heroic American scientist in a mall parking lot. *The American President* (1995), an otherwise agreeable romantic comedy about a widowed president falling for a lovely environmental lobbyist, mentions Libyans who bomb a U.S. weapons system. In this case, at least, writer Aaron Sorkin softens the anti-Libyan dialogue by expressing sympathy for the Arab janitor and other innocents about to be annihilated.

Egyptians are displayed as dirty, hostile, and sneaky in Universal's 1999 version of *The Mummy*, an $80 million remake of the 1932 Boris Karloff classic. In his review, critic Anthony Lane of *The New Yorker* (1999) writes: "Finally there is the Arab question. The Arab people have always had the roughest and most uncomprehending deal from Hollywood, but with the death of the Cold War the stereotype has been granted even more wretched prominence." Adds Lane, "So, here's a party game for any producers with a Middle Eastern setting in mind; try replacing one Semitic group with another—Jews instead of Arabs—and then listen for the laugh" (pp. 104-105).

Motion pictures such as *Not Without My Daughter* (1990) show the Muslim male as a religious hypocrite, a liar abusing Islam and kidnapping his American wife and daughter.

Not only does he imprison and abuse his wife in Iran, he seems to do so in the name of Islam as when he slaps her face, boasting, "I'm a Muslim!" After breaking an oath sworn on the Qur'an he brags: "Islam is the greatest gift I can give my daughter." When he departs the mosque followed by his relatives, the camera cuts to a poster of a grim Ayatollah Khomeini. The editing implies that the offensive actions of Muslims towards American women and the behavior of Iran's late Ayatollah are clearly connected.

Palestinians are characterized by Hollywood as religious fanatics, threatening our freedom, economy, and culture. Producers portray the Palestinian as a demonic creature without compassion for men, women, or children. Palestinian Muslim images reflect a combination of past stereotypes, notably American Indians and Blacks as dark and primitive sexual predators. The "Palestinian equals terrorist" narrative initially surfaced in 1960, in Otto Preminger's *Exodus*. In the 1980s ten features, including *The Ambassador* (1984), *The Delta Force* (1986), *Wanted Dead or Alive* (1987), and *Ministry of Vengeance* (1989), put into effect images showing the Palestinian Muslim as Enemy Number One. Feature films tag him as "scumbag," "son of a bitch," "the Gucci Terrorist," "a fly in a piece of shit," "animals," "bastards," "f—-in' pigs," and "stateless savages" who "massacre children." The slurs are not rebuked by other characters (Shaheen, 1990a, p. 50). Several made-for-television movies also paint the Palestinians as despicable beings, including TV movies such as *Hostage Flight* (1985), *Terrorist on Trial* (1988), *Voyage of Terror* (1990), Cinemax's April 1998 documentary, *Suicide Bombers Secrets of the Shaheed*, and HBO's January 1999 documentary, *Diary of a Terrorist: Mikdad*.

Two 1990s box-office hits, *True Lies* (1994) and *Executive Decision* (1996), also portray Palestinian Muslims as screaming, murderous "terrorists" killing American innocents, including a priest. In *True Lies* Muslims ignite an atom bomb off the Florida coast. Avi Nesher, a former Israeli commando working in the Hollywood film industry, was "incensed by the sick humor of a *Lies* scene in which an Uzi tossed down a flight of stairs inadvertently mows down a roomful of Arabs." Nesher told *Jerusalem Report* correspondent Sheli Teitelbaum (1996): "You were supposed to laugh? I fought Arabs and I had Arab friends, but this was completely dehumanizing a group" (p. 49).

In *Executive Decision*, Muslims hijack a passenger jet, terrorize the passengers, kill a flight attendant, and prepare to unload enough lethal nerve gas to kill millions in Washington, D.C. and along the East coast. Throughout, Islam is equated with violence. Holding the Holy Qur'an in one hand and a bomb in the other, a Palestinian Muslim enters the swank dining room of London's Marriott Hotel and blows up innocent couples. Four days after the film was released, employees of a Denver radio station burst into a mosque and began heckling worshipers while the station broadcast their antics. Twentieth-Century Fox's recent feature *The Siege* (1998) displays stars such as Denzel Washington and Annette Bening as F.B.I. and C.I.A. agents. Their mission? To locate and destroy Palestinian Muslims who terrorize New York City. *The Siege* presents Arab immigrants, assisted by Arab American auto mechanics, university students, and even a Brooklyn college professor, killing more than 700 innocent New Yorkers.

Even the Walt Disney Company, a self-professed family-friendly mega-company, is guilty of the vilification of Arabs and Muslims. Since 1992, Disney has released seven features with harmful caricatures. In December 1995, Touchstone Pictures, a subsidiary of Disney, released a remake of Edward Streeter's 1948 book, *Father of the Bride*. In Disney's *Father of the Bride, Part II*, a sequel to the 1991 Steve Martin remake, disagreeable Mideast

Americans are introduced for the first time. (In the original 1950 Spencer Tracy -Elizabeth Taylor film and all the earlier *Father of the Bride* movies Muslims and Mideast Americans do not appear at all.) Steve Martin and Diane Keaton appear as the happily married George and Nina Banks; they have everything, including a wonderful "Brady Bunch" home. When George convinces Nina to sell the house, the crass Arab family of Habibs is introduced. The rich and unkempt Mr. Habib (Eugene Levy) smokes, needs a shave, and talks with a heavy accent. When Mrs. Habib attempts to speak, her husband barks mumbo-jumbo, a mix of Farsi and Arabic, at her. Cowering like a scolded puppy, Mrs. Habib becomes mute, perpetuating Hollywood's image of the Arab woman as a submissive nonentity. Mr. Habib is portrayed as sloppy, mean, and tight-fisted. After he purchases the house he demands that the Banks be out in ten days, crushing his cigarette on the immaculate walkway. The message is clear: there goes the neighborhood. Interestingly, no one working on *Bride II* denounced the stereotyping, nor did protests emanate from members of the Screen Writers', Actors', or Directors' Guilds of America.

Disney continued to demean Arabs in *Aladdin* (1992), the second most successful animated picture ever made, earning $217 million at domestic box offices. After sensitivity meetings were held between some Arab Americans and Disney executives in July 1993, Disney deleted two offensive lines from *Aladdin's* opening song before releasing the video. That was all. The line, "It's barbaric, but hey, it's home," remains. The storyteller is portrayed as a shifty, disreputable Arab, dastardly saber-wielding villains still try to cut off the hands of maidens, and a wicked vizier still slices a few throats. For generations, these scenes will teach children that Aladdin's home is indeed "barbaric" (Shaheen 1996, p. 7). A *New York Times* ("It's Racist," 1993) editorial complained that "To characterize an entire region with this sort of tongue-in-cheek bigotry, especially in a movie aimed at children, [itself] borders on the barbaric." Professor Joanne Brown (1992) of Drake University agrees that *Aladdin* is racist. The villains display "dark-hooded eyes and large hooked noses," writes Brown. "Perhaps I am sensitive to this business of noses because I am Jewish." Brown explains how she would feel if Disney studios created a cartoon based on a Jewish folk tale that portrayed all Jews as Shylocks (p. 12).

Following the *Aladdin* discussions, Disney executives promised not to demean Arabs in the future, but then went ahead and featured hook-nosed, buck-toothed Arab "desert skunks" in their home-video release of *Aladdin's* sequel, *The Return of Jafar* (1994). *Jafar* sold 10 million copies to rank among the 20 top-selling videos. That same year Disney also produced *In the Army Now*, in which "Glendale reservists" deride Arab cuisine, clobber desert Arabs, and encourage the U.S. Air Force to "blow the hell out of them." Americans of Middle Eastern heritage are again targeted in a Disney children's film called *Kazaam* (1996), starring Shaquille O'Neal, in which Malik, Hassan, and El-Baz, three dark-complexioned Muslim villains needing shaves and speaking with heavy accents, covet "all the money in the world." Sloppy Malik gobbles "goat's eyes" like a pig swallowing corn. He punches good-guy Americans and tosses Max, a twelve-year-old boy, down a shaft presumably to his death.

In 1997, Disney subsidiaries Miramax and Hollywood Pictures released *Operation Condor* and *G.I. Jane*. Set in the Arabian desert, *Condor* displays Jackie Chan battling scores of evil Arabs such as a money-grubbing innkeeper and bedouin white-slavers. Chan also contests two hook-nosed Arabs, "Soldiers of the Faith," who speak fractured English and wear checkered headdresses that look like tablecloths pinched from a pizza parlor. The duo mock Islam by spouting such lines as, "We will never give up the struggle for the holy battle," and, "Praise Allah for delivering you (Chan) to us again." Watching the film, I wondered why the talented Chan, whose 30 films are box-office hits here and abroad, would vilify anyone, especially since Asian performers are still trying to erase the Fu Manchu images. In *G.I. Jane*, viewers cheer as Demi Moore, a macho Navy SEAL officer, "guts it out" and kills Arabs. The Arabs surface only at the end, when the SEALs move to retrieve a U.S. nuclear-powered satellite containing weapons-grade plutonium off the Libyan coast. The camera reveals courageous Moore rescuing her drill sergeant's life, then blasting pursuing Arabs. Since 1986, Hollywood studios have released 22 films showing our military units and agents killing Arabs. As *New York Times* columnist Russell Baker (1997) wrote, Arabs are the "last people except Episcopalians whom Hollywood feels free to offend en masse."

Television

From 1950 until today, one Arab American and one Arab Christian immigrant have appeared as characters in a television series. The first was Uncle Tanoose, the Lebanese patriarch portrayed by Hans Conreid in "The Danny Thomas Show" (1953-71). Tanoose occasionally appeared in episodes, visiting his relatives in the United States. The second was Corporal Maxwell Klinger, an Arab American soldier in "M*A*S*H" (1972-1983), played by Jamie Farr, who tries to get himself discharged by wearing women's clothing. People modeled on such public figures as heart surgeon Dr. Michael DeBakey, UPI's White House correspondent Helen Thomas, or radio's Top-40 celebrity Casey Kasem never appear. This absence is wounding. Since "M*A*S*H" debuted in 1972, there has not been a single series featuring an Arab American character. Surely image makers know what happens to young people when someone in authority portrays their society as one in which they have no public presence. Such an experience, writes Adrienne Rich (1995), can generate "a moment of psychic disequilibrium, as if you looked in a mirror and saw nothing."

Since 1974, when I began to document images on entertainment shows, the rogues have often been Arab Muslims. A selective overview of more than 200 programs, including network newscasts, documentaries, comedies, soap operas, children's cartoons, dramas, and movies-of-the-week yielded the following results. Fanatical Muslims surface in several mid-1980s television movies such as *Hostage Flight* (NBC, 1985), *Sword of Gideon* (HBO, 1986), *Under Siege* (NBC, 1986), *The Taking of Flight 847* (NBC, 1988), *Terrorist on Trial: The United States vs. Salim Ajami* (CBS, 1988), *Hostages* (HBO, 1993), *Freedom Strike* (SHO, 1997), *Path to Paradise* (HBO, 1997), and *Shadow Warriors II: Hunt for the Death Merchant* (TNT, 1999). These TV movies are now constantly rebroadcast on both cable and network systems.

In *Hostage Flight*, the protagonist says, "These [Arab Muslim] bastards shot those people in cold blood. They think it's open season on Americans." In *Under Siege*, the U.S. Secretary of State tells the Ambassador of a Muslim nation: "People in your country are barbarians." The FBI director in this film also scrutinizes Dearborn's large Arab American community for terrorists who have blown up shopping malls and threatened the White House, telling his African American colleague: "Those people are different from us. It's a whole different ball game. I mean the East and the Middle East. Those people have their own mentality. They have their own notion of what's right and what's wrong, what's worth living for and dying for. But we insist on dealing with them as if they're the same as us. We'd better wake up." In *Terrorist on Trial*, a Palestinian Muslim boasts that he ordered the deaths of American women and children and advocates the use of nuclear weapons, saying, "We will strike at them in their home country as well as overseas. Long live Palestine!"

Constantly rebroadcast on 40-plus cable and network systems, these disturbing TV movies show all Arabs, Muslims, and Arab Americans as abhorrent militants at war with the United States. Accomplished Arab American actors are obliged to play terrorists and to demean their heritage. Nicholas Kadi, for example, a competent character actor, makes his living playing Arab Muslim kuffiyeh-clad terrorists. In 1991, Kadi lamented on the news show "48 Hours" that he seldom speaks in films. Instead of talking, directors tell him to impart "a lot of threatening looks, threatening gestures, threatening actions. Every time we [he and others playing heavies] said 'America,' we'd [be directed to] spit." Says Kadi, "There are other kinds of Arabs in the world besides terrorists. I'd like to think that some day there will be an Arab role out there (Kadi, 1991)." Kadi has played stereotypical roles in films such as *Navy SEALS* (1990) and, in TV shows such as "Scimitar," a 1995 NBC *JAG* episode. In "Scimitar" the Iraqi-born Kadi impersonates a Saddam-like colonel holding Meg, an innocent U.S. army officer, hostage. The lusting Kadi tries to force himself on the attractive blond. One screen myth maintains that Arabs consider "date rape" to be "an acceptable social practice." The camera dwells on the drooling Kadi slowly wielding a Damascus scimitar to remove Meg's uniform. The rape is thwarted and Kadi is apprehended just in time. Interestingly, from 1995 to 1999 nine *Jag* episodes produced by Donald P. Bellisario vilified Muslims of the Middle East; with reruns that comes to 25 programs in five years. Programs such as "Embassy," "Act of Terror," and "Code Blue," like "Scimitar," revealed Arab Muslims lusting after American women and blowing up innocents overseas and in a Washington, DC hospital.

The demonization of Arab Muslims is reminiscent of the demonization of American Indians. As commentator Pat Buchanan pointed out at the annual Arab American Anti-Discrimination conference in Washington, DC on June 13, 1998: "The Arabs I see in Hollywood movies are like the movies I used to see with the cavalry and Indians." Clad in strange garb, Arabs are obliged to speak garbled English and to crave blond heroines. Just as screen protagonists call Indians "savages," they call Arabs "terrorists." The closing frames of "Scimitar" show an Iraqi helicopter pursuing Americans. When the chopper goes down in flames, the Marines cheer: "Yahoo. It's just like *Stagecoach* with John Wayne." Puzzled by the reference to Wayne, a motion picture idol, Meg asks the Marine: "John Wayne was killed by Iraqis?" He replies, "No, Indians!" In the Gulf war movie, *Hot Shots Part Deux!* (1994), U.S. soldiers prepare for an Iraqi attack. Warns one G.I., "Indians on the warpath."

A November 1996 segment of *FX: The Series* depicts Rashid Hamadi as a stereotypical Arab drug addict who deliberately runs over and kills a New York City police officer in cold blood. But when policemen move to apprehend him, Hamadi boasts, "I have diplomatic immunity. You can't arrest me." In the end, Hamadi is caught smuggling counterfeit plates into New York City; his "Lebanese" and "Iranian" friends in Beirut fabricated the bills. Final scenes show policemen seizing Hamadi, that "piece of garbage" and "slimeball bastard." In 1998, two *Soldier of Fortune* segments, "Surgical Strike" and "Top Event," surfaced on UPN's television network. Produced by Rhysher Entertainment, the "Strike" episode depicts Arab Muslim "bastards" blowing up a passenger plane, killing all 230 passengers. And in Rhysher's "Event," Arab terrorists move to release three truck loads of poison gas "in the

136

name of Allah," killing thousands of Los Angeles residents. When asked who she works for, the female militant barks, "I work only for Allah."

On the "Jon Stewart Show," U.S. soldier puppets kill white-robed Arab puppets. Waving the American flag, one soldier boasts: "I killed many of them!" Says another: "I decapitated quite a few of them myself." Stewart's audience applauds ("Jon Stewart," 1995). In "Twisted Puppet Theater," Ali, the Muslim puppet sporting a black beard and turban, shouts: "There is only one God and Mohammed is his prophet!" Then he turns and shoots Kukla, the good clown puppet, dead (Showtime, 1995). From December 1991 through early 1992, MTV featured "Just Say Julie" segments, sandwiched between music videos, showing Julie addressing unsavory Moroccan buffoons as "scum" and the "creep with the fez." In one segment the two "fiendish" Arabs armed with explosives move to blow up the television channel.

Cartoons

Over the years I have viewed and studied scores of American cartoons denigrating the Arab, starting with the 1926 animated short, "Felix the Cat Shatters the Sheik." In "Porky in Egypt" (1938), for example, Arab Muslims in prayer suddenly become Amos 'n' Andy shooting craps and a sexy harem maiden removes her veil, revealing an ugly face. Favorite cartoon characters such as Popeye, Bugs Bunny, Woody Woodpecker, Daffy Duck, Superman, and Batman ridicule and trounce Arabs (Shaheen, 1993). Since 1975, more than 60 comparable cartoons have surfaced on television, depicting Arabs as swine, rats, dogs, magpies, vultures and monkeys.

Writers give cartoon Arabs names like "Sheikh Ha-Mean-ie," "Ali Boo-Boo," "The Phoney Pharaoh," "Ali Baba, the Mad Dog of the Desert, and his Dirty Sleeves," "Hassan the Assassin," "The Desert Rat," "Desert Rat Hordes," "Ali Oop," "Ali Mode," and "Arab Duck." While monitoring cartoons on November 23, 1996, I saw "Well-Worn Daffy" on the Nickelodeon channel. Wearing a white kuffiyeh and armed with a shotgun, Daffy shoots at three winsome Mexican mice. The mice call Daffy, among other things, "Arab Duck!" Adult viewers may be able to separate fact from animal, but for many children the animated world of cartoons consists of good people versus bad people, the latter often Arabs. What is particularly relevant about the TV shows/movies, cartoons, and feature films is that they are repackaged and exported back to the Arab world where the youth pick them up and begin to form a negative self-image through antagonistic Western eyes. This has a telling effect on the future of Arab society.

Effects on Children

Viewing these cartoons brings back memories of earlier portrayals of "stupid" African Americans, "savage" American Indians, "dirty" Latinos, "buck-toothed Japs" and "hook-nosed" Shylocks in burnooses. Jewish mothers in Europe of the 1930s and the 1940s, as well as African, Indian, Hispanic and Japanese mothers in the United States during this period, tried to shield their children from such imagery, but such hateful portraits cannot help but promote bigotry toward them. America's Muslim parents are increasingly aware of these dangers and work to counteract or eliminate them. Citing scores of old motion pictures being telecast on cable systems, along with cartoons, re-runs of television dramas and sitcoms, plus newly created TV programs and TV movies-of-the-week, they fear that stereotyping has become more pervasive than ever. Conversely, image makers are now giving children of other ethnic origins positive role models to identify with. Characters appear on the screen that make American children feel good about themselves: American Indians, African Americans, Hispanics, Asians, Jews, Italians, Polynesians, Irish, English, Poles, East Indians, Scots—just about every racial and ethnic group on the planet, except the Arabs. According to the American-Arab Anti-Discrimination Committee (ADC), many parents have complained that as a result of the pervasive stereotype, their children have become ashamed of their religion and heritage. Some have asked their parents to change their Arab names to something more American sounding. A Texas teen told his sister, "I lied about where our parents had come from." Especially alarming are the number of incidents targeting youngsters. After the Trade Center bombing several children of Arab descent in New York were told to "go back where you came from." They went home from school in tears, writes *New York Times'* Melinda Henneberger. "Classmates told them they were responsible for the attack." Muslim girls were taunted; schoolmates pulled off their head scarves (Moghrabi, 1995, p. 3C)." At a suburban Muslim day care center in Texas the driver of a passing car shouted, "Here's a bomb for you, lady!" and threw a soda can at a teacher and her students.

The *Anti-Arab-American Discrimination Hate Crimes* document, published by the American-Arab Anti-Discrimination Committee in November 1994, and the Council on American Islamic Relations' (CAIR) 1996 manual, *A Rush to Judgement: A Special Report on Anti-Muslim Stereotyping*, report many similar incidents. During the heartbreaking experience of Oklahoma City, Suhair al-Mosawia, a Muslim woman seven months pregnant, lost her son after teens pursued her, hammering her home with rocks. Following Muslim custom she gave the stillborn a name, Salam, Arabic for "peace." One Oklahoma City resident suggested putting Arab Americans in internment camps. In a *Cleveland Plain Dealer* op-ed essay, Palestinian activist Hamzi Moghrabi reported that "in Detroit, home of the largest Arab American population outside the Middle East, business owners, including the editor, Osama A. Siblani, of *The Arab American News*, were subjected to bomb threats" and trash was thrown at mosques (ADC, 1994, pp. 12, 14).

Media Images and Prejudicial Responses

Media images, points out media critic Jerry Mander (1978), "can cause people to do what they might otherwise never have thought to do (p. 13)." Following the April 1995 Oklahoma City tragedy, speculative reporting combined with decades of stereotyping encouraged more than 300 hate crimes against America's Arabs and Muslims. Abuses took place even as Muslims mourned, along with other Oklahomans, the disaster (CAIR, 1996). Mohammed Nimer of the Council on American-Islamic Relations told reporter Laurie Goodstein, "Most of these incidents have been completely unprovoked . . . just mere encounters with a person who looks like a Muslim, or a person praying, have prompted bias and violence. That is alarming" (Goodstein, 1996).

In Brooklyn, the police department reported that after the Oklahoma City bombing numerous Arab American businesses received hostile calls and death threats. One caller said, "We're going to put a bomb in your business and kill your family." A San Francisco mosque received 35 bomb threats. In Toledo, Ohio, the St. Francis de Sales High School yearbook, the 1995 ACCOLADE, printed in bold-letter capitals "**KILL ALL THE CAMEL JOCKEYS!**" The remark was part of a 500-word essay by a student. Officials immediately issued apologies, however, and the High School President, Rev. Ronald Olezewski, wrote to parents and friends saying that the "insensitive reference" should never have been either written or published. "We apologize," he said. "Please presume ignorance rather than malice and be assured that all at this institution of learning will learn from the wrong" (Briendel, 1996, p. 3).

The day of the Oklahoma City explosion, Abraham Ahmed, a U.S. citizen of Jordanian origin, boarded a plane in Oklahoma City en route to visit his family in Jordan. Two hours after the bombing, it was reported that Ahmed was a suspect. Immediately, some people in Oklahoma City began dumping trash on his lawn; others spit on his wife. While Ahmed was in Chicago waiting to make connections, FBI authorities escorted him into a room and inter- rogated him for six hours. Missing his flight, Ahmed arrived late in London. There he suffered a humiliating strip-search. After five more hours of interrogation, the handcuffed Ahmed was sent back to Washington, DC for another day of questioning. More than a year after he was cleared, Ahmed, who has lived in Oklahoma City for 14 years, still receives suspicious stares from neighbors.

Persisting in defiance of all evidence, hateful images have their impact on public opinion and policies. There is a dangerous and cumulative effect when repulsive screen images remain unchallenged. The negative images are sometimes perceived as **real** portrayals of Muslim culture, which come back to afflict Americans of Arab heritage as well as non-Arab Muslims in their dealings with law enforcement or judicial officials. For example, in January 1997, a judge in Dearborn, Michigan, was asked to rule whether an attorney could show *Not Without My Daughter* to a jury deciding on a child custody case between an Arab American father and a European American mother. Incredibly, the judge allowed this defam- atory film portraying an Iranian man as a child abuser and child-kidnapper to be introduced in court, influencing the judicial proceeding (*ADC*, 1996-7, p. 33).

The Arab Muslim image parallels the image of the Jew in Nazi-inspired German movies such as *Robert and Bertram* (1939), *Die Rothschild Aktien von Waterloo (The Rothschilds' Shares in Waterloo*, 1940), *Der ewige Jew (The Eternal Jew*, 1940), and *Jud Suss* (1940). Resembling the hook-nosed screen Arab wearing burnooses, screen Jews also dressed differ- ently than the films' protagonists, wearing yarmulkes and black robes. They, too, appeared as unkempt money-grubbing caricatures who sought world domination, worshiped a different God, killed innocents, and lusted after blond virgins (Hull, 1969, pp. 157-177). The simultaneous barrage of stereotypical films, editorial cartoons, radio programs, and newspaper essays helped make Jews scapegoats for many of Germany's problems (Hull, 1969, pp. 157-177).

Concerned that misperceptions might hinder genuine peace in the Middle East, *Newsweek* columnist Meg Greenfield ((1986) wrote, "Actually what I see coming is more like a reversion, a flight back to the generalized, hostile attitudes towards Arabs and/or Muslims as a collectivity that prevailed both as government policy and as public prejudice for so many years" (p. 84). Although progress has been real, Greenfield remains concerned about the kind of blanket, indiscriminate anti-Arab sentiment so often expressed in public, "If anything," she writes, "we should be seeking to sharpen and refine our involvement with those Arabs who are themselves enemies and targets of the violent, hate-filled elements in the region. We should be making more distinctions and discriminating judgments among them, not fewer" (p. 84). Greenfield's telling observations reveal the dangers of stereotyping. The Arab world accommodates peace-loving folk. Most Arabs live not in desert tents, rather in apartments and homes. The majority are poor, not rich; most have never mounted a camel, nor seen an oil well. They do not dally in palace harems, nor do they take vacations on magic carpets. Their dress is traditional or western; the variety of their garb and lifestyle defies stereotyping.

Why vilify people?

No single factor leads to stereotyping. Undeniably, the Arab-Israeli conflict and ignorance, the handmaiden of bigotry, continue to be contributing factors. Most image makers do not have the religious, cultural or language background to understand Islam. To my knowledge, not one university, including those with Middle East and Near East centers, offers courses focusing on Arab and Muslim images in popular culture, and no university actively seeks to recruit faculty members to address this issue, even though comparable subjects are offered for other ethnic groups. In classroom discussions and research works, too few scholars document and discuss media images of Arabs and Muslims. It may take decades of education before misinformation is depleted.

One of the reasons why America's Arabs are not yet able to define themselves may be because none belong to America's "media elite." There are no Muslim communications giants comparable to Disney's Michael Eisner, Fox's Rupert Murdoch, or Time-Warner's Ted Turner. Few work as broadcasters, reporters, or filmmakers. Until Arabs and Muslims achieve some influence, their voices will not be heard. As producer Gilbert Cates (1993) says: "It's axiomatic. The more power you have, the louder your voice is heard (p. 3D)."

Inflexibility and indifference impact the stereotyping. Many Muslim and Arab leaders are reluctant to become involved. Although scores of films and television shows denigrating the Arab are purchased, rented, and screened throughout the Western as well as the Muslim world, Muslim information officials and media syndicators appear to be apathetic. Until very recently they have made little or no attempt to meet with image makers to discuss those images ridiculing them and their neighbors. Politics and fear are other reasons. In spite of many noteworthy accomplishments, American Arabs and Muslims do not yet have sufficient political clout to effect fundamental change. Efforts initiated by various groups, such as the American Muslim Public Affairs Council, the Council on American-Islamic Relations, and the American-Arab Anti-Discrimination Committee (an organization with 25,000 members and 75 campus and city chapters), however, have had some influence. Their efforts have resulted in limited apologies, minor edits, and some altered scenarios.

On June 11, 1998, Attorney General Janet Reno told Americans of Arab heritage attending an ADC conference that stereotypes should never influence policy or public opinion. Yet, when this writer asked CNN's Peter Arnett whether stereotyping had any impact on United States Middle East policies, he said: "The media elite follow U.S. policy," adding that those responsible for shaping policies are influenced in part by the stereotypical pictures in their heads.

Conclusion

Openness to change is an American tradition. There are numerous ways for image makers to humanize the Arab Muslim. They could reveal in television shows, documentaries, and motion pictures the telling effects of hate crimes brought about by stereotyping. They could show the impact of such prejudices on children, especially how some are taunted during the Muslim holy month of Ramadan, the time of purification and abstention. Although Ramadan has "a special meaning for Muslim children, their fasting makes them stand out in school," writes AP's Katherine Roth. Some children are distressed, saying "they often have to contend with anti-Muslim slurs" (1996, p. 4B).

Although harmful caricatures may not disappear soon, those professionals engaged in addressing harmful portraits merit recognition. In early March of 1998, this writer and Dr. Hala Maksoud, President of the American-Arab Anti-Discrimination Committee, informed Dr. Rosalyn Weinman, NBC-TV's Executive Vice President of Broadcast Standards and Current Policy, that the network's soap series, *"Days of Our Lives*, was impugning Arab Muslims. Dr. Weinman followed up immediately on our concerns. For weeks prior to our conversation the soap had displayed a kidnapped blond U.S. heroine held hostage in the "harem" of the Sultan's desert palace. Her kidnapper, a bearded clad-in-black Arab, warned that unless she pleased the Sultan, her head would be "chopped off by an Arabian axe, one of those long, curvy sharp swords." Not only did Dr. Weinman issue an apology, NBC promptly dropped all images and references to Arabs from the soap's plot, and as of March 27, the heroine's captors began appearing as generic villains.

During Jay Leno's January, 1996 appearance on CNN's *"Larry King Live"* he was asked whether he ever apologized to anyone he had made fun of. Leno replied that he had. "I said something about Iran or something. And I said instead of chopping the arm off, they were doing it surgically, or something [like that] now, to criminals. I made some jokes about it and I heard from some Arab Americans. And I called them up and I apologized, admitting that Arab Americans sometimes get a bad rap. When you are wrong, you do apologize. And in that case I was wrong. And I have no problem with that." Though Leno mistakenly assumes Iran to be an Arab country, his insights and candor are refreshing.

In ABC-TV's May 4, 1995, *Nightline* segment, "Muslims in America," host Ted Koppel remarked that "Muslims are the stereotyped religion in the United States" and that Muslims are "often the first we think of when there's a terrorist incident." Koppel displayed news clips from the Oklahoma City bombing containing the speculative statements made by several network correspondents about the connection to Middle East terrorism. His interviews and footage humanized Muslims: like other American Arabs, he reported, those living in Cedar Rapids, Iowa, "home of the oldest mosque in America," were "made to feel like aliens when the bomb went off in Oklahoma City." And on April 18, 1997 Koppel hosted a telling religious segment entitled *The Hajj*, focusing on producer-writer Michael Wolfe's pilgrimage to Mecca. This landmark production, narrated by Wolfe, a Muslim, illustrates the peaceful nature of Islam. Commenting on the success of *The Hajj*, one of the most watched segments in *Nightline's* history, Wolfe says, "I wanted to put front and center a very different view from the distortion that generally attends images of the Muslim world."

Some welcome exceptions to stale Arab caricatures in Hollywood features are beginning to appear. Party Picture's 1995 *Party Girl* represents a first: Mustafa, a Muslim Lebanese school teacher, is the romantic lead. Selling falafel to earn his way through college, Mustafa wins the American heroine's heart and helps her become a responsible person. Independent producer Michael Goldman's 1996 documentary film on singer Umm Kulthum, one of the most important figures in Arab popular culture (*Umm Kulthum: The Voice of Egypt*) was enthusiastically received during New York City's Film Festival at Lincoln Center on October 9, 1996. Fox's 1996 *Independence Day*, a movie depicting earthlings about to be extermi-nated by space aliens, shows the world's armies, including both Israeli and Arab combat units, preparing to repel an alien attack. Following a quick shot of scrambling Israeli soldiers, and the Israeli flag, actor Sayed Bayedra appears as an Arab pilot. Speaking Arabic, Bayedra rushes to his plane to stop the invaders. Coincidentally, during the summer of 1980, when I was interviewing executives and producers for my book, *The TV Arab*, writer Jack Guss told me that perhaps the best way to contest the stereotype would be to show outer-space aliens attacking earth. This way, said Guss, even Arabs and Israelis could be together, fighting off the invaders (Shaheen, 1980).

Two other 1996 features, Paramount's *Escape from Los Angeles* and New Line's *The Long Kiss Goodnight*, briefly display Muslim Arabs as victims of prejudice. The films may solicit mild sympathy for Arabs and Muslims, and though not yet an established trend, the images mark the beginning of a much needed change. In the 1998 feature, *A Perfect Murder*, a remake of the 1954 thriller, *Dial M for Murder*, actor David Suchet appears as a bright soft-spoken Arab American New York City detective, Mohamed "Mo" Karaman. Concluding frames show Mo, sympathetic to the heroine's ordeals, saying in Arabic, "*Allah ma'a kum*" (May God be with you). In English, the heroine replies, "And you, as well."

Daily Variety has reported that actor Patrick Swayze has the lead role in a new film called *The White Sheik*. The story concerns an American boy adopted by an Arab couple who rose to become a prominent sheikh. Also, Disney Studios has produced *The Thirteenth Warrior* (1999), a motion picture based on Michael Crichton's book, *Eaters of the Dead*. The story is set ten centuries ago and stars Anthony Banderas as Ahmed Ibn Fahdlan, a heroic Arab Muslim scholar. "This Arab guy I play," said Banderas, "gets caught by cruel Vikings and their cultures clash completely. But they have a mission to carry out, and that starts pulling them together *(Movie Line,* 1998, p. 50)."

Former Disney Chairman Jeffrey Katzenburg has said, "Each of us in Hollywood has the opportunity to assume individual responsibility for creating films that elevate rather than denigrate, that shed light rather than dwell in darkness, that aim for the common highest denominator rather than the lowest." On December 6, 1996, Katzenburg, who is now one of the three executives in charge of DreamWorks Entertainment, solicited opinions from Arab and Muslim American specialists about DreamWorks' animated feature, the *Prince of Egypt*. The four-hour session included a presentation of the film in progress, followed by a candid question and answer session.

Regional and national Muslim organizations and agencies are beginning to pay increasing attention to the ways in which Arabs, Muslims, and Islam are portrayed in the public media. They point out instances of prejudicial depiction, and are working with non-Muslims in schools and other public arenas to help provide a more balanced, and accurate, picture of persons who have for so long been misrepresented and maligned in the news and in various forms of entertainment media. It seems reasonable to hope that as they become more vigilant, and as image makers and the American public gradually become more aware of the hurt that is caused by such misrepresentations as have been visible through much of this century, Arabs and Muslims may enjoy at least relative immunity from prejudicial

142

portrayal and see themselves depicted at least as fairly as are members of other minority groups in America.

References

American-Arab Anti-Discrimination Committee (ADC). (1994, November). *Anti-Arab-American Discrimination Hate Crimes.*

American-Arab Anti-Discrimination Committee (ADC). (1996-97). *Report on hate crimes & discrimination against Arab Americans.*

Baker, R. (1997, September 1). More killing, Hollywood style. *Jacksonville [WI] Gazette.*

Barboza, S. (1993). *American Jihad.* New York: Doubleday.

Briendel, M. (1996, June 13). School yearbook scandal prompts surprise, anger. *Hills Publications,* p. 3.

Brown J. (1992, December 22). Stereotypes ruin fun of *Aladdin. Des Moines Register,* p. 12.

Cates, G. (1993, January 26). TV women portraying new image. *St. Louis Post-Dispatch,* p. 3D.

Council on American-Islamic Relations. (1996). *A rush to judgment: A special report on anti-Muslim stereotyping.* Washington, DC: Author.

Dart, J. (1996). *Deities and deadlines.* Nashville: Vanderbilt University Freedom Forum.

Downing, S. (Executive Producer). (1996). *FX: The Series.* New York City: UNP-TV.

Esposito, J. (1992). *The Islamic threat.* New York: Oxford University Press.

Goodstein, L. (1996, April 20). Report cites harassment of bombing. *Washington Post,* p. A3.

Greenfield, M. (1986, May 29). A Mideast mistake in the making. *Newsweek,* 84.

Harris, S. (1986, April 11). The world shrinks and stereotypes fall. *Detroit Free Press.*

Hull, D. S. (1969). *Film in the Third Reich.* Berkeley: University of California Press.

It's racist, but hey, it's Disney. (1993, July 14). Editorial, *New York Times.*

Jon Stewart show. (1995, February 25). St. Louis, MO: KMOV-TV.

Kadi, N. (1991, January 30). *48 Hours.* CBS-TV.

Keen, S. (1986, May 15). Speech to the Association of American Editorial Cartoonists, San Diego, CA. See Keen's book, *Faces of the Enemy.* Cambridge: Harper & Row.

Kennedy, J .F. (1962). Yale commencement address, New Haven, CT.

Lane, A. (1999, May 10). [Review of the film, *The Mummy* (1999)]. *The New Yorker,* 104-105.

Leno, J. (1996, January 24). *Larry King Live.* CNN Transcript #1652.

Mander, J. (1978). *Four arguments for the elimination of television.* New York: William Morrow.

Moghrabi, H. (1995, April 23). A rush to judgment,—again. *Cleveland Plain Dealer,* p. 3C.

Movie Line Magazine.(1998, June). p. 50.

Nyang, S. (1996, August 10). Campaign highlights Muslims' quandary. *Los Angeles Times,* p. B10.

Power, C. (1998, March 16). The new Islam, *Newsweek,* 35.

Rich, A. (1995, 1978). *Lies, secrets and silence: Selected prose, 1966-1978.* New York: Norton.

Roth, K. (1996, January 27). Muslims observe holy month of fasting and prayer. *Island Packet*, p. 4B.

Shaheen, J. G. (1980). American television: Arabs in dehumanizing roles. In M. C. Hudson & R. G. Wolfe (Eds.), *The American media and the Arabs* (pp. 39-40). Washington, DC: Center for Contemporary Arab Studies, Georgetown University.

Shaheen, J. G. (1980, July 15). Author's interview with Mr. Jack Guss. Los Angeles.

Shaheen, J. G. (1984). *The TV Arab*. Bowling Green, OH: The Popular Press.

Shaheen, J. G. (1990a). Screen images of Palestinians in the 1980s. In P. Loukides & L. K. Fullers (Eds.), *Beyond the stars: Stock characters in American popular film* (p. 50). Bowling Green, OH: Bowling Green State University Popular Press.

Shaheen, J. G. (1990b, August 19). Our cultural demon: The "Ugly" Arab. *Washington Post*, pp. C1-C2.

Shaheen, J. G. (1993, November 13). Cartoons as commentary. Paper presented at the Chicago Historical Society during the Illinois Humanities Council Festival.

Shaheen, J. G. (1996, February 3). There goes the neighborhood. *Atlanta Journal/Constitution*,

Stone, J. (1996, March 17). Billionaires, bombers and belly dancers. *Ottowa Citizen*, p. 1C.

Teitelbaum, S. (1996, October 17). *The Jerusalem Report*, p. 49.

Twisted puppet theater. (1995, July 23). Showtime.

UNDERSTANDING ASIAN AMERICANS:
BACKGROUND FOR CURRICULUM DEVELOPMENT

by
Shin Kim

Introduction

Asian Americans,[1] including immigrants from Asian countries and their descendants, have experienced an explosive growth since the 1965 revision in U.S. immigration laws. Early in the history of Asian immigration to the United States, severe and explicit restrictions had been placed on their immigration. As a consequence, the number of Asian Americans did not even reach one million by 1965 despite more than one hundred years of history here (Barringer, Gardner, & Levin, 1993). According to the 1980 U.S. census, there were 3.3 million Asian Americans in 1979, 1.5% of the total U.S. population. In a decade since then, the number jumped to 7 million or 2.8% of the population (U.S. Commission on Civil Rights, 1988, 1992). By the middle of the 21st century, projections indicate that one in ten Americans will claim their ancestry in Asian countries (Smith & Edmonston, 1997).

The second notable change in the post-1965 Asian American population is its ethnic diversity. Prior to 1965, Asian Americans generally were identified with only three ethnic groups: Chinese, Japanese, and Filipino. Presently, Asian Americans include Bengalis, Cambodians, Chinese,[2] Filipinos, Hmongs, (Asian) Indians, Indonesians, Japanese, Koreans, Laotians, Pakistanis, Thais, Vietnamese, and several others with different languages and cultures. Some of these ethnic groups, such as the Indian and Chinese, encompass several languages and subcultures. In spite of their remarkable growth in numbers and diversity, the life experiences of Asian Americans have received insufficient attention among serious researchers of race/ethnic relations in the United States.[3] This lack of understanding of Asian Americans' reality greatly hinders the curriculum development appropriate to Asian Americans.[4] The task of developing curriculum relevant to Asian Americans, then, must begin with the effort to understand the Asian American reality.

Another noteworthy yet less apparent change in the 1990s is a growing presence of the children of immigrants in every ethnic community. The first generation of adult immigrants continues to be strong, except for Koreans. Nevertheless, as the history of mass Asian immigration lengthens, more and more children reach adulthood, and their presence in ethnic communities becomes more visible. On the whole, they are well educated and participate actively in various aspects of U.S. society. Whether they will be able to continue their active involvement as they grow older is difficult to predict and is not the task of this article. As their children grow in number and influence, the task of developing curriculum gains heightened urgency.

As mentioned, developing a curriculum appropriate to Asian Americans must begin with the proper understanding of their reality—their life experiences and structural positions—in the United States. I will discuss the similarities and differences among Asian Americans in terms of these experiences as well as their structural position in the U.S.; I begin with a brief discussion on the historical pattern of Asian American immigration.

Historical Pattern of Asian Immigration

Asian immigration historical patterns differ from those of nonAsian groups. Asian immigration to the United States occurred in two distinct stages. In the first stage—from the mid-19th century to the early decades of the 20th century—all Asian immigrations were labor immigrations. Moreover, several groups immigrated in a sequential order, one group at a time. Chinese immigrants were the first; they came from the mid-19th century until the passage of the Chinese Exclusion Act in 1882. As Chinese immigration ended, Japanese laborers immigrated until they too were stopped by legislation, the 1907 Gentlemen's Agreement between the Japanese and the United States governments. For a short three years between 1902 and 1905 during this Japanese immigration, approximately 7,000 Koreans arrived at Hawaiian shores. Japanese immigration was followed by Filipino workers until the Great Depression slowed down the whole immigration flow (U.S. Commission on Civil Rights, 1988).[5]

A pull factor in this sequential immigration was the conflict of interests among members of the dominant group. That is, European American business owners' desire to obtain a cheap and reliable work force and the economic interests of European American labor unions led to a sequential immigration by different ethnic groups (Chan, 1991). This sequential immigration played out in a society with intense prejudice against Asians. Asian ethnic communities were looked down upon or outright despised. Native-born children could not find jobs even with advanced degrees.

From the 1930s to 1965, very little immigration from Asian countries was observed except for a limited number of Filipino workers. It is interesting to note that even though China was a U.S. ally in the second World War, severe restrictions on Chinese immigration were not lessened in any measurable degrees. Descendants of Asian immigrants of this first stage are outnumbered by children of the second stage immigrants in their respective ethnic communities. A notable exception is the Japanese.[6]

As noted previously, the revision of the U.S. immigration laws in 1965 transformed the whole outlook on immigration. Since that revision, which abolished the highly discriminatory 1924 National Origin Act, immigration to the United States has been dominated by people from Asian and Latin American countries. Unlike the first stage, opportunities to immigrate are open to all ethnic groups simultaneously which results in the diversity among Asian immigrants. The society these immigrants migrate to is a society without *de jure* discrimination. Therefore, the push factor of immigration becomes more significant than the pull factor. Almost nonexistent immigration from Japan (in this stage) is a good example of this fact.[7] Additionally, most immigrants in this second stage, especially ones in the early years, are professionals and/or skilled workers. It is a historical irony that the family reunification emphasis of the 1965 revision produced an immigration of highly skilled workers from Asian and Latin American counties.[8] In recent years, the skill level of Asian immigrants has declined like nonAsian groups, as the population base of foreign-born Asian Americans has grown. Still, Asian immigration in this stage (the so-called 'recent', or 'new' immigrants) remains mostly a middle class and high skilled immigration (Smith & Edmonston, 1997).[9] As the number of immigrants increases in most ethnic groups, each group develops its own vibrant ethnic community. Children of the immigrants of this second stage are growing up in different environments from first stage immigrants.

Characteristics of Asian Americans' Reality

Stereotypic Images

The public's stereotypic perception of Asian Americans includes both positive and negative images. Stereotypes are reflected in academic research and in mass media as well. Interestingly, this stereotypic image appears to have swung dramatically in recent years from an overt and summarily negative image to a positive one with subtle disparaging undertones. For example, for a long time—until the mid-20th century—Asian Americans were depicted as "inassimilable," "inscrutable," "cunning," and "filthy." (Chan, 1991; Fugita & O'Brien, 1991; Hurh & Kim, 1990). By the late 1960s, however, a new stereotype of Asian Americans as "successful groups" began to emerge in mass media as the United States was besieged by racial riots. Soon, this success image of Asian Americans became a *fait accompli*.[10] Undoubtedly, stereotypes and changes of stereotypes affect the ethnic identity formation of children and their relationships with others, and, thus, merit further discussion (Min & Kim, 1999).

When Asian Americans were viewed negatively (in summary fashion) as in the past, children were deprived of developing healthy relations with parents and peers. They were prohibited from participating fully in U.S. society. Enduring life with such hardship took a great toll on individuals, and in some cases, created a vicious cycle. The U.S. response to Asian Americans in the past—"there would be discriminatory legislation prohibiting further immigration and for those already here, barriers to equal participation" (Kitano & Daniels, 1988, p. 5)—can be understood in this context as well. Two cases in point: 1) the 1882 Chinese Exclusion Act, the first federal law ever enacted to exclude a specific group, and several anti-Asian state and local laws in western states, and 2) a massive internment of Japanese Americans at the beginning of World War II in sharp contrast to U.S. treatment of German and Italian Americans (Fugita & O'Brien, 1991). In fact, Asian Americans were not allowed to obtain U.S. citizenship until 1952, and were commonly segregated in public facilities including schools (Chan, 1991; Kitano & Daniels, 1988).

The new stereotype of Asian Americans as "successful model minorities" who work hard but quietly, aspire to achieve the American (middle class) Dream, and abide by the law was (and still is) only part reality and part misperception. The post-1965 Asian Americans at the beginning were mostly professional and possessed a relatively high level of human capital. To be sure, this middle-class immigration was not solely an Asian American phenomenon. Immigrations from certain Latin American countries followed a similar pattern. Still, it was much more pervasive among Asian Americans than Latino Americans. In spite of their high level of education, skill, and ability, a majority of Asian immigrants could not find occupations corresponding to their human capital, and many ventured into self-employment in small businesses. Granted, they were quite different from traditional immigrants in terms of earnings and occupations, but perceiving them as a "successful group" is misleading and overlooks the harshness of their lives.

Moreover, since it is only partially based on reality, the success image brings detrimental effects to Asian Americans. For example, suicide rates among Asian American kids are found to be higher than the national average (Rue, 1993). With this image as a successful group, Asian Americans "do not have equal access to a number of public services, including police protection, health care, and the court system" (U.S. Commission on Civil Rights, 1992,

p. 1). This public perception of Asian Americans includes a false idea that Asian Americans receive special favors from the government as well (U.S. Commission on Civil Rights, 1992; Kim, Kim & Gunn, 1997). The tragic killing of Vincent Chin and the 1992 Los Angeles racial disturbance, and their portrayals in mass media vividly illustrate the danger this success image poses to Asian Americans.[11]

Surely, the positive image may boost the psychic ego of some Asian Americans and works as a positive reinforcer on some children. On the other hand, it disguises or ignores Asian Americans' experiences of discrimination in the United States and simplifies the Asian American life experiences. It thereby turns attention away from various social problems such as poverty and school dropouts that currently afflict many Asian Americans (U.S. Commission on Civil Rights, 1992, p. 24). The positive image also carries, erroneously, the message that this country is a land of opportunity open equally to any racial/ethnic group. It is used as a divisive wedge among minority racial/ethnic groups. For example, the attitude expressed in "if Asian Americans can make it, why can't African Americans make it?" (Hurh & Kim, 1990) blames African Americans for their current deprived life condition. At the same time, it arouses envy or jealousy that further aggravates the hostility of African Americans and others toward Asian Americans and results in "Asian bashing" (Kitano & Daniels, 1988).

Whether positive or negative, the stereotypic image conveys a simplistic and distorted picture of Asian American reality without a realistic understanding of their life experiences. All ethnic groups, Asian or nonAsian, suffer from stereotypes. What is unique to Asian Americans is the fact that their stereotypes had been changed somewhat superficially and applied in wholesale fashion. As a result, many children of Asian immigrants must deal with the clear as well as subtle duplicities of positive stereotypes while others suffer from invisibility.

The implications of this for curriculum development are several and revolve around the following considerations. First and foremost, great variance in life conditions among "Asian American" students exists. The success image is only partially correct; some Asian American students are from economically struggling and socially deficient households. Second, this positive image imposes a high expectation on Asian American students' academic accomplishment in general. Some could benefit from it at the same time others could be hurt by it. High expectation originates not only from teachers but also parents. Thus, Asian American students may face an overload of pressures. Third, Asian American students are viewed as "excellent" in mathematics but "not quite good" in humanities and social sciences. Once again, this too simplistic perception could hinder a proper cultivation of talents. Fourth, Asian Americans' peer relationships are much more complicated because of the flip side of the success image—the envy and jealousy it creates. Fifth, this success image may bring an over or false confidence that renders Asian Americans oblivious to possible obstacles they will face later in life.

Common Experience of Mistreatment

Coupled with stereotypes, the public's ignorance of Asian Americans often leads to mistreatment and victimization that grossly violates Asian Americans' civil rights. Recent studies stress that "Asian Americans are frequently victims of racially motivated bigotry and violence" (U.S. Commission on Civil Rights, 1992, p. 1). Due to their general ignorance and insensitivity, to most nonAsian Americans, Asian Americans look alike. Such an unfortunate perception creates numerous serious mishaps. For example, Vietnamese students are placed in Filipino, even in Spanish, bilingual programs. Or Asian students from various language backgrounds, such as Chinese, Vietnamese and Laotian, are placed together in a class so that the language of instruction has to be English (Chung, 1988). The killing of Vincent Chin (see endnote 11) is another good example of this. The trial verdicts—"not guilty" in the first trial and "guilty" with very light sentences in the second trial—are read by Asian Americans as expressions of pervasive ignorance and deep-down institutional racism in the United States.

Even though a significant proportion of current Asian Americans, with the exception of Japanese Americans, are foreign-born, many Asian Americans in the United States are native-born. Furthermore, the number of the native born is rapidly increasing as children of immigrants grow up. But most Americans tend to treat all Asian Americans as foreigners. When Asian Americans mention their home states in response to a question about where they are from, people are usually not satisfied with their answer and keep asking until the countries of the Asian Americans' ancestors are revealed. This kind of conversation, though perhaps unwittingly, carries a subtle message that Asian Americans are less than full citizens of the United States no matter how many generations they have lived here.

Family Life of Asian Americans: Solidarity and Conflicts

Contrary to public expectation, the most prevalent family type among Asian immigrants is the residential and functional nuclear family (Min, 1998; Hurh & Kim, 1988). Without too much generalization, it can be argued that Asian Americans are high in family solidarity. Divorce rates and youth delinquency are still lower among Asian Americans (Smith & Edmonston, 1997), albeit rising, than in other groups. Some scholars trace this solidarity to Confucianism and Buddhism. Regardless of its cause, this strong family solidarity facilitates Asian Americans' economic advancement by easing the pressure to become independent too early, and/or by providing emotional supports. On the other hand, it also can complicate the family life of many Asian Americans.

To be sure, there are the usual generation gaps in Asian American families. Furthermore, there are language and Americanization gaps. Asian American parents (even the native-born) are known for their devotion to children. Children are expected to reciprocate the favor (?) by excelling in life and taking care of their parents in their old age. It is not difficult to imagine how this dimension of family solidarity complicates Asian Americans' family and kinship lives. Moreover, family conflicts are not solely between the native-born children and the immigrant parents. Frictions are observed between the adult children (immigrants) and their elderly parents (Kim, Kim, & Hurh, 1991). To the best of my knowledge, no paper has yet studied how this conflict (between parents and grandparents) affects children. As a matter of fact, the relationship between grandparents and grandchildren is one of the most understudied aspects of Asian American family life.

Another layer of Asian American family life to be mentioned revolves around its male-centeredness and its subsequent traditional gender role expectation. Without question, this male focus affects the self-concept of female children negatively (Min & Kim, 1999). This traditional gender role expectation is evident among the second generation Asian American churches (Chai, 1999) as well as within individual families. Unfortunately, possible adverse effects of this male domination on family life, such as domestic violence, are hushed subjects and receive little study. A great proportion of native-born Asian Americans marry out, that is, marry outside of their own ethnic group. Their marriage partners are as likely to be non-Hispanic whites as other Asian Americans (Kitano & Daniels, 1988).

Religious Activities: Highly Religious in Diverse Religions

Until recently, religious life among Asian Americans, especially among the native-born Asian Americans, had received very little attention. Like immigrants in the past, recent (i.e. post-1965) Asian immigrants brought their religion with them to the United States. Since immigration involves a psychologically upsetting experience of uprooting and re-rooting, immigrants are usually found to be more religious post-immigration than pre-emigration. Thus, it is not surprising to find many Asian immigrant communities religiously active. The unexpected, though, is the intense religious activities of the native-born children of Asian American immigrants, and the significant role a religion plays in their ethnic identity formation (Warner & Wittner, 1998; Kim, Song, & Moon, 1998).[12]

The heterogeneity of specific religions involved in Asian American communities must be stressed. Gone is the overwhelming dominance of western religions such as Christianity among native-born Asian Americans. Protestant religions are predominant among Koreans and Vietnamese, and Filipinos are mostly Catholic. At the same time, however, Hinduism is strong among Indians, and Pakistanis and Bengalis are often Muslims. Among Thais and Chinese, Buddhism is the dominant force (Chan, 1991; Warner & Wittner, 1998).

Socioeconomic Status: Education and Occupation

As expected, current Asian Americans include a high proportion of those who are well educated. Proportionally more native-born Japanese and Chinese Americans have completed a college education than their European American counterparts (Hurh & Kim, 1990; Kitano & Daniels, 1988; U.S. Commission on Civil Rights, 1988). Also, an unusually high proportion of Asian immigrants have completed their college education prior to emigration (Kim, Hurh, & Fernandez, 1989). Asian immigrant parents' emphasis on children's education is well known (Pai, 1993) and helps equip Asian American children to assimilate into the middle-class white United States regardless of their residential location (Zhou & Bankston, 1998).[13] In short, Asian Americans are rich in human capital, especially in formal education on the whole. Even in this respect, though, there are some inter- and intra-group differences. Refugee groups except the Vietnamese are lower in educational attainment, on the average, than non-refugee immigrant groups. Likewise, members of the same ethnic group differ in education, ranging from those who have completed college or post-college education to those without high school diplomas. Due to the aforesaid stereotyping, the latter (the intra-group difference) is hardly acknowledged even among Asian scholars.

Such intra-group differences in education and post-industrial opportunities in the United States result in a high degree of intra-group occupational differentiations. Consequently, members of each Asian ethnic group are distributed among various occupational categories including professional/technical occupations, self-employed small businesses, and low-skill service or manual occupations (Kim, Hurh, & Fernandez, 1989). This occupational difference is exhibited among different ethnic groups, i.e. inter-group difference. One example: The inter-group difference in self-employed small businesses among immigrants, is well documented. For instance, Koreans, South Asians, Chinese, and Vietnamese are active whereas Filipinos are hardly involved in such businesses. Japanese immigrants were once entrepreneurially very active, but their descendants shunned this sector (Fugita & O'Brien, 1991; Kim, Hurh, & Fernandez, 1989). In very recent years, cautious observations are voiced that children, primarily the foreign-born children, of entrepreneurially active Asian immigrants are entering self-employed small businesses in good numbers.[14]

On the whole, Asian Americans are well represented in professional/technical occupations. Once in the professional labor market, though, Asian Americans encounter various kinds of subtle discrimination or difficulty such as peripheralization, underutilization of resources, and the glass ceiling, in spite of their high education levels (Kim, 1993; Hurh & Kim, 1990; U.S. Commission on Civil Rights, 1992). A report of the U.S. Commission on Civil Rights summarizes the problems highly educated native-born Asian males experience in the U.S. labor market as follows:

> For all groups that were studied, American-born Asian men are less likely to be in management positions than their non-Hispanic counterparts. Furthermore, adjusting for occupation and industry, highly educated American-born Asian men in all groups were found to earn less than similarly qualified non-Hispanic white men. These findings raise the possibility that men in all Asian groups face labor market discrimination at the top (1988, p. 7).

Such diverse experiences of Asian Americans present dilemmas to researchers. As Kitano and Daniels observe, "no one model can encompass the experience of all Asian groups" (1988, p. 7) or all members of any one group. Therefore, we need a creative application of the existing theories and development of new labor market models.

Residential Patterns and Locations

Asian Americans are a highly urbanized group. Asian immigrants tend to settle in metropolitan areas rather than rural areas due to economic and ethnic sociocultural opportunities. A very small proportion of Asian Americans is engaged in agricultural production either as owner-farmers or hired farm workers.[15] Most of the post-1965 Asian immigrants also formed ethnic communities of their own in urban areas. Such ethnic communities serve not only as a safe haven for immigrants but also as a vehicle to transmit sociocultural heritage. In other words, the native-born children of Asian immigrants are imbued in both U.S. and ethnic cultures by living in metropolitan areas around the country.

On the whole, Asian Americans are suburbanites more likely than not. Even here, there exists an inter-group difference. Thus, refugee groups are more likely to reside in inner cities than other immigrant groups. With an exception of Chinatown, other ethnic enclaves such as Little Saigon, Koreatown, and Japantown are commercial, not residential enclaves. Ethnic communities, then, are associational gatherings rather than territorially (or geographically) defined ones. Even when they are residing inside cities, Asian Americans tend to assimilate to the suburban middle-class culture (Zhou & Bankston, 1998). One upshot of this pattern is that city and suburban educators must exert concerted efforts to develop an Asian American-appropriate curriculum. In addition, Asian Americans are concentrated heavily in the western states, particularly in California. Estimates of Asian Americans residing in the West (mainly California) range from 40 to 60 percent. One interesting observation: In Asian American circles, the term 'east of California' is uttered frequently to distinguish Asian Americans residing in California and those living outside of California. It succinctly depicts the eminence of California as the choice of residential location among Asian Americans.

Conclusion

Asian Americans can no longer be ignored in the United States. Their number is increasing rapidly and their activities are becoming more visible. So far, the general public's perception of Asian Americans is far from reality and often is based on erroneous stereotypes. Private and public treatment of Asian Americans has its origin in these incorrect perceptions. Developing curriculum that is in tune with Asian American experiences cannot and must not be based on these mis-perceptions. The very first step toward appropriate curriculum development, then, begins with efforts to understand and to appraise the Asian American reality.

As discussed throughout this article, the monolithic "Asian American" experience is nowhere to be found. Asian American groups differ significantly in their immigration history, culture, language, ethnic homogeneity, and other life experiences. Certain groups such as Koreans and Japanese are homogeneous while some, such as Indians and Chinese, are quite heterogeneous. Heterogeneous or homogeneous, each group also exhibits a high degree of intra-group variance in terms of education, occupation, and other socioeconomic factors.

Such inter- and intra-group differences notwithstanding, a common theme runs through various aspects of Asian American reality: the structural position of Asian Americans in U.S. society is that of a minority rather than of the majority. In economic terminology, the difference is micro and the similarity, more macro. To put it differently, Asian Americans are minorities with numerous attributes of the majority. A good proportion of Asian Americans succeed or 'make it' in the U.S. in terms of various observable indicators of success. At the same time, they are mistreated and downright discriminated against in some cases by the nonAsian public because of their racial minority status. This duality creates psychologically turbulent waters for Asian Americans to navigate. Curriculum developers must comprehend this extraordinary environment ordinary Asian Americans face and understand the efforts Asian Americans have to put into their everyday living.

Developing a new inclusive curriculum also requires a refinement of theoretical and conceptual frameworks for racial/ethnic study which goes beyond the traditional bi-racial bias of racial/ethnic studies in the United States. For a long period of time, the study of racial/ethnic relations has been dominated by the black (= the minority) vs white (= majority) polarity. Asian Americans, being neither white nor black, and being minority in some aspects and majority in some others, pose a special challenge. All in all, the case of Asian Americans is historically unique. Thus, developing a curriculum which adequately reflects Asian American experiences is a complicated task. Yes, it is a difficult undertaking. Yet it is an exciting challenge whose time has finally arrived.

152

Endnotes

[1]The classification the U.S. government uses, Asian and Pacific Islanders (API), is a misnomer in my opinion. Pacific Islanders are not included in this analysis.

[2]Chinese here includes those from mainland China, Taiwan, and Hong King.

[3]Some would argue the inattention is due to the diversity among Asian Americans, which certainly appears to be intractable. Yet, there is enough of a base to form pan-Asian solidarity among all ethnic Asian Americans. In addition, Asian Americans are treated as one distinct group by non-Asians and the government.

[4]Since very few first-generation adult immigrants return to school in the U.S., it is assumed in this article that the children of adult immigrants, both the native born (the second generation) and the foreign born (the 1.5 generation), are the target group for curriculum development.

[5]Differences among the three groups are interesting: First, Chinese and Japanese were immigrants whereas Filipinos were more like temporary workers, most of whom returned to the Philippines at the onset of the Great Depression. Second, most Chinese and Filipinos came as single males while the Japanese immigrated as families. Thus, the shortage of marriage partners among the Chinese was acute. Third, the number of Filipino workers was significantly smaller than Chinese or Japanese immigrants.

[6]What are other causes for their invisibility in ethnic communities? Difficult to say. I can propose one more: a good proportion of Chinese were unable to marry and procreate due to a severe sex imbalance. Filipinos returned to the Philippines. Japanese on the other hand had sent their native-born children to Japan either to find a marriage partner or to attend school for a brief period of time. Many of them were crushed psychologically by the internment experience or by the fighting itself though many volunteered to join the fighting. Many remained relatively inactive even after the War. Nevertheless, due to a small number of immigrants in the second stage, the Japanese are the exception here. Oft-speculated high out-marriage rates, in my opinion, were basically speculation.

[7]Push factors push prospective immigrants out of their country of origin while pull factors pull immigrants into the U.S. Since the 1965 revision, push factors in immigrants' countries of origin explain better the variance among immigrant groups in terms of number and composition.

It is also appropriate to mention the inter-group generational differences among children of Asian immigrants here. Japanese Americans are mostly in the third or beyond generations whereas all other groups' native born are mostly the second generation.

[8]It is a perfect historic example of how little understanding of the immigration process existed in U.S. policy making. Some scholars argue that the family reunification was a device the U.S. Congress concocted to discourage nonEuropean immigration (Reimers, 1985). Family reunification gives preference to family members of U.S. citizens. In the 1970s, the preferences of family unification vastly outnumbered the employment preferences. In 1996, about 65 percent of all admissions were family-sponsored immigration (INS, 1996).

[9]The 1960s Cuban immigration is the only nonAsian immigration to be characterized as such.

[10]Discussion in academic circles arrived a bit later. Interestingly, most Asian American scholars argued against, and most nonAsians for, the success image of Asian Americans.

A detailed discussion on the appearance, validity, and implication of the success image of Asian Americans can be found in Hurh & Kim (1990).

[11]On the eve of his marriage, Mr. Vincent Chin, a second-generation Chinese American professional, was randomly picked up without provocation on his part and was bludgeoned to death by unemployed auto workers who blamed their job loss on the Japanese automobile industry. The attackers and the victim were complete strangers. The attackers were found "not guilty" in their first criminal trial. Mass media paid very little attention to his killing and portrayed Mr. Chin as a manual worker with limited English proficiency. On the other hand, the trial of his attackers received a lot more sympathetic attention from the mainstream mass media.

On April 29, 1992, four European American policemen were found "innocent" in their beating of Rodney King, an African American male, in a Simi Valley courtroom. Shortly after the verdict, a violent protest erupted in south-central Los Angeles. As the disturbance became deadly violent, the LA police allowed (by not protecting them conspicuously) Korean Americans in south central LA and the nearby Koreatown to be victimized. In the end, 2,400 Korean-owned small businesses were burned and/or looted. Mass media depicted Korean store owners as "gun toting" vigilantes and the disturbance as a conflict between Koreans and African Americans. Five years since the disturbance, most of the store owners and their family members are unable to rebuild their lives and are still experiencing tremendous mental stress.

[12]Some would argue it is not necessarily unexpected to find that native-born children are also highly religious. This argument is based on the fact immigrant parents are extremely active in religions and on the inheritance of faith. I disagree with them because the inheritance of faith is not automatic. In fact, Chai (2000) describes the desire of children to be different/distinctive from parents in church involvement and illuminates the structural position children occupy in U.S. society.

[13]High college graduation rates among the native-born (grand)children of the pre-1965 Japanese immigrants are used as one of the facts to bolster the cultural argument. The "culture" thesis argues Asian culture (usually Confucianism) puts such an emphasis on formal education. I would argue the culture is a necessary but not a sufficient reason. Once again, it is a combination of culture and Asian Americans' minority position in the U.S.

[14]Personal conversations with officers of the Korean American Merchants Association, Chicago. To my knowledge, no study has documented the incidence of self-employed small businesses among immigrants.

[15]It must be noted that the Japanese were quite active in agriculture prior to the Second World War, especially in California. They were owners, workers, and supervisors of farms. When they were thrown into internment camps, they lost their livelihood. Children of the interned Japanese did not go back to agriculture in most part.

References

Barringer, H., Gardner, R.W., & Levin, M. J. (1993). *Asian and Pacific Islanders in the United States*. New York: Russell Sage Foundation.

Bouvier, L.F., & Davis, G. B. (1982). *Future racial composition of the United States*. Washington, DC: Demographic Information Service Center of the Population Reference Bureau.

Chai, K. J. (2000). Beyond 'strictness' to distinctiveness: Generational transition in Korean Protestant churches. In H. Kwon, K. C. Kim, & R. S. Warner (Eds.), *Korean Americans: Religion and society*. University Park: Pennsylvania State University Press.

Chan, S. (1991). *Asian Americans: An interpretive history*. Boston: Twayne Publishers.

Chung, C. H. (1988). The language situation of Vietnamese Americans. In S. L. McKay & S. C. Wong (Eds.), *Language diversity: Problem or resource? (pp. 276-292)*. New York: Newberry House.

Fugita, S., & O'Brien, D. J. (1991). *Japanese American ethnicity: The persistence of community*. Seattle: University of Washington Press.

Hurh, W. M., & Kim, K. C. (1990, October). The success image of Asian Americans: Its validity, practical and theoretical implications. *Ethnic and Racial Studies, 12,* 512-538.

Kim, K. C., Hurh, W. M., & Fernandez, M. (1989, Spring). Intra-group differences in business participation: A comparative analysis of three Asian immigrant groups. *International Migration Review, 12,* 73-95.

Kim, K. C., & Kim, S. (1999). The multirace/ethnic nature of Los Angeles unrest in 1992. In K. C. Kim (Ed.), *Koreans in the 'Hood* (chap. 2). Baltimore: Johns Hopkins University Press.

Kim, K. C., Kim, S., & Gunn, K. (1997, August 9-13). Self-reliance ideology and the African American view of Korean entrepreneurs: A case study on the South Side of Chicago. Paper presented at 92nd annual meeting of American Sociological Association, Toronto, Canada.

Kim, K. C., Kim, S., & Hurh, W. M. (1991). Filial piety and intergenerational relationships in Korean immigrant families. *International Journal of Aging and Human Development, 33,* 232- 245.

Kim, K. C., Song, Y. I., & Moon, A. (1998, August 19-23). Pluralistic accommodation and young Korean Americans' ethnic identity. Paper presented at 93rd annual meeting of American Sociological Association, San Francisco.

Kim, S. (1993). Career prospect for Korean immigrants' children. In H. Kwon & S. Kim (Eds.), *The emerging generation of Korean Americans* (chap. 5). Seoul, Korea: Kyung Hee University Press.

Kitano, H. L., & Daniels, R. (1988). *Asian Americans: Emerging minorities*. Englewood Cliffs, NJ: Prentice Hall.

Min, P. G. (1998). Korean American families. In R. L. Taylor (Ed.), *Minority families in the United States* (chap. 10). Upper Saddle River, NJ: Prentice Hall.

Min, P. G., & Kim, R. (Eds.). (1999). *Struggle for ethnic identity: Narratives by Asian American professionals*. Walnut Creek, CA: Alta Mira Press.

Pai, Y. (1993). Academic and occupational preferences of Korean American youth. In H. Y. Kwon & S. Kim (Eds.), *The Emerging generation of Korean Americans* (chap. 3). Seoul, Korea: Kyung Hee University Press.

Reimers, D. M. (1985). *Still the golden door: The Third World comes to America*. New York: Columbia University Press.

Rue, D. (1993). Depression and suicidal behavior among Asian whiz kids. In H. Y. Kwon & S. Kim (Eds.), *The emerging generation of Korean Americans* (chap. 4). Seoul, Korea: Kyung Hee University Press.

Smith, J. P., & Edmonston, B. (Eds.). (1997). *The New Americans: Economic demographic, and fiscal effects of immigration*. Washington, DC: National Academy Press.

U.S. Commission on Civil Rights. (1988). *The economic status of Americans of Asian Descent: An exploratory investigation.* Washington, DC: Clearinghouse Publication 95.

U.S. Commission on Civil Rights (1992). *Civil rights issues facing Asian Americans in the 1990s.* Washington, DC.

U.S. Immigration and Naturalization Service. (1997). *Statistical yearbook of the immigration and naturalization service, 1996.* Washington DC: U.S. Government Printing Office.

Warner, R. S., & Wittner, J. G. (1998). *Gatherings in diaspora : Religious communities and the new immigration.* Philadelphia: Temple University Press.

Zhou, M., & Bankston, C. L., III. (1998). *Growing up American: How Vietnamese children adapt to life in the United States.* New York: Russell Sage Foundation.

CIVIC LITERACY, SOVEREIGNTY, AND VIOLENCE: OJIBWE TREATY RIGHTS AND RACIAL BACKLASH IN THE NORTH COUNTRY

by
Gaetano B. Senese

This paper[1] is intended to expand on some dimensions of education which have great consequence for teacher educators, particularly those who train teachers whose pedagogy will impact Native American students and students living in association with American Indian peoples. It focuses on the phenomenon of civic discord, especially on violence as an expression and outgrowth of ill-considered yet legitimate differences between Native people's rights and those of the dominant culture. In order to counteract the potential for social and civic misunderstanding which may lead to discord, it is especially important that teacher educators be familiar with the unique government-to-government relationship between Native Americans and the United States federal government.

First I will discuss the way in which the rationality of native life has been viewed and continues to be viewed by non-Native Americans. As a consequence of this view native life and tribal sovereignty have been driven to the periphery of American consciousness. Yet tribal sovereignty is the lifeblood of American Indians. The education of both the student with roots in the dominant European American culture and the American Indian student is characterized by the marginalization of Native rights. A number of forms of violence, both to property and to persons, is a result.

I will argue that this violence is the result of a socialization process that omits key points of information about tribal and Indian rights, particularly sovereign rights. I then discuss the role for curriculum in this socialization process and suggest a proper notion of "counter-socialization" and the establishment of proper and complete information in curricula as well as the reestablishment of American Indian sovereignty as a key component of pluralist U.S. democracy.

Critical civic literacy, the ability of ordinary citizens to see and secure their legitimate self-determined social policy among competing and often conflicting considerations, plays a crucial role in this countersocialization process. It has far-reaching consequences for the development of both Native American social policy and for the relationship between American Indians and non-Natives.

Traditional socialization and curricula have led to misunderstanding between the Indian and non-Indian interests and indirectly to social policy injurious to Native people and others as well. Donald Fixico (1989) describes well some of the roots of this misunderstanding. He discusses the way the radical individualism of colonial societies clashed with the corporatism of Native peoples. For Native Americans, lands were part of the nature with which individuals and collectivities identified. For settlers nature was an object to be respected but ultimately mastered (p. 13). He cites Reginald Horsman's *Race and Manifest Destiny* as a work which outlines the clash between the mechanistic European view of nature and the organic relationship kept by Native peoples. (p. 15)

Native people have fought, since the European American incursion, to maintain a land base upon which they might live out the meaning of their existence. Today, this dream is kept alive in the lands guaranteed them by treaties made between tribes and the federal government. These lands, reservation lands, are often viewed by non-Natives as concentration camps, holdovers from the 19th century when the military ran out of options for the Native peoples. There is a great deal of misunderstanding about the nature of these lands and their meaning. Indeed, that confusion must become the object of a healing education.

From the early 1980s until the early 1990s, counties in northern Minnesota, Michigan, and especially Wisconsin, were the scene of serious conflict between Native American, principally Ojibwe (Chippewa), fishermen and local European Americans. Serious, sometimes violent protests occurred. These protests were accompanied by racial baiting, racist effigies, rock throwing, and physical threats to Native fishermen. These fishermen were engaged in legal spearing of game fish, a right reserved to them by treaty. These "usufructory" rights enable the Ojibwe to use nonreservation lands for hunting and fishing. They retained these rights on territories they "ceded" to the States and the U.S. government, in exchange for these reserved rights, in 1837 (Wisconsin Advisory Committee, 1989). Indeed, Chippewa often reject the term "treaty rights" since it implies that these rights were awarded by treaty. They remind us that these rights **always** have belonged to the Chippewa and were simply "reserved" by treaty (Strickland, Hertzberg, & Owens, 1990, p. 10).

The following is a poster reprinted in a Northern Wisconsin Ojibwe newspaper, *News from Indian Country*. That it was hung during the mid-1980s reflects clearly the tension between the Ojibwe spearfishers and Wisconsin sportfishing interests. It also suggests the potential for violence in relations between Indian people and whites in this area, a violence which requires a better understanding of Native American civic prerogatives. The poster is a mock invitation to an "Indian Shoot" and reads as follows:

FIRST ANNUAL INDIAN SHOOT
Time: Early spring, beginning of walleye run
Place: Northern Wisconsin lakes
Rules: Open shoot, off hand position only, no scopes, no sling, no tripods, and no whiskey for bait!
OPEN TO ALL WISCONSIN TAXPAYING RESIDENTS
Residents that are BLACK, HMONG, CUBAN or those on WELFARE, A.D.C. FOOD STAMPS or any other government give-a-way program are not eligible.
Scoring:
PLAIN INDIAN—5 POINTS
INDIAN WITH WALLEYES—10 POINTS
INDIAN WITH BOAT NEWER THAN YOURS—20 POINTS
INDIAN USING PITCHFORK—30 POINTS
INDIAN WITH H.S. DIPLOMA—50 POINTS
SOBER INDIAN—75 POINTS
INDIAN TRIBAL LAWYER—100 POINTS
Judges: GOV. TOMMY THOMPSON, REV. JESSE JACKSON
Prizes: FILLET-O-FISH SANDWICHES AND SIX PACKS OF "TREATY BEER"

The contest goes on to offer "Save a Fish, Spear an Indian" bumper stickers as consolation prizes.

While it is wrong to dignify this poster in any way, it does point up the extent to which racist sentiment may develop as an adjunct to what is widely observed to be a violation of the rights of the dominant culture. In this case it is against the Chippewa fishermen, who have, by treaty right, the freedom to use traditional fishing methods for subsistence. This right is clear in all the extant Ojibwe treaties in North Wisconsin. Yet such a level of sovereignty is poorly understood by non-Natives, who have not been educated about the law. In 1984, responding to the escalating threat of violence, the Wisconsin Advisory Committee to the U.S. Commission on Civil Rights conducted a community forum in Superior, Wisconsin. As a result of this forum, the Committee found that non-Indians' lack of information about Indian treaty rights and their legal implications was a major problem. One of the solutions they proposed was the development of a curriculum in which Wisconsin students would be exposed to the concept of Native American sovereignty and to Ojibwe hunting and fishing treaty rights on "ceded" territories. As these materials were developed and piloted, they came with an encouragement, not a requirement, that the districts use them.

For Native Americans, as well as for the understanding of those in the European American culture, reactions to the Native American presence on the nation is of great consequence, and the point is not that sovereignty must be won. We must understand that what is rightfully held must be protected. Multicultural presence in the polity is clear, yet understanding the actual nature of cultural difference has the potential, operating at the edge of the dominant cultural consciousness, to be the scapegoat for violence against person and property. It is my argument that division and destruction are the result of a rationality which cannot accept plural presences and differences which demand positions and places separate from the functional demands of the "uniculture" of property prerogative.

What sort of education is available to help make sense of these issues? Teacher educators must all receive an education that allows them to alert their students to the inadequacies of standard texts in social education, history, civics, and related subjects. They must begin the process of equipping their students to become sensitive critical readers of the curricula they use and to argue for curricular changes and supplementation that give a more accurate picture of the complexities and uniqueness of the American Indian political presence.

In the 1990s several popular high school U.S. government and U.S. history texts were in use in Northern Wisconsin. *American Government Today* (Lewinski, 1980) was used in a high school near the Lac Du Flambeau Ojibwe reservation, Wisconsin. In 768 pages of text, one page is devoted to American Indians in the U.S. In a brief scan of the index I found hundreds of other topics considered more worthy of as much or greater treatment, for example: Calvin Coolidge, 5 pages; Connecticut, 5 pages; The U.S. Secret Service, 5 pages; Dade County, Florida, 2 pages; Dekalb County, Ga. 2 pages; The Export Import Bank, 3 pages; The Fair Credit Reporting Act, 2 pages; Gerald Ford, 16 pages. There is nothing in this civics text on Native American civics.

I examined several U.S. history texts and found only one with more than a few cursory mentions of American Indian people (Smith, 1977). In this text there is nothing about the sovereign nature of treaties. Rather, what little it does contain is misleading information. For example, there is the obligatory map of culture and land use, where tribes covering a territory from southern California to the Rockies are shown as collective "Seed Gatherers" (p. 229). In the obligatory summary section, after having literally no substantive discussion of the nature of tribal sovereignty, students are asked, "In your opinion should the U.S. honor treaty commitments?" It might as well ask in the section on the making of the Constitution, "In your opinion should the federal government follow the Constitution?"

Another text, in a section covering U.S. history since 1945, devotes one page to the changes in Indian America during that period. It mentions nothing of the momentous events at Wounded Knee in 1972, nor the treaty rights victories, the occupation of Alcatraz Island, the B.I.A. occupation, nor the Alaska Native Claims Settlement, the largest land deal since the Louisiana Purchase. Rather it talks about the American Indian Movement setting up "patrol" to protect "drunken Indians from harassment." It uses this negative stereotypical language without mentioning that such harassment came not from thugs but from the Minneapolis police (Nash & Jeffrey, 1986).

During this period, what would a white or a Chippewa student in St. Croix, Wisconsin, learn about themselves or about each other with such guides. There is simply no discussion of the nature of treaty rights that underlie traditional fishing in Northern Wisconsin waters, or of other treaty rights which exist in tribal communities across the nation. In response to the discord emerging during the late 1980s at boatlandings across Ojibwe land and the "ceded" territories, in 1991 the state of Wisconsin passed curriculum reforms as one provision of its Act 31. The Act required the State Superintendent of Public Instruction to develop treaty rights curricula. However, no **implementation** was required to follow this. In 1995 teacher education programs were notified that teaching licenses would not be granted to students who had failed to participate in programs that made the treaty rights materials available. While some teacher education programs were enthusiastic, compliance was left to the discretion of individual colleges, and apparently in several cases professors met their obligation by simply handing out booklets developed by the State Department. Standard L of this legislation requires districts to cover treaty rights twice in elementary school and once in high school. However, these requirements have not been followed by a commitment to fund compliance oversight and evaluation. Indeed, funding for statewide monitoring and compliance regarding curriculum use ended in 1995 (Leary, 1999).

Education in treaty rights is not only fascinating but indispensable for the civic education of Indian people and their neighbors. Yet the complexities are mostly absent from texts used by school districts serving significant Indian student populations or any other population. The progress of the trust relationship has been historically determined by the status of American Indian treaty title to land and compensation for lands used or taken. This compensation has taken a variety of forms, principal of which has been the provision of goods and services to tribal people. The trust relationship identifies the responsibility the federal government has to protect treaty rights in perpetuity. The following issues are central to any Native American multicultural education and should be the basis for any responsible teacher education program selecting, evaluating, and using curricular materials about American Indians.

Evidence for the extent of this trust is to be found in the myriad of treaties and agreements made with Indian peoples from colonial times through the latter half of the 19th century. This extremely large and complex body of law can be found speaking to issues which go beyond trusteeship over land to include education and social development. However, while the nature and extent of trust has been an issue, behind this lies the considerable power of the government to interpret the trust without consulting the beneficiary and, in some cases, to abrogate its responsibility over the protests of those whom the government is treaty-bound to serve.

Until the year 1871, the treaty was employed as the method of establishing the colonial European-Indian and, later, the U.S.-Indian relationship (Cohen, 1945, p.33). Although the method of dealing with tribes by this practice was abandoned with the adoption of the Indian Appropriation Act of 1871, treaties created prior to the Act were not abrogated by its passage (Cohen, 1945). Subsequent to this Act, Congress continued to treat tribes in a fashion similar to that of the Senate under the authority of Article II, Section I of the Constitution. "Agreements" were made and ratified by both Houses which *de facto* operated as the treaties had before. The only substantial change lay in the provision that now the House of Representatives would cooperate with the Senate in ratification of the new "agreements." Along with treaties and agreements, much of the relationship of the federal government to the tribes came by way of special statutes dealing with specific tribes or Indian people generally, and through the adoption of tribal constitutions and charters after the Indian Reorganization Act of 1934 (Cohen, 1945, p. x).

Between the General Allotment Act of 1887 and the Indian Reorganization Act of 1934, the federal government tended to impose regulations and laws upon Indians as a general entity rather than as individual tribes (Cohen, 1945, p. viii). That these overgeneralized statutes and other legal instruments ignored the individual treaty rights of specific tribes prompted a study to be undertaken by the Institute for Government Research. The results of its 1929 study, the "Problem of Indian Administration," helped fuel a decade of governmental, social, and educational "reform" which led to the development of the Indian Reorganization Act and corporatization of tribal entities (Cohen, 1945, p. ix). Regardless of the nature of legal instruments, laws, agreements, and resolutions made subsequent to 1871, however, they carry a concomitant legal weight equivalent to that of the treaties and vice versa. Whether treaties and laws related to Indians receive the same status as other legal instruments dealing with the "general public" is another question, for indeed, the unique place of American Indians in the United States renders problematic their legal status.

A central paradox exists with regard to the status of the Indian which throws Indian policy upon the winds of political fate. On the one hand, Indian people are United States citizens with full guaranteed rights, and with accompanying full responsibilities. On the other hand, the quasi-sovereign nature of the tribes and the recognition of this during the treaty years is ample evidence for special treatment of Native peoples as a polity. In addition, apart from any congressional or court recognition of tribal sovereignty, the Constitution gives Congress "plenary power" over the commerce with Indian people. This plenary power, along with the developing notion of the Indians as "wards" of the government, confuses and dilutes the seemingly polar positions of Indians as sovereign and Indians as full United States citizens. It allows Congress to decide Indian policy unilaterally. A third problem centers around the extent of the government's trust responsibility. While some argue the trust only extends to the protection of Indian material resources, others argue the trust extends to the development of Indian human capital, even to the extent of saying that sovereignty itself is to be protected.

This trust responsibility has itself been a problem for policy makers throughout history. The trust relationship has been called "patronizing" and means have been sought to give more control to Indians. However, when Indians have been shown to be capable of maintaining control, they have been "rewarded" with loss of federal assistance or termination of the relationship between tribe and federal government, including that of limited tribal sovereignty, and a great loss of tribal property through sale and hypothecation.

With all of this, nevertheless, government Indian programs have been geared to preparing Indians to do without special protection in achieving competency for 20th-century life.

161

Indian policy has reflected a spectrum of interpretation, from full sovereignty, through dependence and wardship, to competence, and to citizenship. The discussion of tribal status has often centered on the argument over the degree of tribal sovereignty. Indian legal history turns less on the pull between sovereignty and citizenship than on the issue of "competence" leading to responsibility, with the United States government, from the Civilization Acts to the current era of self-determination, attempting to provide tribes with the social, economic, and educational competencies which will lead from tribal "status" to full citizenship, with all that implies: the responsibility to pay state, sales, and income tax, the abrogation of treaty rights, and the full termination of reservation status. Throughout history this process has been supported by political powers opposed to the legal nature of tribal status. Regardless of the logic supporting the legal status of treaty rights, the plenary power of Congress has been and can be invoked unilaterally to abrogate those treaties.

Federal Indian legal theory takes much of its form and substance from a set of landmark cases adjudicated in the 1830s. The cases began in conflict then as they often do today, although they operated at that time to set a precedent for interpreting dependent sovereign status (U.S. Commission on Civil Rights, 1981). The development of the dependent sovereign concept began with the decision of the Supreme Court in the case of *Cherokee Nation versus Georgia*. Georgia had attempted to impose its state laws on the Cherokee people. The Cherokee filed suit with the Supreme Court under Article III of the Constitution, which provides the court with original jurisdiction in cases involving foreign nations and states. At issue was whether the Cherokee constitute a foreign nation in the Constitutional sense. Chief Justice John Marshall held that the Cherokees and other tribes were not foreign nations but "domestic dependent nations" (U.S. Commission on Civil Rights, 1981).

The domestic-dependent nation concept is important, for it encompasses two key points: 1) that the tribes maintain nation-state, self-governing status, and 2) that they have a special, albeit dependent, relation to the United States government. Marshall relied partially for his opinion on the work of Emerich Vattel, the leading scholar of international law during this period. Vattel held that, "Weaker nations that submit themselves to alliances with more powerful nations are still Sovereign," and quoting Aristotle, "the more powerful [nation] is given more honor, and to the weaker, more assistance"(1860). Later, in *Worcester versus Georgia*, Marshall maintained that all power the federal government held over the tribes was limited to that which represented tribal consent, such as it is expressed in treaties.

In the *Cherokee Nation* case, Marshall argued for the sovereignty of the Cherokee Nation, while claiming that this sovereignty is partial and limited because of the "dependence" of the Cherokee on the United States government (Barsh & Henderson, 1980, p. 140). They are "acknowledged to have an unquestionable and, heretofore, unquestioned right to the lands they occupy, until that right shall be extinguished by a voluntary cession to our government" (Barsh & Henderson, 1980, p. 53). He goes on to argue the limits of this power as due to the "dependent" status of Indian Nations. In the case of *Worcester*, he went further in his determination of sovereign status. Samuel Worcester, a New England missionary, was imprisoned in the state of Georgia for trespassing on Cherokee land in Georgia. At issue was the right of the Cherokee to accept the presence of Worcester without the consent of Georgia. Marshall declared that the laws of Georgia in this regard were "repugnant to the Constitution" (Barsh & Henderson, 1981, p. 56). He argued that tribal status was based only on a "condition" of dependence, not on a decision. Thus, dependence was in no way construed to indicate abdication of inherent political rights. Although dependence of condition was an increasing reality in the 1830s, the "language" of dependence often accepted by the tribes in treaties during an earlier period was, Marshall implied, "A pretense, which tribes had tolerated out of ignorance of its legal implications." They were "not well acquainted with the words [that signify] dependence—nor did they suppose it to be material whether they were called subjects or the children of their father in Europe" (Barsh & Henderson, 1981, p. 57).

For Marshall, then, tribes were politically sovereign, limited by their dependence only to the extent of their admission of dependence at the time of treaty, not the **condition** of their dependence. In most cases, tribes had "never been conquered, but together with Europeans, had yielded and compromised in matters of mutual economic interest" (Barsh & Henderson, 1981, p. 57). They had not forfeited their tribal political authority. Tribes clearly had rights and possessions. In the case of *Worcester*, dependency was redefined as stated in *Cherokee Nation versus Georgia*. United States-Indian relations were clearly related to tribal consent and not to any **condition** of dependence (Barsh & Henderson, 1981, p. 57). These cases laid the groundwork for a relatively broad interpretation of tribal sovereignty and yet, ironically, solidified the "plenary power" of Congress, reinforcing its original jurisdiction over commerce with Indian tribes. However, only the doctrine of the plenary power of Congress survived into the years during which the frontier began rapidly to expand, from shortly before the Civil War into the late 19th century.

Marshall, the ardent federalist, had succeeded in establishing federal power over the state of Georgia with regard to the interpretation of tribal hegemony and immunity from state law. This strong federalist stand and the concomitant broad interpretation of Congressional plenary power are Marshall's legacy in the history of U.S.-Indian power relations from just before the Civil War to the present. Grant's Peace Policy, the Allotment Period after the Dawes Act, the Indian Reorganization Act and the "Indian New Deal," and postwar termination and self-determination were all major policy shifts. Each has a separate character springing from a changing constellation of political and reforming forces. Each, however, reaffirmed the power of the Congress to act with impunity and to impose unilaterally policy change in Indian affairs with little legal recourse on the part of tribes. This emphasis on congressional unilateral plenary power is exacerbated by the concept "dependent sovereign" which evolved from the earlier Cherokee decision, yet in a much weaker form. The **condition** of, rather than the **consent** to, dependence relationship became the leading concept. Sovereignty took a subordinate role in the political relationship due to the growing emphasis on congressional plenary power over its dependent ward, the Indian.

The years during which the European American expanded westward up to and beyond the Mississippi were not characterized by great federal toleration for tribal sovereignty. Tribal sovereignty and political self-determination also meant toleration of tribal custom and habit, along with tribal political will. These were clearly inconsistent with the aims of the European American and his "Manifest Destiny." For only a brief time after the *Worcester* decision were tribes treated as special political entities through the use of special legislation such as that exempting them from federal taxation. However, as early as 1802 and again in 1819, Congress began stipulating this special relationship be contingent upon a federal goal of assimilation—the aim to meld the American Indian, socially, economically, and morally, into the mainstream of the European American life in this country (U.S. Department of Health, Education and Welfare, 1979, p. 19). Indian policy makers began to see tribal dependency, and in some ways the limited sovereignty which remained, as a curable condition.

The "Civilization Acts" of 1802 and 1819 were the first Acts specifically codifying the responsibility of the federal government to provide for "Indian social and welfare programs—to help Indians make the transition from the life of the migratory hunter to that of the self-sufficient farmer" (U.S. Department of Health, Education & Welfare, 1979, p. 19). Prior to the Civilization Act of 1819, federal laws had dealt with or were intended to implement specific provisions of a treaty. The Act of 1819, however, dealt both with treaty and nontreaty tribes and thus established a basis for a federal-Indian relationship apart from, but including, the federal responsibility to treaty tribes.

The federal government's assumption of responsibility for Indian welfare, in addition to specific treaty provisions, begins perhaps in the Civilization Acts. Of paramount importance is the understanding that these government efforts reflect mainly a concern for welfare to the extent that welfare puts the Indian on a path of self-sufficiency and "civilization," or competence. This notion of providing welfare and education until competence is already evident in several early treaty provisions. As Vine Deloria wrote:

> While the removal of the Chippewas, Potawatomies, and Ottawas from the Chicago area was based on the explicit promise that the United States would provide educational services forever, most treaties promised schooling and other federal services for only a limited time. The Menominee (1831) and Pawnee (1833) treaties, for example, provided federal schools for 10 years; other treaties extended the period to 20 years. Officials in Washington believed that these relatively short periods would be adequate to prepare Indians to till the land, become self-sufficient, and be ready for assimilation into the general population. (U.S. Department of Health, Education and Welfare, 1979, p. 15)

The beginnings of Indian welfare as a part of the trust responsibility lay squarely in the effort to "civilize" and assimilate, these being preconditions for a satisfactory Indian social and economic policy. This effort to assimilate is buried not far beneath the surface of the Indian policy of self-determination, a policy promoted as an extension of tribal sovereignty on matters political, economic, social, and educational. Tribal political sovereignty as well as federal rather than state jurisdiction are the legacy of the precedent-setting Supreme Court decisions regarding the Cherokee. Indian material and human capital is held in trust by the federal government. This trust is, however, to be in force only as long as Indians remain in a dependent state as wards of the government. The plenary power of Congress is such that Congress may decide when the condition of dependence is weak enough for the trust to end.

Land is the part of the trust about which there is most agreement. "The U.S. holds technical legal title while equitable title or the right to use the land is held by the beneficiary—the Indian."(Cahn, 1970 p. 170) Indeed, in 1967-1968 fully 90% of the bills which came through the Subcommittee on Indian Affairs dealt with Indian land or land claims money. Regardless of the extent or nature of this trust, however, major Indian legislation has always been written around the notion that Indian material or human capital shall be protected, held in trust, until such time as Indian people gain the "competence" to manage these assets themselves, ending the trust relationship.

Worcester versus Georgia established the notion of treaty federalism with regard to Indian tribes. Tribes are not to be dealt with "within the scope of the federal-state compact, but relate to the United States through separate compacts authorized and enforced under the Treaty Clause: treaty federalism as opposed to constitutional federalism" (Barsh & Henderson, 1980, p. 59)—such as that with states. This interpretation limits the Congress to regulation of "commerce" with Indians, in the same way commerce is regulated with foreign governments. The political relationship flowing from this interpretation must follow a course of mutual agreement. After 1871, unilateral plenary power began to have a broader interpretation, and the government often adopted legislative "agreements" unilaterally. The United States government treated Indian peoples as limited sovereigns for forty years after *Worcester*. But, subsequently the government began to limit its recognition of the tribes to their status as wards rather than limited sovereigns. Indeed, the concept of treaty sovereignty, set by pacts of mutual agreement, became a moot point; in practice, a fiction, for with the total subjugation of the tribes, Indian ward status and capital held in trust through treaty became more and more subject to a broad interpretation of Congressional plenary power.

Because of the sensitive nature of the treaty-trust relationship, a clear education is required for its comprehension. Sadly, much of the requirements for such civic literacy are lacking in the standard curricula at every educational level. This paper points to a need for more study regarding the status of Indian sovereignty studies in our schools, particularly in those near tribal communities. It is particularly important for teacher educators to be conversant with these issues as a way to inoculate their students against the virus of ignorance concerning the special nature of Native American civil life.

It is indeed strange to delineate the strength and complexity of tribal sovereignty while remaining fully aware that neither members of the dominant culture nor most Indian students are educated to appreciate this issue. A recent issue of *News from Indian Country*, an Ojibwe paper, includes the headlines: "Wisconsin Counties Association to Spearhead National Coalition to 'modernize' Indian Treaties." The ensuing story discusses county efforts to begin the abrogation of treaties that allow for traditional Ojibwe fishing practices. It is no surprise, especially in light of the theme of this paper, that the story under that is headlined, "Federal Court Sentences Man for Boatlanding Pipe Bombing." What follows is a story of the indictment and sentencing of a man who ignited a pipe bomb to intimidate some Chippewa fishermen in Solon Springs, Wisconsin. One of the central concerns of this paper is the way political violence, and in this case violence with racial overtones may have roots in both perpetrators' and victims' misunderstanding of civic and economic conditions, of attendant rights and responsibilities.

Horkheimer and Adorno (1972) present an analysis of the nature of reason which works to explain this cultural conflict and begins to unpack some dimensions of the relationship between reason and violence here. They argue that law growing out of the Enlightenment cohabits poorly with realities such as tribal rights, or a Native presence that extends beyond traditional limited concepts of "Native" American which indigenous people do not share. Indeed tribalism itself, when set against the rational state, is mythic, and as such has a weak purchase on legitimacy, as does all reality which survives without an "objective measure." Horkheimer and Adorno argue that the legacy of law in the Enlightenment and after is an extension of power. Public policy is an extension of power, and rights, because they can have no rationality beyond power, exist at the pleasure of the dominant polity, in this case not the tribe. (Horkheimer & Adorno, p. 16)

Harry Girvetz (1974) extends this argument to a notion of violence against property, a type of violence with grave consequences not just for Native property but personhood as well. He talks about economic violence stemming from need. Central to the political security of Indian people is their property. Yet this property, because it is often not recognized or understood, is in constant jeopardy. Tribal lands are held through covenants established between two sovereigns, the tribe and the federal government. This relationship is difficult for those in the dominant culture to understand, much less appreciate. Property ownership is likely to be an individual or family affair in European American culture. The only sovereign recognized is the nation-state because tribal reservation sovereignty is poorly understood, and when tribal rights to land or resources conflict with those of the surrounding communities, the perceived lack of legitimacy can be a source of conflict.

Sherman Stanage (1977), in discussing the nature of violence and civil life, notes that civic understanding is a process of dialogue toward mutual understanding. "Civilization" is **living** dialectically. He cites Collingwood's *New Leviathan* in his discussion of how civic life moves to violence when dialogue cannot happen. In the Native-dominant culture relationship, dialogue is severely restricted because the two sides are often speaking two different languages of reason when discussing property and national sovereignty (p. 212). Hannah Arendt (1970) suggests that we have avoided the study or discussion of violence because study implies a sequence of reason to which violence itself is extremely resistant. Violence, as unreason, refuses to submit to the clear analysis which constitutes reason itself.

Conclusion

It is not only the paucity of textbook information that indicts education, but also the lack of nerve on the part of the education community, including State Departments of Education, to meet the obligation to serve our students with rich material in a manner that promotes reflection. Catherine Cornbluth (1983), in a perceptive essay, cites a number of unsubstantiated myths about the student mind. She argues that these myths perpetuate the teacher's willingness to capitulate to the superficial treatment of a text. She cites fears about student readiness and ability to think critically, wariness about learning "styles," and supposed lack of maturity as convenient excuses to deprive students of a rich reflective experience (p. 175). The kind of education available in the schools and universities is, by its omissions, the precursor to distortion and attendant violence. Dullness and superficiality in the curriculum have more than inert consequences here. Students in the dominant culture have little understanding nor more than shallowly romantic sympathy for a notion of tribal holdings and property rights; American Indian students, unable to crack the codes of privileged literacy, will be helpless in the face of the complex nature of their rights to counter the socialization of their neighbors. What is required is a reemphasis on critical civic literacy both in skills and in material content.

Shirley Engle and Anna Ochoa (1988) have argued that we owe students in a democracy a "countersocialization." I would agree, particularly since latent structures of unexamined prejudice dominate the discourse of rights and do so from arguments of "fairness" and "equal treatment." The legacy of fairness to tribal semi-sovereignty plays poorly in the Enlightenment court where power is tantamount to a certain kind of reason. Indeed, James Leming (1989) has shown that ideals of participatory citizenship and civic literacy are the normal preoccupation of the curriculum theorist rather than the classroom teacher. He cites the two cultures of social studies curriculum—the "countersocialization" culture stemming as far back as Counts and Rugg and the "citizenship socialization" culture, particularly the one which makes its presence known in the National Commission on Social Studies in the School's *Charting a Course* outline for curriculum for the 21st century. Capitulation to a narrow view of civic literacy may well have vicious consequences in the not distant future. In any case this shows a clear path for the teacher educator. Equipping teachers to "counter-socialize" is not only appropriate in many cases, but essential to counteract the misjudgments of ordinary curriculum producers.

If Arendt and others cited here are right, violence can be *expected* to follow on the heels of an education that in not "civic," that is, in Stanage's (1975) words, dialectical. We must have a civic education with full information, students who possess the resources to access that information, and the wisdom to make education dialectical, a dialogue across differences. Throughout the 1990s, Ojibwe leaders and concerned Wisconsin educators, have worked to provide supplemental curriculum materials for treaty rights education. Wildlife biologists have contributed to the effort to show data that indicates the tribal fishery take does not seriously impact the sportfishery. While anti-Indian groups sympathetic to the KKK and other white supremacists continue to organize in the north country, courageous educators have continued to disseminate the truth about treaties (Great Lakes Indian Fish and Wildlife Commission, 1998, p. 28).[2] Public forums, letters to editors, boatlanding "witnesses" are evidence that citizens are exercising the power of peaceful resistance to racism (Masinaigan, 1991, p. 7). Given the lack of legislative support for curriculum reform and the tendency toward textbooks homogenized for the mass market, will appropriately revised textbooks be implemented across the United States or, minimally, in locales with a significant tribal presence? Perhaps educators will take advantage of advances in digital technology to flesh out for their students the historic particulars of tribal sovereignty. Tribes continue to fight to defend their civil rights in courts across the nation, and ongoing popular education is essential if Native Americans are to be equipped with sound information and heard by judges and peers in fairly informed courts of law.

The stakes for a tribal future may be higher than the question of how to prevent seasonal violence over tribal rights to fish and hunt. Felix Cohen (1945) argued that Native American sovereignty, since it is so delicately balanced by history and Supreme Court precedent, is the "miner's canary" of our democracy. Its health is, to invoke a second metaphor, the bellwether of the health of democracy itself. If tribal sovereignty is dissolved in the face of unexamined power, can pluralist democracy, American democracy, endure?

Endnotes

[1] I would like to thank Mr. John Wilmer, of the Bad River Chippewa, for his valuable assistance in preparing revisions for this article.

[2] See the Great Lakes Indian Fish and Wildlife Commission website (www.glifwc.org) for further information on these issues. See also the Wisconsin Department of Public Instruction, Office of American Indian Programs, Madison, WI (608-266-3390).

References

Arendt, H. (1969). *On violence*. New York: Harcourt, Brace, Jovanovich.

Barsh, L. R., & Henderson, J. Y. (1980). *The road: Indian tribes and political liberty*. Berkeley: University of California Press.

Cahn, E. (1970). *Our brother's keeper: The Indian in white America*. New York: World Publishing.

Cohen, F. (1945). *Handbook of federal Indian law*. Washington, DC: U.S. Government Printing Office.

Cornbluth, C. (1983). Critical thinking and cognitive processes. In W. B. Stanley (Ed.), *Review of research in social studies education: 1976-83* (pp. 11-64). #85. Washington, DC.

Costo, R., & Henry, J. (1977). *Indian treaties: Two centuries of dishonor*. San Francisco: The Indian Historian Press.

Engle, S. H, & Ochoa, A. O. (1988). *Education for democratic citizenship: Decision-making in the Social Studies*. New York: Teachers College Press.

Fixico, D. L. (1989). Indian and white interpretations of the frontier experience. In *Native views of Indian-White historical relations* (pp. 8-19). Occasional Papers in Curriculum Series, No.7. Chicago: The Newberry Library.

Girvetz, H. (1975). An anatomy of violence. In S. M. Stanage (Ed.), *Reason and violence: Philosophical investigations* (pp. 183-207). Totowa, NJ: Rowan & Littlefield.

Great Lakes Indian Fish and Wildlife Commission (GLIFWC). (1998). *Treaty rights*. Odanah, WI: GLIFWC Public Information Office.

Horkheimer, M., & Adorno, T. W. (1972). *Dialectic of Enlightenment*. New York: Herder & Herder.

Howe, I. (1991, February 18). The value of the canon. *The New Republic,* pp. 40-47.

Kammer, J. (1980). *The second long walk: The Navajo-Hopi land dispute*. Albuquerque: University of New Mexico Press.

Leary, J. P. (1999). [Telephone interview]. Madison, WI: Wisconsin Department of Public Information. Office of American Indian Programs.

Leming, J. (1989, October). The two cultures of social studies. *Journal of the National Council for Social Studies*.

Lewinski, M. (1980). *American government today*. Glenview, IL: Scott, Foresman.

Masinaigan. (1991, June, July). *Chronicle of the Lake Superior Chippewa,* p. 7.

Nash, G. B., & Jeffrey, J. R. (Eds.). (1986). *The American people: Creating a nation and a society*. New York: Harper & Row.

Smith, L. (1977). *The American dream*. Glenview, IL: Scott, Foresman.

Stanage, S. M. (Ed.). (1975). *Reason and violence: Philosophical investigations*. Totowa, NJ: Rowan & Littlefield.

Stanage, S. M. (1975). Violatives: Modes and themes of violence. In S. M. Stanage (Ed.), *Reason and violence: Philosophical investigations* (pp. 207-240). Totowa, NJ: Rowan & Littlefield..

Stanley, W. B. (Ed.). (1983). *Review of research in social studies education: 1976-83*. #85. Washington, DC.

Strickland, R., Hertzberg, S. J., & Owens, S. R. (1990). *Keeping our word: Indian treaty rights and public responsibilities.* Odanah, WI: Great Lakes Indian Fish and Wildlife Commission.

U.S. Commission on Civil Rights. (1981). *Indian tribes: A continuing quest for survival.* Washington, DC: U.S. Government Printing Office.

U.S. Department of Health, Education and Welfare, Office of Education. (1979). *A brief history of the federal responsibility to the American Indian.* Washington, DC: U.S. Government Printing Office.

Vattel, E. (1860). Law of Nations, or principles of the law of nature: applied to the conduct and affairs of nations and sovereigns. [Microform]. New York: Printed for Messrs. Berry and Rogers, Hanover-Square.

Wisconsin Advisory Committee to the U.S. Commission on Civil Rights. (1989). *Discrimination Against Chippewa Indians in Northern Wisconsin.*

THE CONCEPT OF *EDUCACIÓN*: LATINO FAMILY VALUES AND AMERICAN SCHOOLING

by
Leslie Reese, Silvia Balzano, Ronald Gallimore, and Claude Goldenberg

Introduction[1]

In North America, family values influence children's success in school across racial and ethnic groups (Ginsburg & Hanson, 1985; Weisner & Garnier, 1992). Some specific value commitments predict school performance. These include the importance a family attaches to children's education and to schooling-directed efforts. There may also be a more general effect of family values on school achievement that is relatively "content-free." Weisner and Garnier's (1992) longitudinal study of conventional, nonconventional, and countercultural families indicated that diverse value commitments "protect" children from threats such as marital instability, which can otherwise reduce academic achievement level. Weisner and Garnier concluded that families reporting sustainable, and meaningful values of many kinds were more likely to sustain a home environment conducive to a child's academic development.

Not all family values may have a clearly positive impact on school achievement. In particular, there has been a persisting view among educational researchers that some traditional family value commitments have a negative impact on school performance of minority culture children living in North America. The "traditional" values to which many educational researchers refer are part of what LeVine and White (1986) term an "agrarian model" of human development. In contrast to industrialized societies characterized by an "academic occupational" model of child development, agrarian societies

> evolve moral codes favoring filial piety and intergenerational reciprocity, gender-specific ideals of social and spiritual values rather than specialized intellectual ones, concepts of childhood learning that emphasize the acquisition of manners and work skills without competitive evaluations, and concepts of the adult years as the prime period for significant cognitive development. (p. 3)

Obedience and respect for elders are adaptive values in contexts in which a whole family works together as an economic unit and where child labor is necessary for survival.

Although "agrarian" values may have their origins in rural economies, commitment to them is not limited to agricultural workers and their families. This is clear in many Latin American societies (Mexico included). These societies include industrialized centers and populations, where the precariousness of life in urban settings often demands adaptive behaviors, in terms of the family as the basic unit of production and kin networks as the source of services, which are similar to those required in an agrarian setting. Availability of agrarian values is partly a result of the sizable portion of the population in many Latin nations that still participate in a rural, agrarian economy and lifestyle. Similarly, immigrants from Latin societies are often from agrarian backgrounds and may continue to rely on kinship networks in similar ways in North American urban areas. Thus, the agrarian cultural model in Latin American countries or for newly-arrived immigrants to the U.S.

is not a disappearing inheritance from the past but a continuous source of meaning and guidance . . . (LeVine and White, 1986).

Even Latino immigrants to America's great urban centers who do not come from a rural or agrarian background themselves may confront adaptive challenges in the U.S. to which "traditional" values may contribute to the construction of sustainable, coherent, and meaningful responses.

Do traditional, agrarian values put minority culture children at a disadvantage in North American schools? The impact of traditional values on the educational adaptation and achievement of minority culture children is not a simple matter. Available findings are mixed for some groups such as some Latino/Hispanic communities.

Some studies conclude that traditional, rural-origin families endorse values putting their children at a disadvantage in individualistic and competitive school contexts. For example, for Mexican-Americans, "traditional" as opposed to "modern" family values have been hypothesized to complicate adaptation to urban life in general and to American schools in particular (Chandler, 1979). Rural-born Hispanics have been characterized as present-time oriented, and family-oriented rather than individual achievement-oriented (LeVine & Padilla, 1980). Mexican-American parents have been described as having low aspirations and expectations for their children's achievement and assigning more value to family unity and obedience to authority (Grossman, 1984). Such results have led some to conclude that "traditional" Latino values put children at a disadvantage in individualistic and competitive school contexts (e.g., Cabrera, 1963; Coles, 1977).

However, some findings suggest traditional agrarian values are not necessarily obstacles to educational achievement. For example, family ties within a traditional agrarian value system can be a source of emotional support and personal identity, and family unity can constitute a strong motivational force for individual school attainment and personal achievement (Abi-Nader, 1990; Suarez-Orozco, 1989).

In this chapter we attempt to "unpack" some of the effects of traditional Latino family values on their children's early school adaptation and achievement. Our research suggests that, while recent immigrants from Mexico and Central America hold agrarian-origin values which differ from the academic-occupational orientation of school personnel, these differences do not necessarily work to the disadvantage of students. To the contrary, under certain conditions, these values may be complementary to those of the school and in fact serve to support educational adaptation and achievement.

A key to our findings and analyses is the concept of *educación* often referenced by the immigrant Latino parents who participated in our study. On the surface, *educación* appears to be a direct translation of the English word "education." Although they are related etymologically, the Spanish term carries with it a set of inferences and behaviors that are not referents of its English cognate. In this chapter, one of the principle aims is to analyze the Latino parents' concept of *educación* and identify the belief components which it encompasses.

A second major objective of this chapter is examination of parental actions stemming from *educación* beliefs among the parents in our sample. Not all strongly endorsed cultural beliefs are instantiated in ways that impact children's experiences and development (Weisner, Bausano, & Kornfein, 1983; Weisner, Beizer, & Stolze, 1991). Some cultural beliefs lead to instantiation into everyday routines of families, while others seem to be readily available, expressed, and endorsed but not reliably acted on (D'Andrade & Strauss, 1992). Those beliefs that are instantiated into the daily routine are more likely to produce detectable effects on children's development, a conclusion supported by cross-cultural evidence (Weisner, 1984).

Finally, in this chapter we examine the impact on students' academic performance of the parents' beliefs and actions. This analysis brings us full circle back to the question of the impact of Latino family values on student achievement. Thus, three major questions frame this chapter:

(1) What *educación* values about education and learning do immigrant Latino parents endorse?

(2) In what ways do these beliefs shape parent actions that affect children?

(3) In what ways are parent beliefs and actions related to student academic performance?

In the Discussion section, we return to the larger issue—Do the values of immigrant Latino families put children at a disadvantage in American schools, or are they complementary and supportive in ways that are not always recognized and acknowledged?

Methods

<u>Sample</u>

The data reported here were collected as part of a longitudinal study of children's literacy development from ages five to nine. A cohort of 121 Spanish-speaking Latino families of kindergarten students was randomly selected from classrooms in two school districts in the Los Angeles area. Families from one district (N = 91) have children who attended school in Lawson (all names are pseudonyms), an unincorporated area of approximately 1.2 square miles in metropolitan Los Angeles. School enrollment in the Lawson District is approximately 90% Latino. Another group of children (N = 30) resides in a racially mixed neighborhood (Sandy Beach) and attend school in a large urban district.

From these 121 families, a subgroup of 32 families was selected at random to form part of an "Ethnographic Subset." In addition to the interviews, tests and teacher ratings described below, more in-depth information was collected from these families through a set of extended interviews at home and at school. The open-ended interviews carried out with these families provided the bulk of the data used for the present chapter. In the analysis which follows, much of the descriptive statistical data is taken from the longitudinal sample, while the ethnographic case studies provide the material necessary to interpret trends.

<u>Sample Description</u>

Information gathered from the longitudinal sample in the fall of 1989, when the focal children (child that was focus of our data collection in each family) were beginning kindergarten, provides a thumbnail sketch of the population. Table 5.1 summarizes the characteristics of both the longitudinal and case study samples.

Overall, the great majority (84%) of the parents in both communities came to the United States from Mexico; the rest are from Central America. The Mexican-origin parents in our sample tend to follow an earlier migration pattern identified by Cornelius (1989-1990): About 55% of the women and over 60% of the men are from the states of Jalisco, Michoacan, and Zacatecas. A majority (75.2%) of the focal children were born in the United States, 94%

of these in California. Close to 22% of the children were born in Mexico; 3.3% were born in Central America. Mothers average 9.6 years (range = 1-27) living in the United States; fathers average 11.7 years (range = 1-53). The average number of years of education for both mothers and fathers is 7.0 years (range = 0-16).

Table 1
Demographic description of the ethnographic subset and longitudinal sample

	Ethnographic subset ($n = 32$)	Longitudinal sample ($n = 89$)
Mother's number years of education	7.56	7.0
(mean/range)	0–15	0–16
Mother's number years in U.S.	10.19	9.45
(mean/range)	1–27	1–25
Mothers born in Mexico (%)	78.1%	84.3%
Father's number years of education	6.48	7.1
(mean/range)	0–13	0–14
Father's number years in U.S.	12.3	11.5
(mean/range)	3–21	1–53
Fathers born in Mexico (%)	78.1%	87.6%
Father's work status (%)		
White collar	0%	5.88%
Skilled	50%	48.24%
Unskilled	50%	45.88%
Target children born in U.S. (%)	78.13%	71.91%
Target children* attended preschool (%)	56.25%	58.43%

(There are no significant differences between groups. Analyses included t-tests chi-square tests as appropriate.)

Although all census categories are represented, the parents' occupations in our sample tend to be clustered in the lower levels of occupation within each category: service (30.4%), repair (23.2%) and laborer (34.4%). Only 3.2% of the fathers reported being unemployed when the project began in 1989. Parents with jobs in the service industries work as cooks, waiters, maids and housekeepers, janitors, bartenders, bus boys, parking attendants, childcare workers and cafeteria workers. Also included are two teacher's assistants. There were also skilled workers, such as mechanics, electricians, carpenters, welders, construction workers, as well as a dressmaker. The largest percentage of both men and women are employed as laborers in factory jobs such as assembly, packing, machine operation, and loading. Other jobs include factory supervisor positions, as well as drivers of various types of vehicles.

Approximately 43% of the mothers work outside the home. Many mothers not working outside of the home cite the care of small children as a major reason for their not seeking employment at the present time. Of those employed in the Lawson area, 48% are found in service occupations and 30% in factory work. For Sandy Beach, the percentages are 23% and 54% respectively. Although we did not collect income data directly, we know from school records that these are overwhelmingly low-income families. Nearly 70% of the students qualify for free meals, and another 19% qualify for reduced-price meals.

Procedures

Families were interviewed in their homes in the fall of their child's kindergarten year by Spanish-speaking interviewers who followed a standard protocol. The interview included questions on family characteristics and demographics, parental views on their children's projected academic progress, and their aspirations and expectations with regard to their children's educational and occupational future. Parents were asked about factors they considered important for student academic success and the role parents play in school achievement. (See Appendix for some of the interview questions that provided data for this chapter.)

Three more telephone interviews of approximately 20 minutes were carried out with each family in the spring and fall of 1990 and in the spring of 1991. These interviews updated parent views of student progress and their short- and long-term expectations for student performance, as well as data on specific learning activities which take place in the home, parent beliefs regarding how children learn, and their views regarding parent and teacher responsibilities in the learning process.

In addition to data collected through parent interviews, information was also gathered on students' literacy achievement. All children in the longitudinal sample were tested in the spring of their kindergarten year on a number of literacy measures which assessed a range of early literacy skills and knowledge. At the end of first grade, the children's scores on district-administered standardized tests were collected. Teachers, in the spring of each year, rated all participating children's performance over the course of the year in learning to read, in academics in general, and in interest in and motivation to learn.

The 32 "ethnographic" case study families were visited on twelve occasions over the course of four years. During each visit, fieldworkers conducted "conversational" open-ended interviews covering the topics listed above. Special attention was devoted by fieldworkers to the terms of reference and nature of actions parents reported taking to help their children succeed in school. When possible, fieldworkers observed these actions. The children were also observed in the classrooms, and their teachers interviewed on at least five occasions in four years.

Shortly after each visit extended narrative fieldnotes were prepared. At the end of each year, a comprehensive summary fieldnote was prepared for each case study family.

Coding of Ethnographic Data

Each case was coded for a number of specific quantitative indices. Each family was rated by the fieldworker who had made repeated visits to the home. Two of these ratings which will be used in the subsequent analysis of data are the *home literacy rating* and the *father participation rating*. Fieldworkers rated the general literacy environment of each family on a scale of 1 to 7. This "home literacy rating" indicates how supportive the family literacy environment is of school success by including such factors as the amount of printed material in the home, the opportunities that exist for children to observe or experience literacy activities of different types, and the responsiveness of adults and siblings to children's interests and initiation of literacy events. The presence in homes of young children of such literacy/learning events are known to predict early reading achievment (Durkin, 1966; Mason & Allen, 1986).

Fieldworkers also rated father participation in family activities. In each Ethnographic Subset family, the father was categorized as (1) actually participating in learning activities with the children, (2) supporting these activities (usually providing motivation or supporting the mother in her participation), (3) being present and socially responsible as a breadwinner, or (4) being largely absent and not involved in family activities.

Other Data Coding

Using parents' responses to Question 6, Appendix, each case received 3 scores—one each for the extent to which children are helped with school-related tasks by (1) mothers alone, (2) fathers alone, or (3) both mothers and fathers. The scores were simply the number of tasks a family reported being done by mothers alone, fathers alone, or both parents (the possible range of scores for each family is 0-9).

Data Analysis

Our analysis of the folk model of *educación* relies on the tradition of cognitive anthropology initiated by Goodenough (1957) and followed by Frake (1977), Lakoff and Johnson (1980), D'Andrade (1985), Holland and Quinn (1987), and D'Andrade and Strauss (1992). It assumes that cultural models are taken-for-granted cultural constructions of the world, widely shared by the members of a society, and that they play an enormous role in their understanding of that world and their behavior in it. In this sense, the term *educación*, and the numerous metaphors which immigrant Latinos use to refer to it, provide a window to the cultural understandings on which immigrant Latino parents base their understanding of childrearing in general and American school "education" in particular, and to the actions they take to achieve their goals.

Our construction and interpretation of the folk model of *educación* is taken from the review and synthesis of fieldnotes for each case study family. Since the longitudinal study was designed to focus on the connection between home and school, parents were not asked questions about *educación per se*. Rather, the fieldworkers focused on a more circumscribed set of questions regarding children's schoolwork and parents' role in children's school activities and progress. Aware that the term *educación* was not equivalent to the English "education," we used the parents terminology to refer to schooling or academics (*preparación, preparación formal o escolar, estudios*) when discussing these issues. Inevitably parents referenced the broader concept of *educación* in any discussion of schooling, the parents' role in homework, and the expectations that parents had for their children's academic futures. This theme, therefore, was one which emerged from the parents' own comments and explanations and was found, although not always with the explicit label by the parents of "*educación*," across all of the cases.

Results

The Folk Model of *Educación*

Parents do not spontaneously make the distinction between schooling (academics) and upbringing (morals) that is made in English. Instead, both are part of a larger whole that leads to becoming a good person. One mother, for example, when asked what she would like for her son's future occupation, replied:

> Me gustaría que estudiara, y sobre todo que fuera recto, que tuviera buenas costumbres, que llegara a ser una persona de respeto y que también fuera respetuoso con las personas. (I'd like him to study, and above all to be upright, to have good behavior, to become (literally: to arrive at being) a person of respect and to be respectful of others too.) (Case #91).

Study and formal schooling accompany the notion of being a "good person" but are not its only components.

In a different context, another mother gave as the reason for helping her child with his homework,

> para que tenga una idea de lo que es bueno y lo que es malo (so that he'll have an idea of what's right and what's wrong.) (Case #23).

Another mother illustrates the lack of distinction made between academics and morals within the concept of *educación* when she referred to both as "study":

> Todo es estudio, todo es estudio. Saberlos educar también es estudio. ¿De qué sirve tener una carrera grandísima si son borrachos, ni van al trabajo? (Everything is study; everything is study. Educating them at home is also study. What is the use of having a great career if they're drunks or if they don't go to work?) (Case #53).

And another mother states succinctly,

> Si no son educados en la casa, son un desastre en la escuela. (If they aren't educated (i.e., well brought up) at home, they are a disaster at school.) (Case #56).

The blending of academic and moral development in their comments led us later in the fieldwork to interview parents more closely. However, even extended attempts to get parents to distinguish the two aspects of *educacíon* separately and to speculate on which was more important to a child's schooling success did not result in differentiation. The comment of one father was the typical response:

> Las dos cosas van de la mano. Uno tiene que estar siempre tratando de caminar un camino recto. Sería imposible llegar a la universidad si no tiene buenos modales, si no se enseñe a respetar a los demás. Llegaría a ser pandillero, si no. (The two things go hand in hand. One always has to try to walk a straight path. It would be impossible to get to the university if one doesn't have good behavior, if one isn't taught to respect others. One would end up as a gang member otherwise.) (Case #64).

The term "buenos modales," often translated as "good manners," has been translated here as "good behavior" in an effort to accurately convey the usage of the parents who, more than to etiquette, seem to be referring to fundamentally correct behavior. For example, a father states,

Si no tienen buenos modales, buenos fundamentos, ¿qué van a hacer ellos? (If they don't have good behavior, good fundamentals, what will they do?) (Case #63).

Moral Learning as the Bedrock for Academic Learning

The immigrant Latino parents in our sample believe that their primary responsibility with regard to their children is

hacerles saber lo que es bueno y lo que es malo (to make them know what is right and what is wrong.) (Case #92).

An oft-repeated expression is that this knowledge is the foundation for all learning that comes later. Therefore, some parents, when pressed to distinguish between academic and moral education as described above, expressed the view that the moral education of the home served as the groundwork for the academic instruction that the school would provide. For example,

Es más necesario más bien educarlos moralmente que academicamente. Para poder educar, si a un maestro le dan un niño que no tiene principios morales, ni está preparado moralmente, va a ser bien difícil de enseñarle cosas académicas. Un niño va a aprender más fácil si ya sabe respetar y tratar. (It's more necessary to educate children morally than academically. In order to educate, if a teacher is given a child who doesn't have moral principles, or who isn't morally prepared, it will be difficult to teach this child academic things. A child will learn more easily if he already knows how to respect and treat others.) (Case #33).

Thus, parents might express the view that academics and morals were intertwined and indistinguishable, or that morals were actually the basis for academics. In any case, they were consistent in associating both with the idea of what it is to "educate" a child.

Knowledge of Right and Wrong

Parents in our sample see as their principal responsibility the rearing of a moral and responsible child, a child who will become what is often referred to as a "*persona de bien*," a good person. For example, one father stated emphatically that the most important thing for his children is

básicamente la moralidad, la honestidad. Son las cosas fundamentales de la familia, hacerlos personas de bien. (basically morality, honesty. These are the fundamental things of the family, to make them good people.) (Case #63).

A mother reaffirms,

Tiene uno que enseñarles a ser buenos, aparte del estudio. Enseñarles a ser correctos. Enseñarles moralidad, enseñarles a ser buenos, pues pueden estar muy estudiados y todo, pero si uno no les enseñan a ser correctos de últimas de nada les sirve. (One has to teach them to be good, aside from schooling. Teach them to be correct [in behavior]. Teach them morals, teach them to be good, because they can have studied a lot, but if one hasn't taught them correct behavior, in the end it [study] doesn't help them.) (Case #1).

The term referenced by parents for this task of orienting their children and inculcating firm moral precepts is *"educación."* One mother states that what she expects to be important for her children in the future is

la *educacíon* que nosotros les damos. Es algo que necesitan para progresar también. Lo que ven en la casa les sirve para saber lo que está bien y lo que está mal. (the *educación* that we give them at home. It is something that they need to progress too. What they see at home helps them know what is right and what is wrong.) (Case #113).

Teaching Respect and Correct Behavior

Not only do parents feel they must teach children to distinguish between right and wrong, but they must also teach them to act accordingly, in other words, to demonstrate good behavior. Both the knowledge of right and wrong and knowing and practicing the behaviors and manners which are the result of such knowledge are key aspects of the concept of *educación.*

Teaching respect for parents and others is one of these behaviors and one which forms an essential part of *educación.* As one parent explains,

Todos nosotros, los mejicanos, venimos de una tradición antigua, de ranchos donde se respeta al padre y a la madre. Tratándose de hermanos, los menores respetan a los mayores. (We Mexicans come from an old tradition, a tradition of the 'ranchos,' where the father and mother are respected. Regarding siblings, the younger ones respect the older ones.) (Case #23).

Respect for all members of the family, taught by the parents and demonstrated by the children, is what causes one father to conclude that all is well with his family:

Ella, él [he gestures to the focal child's brother and sister] son hermanos; es lo más importante. Respetar a los prójimos y a ellos mismos. Ahorita yo veo que mi familia va bien. No tengo problemas. Respetamos las opiniones de cada persona. (She. he [he gestures to the brother and sister of the focal child] are siblings; that is the most important thing. Respecting those close to them and themselves. Right now I see that my family is doing well. I don't have problems. We respect the opinions of each person.) (Case #2).

This same father describes the respect that he was taught at home by his parents as a *"bonita herencia"* ("beautiful inheritance") that he was given by his parents, and which he is giving his own children. As they educate (*educar*) their children, then, one of the good behaviors which parents seek to inculcate is that of respect.

Summarizing to this point, the term *educación* encompasses, but is not limited to, the formal academic training the child receives. Although *educación* and the English term "education" overlap in important ways, *educación* has a broader meaning. The term invokes additional, nonacademic dimensions, such as learning the difference between right and wrong, respect for parents and others, and correct behavior, which parents view as the base upon which all other learning lies.

The Importance of Family Unity

The key beliefs of *educación* discussed above are inculcated by parents in the home in an environment in which the importance and unity of the family are expressed values. The teaching of right and wrong and correct behaviors such as respect constitute the parents' responsibilities for the correct upbringing of their children. Closely associated with these values of *educación* is that of the importance of family unity. One father stated,

Somos pobres pero tenemos nuestra familia. (We are poor but we have our family.) (Case #2).

Another mother revealed,

Yo pienso que estar unidos, tanto mi esposo como mis hijos, tener la comunicación, es muy importante. Yo pienso que no hay otra cosa tan importante. Entonces, por buscar dinero, para tener dinero, para tener riqueza, uno trabaja y pierde uno lo que es lo más importante. Para mí, lo más importante es los hijos, el esposo, para mí. (I think that being together, with my husband as well as my children, having comunication, is very important. I don't think there is anything else as important. Because in order to seek money and riches one goes to work and loses sight of what is the most important thing. For me the most important thing is my husband and children.) (Case #92).

Thus, the teaching of respect and obedience takes place in the atmosphere in which the family, and the child's place in the family, is highly valued.

El Buen Camino

In talking about their children's development and education, parents make statements which indicate that the concept of *educación* is structured metaphorically according to the idea of a road down which children travel under the guidance and orientation of their parents. For example, parents say:

Desde que son chiquitos, uno trata de encaminarlos. Ya cuando son más grandes, las malas compañías los echan a perder. (From the time they [children] are young, one [as a parent] tries to put them on the right road. When they are older, bad associates ruin them.) (Case #78).

A la edad de doce años, muchas veces las criaturas se descarrilan. (Sometimes, at the age of 12, children go off the rail [go astray].) (Case #53).

Yo no fui criada 'a la moda', ni mi marido tampoco. Nosotros queremos enseñarles [a nuestros hijos] ese camino. Como nos criaron a nosotros. (I was not brought up to follow the new wave, neither was my husband. We want to teach our children that road, the way we were brought up.) (Case #54).

Parents see their responsibility as that of giving their children the knowledge necessary for them to follow the "good path" in life; however, children make the decision for themselves. Eighty-one per cent of the Ethnographic Subset families stated that children make these life-course decisions between the ages of 12 and 18.

As parents describe the characteristics of *"el buen camino,"* the "good path," they place school on the good path and dropping out of school on the bad path. Thus, schooling and academic achievement are not seen as separate from moral development, but are rather imbued with virtue as part of the good life for which one aspires and prepares one's children.

<u>High Educational Hopes for the Child</u>

The responsibility of the parents for the moral upbringing and instruction of the child, which is at the heart of the concept of *educación*, is a commonly expressed belief in families across the sample. But also common to the sample at large are high hopes for their children's academic achievement. Indeed, as described above, most of the parents do not separate academic and moral goals for their children; continued schooling is part of the good path in life that is desired and worked towards for their children.

When asked directly about the level of schooling that they aspired to for their children at the beginning of kindergarten, 80% of the parents in the longitudinal sample responded with finishing college or university (with an additional 12% desiring at least some college or university attendance). When asked how far they thought their child would actually go in school, 44% continued to give finishing college or university as the level of expected attainment.

When not responding to specific questions about educational aspirations and expectations, however, parents often make comments about their dreams and goals for their children's futures which link elements of "moral education" (*educación*) with formal schooling. For example, one mother states that she wants her children to "be someone" when they grow up, which she describes as

que no sean de la calle, que tengan un título, que no anden robando. (that they are not bums, that they have a title [degree], that they don't rob.) (Case #111).

Many link staying in school with staying out of trouble; as one parent says,

Al niño uno tiene que inculcar lo bueno, que tienes que estudiar, que no andes sucio, así se hace la ilusión. (One has to inculcate into children what is good, that you have to study, not to go around dirty, that way they get the idea.) (Case #113).

Links Between Beliefs about *Educación* and Parents' Actions

<u>Moral Teaching</u>

Given the centrality of *educación* and the beliefs it encompasses, it is not surprising that parents describe taking actions for and with their children that feature issues of morality and proper behavior. When asked what actions parents should take to help their children succeed in school (Appendix, Question 1), only rarely did parents cite promoting early literacy, preschool preparation, or other academically oriented activities. Rather, the action most commonly reported by parents was to talk with or counsel their children concerning correct and incorrect behavior. One mother reports,

Siempre le estoy diciendo: 'Tú tienes que ser un niño bueno y usar tu inteligencia en lo bueno y no en lo malo.' (I'm always telling him: 'You have to be a good boy and use your intelligence for the right things and not for the wrong ones.') (Case #26).

Parents use the terms *evitarles* and *prevenirles* to describe the ways in which they let children know about the probable future consequences of bad behavior or of being influenced by a bad crowd.

Use of dramatic examples is a common technique parents use to teach right and wrong and discourage misbehavior. One mother says that she uses books and magazines for this purpose. She reads a story to her children and then she says, for example, "Look what happened to that boy. He got run over because he didn't listen to his parents" (Case #111). Another mother reported pointing out a woman on the street as an example for her five-year-old daughter of what happens when you use drugs (Case #113).

Because children are believed to learn principally through example and imitation, a common strategy for ensuring proper behavior is restricting children's peer contacts and their play areas. For example, when parents in the longitudinal sample were asked what they do to minimize the dangers to their children of the neighborhood in which they live, of the 28 parents who rated their neighborhood as more dangerous than average, 57% reported that they kept their children inside the house (21% reported that they counseled their children about the dangers; 14% said that there was nothing that they could do.) (See Question 5, Appendix). One mother will only let her young daughters play outside of their one-room apartment when she sits in the window to watch them. She gives as an explanation of her behavior that children learn bad things when they see them, "*sin que nadie haga nada en especial para enseñarles*," ("without anyone's needing to teach them") and she wants to be very careful about what they are exposed to (Case #113).

An extreme example of restricting children's friends, but one which is not uncommon, is to send a child who is having problems and following the "wrong path" to stay with relatives in Mexico.

Como usted sabe, al pueblo que fueras, hacer lo que vieras. Aquí ven puro cholo, pura cosa de esas, pues. Les hace mal. Donde no lo ven, pues, no lo hacen. (As you know, wherever you go, you do what you see the people doing there [referring to a well-known saying in Spanish]. Here they see only "cholos" and things like that. It is bad for them. If they don't see these things, they won't do them.) (Case #53).

Keeping children inside and away from bad influences can have the additional benefit of supporting academic and learning activities. For example, one father tells a high-school-aged daughter to study so that she will not be interested in having a boyfriend (Case #2). Other parents state that they wish the school would give more homework so that they can then keep the children busy ("*entretenidos*") inside the home (e.g., Cases #111 & 112).

Academic Learning and Preparation

In contrast to teaching their children good manners, respect for elders, and about right and wrong, less emphasis was reported on arranging or encouraging academic activities that might prepare a preschool child for school. Ethnographic Subset families were asked to rank in order of importance a set of twelve statements regarding parent responsibilities before a child enters school (see Table 2). Thirty percent chose teaching respect for parents as the most important task. In order of frequency of choice, the other statements chosen "most important" were: teaching the child the difference between right and wrong (22%), teaching good manners and behavior (17%), and engaging in dialogue with the child (13%). Preparing the child for school by teaching such things as the alphabet and numbers was ranked ninth of the 12 statements and reading to the child was rated tenth. Not surprisingly, at the beginning of the kindergarten year during our first interview with the longitudinal sample, only 25% of the families reported reading to their children.

Table 2
Parents' rank order of parental responsibilities in the preschool years

Rank	Description of responsibility	% choosing as #1	Total rank value*
1	Teach respect for parents	30	209
2	Teach difference between right and wrong	22	200
3	Teach good manners	17	199
4	Dialogue with child	13	199
5	Respond to child's questions	0	177
6	Motivate child to do his best	0	171
7	Provide learning experiences	4	170
8	Provide model of a good person	4	159
9	Prepare child for school	4	146
10	Read to child	0	95
11	Teach new words	4	57
12	Make sure child learns English	0	50

*Each item was ranked by parents from 1 to 12. The total values were obtained by assigning each rank of 1 a score of 12 (2=11, 3=10, and so on), so that the highest value would be given to the item ranked as of greatest importance to the parents.

Parents do relatively little to specifically prepare their children for the academic tasks of school during the preschool years. Once the children begin school, however, parents assist children with homework and give additional practice on concepts being taught at school. For example, by the spring of the first grade year, 91% report that children are assisted with homework (53% daily and 38% sometimes/often) and 61% (46% daily and 15% sometimes/often) report they review completed schoolwork with the child. (These percentages include help and reading provided by siblings, relatives, and nonrelatives as well as by parents.)

By the end of first grade, 85% of the parents report that their children are read to (25% report that this takes place "daily" and 60% report "sometimes" or "often"). In discussing the reasons that reading to children is important, none of the parents in the Ethnographic Subset families stated that he or she read to the child in order to help the child learn to read. One-third of the parents stated that reading served to foster interest in the child's reading. Other common answers included entertaining the child (24%) and teaching the child about morals (20%). One parent saw that reading together was part of building family unity:

Los niños cuyos padres no les han leído se crían o se desarrollan un poquito retirados de sus padres o de su papá. (Children who are not read to by their parents grow up or develop a little separated from their parents or their father.) (Case #26).

Other parents reported reading Bible stories to their children so that they would know the difference between right and wrong (Case #92) or reading magazine selections to their children and discussing what could be learned from the behavior of the characters in the stories (Case #111).

<u>Use of Punishment and Conflicts with the School</u>

Finally, a set of actions that appear to be common to the population and associated with the concept of *educación* is the use of corporal punishment to discipline children and keep them on the "right path." Most parents say that they are strict with their children. One states that it is necessary to control children when they are young, sometimes with "*cinturazos*" ("whippings") (Case #113). Another contends that it is necessary for parents to hit children so that they will "*hacer caso al papá y a la mamá*" ("pay attention to their father and mother") (Case #91). Another father asked how better to educate a child than by disciplining him (Case #2).

These beliefs and practices can bring the parents into direct conflict with the school. That this issue is of great concern to parents is indicated by the number of times it surfaced without prompting in the interviews and by the passion with which the views were expressed. Parents of both higher and lower achieving students express emotions ranging from concern to outrage about what they regard as school interference with family discipline practices.

These emotional reactions arise in part from instruction on child abuse that is currently required of students in California public schools. Florid tales about authorities removing children from their families circulate freely in the community. Parents are told by their children that they have been instructed to report to school authorities any time that their parents hit them. Parents feel that this directly undermines the respect that they are trying to instill in their children:

Principalmente aquí no quieren que uno los castigue, no quieren que uno les pegue. Entonces ¿qué va a hacer uno [como padre]? Por eso es que hacen lo que hacen. (Mainly, here [in the U.S.] they don't want one to punish [children]; they don't want one to hit them. So then what is a parent supposed to do? That's why [children] do the things they do. (Case #53).

Another parent describes her niece being punished when she wanted to go out with her boyfriend instead of going to school. Because a visible mark was left on the girl's arm, her father was called to school to explain. Our informant concluded,

En la escuela los consejeros son de una manera, pero ya en casa el trato es otro, en los hijos es otro. Porque hay niños que con palabras no entienden, aunque sea un jalón de orejas o una guantada, sí necesitan. (At school the counselors act one way, but at home, with children, our treatment is different. Because some children just don't understand with words; they need their ears pulled or a slap.) (Case #26).

Another parent directly links children's bad behavior with their knowledge that their parents cannot punish them; she states that children are out of control because

184

desde chiquitos oyen que los papás no deben de tocar a los niños. Ni pegarles. Uno tiene que hablar, hablar. Pero como ellos no entienden si uno no les da una nalgada. (From the time that they're small children they hear that their parents can't touch their children. Or hit them. One is only supposed to talk and talk. But since they don't understand unless one gives them a swat.) (Case #24).

As a result, many parents feel that they are or will be prevented from fulfilling their childrearing responsibilities by the very institution that they would have expected to support them. Whereas American school personnel often tell parents that they are the children's "first teachers," a common expression used by Latino immigrant parents is "*la maestra es la segunda mamá.*" ("The teacher is the second mother.") It is, therefore, a source of confusion for parents, who cannot understand why the teacher/mother is calling into question a family's teachings about right and wrong. Far from viewing their own actions as child abuse, many parents see the school response as lack of concern for children's "*educación.*"

These contradictory feelings about school can influence parents' decisions about children's academics. One of the mothers (Case #26) described an eleven-year-old daughter's being selected to attend a special, advanced math class at a local high school campus. The girl, at sixth grade in middle school, was already taking eighth grade level classes. Although she was very proud of her daughter, the mother stressed the undesirability of letting her be in contact with older children in a bigger school. She felt that, through inter-action with older students, María would be exposed to attitudes and behaviors that were contrary to home teachings, and that María was too young to clearly distinguish between right and wrong. María was not allowed to take the advanced class.

Other Potential Conflicts with the School

Discipline issues are not the only source of conflict with the school. Although parents hold high educational and occupational hopes for their children, see school as necessary to get ahead in life, and include schooling as one of the elements of the "good path," they also see school as a potential source of bad influence. This is especially true for junior and high school students who, parents believe, might be exposed to the bad influences of their peers ("*las malas amistades*"). Parents fear these influences can then lead to getting involved with gangs and drugs, dropping out of school, and generally making nothing of oneself. Some families take steps to remove children from these bad influences. For example, when one family's older son began to be involved in gang activities, his schooling was interrupted by his being sent to Mexico (Case #114). Another mother kept an older child out of school altogether rather than risk further involvement with the bad influences there (Case #53).

Not only is school the place where peers may influence the child for the worse, but it is the place where topics are taught and discussed which some parents feel are not appropriate for their children's level of moral development and are thus damaging to them. By the age of nine or ten, children start receiving specific information about the deleterious effects of drugs and the danger of contagious diseases such as AIDS. Although parents agree that knowing about "drugs and sex" is necessary in this society, they often think that children are introduced too quickly to these matters:

Pero a veces esto los desorienta y la juventud no agarra la orientación correcta y se van para el otro lado . . . Porque no tienen su mente capaz de distinguir lo bueno y lo malo.

Su mente no está tan preparada, tan capacitada, porque ellos son niños. (But sometimes [these teachings] disorient them and young people don't take the right orientation and they go astray . . . Because their mind is not prepared enough, because they are still children.) (Case #54).

In summary, the values of *educación* are much in evidence in our sample, and there are many indications of continuing and robust commitment to them. These values are seen by parents to underlie formal schooling and to support academic progress. Although in many ways parental beliefs are congruent or complementary to those of the schools, this is not always the case. Parents in our sample have revealed contradictory feelings with regard to children's school attendance and its impact on their children's lives, as they define and envision them.

Links Between Parent Values and Action and Children's School Performance

Do parents' *educación* values, and the actions based upon them, influence children's school performance in kindergarten and first grade? Is there any relationship between parents' subscribing to the values of *educación* and their children's school achievement? For this analysis, we made use of the Ethnographic Subset. We analyzed and coded case fieldnotes, used individual tests of early literacy at the end of kindergarten and first grade reading achievement test scores, and obtained teacher ratings of children's academic progress and motivation at the end of kindergarten and the end of first grade. We also used data from the interview questionnaire, asking parents what they did to help their children in school and who did it (Appendix, Question 6).

Values and Achievement

The expressed values and beliefs of *educación* were **unrelated** to children's school achievement. Examination of fieldnotes for all families indicated that endorsement of *educación* values is so common and uniform that there was no possibility of a differential between families with high and low achieving children. Virtually without exception, the parents see their primary responsibility being the moral upbringing of the child. Similarly, beliefs about the need to guide children along the "good path," to teach children to respect their parents, and to maintain family unity are expressed by parents of both academically successful and unsuccessful children.

To test this conclusion more systematically, we examined separately the field notes of families of the 7 most and 7 least academically successful children in the Subset of 32 cases. ("Most" and "least" successful students received teacher academic ratings .5 standard deviation above or below, respectively, the mean in the study.) Parents of **both** groups of children are virtually identical in their endorsement of *educación* values.

Moreover, **endorsement** of *educación* values was so invariant that it did not distinguish between families providing home environments that were more or less supportive of literacy and academic development. In other words, endorsement of these values—aspects of which potentially conflict with the school or with values presumed important for children's school success (see section above)—did not appear to hinder or help students' achievement, at least in the early years of schooling. These stated values, uniform throughout our sample, did not influence family literacy practices, even among the extremes of our cohort. On the contrary,

186

all the parents viewed moral upbringing—which they refer to as *educación*—as encompassing and supporting academics.

Father Participation, Home Learning Environment, and Early Academic Achievement

If verbally subscribing to the values of *educación* had no bearing on home literacy environment or early achievement, what did distinguish families of better achieving students? The fieldnotes and fieldworker ratings suggested that (1) children whose fathers took an active role in the domestic routine and were more involved in child literacy/learning activities enjoyed home environments that were more supportive of literacy learning, and (2) children with more favorable home learning environments did better academically in school.

The father involvement variable was based on Question 6 (see Appendix) which was asked as part of an interview conducted at the end of first grade (for the focal child). For each of nine different kinds of academic/learning help, families (mothers usually were informants) were asked who provided help (if help was provided). In a few cases, fathers did these kinds of tasks alone with their children. But mostly families either reported it was mother alone who helped, or that both mother and father helped. We correlated three home academic help variables (mother alone, father alone, both) with fieldworkers' ratings of the home environments' support for school learning while the child was in kindergarten. We found a robust correlation (.52; p<.01) between the extent to which **both** parents participated in activities to help children in school and the degree of home support for academic achievement. There was a marginally significant **negative** correlation (-.33; p = .09) between mothers helping alone and the quality of the home learning environment; fathers' help alone was not significantly related to home learning environment. Having both father and mother engaged in home learning activities was extremely important for the creation of a home environment that supports academic learning. Neither the help of mother nor father alone was sufficient.

Furthermore, ratings of the home literacy environment in kindergarten were strongly correlated with kindergarten literacy achievement (.49; p<.01), first grade home literacy environment (.80; p<.0001), and first-grade teachers' academic ratings of the child (.58; p = .001). First grade home literacy environment, in turn, is related to first-grade teachers' academic ratings of children (.54; p<.01) and first grade reading achievement, as measured by nationally normed standardized tests (.42; p<.05). In short, involvement of both parents in children's home learning helps create conditions in the home supportive of academic achievement; these conditions, in turn, seem to promote higher levels of school achievement.

Father Participation and the Implementation of *Educación* Values

Why does father participation influence the home learning environment, which in turn predicts high and low achieving children? The case materials suggest that active involvement of the father (and mother) in the domestic routine, in childrearing, and in literacy/learning activities greatly increases the chances that the *expressed* values of *educación* will be *implemented*. Among low achieving children, fathers were often physically and/or emotionally absent from the home and were not, therefore, supporting the mother in her efforts to work with and discipline the children. From this lack of control followed the inability of the

187

household to follow through on the beliefs and values of *educación* by implementing them into a child's daily routine.

For example, in the family of one high achieving child, both parents work outside the home and co-ordinate their schedules so that one parent is always at home with the children. The father is the one whose schedule permits him to take the children to school and make daily contact with their teachers. Both parents assist the kindergarten child with schoolwork as necessary (Case #64). In another family with a high achieving child, it is the father who co-ordinates home academic efforts, encouraging an older sibling to help the focal child with schoolwork and urging the mother to go to school when the child is sick to pick up additional practice work for her (Case #2). In yet another case, the family reads the Bible together. These literacy events are used by both parents to teach their daughter the syllables for reading, and the father gets involved by purchasing additional book sets for a home library (Case #92).

In the families of low achieving children, various ecocultural factors contribute to a high degree of absence of the father from the home and to a lack of his involvement in children's activities. In one family, the father's very precarious work status, which the mother describes as *"por contrato en vez de por hora"* ("piece work instead of hourly"), results in his spending long hours away from the family and coming home too tired to interact much with his daughters (Case #113). One father's truckdriving job takes him out of the home for as much as a week at a time (Case #91), and another father's alcoholism-related absences cause his wife to lament on different occasions,

> Van a pensar que no tienen papá estos niños and Yo estoy sola para esto, él casi no tiene tiempo para nada. (They're going to think that these children don't have a father and I'm alone in this; he hardly has time for anything.) (Case #94).

In yet another family, the father's alcoholism and drug use are cited by the mother as the reason that they are no longer together; the father visits his children but is not present in day-to-day activities and is not reported to engage in school-related assistance or discussions with his children (Case #114).

The case materials suggest that father participation and engagement in the household is related to the degree of control that the mother feels that she can exert over child behaviors and activities. From the mothers of low achieving children we heard many statements about their inability to secure child compliance: One mother wanted her son to attend preschool, but since he did not like it she gave in and let him stay home (Case #91). Another mother reported that she would sit down with her son to do the homework, but if she got up for even an instant, *"él ya se arrancó y se fue."* ("he was already up and gone") (Case #24). A mother who is separated from her husband is raising three children older than the child who is part of our sample. Her unmarried ninth-grade daughter is expecting a child, and the fifth-grade son was sent to Mexico at the end of the last school year because he refused to attend school here. The mother plans to move to an apartment near her brother's family. She states about her older son,

> Tal vez se necesite que un hombre, como dice mi hermano, le ponga consejos y le jale las riendas. El es más estricto. Como yo le hablo y le doy consejos y no me hace caso. Necesita de un hombre. (Maybe a man is needed, as my brother says, to give him advice and pull in the reins on him. He is stricter (than I). Like I talk to him and give advice and he doesn't pay any attention to me. He needs a man.) (Case #114).

188

Educación, Parent Education, Single Parents, and Family Literacy

Our cohort presents a mixed picture of relationships between child achievement and parental education, with mother's education largely unrelated, and father's education related in different ways at different grade levels. The ethnographic materials suggest that it is not fathers' education that directly influences children's achievement. The pathway of influence is indirect—better educated fathers assist mothers to implement a home routine that includes sustainable literacy/learning activities. Put another way, these fathers act on the *educación*-related emphasis on family and family unity by participating in the domestic routine and by collaborating with their wives. This is consistent with Ortiz's (1993) conclusions that fathers who shared childcare functions with their wives engage in more literacy activity themselves and with their children than men who divide such functions. Thus, one aspect of our finding that father participation distinguishes families of high and low achieving children may relate to an adaptation of the *educación*-related emphasis on family and family unity. Couples living in the U.S.A. who are adapting their values to foster school achievement adopt a couple relationship characterized by sharing and collaboration regarding children's early schooling that may not be characteristic of families endorsing traditional, agrarian value systems.

Single parent homes *per se* do not necessarily produce less supportive literacy environments and lower achieving children. Across the sample, mothers are the ones who carry the heaviest domestic and childcare workload, including participating in and assisting the children with learning and schooling activities. These activities in particular and the home environment in general are more supportive of literacy development when the mothers are supported in their endeavors by another adult, in most cases the father. A study of higher and lower achieving fifth-grade students from the same community found that, in fact, single parent families were found in the higher and not the lower group. However, these single parents, in both cases, were supported by grandparents in the home, one of whom took on many school-related tasks while the mother worked outside the home (Reese, 1992).

Implementation of *educación* values is not the only family factor influencing student achievement. Another factor is family history of literacy. For example, in one case of a high achieving child, the mother reported getting ideas for helping her children from things that her parents did with her. Both of her parents read to their children and told them legends, and so she does the same thing (Case #64). By way of contrast, a low group mother states,

Yo nunca les había leído hasta ahora que están en la escuela. Como yo me crié así que nunca me leían, yo tampoco les leí. (I never read to my children until they were in school. In the same way that I was brought up where no one read to me, I didn't read to [my children] either.) (Case #24).

Parents with relatives who have attended the university have more specific plans for their children's receiving a scholarship or working while attending than do parents without this source of information (Cases #2 and #111). Thus, there is a tendency for higher achievers to come from families in which some members (not necessarily the parents) have higher levels of education and professional careers. These families possess and are able to transfer to their children relatively greater "cultural capital" (Bourdieu, 1977) than those families without this literate history.

Discussion

Most of the immigrant Latino parents in our sample see their primary responsibility as guiding their children along the "right path" in life by instilling in them the values of respect, family unity, good manners, and knowledge of right and wrong. These values correspond to what LeVine and White (1986) term an "agrarian model," as opposed to an "academic occupational model," of educational development.

Some have suggested that success in U.S. schools will come as families leave behind the values which were adaptive in more traditional, rural contexts and adopt those of the academic occupational model, characterized by a competitive labor market, social mobility, schooling as preparation for economically specialized occupations, and mass participation in national government. However, our results suggest a more complex account is required: many of the values embedded in the agrarian model lead to actions that in fact support school achievement.

In addition, many of the families in our study community are taking a third path. As they come into contact with American institutions and adapt to ecocultural forces in the urban American niche, they are constructing cultural patterns that fuse elements of the agrarian and the academic occupational models. In contrast to practices in their home countries when they were growing up, some families are limiting the number of children they have in order to better raise them (Case #64). The roles of women are changing in some families, as are marital relationships. The latter is reflected in the finding that it is the sharing of responsibility for home literacy activity that is associated with higher achievement, not mother or father dividing the tasks (Ortiz. 1993). Some families are adopting new practices which have been suggested by teachers or modeled by schoolwork. For example, one mother remarks that her preschool child is benefiting from the focal child's school experience, because she now sees the benefit of having a lot of learning materials at home for the children to write with (Case #24). Others are assisting the children with schoolwork and rewarding them for getting good grades, even though these things might not have been done by their own parents (Case #112).

At the same time, parents are not leaving behind (at least not at this point in their stay in the U.S.) the values of the agrarian model. Most are proud to say that they are raising their children with the same values with which they were raised. Yet, in their lives in a new country, many state that they want more educational and occupational opportunities for their children than they themselves had, and that they do not want to foreclose these opportunities for their children as their parents may have done for them. In spite of adopting possibly new goals outside the agrarian tradition, the conditions under which the immigrants live and work at the same time serve to strengthen or re-activate agrarian values of family unity and filial respect. Jobs are often obtained through the contacts of relatives, and homes and other resources are shared with relatives and their families as the need arises. Under pressure, the old ways can solve problems for which there are no new solutions available to poor, blue-collar workers with little job or economic security.

Blending the old ways with new ones was most evident in our examination of family values, schooling, and children's academic performance. The emerging third way rests on a foundation of the traditional values of *educación*, which blends values and activities that foster academic success. Some families are more successful than others in integrating the old and new and instantiating them into daily life. This is one reason why, in such an appar-

190

ently homogeneous group, there is so much variance in family practices and child achievement. These results suggest that, as predicted by ecocultural theory, articulation or endorsement of *educación* beliefs alone has no impact on child development or achievement (Weisner, 1984). A relationship is observed, however, when specific *educación* values are instantiated in activities—such as father involvement in child learning/schooling tasks which we believe reflects an *educación*-linked emphasis on family and family unity.

Clearly, a complex relationship exists between the values of Spanish-speaking immigrant families and the values that influence the U.S. schools their children attend. The concept of *educación* that guides immigrant Latino parents' child-raising practices is in many ways complementary to the process of formal education their children receive in U.S. schools. Parents see a strong moral foundation as the underpinning of formal education and later success in life. Parents are supportive of teachers' efforts to instill good behavior in the students and are generally responsive to teacher requests for help with schoolwork when they feel able to assist. Different as they may be, we found no evidence that the traditional values create serious disadvantages that outweigh some considerable advantages for those families who can successfully implement their beliefs into their children's daily routines.

Still, there are some discontinuities between home and school that are potentially conflictive. One emerged in those instances in which parents perceive a threat to their child's moral development (very often taking place at school itself). When threats are seen, parents make choices which strengthen morals at the expense of academics. Thus, a child might be denied a more challenging math course, will be taken out of school, or will be sent to Mexico, actions which undermine the child's academic progress, when parents fear the child's contact with bad influences. Even more problematic are differences in views regarding discipline, and the parents' reaction to reported or actual government intervention by child protective service agencies.

Is it necessary for a value system and the actions and practices associated with it to be *identical* to those of the school in order to foster the school success of minority culture students? Or can the family values *complement* those of the school, that is, can they overlap in some important ways while differing in others? There is evidence that what matters in terms of student academic success is not a particular content of beliefs, but the fact that a family has a coherent set of beliefs which they teach their children and which they use to construct an environment for children (Weisner & Garnier, 1992; Gallimore, Goldenberg, & Weisner, 1993). This view also holds that in human history a number of value systems have emerged, for example the agrarian and academic/occupational models, and that each has advantages and disadvantages depending on the circumstances to which a family is adapting (Weisner, 1984).

Given the threats facing their children and families, parents' fidelity to the beliefs encompassed by *educación* may maximize long term outcomes at the cost of some short term opportunities. Rather than being a problem, continued adherence to their traditional, agrarian-origin values may in fact be fused with new ideas and practices that have long-term protective and adaptive value. In other words, despite their differences, U.S. schools and immigrant Latino families may have more in common regarding long-term children's academic achievement than either might realize. Rather than creating irreconcilable differences, their respective values provide opportunities for co-operation and collaboration— for the benefit of the children, the families and the teachers.

Endnote

[1]This research was funded by grants from the Spencer Foundation and the National Institute of Child Health and Human Development, with additional support provided by the Sociobehavioral Research Group, Mental Retardation Research Center, UCLA. Special thanks to the families and school personnel who made this work possible. This chapter is based on a paper presented at the Annual Meetings of the American Anthropological Association, 1991.

References

Abi-Nader, J. (1990). A house for my mother. *Anthropology and Education Quarterly, 21*(1), 41-58.

Bourdieu, P. (1977). Social class, language and socialization. In J. Karabel & A. H. Halsey (Eds.), *Power and ideology in education*. New York: Oxford University Press.

Cabrera, Y. (1963). *A study of American and Mexican-American culture values and their significance in education*. San Francisco: R & E Research Associates.

Chandler, C. (1979). Traditionalism in a modern setting: A comparison of Anglo- and Mexican-American value orientations. *Human Organization, 38*(2), 153-159.

Coles, R. (1977). Eskimos, Chicanos, Indians. *Children of Crisis, 4*. Boston: Little, Brown.

Cornelius. W. A. (1989-1990). Mexican immigrants in California today. *ISSR Working Papers in the Social Sciences, 5* (10). Los Angeles: Institute for Social Science Research, UCLA.

D'Andrade, R. G. (1985). Character terms and cultural models. In J. Dougherty (Ed.), *Directions in cognitive anthropology* (pp. 321-344).

D'Andrade. R. G., & Strauss, C. (1992). *Cultural models and human motives*. Cambridge: Cambridge University Press.

Durkin, D. (1966). *Children who read early: Two longitudinal studies*. New York: Teachers College Press.

Frake, C. O. (1977). Plying frames can be dangerous: Some reflections on methodology in cultural anthropology. *Quarterly Newsletter of the Institute for Comparative Human Development, 1*(3), I-7.

Gallimore, R., Goldenberg, C. N., & Weisner, T. S. (1993). The social construction and subjective reality of activity settings: Implications for community psychology. *American Journal of Community Psychology, 21*(4), 537-559.

Ginsburg, A., & Hanson, S. (1985). *Values and educational success among disadvantaged students*. Washington, DC: U.S. Department of Education (ERIC # ED 268 068).

Goodenough, W. H. (1957). Cultural anthropology and linguistics. In P. Garvin (Ed.), *Report of the seventh annual round table meeting in linguistics and language study*. Monograph Series on Language and Linguistics, No. 9 (pp. 167-173). Washington, DC: Georgetown University.

Grossman, H. (1984). *Educating Hispanic students: Cultural implications for instruction, classroom management, counseling and assessment*. Springfield, IL: Charles C. Thomas.

Holland, D., & Quinn, N. (1987). *Cultural models in language and thought*. Cambridge: Cambridge University Press.

Lakoff, G., & Johnson. M. (1980). *Metaphors we live by*. Chicago: University of Chicago Press.

LeVine, E. S., & Padilla, A. M. (1980). *Crossing cultures in therapy: Pluralistic counseling for the Hispanic*. Monterey, CA: Brooks/Cole.

Levine. R., & White. M. (1986). *Human conditions: The cultural basis of educational development*. New York: Routledge & Kegan Paul.

Mason, J. M., & Allen. J. (1986). A review of emergent literacy with implications for research and practice in reading. *Review of Research in Education, 13*, 3-48.

Ortiz, R. W. (1993). *The unpackaging of generation and social class factors: A study of literacy activities and educational values of Mexican American fathers*. Unpublished Ph.D. dissertation, Department of Education, University of California, Los Angeles.

Reese. L. (1992). *Ecocultural factors influencing the academic success of young Latino students*. Unpublished Ph.D. dissertation, Department of Education, University of California, Los Angeles.

Suarez-Orozco. M. (1989). Psychosocial aspects of achievement among recent Hispanic immigrants. In H. Trueba & L. Spindler (Eds.), *What do anthropologists have to say about dropouts?* New York: The Falmer Press.

Weisner, T. S. (1984). Ecocultural niches of middle childhood: A cross-cultural perspective. In W. A. Collins (Ed.), *Development during middle childhood: The years from six to twelve* (pp. 335-369). Washington, DC: National Academy of Sciences.

Weisner, T. S., & Garnier, H. (1992). Nonconventional family life-styles & school achievement: A 12-year longitudinal study. *American Educational Research Journal, 29*(3), 605-632.

Weisner, T. S., Bausano, M., & Kornfein, M. (1983). Putting family ideals into practice: Pronaturalism in conventional and nonconventional California families. *Ethos, 11*(4), 278-304.

Weisner, T. S., Beizer, L., & Stolze, L. (1991). Religion and the families of developmentally delayed children. *American Journal of Mental Retardation, 95*(6), 647-662.

Appendix

Selected Interview Questions

1. What things do you think should be the parents' responsibility to teach children? What things should the teachers be responsible for teaching them?

2. How far do you want your child to go in his/her education?

   a. finish elementary school   b. finish junior high school   c. finish high school
   d. trade/vocational school   e. at least some college   f. finish college
   g. don't know or can't say

3. How far do you think he/she will go in school? (Answers a–g above)

4. If you could choose, what occupation would you like for your child?

5. On the scale of 1 to 7, how would you rate the neighborhood where you live? Would you say that it is a dangerous area and not very favorable for bringing up children; is it just about average; or is it a good environment for bringing up children?

(Those who rated the neighborhood 4 or below were also asked, "Since the area that you live in is (very dangerous/dangerous/average), how can this affect your children? Do you think that parents can do anything to prevent such situations?")

6. There are many things that parents may do with their children to help them in school. We'd like to know in your home, is there someone who does these things with _(child)_? Who is it? How often?

   a. helps with homework
   b. attends conferences with the teacher
   c. makes sure child attends every day
   d. reads to child
   e. gives advice about doing well in school
   f. gives reward if child does well in school
   g. buys additional learning materials
   h. helps child with English
   i. goes over schoolwork (completed papers)

If not noted above, ask: What is the role of the father in the activities we just talked about?

OPENING CLASSROOM CLOSETS: TEACHING ABOUT LESBIANS, GAY MEN, AND BISEXUALS IN A MULTICULTURAL CONTEXT

by
R. Jovita Baber and Brett Beemyn

The following article was originally written by R. Jovita Baber in 1993 and updated by Brett Beemyn in 1999 to incorporate more recent studies and examples. Sadly, many of the arguments about the failure of schools to foster acceptance of lesbians, gay men, and bisexuals remain as valid today as they were six years ago.

Family, the mass media, and formal education are probably the most powerful institutions influencing and maintaining our present culture. The family in the United States has undergone dramatic changes in the last century. The media reflects these changes, while education is caught in a political battle over its role in teaching about them. Among the most contested changes are those related to the place of lesbians, gay men, and bisexuals within our society. Educational institutions need to teach acceptance of lesbians, gay men, and bisexuals, since they are members of our pluralistic society but are subject to discrimination and harassment based on their sexual and gender identities.

In the early sixties and seventies, the traditional nuclear, heterosexual family came under critical examination with the rise of the women's liberation movement. The release of Betty Friedan's book *The Feminine Mystique* (1963)—in which she wrote about "the problem that has no name"—helped spark a change in attitudes. Instead of asking, "What's wrong with women who can't adjust to marriage?" people started to ask "What's wrong with marriage that so many women can't adjust to it?" Thereafter, many studies of marriage placed the traditional nuclear family under closer scrutiny (Tavris & Wade, 1984).

Our society's ideas about what defines a family and the roles of men and women in families have been revolutionized since the early sixties. For example, the rate of divorce has doubled since 1960, and the Census Bureau now projects that 40% of new marriages will fail (National Center for Health Statistics, 1995; Vobejda, 1998). As of 1998, there were nearly 12.5 million single mothers in the U.S., and 72% of all mothers were in the paid work force (Bureau of Labor Statistics, 1999a; 1999b). The number of children born out of wedlock increased from under 4% in 1950, to 11% in 1970, to more than 32% in 1997 (Magnet, 1992; National Center for Health Statistics, 1998). At the same time, the number of lesbian, gay, and bisexual parents has grown tremendously in the 1980s and '90s; studies estimate that from four to 14 million children are currently being raised by two to eight million lesbian/gay/bisexual parents (Patterson, 1995). As a result of these changes, the "traditional" family, with the father going off to work and the mother remaining at home to take care of the children, represents just 10% of U.S. families today (Bates, 1992). Educational institutions need to acknowledge these new realities in their policies and curricula.

Many of these changes are related to changing ideas about sexuality. We have inherited many of our sexual mores from the Victorian era, when sex was considered "dirty, dangerous and disgusting." A Victorian female was expected to "save herself" for her husband. But since the 1960s, several studies on sexual behavior have shown that the number of women having pre-marital sex is increasing and that people's attitudes and behaviors about sex in

195

general have become more liberal. As a result, sex is no longer seen as something dirty, but rather, as a natural part of intimate relationships.

At the beginning of the century, the idea of contraceptives was a radical notion. Today, though, most people do not question an adult's right to use birth control. Contraceptives and their acceptance have allowed people to separate sex as a pleasurable, intimate activity from its reproductive function. When this occurred, lesbian, gay, and bisexual relationships were increasingly able to assume a more logical place as part of a new understanding of sexuality.

Within the context of society's changing attitudes around family and sexuality, the lesbian, gay, bisexual, and transgender (LGBT) rights movement has grown and developed. Those who oppose equal protection for lesbians, gay men, and bisexuals generally want to maintain traditional sexual mores and the nuclear family. The Reverend Pat Robertson has charged that laws that limit discrimination against lesbians, gay men, and bisexuals would legitimize their lifestyle and "would destroy the American family." This argument is often part of a larger philosophy that equates the erosion of the traditional family with the demise of our society: "this revolution [the result of an epidemic of divorce, remarriage, illegitimacy, and new strains within intact families] . . . has deeply troubling implications for the American social order" (Magnet, 1992).

People who are more accepting of the changes in the family are often more receptive to lesbians, gay men, and bisexuals. They typically argue that the family is a flexible institution that has always changed with the times and will continue to do so. Doherty (1992) describes today's family arrangements as the "pluralistic family":

no single family arrangement . . . [but] a plethora of family types . . . including dual career families, never-married families, post-divorce families, step families, and gay and lesbian families. Legislative bodies and courts are beginning to codify the Pluralistic Family by redefining the terms to include arrangements considered deviant, non-family forms in the past. Tolerance and diversity, rather than a single family ideal, characterizes the Pluralistic Family. (p. 35)

Although some of these new arrangements have become embedded in society's perceptions of family, Doherty acknowledges that the plethora of family types has left many people feeling very ambivalent. "Surveys indicate that most Americans still believe in the traditional family values . . . that the stable two-parent family is the best environment for raising children." However, she cites family sociologist Dennis Orthner, who points out a difference between family "values" and family "norms." While our values and ideals have remained traditional, our norms and expectations have changed remarkably, as indicated by the earlier statistics on families in the U.S.

Similar ambivalence is felt toward acknowledging lesbian, gay, and bisexual relationships. Polls in the last few years have consistently shown that large majorities support equal rights for gays in job opportunities (84%) and housing (80%), but oppose same-sex sexuality itself. For example, 56% of the respondents to a 1996 survey said they believed sexual relations between two consenting adults were "always wrong," while 46% of those polled in another survey thought such relationships should be illegal (Yang, 1997; Yang, 1998). Even higher numbers believe that same-sex marriage should not be legalized—about two-thirds of respondents to recent polls. Although the level of disapproval for same-sex relationships is down from highs of 70-75% in the 1980s and early '90s (Yang, 1997), these findings demonstrate that while people may ideally believe in equality for all, they are not ready to give up their conviction that nuclear families are better than other family arrangements. They will not "endorse homosexuality as equal to heterosexuality" (Shapiro, 1993). The conflict that arises when schools want to teach about lesbians, gay men, and bisexuals is embedded in the differences between family "values" and family "norms," and sexual "values" and sexual "norms."

Social trends indicate that our society will probably not return to the traditional nuclear family as the dominant family arrangement (Wallis, 1992). Doherty (1992) writes: "The forces of gender equality, diversity, and personal freedom may never again permit a single ideal family structure. . . ." Doherty further states that the "Pluralistic Family has redefined our notions about relationships, parenthood, and homelife. Increased tolerance for multiracial and single-sex couples who are raising children will be necessary as this type of family is here to stay for an indefinite future." Thus schools need to play an active role in encouraging acceptance of multiracial and same-sex relationships.

The mass media is already giving greater and often more positive attention to lesbians, gay men, and bisexuals. For example, searches of *The New York Times* and *The Washington Post* for stories that mention "lesbian and gay" resulted in 267 and 214 articles, respectively, for the past twelve months alone. Whether it is features on brain studies that seek to unravel the mysteries of sexual orientation, news reports about the Senate's refusal to confirm an openly gay man to an ambassadorship, or the critical treatment of the assertion by Jerry Falwell's group that one of the Teletubbies is gay, stories involving gay people have become a regular feature of the national print media. In popular magazines, lesbians, gay men, and/or bisexuals were the cover stories of the June 21, 1993 and July 17, 1995 editions of *Newsweek*, the July 5, 1993 edition of *U.S. News and World Report*, and the July 19, 1993 edition of *Christianity Today*. In 1998, the press gave unprecedented coverage to the hate-motivated murder of Matthew Shepherd, and many newspapers and magazines responded to his death by calling for passage of a national hate crimes law that would increase penalties for attacks motivated by someone's actual or perceived sexuality. Undoubtedly, part of the reason the story received so much attention was because Shepherd was a white, middle-class gay college student. (In the six months following Shepherd's death, six transgendered people, most of whom were people of color and poor, were killed because of their gender identity, but their murders were entirely ignored by the mainstream media, even in some of the places where the attacks occurred [Meyer, 1999].) Nevertheless, the story of Shepherd's death would not have been considered as newsworthy if lesbians, gay men, and bisexuals were not becoming more accepted.

Human sexuality, in its many forms, is also increasingly being represented on television and in movies. In 1997, there were a record 30 lesbian, gay, and bisexual television characters, led by the show *Ellen*, which became the first prime-time series to have its lead character come out (Gay and Lesbian Alliance Against Defamation, 1997). Although it was canceled after the 1998 season, the widespread coverage given to *Ellen* demonstrated the growing visibility of gay people on television. Likewise, Hollywood movies are including more—though not necessarily more realistic—depictions of lesbians, gay men, and bisexuals, with recent popular films ranging from *The Silence of the Lambs* (1991) and *Basic Instinct* (1992) to *The Birdcage* (1996), *In and Out* (1997), and *As Good As It Gets* (1998).

Historically, the few lesbian, gay, and bisexual personalities in the entertainment media were often characterized negatively. More recently, they are included because their sexuality is key to the story line: "The story focuses on their sexuality rather than their day-to-day nonsexual lives" (Herek & Berrill, 1992). While the images of lesbians, gay men, and bisexuals are increasing and becoming less hostile, they are still seldom portrayed as compassionate, whole (sexual and nonsexual) people. This is no small matter, for the mass media affect how people perceive lesbians, gay men, and bisexuals. In a *U.S. News and World Report* poll, 56% of voters worried that media portrayals of gays had had a negative influence on society (Shapiro, 1993). Schools need to balance the continuing stereotypical depictions of lesbians, gay men, and bisexuals in the media with more realistic representations.

Teaching about lesbians, gay men, and bisexuals is riddled with the political controversies surrounding the changing family and sexual morality. Schools throughout the nation are cautiously beginning to question when and where to teach children about lesbians, gay men, and bisexuals (Lacayo, 1992). One of the most heated debates erupted in New York City in 1992 when the "Children of the Rainbow" curriculum suggested that first graders read the gay/lesbian-positive books *Daddy's Roommate*, *Heather Has Two Mommies*, and *Gloria Goes to Gay Pride*. Half of the 32 local school boards balked. The borough of Queens had an outright revolt, as sexual morality and "traditional family values" became the focus of debate (Tucker, 1993).

Other places have avoided this kind of political battle by introducing lesbians, gay men, and bisexuals into the curriculum at a later grade level and by including community leaders in the process of policy development (Celis, 1993; Ribadeneira, 1992; Tucker, 1993). Massachusetts created the nation's first Governor's Commission on Gay and Lesbian Youth in 1992 to work towards the creation of a safe, supportive environment for lesbian, gay, and bisexual students in the state's public schools, which led the following year to Massachusetts banning sexual orientation discrimination in its educational institutions (Massachusetts Governor's Commission on Gay and Lesbian Youth, 1997). Most changes, though, are occurring on the city or county level: Fairfax County in Virginia, Broward County in Florida, Houston, San Francisco, and Seattle have begun to include lesbians, gay men, and bisexuals in various areas of their curricula (Celis, 1993; Tucker, 1993).

At the same time, a growing number of colleges and universities are establishing sexuality or lesbian and gay studies programs and offering courses in the field. At least fourteen schools currently have a minor, concentration, or certificate in sexuality/lesbian and gay studies, San Francisco City College provides a bachelor's degree, and Brandeis University and Barnard College are currently planning degree programs (Younger, 1999). More than a hundred colleges and universities now offer regular classes on lesbians, gay men, and bisexuals, and numerous others are incorporating such material into more general courses. Why are so many schools integrating lesbians, gay men, and bisexuals into their curricula when their inclusion often sparks controversies over the family and sexual morality?

The Importance of Integrating Lesbians, Gay Men, and Bisexuals into the Curriculum

The primary reason for including lesbians, gay men, and bisexuals in the curriculum is because they are members of our pluralistic society. Some people argue that 10% of the population is lesbian and gay, citing the Kinsey studies (Kinsey, Pomeroy, & Martin, 1948; Kinsey, Pomeroy, Martin, & Gebhard, 1953). More recently, surveys conducted by the Alan Guttmacher Institute and the National Opinion Research Center found that only 1% and

2.8% of men, respectively, were **exclusively** gay. These figures are in line with the 1-3% findings of surveys in Britain, France, and Denmark (Barringer, 1993a; Schmalz, 1993). But a distinction has to be made here between behavior and identity; many people who are involved in same-sex relationships don't consider themselves lesbian, gay, or bisexual. Another recent study reported that 22% of men and 17% of women had had same-sex sexual experiences, but just 9% of the men and 5% of the women self-identified as homosexual or bisexual (Keen, 1993). The fact that people tend to underreport behavior that might be considered anti-social and overreport behavior that is socially sanctioned makes it even more difficult to assess the exact number of lesbians, gay men, and bisexuals in our society (Barringer, 1993b). But whether lesbians, gay men, and bisexuals make up 1%, 10%, or 20% of the population, they are members of our society and should receive the same benefits, rights, and respect as other people.

In a pluralistic society such as the United States, we must teach the acceptance of difference. One can see the results of social intolerance in the 1990s by observing the ethnic cleansing in Bosnia, Rwanda, and Kosovo, the neo-Nazi attacks on Turkish people in Germany, the Iraqi treatment of the Kurds, and other international crises (Breslau, 1992; Lief, 1992; Lane & Breslau, 1992). Similar violence created by social intolerance is seen within the U.S. In 1997, 8,049 hate-crime incidents were reported to the FBI by local law-enforcement agencies. The actual number of incidents was undoubtedly even higher, as jurisdictions representing 17% of the U.S. population did not provide any information and many others submitted inadequate reports. For example, not a single hate crime was recorded for the year in the entire states of Alabama, Mississippi, and Arkansas. Crimes motivated by race made up the largest category of the incidents that were reported (58%), followed by religion (17%), sexual preference (14%), and ethnicity (11%) (Freiberg, 1998).

Groups whose mission is to monitor hate crimes against lesbians, gay men, bisexuals, and transgendered people receive many more reports of violence. The National Coalition of Anti-Violence Programs documented 2,445 hate crimes against individuals who were known or perceived to be lesbian, gay, bisexual, or transgendered in 1997, more than twice as many incidents as were submitted to the FBI. But even these statistics are incomplete, as they are based on reports from only 14 violence tracking programs, and many areas of the country lack any means to document such crimes (Freiberg, 1998). A 1998 study of nearly 500 college students in the San Francisco Bay area conducted by psychologist Karen Franklin found that the majority had participated in or witnessed anti-gay incidents. Half of the male respondents admitted to some form of anti-gay attack; 18% said that they had engaged in physical violence or threats against people whom they believed were lesbian, gay, or bisexual, and another 32% had taken part in anti-gay name calling. And far from being guilty over their involvement in hate crimes, nearly half of the assailants said they would likely assault again in similar circumstances. "Indeed, assaults on gay men and lesbians were so socially acceptable that respondents often advocated or defended such behaviors out loud in the classrooms, while I was administering my survey," Franklin states. Many of the students who had never assaulted or harassed someone perceived as gay were not more tolerant so much as they were concerned about getting into trouble or experiencing retaliation. Franklin argues that "[a]s long as the schools are breeding grounds for intolerance and abuse, hate crimes will continue" (American Psychological Association, 1998; Ness, 1998).

Because of their power to influence society, educational institutions can help limit the number of hate crimes committed by teaching acceptance of diversity. The majority of these crimes are committed by youth and young adults. The general profile of the "gay basher" is a young male acting alone or with other young men. One study indicated that 54% of the assailants were under 21 years of age, and 92% were male. Another report, by the Governor's Task Force on Bias-Related Violence, revealed that high school students were more prejudiced against gays than any other group (Herek & Berrill, 1992). Franklin concludes from her research that "the majority of young people who harass, bully, and assault sexual minorities do not fit the stereotype of the hate-filled extremist. Rather, they are average young people who often do not see anything wrong with their behavior. And the reason they do not see anything wrong is simple—no one is telling them that it is wrong" (American Psychological Association, 1998; Ness, 1998). Educators must attempt to reduce the fears, intolerance, and ignorance behind violent attitudes such as these by teaching about difference. In U.S. society, opposing opinions—even hatred—are and should be admissible by the First Amendment, but violent acts that stem from intolerance cannot be permitted.

Either lack of policies or the lax enforcement of policies has permitted much of the harassment and hate crimes against lesbians, gay men, and bisexuals to happen in our educational institutions. A study conducted by psychologist Anthony D'Augelli found that 17% of lesbian, gay, and bisexual youth had been assaulted, 44% had been threatened with physical attack, and 80% had been subjected to direct verbal abuse (Gay, Lesbian and Straight Education Network, 1999b). Another survey found that they were seven times more likely than their nongay classmates to be threatened with a weapon while at school. In one Des Moines high school, students found that their classmates experience anti-gay epithets 25 times a day on average, and teachers who overhear such slurs fail to respond to them 97% of the time. Given such an atmosphere, it is not surprising that the most recent Youth Risk Behavior Survey of the Massachusetts Department of Education revealed that the state's lesbian, gay, and bisexual students are more than five times as likely as other students to skip classes because they feel unsafe at or en route to school (Gay, Lesbian and Straight Education Network, 1999a).

The same intolerance is found at colleges and universities. In 1989 alone, a total of 1,329 anti-gay episodes were reported to the National Gay and Lesbian Task Force by lesbian, gay, and bisexual student groups on just 40 campuses (Herek & Berrill, 1992). Such acts of violence and harassment have led a number of institutions to investigate their campus climate for LGBT students, staff, and faculty in recent years. Examining the results of investigations at 30 colleges and universities, diversity specialist Sue Rankin found that anti-gay incidents were prevalent at all of them:

> For example, in studies where surveys were used as the primary tool, the data indicated that LGBT students are the victims of anti-lgbt prejudice ranging from verbal abuse (2%-86%) to physical violence (6%-59%) to sexual harassment (1%-21%).
>
> In those investigations that utilized qualitative data, analogous findings were reported indicating the invisibility, isolation, and fear of LGBT members of the academic community. Their lives are filled with secret fears. For the professor, counselor, staff assistant or student who is gay, lesbian, bisexual or transgendered, there is the constant fear that, should they be found out, they would be ostracized, their careers would be destroyed, or they would lose their positions (Rankin, 1999).

200

To cite just one campus study, a survey at the University of Oregon found that 61% of lesbian, gay, and bisexual students feared for their personal safety (Herek & Berrill, 1992). An environment in which nearly two-thirds of a group of people feel threatened does not nurture tolerance, pluralism, or democratic ideals. Educational institutions need to encourage the exploration of new and opposing ideas, while penalizing violent and bigoted behavior. Policies that clearly state a punishment for harassing or victimizing a person because of their minority status should be implemented and enforced.

A second reason for schools to integrate lesbians, gay men, and bisexuals into the curriculum is because they are likely to have students, including lesbians, gay men, and bisexuals, who are struggling with their sexuality. Lesbian, gay, and bisexual youth often take to heart the hatred that is directed at them through harassment. They internalize the rejection they receive from peers and family and find few available role models to assist them in developing positive self-images. These factors put lesbian, gay, and bisexual youth in a high-risk group for dropping out of school, committing suicide, and abusing drugs and alcohol (U.S. Department of Health and Human Services, 1989; Uribe & Harbeck, 1992).

The U.S. Department of Health and Human Services' "Report of the Secretary's Task Force on Youth Suicide" (1989) states that "gay youth are 2 to 3 times more likely to attempt suicide than other young people. They may comprise up to 30 percent of completed youth suicides annually." Subsequent studies have confirmed these results. A 1995 survey of public high school students in Massachusetts found that lesbian, gay, bisexual, and questioning youth were 3.41 times more likely to report a suicide attempt than their peers, and one-third had attempted suicide in the previous year. Among adolescent males, being gay or bisexual was the strongest independent indicator of suicide risk (Sun, 1998; Garofalo et al., 1999). In a similar study of Minnesota middle and high school students, 28.1% of self-identified gay and bisexual males reported making at least one suicide attempt, compared to 20.5% of self-identified lesbians and bisexual females, 14.5% of heterosexual females, and 4.2% of heterosexual males (Boodman, 1998).

Self-destructive behavior and unhealthy coping skills are also seen in the high level of alcohol and drug addiction among lesbians and gay men, with estimates suggesting that "about 25% of such persons suffer from definitive drug and alcohol abuse problems, while an additional percentage experiences 'suggestive or problematic' abuse patterns" (Bickel-haupt, 1995). The messages of our society have distorted some of the self-perceptions of lesbians, gay men, and bisexuals. Educators at all levels of academia are in a position to provide information and support that can help end these abuses. "We have a moral obliga-tion to combat a devastating trend," says Gerald Newberry, coordinator of the Fairfax County's family-life education programs. "We need to communicate to our kids [and young adults] that people are different, and that we don't choose our sexual feelings—they choose us" (qtd in Lacayo, 1992).

Lastly, schools need to integrate lesbians, gay men, and bisexuals into the curriculum because an increasing number of children are being raised by lesbian, gay, and bisexual parents. Research has shown there are no disadvantages to being raised by a same-sex couple: no impact on gender identity, self-esteem, self-concept, or sexual orientation (Goleman, 1992; Bliss & Harris, 1999; Freiberg, 1999). Developmental psychologist Virginia Casper says that school is probably the most difficult arena for children raised by same-sex parents, as peers and staff retain traditional ideas about family arrangements and sex-role models. Casper and her colleagues argue that teachers and administrators should acknowledge that some children and young adults have lesbian, gay, or bisexual parents (Goleman, 1992). To do this effectively, not only should the curriculum be integrated to teach students acceptance, but staff development needs to include acceptance education for teachers.

There are many humanitarian reasons for teaching about lesbians, gay men, and bisexuals in academia, yet the process of integrating them into the curriculum will be neither easy nor quick. A *U.S. News and World Report* poll indicates that 52% of respondents oppose teaching about lesbians and gay men in public schools, while 44% favor it (Shapiro, 1993). Attitudes toward lesbian, gay, and bisexual teachers are also very ambivalent. A 1996 survey found that respondents were almost equally divided over whether gays should be hired as elementary school teachers (although this was much improved over the nearly two-to-one opposition of a decade ago), and just 60% felt that they should be allowed to instruct high school (Yang, 1998). Lesbians, gay men, and bisexuals may be more visible, but ignorance about their lives still exists among the general public. Frances Kunreuther, executive director of the Hetrick Martin Institute, says, "This is not the first issue this country has faced that has been emotional. I expect it to be painful. But fortunately in this country, we just don't protect the majority" (qtd in Ribadeneira, 1992).

Including Lesbians, Gay Men, and Bisexuals in the Classroom

Lesbians, gay men, and bisexuals should be included in multicultural education. While lesbian, gay, and bisexual communities are extremely diverse, and critics say that the only commonality is attraction to the same sex, lesbians, gay men, and bisexuals share a history of being oppressed as members of a sexual minority. This common experience pulls lesbians, gay men, and bisexuals together throughout the world, as seen by the emergence of international lesbian, gay, and bisexual organizations. While internal rifts exist, lesbians, gay men, and bisexuals have learned to celebrate their commonality by creating communities and cultures that include their own newspapers and magazines, literature, music, radio and cable television programs, web pages, and internet chat rooms. These communities and cultures need to be integrated into multicultural studies.

Lesbians, gay men, and bisexuals together constitute a cultural group that can be identified and studied, but their experiences vary widely according to such factors as nationality, gender, race, religion, class, and age. For example, while some in the U.S. see same-sex couples as threatening to the nuclear family, they enjoy many of the same rights as heterosexual couples in Denmark and Sweden and have won major victories in Canada (Wright, 1999). In a study of 77 cultures, C. S. Ford and F. A. Beach found that 28 of them condemned same-sex sexuality with punishments ranging from mild sanctions to death, while in the remaining 49, "homosexual activities . . . are considered normal and socially acceptable for certain members of the society" (qtd in Blumenfeld & Raymond, 1992). Since one's perceptions of homosexuality and bisexuality are highly culturally bound and often linked to how family and sexuality are defined within the culture, a full discussion of lesbians, gay men, and bisexuals is appropriate in the context of studying cultural groups.

James Banks (1989) defines four distinct levels at which teachers can integrate multicultural perspectives and information into the curriculum: contributions, additive, transformation, and decision making and social action. When applying Banks's theory to lesbians, gay men, and bisexuals, one should not necessarily assume that one level of curriculum integration is inherently better than another. The approach educators use should be carefully selected after considering the political environment in which the curriculum will be taught, the educators' level of comfort with discussions of sexual and gender identities, and the educators' security in their own sexuality. These factors will play a role in the level of success attained.

The contributions level does not alter the traditional curriculum a great deal, but rather, systematically inserts underrepresented cultures into the course. Since, as is commonly stated, lesbians, gay men, and bisexuals are everywhere, every field of study has famous lesbian, gay, and bisexual people already within it. If an English professor traditionally gives background information about the authors being read, the teacher should include the fact that numerous famous writers, such as Gertrude Stein, Walt Whitman, Herman Melville, Virginia Woolf, James Baldwin, and Alice Walker, had or have relationships with people of the same sex. If biography is an important aspect of an art history course, one might mention that Michelangelo and Leonardo da Vinci, as well as more contemporary artists like Andy Warhol and Robert Mapplethorpe, had same-sex relationships. Or political science and history courses could discuss the same-sex sexuality of monarchs such as King Richard II, Pope Julius III, Queen Christina, and King James I, or of more recent leaders such as Susan B. Anthony, Eleanor Roosevelt, and Bayard Rustin (Blumenfeld & Raymond, 1992; Folliard, 1999).

Including lesbians, gay men, and bisexuals in the curriculum through a contributions approach allows for the identification of some famous gay people. This approach does little to break down stereotypes and myths about lesbians, gay men, and bisexuals as a group, however, since an educator is simply acknowledging the same-sex relationships of individuals, most of whom are already part of the curriculum. To take a more proactive stance, a teacher could adopt Banks's additive approach. This method would modify the traditional curriculum slightly by including material that describes the wider experiences of lesbians, gay men, and bisexuals and the concepts and themes unique to gay communities. In a discussion of the literary and historical figures mentioned above, for example, a teacher could address how same-sex sexuality was viewed during their lives and the impact it might have had on their work. If the class was considering the ongoing struggle for women's reproductive freedom, an educator could bring in information on the legal battles that lesbians have fought in order to conceive and to keep their children. In a unit on civil rights movements in the United States, one could present material on the LGBT movement for equal rights.

The additive approach allows teachers to introduce their students to lesbian, gay, and bisexual issues without making tremendous waves in a school system. But the approach is limited in that it reinforces the idea that lesbian, gay, and bisexual history is not an integral part of U.S. history, as people are viewing lesbians, gay men, and bisexuals from a heterosexual point of view. Further, it does little to explain the tensions, relationships, and connections among lesbians, gay men, bisexuals, and heterosexuals.

In contrast, a transformative approach would critique stereotypes and myths by asking students to question why we take for granted what we do. They begin to see how concepts of sexuality, family, and gender have shaped our society and to explore their heterosexual assumptions through being presented with material from lesbian, gay, and bisexual world views. A direct application of Banks's transformation approach could, however, be unsuccessful, for a mainstream community might rebel if an educator offered only lesbian/gay/bisexual perspectives. Exposing students to all sides of any argument would be important. Heterosexual students would be faced with the dilemma of resolving the internal conflict that arises when world views collide. If students truly take on the challenge of resolving this conflict, they can recognize their own world views and the subjectivity of their positions. At the same time, lesbian, gay, and bisexual students would be empowered by having their perspectives validated.

In adapting Banks's transformation approach, the educator could pose difficult questions, such as how the United States should react to lesbians, gay men, and bisexuals. When the question is posed, the teacher must be very careful to provide the students with sufficient information from all sides to enable critical thinking about the issue. For background material, the teacher should present the students with information arguing that homosexuality is an immoral **decision** that will destroy the nuclear family and information arguing that homosexuality is an **orientation**, not a choice, and a legitimate alternate family arrangement. Then students could be shown the contradictions within our own legal system that reflect the various attitudes toward homosexuality. The 14th Amendment says that no state can deny any person equal protection under the law. However, 18 states currently have enforceable sodomy laws against people who pursue same-sex relationships, with penalties of up to ten or more years in prison in six states, including a possible sentence of five years to life in Idaho (American Civil Liberties Union, 1999). On the other hand, nine states and the District of Columbia prohibit discrimination against lesbians, gay men, and bisexuals in employment, housing, and public accommodations, and two others ban anti-gay bias just in employment (Roundy, 1999). How is it that in one country, different states can have such opposite interpretations of how the Constitution should or should not be applied?

In order for the transformation approach to work, an environment must be established in which students are able to honestly explore their beliefs, feelings, and reactions to the material. Finding and creating materials that provide lesbian/gay/bisexual perspectives and making sure points of view are equally represented is more time consuming than adopting a contributions or additive approach, especially if one considers the need for ongoing staff development to make the approach truly effective. Banks suggests this kind of training be institutionalized, even though this can be costly as well as time consuming.

The last level Banks mentions is the decision making and social action model of curriculum integration. This approach is organized around the students' identifying an important social problem, learning about the issue, and taking action. There are many advantages to this method. The students interact directly with the material presented in the process of developing their thinking, research, decision making, and social action skills. Students would also be called upon to analyze their own values and to improve their cooperative skills as they work together on a final project. One of the drawbacks to this approach when applied to lesbians, gay men, and bisexuals is the extent of controversy that could erupt. The students may find that they do not have political efficacy, for example, if the status quo is too threatened by the action they decide to take.

The students in a class organized around a decision making and social action agenda could study homophobia and biphobia and then resolve to start a project to raise awareness and limit the number of homophobic and biphobic incidents on campus. The students could also research the extent of discrimination and anti-gay related incidents at the institution and work to have sexual orientation included in the school's non-discrimination clause or sexual harassment policy.

Teachers need to consider their situation carefully to create a curriculum that can be effectively and successfully implemented within their own classrooms and institutions. As educators and administrators, we need to examine our own attitudes for ways we are maintaining the ignorance and hatred that have oppressed lesbians, gay men, bisexuals, and other persons in underrepresented groups. We need to work toward a time when we stop simply talking about integrating underrepresented groups into the curriculum and actually begin to teach students, as a matter of course, about the increasingly complex and pluralistic society in which we live. As key persons in institutions that have the power to influence society, we have a responsibility to educate our students about our shared humanity.

References

American Civil Liberties Union. (1999, January). Status of U.S. sodomy laws. http://www.aclu.org/issues/gay/sodomy.html.

American Psychological Association. (1998, August 6). Anti-gay aggression: Expressions of hatred or of perceived cultural norms? News release. http://www.apa.org/releases/react.html.

Anderson, J. (1993, January 10). Portraits of gay men, with no apologies. *New York Times,* p. M5.

Banks, J. A., & Banks, C. A. M. (Eds.). (1989). *Multicultural education: Issues and perspectives.* Boston: Allyn & Bacon.

Barringer, F. (1993a, April 15). Sex survey of American men finds 1% are gay. *New York Times,* p. Al.

Barringer, F. (1993b, April 25). Polling on sexual issues has its drawbacks. *New York Times,* p. L23.

Bates, T. D. (1992, October 9). Paying for values: The real needs of real families. *Commonweal,* 6-7.

Bickelhaupt, E. E. (1995). Alcoholism and drug abuse in gay and lesbian persons: A review of incidence studies. *Journal of Gay and Lesbian Social Services, 2,* 5-14.

Bliss, G. K., & Harris, M. B. (1999). Teachers' views of students with gay or lesbian parents. *Journal of Gay, Lesbian, and Bisexual Identity, 4,* 149-71.

Blumenfeld, W., & Raymond, D. (1992). *Looking at gay and lesbian life.* Boston: Beacon Press.

Boodman, S. G. (1998, March 3). Gay teen boys likelier to commit suicide. *Washington,* p. Z5.

Breslau, K. (1992, August 3). The push for national purity. *Newsweek,* 36-7.

Bureau of Labor Statistics. (1999a). Employment characteristics of families in 1998. http://stats.bls.gov/news.release/famee.nws.htm.

Bureau of Labor Statistics. (1999b). Families by presence and relationship of employed members and family type, 1997-98 annual averages. *Labor force statistics from the current population survey.* http://stats.bls.gov/news.release/famee.t02.htm.

Celis, W. (1993, January 6). Schools across U.S. cautiously adding lessons on gay life. *New York Times,* p. A18.

Doherty, W. J. (1992, May/June). Private lives, public values: The future of the family. *Psychology Today, 25,* 32-37.

Folliard, P. (1999, April 16). Love letters: Historian looks at a first lady and the most important person in her life. *Washington Blade,* pp. 39-40.

Freiberg, P. (1998, December 4). Gay hate crimes rise 8 percent: Annual FBI statistics document 1,102 incidents nationwide. *Washington Blade.*

Freiberg, P. (1999, February 26). Study finds lesbian parents as good as straights: Researchers say sharing partnering duties allows more time to spend with children. *Washington Blade.*

Friedan, B. (1963). *The feminist mystique.* New York: Norton.

Garofalo, R., et al. (1999). Sexual orientation and risk of suicide attempts among a representative sample of youth. *Archives of Pediatric and Adolescent Medicine, 153,* 487-93.

Gay and Lesbian Alliance Against Defamation. (1997). '97 Television lineup includes record number of "out" characters: 23% increase in gay characters over last season. http://www.glaad.org/glaad/press/970813.html.

Gay, Lesbian and Straight Education Network. (1999a, June 6). GLSEN expresses disappointment over loss of California's AB 222. News release. http://www.glsen.org/pages/sections/ library/news/9906-1.article.

Gay, Lesbian and Straight Education Network. (1999b). What's it like to be young and gay in American schools today? http://www.glsen.org/pages/sections/library/reference/014.article.

Goleman, D. (1992, December 2). Gay parents called no disadvantage. *New York Times,* p. C3.

Herek, G., & Berrill, K. (1992). *Hate crimes: Confronting violence against lesbians and gay men.* Newbury Park, CA: Sage Publications.

Keen, L. (1993, March 5). Study finds 20% report same-sex experiences. *Washington Blade,* pp. 1, 23.

Kinsey, A., Pomeroy, W. B., & Martin, C. E. (1948). *Sexual behavior in the human male.* Philadelphia: W. B. Saunders.

Kinsey, A., Pomeroy, W. B., Martin, C. E., & Gebhard, R. H. (1953). *Sexual behavior in the human female.* Philadelphia: W. B. Saunders.

Lacayo, R. (1992, December 14). Jack and Jack and Jill and Jill. *Time,* 52-53.

Lane, C., & Breslau, K. (1992, December 7). Germany's furies. *Newsweek,* 30-32.

Lief, L. (1992, July 27). Europe's trail of tears: 'Ethnic cleansing' threatens to unleash another holocaust. *U. S. News & World Report,* 41-43.

Magnet, M. (1992, August 10). The American family, 1992. *Fortune,* 42-47.

Massachusetts Governor's Commission on Gay and Lesbian Youth. (1997). Mission and history. http://www.magnet.state.ma.us/gcgly/mssn.htm.

Meyer, L. (1999, May 25). The hidden hate epidemic: Violence against the transgendered is widespread, brutal—and often unnoticed. *Advocate,* pp. 61-63.

National Center for Health Statistics. (1995, March 22). Divorces and annulments and rates: United States, 1940-90. *Monthly Vital Statistics Report,* p. 9. http://www.cdc.gov/nchswww/fastats/divorce.htm.

National Center for Health Statistics. (1998, October 7). *National Vital Statistics Report,* p. 15. http://www.cdc.gov/nchswww/fastats/pdf/47_4t6.pdf.

Ness, C. (1998, August 15). Survey: Alarming rate of anti-gay violence. *San Francisco Examiner.* http://www.examiner.com/980816/0816antigay.shtml#top.

Patterson, C. J. (1995). Lesbian mothers, gay fathers, and their children. In A. R. D'Augelli & C. J. Patterson (Eds.), *Lesbian, gay, and bisexual identities over the lifespan: Psychological perspectives* (pp. 262-90). New York: Oxford.

Rankin, S. (1999). Queering campus: Understanding and transforming climate. *Metropolitan Universities: An International Forum, 9,* 29-38.

Ribadeneira, D. (1992, December 13). Gay, lesbian students live with harassment. *Boston Globe,* p. 49.

Roundy, B. (1999, May 28). Nevada passes civil rights law: State poised to be 11th to ban sexual orientation bias. *Washington Blade,* pp. 1, 29.

Schmalz, J. (1993, April 16). Survey stirs debate on number of gay men in U.S. *New York Times,* p. A20.

Shapiro, J. P. (1993, July 5). Straight talk about gays. *U. S. News & World Report,* 42-48.

Sun, L. H. (1998, July 20). As gay students come out, abuse comes in: Changing attitudes, new laws push ambivalent schools to confront harassment. *Washington Post,* p. A8.

Tavris, C., & Wade, C. (1984). *The longest war: Sex differences in perspective.* Chicago: Harcourt Brace Jovanovich.

Tucker, W. (1993, February). Revolt in Queens. *The American Spectator,* 26-31.

Uribe, V., & Harbeck, K. M. (1992, October). Project 10 addresses needs of gay and lesbian youth. *The Education Digest,* 50-54.

U.S. Department of Health & Human Services (1989). Report of the Secretary's Task Force on Youth Suicide. Washington, DC: Public Health Service, Alcohol, Drug Abuse, and Mental Health Administration.

Vobejda, B. (1998, May 28). Traditional families hold on: Statistics show a slackening of 1970s, '80s social trends. *Washington Post,* p. A2.

Wallis, C. (1992, Fall). The nuclear family goes boom. *Time,* 42-44.

White, B. (1992, October 16). Advisory panel urges Ga. schools to broaden definition of a family. *Atlanta Constitution,* p. D2.

Wright, K. (1999, May 28). Couples win in Canada: Ruling expected to change laws that exclude gays. *Washington Blade,* pp. 1, 12.

Yang, A. S. (1997). The polls—trends: Attitudes toward homosexuality. *Public Opinion Quarterly. 61,* 477-507.

Yang, A. S. (1998). *From wrongs to rights: Public opinion on gay and lesbian Americans moves toward equality.* Washington, DC: National Gay and Lesbian Task Force Policy Institute.

Younger, J. (1999). Academic programs and opportunities for LGB study in the U.S. and Canada. http://www.duke.edu/web/jyounger/lgbprogs.html.

THE MICROCULTURE OF DISABILITY

by
Jacqueline C. Rickman

Freak shows are not about isolated individuals, either on platforms or in an audience. They are about organizations and patterned relationships between them and us. "Freak" is not a quality that belongs to the person on display. It is something that we created: a perspective, a set of practices—a social construction.

(Bogdan, 1988, p. x)

Higher education has a unique opportunity to assume a leadership position in the preparation of a generation of citizens with disabilities who have positive images of themselves and who are socially engaged, rather than socially estranged. To accomplish this task, postsecondary institutions must recognize the characteristics of students with disabilities as well as the level of disability stereotypes and misconceptions operating on campus. They must assume responsibility for meeting the needs of students with disabilities and for countering the stereotypes and misconceptions. Increasingly, postsecondary educators and administrators are assuming that responsibility; they are learning to respond resourcefully to a growing demand that the needs of students with disabilities be met and that they be helped in their efforts to develop positive self images and become socially engaged citizens.

Characteristics of Postsecondary Students with Disabilities

At present, approximately 10% of students enrolled in U.S. institutions of higher education report that they have a disability. The microculture of disability is comprised of subcultures consisting of specific disabilities such as hearing impairment. Within each subculture are further subsets such as the totally deaf and the partially deaf. Individuals within these subsets reflect a great variety of medical diagnoses and are representative of the population at large in their heterogeneity.

Four major disability subcultures and five onset categories exist in postsecondary institutions. The most common disability subcultures and their subsets include: 1) learning disabilities (perceptual, perceptual-motor, and general coordination problems, disorders of attention and hyperactivity, disorders of memory and thinking, language disorders), 2) physical disabilities and other health impairments (neurological impairments, musculoskeletal and chronic medical conditions), 3) visual disabilities (totally blind, partially sighted), and 4) hearing impairments (totally deaf, partially deaf). Onset categories include: a) special education early onset, b) special education adventitious onset, c) recently diagnosed, d) self referral, and e) other referral. These categories can be differentiated further depending on whether the conditions are permanent or uncertain and degenerative.

Although it would be illogical to assume that all students with disabilities have the same levels of independence and productivity or that they have identical needs for adaptations and services, all share the experience of interacting on a regular basis with social stigmas based on inaccurate assumptions and ambivalence. At present, many drop out of college, and those who stay perceive themselves in a distinct marginal status with inequitable access to programs and services.

Reported stigmatic reactions from nondisabled faculty and peers have included: discomfort, admiration, patronizing or pitying attitudes, avoidance, fear, an assumption of low intelligence, an assumption of talent, treatment like that of a child, an assumption that all members of a disability subculture are alike, a public disclosure of special accommodations needed, and simply ignoring the situation. Most students practice self-advocacy and do not expect preferential treatment; most want faculty to ask about their disability and to collaborate with them for appropriate environmental and academic accommodations. Their expectations parallel those of their collegiate peers. They expect their postsecondary experience to provide them with the tools to achieve rewarding, productive, and integrated adult lives. They expect the institution to respect them and to be sensitive to their beliefs and experiences. I would like to examine the sources of disability stereotypes before discussing current stereotypes and misconceptions about postsecondary students with disabilities and then suggesting ways educators can help meet their needs.

A Chronology of Evolving Disability Stereotypes

In his book, *Freak Show: Presenting Human Oddities for Amusement and Profit*, Robert Bogdan (1988) suggests that "whenever we study deviance, we must look at who are in charge—whether self-appointed or officially—of telling us who the deviant people are and what they are like" (p. 279). Through the years, those who have been in charge of people with disabilities as well as the media have misunderstood, incorrectly categorized, and stigmatized individuals within the microculture of disability. Bogdan's pioneering text explores and evaluates the gradual evolution of those who were in charge of people we would identify today as having disabilities—from the managers, promoters, and audiences of "freak shows," through the administrators of professional organizations and charities, to medical practitioners, to present-day professionals and human service providers.

Freak Shows (circa 1840-1940)

Barbara Baskin sought to ban freak shows from the New York State Fair in 1939 contending that they were to disabled people as *Amos 'n Andy* was to African Americans and as the striptease show was to women (Bogdan, 1988). In the carnival culture, people with differences were seen as valuable presentations; indeed, their abnormalities and human variations translated into meal tickets and security. As exhibits, these individuals were part of the public domain. They were presented in two unique modes to their audiences: the exotic mode that exploited the public's curiosity about the unusual or sensational and the aggrandized mode that capitalized on the public's need for superior status and power.

The exotic mode was rooted in racism, imperialism, and handicapism. It presented people with disabilities as human curiosities—specimens to be feared and held in contempt. As exhibits, they were the devalued victims of institutionalized discrimination, hopelessly stigmatized and devoid of human dignity. Paradoxically, Bogdan's research revealed that these marginal citizens thought of themselves as having high status and as very elite carnival insiders who arrogantly viewed their audiences with disdain and contempt.

The aggrandized mode exploited the exhibits, that is the persons on display, as mere objects in a tainted amusement world. In doing so, it capitalized on the audience's need to maintain a sense of superior status and power. It contended that people with disabilities were not competent enough to be part of society. They were to be excluded and kept with their own kind. The most insidious features of this mode were the underlying contentions that exhibits were not capable of achieving, and that normal accomplishments by people with disabilities were to be flaunted as extraordinary. The aggrandized mode thereby served as the foundation for the perceptions of not only **Jerry Lewis's pitiful poster child**, the indigent **idiot**, and the blind **beggar**, but also the disabled **wonder-kid**, the **amazing crippled prodigy**, and the blind **genius**. All of these images were manufactured when audiences determined that people with disabilities were exhibits who were amusing, but tainted, incompetent, disgusting, and ultimately unworthy of inclusion in the larger world.

The Medical Establishment and Charities (circa 1940s-1960s)

A later conception of disability was basically **pathological** in that people with disabilities were seen as **patients**. Several premises were operant within this philosophy. They were: (1) people with disabilities could be treated and possibly cured; (2) people with disabilities were to be secluded from the public; and (3) people with disabilities were to be feared, and in many cases locked away to protect the **normal** citizenry from danger. The trend was followed by the emergence of organized charities, professional fund raisers, and poster children. It is likely that freak shows are perceived as repulsive today because members of society, including many with disabilities themselves, have embraced the pathological disabled imagery of pity as an artifact of the medical establishment's monopoly over the presentation of people with disabilities.

Freedom Movements: Rehabilitation Reform (circa 1960s-1970s)

Beatrice Wright (1960) was a pioneer in the provision of counseling and rehabilitation services for people with disabilities. Her mentor was Carl Rogers, who emphasized the importance of investigating the perspective of individuals with disabilities, of valuing what they were saying about their experiences. Her sensitization developed into an awareness of and objection to the presence of gross societal distortions and misconceptions about this population. Wright observed the medical establishment's presentation of people with disabilities as pathological cases and formulated the "fundamental negative bias" as a powerful source of prejudice that steers perception, thought, and feeling along negative lines to such a degree positives remain hidden. She reports that one's perception, thinking, and feeling regarding deviance will be negative if three conditions for the functioning of the fundamental negative bias are met. These conditions are saliency (what is observed stands out sufficiently), value (it is regarded as negative), and context (it is vague or sparse). Her view appears to be based on an integration of Heider's (1958) balance theory of sentiments and Sherif, Sherif, and Nebergall's (1965) social judgment theory. This theoretic combination suggests that when similarity with the self is perceived, the similarity will be exaggerated and liking and belonging will be induced; when differences are perceived, however, the dissimilarity will be exaggerated, resulting in a host of complex rejection reactions Dembo, Wright, and Leviton (1975) identify as negative spread effects.

Perhaps an indication of these negative spread effects can be found in Zimbardo and Ebberson's (1970) observation that "the United States has spent millions of dollars on unsuccessful information campaigns to correct stereotypes about minority groups, to present the facts, and to help people get to know one another" (p. 101). Though U.S. universities were becoming beacons of protest against structural exclusion during the 1960s and 1970s, the fundamental negative bias against people who differed from the norm was too strong to overthrow, as evidenced in the spread effects of bigoted and prejudicial attitudes held by many postsecondary personnel and students. Many with disabilities were denied admission; those who were admitted were perceived as dependent, unattractive, and not eligible for special services or adaptations.

Unawareness and Ambivalence as Sources of Negative Attitudes Toward Persons with Disabilities (circa 1980s)

During the 1980s, researchers began to report that the origins of conscious and unconscious negative attitudes toward disability range from full awareness to total unawareness. They emphasized that unawareness, or mindlessness, was the overwhelming determinant of negative societal attitude formation (Livneh, 1988; Langer & Chanowitz, 1988). At postsecondary institutions, an increase in mindfulness about the situations of students with disabilities was noted in females, younger personnel, faculty at institutions with disability service programs, faculty within education and the social sciences, and in faculty with previous extended contact with students with disabilities (Fonosch & Schwab, 1981; Yuker, 1987; Amsel & Fichten, 1990). Less supportive attitudes were held toward students with learning disabilities and socioemotional problems than for those with hearing, visual, or physical disabilities (Leyser, 1989).

In contrast, other findings during the 1980s discounted the notion of discriminatory practices based on a fundamental negative bias in favor of ambivalence. Ambivalence is best described as confusion about enduring cultural myths derived from freak show, medical, and rehabilitation images. Among those myths is the idea that disability and mainstream cultures exist without conflict within a harmonious world family, its Woodstock imagery reinforcing the false belief that interactions between members of mainstream and marginal cultural groups are easy. Ambivalence results when normal interpersonal discomfort and miscommunication occur, as they most certainly will, and mainstream individuals revive other myths that suggest persons with disabilities are eccentric (according to Bogdan's exotic mode) or inferior (as in Bogdan's aggrandized mode).

Sources of Stigma Identified by Consumers with Disabilities (1980s-present)

In the late 1980s and early 1990s, the seeds of Wright's client-centered emphasis began to blossom. Consumers with disabilities themselves began to speak on their own behalf. They presented intriguing arguments such as the idea that even a focus on disabled superstars, which implies more respect for disabled persons' accomplishments, can be a prejudicial reaction rather than a recognition of the person as an individual (Yuker, 1987). In contrast, protests against current counseling practices were illustrated in Kalter's (1991) caution against the treatment of disability exclusively as a drama of personal adjustment with no social context since the consequence would be the reduction of the issue to one of individual character and courage rather than of societal stigma and discrimination.

Legislation such as the 1990 Americans with Disabilities Act (ADA) has increased environmental and academic accessibility in both public and private postsecondary institutions and has enhanced employment opportunities for people with disabilities. However, negative attitudes towards students with disabilities on the part of faculty, administrators, and peers remains a challenging enigma. Unfortunately, current investigations have revealed that nondisabled students attributed fewer socially desirable and more undesirable traits to students with disabilities than to their nondisabled peers (Fichten & Bourdan, 1986). In fact, circumplex scales that tested for sameness and difference disclosed that the perception of traits of students with disabilities and their nondisabled peers were clearly opposite. Persons with disabilities were characterized as aloof-introverted, lazy-submissive, and unassuming-ingenuous, while nondisabled persons were seen to be more gregarious-extroverted, ambitious-dominant, and arrogant-calculating (Fichten & Amsel, 1986).

The microculture of persons with disabilities perceives social isolation and underparticipation in campus life as common and all-encompassing problems (Hanna & Rogovsky, 1991; Oakes, 1990; Jenkins, Amos, & Graham, 1988). A hypothesized cause for this exclusion can likely be found within the intersection of self-concept and a sociocultural system that encompasses the attitudinal barriers of apathy, paternalism, fear, curiosity, stereotyping, need for stability, and focus on disabled superstars (Pati & Atkins, 1981; Levi, 1975; Lenhart, 1976/1977). Low self-esteem resulting in social isolation as well as gross societal misconceptions and deep-seated discrimination must be addressed.

Assuming Responsibility for Meeting the Needs of Students with Disabilities

Higher education administrators, faculty, and staff must take responsibility to insure awareness and communication between nondisabled and disabled students and between university personnel and students with disabilities. Programming to counteract negative stereotypes and misconceptions can help. Fragmented and destructive interactions will continue, however, without vigorous and consistent upper administrative support. At the grass-roots level, formal in-services and workshops will be exercises in futility unless every participant believes he or she can be a change agent with the individual and collective power to make a difference. Fortunately, the higher education community has a history of solving problems, and student interest in social values is growing (Astin, 1991; Fichten & Bourdon, 1986; McLoughlin, 1982).

Higher Education Administrators, Faculty, and Staff

Disability awareness is now the responsibility of professionals in postsecondary settings who enjoy easy access to "a broad and rich literature on the lived experience of persons with disabilities, attitudes toward disability, stigma and discrimination, the disability rights movement, and laws and public policies affecting citizens with disabilities" (Hahn, 1991, p. 18). They are privy to action research from sociological, historical, philosophical, psychological, legal, educational, and scientific perspectives. But are universities willing to develop solutions to the marginal status of their students with disabilities? The facilitation of such opportunities means the surrender of the comforts of tradition and prejudice to close analysis, systematic evaluation, collaborative research efforts, and creative innovations (Feldman & Newcomb, 1969).

Campuswide assessment of needs and problems is the first priority. Recommended mechanisms are town meetings, surveys, interviews, and other interpersonal strategies designed to gather information from as many stakeholders as possible. Yuker's Attitudes Toward Disabled Persons Scale (ATDP) (see Yuker & Block, 1986) is one example of a survey that has been used effectively to reveal the level of disability stereotypes held in specific institutional contexts. Demographics should be investigated for retention rates and resiliency factors related to successful completion of studies on the part of students with disabilities. Former students should be surveyed for information on what worked for them. Myers' (1994) investigation, designed to reveal communication patterns and preferences of college students with visual disabilities, offers an excellent research base for a parallel inquiry.

The next priority is the generation of strategies to counteract the campus community's identified miscommunication patterns and misconceptions. Implicit in such counteraction is the need to adjust and refocus attitudes at every level: student workers, receptionists, custodial staff, faculty, and administrators, as the following case study illustrates.

Donna was a first-year student with learning disabilities (LDs) enrolled at an eastern university with a well known disability support service program. The legal documentation of her condition with an explanation of prescribed adaptations had been sent to her professors. She had forgotten to attend the orientation meeting for new students with disabilities, so she did not know the procedures for accessing accommodations. Her specific learning deficit, like that of the majority of adults with LDs, was in written language and necessitated a word processor with a spell check for written assignments and exams. She affirmed this need with each of her professors, including the one she had for U.S. history. He verbally agreed to allow her to take his essay exams using a word processor at the disability service center. On the day of the first exam, a graduate student was filling in for the professor. Nervously, Donna explained her circumstances to him and he reluctantly gave her a copy of the exam and excused her.

When she arrived at the disability service center, she asked the receptionist for directions to the word processors explaining she had to take an exam. The receptionist scolded her for not having faculty authorization to take the test under special circumstances. The student attempted to protest but the receptionist threw a faculty authorization form at her, frowned, and went back to his typing. The student meekly trekked back to get the required signature. The graduate student, however, was confused and unsure of what to do and ended up refusing to sign, stating he hadn't been given the authority. He suggested she return to the disability service center. When she arrived at that office, the clerk was on the phone and chose not to acknowledge her presence. She broke into tears, dropped the exam, and fled. When she returned to class the next week, the professor refused to give her a makeup exam. She dropped out shortly thereafter.

The smugness of one clerk, the lack of concern of a faculty member, the ignorance and confusion of a graduate student, forgetfulness, and inadequate procedural communication between a student and disability service personnel were combined factors culminating in one student's failure to make it through the maze of higher education. Could these causative variables have been avoided? Are proactive strategies possible for counteracting negative stereotypes and discriminatory interactions? I believe so.

Receptionists and Other Front-Desk Personnel

Anti-discriminatory procedural safeguards need to be built into job descriptions and monitored and evaluated on a regular basis. Because of their highly visible interactive positions, receptionists and other front-desk personnel merit extensive training in how to guide and direct students who may not do things the way they do. To practice creative resourcefulness and sensitive responsiveness, they would ideally possess flexibility, interest in problem solving and networking, and openness to new strategies for meeting students' needs. It is absolutely critical their success be acknowledged and rewarded by superiors to generate respect for themselves and those they were hired to serve. If the first priority of the receptionist Donna met was the student, an alternative scenario would have included his timely and undivided attention to her specific problem. While Donna did not fulfill her own responsibilities to learn and follow through on test-taking procedures, her unawareness did not warrant the treatment she encountered.

Faculty and Graduate Assistants

While large scale institutional reform is underway, specific changes can be made by faculty that will make a major impact on students. Attention needs to be given to the way language, environment, and course methodology perpetuate myths. Language in course descriptions and lectures must not isolate people who are not in the mainstream. Consider, for example, the following course description for an introductory U.S. history course:

. . . investigate the great heterogeneity of the population in the U.S. in the 1960s, from powerful citizens like those in positions of medicine, politics, and business to the disabled and infirm who struggled in less fortunate situations.

Discussing those in successful positions and those who were struggling without considering the impact each had on the other is aggrandizing behavior. Those who struggled did not suffer oppression in isolation; those who succeeded did not acquire power through natural giftedness and physical inheritance. We need to talk about the balance sheet—to note that social disadvantage not only limited some individuals, it also enhanced the self-esteem and opportunities of others.

Like language, environment can help or hinder the interaction among students with disabilities and those without. According to Sherif, Sherif, and Nebergall (1965), students are likely to sit and socialize with those who most resemble them. By changing the seating arrangement purposefully and often, faculty can build in opportunities for a variety of interactions that provide extended contact among nondisabled students and students with disabilities and opportunities for them to learn from each other. Carefully facilitated classroom interactions may have afforded Donna a more focused and proactive test-taking action path.

Recommended course adaptations to access individual abilities (versus deficits) fall into two categories: methods utilized to disseminate course content and methods used to measure subject mastery. The case of an educator at a large Midwestern university illustrates both.

The faculty member observed nonverbal reactions to the peer-tutoring method she routinely used in her political science course. Students who achieved mastery over specific content were paired up to drill those who were struggling. She saw an attitude of superiority developing in the tutors and a concurrent lack of confidence and helplessness in those being tutored, many of whom were students with learning disabilities. It became apparent the tutors perceived themselves as solutions to the "problem" of inept students.

Because grouping for the learning of rote facts and principles was the only type of peer tutoring within her course, the industry of the tutors, who were very capable in the sequential organization of information, was operationalized at the expense of the academic identity of the tutorees whose ordering tendencies were less linear. She did not consider the tutorees incapable of the work, having observed their streaks of brilliance in class discussions and their creativity in problem solving and relating real-life case studies. She also noted untapped abilities in role playing, technological aptitude, critiquing films and readings, debate, research, interviewing, mediation, and oral presentations. Once aware of this, she began using a variety of creative pairings and team work to recognize and exercise the strengths of all the students.

Similarly, to level the playing field of evaluation, faculty who always use timed, computer-scored, multiple-choice tests may want to add alternate evaluative formats. The heterogeneity of students' learning styles are responsive to taped, project, portfolio, self-paced, developmental, collaborative, computer assisted, oral, short answer, and untimed assessments. These types of course adjustments do not necessitate additional cost or extreme revisions in planning or teaching style for most faculty, yet they benefit all students, not just those with disabilities.

Disability Support Service Personnel

The directive to disability support administrators is clear. While one might expect them to be directly responsible for programs counteracting identified miscommunication among students, faculty, administration, and staff, it must be stated it is no easy task to combat rampant negative bias, arrogance, mindlessness, ambivalence, and delivery system breakdowns. In order to implement effective interventions, collaboration with students with disabilities and representatives from all campus departments and services is imperative.

The content of disability awareness interventions should be innovative and include: a) the college's legal responsibilities, b) characteristics of disabilities, c) methods of providing reasonable architectural and academic adaptations, and d) ways to gain and maintain productive communication and collaboration. They should contain clearly defined short- and long-term anticipated outcomes to be used for formative evaluation. Additionally, a chorus of researchers recommends campus interventions that attend to the credibility of the presenter. Successful attitude modifying in-services have included talk show, panel discussion, and interview formats featuring qualified students with disabilities, expert speakers from off-campus sites, and university personnel who have effectively collaborated with students to achieve productive academic and physical accommodations (Gerber, 1990; Wright, 1988; Yuker & Block, 1986; Cortez, 1983; Pomerantz, 1983; Donaldson & Martinson, 1977; Dembo, 1970).

Summary

Assessing campuswide needs and problems, building in procedural safeguards, and recommending changes are the first steps toward the successful inclusion of students with disabilities within the campus community. Subsequently, campuswide programming must be designed as a direct response to identified institutional exclusion since every communication, environmental, and attitudinal barrier has a critical effect on students with disabilities. It is only when we gain a comprehension of the inherent challenges in our interactions with students with disabilities that we can engage in the construction of images of disability that dismantle the shameful and destructive freak show and pathological patterns. Bogdan (1988) has identified and contributed to the growth and success of all our students in his imperative to move beyond appearances, first impressions, stereotypes, and misconceptions to get to know our students, not as they have been presented but as they **are**.

References

Amsel, R., & Fichten, C. S., (1990). Interaction between disabled and nondisabled college students and their professors: A comparison. *Journal of Postsecondary Education and Disability, 8,* 125-140.

Astin, A. (1991). The changing American college student: Implications for educational policy and practice. *Higher Education, 22*(2), 129-144).

Bogdan, R. (1988). *Freak show: Presenting human oddities for amusement and profit.* Chicago: University of Chicago Press.

Cortez, D. M. (1983). A study of the effects of an in-service program for postsecondary faculty on mainstreaming handicapped students (Doctoral dissertation, New Mexico State University, 1983). *Dissertation Abstracts International, 39,* 2865 A.

Dembo, T. (1970). The utilization of psychological knowledge in rehabilitation. *Welfare Review, 8,* 1-7.

Dembo, T., Leviton, G. L., & Wright, B. (1975). Adjustment to misfortune: A problem of social and psychological rehabilitation. *Artificial Limbs, 3,* 4-62. (Original work published 1956)

Donaldson, J., & Martinson, M. C. (1977). Modifying attitudes toward physically disabled persons. *Exceptional Children, 43,* 337-341.

Feldman, K. A. (1972), & Newcomb, T. M. (1969). *The impact of college on students.* San Francisco: Jossey-Bass.

Fichten, C. S., & Amsel, R. (1986). Trait attributions about college students with a physical disability: Circumplex analyses and methodological issues. *Journal of Applied Social Psychology, 16*(5), 410-427.

Fichten, C. S., & Bourdon, C. V. (1986). Social skill deficit or response inhibition: Interaction between disabled and nondisabled college students. *Journal of College Student Personnel, 27,* 326-333.

Fonosch, G. G., & Schwab, L. O. (1981). Attitudes of selected university faculty members toward disabled students. *Journal of College Student Personnel, 22,* 229-235.

Gerber, D. A. (1990). Listening to disabled people: The problem of voice and authority in Robert Edgerton's *The cloak of competence. Disability, Handicap, and Society, 5*(1), 3-23.

Hahn, H. (1991). Alternative views of empowerment: Social services and civil rights. *Journal of Rehabilitation, 57*(4), 18-20.

Hanna, W. J., & Rogovsky, B. (1991). Women with disabilities: Two handicaps plus. *Disability, Handicap, and Society, 6*(1), 49-63.

Heider, R. (1958). *The psychology of interpersonal relations.* New York: Wiley.

Jenkins, C., Amos, O., & Graham, G. (1988). Do black and white college students with disabilities see their worlds differently? *Journal of Rehabilitation, 54*(4), 71-76.

Kalter, J. (1991). Good news: The disabled get more play on T. V. Bad news: There is still too much stereotyping. In E. Lessen (Ed.), *Exceptional persons in society* (pp. 55-6). Needham, MA: Ginn.

Langer, A. L., & Chanowitz, B. (1988). Mindfulness/mindlessness: A new perspective for the study of disability. In A. Yuker (Ed.), *Attitudes toward persons with disabilities* (pp. 69-81). New York: Springer.

Lenhart, L. C. (1977). The stigma of disability (Doctoral dissertation, The University of Oklahoma Health Services Center, 1976). *Dissertation Abstracts International, 37,* 5439B.

Levi, V. (1975). *Disabled persons; attitudes formation and the effect of the environment: An experimental research.* Unpublished manuscript, York University, Toronto.

Leyser, Y. (1989). A survey of faculty attitudes and accommodations for students with disabilities. *Journal of Postsecondary Education and Disability, 7,* 97-108.

Livneh, H. (1988). A dimensional perspective on the origin of negative attitudes toward persons with disabilities. In A. Yuker, (Ed.), *Attitudes toward persons with disabilities* (pp. 35-47). New York: Springer.

McLoughlin, W. P. (1982). Helping the physically disabled in higher education. *Journal of College Student Personnel, 23,* 240-246.

Myers, K. (1994). *Preferences of communication styles and techniques of persons with visible visual disabilities: Implications for higher education.* (Doctoral dissertation submitted for publication, Illinois State University, 1994).

Oakes, J. (1990). *Lost talent: The underparticipation of women, minorities, and disabled persons in science.* Santa Monica, CA: Rand.

Pati, G., & Atkins, J. (1981). *Managing and employing the handicapped: An untapped potential.* Chicago: Brace & Jovanovich, Human Resource Press.

Pomerantz, R. M. (1983). *The effectiveness of training modules designed to improve the attitudes of college faculty toward students with disabilities: An evaluation study* (Doctoral dissertation, Temple University, 1983). *Dissertation Abstracts International, 44,* 1604B.

Sherif, C. W., Sherif, M., & Nebergall, R. E. (1965). *Attitude and attitude change: The social judgment-involvement approach.* Philadelphia: Saunders.

Wright, B. A. (1960). *Physical disability—A psychological approach.* New York: Harper & Row.

Wright, B. A. (1988). Attitudes and the fundamental negative bias. In A. Yuker (Ed.), *Attitudes toward persons with disabilities* (pp. 3-21). New York: Springer.

Yuker, H. (1987). Labels can hurt people with disabilities. *Et Cetera, 44*(1), 16-22.

Yuker, H., & Block, J. R. (1986). *Research with the attitudes toward disabled persons scales (1960-1965).* Hempstead, NY: Hofstra University, Center for the Study of Attitudes Toward Persons with Disabilities.

Yuker, H. E. (1988). *Attitudes toward persons with disabilities.* New York: Springer.

Zimbardo, P. G., & Ebberson, E. (1970). *Influencing attitudes and changing behavior.* Reading, MA: Addison-Wesley.

USING HUMOR TO PROMOTE
MULTICULTURAL UNDERSTANDING

by
Samuel Betances

As keynoter, workshop leader, teacher, and guide on issues related to diversity and multi-cultural concerns I have been approached with increasing frequency by people who have participated in one or more of my presentations and found them both engaging and enter-taining. They earnestly desire to do what I do: engage an audience through humor while discussing critical issues. My effective use of humor creates bonds among workshop partic-ipants, audience members, and students and helps release tension, making humor an essential tool in the consciousness raising that is my goal.

What follows is a series of reflections and suggestions about humor that provide both a philosophy and a point of view teachers and presenters can use in promoting collaboration among diverse groups. Since my quest is to educate and to promote critical thinking through the use of humor, I like to think of myself as an "edutainer." What makes the performance of an "edutainer" memorable and significant has to do with both the nature of a diverse society and the process of teaching itself. The burning and controversial issues of diversity cannot be discussed, presented, or analyzed unless students are fully attentive, but competing for students' attention in our technological media age is very demanding.

No matter how poor or humble the origins of a student may be or how lacking in resources a rural or urban sector may be, our students have an awareness of what quality is in the world of highly polished, technically sophisticated media performances. Competition for their attention by advertising, general entertainment, news broadcasting, and cultural events has familiarized them with an array of mind-grabbing techniques and frequently left them with little patience for carefully paced, logically developed formal expository lectures. Students quickly distinguish a boring presentation from a lively one. However, as educators we are not likely to have access to the media techniques familiar to students weaned on HBO, sitcoms, sports broadcasting, MTV, soap operas, CNN, the Discovery Channel, Nintendo games, and rock concerts. To capture and hold our students' interest we need look for other tools. One of the most powerful I have found is humor. The effective use of humor contributes to good communication and to understanding. It can help us make our society safe for differences.

I am not suggesting we become comedians or buffoons and make a mockery of our profession or trivialize serious subject matter. Rather, I am suggesting that we as profes-sionals learn to pay attention to how we present ourselves, that we exhibit a profound respect for our students by bringing them into the learning process through experiences that make us human. We are, after all, more similar than different and nowhere is that more likely to be exhibited than in our common human—and frequently humorous— experiences.

I've learned to poke fun at myself about issues related to my body, social identity, gender relationships, absurd assumptions and fears, and how I have grown and unlearned bad lessons while learning new good ones. I walk my students through my own personal journey to understanding, and I have fun while I do it. Powerful personal lessons can make a message memorable and motivate students to want to hear more. Entering into a dialogue with them about my personal struggles while respecting myself enough to reject rejection allows me to guide them to discover better ways of avoiding their own potential pitfalls. Accomplishing this with humor both catches their attention and encourages them to remember the lessons.

Through humor we can recognize our collective human experiences and can share, in a spirit of respect and fun, the insights born out of each other's social realities. Laughter creates bonds through which students and teachers agree to suspend certain rules of authoritative behavior that may prevent trust and real learning from taking place. Often students have the idea that abstract knowledge or information learned in a classroom cannot be useful in their world. Humor based on the teacher's experiences can convince them otherwise. When a teacher uses humor in the classroom, especially when sharing personal stories to illustrate points, students learn very quickly that their instructor is a "real" person who trusts them with personal information and who does not reside in an unattainable or irrelevant "ivory tower."

My sense is that John Dewey was correct in arguing that one cannot become a great teacher unless the abstract and theoretical lessons being taught are connected by illustrations to the concrete experiences of students. Whether we begin with their experiences or our own to achieve this, we are likely to find humor in the telling appropriate and satisfying. By knowing very well what is going on in the lives of students, we can bring their experiences to the classroom and integrate them into our presentations in a humorous fashion so students not only understand and relate to what is being taught but relate to us as well. Successful comedians, in touching on situations to which their audiences can relate, establish connections with them. The same principle applies in the classroom as shared humor increases teacher-student rapport. Accomplishing this, the journey into new areas of knowledge is made easier because of the attachment and trust established through laughter and common threads of experience.

Does learning **have** to be fun? Not always. Many of us learn our most important lessons in life at "Hard Knocks University." Through painful experiences we learn to avoid certain things and embrace others. But learning in the classroom can be fun. Certainly teaching can be. The challenge of teaching students in a diverse society is teaching important lessons about getting along with each other as individuals and as members of various groups: engaging human beings so they recognize their common humanity and identify with a collective "we." Reaching this experience of our shared humanity becomes more important than teaching facts and figures. We must think of ourselves more as teachers of human being than as experts in our field. From this perspective, humor is indispensable. It allows students to let down their guard in a spirit of family.

We cannot, of course, ignore facts and figures or overlook the ideas and critical thinking skills that will form the basis of students' understanding of our multicultural society. We cannot fulfill our intellectual duty of sharing new and important information or of stimulating our students to think, however, unless their minds are open and ready to engage the ideas and perspectives we offer them. I've learned that using humor in an intelligent and respectful way is the key to bridging the chasm that often separates seemingly esoteric concepts from daily living.

I've read books on humor and comedy to learn to uncover the humor in situations. Used book stores have proven to be an invaluable resource for materials about humor, and the lives of great comics have enhanced my comedic repertoire. I've learned a lot about telling stories in an entertaining fashion and about the importance of timing and sequencing. I've also become aware of pitfalls to avoid. My teachers have included Steve Allen, Bill Cosby,

Joan Rivers, and Hal Roach. From Bill Cosby, for example, I learned to embrace the obvious lessons of day to day middle-class family life. Reading his *Fatherhood* sparked my memory of my family life in a barrio and uncovered the humor in many family situations. It prompted me to explore humor across socioeconomic classes and to incorporate my own family experiences into my presentations on the family. Studying Cosby's vision and humor expanded my vision and has led me to become a bit more pleasant, interesting, and entertaining in my teaching.

Because of his interest in education as well as entertainment, comedian Bill Cosby fits into the category of edutainer I suggested for teachers. Comedians who identify themselves exclusively or primarily as entertainers frame their messages and their insights into human experience to lead people to laughter and to establish their reputations as comics—sometimes with a reckless disregard for certain groups. Educators—edutainers—need to frame their knowledge of humanity in humor to lead students to understanding and to become great teachers, explicators of social reality and of the human spirit. And in the sensitive area of diversity, we must avoid being reckless with the reputation of any group. This does not, of course, mean that we can never refer to the ethnicity, gender, or other determinants of a group's identity. For example, my Puerto Rican heritage allows me to heighten consciousness of the media's use of scripts that recycle debilitating stereotypes of Puerto Ricans.

For instance, "The West Side Story could not have been written by a Puerto Rican," I tell my students.

Why?" they ask.

"Because you cannot call for María at three o'clock in the morning in a Puerto Rican neighborhood and have only one window open!"

The spontaneous laughter this elicits is partly inspired by the punch line and partly by my respect for timing and a careful attention to setup that allow me to push the students toward the unexpected finish and then lead them to a discussion about the scripts Hollywood uses to portray not only Puerto Ricans but also women, African Americans, or people who are librarians or "absent minded professors." Diversity discussions come out of the powerful illustration from my own heritage group without dumping on it. My real target is not even the media but the uncritical scripts and forces that have shaped our world view and may cause us to internalize limiting or destructive visions of ourselves or others. Humor helps dissolve the tensions associated with group conflict and the "isms"—such as racism and sexism—that prevent cohesion and collaboration in a diverse society.

As a professor of sociology, my greatest challenge is to motivate and teach students about classism. Sociologists identify that process in our lectures and readings as "stratification." As successful professionals we enjoy positions of relative security and comfort. Poverty is a concept very hard to comprehend in our status within the middle class or what many of our students identify as a sea of plenty. Using humor based on my personal life helps me utilize my present socioeconomic status to promote concepts of social justice and to make the transition between the abstract sociological literature and concrete examples more smoothly and clearly. As a former welfare child from a broken home and as a member of a stigmatized group, I could be very angry, and perhaps alienating, because of this background, but I choose instead to use humor to evoke the sympathy of my students, whatever their class background, and to help them recognize the abuses of higher socioeconomic classes against those in lower stratums of society.

"I was very poor," I share with them. My students' interest is sparked since I also attended Harvard University. "So poor, that once someone broke into our little apartment on the west side of Chicago and didn't take anything." Out of the smiles and chuckles that come out of the tale, come precious teaching moments as I explain how some victims of break ins feel very bad when they lose jewelry, a VCR, money, a camera, or other quick-sell items. "But real victims may very well be persons like those in my family on the day thieves broke in and did not take anything."

Powerful insights about the meanings of material things and how the criminal justice system operates in neighborhoods where some of us are often overpoliced but underprotected follow. Humor allows the students and instructors to share laughter and to create a "we" climate that promotes understanding. The tragic consequences of our inhumanity to each other can thus be countered or offset. Academicians from groups that have experienced oppression may be in a unique position to help students understand that oppression. But without humor, those lessons can be lost to a classroom of middle-class students bombarded with so much sober and serious criticism they feel they are the target of an inappropriate radical agenda.

Humor is the sugar that helps the medicine go down. Students will laugh at an experience, an event, or a story meant to be funny by those orchestrating, performing, or swapping tales to the degree that they are in humor. To be in humor requires a mind-set which is distant enough to the absurd situation described so as to be in fun. If a listener is too emotionally attached to the person or group that is the subject of humor, the listener will not be in fun and will view the experience as offensive, injurious, and debilitating. A similar response can be evoked by "going too far." Victimized by the situation, what is the person to do? Since the victim may not fully know how to protest, she/he may experience peer pressure at that moment and actually laugh and thereby cooperate in an inhumane, hostile encounter packaged in laughter.

Some circumstances make it impossible to be in humor. For example, one cannot be in fun about death while still in mourning. Promoters of healthy relationships cannot be in fun about child molestation, the tragic consequences of airplane crashes, or the ravages of an ongoing war. Women and men, having had an experience of sex as a powerful weapon of assault, may never be in humor about rape. Members of groups labeled minorities will not be in fun when they are set up by jokes that demean and debilitate them through stereotypes depicting them as worthless, criminal, dirty, stupid, lazy, drunken, cheap, or as sexual animals.

Respect for people with different life styles, who speak different languages and whose physical condition is not the same as that of the majority population, must never be undermined through dysfunctional humor. If a teacher is ever in doubt as to whether a "funny" situation might offend students, the rule is don't tell it. Sit on the urge. Better to miss out on some laughter and be inclusive and respectful than to alienate and cause injury in one's quest for a laugh. Every joke that recycles a stereotype about a group contributes to frustration and sets up barriers to collaboration, respect, and coalition building. The classroom must be freed from such oppression.

While I do not want to discourage the use of humor and laughter or teaching that incorporates jokes and humorous insights, I do want to prevent uncritical people from using such tools to cause injury. For example, ethnic jokes and the like can be weapons that assault the dignity of groups with little power to defend themselves. How often do people in public life, responding to criticism for telling ethnic jokes, explain that no harm was intended. Yet harm was done. By choosing affirming rather than debilitating humor, our efforts to educate and entertain simultaneously will be rewarded without sacrificing laughter and fun in the process.

Laughing with people of a certain interest group is very different from laughing at them. The real edutainers, who are committed to communicating diversity, can present insightful, entertaining presentations where laughter bonds, helps to release tension, and promotes understanding by exposing apparent contradictions not easily revealed or readily accepted when presented through a didactic lecture. The sugar of humor can indeed help make difficult truths palatable, but the humor must be a humor grounded in tolerance and respect. This is the opposite of a humor of intolerance and bigotry. Bigotry, whether by lynching or by laughing, is wrong.

We do not tolerate the extreme bigotry of physical assaults in our institutions, yet we still sometimes enjoy a joke at the expense of a socially defined "inferior" cultural group. At the core of the evil in the humor of intolerance is a philosophy, a mindset, that certain groups are less than human. Such groups, the popular culture says, do not deserve to be viewed with awe and respect. They can be ridiculed through laughter, through ethnic jokes. What gets packaged as ethnic humor in our society often promotes stereotypes and carica-tures that dehumanize. We recognize those stereotypes as reflected in jokes about the stupidity of Poles, the drunken behavior of the Irish, the homosexual tendencies among Greeks, the uncontrolled sexual appetites of men, the money hungry Jews, the criminal behavior among African Americans, the laziness of Mexicans, the graffiti prone Puerto Ricans, the Mafioso Italians, the brutal Germans, the sly Oriental, the bimboism inherent in females or the terroristic, belly-dancing Arabs. There are others to be sure. Each group is laughed at by others.

Group cohesion among those sharing the "in fun" experience occurs at the expense of the group victimized through debilitating humor. The outgroup may counter by staying away from the people expressing such hostilities. The outgroup may also enjoy its own "anti-other" group humor. Social distance results and the social disease of the "isms," fed on stereotypes perpetuated through humor, runs rampant and strangles any hope of unity. Fragmentation is heightened and the possibility of establishing goodwill in schools by creating winning diversity teams is thwarted. Hostility feeds counter hostility. Yet, ironi-cally, everyone is smiling. When people are forced into laughter through jokes at their expense, they may grin and bear it, but sensing danger or hostility they will also strengthen their defenses against the pain of the situation.

In some contexts laughter can help dissipate the pain of oppressive situations. Much of life involves suffering, abuse, and conflict. This is certainly true in situations defined by intolerance based on ethnicity, gender, class, sexual orientation, or religion, but a wise teacher can use humor to expose the absurdities underlying and surrounding such bigotry—as in the arguments dominant groups offer to justify oppressive behavior—and to release the tension discussions of controversial issues sometimes create. The principle guiding our intro-duction of humor into these or any discussions must be that the humor be affirming.

Multicultural leaders must be consistent and vigilant in "walking the talk" by using humor only to move towards a freer and healthier society. The classroom and campus must be safe for students who are eager to contribute to the collective well-being. All too frequently, however, colleges and universities are places where social, yet dysfunctional, values that tolerate selected group bashing through humor are allowed to flourish. Still, we need more, not less laughter on campus and in the classroom because laughter can be healing and bring people together.

Diversity cannot be achieved without humor. This is my deepest personal conviction. We must have fun and not take life so seriously that we miss opportunities to share in the common emotion of bonding through laughter. Laughter is a great human attribute. It brings joy and contentment. Some of us may be more gifted than others in being able to generate this most precious of human responses but most of us can learn styles of storytelling and presentation that incorporate humor. As noted above, however, that humor must be affirming. Injecting debilitating humor only leads to alienation, and the building of barriers to good relations and effective communication.

Clearly, we must transform barriers to understanding into bridges of understanding in our diverse society. Laughter and humor are wonderful resources to promote a healthy vision of a heterogeneous society. But to be effective, multicultural teachers must learn to take humor seriously. Edutainers must be literate about the potential of humor as a force for good or evil. They must reject negative uses of humor and, in a spirit of fun, with compassion and enthusiasm, embrace its healing and liberating potential. This, of course, is the real challenge of using humor in the classroom: to make it a resource in our efforts to help our students become full partners in the building of a society that is stronger, healthier, and freer than we found it. Comedians may use humor simply to be funny. As educators we need to use humor to make the dream of wholeness in diversity a reality. Teachers committed to the realization of this dream must be gifted with a passion for social justice, genuine depth of knowledge, and a sense of humor that facilitates collaboration and coalition building.

Suggested Readings

Allen, S. (1987). *How to be funny: Discovering the comic you.* New York: McGraw Hill.

Apte, M. L. (1985). *Humor and laughter: An anthropological approach.* Ithaca, NY: Cornell University Press.

Cosby, B. (1991). *Childhood.* New York: Putnam.

Cosby, B. (1987). *Fatherhood.* New York: Berkley.

Hendra, T. (1987). *Goin too far.* New York: Dolphin.

Moody, Jr., M.D., R. (1978) *Laugh after laugh: The healing power of humor.* Jacksonville, FL: Hedwaters Press.

Reader's Digest Editors. (1982) *Laugher, the best medicine.* New York: Berkeley Books.

Rivers, J. (1986). *Enter talking.* New York: Delacorte Press.

Roach, H. (1983). *His greatest collection of Irish humor and wit featuring the "unnecessary sayings" of the Irish in conversation.* Dublin, Ireland: Tallaght Co.

CURRICULUM AND INSTRUCTION

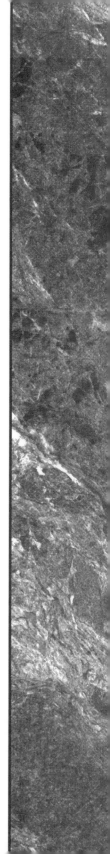

THE POINT OF THE STORY

by
Joan Livingston-Webber

In 1983, 1 was teaching writing and reading to high-risk, first-year students at Indiana University. There were fifteen students and two teachers who met for six hours a week. In this class was a young African American man. He came to class faithfully and turned in his work on time. His writing was imaginative and imagistic, but it never showed even the germ of the structure of an academic paper. I too was faithful and prompt, but I was frustrated with him during class time. He got an "F" in the course, and he may very well have left school. I had done what I could.

Later I was in the library browsing through journals and ran across an article about African American ghettos. I don't remember the journal or the author. I was struck by one bit of information only. In the ghetto, the article said, to look someone in the eye is to issue a challenge. To keep your eyes down is to show respect. I revised the narrative of my inter-actions with the student. The revisionist narrative has to include a finer level of detail about habitual practices. It goes like this:

I would return papers in class and sit down in a student desk to discuss the papers with each student. *Original version: This young African American man never paid attention.* **Revised version: This young man didn't make any eye contact.** I wanted to help him. He clearly wanted to pass the course. *But he wouldn't take advantage of the help I offered.* **He respected me or my power enough to signal that respect by not looking at me.** I had 14 other students who would use the time. I signaled to him that he wasn't as worth giving help to as the other students. I don't know why he kept being faithful and prompt all semester.

Narrative works its way through multicultural texts, from the anecdotes teachers swap to the stories in which students' lives are embedded. Being multicultural, in part, means being able to recognize the intentions encoded in the stories we live by and tell each other, stories by which we make ourselves and our lives known. One part of university education is a press toward constructing certain commonalities in our storytelling. College graduates will meet somewhere and tell each other college stories, stories about fraternity brothers, student government power mongers, the teachers who used 20-year-old syllabi or whom we only appreciate now years later, all stock characters in the nation's college story. Through these stories, former college students come to feel like they belong to at least one group in common, the group of people who share just these topics for stories.

As educators, we also want to see students using stories for purposes that match our own, for example, to exemplify abstract generalizations about human behavior or to illus-trate a point made in an argument. We know how much the narrative that illustrates is part of getting the point, of understanding a communication. Students from all cultures will complete college, then, with stories about their lives that share some content and with a tendency to tell some of their stories for the same purposes—to exemplify or to illustrate a larger point.

This description of the role of narrative in university life is obviously simplistic. I want to complicate the circumstances of narrative and college that I have just invoked. I want to describe ways that the multicultural classroom problematizes narrative, intending to imply that there are many more ways I could have chosen to present narrative as problematic. Then I want to suggest that an appropriate, teacherly response—a response, **not** a solution—is to adopt an anthropological turn of mind, to understand our feelings as something other than an unmediated reflection of reality.

Narrative varies along cultural lines and may do so in the functions it serves and in the forms it takes. For example, stories appear to have a functional role in the development of women's intellectuality that they apparently do not have in men's. According to the work of Mary Belenky and her colleagues (1986), narrative plays a primary role in the intellectual functioning of some women, with no comparable role for men.

We have to examine for a moment what constitutes formal knowledge as it is most frequently understood. Formal or procedural knowledge is an intellectual perspective in which the concern is with the form of things. It relies on procedures, skills, techniques, and strategies—on methods whose steps can be specified in advance. The product of these methods is a knowledge of structure, of how a reality is shaped, of its form. Using the right method guarantees the validity and reliability of the results; method guarantees the knowledge and its truth. Form is, in this sense, more relevant to truth than content is (Belenky, Cunchy, Goldberger, & Tarule, 1986, p. 95; see also Perry, 1968). If a person has followed the proper formal procedures to a result, then that knowledge comes with a kind of guarantee. Generally, academics recognize scientific method as a right form, particularly in adopting an objective stance and an analytic framework.

Though otherwise displaying this familiar kind of objectivity, women may use an alternate method to arrive at formal knowledge, one that uses the form of personal and emotional experience to arrive at truth. A woman may project herself by empathy into the form or shape of another's experience. Empathy leads her to "share [the] experience that has led a person to an idea" (Belenky et al., 1986, p. 113) rather than to follow the analytic steps that result in the idea as the logical conclusion in an argument structure. In other words, the most appropriate answer to the question "why" may be a narrative rather than a set of reasons. "Why" asks something like, "What was the experience that led you to this belief?" Our academic values may lead us to judge this responsive narrative as merely anecdotal. Simply repeating the question "why" more forcefully, though, is not likely to elicit a set of reasons rather than a narrative. And when we, in turn, answer this woman's "why" with a set of reasons, she may feel that we are putting her off, keeping our distance, or refusing to answer her honestly.

Just as it is for formal analysis and objectivity, the focus of this kind of narrative knowledge is form and method: the form is narrative; the method is empathy. In a sense, connected knowers, these narrative-seeking women, are phenomenologists; they want to understand the structures of experience. Separate knowers and relativists, the reason-seeking academics, are more like epistemologists; they want to understand the structures of knowledge and language. A connected knowing will understand a text or a problem the way it understands people, seeking experiential structures; a separate knowing will understand people the way it understands texts and problems, seeking epistemological structures. We should not make this distinction absolute, between ways of knowing and between men and women, but we should wonder what is involved when a female student seems stuck in anecdotal responses to questions we believe ask for a set of reasons.

Some women some of the time, thus, use narrative for a purpose—explaining why—different from the purposes academics conventionally associate with narrative. Narrative may also take forms different from those we are accustomed to. Let me complicate the problematics of narrative further by explaining how some of the narratives of African Americans and European Americans observe different formal conventions, leading many, especially European Americans, to fail to understand the narratives of even our gender peers. For this part of my explanation, I want to rely on Courtney Cazden's work (1988) with primary school students and Thomas Kochman's work (1981) with community blacks.[1]

Cazden (1988, pp. 8-27) compiles research done in California and New England schoolrooms on the sharing-time narratives of primary school children. She found that most black girls' sharing-time narratives were formally different from their white classmates' narratives in ways that left their teachers bewildered. White children's stories were "topic-centered"; most black girls' stories were "episodic" (p. 11). Topic-centered stories had one time, one setting, one event, and very few, perhaps three, characters. The topics of these stories were "publicly familiar scripts" (p. 22). Episodic stories, on the other hand, were longer and formally more complicated, with three to nine temporal shifts, changing scenes, and a larger cast of characters. The topics were often public scripts from a different (African American) culture (p. 22). Even with culturally shared topics (a puppy being put to sleep), teachers had a hard time understanding basic information (that the puppy was dead) (p. 15).

The examples of episodic stories that Cazden includes in her book seem to me to be organized in this way: Three or more incidents are told whose relationship to each other must be inferred. Sometimes, they seem to be instances of an overarching type of event which is not named. European Americans (like me) are not used to being expected to do this particular kind of inferential work with narratives, automatically filling in the conceptual links among episodes. Most European Americans cannot do so for episodic narratives; we expect at least a minimally explicit link verbalized by the teller, something on the order of "meanwhile back at the ranch" or "another time when." An enculturated person fills in those links inferentially without conscious thought. Six-year-old black girls do not verbalize the properly implied links of their stories for their white teachers, and they end up with bewildered and frustrated teachers. The girls themselves must also feel bewildered and frustrated. Cazden's work with five black and seven white Harvard graduate students in education suggests that this negative response derives from the white teachers' inability to understand the episodic narrative form (p. 17).

Of course, children who never tell topic-centered stories probably won't make it into our college classrooms. Even so, for some of our students, telling narratives in the form we like them told will be a more carefully learned and less natural competence. For example, African Americans (and some other cultural groups like Greeks and Jews) may feel they have terribly belabored a story, ruined it, if they explicitly state the point or name the overarching type that the episodes are exemplars for (see Tannen, 1984; see also Kochman, 1981). Some especially sensitive individuals might indeed be willing to ruin their narratives to accommodate the thick-headedness of their listeners, if they perceive these listeners aren't getting it. Most European Americans, especially midwesterners, expect narratives to be topic-centered with the point explicitly stated (see Johnstone, 1990). They will wonder what the point is when told an episodic story or sometimes even a topic-centered one with the point implicit. A common European American response would be, "So what?" or "What's the point?" or "I don't get it."

Midwestern, European American narratives are not participatory in the sense that the teller is held responsible for making the narrative intention explicit, stated in so many words. It is almost as though some sentence must always begin with an implicit, "And the moral of the story is." African American stories may demand the participation of the listener to construct the narrative intentions inferentially. Basically, very different elements go without saying in episodic and topic- centered narratives. African American culture finds episodic narratives well-formed whose intentions go without saying.

When an African American student in my class—or any student for that matter—seems to be going on and I don't get it, when I can't find the storyline, I have to ask if my competence is sufficient to the task. I have to ask if one plot-driven story "line" carries the significance of the narrative, if it is the structural key to getting it. Do I know how to hear the narrative? When I read Gloria Naylor's novel, *Mama Day* (1989), and do not realize until the end that one of the main characters has been dead for a long time, I have to wonder if I am reading the book the way that European American teachers listen to the sharing-time stories of six-year-old African American girls—with inappropriate structural expectations. When one student interrupts another student mid-narrative, I want to say, "Wait. Let her finish."—even when I'm not sure that I understand myself what's going on with the narrative.

What we've seen so far are cultural differences surfacing in the forms and functions of narrative for mainstream men and women and for African Americans and European Americans, particularly those European Americans in the midwestern states. We should assume differences will show up as well between other cultural groups and our own. For example, Native Americans certainly shape stories differently from those we academics have been trained to understand and validate. Some Native American cultures tell stories that have no endings as mainstream U.S. culture would recognize an ending. We do not get the sense of closure we require to recognize an ending (Cazden, 1988, p. 12). Athabaskans elaborate what appear to be lengthy digressions in their stories when their listeners provide inappropriate responses, since listener responses always influence the organization of Athabaskan stories in formally specifiable ways (Scollon & Scollon, 1981, p. 114). Vietnamese students writing stories in English elaborate on setting and on the reflective mental processes of characters while their native-speaker peers are writing clearly forward-moving plot lines (Söter, 1988, pp. 188, 195, & 198).

Narratives don't come in uniform shapes nor do they serve one purpose only, and we tend to feel bewildered by or impatient and frustrated with tellers whose stories have a shape or purpose that we do not intuitively understand. Even if I, as a woman, intuitively understand the narratives of intellectual import that North American women tell, it's clear that I cannot presume that I will automatically understand all of the stories told by African American women—or African American men or Vietnamese Americans or Native Americans.

Students will always tell stories to their teachers. Even if I'm not asking students for narratives about course content, I may be heard as asking for them. Students and teachers use narratives to exemplify concepts and to illustrate abstract points. We also use stories to interact with each other. Students use narrative to explain absences and to get extensions. These stories will irritate us if we believe that excusing is not an appropriate function for student-teacher narrative, although the functions of narrative vary culturally just as the forms do. We ourselves may use narrative to explain to the class why the tests aren't done or, one-on-one, to explain why the student failed the oral report or excelled in the lab component.

The possible meanings of narrative become decidedly complicated in our multicultural classrooms—far too complicated for each of us to respond by analyzing every student narrative for its form and function. We don't have the skills. We don't have the time. Such a comprehensive analysis is in fact, an impossible task even for the most committed sociolinguist. But I believe, anyway, it is less important that we understand every story on our own than that we recognize when we're not getting it and take remedial action.

I suggest a multicultural teacher must develop an anthropological attitude about herself. In fact, I implore that we do so. This attitude is a means for identifying when we're just not getting it. We must adopt an anthropologist's approach to our feelings and judgments. We must learn a kind of detachment from our own feelings, a kind of objectivity in which our negative feelings, of confusion as well as of anger, are clues to the existence of cultural difference, practicing what Deborah Tannen has called "a rhetoric of good intentions" (1990), a rhetoric in which we judge people's intentions or people themselves negatively only as a last resort and never as a first recourse.

The forms and functions of narrative, how we tell stories and why we tell them, are such a basic part of our cultural makeup that we have to really slow down our responding process even to notice that someone else's narrative is rubbing us wrong because of its form or function. We may only be aware that the story seems out of place or doesn't seem like a real story. I want to borrow the first ingredient of Raymonde Carroll's "recipe" for avoiding cultural misunderstanding (1988, p. 5) to explain an appropriate way, an anthropological way, to use those judgments. What is this anthropological attitude and how do we practice it?

An anthropological attitude sees our negative feelings and value judgments as signals that we may be encountering cultural variation (Carroll, 1988, p. 6). We might simply feel dislike for the person who is talking or we may have stronger negative feelings of anger or fear. We may be making judgments about the teller: that he or she is rude, an airhead, stuck in orality, from a deficient culture, childish, arrogant, and so on. A reorientation regarding these feelings and judgments is crucial. We don't deny them; they are valuable clues. What we do is reorient ourselves to them. This reorientation requires that we deal with our own emotional responses and judgments not as truths about other people and their intentions, but as data, as clues that can lead us to insight about truths of our multicultural circumstances.

I want to stress the difficulty and importance of this shift in our relationship to our own feelings. Carroll (1988) says that this sort of effort "can be more painful than psychoanalysis" (p. 11). It requires careful self-monitoring and a detachment toward our inner selves that few, if any, of us, come to in the general course of things. Regarding our automatic feelings and judgments in this way forces us to trust them for different information than we are accustomed to. In a homogeneous culture, I can trust that my natural (that is, cultural) responses are valid, that they reflect the reality of what's happening around me. In a multicultural setting, I simply cannot trust them in the same way.

For example, when I am interacting with a European American female student and she is telling me stories about herself, I can trust my gut feelings to know, with good assurance, how to respond appropriately and need to give little thought to how I have come to that response. I am even fairly confident of trusting my immediate responses to the stories of self told me by a midwestern European American male student. I am not and ought not be so sure of my judgments, however, when a student of another culture tells me stories about

231

herself or himself. I may not comprehend the form of the narratives or their function. Narratives of self between the sexes and between student and teacher function for purposes other than they do for my European American cultural self.

As teachers, what should we do? As teachers, we may feel our authority challenged by someone who means no challenge. Eye contact and physical proximity may signal conventional cultural meanings quite different from the ones we understand when we rely on our own unanalyzed judgments to interpret reality. As teachers, we may also make incorrect judgments about the meaning of a student's silence when we expect narrative. ("She's shy." "He's aloof.") We often judge narratives that we do not understand as a kind of acting up, and we often judge the absence of a narrative we expect as a refusal to participate, as withholding the self. We must begin to see these kinds of judgments as data for further processing and not as necessarily correct interpretations of another's meaning.

A teacher's judgments are part of the context in which students work and easily affect the performance of both students and their teachers. Each of the judgments we make about a student is in a sense, the point to a story that we have composed about that student. The point of my original story about the young African American student in my reading and writing class was that he defied my attempts to help him learn to write for college. He was defiant. The point of my revised story, though, is more about me than about him. The point of my revised story is that I missed the point, that I misinterpreted his body language and wrote him into a story which absolved me of my misinterpretation. I need to remember that I am the teacher. I am the one who, if I do not know, should at least be able to recognize that I do not know. The only way I have found to do so is not to mistake my feelings and judgments for literal reflections of reality but to take them as clues about a more complex reality than my acculturated emotional responses would allow.

I have since learned many specific ways that my automatic interpretations of students' stories may be wrong. I have learned even to enjoy some forms of narrative that I couldn't have recognized five or ten years ago. But even with this knowledge and ability, I am far from being able to understand correctly all of the narratives that get told around my classroom at the moment they are being told. I have learned to ask, to say that I am bewildered, to share my frustrated interpretations as conceptual drafts that need correcting. This process can slow down a class. But this process is one my students need to have modeled and I need to practice. Going through this process is integral to my identity as a multicultural teacher. It is crucial for navigating in the multicultural society of the classroom.

Endnote

[1]Let me add one note on terminology. Both Cazden (1988) and Kochman (1981) use the terms black and white to talk about features of culture. This usage is a function of their publication dates. Where I am drawing on their work, I maintain their language. Cultural features, as we know, are aspects of culture not of race (whatever "race" may mean). Where I am not misrepresenting someone else's language, I have mostly chosen ethnic labels rather than color ones. Someday, perhaps, our cultures will correlate with something other than ethnicity. I would have very mixed feelings about that day. In any case, I have selected what I believe is acceptable usage.

References

Belenky, M., Clinchy, B., Goldberger, N., & Tarule, J. (1986). *Women's ways of knowing: The development of self, voice, and mind.* New York: Basic Books.

Cazden, C. B. (1988). *Classroom discourse: The language of teaching and learning.* Portsmouth, NH: Heinemann.

Carroll, R. (1988). *Cultural misunderstanding: The French-American experience.* Chicago: University of Chicago Press.

Johnstone, B. (1990). *Stories, community, and place: Narratives from middle America.* Bloomington: Indiana University Press.

Kochman, T. (1981). *Black and white styles in conflict.* Chicago: University of Chicago Press.

Naylor, G. (1989). *Mama Day.* New York: Vintage Books.

Perry, W. (1968). *Forms of intellectual and ethical development in the college years.* New York: Holt.

Scollon, R., & Scollon, S. B. K. (1981). *Narrative, literacy and face in interethnic communication.* Norwood, NJ: Ablex.

Söter, A. O. (1988). The second language learner and cultural transfer in narration. In A. C. Purves (Ed.), *Writing across languages and cultures: Issues in contrastive rhetoric* (pp. 177- 205). Newbury Park, CA: Sage.

Tannen, D. (1984). *Conversational style: Analyzing talk among friends.* Norwood, NJ: Ablex.

Tannen, D. (1990). *You just don't understand: Women and men in conversation.* New York: William Morrow.

CONFLICT AND RESISTANCE IN THE MULTICULTURAL CLASSROOM

by
Linda Dittmar

For all my thirty years of teaching at an urban university which serves a diverse, commuting, working-class and lower middle-class student population, and for all my long-standing commitment to considering multicultural issues in all my courses, I still find it hard to generalize about multicultural teaching. We, faculty, may design courses and develop programs that address a range of multicultural concerns, but the test of such plans is in the classroom. What actually happens in a particular class depends on the teacher and students on hand as they give theory its concrete application. If there is one lesson I did learn in this regard, it is that one cannot approach a new class feeling assured that a carefully thought-out syllabus or a fully reasoned pedagogy will necessarily prove successful.

Some years back, for example, I redesigned my section of Freshman Composition around a multicultural reader, *Across Cultures* (Gillespie & Singleton, 1991), which includes a variety of short pieces concerning diverse cultural identities and cross-cultural encounters, mostly within the United States but also outside it.[1] For two consecutive semesters students read, discussed, and wrote about the same selection of essays, and for two semesters I facilitated this work by teaching in a similarly informal, friendly, and supportive manner. Still, while on their face these two courses were identical, the actual classroom experiences were vastly different. The first offering was so successful that I left the class buoyed by a feeling that a multicultural perspective is ideally suited for first-year composition courses, especially at an urban university such as the University of Massachusetts-Boston (UMB). The second offering was so labored and strained that it left us, students and teacher alike, wondering whether the thematics of multiculturalism do in fact offer a meaningful infrastructure for such a course.

In the first instance the readings sparked stimulating discussions of difference, identity, social inscription, and social change. Students' essays became progressively more thoughtful, complex, and honest. The collection of strangers we call a "class" gradually turned into a community, and some students would adjourn to the campus coffee shop after class to continue their discussions. In the second instance students resisted the material. They found it too repetitive (even though, with one exception, no two writers came from the same cultural community) and not particularly engaging or relevant to their experience. They were relatively silent in class, trudging in their essays, and happy to disperse as soon as class ended. There were more absences, more late papers, and fewer efforts at optional assignments and revisions in this class than in the preceding one. By the end of the first semester I believed that I had finally landed on an engaging and empowering model for teaching college composition; by the end of the second course I became skeptical again.

What, then, made such a difference? To my mind the key was the substantial difference among the students enrolled in a given course and, therefore, the character of each class as a whole. This difference emerged during the second week of the semester, when we went around the room (we were sitting in a circle) and introduced ourselves. In keeping with the supportive, friendly tone I was trying to establish right away, these introductions occurred through the protective mediation of people interviewing and introducing one another around questions generated by the class and included me as an equal participant. The first class represented an array of backgrounds, ages, and life experiences. In fact, we had among us a cultural diversity that far exceeded what one might have guessed by simply looking at our faces. Among us were Greek as well as Vietnamese immigrants, a female Karate teacher and a Russian high school senior, an Israeli armed services veteran (male) studying alternative Chinese medicine, a U.S. armed services veteran (female), an ex-marine who recently saw action in Kurdish Iraq (late 1980s), a French Canadian woman who spent a year in an Egyptian village, a young African American Moslem mother, an Irish American engaged to a Salvadoran, and a small cluster of recent high school graduates of diverse ethnicities. No one age group or ethnicity prevailed, though the overall impression the group gave was European American. The second class had more people of color in it, but the mix proved more bifurcated. Here we had five African Caribbean students from different Francophone and Anglophone islands as well as students from other cultural backgrounds, and about half the class consisted of recent parochial high school graduates, mostly of one European ethnicity. This group was shy and quiet, while the more mature students on whom I would normally depend for lively in-class participation happened to be uncommonly beleaguered by crises at home and at work. This second group included all but one of the Caribbean students, a Vietnam veteran who was on drugs and on the verge of homelessness, a Turkish immigrant, and a latter-day "hippie" and Grateful Dead follower.

It is easy enough to blame the defensive silence and apparent disinterest of that second class on the immaturity of some and on the personal travail of others. At our university such a student population is not uncommon. However, when it comes to teaching a course that includes attention to social diversity as an important thematic focus, each class will experience differently the tensions this subject matter inescapably brings to the surface. In this respect the first class was energized by the optimism of people using their education in what they considered a positive new step in their lives. For them diversity was a strength. The second class seemed paralyzed by its young members' distrust of education as a means to fulfillment, and by its adult members' barely keeping a foothold in the academy even as they were experiencing increasing personal, social, and economic marginality. In so far as the first class believed it had a chance of living "the American dream," it was learning about multiculturalism as a riches, and doing so while moving away from marginality towards the mainstream. In contrast, the second class was a living laboratory of the injuries of difference as these get played out in the United States. Its students clearly entertained some sense of aspiration, but aspiration attenuated and qualified by disaffection.

Overall, my experience teaching and team-teaching at UMB suggests that it is easier to teach about multiculturalism to students who feel less implicated in the social strife the concept so readily entails than to students who relate this subject matter to their own social and economic positions in embattled ways. Students who feel empowered by multicultural understanding will be more open to it than those whose anxieties are aggravated by such knowledge. For me, such teaching is easier in advanced and graduate courses, where a winnowing process leaves us with relatively goal-oriented, forward-looking students who are freed by their emergent strength to appreciate diversity without feeling implicated in the inequities our society rationalizes as a function of difference. In my experience a multicultural focus has more often elicited defensiveness, resistance, or outright antagonism in lower-division and introductory courses, where a student's sense of personal strength and collective enrichment is likely to be particularly vulnerable.

236

It is precisely for this reason that attention to multiculturalism belongs most urgently in lower division courses. After all, to the extent that introductory courses, core programs, and other distribution and general education requirements are the gateway to higher education, they should raise questions concerning the social use of the academic enterprise, including its relation to our increasingly multicultural society. Yet students entering such courses and programs are not always prepared to embrace them. How and why they are "not prepared" may vary across different colleges and universities, but at a school like UMB this lack of preparation includes a worry that the much touted benefits of education cannot be taken for granted. Many families, employers, and an increasing number of policy-setting administrators view higher education pragmatically as offering necessary training for the workplace. In this context, the notion that college level education might be an opportunity for personally enriching and socially transforming inquiry comes across as a luxury.

At work here are the "injuries of class" (Sennet & Cobb, 1973) inflected through diverse cultural disenfranchisements. The pragmatic view of a college degree as a meal ticket ends up tangled in "multiaxial" constructions of identity (Fiske, 1996; Lippman 1998)—race and ethnicity, class, age, gender and sexuality, or disability, for example—where difference entails inequality. In this context, multiculturalism stirs up much more than a broadly receptive understanding of cultural diversity. While it can give certain individuals a voice and heighten the group's positive awareness of the multiple histories that shape our evolving national plurality, it also acts as a reminder of constraints, obstacles, and humiliations. The problem with teaching a young and economically disenfranchised student body about multiculturalism is that it can aggravate their entirely justified sense of their own uncertain futures.

This observation is born out by a review of difficult teaching situations I have encountered, where a given session or an entire course was steeped in pain. Examples include the occasion where an African American student chose to speak out in support of affirmative action and collapsed in an asthmatic attack under the stress of confronting racist classmates. On another occasion a working-class Italian American woman who was just venturing into class participation panicked at the prospect of discussing the virulently anti-Italian gangster film, *Scarface* (Hawks, 1932). In another situation a male student of an unspecified sexual orientation found himself shakily reminding a largely female women's studies class that gay bashing occurs alongside violence against women, while in yet another offering of this same course a young male, near tears, shared his difficulties as a single father. In none of these cases did social construction and cultural identity invite detached academic contemplation. Each instance invoked awareness of disenfranchisement along the multiaxial lines mentioned above, with gender, sexuality, race, age, and class slipping and sliding in and out of view as the primary locus of pain. Furthermore, at each turn it was a member of a hurt group who testified to injuries incurred personally in the name of difference.

On such occasions, teacher support to the courageous student is essential, though it does not guarantee that fellow students will come around. The debate on affirmative action was not resolved; students have been known to complain about the "predominance" of African American materials in literature courses where such materials amounted to less than half the course; and mention of sexual orientation continues to stir homophobic tensions. In the situations described above, individuals felt able to speak up because preceding sessions made the class seem relatively safe, but in each case such venturing forth nonetheless took courage. However supportive the teacher and however respectful the class community, one cannot guarantee a positive reception. Inevitably such discussions uncover injuries that countermand the notion that education is an impartial pursuit of pure knowledge. Rather, vulnerable individuals find themselves bearing the undue burden of enlightening others whom they see as the majority in power. My own response as a teacher is to acknowledge openly the courage and difficulty of the situation, to share an analogous pain or acknowledging relevant details about my own social position, to support other students who do likewise, and to refrain from calling on those who remain silent.

As these examples suggest, multicultural education is likely to uncover the inequities bound up in difference. It foregrounds the uniqueness of cultures, but as a comparative project, it also foregrounds the assessment of differences across cultures, including the injustices and strife such differences entail. "Culture," in this respect, includes much more than modes of representation, understanding, and articulation. It functions ideologically, in that cultural constructions of identity directly affect people's positions within economic, political, and other social relations, that is, within power relations. Thus "race" turns out to concern much more than genetics.[2] It is a social and cultural construct that has material and ideological consequences. In the case of race, ethnicity, gender, region, age, religion, sexuality, nationality, physical ability, and the like, identity repeatedly proves to be tied to the distribution of material goods. It is tied to jobs, housing, and educational access, for instance, but also to such crucial intangibles as dignity, respect, freedom, mobility, and choice. When students such as mine struggle to either break through barriers of silence or keep them intact, they are acting on their awareness, conscious or not, that relations across cultures implicate each of us in the consequences of his or her cultural position.

In short, the resistance and conflict multiculturalism can draw to itself are neither abstract nor impersonal. They are rooted in pressing life situations. The pedagogy they require involves finding ways to reduce anxieties, encourage openness, and foster hope that this undertaking can actually lead to personal and collective amelioration. While such pedagogy is filtered through the ineffable resonance of individual teaching, it also rests on our modeling of the qualities we hope attention to cultural diversity will foster in our students: openness, tolerance, respect, generosity, understanding, compassion, and optimism, for instance. Each class is a community that can work with or against the values posited by multicultural education, and faculty can enact these values across the daily operations of their courses. They can have students collaborate in dyads or small groups in or out of class; lead discussions in a circle; work collectively with the chalkboard; team-teach; have everyone on a first name basis; make a point of validating individual viewpoints and identities; use role playing; hold conferences or group tutorials; and set aside time to share a snack, celebrate a particular accomplishment, or recognize someone's national holiday. These and similar steps enact the ideals of cross-cultural awareness: they democratize the ownership of knowledge, diffuse the insularity of individuals, and affirm the pleasure of learning and the growth made possible through an exchange across differences.

The improvisation and intuition that go into this approach to teaching strain one's memory and energy beyond the familiar demands of what Paulo Freire (1970) calls "the banking model of education" (p. 58). In this model faculty do not simply deposit nuggets of knowledge into the supposedly empty minds of learners. To acknowledge students' particularities and incorporate them into the course work, we must pay attention to each individual in ways that exceed the standard delivery of services our job descriptions imply. To remember enough of each student's interests, in-class comments, or writing so as to refer to it weeks later is indeed taxing, and great concentration is needed to turn the chalkboard into a repository of the class's collective thinking. Still, while it is unrealistic to expect any of us constantly to juggle all of the above, to be aware of these options and open to experimentation is to invite fresh possibilities.

In my experience, joint chalkboard work is particularly and consistently engaging and useful. While I act as scribe, we use this work not just to solicit and record contributions, but as a means of organizing these contributions and developing ideas in a more sustained way. Anything can send us to the chalkboard: some concept or word in need of definition, a topic in search of a thesis, or a thesis ready for explication. Culling ideas from the entire class, we record concepts, note synonyms and antonyms, generate lists, debate digressions, or diagram contrasts and parallels. Once such raw materials are visibly in place, we use the eraser and chalk to reorganize them into sequences, clusters, or other units that allow us to reconceptualize the issue at hand. Key here are the shared processes of generating and shaping thought and knowledge, the evident adaptability of ideas that this process demonstrates, the recognition that each person's contributions acquire meanings in relation to others' contributions, and the critical awareness fostered by all of these.[3] Such teaching tools are not inherently multicultural, of course. What makes them useful in the resistant classroom, and symbolically resonant in the multicultural classroom specifically, is their collective nature. Beyond providing fresh opportunities for insight, the techniques I describe above are valuable as models of social well-being. Creating a situation where just about everybody has something to contribute to an accumulating body of ideas, and where no one person needs to worry about being singled out, this pedagogy affirms that many minds are better than one, and that knowledge is perpetually open to redefinition. Key here is a democratic, egalitarian approach that decenters ownership of knowledge and values collaboration and exchange. The idea is not to promote an uncritical acceptance of any and all views, but to treat all ideas with respect, to be aware that on different occasions different views may emerge as compelling, and to understand that this deserves critical attention. The inclusiveness and dialogue implicit in the concept of multiculturalism get enacted in class, but so do its comparative and evaluative implications. On the one hand, our pedagogy supports the investment of multicultural education in the coexistence of the many. On the other, it uncovers the existence of differences and the necessity of working productively within that reality.

It takes considerable honesty to allow the conflicts and anxieties which seep into the discourse of multiculturalism to surface. For me as a teacher—that is, as a person invested in planning and guiding my students' discussions, not just facilitating them—some challenging moments have occurred when students took the discussion in unexpected directions that nonetheless opened up for us new perspectives on the issue of multiculturalism. One such incident occurred when a Puerto Rican student called me on my use of "America" to mean the United States. Her point was well taken, of course, but for a brief moment I hesitated between feeling put out about my own hegemonic practice and the problem of whether to take the time out of a totally different topic to pursue this apparent digression. On another occasion an African American woman, angry with one of Hollywood's predictably racist representations of an African American "mammy," interrupted the discussion of some other aspect of the film and had us address the issue of racism right then and there. My own plan was to lay the groundwork gradually and build up to this climax later in the hour. I was miffed at having my neatly laid plan jostled, but I was also aware that the student did not trust me, a white instructor, to address the film's racism adequately.

In another situation, an outspoken gay student acted similarly; ever alert to the possibility of erasure, his refocusing us on "queer" issues exceeded my plans and tried some students' patience.

In each of these instances, students who are particularly impacted by the inegalitarian consequences of cultural difference opened up for us new and unanticipated topics, and in each case I had to decide on the spur of the moment whether or not to let this new agenda work its way though our valuable class time. Though I was sometimes rattled by such sudden developments, including students' evident expectation that, left to my own devices, I would not give their concern due consideration, I was ultimately not worried about my authority in class or about my being unable to address the issue. Of course such situations are unsettling. They signal distrust regarding particularly sensitive moral, political, and personal aspects of identity, on top of their challenging a teacher's ability to suddenly reshape the focus of a given hour without getting off track. They make the most seasoned, self-aware teachers, let alone less experienced ones, face the reality of students' divergent agendas, grievances, fears of erasure, and distrust, but the classroom management skills they suppose are ones we can develop.

For me personally, the first step has been to consider empathetically students' stake in redirecting the discussion. Ultimately, I do not see it as disruptive, even if it impedes my original plan. My choice is usually to go with the students, and when in doubt I consult them. For example, when a racist film representation drew fire on the first day of class one semester, I explained that though I had planned to address it differently I thought the matter important enough and student involvement strong enough for us to suspend a business-as-usual approach. We ended up skipping another topic altogether, simply for lack of time, but we felt good about redirecting our discussion to the more immediate concern. I do recognize that teachers less experienced or less sure of their own pedagogy or politics may not feel confident about navigating such situations. An alternate option might be to acknowledge the urgency of the issue, to promise to return to it at a specified point in the near future, and to keep that promise generously.

My own flexibility is backed up with assertiveness and an ability to guide a discussion authoritatively, the result of much experience, including several disasters. To this day my sure-handedness is also tenuous. Thinking of the students' stake in a question, however out of step with me or fellow students it might be, I have learned to suspend concern over how I come across, to acknowledge the need behind such interruptions, and to go on to consider the practical question of how to use our precious class time. In practice, the students' points have often been substantive, discussing them has been informative to the class as a whole, and their courage in risking a critique of our joint work deserves support, especially given their personal vulnerability as people who share in the cultural oppression they are protesting. In a classroom that attempts to model collaborative learning such openness is extremely important.

A reshuffling of lesson plans can occur not only on a particular day but may extend across an entire course. I have learned, after several miscalculations, that to downplay sensitive cultural issues is to create new problems while solving none. Euphemisms for the politics of hate (using "racial" or "race" where "racism is more accurate, for example, or postponing attention to homophobia until the class is "ready" for it) are evasions, not instances of diplomacy. Years ago I made the mistake of downplaying lesbianism in a course on women and film. Our sole treatment of this subject was *Queen Christina* (Mamoulian,

1933), where the Greta Garbo character's lesbianism is so toned down that at least one student insisted that she wore pants only because they were a comfortable riding habit. Students who found this film's equivocation on sexual orientation frustrating ended up repossessing another film, *Ramparts of Clay* (Bertucelli, 1971) as speaking to this issue, even though this film's marginalized female protagonist is not presented as a lesbian. Set in a remote Tunisian village, the woman's opposition to patriarchy proved a model of strength and resistance they needed. Realizing that my syllabus was not dealing with lesbian issues forthrightly, in the next offering of this course I moved *Queen Christina* to an earlier place in the syllabus and countered it with the lesbian-positive, anti-authoritarian film, *Mädchen in Uniform* (Sagan, 1932). Here the choice of materials as well as their place in the syllabus proved important. Focusing on potentially controversial material early on in the term helped me integrate it into the course as a legitimate topic for discussion and set as our ground rule a respectful tone for this discussion.

As I suggest elsewhere in greater detail (Dittmar, 1985) our challenge is to find ways to avoid marginalizing or being defensive about multicultural concepts and materials. In courses where a multicultural perspective is not an announced goal (e.g. my Narrative Form in the Novel and Film, Literature and the Political Imagination, Woman's Image on Film, and Women Film Directors), including multicultural materials early on in the course helps establish a receptive atmosphere. In situations where postponement is advisable, one can still establish a receptivity to multicultural analysis from the start. For example, in my American studies course, America on Film, I delay an extended unit on race and racism but prepare for it during the preceding weeks. As we view a chronologically organized sequence of Hollywood films, we learn to ferret out instances of ethnic and class bias, sexism, racism, and homophobia across an array of decades and genres—the western, the gangster film, film noir, and the like. That is, in the course of surveying U.S. cinema's construction of "American" ideals, we gradually build up an awareness of the politics of cultural specificity that, in its turn, makes a five weeks' unit on African American representations not a digression but a case in point. Though a 14-week course cannot afford several such units, the earlier material helps me situate this unit in the context of a more inclusive identity-related discourse. I share this thinking with the class, noting ways a semester's time constraints preclude similar attention to other facets of cultural identity, and cautioning against using African American experience as a token for diversity and difference.

The decisions we make about how much time to allocate certain topics, how to sequence them, and when to discuss them (be it within a single hour or across an entire semester) involve more than curricular planning. Teaching about multicultural issues also requires awareness of students' intellectual and personal investments in the learning process, and flexibility about our plans, even the best laid ones. As the discussion above suggests, we do so, or at least I do so, with varying success. In my two sections of freshman composition this recipe was not foolproof; it worked well in the class that was vibrantly engaged to begin with, but not in the class which was bifurcated by a mix of shyness and crises. Most students I know approach their courses with considerable good will, but some challenges are hard to surmount. While sharing with students our thoughts about class process or a course's structure (as I do regarding the African American unit, above) is always useful, it is not a cure all. My own difficulty with such teaching is greatest when the pain associated with questions of identity turns into hostility, be it passive or aggressive, personal or ideological.

241

Beyond the problems of an atypically dysfunctional class, I have since encountered another, more systemic opposition to the goals of multicultural teaching. As long as we treat "difference" (or "diversity," or "multiculturalism") as a plurality, as a co-equal range of possibilities, something like the Dr. Seuss account of creatures who did or did not have stars on their bellies, we are on safe ground. Seen this way, multiculturalism can be celebrated as an update of the "melting pot" ideal. But once this discourse includes recognition that "different" does not mean "equal," we head for trouble. In my own career, such trouble included a hostile neo-Nazi "skinhead" in a first-year literature class and an actively hostile conservative in a sophomore film course, both apparently "white." In the first instance, body language, leather and hardware attire, demonstrative silence in class, and repeated delays in completing assignments and refusals to confer with me, all exuded disaffection. In the second instance the student was disruptively attention-seeking, interrupting both me and fellow students, and attempting repeatedly to bait me—most memorably when he announced that California's anti-immigrant legislation was a good idea because "those people" bring AIDs from "over there."

This was no innocent declaration of views; by the fourth week into the term he knew that I would wince at such words. On this occasion he was countering my comments about anti-Indian and Mexican racism in John Ford's classic western, *Stagecoach* (1939), in the course, America on Film, where such comments were to lay the groundwork for an extended discussion of racism later on. Ironically, this happened in the same course where, some years earlier, an Italian American student cringed at the racist treatment of her ethnicity in *Scarface*, except that now the student was feeling aggrieved as a member of white America's mainstream. Along similar lines, in another class a Cuban American student protested sympathetic discussion of El Salvador's peasants in Manlio Argueta's novel *One Day in Life*, claiming they were the ones guilty of massacres, not the government's Special Forces. Whatever the historic record, his views were shaped by a tangle of beliefs and anxieties to which truth seemed irrelevant—a situation not unlike the anti-immigrant sentiments which countered our discussion of racism in *Stagecoach*. In each case self-interest became an ethics, dictating a hegemonic "rightness."

Such incidents will take on different forms and occur with varying degrees of intensity in different parts of the country and with different student populations. My own experiences may be specific to UMB, but one general point they do suggest is that at issue is more than curriculum design or class management. The discourse of multiculturalism can open wounds likely to need some accommodation in class, including grievances that can edge into hate speech. While teachers can register this fact with a measure of empathy, the question of how to deal with its consequences constructively is not easy to answer, especially considering that faculty, too, may feel assaulted by category: as a minority, a woman, a queer, a young person, a white male, for example. My colleagues report a range of such difficulties, with gender and multiculturalism heading the list. With many of us women, some people of color, and some quite young, our own subaltern identities as well as our students' can themselves be a magnet for conflict.

Amidst much discussion of the social usefulness and humanizing potential of multicultural teaching, what remains under-discussed is the antagonism which it can elicit. Such antagonism has colored even relatively civil academic debates about the canon (sometimes erroneously coupled with post-structuralism), but we need a more extended discussion of situations where disagreement turns into hate, especially as education is an arena where

American ideals and ideology get debated and forged. Much of this essay reflects positively on ways educators may pursue the collaborative, pluralistic, and ameliorative goals of multicultural education. In my own pedagogy, this is a matter of accountability—to our students and to society at large. But haunting it are certain loose ends, questions I have not resolved yet, perhaps because the need to address them has been, in my experience, too sporadic. You may have a different student body than I; you may prefer to rein in your classes to avoid chaos; you may also be too new to multicultural teaching to feel comfortable about improvising on short notice. The pedagogy I discuss here evolved out of experiences and priorities you may not share. But I do believe that anyone undertaking multicultural teaching risks a tension between utopian aspirations and resistance.

For me, at least, open discussion works best. When my intentions get derailed, when students chafe or pull in other directions, I invite self-reflection, be it in class discussion or in anonymous course evaluations. Critiquing our work helps students understand how faculty chart the learning process and what active roles they can play in it. Much like our use of the chalkboard, shared attention to course design and to the meanings implied in its organization allows students to assess their work and envision alternatives to it. Recognition that the production of knowledge and processes of learning are constructs, products of choices, complements my efforts to demystify cultural constructions in general. It is a pedagogy that reflects in practice what we teach in theory. Dispersing authority and decentralizing the management of ideas, it lets students experience the possibility of collaborative exchange—not necessarily harmonious exchange, and certainly not a bland melding of cultures so as to drain multiculturalism of the struggles it entails, but at least a dialogue that reflects the dynamic existence of diverse cultures, ones that connect and diverge again and again.

Endnotes

[1] The early 1990s saw a burgeoning industry in multicultural readers. Bearing titles such as *American Mosaic* (Song & Kim, 1991), *American Voices* (LaGuardia & Guth, 1993), *Connections* (Stanford, 1993), *Encountering Cultures* (Holeton, 1992) *Side by Side* (Wiener & Bazerman, 1993), and *One World, Many Voices* (Hirschberg, 1992), their rapid accumulation on my shelves testifies to a growing push to introduce multicultural perspectives into the curriculum, though several of them fail to problematize the notion of "America" as itself a form of cultural hegemony.

[2] For a critique of the use of the concept "race," see B. P. Allen and J. Q. Adams (1991), "Why 'Race' Has No Place in Multicultural Education." Though I agree with the authors' view that our "notions of 'race' are confused, inconsistent, and scientifically unsound" (48), I nonetheless believe that this ambiguous and unstable concept has a functional existence and virulent effects that require that we keep this label as long as it has practical consequences.

[3] New technologies now make possible doing this work on a computer screen, too, though I prefer the "thought in progress" that chalkboards register, including the roughness of writing and lingering erasures.

References

Allen, B. P. & Adams, J. Q. (1991). Why 'race' has no place in multicultural education. In J. Q.Adams & J. R. Welsch (Eds.), *Multicultural education: Strategies for implementation in colleges and universities, Vol. 2.* (pp. 45-50). Macomb, IL: Illinois Staff and Curriculum Developers Association.

Argueta, M. (1983). *One Day in Life*. New York: Vintage.

Bertucelli, J. L. (Director). (1971). *Ramparts of Clay* (Algeria-France).

Dittmar, L. (1985, Fall). Inclusionary practices: The politics of syllabus design. In B. H. Davis (Ed.). [Special issue] *The Journal of Thought, 20*(3), 37-47.

Fiske, J. (1996). *Media matters: Race and gender in U.S. politics*. Minneapolis: University of Minnesota Press.

Ford, J. (Director). (1939). *Stagecoach*. Wanger/United Artists.

Freire, P. (1970). *The pedagogy of the oppressed*. New York: Continuum.

Gillespie, S., & Singleton, R. (Eds.).(1991). *Across cultures: A reader for writers*. Boston: Allyn & Bacon.

Hawks, H. (Director). (1932). *Scarface*. United Artists-Atlantic.

Hirschberg, S. (Ed.). (1992). *One world, many voices*. New York: Macmillan.

Holeton, R. (Ed.) (1992). *Encountering cultures: Reading and writing in a changing world*. Englewood Cliffs, NJ: Prentice Hall.

LaGuardia, D., & Guth, H. P. (Eds.). (1993). *American voices: Multicultural literacy and critical thinking*. Mountain View, CA: Mayfield.

Lippman, D. (1998). Who's on third?: Poaching in the culture wars. In *Socialism and Democracy, 12*(1-2), 123-133.

Mamoulian, R. (Director). (1933). *Queen Christina*. Metro-Goldwyn-Mayer.

Sagan, L. (Director). (1932). *Mädchen in uniform*. Deutsche Film Gemeinschaft.

Sennet, R., & Cobb, J. (1973). *The hidden injuries of class*. New York: Vintage.

Song, Y. I., & Kim, E. C. (Eds.). (1991). *American mosaic: Selected readings on America's multicultural heritage*. Englewood Cliffs, NJ: Prentice Hall.

Stanford, J. A. (Ed.). (1993). *Connections: A Multicultural reader for writers*. Mountain View, CA: Mayfield.

Wiener, H. S., & Bazerman, C. (Eds.). (1993). *Side by side: A multicultural reader*. Boston: Houghton Mifflin.

SELF-REGULATED LEARNING AND TEACHING: AN INTRODUCTION AND OVERVIEW

by
Reinhard W. Lindner

The construct of self-regulated learning has varied origins and flies under the banner of several theoretical frameworks. The basic issue addressed, however, is focused on the notions of volition and (internal) control. While not entirely ignored, these represent relatively neglected topics within the discipline of psychology, particularly learning related psychology. Nevertheless, a growing body of literature suggests that optimal academic performance is strongly tied to the degree of self-regulation the learner is capable of exercising (Borkowski, Carr, Rellinger & Pressley, 1990; Jones & Idol, 1990; Lindner & Harris, 1992b; Zimmerman & Martinez-Pons 1986; Zimmerman, 1990). Although the self-regulated learning perspective is not, at present, a theoretically unified one, according to Zimmerman (1990, p. 4), "a common conceptualization of these students has emerged as metacognitively, motivationally, and behaviorally active participants in their own learning." In other words, whether one espouses a social-cognitive, information processing, or socio-cultural orientation, there nevertheless appears to be general agreement that self-regulated learners are purposive and goal oriented (proactive rather than simply reactive), incorporating and applying a variety of strategic behaviors designed to optimize their academic performance.

While many students, barring those who are totally tuned out, are, to some degree, and on some occasions, active in the manner Zimmerman describes, self-regulated learners have been found to be both more keenly aware of the relation between specific behaviors and academic success and more likely to employ such behaviors systematically and appropriately (Zimmerman & Martinez-Pons, 1986). In short, they evidence far higher executive or metacognitive processing than their fellow students. Self-regulated learners control learning outcomes, that is, primarily from within; they are intrinsically motivated, self-directing, self-monitoring, and self-evaluating. They also appear, however, to be more finely tuned than their less successful counterparts to situational demands, hence exhibiting greater flexibility in adapting to the variable and sometimes uncertain challenges that exist in the classroom, particularly at the high school and college levels. The question, of course, is: how did they get to be this way?

My own approach to this issue has been to first seek to define, on the basis of the literature surrounding this topic as well as my own investigations, the components of self-regulated learning and then to attempt to capture the dynamics of the learning process from a self-regulated perspective. The model that has resulted from this effort reflects an information processing orientation. With regard to the question of origin, or developmental dynamics, however, I favor a sociocultural approach (Rogoff, 1990).

Components of Self-Regulated Learning: An Information Processing Model

In terms of the self-regulation of cognition the basic mechanism involves: 1) analysis of the task, 2) construction of a plan or strategy, 3) implementation, 4) monitoring by periodically comparing execution to an internal standard, and 5) modification of the plan, when necessary. The entire process should be thought of as recursive rather than as simply linearly executed. The working information processing model of self-regulated learning which I have developed consists of six dimensions: A) epistemological beliefs, B) motivation, C) metacognition, D) learning strategies, E) contextual sensitivity, and F) environmental utilization/control (see Appendix A). In short, in seeking to understand the dynamics of self-regulated learning I argue that it is best to view each individual as bringing to a learning situation:

- a largely unconscious frame of reference (informal epistemology) comprised of beliefs about the nature of knowledge and the process of knowing (Kuhn, 1991; Perry, 1988; Schommer, 1990);
- a particular motivational orientation and set of values (Dweck, 1989);
- the capacity (present in all, but more or less developed in a given individual) for monitoring, evaluating, and, generally, reflecting over one's cognitive activity (Flavell, 1979; Brown, 1987);
- a specific (to the individual) body of strategic knowledge about how to process information effectively and efficiently (Derry 1990; Pressley, Woloshyn, Lysynchuck, Martin, Wood, & Willoughby, 1990);
- a characteristic degree of sensitivity to contextual cues that facilitate, or afford, learning or problem solving; and
- a specific level of understanding of how to utilize and/or control environmental conditions effectively such that learning goals are most likely to be achieved (Nelson-Le Gall, 1985; Zimmerman & Martinez-Pons, 1986).

Most of the various self-regulated learning strategies reported in the literature (see, for example, Pintrich, Smith & McKeachie, 1989; Weinstein, Zimmerman & Palmer, 1988; Zimmerman & Martinez-Pons, 1986) fall into one or another of the categories I have constructed.

Contextual sensitivity, I should note, although implicit in much of the published literature, is not an area typically identified explicitly as an independent aspect of self-regulated learning. However, the theme that cognitive processes are contextually bound, or "situated" (Rogoff & Lave, 1984; Rogoff, 1990) is becoming increasingly general in the contemporary literature on learning and cognition, particularly as it occurs in educational settings. I therefore decided to define it as a separate dimension of self-regulated learning. Also unique to this model of self-regulated learning is the inclusion of epistemological beliefs as a moderating factor. The particular epistemological orientation (absolutist, relativist, evaluative) or set of beliefs that characterize a given individual imposes powerful constraints on the nature and degree of self-regulation a learner is likely to exhibit (Perry, 1988; Schommer, 1990).

In developing this model, I reasoned that the self-regulated learner must be able to both internally regulate, monitor, evaluate, and modify, when necessary, the learning process and be alert to and utilize or manage contextual (external) factors such as course and instructor demands, where and when to study, who, when, and where to go for assistance. It is also evident that motivational factors mediate the utilization of both cognitive and environmental resources (Borkowski et al., 1990). Individuals high in self-efficacy, for example, are more likely to use cognitive and metacognitive strategies and to seek appropriate (instrumental) forms of assistance when needed (Karabenick & Knapp, 1991; Schunk, 1991). At the same time, there is a positive relationship between a sense of personal control over learning outcomes and subsequent motivation (Dweck, 1989; Schunk, 1991) to undertake learning related challenges. Furthermore, self-regulated learners must not only be motivated, they must know how to **sustain** motivation over time and in the face of competing alternatives or demands (Kuhl & Beckman, 1985). Despite the many elements that enter into it, there is sound reason to believe that self-regulated learning is a unified process which involves the integration and utilization of cognitive, metacognitive, motivational, perceptual, and environmental components in the successful resolution of academic tasks (Lindner & Harris, 1992a; Zimmerman & Martinez-Pons, 1986).

Figure 1
Conceptual model of the self-regulated learning process

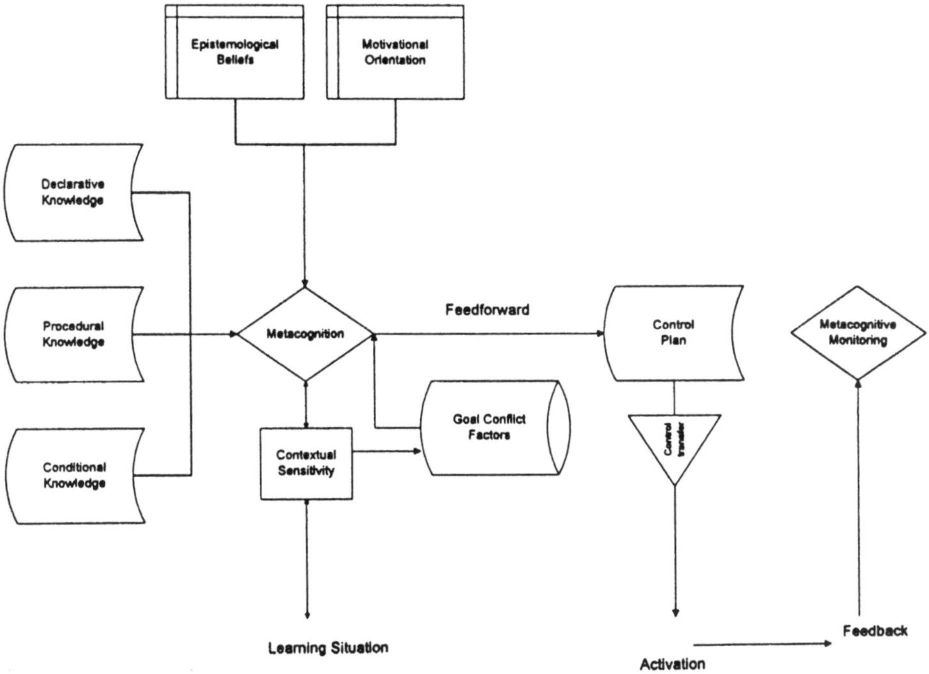

Perhaps the interworkings of the model in action can best be grasped by way of an example. Using Figure 1 as a guide, consider a student faced with the typical task of preparing for a quiz. For purposes of discussion let us assume it will be a written (rather than multiple choice) quiz. Let us also assume the quiz has been announced one week in advance and the subject is world politics. A number of decisions face the learner even in this simple situation. The strategy the learner eventually pursues depends both on factors internal to the learner and external factors present in the larger situation in which the learning task is set. First of all, the learner brings at least three kinds of knowledge to any task: declarative (knowing that or what), procedural (knowing how), and conditional (knowing when and where to do what). As the learner encounters a particular task, the eventual strategy developed will depend both on the knowledge she possesses and how well she reads the nature and demands of the task (contextual sensitivity). If background knowledge is strong (the task is familiar), the solution path may appear simple and straightforward. If specific knowledge is lacking (regarding the subject matter or the situation or because the teacher is new to the student), a general strategy or plan must be developed. For such a plan to be effective, metacognitive or executive processing will be required. However, the nature of the decisions made at this point will also be driven internally by the largely unconscious epistemological beliefs and motivational orientation the learner brings to the task. If, for example, the learner's epistemological orientation is absolutist in nature, she will interpret the task as primarily a matter of acquiring the "facts," memorizing them and regurgitating them exactly. A relativist, on the other hand, is likely to interpret the task as asking for her opinion on the facts or issue in question.

Motivational orientation too will affect the course of action selected by the learner. If, for example, the learner is **performance** oriented (Dweck, 1989), and the task is challenging (the risk of failure is relatively high), she may choose to minimize effort in order to have a ready-made explanation in the case of failure (I didn't try). Both one's epistemological and motivational orientation exert a tacit but powerful influence on the learner's executive decision-making process. These factors are particularly crucial to investigate if the learning process in a specific individual's case is or becomes maladaptive.

Let us assume, for the purposes of discussion, that our hypothetical learner's epistemological and motivational orientations are relatively salutary. The executive component must effectively define and analyze the learning situation and devise an appropriate action strategy. The efficacy of the strategy devised will be dependent upon the depth of the learner's repertoire of learning tactics and conditional knowledge. Performance will also vary as a function of the number and attractiveness of goal conflict factors (social and other extracurricular activities) present in a situation relative to the effort and actions necessary if the goal of passing the quiz is to be achieved. The stronger the drive to succeed, and the fewer the number and attractiveness of goal conflict factors present, the greater the likelihood that the learner will persist in carrying out the strategy in pursuit of goal attainment. In any case, metacognitive reflection and processing subsequently generates feedforward in terms of a learning plan and goal selection. The plan will next be transformed into action. Action, of course, produces feedback which, if carefully monitored, allows adjustments to the plan over the course of action. Feedback of a different kind also comes upon task completion. Such feedback not only informs the learner if she succeeded but provides a source of conditional knowledge allowing for future construction of more appropriate and adaptive strategy building. Teaching can play a crucial facilitating and informative role at this point in insuring that proper connections between behavior and outcome are made on the part of the student.

The Development of Self-Regulated Learning

In approaching the question of development, as previously noted, I favor a sociocultural approach in the spirit of Vygotsky (1978). That is, I assume that cognition is first other-regulated within the context of the individual's social and cultural relationships. Through social interaction over time, cognitive structures and processes peculiar to each individual arise which come to characterize her conceptual and procedural interaction with the events and individual actors of her world. Ideally, the individual, moving through the **zone of proximal development** (Vygotsky, 1978), gradually becomes increasingly self-conscious and self-regulating. In Vygotsky's (1981) terms: "Any function in the child's cultural development appears twice, or on two planes. First it appears on the social plane, and then on the psychological plane. First it appears between people as an interpsychological category, and then within the child as an intrapsychological category." It is important to note that, from this perspective, the degree to which one self-regulates behavior and thought is primarily a function of the nature and quality of one's interpersonal relationships. I want to also emphasize, however, that self-regulation of **academic** cognition, in the sense that I have been depicting it, is neither a necessary or natural outcome of development. This is not meant to suggest, however, that the contents of one's mind and the nature of one's interactions are strictly determined by sociocultural experience. Individuals clearly play a role in determining their developmental routes and outcomes. Nevertheless, sociocultural experience imposes powerful constraints (for good or ill) on individual development.

The issue of the development of **academic** self-regulation raises not only the question of origin but of individual and group differences. That is, are some individuals and/or groups (for example, socioeconomic, ethnic) more or less likely to develop the skills and attitudes of a self-regulated learner than others, and why?

Self-Regulated Learning and Multicultural Education

I have thus far provided a description and evidence for the general characteristics and development of self-regulated learners. The question many readers will want addressed, however, is: are some learners more or less likely to be self-regulating due to differential cultural or subcultural experiences? The answer (although too complicated to address fully here) would seem to be, yes. This appears particularly true with groups who have traditionally not performed well in our schools and whose status is "castelike or involuntary" (Ogbu, 1992, p. 8). This involuntary status as a minority leads many members of such groups to identify the adoption of certain behaviors (for example, those associated with success in school) as requiring a rejection of their own unique cultural identity and sense of community. The result is an inability or unwillingness to accommodate their behavior to the demands of classroom culture which would facilitate success in that setting. In fact, such individuals are likely to enter the classroom setting with a cultural identity that has been formed in significant ways in opposition to that of the dominant culture (Ogbu, 1992). The problem is further exacerbated by peer pressure and the lack of clear incentives within the context of a social reality that is less than encouraging in terms of future social and/or economic success. Ogbu has done much to clarify the nature of the different cultural frames of reference such groups bring to the classroom context. I suspect that this issue plays out, in terms of the issue of self-regulation of learning, in several ways.

In the first place, I suspect that some minority groups not only operate from a different **cultural** frame but (perhaps, partly as a consequence) a different **epistemological** frame of reference. In terms of my own research (Lindner, 1994), the evidence suggests that certain epistemological beliefs antithetical to academic success are dominant among, for example, African Americans who have been incarcerated. I hesitate to generalize from such data. However, I do think it indicates that this question demands further investigation. Certainly differences in epistemological criteria on a variety of issues is implicit in the many debates between minority and dominant group members that appear to talk past one another.

Secondly, an individual possessed of an oppositional orientation to behaviors and attitudes that promote success in the classroom seems unlikely to develop either the motivational orientation or processing strategies likely to facilitate academic success. In short, I strongly suspect that members of minority groups of an involuntary status are less likely to demonstrate the kinds of attitudes and behaviors I have defined as underlying academic self-regulation. I have no doubt, however, that if convinced that a strategy of "accommodation without assimilation" (Gibson, 1988) were in their best interest, such individuals could be taught to develop and utilize such skills. Indeed, the (admittedly limited) data we have on **successful** minority students at the college level (Harris & Lindner, 1993) indicates that they utilize self-regulated learning skills to a higher degree than less successful students, regardless of status.

Applications of Self-Regulated Learning Theory to Instruction

Since experience, and in particular social experience, plays such a powerful role in the development of self-regulation, it should not be surprising that school experiences are crucial in the development of the cognitive tools available to individuals. The school setting is at once a cultural artifact and a living social and experiential context in which the primary

Figure 2
The self-regulated learning/teaching cycle

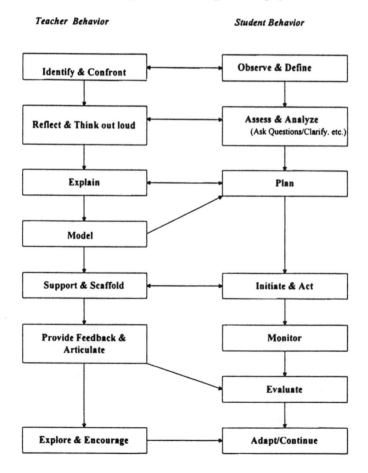

250

focus is literacy-based learning. Some forms of teacher-learner (as well as peer) interaction, however, are clearly more facilitative of self-regulation of the learning process than others. Teaching can be primarily presentative and corrective (focused on what Howard Gardner (1991) has termed the "correct answer compromise"), wherein the teacher regulates the learning; or dialogic and facilitative, wherein the teacher actively seeks to foster student regulation of the learning process.

The particular instructional model I have been developing incorporates the basic assumptions of the **cognitive apprenticeship** approach (Rogoff 1990) and tailors them such that they specifically foster the emergence and development of self-regulated learning. As Rogoff, (p. 39) notes, cognitive apprenticeship occurs when "active novices advance their skills and understanding through participation with more skilled partners in culturally organized activities." Cognitive apprenticeship is, in other words, a form of socially mediated instruction wherein 1) to-be-learned skills are modeled by a more experienced [adult or peer] "expert," 2) made explicit by the "expert" through think-aloud demonstrations in the application and regulation of the component skills, and 3) over the course of learning the "novice" is induced to accept increasing responsibility for his/her performance of the target skill (Englert & Raphael, 1989). Also crucial to the cognitive apprenticeship model is the notion that socially mediated learning is most effective when occurring within the zone of proximal development (Vygotsky, 1978; Rogoff 1990). That is, such instruction attempts to enter a student's optimal region of sensitivity to social guidance in order to facilitate cognitive growth. While space does not permit a complete explication of a self-regulated teaching model, let me attempt to describe its basic skeleton and, on the student side of the process, what it seeks to promote.

Before I begin, allow me to state some preliminary conditions and concerns. It is important to realize that if self-regulated learning is the desired outcome of instruction, then the conditions of learning and instruction must be designed to insure its development. That is, self-regulated learning must be the explicit goal of instruction. Furthermore, instructional policy and the institutional support system that regulates its day-to-day affairs must be such as to facilitate this educational goal. This point may appear obvious. However, it is crucial to emphasize at the outset that traditional schooling in this country, though well intended, has inclined toward fostering learning that is teacher and policy (other) regulated rather than seeking to foster student self-regulation of the learning process. Unfortunately, programs that have set out explicitly to promote self-regulated learning, at this juncture, remain largely experimental in nature (see, for example, Paris, Cross, & Lipson, 1984). Having said this, the question of how, in practical terms, to go about the business of nurturing self-regulated learners remains to be addressed.

First of all, it is recommended that teaching for self-regulated learning take place in conjunction with the teaching of content rather than as a separate set of skills. Emphasizing self-regulated learning in the context of content and skill acquisition ensures the greater likelihood of transfer. Secondly, it is crucial that instruction begin at the level of the student. Simply informing students about powerful learning tools will only produce, at best, confusion and discouragement. Thirdly, it is crucial that the collaborative and reciprocal nature of the teaching-learning process inform the entire cycle. Teaching and learning are not two separate activities with entirely independent aims and responsibilities. Rather, they are highly complementary activities with a single aim: the promotion of informed, independent and skillful information processing and decision making. In order to accomplish this overarching goal, it is critical for the teacher to take the mystery out of the learning process by making his thinking visible (by thinking out loud) and through modeling the learning cycle for the student. The ultimate aim, it must be kept in mind, is to transfer control of the performance sought from the teacher to the student. This deceptively simple point is a difficult one for many teachers, particularly those who feel they must always be in control of all that occurs in their classroom. In sum, the teacher's task is to move the student from other-regulation, through the zone of proximal development, to self-regulation.

One begins the cycle by **identifying** for and **confronting** the learner with the problem to be solved, or skill to be taught. In so doing, one should pause and **reflect**, considering (out loud) the reason(s) behind the identification of the problem or the skill to be learned. For example, a highly effective strategy for learning from text involves generating and answering crucial questions such as what, when, who, where, how, and why with regard to text content. Teaching the effective use of this strategy would include explicit identification of the learning goal and the reasoning behind its use. In an effort to clarify and promote comprehension, the teacher may wish, at this point, to have students generate, discuss, and compare possible alternative strategies. The next step involves **explaining** how to effect the strategy followed by explicit and detailed **modeling** of the strategy on the part of the teacher. In the process, the teacher should **articulate** what is being done and why. Once these five steps have been carried through, time should be taken to **encourage and explore** questions or consider strategies generated by students and to explicitly consider other situations in which the strategy or skill being taught could effectively be employed.

At this point, students should be allowed to attempt to apply the strategy or skill on their own under the careful **scaffolded guidance** of the teacher. The basic idea is to provide as much, and only as much, guidance as the student requires. A crucial element in the successful internalization of the learning process is provision of explicit and detailed **feedback** from teacher to student. Finally, the learner's independent action and taking control of the learning process must be carefully nourished and **encouraged**. That the entire cycle I have described is in the form of a dialectic (dialogue) between teacher and learner (designed to regulate learning and cognition) is hopefully transparent. Its aim is to promote an approach and attitude toward learning and behavior that is self-reflective, self-evaluative, and, ultimately, self-regulative. If attained, transfer, in the sense of the regulation of cognition, will, I think follow rather naturally. In fact, such transfer can be viewed as the hidden goal of the self-regulated teaching-learning sequence. The learning/teaching cycle, however, does not end at this point. In fact, there is no real end point to the sequence, just as there is no true end point in learning. At the closing of a particular teaching/learning event, time should, once again, be taken to **encourage and explore** questions or consider alternative strategies generated by students, now that they have applied the strategy or skill on their own. It would be wise, I think, as a particular portion of the cycle is brought to closure, to also consider the possible limitations of a specific skill, concept, or strategy.

I believe it worth noting at this point that what I have been describing as a teaching model for promoting self-regulated learning falls within a family of approaches to instruction called **constructivist** models. A persistent criticism of constructivist approaches to instruction is they place too much of a burden on the learner without sufficient consideration of the kinds and complexity of entry level skills they presuppose (Dick, 1991; Perkins, 1991). Such criticisms have a grain of truth in them. That is, the cognitive demands of complex tasks can be overwhelming and frustrating for a novice learner. As Perkins (1991,

p. 18) puts it: "Constructivist pedagogy often imposes sharp demands on learners." It is tempting, therefore, for both teacher and learner to succumb to the allure of a more direct approach to instruction. The answer to this dilemma, however, is not to abandon the constructivist approach. Rather, the answer lies in a pedagogical approach that stresses the crucial role of the **scaffolding** (a pedagogical technique that seeks to temporarily reduce the cognitive load imposed on the learner when confronted with new and complex tasks or concepts) of the learning process by a sensitive and flexible teacher.

The model I have described above is, admittedly, abstract and sketchy in nature. The main point, again, involves an emphasis on taking the mystery out of learning and the fostering of volitional control on the part of the learner. Since gaining such control is a complex process, such instruction needs to occur early and often in the learning career of students. A specific technique, primarily a form of scaffolding, which I use with my students (many of whom are the products of schooling that fostered other-regulation of learning!), is represented in Appendix B. Basically, prior to entering a new content area in my classes, I pass out this sheet and ask students to begin filling it in. I begin by asking them to clearly define and differentiate (as far as they can, at this point) the topic we will be examining, and to set some specific goal(s) with regard to learning it. Next, I attempt to lead them to draw out whatever knowledge (accurate or inaccurate) they already possess concerning the topic at issue. In this manner, active learning is initiated. Once they have read their text and the topic has been covered in class, I ask students to consider: 1) what questions they have, 2) how confident they would be about taking a test, and 3) what specifically they could do to improve their understanding. That this form of instruction is designed to promote taking charge of the learning process on the part of the student is, hopefully, transparent. It represents a type of **dialogue** between teacher and learner that, if all goes well, will be internalized by the student and become a normal aspect of her learning *modus operandi*. The technique allows for flexibility and for working through the various steps (as needed) of the teaching process previously articulated. This is, of course, only one way to actualize teaching for self-regulated learning. The specific technique employed is, I believe, not nearly as important as the fact that a deliberate, conscious effort is made on the part of teachers to foster self-regulated learning in the classroom.

References

Borkowski, J. G., Carr, M., Rellinger, E., & Pressley, M. (1990). Self-regulated cognition: Interdependence of metacognition, attributions, and self-esteem. In B. F. Jones & L. Idol (Eds.), *Dimensions of thinking and cognitive instruction*. Hillsdale, NJ: Erlbaum.

Brown, A. (1987). Metacognition, executive control, self-regulation and other more mysterious mechanisms. In F. E. Weinert & R. H. Kluwe (Eds.), *Metacognition, motivation, and understanding*. Hillsdale, NJ: Erlbaum.

Derry, S. J. (1990). Learning strategies for acquiring useful knowledge. In B. F. Jones & L. Idol (Eds.), *Dimensions of thinking and cognitive instruction*. Hillsdale, NJ: Erlbaum.

Dick, W. (1991, May). An instructional designer's view of constructivism. *Educational Technology, 31*, 31-44.

Dweck, C. S. (1989). Motivation. In A. Lesgold & R. Glaser (Eds.), *Foundations for a psychology of education*. Hillsdale, NJ: Erlbaum.

Englert, C. S., & Raphael, T. E. (1989). Developing successful writers through cognitive strategy instruction. In J. Brophy (Ed.), *Advances in research on teaching, Vol. 1.* Greenwich, CT: JAI Press.

Flavell, J. H. (1979). Metacognition and cognitive monitoring: A new area of cognitive-developmental inquiry. *American Psychologist, 34,* 906-911.

Gardner, H. (1991). *The unschooled mind.* New York: Basic Books.

Gibson, M.A. (1988). *Accommodation without assimilation: Sikh immigrants in an American high school.* Ithaca, NY: Cornell University Press.

Harris, B. R., & Lindner, R.W. (1993). *Cultural influences on self-regulated learning.* Unpublished manuscript.

Jones, B. F., & Idol, L. (Eds.). (1990). *Dimensions of thinking and cognitive instruction.* Hillsdale, NJ: Erlbaum.

Karabenick, S. A., & Knapp, J. R. (1991). Relationship of academic help seeking to the use of learning strategies and other instrumental achievement behavior in college students. *Journal of Educational Psychology, 83*(2), 221-230.

Kuhl, J., & Beckman, J. (Eds.). (1985). *Action control: From cognition to behavior.* Berlin: Springer-Verlag.

Kuhn, D. (1991). *The skills of argument.* New York: Cambridge University Press.

Lindner, R. W. (1994). Self-regulated learning in correctional education students and its implications for instruction. *The Journal of Correctional Education, 45*(3), 122-126.

Lindner, R. W. & Harris, B. (1992a). *Self-regulated learning and academic achievement in college students.* Paper presented at the April, 1992, American Educational Research Association annual convention, San Francisco.

Lindner, R. W., & Harris, B. (1992b). Self-regulated learning: Its assessment and instructional implications. *Educational Research Quarterly, 16,* 2.

Nelson-Le Gall, S. (1985). Help-seeking behavior in learning. *Review of Research in Education, 12,* 55-90.

Ogbu, J. U. (1992). Understanding cultural diversity and learning. *Educational Researcher, 21*(8), 5-14.

Paris, S. G., Cross, D. R., & Lipson, M. Y. (1984). Informed strategies for learning: A program to improve children's reading awareness and comprehension. *Journal of Educational Psychology, 76,* 1239-1252.

Perkins, D. N. (1991, September). What constructivism demands of the learner. *Educational Technology, 31,* 19-21.

Perry, W. G. (1988). Different worlds in the same classroom. In P. Ramsden (Ed.). *Improving learning: New perspectives.* London: Kogan Page.

Pintrich, P. R., Smith, D. A., & McKeachie, W. J. (1989). *Motivated strategies for learning questionnaire.* Ann Arbor: University of Michigan.

Pressley, M., Woloshyn, V., Lysynchuck, L. M., Martin, V., Wood, E., & Willoughby, T. (1990). A primer of research on cognitive strategy instruction: The important issues and how to address them. *Educational Psychology Review, 2,* 1-58.

Rogoff, B. (1990). *Apprenticeship in thinking: Cognitive development in cultural context.* New York: Oxford University Press.

Rogoff, B., & Lave, J. (Eds.). (1984). *Everyday cognition: Its development in social context.* Cambridge, MA: Harvard University Press.

Schommer, M. (1990). Effects of beliefs about the nature of knowledge on comprehension. *Journal of Educational Psychology, 82*(3), 498-504.

Schunk, D. H. (1991). *Learning theories: An educational perspective.* New York: Merrill.

Vygotsky, L. S. (1978). (M. Cole, V. John-Steiner, S. Scribner, & E. Souberman, Eds.). *Mind in society: The development of higher psychological processes.* Cambridge, MA: Harvard University Press.

Vygotsky, L. S. (1981). The genesis of higher mental functions. In J. V. Wertsch (Ed.), *The concept of activity in Soviet psychology.* Armonk, NY: M. E. Sharpe.

Weinstein, C. E., Zimmerman, S. A., & Palmer, D. R. (1988). Assessing learning strategies: The design and development of the LASSI. In C. E. Weinstein, E. T. Goetz, & P. A. Alexander (Eds.), *Learning and study strategies: Issues in assessment, instruction, and evaluation.* New York: Academic Press.

Zimmerman, B. J. (1989). A social cognitive view of self-regulated academic learning. *Journal of Educational Psychology, 81*, 329-339.

Zimmerman, B. J. (1990). Self-regulated learning and academic achievement: An overview. *Educational Psychologist, 25*, 3-17.

Zimmerman, B. J., & Martinez-Pons, M. (1986). Development of a structured interview for assessing student use of self-regulated learning strategies. *American Educational Research Journal, 23*, 614-628.

Zimmerman, B. J. & Martinez-Pons, M. (1988). Construct validation of a strategy model of student self-regulated learning. *Journal of Educational Psychology, 80*, 284-290.

Zimmerman, B. J., & Schunk, D. H. (Eds.). (1989). *Self-regulated learning and academic achievement: Theory, research and practice.* New York: Springer-Verlag.

Appendix A
Self-regulated Learning
(Lindner & Harris, 1992)

General definition: A) The ability to monitor, regulate, evaluate, sustain, and strategically modify, when necessary, the learning process and B) sensitivity to, and ability to exercise control over, contextual factors that affect learning outcomes. The basic components of self-regulated learning include 1) **epistemological beliefs**, 2) **motivational processes**, 3) **metacognitive processes**, 4) **learning strategies**, 5) **contextual sensitivity**, and 6) **environmental control and/or utilization**. Self-regulated learners are possessed of a belief system that views knowledge as complex and evolving, rather than simple and fixed, and the knower as capable of self-modification. An individual is a self-regulated learner to the degree that she/he is able to effectively monitor and regulate (control) and sustain the learning process; apply a variety of appropriate and efficient strategies to learning problems encountered; maintain a sense of competence, (intrinsic) motivation, and personal agency; accurately diagnose the character and demands of particular learning challenges; and effectively utilize and control environmental factors that have a bearing on learning outcomes.

Six Dimensions of Self-Regulated Learning

A. **Epistemological Beliefs**: Defined as relatively enduring and unconscious beliefs about the nature of knowledge and the process of knowing (i.e., the source, certainty, speed of acquisition, etc., of knowledge).

B. **Motivation**: Refers to goal oriented effort that is a complex function of goal value, goal accessibility, learning orientation, perceived likelihood of success, one's sense of self-efficacy and the factor(s) to which one habitually attributes success and/or failure.

C. **Metacognition**: Defined generally as 1) knowledge about cognition and 2) awareness and conscious regulation of one's thinking and learning. The executive engine of cognition.

D. **Learning Strategies**: Refers to both operative knowledge of specific learning tactics (highlighting, summarizing, etc.) and the ability to combine various tactics into an effective learning plan.

E. **Contextual Sensitivity**: Refers to the ability to "read" the learning context for what it specifies regarding the demands of a particular problem setting and what it affords in the way of problem resolution.

F. **Environmental Utilization/Control**: Refers to the utilization and management of circumstances and resources external to the self in the pursuit of learning related goals.

Appendix B
What I Know Metacognitive Worksheet

TOPIC/SECTION: _____

_____

LEARNING GOAL(S): _____

_____

Before you begin, consider:

What do I know about this topic already (activate prior knowledge):

    First: Ask yourself, have I read/heard about this topic before?
    Then: Briefly review mentally your prior understanding of the topic.

    NEXT, begin studying. After each major section of text, STOP and ASK:

What do I know about this topic after studying/learning:

    First: Outline or map out the main concepts as presented in your text.
    Then: Summarize the main concepts presented in your own words.

What do I still not know or understand (questions I have):

    First: Return to your text and list concepts which you missed or which are still unclear.
    Then: Try to specify what is confusing you about the concepts you identified as unclear.

If I had to take a test on this topic right now, what grade would I expect?

    Circle one: A B C D F

FINALLY, ask yourself:

What could I do to improve my knowledge and understanding?

    First: Review and evaluate your previous strategy.
    Next: Revise your strategy to enhance your progress toward your goal(s).

ENDING THE SILENCE:
ENCOURAGING DISSENSUS IN THE CONTACT ZONE

by
Hallie S. Lemon

"Silence is the weapon of hostility and has a way of breeding violence, first of the body and then the soul."

—Jerry Hazen

This quote cannot be found in a textbook on pedagogy but is remembered from a Sunday sermon; the minister added that we can best end prejudice not by realizing that the objects of prejudice are just as good as we are but by realizing that they can be as human as we are, too, and have their dark moments. In our collaborative classrooms, silence among class-mates has been replaced by dialogue. Linda Dittmar (1993) recognized this silence as a barrier which students either struggle to break through or keep in place. Breaking silence without conflict in a multicultural classroom appears impossible and, as I hope to show, may even be undesirable. In a classroom of students from diverse cultures, which Mary Louise Pratt (1991) describes as a contact zone, fostering honest dialogue requires structured teaching strategies as well as an understanding of four terms: **dissensus, consensus, confrontation/problem solving**, and **groupthink**.

Kenneth Bruffee (1993) concentrates on redefining higher education as helping students "reacculturate themselves and one another into the community that the teacher represents" (p. 225). He defines reacculturation as switching membership from one culture to another; it involves:

. . . giving up, modifying, or renegotiating the language, values, knowledge, mores, and so on that are constructed, established, and maintained by the community one is coming from, and becoming fluent instead in the language and so on of another community. (p. 225)

College teachers should recognize the learning process as a reacculturation and acknowledge that students will be negotiating from many primary cultures brought with them into the classroom.

Definition of *Dissensus*

Bruffee's definition of learning as reacculturation provides a theoretical foundation for John Trimbur's (1989) description of **dissensus**, Pratt's (1991) contact zone, and the conver-sation which occurs at the boundaries of knowledge communities. Boundary discourse is the most positive term for the language of negotiation; it has also been referred to as abnormal discourse and non-standard discourse. However, it is more correctly seen as a complete and acceptable language of one culture negotiating with the language of another culture. In our college classrooms because no single voice can speak for all the students, the multicultural heritage of the students affects the negotiations.

Trimbur (1989) discusses two main criticisms of collaborative learning: first, that consensus stifles the individual voice, and second, that it focuses on the conversation of knowledge communities but fails to realize they are embedded in an "unequal, exclusionary social order" with "hierarchical relations of power" (p. 603). We are teaching our students to participate in the more knowledgeable conversations of our disciplines, to recognize that we all belong to many communities each with its own vernacular language. But "the term vernacular cannot be understood apart from the relation of domination and subordination that it implies" (p. 609).

Given these criticisms, Trimbur (1989) wants us to consider the collaborative learning occurring in our college classrooms from a new perspective:

> We will need . . . to look at collaborative learning not merely as a process of consensus-making but more important as *a process of identifying differences and locating these differences in relation to each other* [italics added]. The consensus that we ask students to reach in a collaborative classroom will be based not so much on collective agreements as on collective explanations of how people differ, where their differences come from, and whether they can live and work with these differences. (p. 610)

Trimbur (1989) suggests that we remind our students that consensus does not often happen in daily situations involving conflicting points of view; often, nobody takes the time to hear all sides of an issue to try to reach a solution that all parties can accept. Therefore, our students should be encouraged to interrupt the conversation "in order to investigate the forces that determine who may speak and what may be said, what inhibits conversation and what makes it possible" (p. 612). Which people are being excluded from the conversation and how are they being excluded? These discussions can serve as, "a critical measure to understand the distortions of communication and plays of power in normal discourse" (p. 615).

The second term in my title, **contact zone**, is closely related to Trimbur's ideas and was illustrated by Pratt (1991). Pratt urges us to think of our classrooms as contact zones where "cultures meet, clash, and grapple with each other, often in contexts of highly asymmetrical relations of power" (p. 34). Pratt wants us to establish "safe houses" in our curriculum where dissensus is tolerated and valued: "intellectual spaces where groups can constitute themselves . . . with high degrees of trust, shared understandings, temporary protection from legacies of oppression" (p. 40). When cultures are discussed and objectified in a multicultural course, "all students [will see] their roots traced back to legacies of both glory and shame; all the students [will experience] face-to-face the ignorance and incomprehension, and occasionally the hostility, of others" (p. 39).

Richard Miller (1994) notes, "Required self-reflexivity does not, of course, guarantee that repugnant positions will be abandoned. . . . [It] does not mean that this approach wields sufficient power to transform the matrix of beliefs, values, and prejudices that students (and teachers) bring to the classroom" (p. 407). We still need strategies for dealing with resistant students, but Miller believes that close attention to what our students say and write in the contact zone may provide "the most promising pedagogical response" (p. 408). Pratt also notes "moments of wonder and revelation, mutual understanding and new wisdom—the joys of the contact zone" (p. 39).

How does the notion of dissensus, which exists within the contact zones of our multicultural classrooms, affect our understanding of collaborative learning itself?

Dangers of Consensus

Teachers have viewed consensus as the ultimate outcome of collaborative work and feared conflict in group discussions, perhaps intervening to stop any heated verbal disagreement. Weiner (1986) uses Trimbur's earlier definition of consensus to show how important it has been thought to be to the nature of collaborative work: "intellectual negotiation which leads to an outcome (consensus) through a process of taking responsibility and investing collective judgment with authority" (p. 55). In fact, Weiner asserts that this attempt to reach consensus is the main element which "distinguishes collaborative learning from mere work in groups" (p. 54). Consensus or ". . . collective judgments in groups" (p. 55) is necessary for the groups to accomplish the goal of the activity; Weiner describes a successful task description as one which contains instructions to . . . "require a member of the group to record this consensus in writing" (p. 56).

In the same article, however, Weiner quotes a letter from Trimbur warning new practitioners of collaborative learning to understand, "the process of social negotiation that underwrites consensus" (p. 54). In this letter, Trimbur already seems to be working toward the concept of dissensus defined in his 1989 article. Noting that most successful collaborative activities allow students to understand the underlying causes of differing views, he would have us teach students that they can "agree to disagree" (p. 54).

Dittmar (1993) is another who warns a harmonious exchange might indicate a "bland melding of cultures" (p. 36). Allan Cox (1991) in "Consensus as a Killer of Creativity" argues we don't want consensus, which he defines as an "attempt to secure virtual unanimity among a group of people," because it wastes time, leads to "mediocre options," and discourages commitment to the decision. "Something that is everybody's task becomes nobody's task" (p. 15). He defines effective teamwork as "managing diversity"; today's corporations now have access to new viewpoints and ways of meeting problems because of the past experiences and traditions of their multicultural work force. The team members realize sometimes their ideas are implemented, sometimes not, but they are always solicited and considered. Cox encourages confrontation between these often conflicting ideas; the leader needs to be one who "chooses between the competing options he has spurred through vital exchanges among his [or her] team members" (p. 15).

Confrontation/Problem Solving

Learning how to value and manage conflict successfully is another skill we should be teaching our students in a multicultural classroom. Wilson and Hanna (1986) acknowledge conflict can be dysfunctional or functional and can at times provide benefits. When used effectively, the advantages of conflict may include: 1) increased involvement of members, 2) an outlet for hostility, 3) greater cohesiveness of the group, and 4) a greater chance for commitment to the decision (p. 268). They explain both poor and effective conflict-management strategies labeling **confrontation/problem-solving** as a win-win strategy while compromise is considered a lose-lose method. What do these labels tell us about forcing compromise on our students to achieve consensus?

Wilson and Hanna's key is to focus on long-term goals rather than solutions to individual problems. Blaming the other person involved will not help; energies need to be directed toward defeating the problem. One example comes from management efforts to keep health

261

insurance costs down. Workers had full coverage with no deductible, but the company was concerned about yearly increases averaging 15%; workers, forced to pay the same percentage increase each month to cover their dependents, wanted the company to pay part of this. A compromise would have split the difference and given employees half of what they were asking. However, an integrated solution, like those favored by Wilson and Hanna, resulted when the overall insurance picture was studied. In this instance, the employees accepted a $100 deductible that brought the total cost down for both the company and employees and allowed the company to pay a portion of dependent coverage while the employees' $100 deductible was made up through reduced dependent payments.

One way to arrive at an integrated solution such as this one is to employ good listening skills (something that can be taught) as well as to confirm understandings and conclusions being discussed; participants should be encouraged to come to the group with tentative solutions and answers, even researching them beforehand. Obviously in my example, both sides had to understand the effects of a deductible in reducing insurance costs before discussing it.

Current studies are being done to learn more about the ways learning groups function and about conflict in groups. Some of the findings may be surprising to many teachers. Thia Wolf (1990) has noted that the litany of complaint heard when the students begin to work is actually part of the process; it unites the group as they begin to relate to the assignment. Some of the comments a circulating teacher may hear as off the task may be part of the necessary socialization process that goes on, or they may be used deliberately to break the tension that occurs when the groups are on track, either negotiating ideas or evaluating each other's work. A membrane is established, and neither the teacher nor a student should break it.

Theodore F. Sheckels (1992) outlines the types of talk in collaborative groups into Task Talk, Role Talk, Consciousness-Raising Talk, Encounter Talk, and Non-Verbal Dimensions. The teacher's attitude toward encounter talk is often hostile, but Sheckels suggests it shouldn't be because conflict often indicates boundary-seeking and is positive. He identifies only three behaviors as negative: dominating (not allowing other people to speak), clowning (undermining the seriousness of the lesson), or blocking (preventing discussion of the issues). Robert Brooke (1987) defines the activities students "engage in to show that their identities are different from or more complex than the identities assigned them by organizational roles" as the students' **underlife** (p. 142). He suggests that what appears to the teacher to be disruptive behavior is actually students ". . . actively connecting ideas in the classroom to their own lives outside the classroom" (p. 145).

Geoffrey A. Cross (1993), in a book-length ethnography of a collaborative writing group, suggests teachers train students to understand and manage conflict. He defines confrontation as "the meeting of mutual needs" (p. 135). Students should be encouraged to elicit information from the dissenters and keep a **conflict-process log** to identify group conflicts and ways of managing them. Discussion of these process logs may be one way to deal with resistant students. He warns that groups, knowing a compromise will always be reached, will begin discussion with expanded demands; some compromise solutions "may be so weakened as to be ineffective" (p. 135). Although a decision must eventually be reached, Wolf notes that controversy is very much a part of euphoria in groups; teachers should be more wary of groupthink.

Groupthink

In my own classrooms, I am worried about groups that reach conclusions too soon, so I often deliberately try to complicate matters for them. If, for example, a group reaches a complete interpretation of a complex essay in a few minutes, I will ask questions about aspects that they have not considered. Usually, one student has noted at least some of the complexity but has been silenced by fear of a confrontation. These groups who find the easy consensus may exhibit characteristics of **groupthink**, a term outlined by Irving Janis in 1972 and charted in a subsequent book by Janis and Leon Mann (1977). They have outlined the antecedent conditions for groups guilty of groupthink and subsequent poor decision making, among them: 1) high cohesiveness, 2) insulation from others, 3) lack of good procedures for finding information, 4) directive leadership.

Janis and Mann claim these conditions lead a group to believe itself to be invulnerable. Such a group tends to rationalize its decisions, to stereotype other groups, and to believe it is in the right. It censors itself, not allowing in ideas that would alter its views. The results often show an incomplete survey of choices and objectives, a biased processing of information, and a failure to work out alternative plans or scenarios. Janis (1972) offers suggestions to prevent groupthink including regularly appointing someone from the group to challenge all ideas that are proposed; this role could be added to that of discussion leader and/or recorder.

When our groups are too homogeneous and reach conclusions too quickly, we should look for the signs of groupthink. Dittmar (1993) cites the diversity of views in a successful class in direct contrast to a second class that was less successful: "about half the class consisted of young high school graduates, all European American graduates of parochial schools, and mostly of one ethnicity" (p. 30). However, heterogeneous grouping may not always be possible in our classrooms, so what other strategies could we employ to encourage dissensus in our classrooms?

Strategies to Encourage *Dissensus*

Reither and Vipond (1989) provide successful ways to use collaborative strategies which might encourage the type of discussion Trimbur is calling for in his article. They focus on the knowledge-making aspects of collaboration. "We make our meanings not alone, but in relation to others' meanings, which we come to know through reading, talk, and writing" (p. 862). They suggest structuring entire courses so "students collaboratively investigate a more or less original scholarly question or field" (p. 863). "The teacher is responsible for orchestrating and acting as an expert co-researcher, modeling the process" (p. 863). Reither's senior Shakespeare class investigated what Shakespeare had to know to write his plays; Vipond's introductory psychology class investigated the psychology of humor. On the basis of numerous studies, Slavin (1989-1990) has concluded "when students of different racial or ethnic groups work together toward a common goal, they gain in liking and respect for one another" (p. 53).

My example in NCTE's *Talking to Learn* (1990) was developed for a sophomore composition class; for their final project, the groups of students choose an art form illustrating the topics we have been discussing all semester. When allowing students to choose the material from their culture (underlife) they will teach to the class, we can discuss the forms that are "accepted," those that are considered "unacceptable," and the forces that determine acceptance, thus acknowledging the dissensus of our classroom community.

A demonstration of Trimbur's own use of collaborative learning to encourage dissensus comes from his 1993 workshop at the University of Chicago's Critical Thinking Seminars. First, he asked us to view a short clip from Spike Lee's film *Do the Right Thing* (a yuppie character had ridden his bicycle over the new shoes of one of the neighborhood youths causing a loud confrontation). The workshop participants watched the clip three times and responded in writing each time: 1) what did we see; 2) how did it make us feel; and 3) what did the scene mean. He encouraged us to interpret the scene in terms of our own experience. Then he arranged the participants into groups of five with a discussion leader and recorder. The three writings we had done (five minutes each) were our admission ticket to the discussion; we couldn't participate in the groups unless we were prepared. After each person had read aloud the last writing he or she had done, we tried to reach a consensus in responding to three questions. We were asked to 1) explain how the responses were alike and different and describe the similarities and differences; 2) explain the similarities and differences and identify the assumptions members of the group seemed to be making in their responses; and 3) finally, if we had time, decide whether we could agree on the meaning of the sequence. These directions were asking us to look for ways our responses varied and to find explanations for the differences.

Since I was the recorder for our group at Trimbur's workshop, I still have my notes and can describe how the five of us differed in our reactions to the same film clip. One felt anger at the failure of the characters to get along; another identified with the "Mouthy One" who had to back down; a third felt racism is a disease and is getting worse; a fourth didn't like noisy confrontations; and the fifth feared the verbal conflict because verbal conflict was threatening to him. We discussed why we reacted differently; some of us assumed ways of disagreement that don't involve so much noise; some reacted the ways we are accustomed to in our disciplines. The English teacher started a thesis/proof response based on the characters while the economist saw the economic theories involved in the effects of racism. We did not have time in the seminar session to answer Trimbur's third question; however, in planning this activity for a semester's course, teachers can schedule in sufficient time.

Although gender did not come up in our particular discussion, it is often the first difference groups discover in the way they react to material. Cross (1993) encourages members of groups to be conscious of gender and job-role influences on the way decisions are made. Instead of ignoring the feminine point of view as being too emotional, for example; groups should listen to this voice. He notes that intended audiences are likely to be both male and female; therefore, writers must "identify and analyze previously tacit gender perspectives . . . [so] **androgenous prose** will result" (p. 137).

We can incorporate dissensus into our classrooms in many ways. Besides those indicated above, Bruffee (1993) suggests assigning questions to which there are no clear or correct answers (Task A) or assigning questions to which there are answers accepted by the prevailing knowledge community and asking the group to explain how these answers were reached (Task B). A third possibility is to allow the groups to find an answer, present the prevalent answers of the academic community, and then negotiate between the two.

Collaborative pedagogy is also an effective teaching strategy; in Volume 2 of *Multicultural Education*, Teri Faulkner and I reviewed thirty-seven studies showing how collaborative strategies have been proven to be especially valuable in diverse classrooms. Four of those studies showed that content mastery is indeed enhanced by collaborative learning strategies, the minority students gaining more in cooperative classrooms than they did in traditionally structured classrooms. The non-minority students also learned more in cooperative classrooms, even though their growth in learning was not as striking as that of the minorities (Kagan, 1992). Although domination by the higher status social group in multiracial student groups has raised questions, Kagan insists after using cooperative learning, there is a decrease in self-segregation: "students choose more friends from the other races and interact in a more integrated pattern." Sometimes the improvement in race relations is striking: "For example, in one study in traditional classrooms, students listed 9.8% of their friends from a race other than their own; in contrast, students in cooperative classrooms listed 37.9%" (p. 2:9). These collaborative structures, even when and maybe even *especially when* conflict is present, are a mechanism for people to talk with each other and begin building connections across differences (Hulse-Killacky, 1990; Russo & Allsup, 1989).

Designing curriculum based on the theories of collaborative learning requires us to help students recognize that they are already members of many communities of knowledgeable peers (Bruffee 1993). David Jaques (1984) reminds us that many of the goals of a college education such as developing a critical and informed mind, developing an awareness of others' interests and needs, and developing a social conscience are all "processes which are experienced mostly if not totally within well-organized study groups" (p. 64). The process itself is what is important: "The end is the means" (p. 63). We should not try to short-circuit this means by eliminating all conflict or dissensus from our classrooms.

References

Brooke, R. (1987). Underlife and writing instruction. *College composition and communication 38*, 141-153.

Bruffee, K. (1993). *Collaborative learning: Higher education, interdependence, and the authority of knowledge*. Baltimore: Johns Hopkins.

Cox, A. (1991, July 2). Consensus as a killer of creativity. *Chicago Tribune*, p.15.

Cross, G. (1993). *Collaboration and conflict: A contextual exploration of group writing and positive emphasis*. Cresskill, NJ: Hampton Press.

Dittmar, L. (1993). Conflict and resistance in the multicultural classroom. In J. Q. Adams & J. R. Welsch (Eds.), *Multicultural education: Strategies for implementation in colleges and universities, Vol. 3* (pp. 29-37). Macomb, IL: Illinois Staff and Curriculum Developers Association. [See this volume, pp.235-244]

Faulkner, T. M. & Lemon, H. S. (1992) Collaborative learning: Building community in a culturally diverse classroom. In J. Q. Adams & J. R. Welsch (Eds.), *Multicultural education: Strategies for implementation in colleges and universities, Vol. 2* (pp. 3-11). Macomb, IL: Illinois Staff and Curriculum Developers Association.

Hulse-Killacky, D. (1990, May). *Effective group work in community colleges.* Paper presented at the Annual Conference of the Association of Canadian Community Colleges, Charlottetown, Prince Edward Island, Canada.

Jaques, D. (1984). *Learning in groups*. Beckenham, Kent: Croom Helm.

Janis, I. L. (1972). *Victims of groupthink*. Boston: Houghton-Mifflin.

Janis, I. L. & Mann, L. (1977). *Decision making*. New York: Free Press.

Kagan, S. (1992). *Cooperative learning*. San Juan Capistrano, CA: Resources for Teachers.

Lemon, H. S. (1990). A speaking project about the arts that acknowledges the students' underlife. In *Talking to learn: Classroom practices in teaching English, Vol. 24*, Urbana, IL: National Council of Teachers of English.

Miller, R. E. (1994). Fault lines in the contact zone. *College English 56*, 389-408.

Pratt, M. L. (1991). Arts of the contact zone. *Profession 91*. New York: Modern Language Association, 33-40.

Reither, J. A. & Vipond, D. (1989). Writing as collaboration. *College English 51*, 855-867.

Russo, T., & Allsup, C. (1989, November) *Teaching diversity through pluralism: A model for teaching about racism.* Paper presented at the Challenge of Diversity: Curriculum Development for the 21st Century Conference, Madison, WI.

Slavin, R. E. (1989-90). Research on cooperative learning: Consensus and controversy. *Educational Leadership, 47* (4), 52-54.

Sheckels, T. F. (1992). Research in small-group communications: Implications for peer response. Paper presented at the Conference on College Composition and Communication, Cincinnati, OH.

Trimbur, J. (1989). Consensus and difference in collaborative learning. *College English, 51*, 602- 616.

Trimbur, J. (1993). Workshop presented at the University of Chicago's Bringing the World into the Classroom Conference, Chicago, IL.

Weiner, H. S.(1986). Collaborative learning in the classroom: A guide to evaluation. *College English, 48*, 52-61.

Wilson, G. L. & Hanna, M. (1986). *Groups in context*. NY: Random House.

Wolf, T. (1990). The teacher as eavesdropper: Listening in on the language of collaboration. In D. A. Daiker & M. Morenberg (Eds.), *The writing teacher as researcher* (pp. 277-289). Portsmouth, NH: Boynton.

MULTICULTURAL MATHEMATICS

by
Melfried Olson, Judith K. Olson, and Howard L. Hansen

Introduction

"What does it mean to do mathematics?" Before trying to provide an answer to this question two comments are in order. First, to say that a person learns mathematics by doing mathematics brings several assumptions to the forefront: that learning mathematics is an active pursuit; that mathematics is learned in a contextual framework; and that mathematics is a pattern of communication. Second, each of these assumptions brings us to the role of culture in the teaching and learning of mathematics. In every culture there are ways of knowing mathematics. These ways of knowing may differ from culture to culture and certainly impact the manner in which students engage in, value, and learn mathematics. That is, these differences may influence how mathematics is valued, how learners interact when learning mathematics, or what it means to **know mathematics**. Each of these ideas has implications for interaction with students in the mathematics classroom.

Why is the multicultural question in mathematics important? According to Banks (1994), "Multicultural education, as its major architects have conceived it during the last decade, is not an ethnic- or gender-specific movement. It is a movement designed to empower all students to become knowledgeable, caring, and active citizens in a deeply troubled and ethnically polarized nation and world" (see this volume, p. 3). The National Council of Teachers of Mathematics (NCTM) addressed this issue for school mathematics. Under the topic of *Opportunity for all*, NCTM (1989) states:

> The social injustices of past school practices can no longer be tolerated. Current statistics indicate that those who study advanced mathematics are most often white males. Women and most minorities study less mathematics and are seriously underrepresented in careers using science and technology. Creating a just society in which women and various ethnic groups enjoy equal opportunities and equitable treatment is no longer an issue. Mathematics has become a critical filter for employment and full participation in our society. We cannot afford to have the majority of our population mathematically illiterate. Equity has become an economic necessity. (p. 4)

Similar issues in mathematics education are addressed by the National Center for Research in Mathematical Sciences Education (NCRMSE, 1994):

> Mathematics instruction has been more accessible to students who are members of society's dominant racial, cultural, social class, and gender groups than to those who are not. From a perspective of equity and fairness, all student groups need access to mathematics instruction and opportunities to excel in mathematics. The reform of school mathematics provided the educational community with possibilities for addressing the needs of an increasingly diverse student population. As they develop policy, research, and practice, educators will need to combine concerns for both equity and reform. If they fail to do so, students who do not come from dominant groups may, once again, be denied full participation. The options educators have and the choices they can make are

in the areas of curriculum pedagogy, assessment, and school contexts that facilitate student learning. (p. 1)

While Lynn (1994), NCRMSE (1994), the Federal Coordinating Council for Science, Engineering, and Technology (1993), and NCTM (1989) discuss the equity issue in pre-college mathematics and science, many believe that the issues of equity, especially in mathematics and science, for higher education are just as valid. Olson and Olson (1991) give three principles from which faculty members can try to build success: all students can learn mathematics; all students should be given the opportunity to learn mathematics; and ideas and programs should not be discarded because they are not perfect. No matter what mathematical concepts and skills they possess, students in higher education generally are more academically successful than those who do not access higher education. Faculty in higher education must face the reality that they get the best students who complete high school. They must decide how to deal with these students. If this group is multicultural, the problem may even be more difficult. What can be done? As indicated above, no perfect answer to this challenge exists. However, the following three ideas may be useful: developing meaningful mathematical tasks, establishing high expectations, and providing student mentoring.

Meaningful Mathematical Tasks

Among the dimensions of multicultural education identified by Banks (1994) that can be addressed by mathematics teachers are content integration and the knowledge construction process. Content integration is concerned with how teachers use examples from a variety of cultures to illustrate key concepts and generalizations in their discipline. While mathematics teachers can insert multicultural content into their instruction, this can also reinforce stereotypes if it is the only attempt made to include multiculturalism. An analysis of the knowledge construction process is probably of more importance to mathematics teachers. According to Banks (1994), "A multicultural focus on knowledge construction includes discussion of the ways in which the implicit cultural assumptions, frames of reference, perspectives, and biases within a discipline influence the construction of knowledge" (see this volume, pp. 7-8). In general, the issues of multicultural mathematics education demand a review of significant concerns in mathematics teaching. A critical area is personal/cultural knowledge: the concepts and interpretations that students derive from personal experiences in their various cultural settings. For example, Slavin (1983) indicates that many African American and Mexican American students are more likely to succeed in a cooperative learning environment.

College instructors of beginning level classes often face a challenge concerning meaningful mathematical tasks. Many textbooks are written from a skills-to-application basis rather than a skills-from-application basis. This often means that students must wait to see the significance of the applicability of the mathematics they are learning. The appropriate choice of a meaningful mathematical task should assist the student in making use of mathematics while simultaneously learning more about the content of mathematics. According to NCTM (1991) these mathematical tasks should

engage students' interest; develop students' mathematical understandings and skills; stimulate students to make connections and develop a coherent framework for mathematical ideas; call for problem formulation, problem solving, and mathematical reasoning; promote communication about mathematics; represent mathematics as an ongoing human activity; display sensitivity to, and draw on students' diverse background experiences and dispositions; [and] promote the development of all students' dispositions to do mathematics. (p. 25)

The tasks chosen by instructors frame students' opportunity to learn, structure thinking about concepts and procedures, convey messages about the role of mathematics, help define what doing mathematics means, and assist in the development of students' problem-solving ability. "In selecting, adapting, or generating mathematical tasks, teachers base their decisions on three areas of concern: the mathematical content, the students, and the ways in which students learn mathematics" (NCTM, 1991, pp. 3-4).

The selection of mathematical tasks to achieve all of the goals described above is not trivial. However, it is significant that the selection of meaningful mathematics tasks clearly includes the concepts described for a multicultural education. The selection of an appropriate mathematical task is just the beginning of the process. Implied in the descriptions of mathematical tasks is the need for pedagogy different from the traditional methods. This, too, meets the criteria for a multicultural education. The instructor must be more of a director of instruction, one who poses questions, asks students to clarify and justify ideas, monitors discussions, and determines when to expand on ideas presented by students. An instructor who chooses to operate in this manner must also begin to analyze teaching and learning. Instructors must observe, listen, and gather information to assess students differently. Instructors must give more meaningful direct feedback to students, which helps to begin the mentoring process described later.

The focus on meaningful mathematical tasks suggests that an alternative to the traditional classroom culture would be developed. It can be argued that, largely as a result of traditional instruction, students have developed beliefs about mathematical classroom culture that are often counterproductive. For example, students often view mathematics as a collection of rules to be memorized and look to the teacher as the authority figure who has the one right answer. Several current practices need to be reexamined to change these cultural beliefs. One must think about such matters as what students already know and what they can work on next, the issue of prerequisite skills, who should do the talking, and how students should work together. One quick classroom culture check for an instructor is to answer the following question upon teaching a class, "What did you do in class today?" If the response begins with "Today, I covered ..." much is said about classroom culture. If this is a consistent response, the instructor may be creating a classroom culture that reinforces counterproductive beliefs about the learning of mathematics. Classrooms must become places where **students and instructors** work together.

The following statement by Woodrow (1988) shows the significance the choice of task has in the learning environment. He states:

It is a commonly held belief that mathematics is an essentially acultural subject. It is arguable whether this is a valid statement—the nature of argument and the language of implication are both culturally determined—but it is certainly not true that the teaching of mathematics can be acultural. The attempt to convey the ideas and concepts to the learner must take place using the metaphors and imagery available to the learner, and these are clearly the consequence of the society and culture within which the learner lives. (p. 229)

It is not surprising that those persons who hold the view that mathematics is culture free find it difficult to consider that differing pedagogical methods may be needed to reach a larger number of students. However, if one accepts the notion of socially constructed mathematical knowledge, both individual and broader cultural influences can be recognized. A person with this perspective will go beyond the quasi-trivialized inclusion of multiculturalism through historical remnants to the realization that cultural perspective may affect ways of thinking mathematically.

Usiskin (1994) provides a definite challenge to any mathematics teacher when he states, "Every mathematics course should allow for individual differences in **interest** by including a wide variety of activities and contexts which bring out the brilliance, surprise, applicability, and structure of mathematics, and in which students are given choices" (p. 12). While his comments are aimed at pre-college mathematics courses, the comments apply to college mathematics courses as well. This calls for mathematics instructors to bring out the interesting aspects and applicability of mathematics that drew many faculty members to the study of mathematics in the first place.

A perceived difficulty associated with the use of meaningful mathematical tasks is that to explore topics in depth usually means fewer topics are covered. The predicament—one can only know something about which one has thought, yet can only think about something one knows—is real. An instructor must decide whether to provide students with a large volume of topics less well connected or a small volume of more connected topics.

In summary, those who teach mathematics must wrestle with a new paradigm of teaching. Teachers must recognize that individuals investigate and internalize their world and the role of mathematics in that world in a relationship unique to their cultural setting. Teachers must be prepared to teach mathematics beyond the dualistic approach that continues to be fostered by almost all societies. Almost every teacher of mathematics has heard, or, heaven forbid, stated, "At least in mathematics there is a right answer." Mathematics instructors interact with students who bring a dualistic view of mathematics to the learning situation. If the students are reinforced in that idea by the manner in which the subject is taught, instructors should not be surprised students have questions about the use and value of mathematics.

High Expectations

The selection of meaningful mathematical tasks begins with a focus on sound and significant mathematics. Naturally, this implies high expectations for students and, perhaps more significantly, high expectations that **all** students can engage in and are capable of learning mathematics. Advocating higher academic expectations is consonant with the expectations of the population in general as well as of traditionally underrepresented groups. When the public was surveyed concerning standards for high school academic work, 61% of Americans agreed standards are too low. Seventy percent of African American parents with children in school share this view (Johnson & Immerwahr, 1994-95). Clark Atlanta University has eliminated remedial mathematics courses in an effort to demonstrate a commitment to higher expectations (Morgan, 1993). Of course, along with these higher expectations, faculty members must commit to diligently working with students and must receive administrative support for their efforts. Higher education must not succumb to the institutionalization of lower expectations through tracking.

At the high school level, Mirel and Angus (1994) report that the effect of increased academic coursework in the public schools between 1973 and 1990 contributed to improved student outcomes, especially among minorities, and did not lead to an increase in the dropout rate. "Unfortunately, the increases in academic coursetaking by minority students have not resulted in subsequent increases in college enrollments, especially on the part of black students" (p. 41).

The connection between questioning and expectations is significant. Teachers enhance the academic integrity of their courses by asking meaningful questions and allowing students opportunities to explore the questions before expecting a response. Questions can frame a situation so that it forms the basis of a meaningful mathematical exploration. Raspberry (1994) reported about a university summer program for engineering students from under-represented groups that started to show remarkable results, but only after a ten-year period. Project staff made a simple adjustment. They quit treating the students as if they would have academic problems and treated them like the capable students they were.

As students are confronted with meaningful questions, are given enough time to respond, and are allowed alternative methods of explanation, achievement levels improve. Questioning sets an expectation of academic achievement and enhances the personal connection between teacher and student as well as between students. Nelson-Barber and Meier (1990) report that the type of questions asked in classroom settings, and the narrow range of acceptable answers, keep poor and traditionally marginalized students from active engagement and lead to negative perceptions of student abilities. This is clearly an area in which teachers can have an impact on instruction. Mathematics instructors who focus on teaching concepts find it easy to begin the questioning process. Waiting for students to respond, being non-judgmental in handling responses, and nurturing all students so they feel free to respond are other matters. Instructors using this approach find it rewarding because of the increased student involvement and higher-order thinking. This journey, once started, is irreversible.

Mentoring

Discussing the success of women in the sciences, Tobias (1990) and Buerk (1986) cite strong mentoring and personal involvement as key factors in that success. Faculty mentoring is frequently seen in its most positive context in graduate studies, especially at the doctoral level. A doctoral student often works closely with one professor. This professor becomes the model from which professionalism as well as content is learned. The importance of professionalism is seen in the connections doctoral students make when seeking funding or responding to postdoctoral opportunities.

Mentoring at this level of intensity for all undergraduate students is likely impossible. However, some aspects of mentoring are possible. As there are not enough African, Asian, Latino, or Native American mathematics faculty members to serve as mentors and role models, all members of the profession must actively engage in this endeavor. Mentoring students in the major, especially in mathematics, is possible due to the relatively small number of mathematics majors at most institutions of higher education. Mentoring all students who take mathematics classes is more difficult. Yet some possibilities exist in addressing this. For example, many majors require students to take a sequence of two mathematics courses. Arrangements can be made for the same instructor to teach a sequence thus creating an opportunity for two-semester involvement with students.

Mentoring can also be connected to the idea of meaningful mathematical tasks and the associated pedagogy. In a broad sense, mentoring includes extended communication opportunities between students and teachers. When appropriate tasks demand students prepare projects, make presentations in class, write about conceptual ideas, and actively engage in problem solving, the opportunity for mentoring is available. In fact, when instructors provide appropriate verbal or written feedback, engage students in problem solving, or ask for reflective action on the part of the student, mentoring exists. Instructional strategies that require students to reflect on the teaching and learning of mathematics, that build upon the experiences of the learner, that involve decision making in context, and from which the student must construct meaning connect well with multicultural education. Banks (1994) states,

> Reflective action by citizens is also an integral part of multicultural theory. Multicultural education . . . links knowledge, values, empowerment, and action. Multicultural education is also postmodern in its assumptions about knowledge and knowledge construction . . . . Multicultural theorists maintain that knowledge is positional, that it relates to the knower's values and experiences, and that knowledge implies action." (see this volume, p. 4)

These strategies are the foundation upon which students can build mathematical power.

Summary

This article describes three possibilities for meeting the multicultural realities and challenges of the mathematics classroom: developing meaningful mathematical tasks, establishing high expectations, and providing mentoring. These ideas, together with the following three thoughts, are important for mathematics teachers with respect to multicultural education. One, teachers need to restructure their thinking about who is capable of learning mathematics. Habits of mind are hard for teachers to break, especially when teachers can cite examples to support their way of thinking. Being able to cite examples of students from underserved populations who were not successful should not be a reason to conclude that no students from underserved populations can be successful. Similarly, citing examples of students from underserved populations who are successful in mathematics is no reason to conclude the task is complete. Two, all students need to know the part they and their culture have played in the creation and development of mathematical knowledge. We must look to current cultural usage and development as well as to historical examples. Three, instructors should come to know and respect all of their students just as they respect students majoring in their own field of study. Students must be taken as they come and assisted to where they want to go, whether or not they are planning to major in mathematics or a closely related field. Students should not be blamed or have their self-esteem attacked due to lack of knowledge and understanding. The task of the instructor is to move them to knowledge, understanding, application, synthesis. This may be difficult but it is not impossible.

References

Banks, J. A. (1994). Multicultural education development, dimension, and challenges. In J. Q. Adams & J. R. Welsch (Eds.) *Multicultural prism: Voices from the field* (pp. 1-14). Macomb, IL: Illinois Staff and Curriculum Developers Association. [See this volume, pp. 3-14]

Buerk, D. (1986). *Carolyn Werbel's journal: Voicing the struggle to make meaning of mathematics*. Wellesley, MA: Wellesley College, Center for Research on Women.

Federal Coordinating Council for Science, Engineering, and Technology. (1993). *Pathways to excellence a federal strategy for science, mathematics, engineering, and technology education*. Washington, DC: Author.

Johnson, J., & Immerwahr, J. (1994-1995, Winter). First things first: What Americans expect from the public schools. *American Educator, 18*(4), 4-13, 44-45.

Lynn, E. (1994, Spring). Science and equity: Why it's important. *Dwight D. Eisenhower Mathematics and Science Education Newsletter, 4*, 1, 4-5.

Mirel, J., & Angus, D. (1994, Summer). High standards for all. *American Educator, 18*(2), 4-9, 40-42.

Morgan, J. C. (1993, January 28). Shabazz works math wonders at Clark Atlanta University. *Black Issues in Higher Education Special Report: Recruitment and Retention*, pp. 15, 17.

National Council of Teachers of Mathematics. (1989). *Curriculum and evaluation standards for school mathematics*. Reston, VA: Author.

National Council of Teachers of Mathematics. (1991). *Professional standards for teaching mathematics*. Reston, VA: Author.

National Center for Research in Mathematical Sciences Education. (1994, Fall). Equity and mathematics reform. *NCRMSE Research Review: The Teaching and Learning of Mathematics, 3*(3), 1-5.

Nelson-Barber, S., & Meier, T. (1990, Spring). Multicultural context a key factor in teaching. *Academic Connections*, pp. 1-5, 9-11.

Olson, J. K., & Olson, M. (1991). Including the unincluded in mathematics. In J. Q. Adams, J. Niss, & C. Suarez (Eds.), *Multicultural education: Strategies for implementation in colleges and universities* (pp. 41-45). Macomb, IL: Western Illinois University Foundation.

Raspberry, W. (1994, July 19). Setting the highest goal for the brightest—they will achieve. *Chicago Tribune*, p. 17.

Slavin, R. E. (1993). *Cooperative learning*. New York: Longman.

Tobias, S. (1990). *They're not dumb, they're different: Stalking the second tier*. Tucson, AZ: Research Corp.

Usiskin, Z. (1994, Winter). Individual differences in the teaching and learning of mathematics. *UCSMP Newsletter, 14*, 7-14.

Woodrow, D. (1988). Multicultural and anti-racist mathematics teaching. In A. J. Bishop (Ed.), *Mathematical enculturation: A cultural perspective on mathematics education* (pp. 229-235). Boston: Kluwer Academic.

A MULTICULTURAL PERSPECTIVE IN THE WOMEN'S STUDIES CLASSROOM

by
Martha E. Thompson

This essay is intended as a contribution to the on-going discussion about how to integrate a multicultural perspective into women's studies courses. The approach I will discuss grew out of my experience in teaching at Northeastern Illinois University, a state-supported university of 10,500 with an established women's studies program. Northeastern has a female majority with a student body highly diversified by age, ethnicity, literacy skills, race, religion, physical ability, political perspectives, sexual orientation, and social class. Most of the students live and work in highly segregated neighborhoods or communities.

In recent years, the greater availability of books, articles, films, and research centers analyzing the interrelationship of race, class, and gender has made it possible to integrate a multicultural perspective into every aspect of women's studies courses (e.g. Amott & Matthaei, 1996; Andersen & Hill Collins, 1998; Cyrus, 1997; Disch, 1997; Kendall, 1997; Kirk & Okazawa-Rey, 1997; Naples, 1998; Richardson, Taylor, & Whittier, 1997; Zinn, Hondagneu-Sotelo, & Messner, 1997).

Materials which integrate race, class, and gender are necessary for multicultural education, but are not sufficient (Dines, 1994; Belkhir, Griffith, Sleeter, & Allsup, 1994). The process of creating a multicultural classroom in women's studies must also include structuring a supportive environment in which students can experience the benefits of a multicultural classroom for grappling with women's studies issues. Creating a supportive classroom environment is important because of the prejudices most students bring into the classroom. Many students, including feminists, often use racist and classist arguments to explain the situations of different groups of women. For instance, after viewing a film about a racially and ethnically diverse group of women organizers, an Anglo feminist proposed that if Latinas and African American women would learn to speak "proper English" they could increase their chances for success.

There is enormous potential in a multicultural classroom for developing an understanding of the intersections of gender, race, and class. Abstract ideas can be developed, discussed, or tested from different sets of social experiences. Complexities and contradictions, suggesting new directions, can more easily be revealed and explored. Having the opportunity to communicate ideas to a multicultural audience can sharpen students' speaking, writing, and thinking skills. However, for a diverse group of people with varying interests in women's studies and varying skills to work in such a way, they need a supportive classroom environment and the opportunity to develop relevant knowledge and skills. In the following pages, I will discuss strategies I have used for creating a supportive classroom environment and nurturing people's abilities to analyze concrete experience, discuss complex ideas, and formulate effective social action.

Structuring a Supportive Classroom

To structure a supportive classroom, I use techniques which encourage students to empathize with each other. To develop empathy, students need an opportunity to encounter the unique experiences of each individual in the classroom, to witness the feelings generated by these experiences, and to discover the influence of social forces on each individual's experience. Almost all of the strategies I use begin with students' writing and then reading or summarizing what they have written to a small or large group. Sometimes students work in pairs reading and commenting on what the other has written. Writing assignments give students an opportunity to practice a particular skill and to receive feedback. Students indicate that routinely writing before speaking gives them an opportunity to formulate their thoughts, makes them more confident in participating in class discussion, and improves their writing.

One strategy I have found consistently successful is to ask students to write about their own experiences with the assigned reading topic and then to read their essay to the rest of the class. For example, if students have done reading concerning race, gender, and class, their assignment might be the following:

> Write an essay in which you describe an incident or experience which first made you aware of race, class, or gender. Describe what you were doing, who you were with, what happened, how you felt about the experience, and what you did in the situation. Reflect on how this experience may have influenced you.

I ask for volunteers to share what they have written. When people share their stories, race, class, and gender are no longer abstract concepts but become key words to describe a variety of unique experiences and feelings.

Another strategy for building a sense of common purpose is to create small groups based on some combination of similar knowledge and experience (Thompson, 1992). For example, in creating groups for a discussion of feminism, I asked students to write about their familiarity with feminist literature and their experience with feminist groups. Based on individuals' self-assessments, groups were created by identifying clusters of people along the two dimensions of knowledge and experience. One group consisted of individuals who had read feminist literature prior to the course and had participated in at least one feminist group; another group was comprised of individuals who had not read any feminist writing prior to the course and had never participated in a feminist group; another group consisted of individuals familiar with feminist literature, but who had never participated in a feminist group; an additional group consisted of people who had participated in a feminist group, but had not read any feminist writings. All the groups were mixed by age, ethnicity, gender, and race.

Groups were asked to draw upon their reading and their own experience to discuss how gender, race, and class might affect people's involvement in feminism. For students to be able to begin to talk with each other, I have found it effective to give small groups a specific task to accomplish. For instance, to initiate a discussion of how gender, race, and class might affect involvement in feminism, I might ask each group to come up with five to ten images or ideas their reading associates with feminism. Once they have a list, they pick one or two images or ideas and then discuss how these images or ideas (e.g. women are discriminated against; patriarchy is the root of women's oppression; women's liberation is central to all struggles for revolutionary change) help explain the experiences of two or more groups which differ by class, gender, or race (e.g. middle-class African American men and middle-class African American women; poor white women and poor Latinas). The idea is to encourage students to discuss feminism in the context of specific groups.

Following small group discussions, a representative selected by the group presents the highlights of the discussion to the rest of the class. This process of reporting reveals that people with different levels of knowledge and experience can contribute to a common effort if able to work at their own level of competence. Feedback from students indicates that the collective description, analysis, or evaluation is always more complex and thought-provoking than what any individual initially brought into the classroom or what a single group developed.

Creating groups with commonalities takes careful planning before class to arrive at questions which will allow real commonalities and differences to emerge and takes class time to organize. I have found the results well worth the effort. When groups consist of people with similar self-assessments of knowledge and experience, participation is greater, the quality of the work is higher, and students are more likely to feel connected to each other than when groups are randomly created.

Students who are knowledgeable, experienced, or skilled have indicated that they can freely participate in these small groups without dominating them or getting bored. Students with less knowledge, experience, or skills have indicated that they are not embarrassed or lost, but can freely participate in the group discussion at their level of competence. Throughout the course, the membership of groups changes, giving students the opportunity to work with almost all other class members at one time or another.

Nurturing Effective Thinking

To encourage students to think effectively about the intersection of race, class, and gender, students need not only a structured, supportive environment, but the opportunity to develop their thinking skills. To assist students, I break the process into stages of analysis, theory, and action (Freire, 1968; Hartsock, 1979; Sarachild, 1975) and work with students to develop the knowledge and skills required for each stage. I describe each of these stages below.

Analyzing Personal Experience

The first step is to gather and analyze information about women's lives. The knowledge required for this step includes knowing how women's lives have been trivialized and ignored by traditional sources of information and understanding that we must actively seek information about women from different social strata and life circumstances. The skills essential for this step include gathering information systematically, identifying patterns and variations, and developing or identifying concepts which reflect what has been observed. To gather and analyze this information requires an assumption that the lives of ordinary people are an important source of information and insight.

To increase the likelihood that students will view ordinary people as important information sources, I select materials in which writers or speakers discuss the complex forces in their lives with intellectual and emotional depth and acknowledge the contradictions they experience in behavior, feeling, and thought. Whenever possible, I use materials which describe the experiences of women and men who differ by age, class, disability, ethnicity, race, religion and/or sexual preference (e.g. Amott & Matthaei, 1996; Anderson & Hill

Collins, 1998 ; Cyrus, 1997; Disch, 1997; Kendall, 1997; Kirk & Okazawa-Rey, 1997; Richardson, Taylor, & Whittier, 1997; Zinn, Hondagneu-Sotelo, & Messner, 1997).

Regardless of the work used, students need an opportunity to learn how to collect and analyze the information offered. Grounded theory (Glaser & Strauss, 1967) is an inductive strategy of theory-building in which information is gathered, grouped into categories, and compared and contrasted with information from different groups or situations until no new information is gathered.

In adapting this approach to a classroom, I ask students to list key words or phrases from their reading to describe the experiences, emotions, or behaviors of a group of women. For example, when talking about feminism, I might ask students to identify words or phrases people use to describe feminism. Students have come up with words and phrases, such as, "woman-centered," "equality," "man-hater," "empowerment of women," "lesbian," "humanism," "moving into action," "women's liberation." After words and phrases are listed, we go through the list item by item to group them. For instance, in working with the above list, students are likely to group "man-hater" in a different category than "woman-centered." Though different groups of students come up with different combinations of words and phrases, most students understand that the idea is to explore the relationship the words have to each other. Any set of words can be grouped into different categories. One possible grouping of the list above is **stereotypes** (e.g. man-hater), **focus on women** (e.g. woman-centered, lesbian, women's liberation, empowerment of women), **focus on female-male relationships** (e.g. equality, humanism), **action-oriented** (e.g. moving into action). From this grouping, we see that to explore feminism, we will need to focus on women only as well as consider relationships between women and men; we will need to consider social action and be prepared to grapple with stereotypes.

I make it clear these labels are concepts, words representing a general idea, that we can use to guide our discussion of ways in which feminism applies to different groups of women or situations. At this point, I might give students an assignment to re-read earlier selections or new selections to compare and contrast different groups or situations in relationship to the concepts we have just identified. For example, what **stereotypes** about feminists, women, or other groups do they find in their reading? Do they find a discussion of **relationships between women and men**? In what ways does a writer **focus on women**? What **actions** does the writer suggest?

Through this process of comparison and contrast, students see the utility of a concept which applies to a diversity of experiences and can also see the variations in the ways different groups of women experience what the concept is attempting to describe. For instance, students find, of course, that feminists are not the only group stereotyped; they also find that feminist writers differ in the extent to which they focus on women and on the relationships between women and men; and they also discover that feminists differ in their orientation to action. Once we have discussed these initial concepts, we generate a list of questions we have regarding the topic or issue we have been addressing. This sets the stage for evaluating others' ideas about the topic or issue. For instance, what stereotypes are associated with different groups we are studying? Is the primary focus of a writer or a group on women only or on relationships between women and men? Does a writer or group propose social actions? What kinds of actions?

Evaluating Ideas

Students generally enjoy analyzing people's experience, but have a more difficult time evaluating ideas they read. Students need support and guidance to read carefully, systematically, and critically. I assign works that use everyday language, not jargon or unnecessarily complex vocabulary or sentence structure and that have many concrete examples and illustrations. I also work with students to develop an approach for reading. Initial assignments explicitly identify what to look for in the reading, for example,

- What is the main point of the essay?
- What are the key concepts and how are they defined? How do they relate to each other?
- What does the writer say about how her or his writing fits with other writing on this topic? Is it a new area of discussion? Is it an addition to an on-going discussion? Is it a challenge to another point-of-view?

I also introduce students to ways to evaluate ideas using their earlier analyses of women's lives. One approach is to ask students to see how many of the questions raised earlier by the class are answered. For example,

- Does the writer consider any concepts similar to those we developed from our analysis of women's experience? How does the writer define the concept? How similar is it to the understanding we developed?
- Does the writer address the intersection of gender, race, class? How does the writer deal with the intersection?

I usually lead the first evaluation discussion with the whole class. Later evaluation discussions typically occur in small groups followed by reporters sharing the highlights of each small group discussion with the rest of the class. This strategy for evaluating feminist scholarship is generally well-received by students. Because their own analysis of women's experience is part of the standard of evaluation, students do not feel manipulated or coerced into accepting a particular viewpoint.

Formulating Social Action

The process of bringing a multicultural perspective into the women's studies classroom also involves formulating effective social actions. To develop and evaluate effective feminist actions, students benefit from knowing about historical and contemporary visions, the current state of the issue under discussion, a range of actions with which activists have experimented, and the consequences of those actions. Key skills for students to learn are translating abstract ideas into concrete realities and implementing a concrete idea.

Using the skills developed earlier, students can draw on the writings of activists to develop familiarity with visions and strategies for change (e.g. Kirk & Okazawa-Rey, 1997; Naples, 1998). For students, translating abstract ideas into concrete realities and developing attitudes supportive of a range of actions requires special attention. One strategy I have used is to have small groups brainstorm ways an individual, a particular group (e.g. our class), or society could implement an idea; I then have each group share its ideas with the rest of the class. The small groups are typically comprised of people with similar knowledge about the topic under discussion and similar experience in taking risks (see earlier discussion of creating a supportive classroom). For example, in a class session on building bridges among diverse groups, the class was divided into groups based on their familiarity with readings about racial prejudice and discrimination and their experience with taking public action against racism. The task was to identify how they could individually and in a group implement the idea of building bridges in their everyday lives. Because groups had a different set of knowledge and experiences to draw upon, the class identified a long list of immediate actions that included options for the least to most experienced bridge builders in the classroom. Asking students to try one of these strategies for bridge building and then to report on it to the class encourages students to take risks and to develop a deeper understanding of social action.

Another strategy I have used to encourage students to implement their ideas is to ask students to write a letter to a particular audience (e.g. the student paper, a local newspaper, a family member, a friend) about an issue related to one we have discussed. Students can be encouraged to deal in some way with the impact this issue may have on women from diverse backgrounds or experiences.

Even if students do not send the letter, writing to an outside audience about a contemporary issue gives class members a concrete focus for discussing how they feel about taking risks and the possible consequences of action or nonaction. Seeing the variety of audiences and strategies students choose to address issues also expands students' appreciation for the strengths of a multicultural group for formulating social actions.

Conclusion

In this essay, I have discussed an approach to creating a multicultural perspective in women's studies courses. Diversity can be an asset in the classroom if women's studies teachers consciously create opportunities for the uniqueness of each student to be revealed while simultaneously building on commonalities and differences to involve students in the process of analyzing women's experience, evaluating ideas, and formulating social actions. For students to develop their skills and confidence they must begin by working at their level of competence with others who have similar levels of knowledge and experience. Encouraging groups to combine their work with others builds solidarity among the diverse groups while simultaneously contributing to a more complex understanding of society.

Involving students in collectively analyzing experience, evaluating ideas, and formulating actions requires that women's studies teachers genuinely view students as rich resources of insight. To assist students in discovering their abilities, we need to create opportunities for students to develop their knowledge and skills.

Since I began to work constructively with diversity in the classroom, I have been richly rewarded by the work students have done, supportive and stimulating classes, and improvements in students' reading, writing, and thinking skills. My own enjoyment of and commitment to teaching have been renewed and enhanced.

Acknowledgments

Thanks to students in women's studies courses for their ideas, feedback, and inspiration. Thanks also to J. Q. Adams and Janice R. Welsch for their helpful comments on an earlier version of this essay and to Shelley Bannister, Diane Haslett, and Susan Stall, members of my writing group for their encouragement, suggestions, and insights.

References

Amott, T., & Matthaei, J. (1996). *Race, gender, and work: A multi-cultural economic history of women in the United States.* Boston, MA: South End Press.

Andersen, M., & Hill Collins, P.H. (Eds.). (1998). *Race, class, and gender: An anthology* (3rd ed.). Belmont CA: Wadsworth.

Belkhir, J., Griffith, S., Sleeter, C., & Allsup, C. (1994). Race, sex, class and multicultural education: Women's angle of vision. *Race, Sex, & Class 1*(2), 7 -22.

Cyrus, V. (Ed.). (1997). *Experiencing race, class, and gender in the United States* (2nd ed.). Mountain View, CA: Mayfield.

Dines, G. (1994). What's left of multiculturalism? *Race, Sex, & Class 1*(2), 23-34.

Disch, E. (Ed.). (1997). *Reconstructing gender: A multicultural anthology.* Mountain View, CA: Mayfield.

Freire, P. (1968.) *Pedagogy of the oppressed.* New York: Seabury.

Glaser, B. G., & Strauss, A. L. (1967). *The discovery of grounded theory.* Chicago: Aldine.

Hartsock, N. (1979). Feminist theory and revolutionary strategy. In Z. R. Eisenstein (Ed.), *Capitalist patriarchy* (pp. 56-77). New York: Monthly Review.

Kendall, D. (Ed.). (1997). *Race, class, and gender in a diverse society: A text reader.* Boston: Allyn & Bacon.

Kirk, G., & Okazawa-Rey, M. (Eds.). (1997). *Women's lives: Multicultural perspectives.* Mountain View, CA: Mayfield.

Naples, N. (Ed.). (1998). *Community activism and feminist politics: Organizing across race, class, and gender.* New York: Routledge.

Richardson, L., Taylor, V., & Whittier, N. (Eds.). (1997). *Feminist frontiers IV.* New York: McGraw-Hill.

Sarachild, K. (1975). Consciousness-raising: A radical weapon. In Redstockings (Eds.), *Feminist revolution* (pp. 131-137). New Paltz, NY: Redstockings.

Thompson, M. E. (1992). Building groups on students' knowledge and experience. *Teaching Sociology, 21*(1), 95-99.

Zinn, M. B., Hondagneu-Sotelo, P., & Messner, M. (Eds.). (1997). *Through the prism of difference: Readings on sex and gender.* Boston: Allyn & Bacon.

NATIVE NATIONS AND AMERICAN INDIANS: CULTURE, CURRICULUM, AND SOCIAL JUSTICE

by
James V. Fenelon

"You, who are wise must know that different Nations have different Conceptions of things and you will therefore not take it amiss, if our Ideas of this kind of Education happen not to be the same as yours."

Canassatego, 1744
Leaders of the Six Nations
Lancaster, Pennsylvania

"Mitakuye Oyasin" is used by many Lakota and Dakota traditionalists, and increasingly other Native peoples, to express "all our relations" within "the people" as a whole, like a nation, related to all others, Native and non-Indian alike. As the 20th century ends, indigenous people have re-appropriated the term "nation" as used by leaders in the centuries around 1744 and have reverted to using both resistance and survival ideologies.

This essay illustrates these issues by emphasizing indigenous cultures, curricula, and conflicts over social justice, historical perspectives, and the current "voice" of Native Nations and people, all existing long before and certainly since Columbus and other Europeans first arrived in the Americas (Cleary & Peacock, 1998). Underlying themes underscore that previous forms of education in the United States and colonial North America were for the purposes of cultural destruction (Adams, 1995) and social domination that included institutional racism (Huff, 1997) and deep struggles over the meaning of life itself (Locust, 1988). Therefore we begin an understanding of Native Americans and systems of Indian education, at the beginning of "contact" between western Europeans and indigenous peoples of the Americas.

Introduction

The Arawaks were a peaceful, well-organized society living in the area of present-day Haiti in 1492, when Christopher Columbus arrived and from the myopic view of the Europeans "discovered" them and other Caribbean people (Zinn, 1980). He promptly dubbed these indigenous peoples "Los Indios" after his monumental miscalculation on where in the world he was (Josephy, 1994). The rest, as "they" say, is history.

But whose history is it? Are scholars and students aware that the indigenous people throughout the Americas, those whom Columbus carelessly dubbed "Indians," represent a great diversity in language and culture throughout the continent? Have we stopped to consider the implications of the fact that within fifty years after Columbus arrived in the "New World" the Arawaks on Hispaniola would be wiped out (Las Casas, 1974) and the great Aztecan empire of Mexico would be destroyed (Josephy, 1994); that within another three centuries whole nations such as the Cherokees would be struggling for existence and forcibly "removed" over half a continent (Dippie, 1982; Wallace, 1993), and that five hundred years later Lakota "Takini" (survivors) and other Natives would end the hundred years of mourning for the Ghost Dancers and families killed at Wounded Knee (Fenelon, 1998; Brown, 1970), symbolizing the end of the western "frontier" for the United States? We must answer these and other questions in order to produce a more relevant and truthful curriculum about the make-up of American culture, what we teach in our schools as well as the research and knowledge presented in colleges and universities. In this light, we can view integrating Native American perspectives within four broad arenas: 1) history, 2) cultural understanding or world view, 3) contemporary sociological structures, and 4) the struggle for social justice and voice.

History

Integrating the history of Native American people more fully into the curriculum involves much more than including simple factual accounts. It is the **Indian perspective**, historical and philosophical, that requires inclusion whenever possible. What did the Wampanoags think about the Puritan enclave at Plymouth? Could they have tolerated and assisted the newcomers (Peters, 1987), only to be shocked at the barbarity of the New Englanders' response to religious differences? The United States history is replete with Indian Wars looked at only from the conqueror's point of view. Does the Trail of Broken Treaties, extending from one continent to the other, support the concept of Manifest Destiny or the power of the sword leading to the Termination Policy of the 1950s (Deloria, 1990, 1984)? In more recent history there are fewer indications of genocidal actions, and more of purposeful "culturicide" (Fenelon, 1998) through coercive assimilation that wipes out Native American cultures, especially through educational policy, as when:

> The (Navajo) children are caught, often roped like cattle, and taken away from their parents, many times never to return. They are transferred from school to school, given white people's names, forbidden to speak their own tongue, and when sent to distant schools are not taken home for three years. (Coolidge, 1977)

Most Native American families have stories from the boarding school period of Indian education policy (Hamley, 1994), the fall-out extending into modern times for reservation and urban Indian populations (Fixico, 1986; Prucha, 1978). A poignant example of historical perspective is the observance of the previously mentioned hundred years passing since the slaughter of the surrendered Ghost Dancers on Pine Ridge (Oglala "Sioux") Reservation in South Dakota. The military and frontier states recorded it as the last battle with "hostiles" in the name of civilization, while Lakota and other Native American Nations remember it as the purposeful killing of hundreds of women and children because they practiced an outlawed religion (Miller, 1985), because they wished to move about in cultural freedom, or perhaps because they had defeated Custer in battle over twenty years earlier (Fenelon, 1998).

Inclusion of Native American historical perspectives means a much broader horizon of who Indian people were and are—the accomplishments and contributions as well as the conflicts and conquests. The United States Constitution was at least partly based on the Iroquoian Confederacy of Nations (Johansen, 1982). Many states and other place-names are from indigenous languages, such as Chicago, Illinois. Small and mid-sized cities existed in the Ohio River Valley all the way westward to the upper Missouri (Forbes, 1998;

Silverberg, 1986). Food, plant and animal lore, natural sciences, and even medicines are derived from Indian knowledge.

Over the past five hundred years, human beings have sculpted a new worldwide society, a new political and economic order as well as a new demographic and agricultural order. Indians played the decisive roles in each step to create this new society. However, the modern world order came to be viewed as the product of European, not American, history. (Weatherford, 1988, p. 253)

In viewing the history of the United States, a key element of multicultural development is the inclusion of Native American contributions on every level. Besides bringing this history to the curriculum with equal weight—both in generic forms and in specific regional and community history, we need to include the Native American perspective of being conquered and cheated out of their lands (Deloria, 1984). This will benefit all students of our country's past, indigenous and "immigrant" Americans alike.

Cultural Understanding

Awareness, appreciation, and respect for cultural differences and similarities is critical to integrating any Native American perspective into the curriculum effectively. One way of addressing these needs is to use existing works, such as the book and guide *People of the Three Fires* (Clifton, Connell, & McCluken, 1986), which, through historical representation of the Ottawa, Potawatomi and Ojibway of the greater Michigan area, shows how the indigenous societies changed as they came into contact with Anglo Americans, and how the United States government ultimately possessed all their lands.

Even within distinct Native American groups, nations, or "tribes," cultural perspectives have many variations, including "traditional," bicultural or multicultural, coercively assimilated, and acculturated. Using local and regional materials or content allows students to see the sweep of these changes, and the connections to their own community development.

Another effective means for building cultural understanding is to present Native American philosophy and thought through the words of some of the many great indigenous orators of the past and present.

The man who sat on the ground in his tipi meditating on life and its meaning, accepting the kinship of all creatures and acknowledging unity with the universe of things was infusing into his being the true essence of civilization. . . .

The white man does not understand the Indian for [the] reason that he does not understand America. In the Indian the spirit of the land is still vested, it will be until other men are able to divine and meet its rhythm. (Standing Bear, 1933)

This approach has the additional benefit of developing discussion of the legitimacy of different "world views" (Whorf, 1956) on issues such as what civilization is or the relationship of peoples to the land and environment. Vine Deloria Jr. points out that "Traditional people preserve the whole vision and scientists generally reduce the experience to its alleged constituent parts and inherent principles." (Deloria, 1990)

A third effort to make toward cultural understanding is to develop empathy by reading and talking to Native American artists and scholars, visiting nearby reservations or Indian centers, and attending Indian social and cultural events. This kind of contact, sought after by ethnographers and anthropologists, can lead to scientific and ecological insights remarkably similar to those of the academic community (Green, 1995; Willis, 1983).

Native peoples view the world as complex, interconnected in non-linear relationships (heterarchic), dynamic, unknowable (indeterminant), changing/moving in several simultaneous cycles (mutual causality), growing as a whole (morphogenesis) and consisting of many perspectives. (Nichols, 1991)

Many of these qualities are the same needed in developing multicultural curricula for higher education and are the basis for research on whole mind, accelerated learning, and multiple intelligences theory (Gardner, 1987).

In developing and integrating Native American content into the curriculum, the problem of stereotyping surfaces again and again. With mainstream Americans, this stereotyping of Native peoples tends to fall into two categories: the romantic "warrior/princess" of the past and the wild "savage" associated with drunken laziness in modern times (Riding In, 1998). In an unpublished research study I conducted with Native American graduate students at Harvard University in 1991, the "Noble Savage" syndrome in conjunction with pan-Indian generalities (i.e. feathers and tipis, Custer and Crazy Horse, "chiefs" and "tribes") was stated most often to be the main problem with conventional curriculum. But culture refers to the mechanisms of social control and organization as much as clothing, singing, and dancing. "Culture" is 1) the cognitive paradigms through which people define and communicate the proper and the possible, and 2) the corresponding informal norms and implicit contracts by which a group of people reward and penalize each other (Cornell & Kalt, 1992).

When Western schools only address the surface features of culture and attempt to break down "deep" cultural interactions through forced assimilation to the dominant culture's secular institutions (Fuller, 1991; Fenelon, 1998), traditional communities are threatened and Indian children experience direct conflict with the modern, civic world (Hornett, 1990; Locust, 1988). Only through comprehensive and meaningful content sensitive to Native Americans can the "Indian" students' self-esteem and the Anglo students' sense of balance be maintained in today's diverse educational systems.

Sociological Structures

Native Americans represent an incredible diversity of indigenous nations, "tribal" societies, languages, cultural practices, local environments, and histories. Wide-ranging topics such as anthropology, architectural design, geography, sociolinguistics, and history can be drawn from simply studying a few reservations in the United States. For example, spatial and directional orientation are more common in Native American philosophy than hierarchy and binomialism (Deloria, 1979; Fenelon & Pugh, 1988; Hornett, 1990). From es-Chikag-o, let us look to the four directions of Native America: West, with the Puyallups, northwest coastal fishermen, living in longhouses when explorers met them, now an urban "tribe" recently winning their treaty settlement in Tacoma; North, the Lakota and Dakota "Sioux," hunters of the plains buffalo, living in tipis and earth lodges when fighting soldiers, and now defending arid reservation lands in the Dakotas in the shadow of the Black Hills; East, the Wampanoag, East Coast fishing and farming people, living in wickiyup longhouses when the Puritans arrived, now rebuilding on their island and peninsula areas of Massachusetts; and South, the "Navajo" Dine, ranchers and farmers of the southwest mountains and desert, living in hogans when pioneer wagon trains invaded, now managing the largest land-base reservation in the United States. "Curriculum should be localized to reflect the historical experience, culture and values of the local and regional Native communities" (Indian Nations at Risk, 1991).

Each Indian Nation and reservation has to deal with complex questions of sovereignty and cultural maintenance. Throughout many shifts of federal policy the belief of Native people has been that education should integrate goals of both cultural sustenance and self-sufficiency (Nichols, 1991), while non-Natives have viewed these goals as incompatible. In fact, both viewpoints are valid:

There is much to be learned from a traditional education and we must see it as the prereq-uisite to any other kind of education or training. Traditional education gives us an orien-tation to the world around us, particularly the people around us, so that we know who we are and have confidence when we do things. (Deloria, 1990, pp. 12-18.)

In respect to the origination of the curriculum, the Indian Nations at Risk Task Force (INAR) has stated that "Native communities must be the producers of Native education materials that reflect the language and culture of the local area." INAR has noted the importance of working on language development, cultural background (history, curriculum change), partnerships with community organizations, and accountability (Demmert, 1991). These elements of Native American curriculum development are likewise needed for mainstream higher education.

Finally, in discussing such cultural paradigms as knowledge, Kalt and Cornell (1989) tell us that "Indian tribes can provide answers to such questions as whether or not public ownership of enterprises is acceptable, or whether a separation of political authority and judicial authority is appropriate . . . selecting for activities that best fit with indigenous conceptions of self and appropriate intragroup relations."

Social Justice and Voice

As explained in the previous passages, Native Americans as individuals, nations, and as peoples have lived through great injustices (Noriega, 1992). It is only through changing the dominant Anglo-Eurocentric curriculum content and perspectives that higher education, and then public schooling, can begin to redress these wrongs. The role of both U.S. government and "tribal" courts, the numbers and placement of Native Americans throughout the country, their sense of nationality, the causes of the dire poverty and victimization of Indian people, and their vast contributions to society should be noted in the curriculum whenever possible and appropriate. "The study of Native American language, law, history, culture, art, and philosophy should be required of students. . . " (Indian Nations at Risk, 1991).

Cultural capital theories (Shamai, 1990) demonstrate that monocultural curricula perpetuate inequality as a social hierarchy in the face of significant and lasting Native American contributions to the development of the United States (Weatherford, 1988). A direct connection exists between redressing issues of justice through curriculum and whose voices are heard in that dialogue. Native Americans deserve to be the authors of such curricula since it is their voices that have been missing and are needed. An excellent example of voice, based primarily on the oral tradition of storytelling found in nearly every Indian Nation is

287

Keepers of the Earth (Caduto & Bruchac, 1990), which integrates natural science, tribal authenticity, regionalism, and Native American world views. When Indian-inspired curricula such as these are combined with local, regional and national histories of indigenous people, a comprehensive Native American curriculum becomes possible.

If we redefine Indian education as an internal Indian institution, an educational process which moves within the Indian context and does not try to avoid or escape this context, then our education will substantially improve. It will originate as part of the tribal perspective about life and pick up additional information on its return to Indian life. (Deloria, 1990)

Curricular Integration

Out and out assimilation has proven to be disastrous for Native Americans (Deloria, 1984; Wax, 1971) and produces a very distorted picture of the United States for other Americans. We are at a point when we must integrate Native American content into the curriculum, not only for the self-esteem and continuance of Indian students (Hornett, 1990), but for the benefit of all students and all schools, especially in light of the multicultural world in which we live, in contrast to a hegemonic curriculum which legitimates only part of the overall cultures of our nation (Giroux, 1983). Inclusion of Native Americans will enhance oral traditions and identity, both personal and national, bringing forth rich and varied backgrounds in storytelling and cultural histories. As Cazden (1987) points out, in educational institutions "spoken language is an important part of the identities of all the participants."

We can approach the integration of Native American curriculum from many entry points, including adding history and cultural knowledge to the established curriculum; replacing key areas with Native American perspectives; and infusing historical and cultural knowledge and perspectives as alternative ways to view "mainstream" perspectives (Banks, 1989). Adding to the curriculum has the problem of being "in addition to," an afterthought, the first element to be cut out under time or resource constraints. Replacing brings elements of the curricula into opposition with each other, a conflict the minority-culture perspective will either lose outright or that will cause resentment (Corrigan, 1988; Locust, 1988). Infusing, while healthier than the other two, continues with the world view of a "mainstream" and the implication of lesser tributaries (McCarthy, 1990), reinforcing cultural dominance (Smelser, 1992). While such an approach may be useful in the short run, it does not accord the respect and prominence that other cultural perspectives deserve, most pointedly Native American "Indian" Nations, the first stewards of North American lands (Snipp, 1989). Therefore, I propose we view Eurocentric curriculum as one stream, currently in dominance, that we need to balance with many other cultural streams, first and foremost with Native Americans. A more global curricular metaphor would be a "River of Nations and Cultures."

When I took Harvard Law School's Federal Indian Law course, one intelligent yet perplexed student could not grasp the concept that enrolled American "Indians" were members of their respective tribe's National society, including its law and order system, and were both State and Federal citizens of the United States (Deloria, 1984) with all its sovereignty underpinnings (Fenelon, 1998). An either-or dichotomous mentality (Rosenblum & Travis, 1996) had been indoctrinated in him through his schooling, right on through to the graduate level. Realistic and effective multicultural education concerning Native Americans

288

will take place when majority-culture students are brought to realize, first through the curriculum, that history, knowledge, and people can belong to more than one culture, (Cajete, 1994; Cleary & Peacock, 1998) and that we are better off when more inclusive and diverse.

Conclusions

The first settlement within the present borders of the United States sees the first slave revolt. About five hundred Spaniards bring with them one hundred African slaves. The slaves revolt, and the Spaniards are so discouraged and beaten that they return to Haiti, leaving the Africans living with the indigenous population, the first of several black and native acts of solidarity. (Bennett, 1984; in Chicago Religious Task Force on Central America, 1991:95)

Within *Dangerous Memories, Invasion and Resistance since 1492*, developed by the Chicago Religious Task Force on Central America, (1991), these issues of differing "racial" histories literally show how knowledge, history, world view and intercultural understanding in higher education are constructed and then reinforced to the dominant group's interests. The title *Dangerous Memories* ". . . is meant to challenge us to understand and appreciate the last five hundred years in American history from vantage points to which many of us have not been privileged" (p. 9).

Native American content materials, with historical and cultural perspectives, must be integrated into the curriculum of all schooling in the United States, elementary through university. This should be done with Native American people as the primary resource specialists for the benefit of everyone. For the short term, this Native American curriculum should be infused into curricula already being taught. The final goal should be to develop, wherever appropriate, balanced "cultural streams" which minimally address the four major areas of history, cultural understanding, sociological structures, and issues of social justice and voice for Native American "Indian Nations" and people.

This integration will achieve four basic objectives:

• to reinforce and sustain Native American societies and culture: since these societies are more than just of value to their members, or to accurate history and ethnography, but can provide alternative world views useful in solving world problems, (Fishman, 1991);

• to make "Americans" in general more informed about their roots: since current monocultural histories increase the often isolated and, therefore, distorted perspectives Americans have about North America, (Wolf, 1982; Fenelon, 1998; Josephy, 1994);

• to build the basis for a truly multicultural society in the U.S.: since understanding the historical and current cultures of Native Americans assists the development of similar processes for other cultural, racial/ethnic groups in the United States, (Deloria, 1990; Weatherford, 1988; Crawford, 1995); and

• to provide equity and hope for the disenfranchised in "America": since recognizing the contributions of and injustices toward Native Americans through an intercultural understanding is the first step, in curriculum, on the path to equal opportunity through education, (Riding In, 1998; Wax, 1989; Begay, 1997).

Infusing, integrating, and ultimately streaming Native American cultures into curricula as valid contributors to United States society will benefit all people in our country, not only indigenous people and "minority" groups. Basic understanding of slavery, genocide, domination, conquest, resistance, and survival ultimately liberates "us" all as Americans. When colleges and universities, and schools and communities, achieve this in the curriculum taught each and every learner, Native American people, other traditionally underrepresented groups and majority-culture students will all benefit with an increased awareness and more knowledge of the world we live in. Then we can truly say "Mitakuye Oyasin."

References

Adams, D. W. (1995). *Education for extinction: American Indians and the boarding school experience,* 1875-1928, Lawrence: University of Kansas Press.

Banks, J. (1989). *Multicultural Education: Issues and Perspectives,* Boston: Allyn & Bacon.

Begay, M. (1997). Leading by choice, not chance: Leadership education for Native chief executives of American Indian Nations. Doctoral dissertation, Harvard University.

Bennett, L., Jr. (1984). *Before the Mayflower.* New York: Penguin Books.

Brown, D. (1970). *Bury My Heart at Wounded Knee.* New York: Holt, Rhinehart and Winston.

Caduto, M., & Bruchac, J. (1988). *Keepers of the Earth,* (w/teacher's guide) Golden, CO: Fulcrum.

Cajete, G. (1994). *Look to the mountain: An ecology of indigenous education,* Durango: Kavaki' Press.

Canassatego. (1744; 1971) In T. C. McLuhan (Ed.), *Touch the Earth.* New York: Simon & Schuster.

Cazden, C. (1987). *Classroom discourse: The language of teaching and learning.* Portsmouth, NH: Heinemann.

Chicago Religious Task Force on Central America. (1991). *Dangerous Memories: Invasion and Resistance Since 1492,* (Golden, McConnell, Mueller, Poppen, & Turkovich, Eds.). Chicago, IL: Author.

Cleary, L. M., & Peacock, T. D. (1998). *Collected wisdom: American Indian education.* Boston: Allyn & Bacon.

Clifton, J., Cornell, G., & McCluken, J. (1986). *People of the three fires,* (w/guide & workbook), Grand Rapids: University of Michigan Press.

Coolidge, P. (1977). *"Kid catching" on the Navajo Reservation: 1930.* New York: Association on American Indian Affairs.

Cornell, S., & Kalt, J. P. (1992). *What can tribes do? Strategies and institutions in American Indian economic development,* Los Angeles: American Indian Studies Press.

Corrigan, P. (1988). Race/ethnicity/gender/culture: Embodying differences educationally: An argument. In J. Young (Ed.), *Breaking the Mosaic.* Toronto: Garamond Press.

Crawford, J. (1995, Winter). Endangered Native American languages: What is to be done, and why? *The Bilingual Research Journal, 19*(1), 17-38.

Deloria, V. (1990, Autumn). Knowing and understanding 5(1); Traditional technology 5(2): 12-17; Transitional education 5(3): 10-15; Property and self-government as educational initiatives 5(4), 26-31. *Winds of Change.* Boulder, CO: American Indian Science & Engineering Society (AISES) Publishing.

Deloria, V. (1979). *The metaphysics of modern existence.* San Francisco: Harper & Row.

Deloria, V., Jr. (1984). 'Congress in its wisdom': The course of Indian legislation. In S. Cadwalader & V. Deloria, Jr. (Eds.), *The aggressions of civilization, federal Indian policy since the 1880s.* Philadelphia: Temple University Press.

Demmert, W. (1991, March). Status of the Indian Nations At Risk Task Force. Unpublished presentation at Harvard Graduate School of Education. (Also in INAR, 1991)

Dippie, B. W. (1982). *The vanishing American.* Middletown, CT: Wesleyan University Press.

Fenelon, J. (1998). *Culturicide, resistance and survival of the Lakota ("Sioux" Nation).* New York: Garland Publishing.

Fenelon, J., & Pugh, S. (1988, January). Integrating learning, language and intercultural skills for international students. *Journal of Reading, 31*(4), 310-319.

Fishman, J. A. (1991). *Reversing language shift: Theoretical and empirical foundations of assistance to threatened languages.* (Clevedon) Philadelphia: Multilingual Matters.

Fixico, D. (1986). *Termination and relocation, federal Indian policy 1945-1960.* Albuquerque: University of New Mexico Press.

Forbes, J. (1998). The urban tradition among Native Americans. *American Indian Culture and Research Journal, 22*(4), 15-42.

Fuller, B. (1991). *Growing up modern.* London: Routledge.

Gardner, H. (1987). The theory of multiple intelligences. *Annals of Dyslexia, 37,* 19-35.

Giroux, H. (1983). Theories of reproduction and resistance in the new sociology of education: A critical analysis. *Harvard Educational Review, 53*(3).

Green, M. K. (1995). Cultural identities: Challenges for the twenty-first century. In M. K. Green (Ed.), *Issues in Native American cultural identity.* New York: Peter Lang Publishing.

Hamley, J. (1994). Cultural genocide in the classroom: A history of the federal boarding school movement in American Indian education, 1875-1920. Doctoral dissertation, Harvard University.

Hornett, D. (1990, Fall). Elementary-age tasks, cultural identity, and the academic performance of young American Indian children. *Action in Teacher Education, 12*(3).

Huff, D. J. (1997). *To live heroically: Institutional racism and American Indian education.* Albany: State University of New York Press.

Indian Nations at Risk. (1991, October). An Educational Strategy for Action. In M. Charleston & G. L. King (Eds.), *Final Report of the Indian Nations At Risk Task Force.* Conference Publishing Title: Indian Nations at Risk Task Force: Listen to the People. Washington, DC: U.S. Department of Education.

Johansen, B. E. (1982). *Forgotten founders.* Boston: Harvard Common Press.

Josephy, A. M. (1994). *500 Nations.* New York: Knopf.

Kalt, J., & Cornell, S. (1989, December). Pathways from poverty: Economic development and institution-building on American Indian reservations. Harvard Project on American Indian Economic Development. John F. Kennedy School of Government, Cambridge, MA.

(de) Las Casas, B. (1974). *The devastation of the Indies: A brief account* (H. Briffault, Trans.). New York: Seabury Press. (Original work published 1538)

Locust, C. (1988, August). Wounding the spirit: Discrimination and traditional American Indian belief systems. *Harvard Educational Review, 58*(3).

McCarthy, C. (1990). *Race and curriculum: Social inequality and....* Philadelphia: Falmer Press.

Miller, D. (1985). *The ghost dance.* Lincoln: University of Nebraska Press.

National Advisory Council on Indian Education. (1989). Educating the American Indian/Alaska Native family. 16th Annual Report to the United States Congress. Author.

Niehardt, J. G. (1959). *Black Elk speaks.* New York: Pocket Books.

Nichols, R. (1991, October). Continuous evaluation of Native education programs for American Indian and Alaska Native students (#8). (U.S. Department of Education Task Force, Co-Directors W. Demmert & T. Bell) Indian Nations at Risk Task Force: Listen to the People Conference Publication. Washington, DC: U.S. Department of Education.

Noriega, J. (1992). American Indian education in the United States: Indoctrination for subordination to colonialism. In M. Annette Jaimes (Ed.), *The State of Native America.* Boston: South End Press.

Peters, R. (1987). *The Wampanoags of Mashpee.* Jamaica Plain, MA: Inter-tribal Press.

Prucha, F. P. (1978). *Americanizing the American Indian.* Lincoln: University of Nebraska Press.

Riding In, J. (1998). American Indians in popular culture. In C.R. Mann & M. Zatz (Eds.), *Images of color, images of crime* (pp. 15-29). Los Angeles: Roxbury.

Rosenblum, K. E., & Travis, T. M. (1996). *The meaning of difference.* New York: McGraw-Hill.

Shamai, S. (1990). Critical sociology of education theory in practice: The Druze education in the Golan. *British Journal of Sociology of Education, 11*(4).

Silverberg, R. (1986). *The mound builders.* Athens: Ohio University Press.

Smelser, N. (1992). Introduction. In R. Munch & N. Smelser (Eds.), *Theory of culture.* Berkeley: University of California Press.

Snipp, M. C. (1989). *American Indians: The first of this land.* New York: Russell Sage Foundation.

Standing Bear, L. (1933). *Land of the Spotted Eagle.* Boston: Houghton Mifflin.

Wallace, A. (1993). *The long and bitter trail.* New York: Hill & Wang.

Wax, M. (1971). *Indian Americans: Unity and diversity.* Englewood Cliffs, NJ: Prentice Hall.

Wax, M. (1989). *Formal education in an American Indian community: Peer society and the failure of minority education.* Prospect Heights, IL: Waveland Press.

Weatherford, J. (1988). *Indian givers: How the Indians of the Americas transformed the world.* New York: Ballantine.

Whorf, B. L. (1956). *Language, thought, and reality.* Cambridge, MA: M.I.T. Press.

Willis, P. (1983). Cultural production and theories of reproduction. In L. Barton & S. Walker (Eds.), *Race, Class and Education.* London: Croom Helm.

Wolf, E. R. (1982). *Europe and the people without history.* Berkeley: University of California Press.

Zinn, H. (1980). *A people's history of the United States.* New York: Harper & Row.

TEACHING ABOUT RACE IN THE RACE-CONSCIOUS UNITED STATES

by

J. Q. Adams

Race continues to be one of the most compelling issues in the pursuit of the democratic ideals of the United States of America. Always a critical factor in the social relationships of people in this country, it becomes even more critical when we consider the continually changing mosaic of our nation's population. Because of these changes the demand on colleges and universities to develop courses dealing with this and other issues associated with a multicultural society are increasing.

This chapter will deal with some of the complexities involved in teaching about race and racism in this country. It is divided into four sections and reflects the experiences of my 25 years of teaching courses and presenting workshops on this topic.

Course Preparation

Serious consideration must be given to the scope, sequence, and placement of this course within the university's curriculum. Much thought should also be given to who will teach this course, the materials to be used, the number of students per class, the location of the classroom, and the level at which the course will be taught.

A. One of the first things an instructor should do in teaching a class of this nature is to take some time for personal introspection. The instructor should ask him/herself: Why am I teaching this class? What are my qualifications? Have I examined my strengths and weaknesses in relation to the course content and the classroom dynamics the course is likely to generate? Do I have any hidden agendas? If I have content weaknesses, what can I do to turn them into strengths? Do I have a contingency plan for dealing with the unexpected?

B. Probably the most important class of the semester for a course of this nature is the first class. It is critical because it will set the tone for the rest of the semester. Each student should receive a syllabus and ample time should be allotted to discuss it in detail. The syllabus should contain the standard components, including the instructor's office hours, course description, materials, test and assignment information, as well as the grading scale. In addition to this and any other information you feel is necessary, there should be a section that specifically discusses class conduct. This is essential, given the sensitive nature of the course content. Students should be informed that some of the material in this class may evoke intense feelings, in themselves and among their classmates, but that the discussion and debate of the issues are an essential part of the learning process. At the same time it should be made crystal clear the class will be conducted with respect for a variety of opinions, a tolerance for difference, and openness to cooperation in order to achieve the common goal of a greater understanding of how race functions in our society.

Curriculum Issues

Obviously, innumerable approaches to designing a course about race in the U.S.A. are possible, but a few fundamental ideas and historical cases demand to be included in any fair approach to this issue. In the following sections some of these concepts and cases will be identified and discussed.

A. Global and national demographics are critical to understanding the tremendous changes taking place in this country and around the world. Students of color easily see themselves as minorities in this country while European American students see themselves in the majority. Our emphasis on a European-centered curriculum reinforces those perceptions. Therefore, it is critical for students to learn—as far as this is possible given the slipperiness of the term race—the actual racial composition of the world's population as well as the current racial composition of our own country. This can be a powerful learning experience for students and a beginning stage for changing some of their existing paradigms about race.

The instructor should also be conscious of generalizations that can be drawn from this kind of information. It is not uncommon for some European American students to feel that the race with which they identify is in trouble because it is so outnumbered by people of color and that this will render them vulnerable in some way in the 21st century. Students of color may find this situation very empowering and demonstrate a kind of pan-colorism that some European American students may find threatening and inappropriate. If either or both of these situations occur they can be turned into excellent learning examples that demonstrate the impact majority/minority relationships can generate in a cultural scene such as the classroom. Two excellent simulations that can be used to challenge students are *BaFa BaFa* and *Star Power* (1999).

Among many good resources that explore global and national demographics and their implications is James Banks' *Teaching Strategies for Ethnic Studies* (1996). *The World Almanac and Book of Facts 1999* (1998) is also a readily available and relevant resource. In addition, the U.S. Census Bureau, United Nations, Central Intelligence Agency, Federal Bureau of Investigation and the American Demographic have excellent web sites available on the Internet.

B. In order to discuss race, we must be able to define it. This is by no means an easy task, but the concept must be dealt with on at least two levels of understanding. The first involves the scientific understanding and use of the term. Students should be knowledgeable about the morphology and genetics of race. In addition they should know of the different classification systems developed to describe human beings in race-related terms (Omi, 1997; Gain, 1971; Coon, 1962; Baker, 1974). Instructors should especially be aware of Cavalli-Sforza's *The History and Geography of Human Genes* (1994) which is probably the most comprehensive effort of its kind in the world today.

Secondly, the students should have some knowledge of the sociological view of race and its implications in contemporary society. This should encompass both the negative and positive connotations of the concept (Montagu, 1998 & 1999; Cose, 1997; West, 1994; Jensen, 1973; Simpson & Yinger, 1985). Most students do not have a clear understanding of either meaning of race and, therefore, tend to misrepresent themselves whenever they are using the term. By the end of the class each student should be able to demonstrate a clear understanding of this concept in either context.

Many students have well developed belief systems about race even though they may be faulty in their construction or based on unexamined assumptions. An instructor should not be surprised to find students quoting religious justifications to support the differences they perceive in races. It is important to tread lightly here but at the same time present the students with factual material that allows them to explore their beliefs and to make up their own minds without becoming stuck in an "I am Right; you are Wrong" dynamic. Two excellent sources to help students explore their perceptions are Peggy McIntosh's (1988) work on white privilege and Olsson's (1997) short handbook *Detour Spotting: For White Anti-Racists.*

C. This course is about race relations in the U.S.A. In order to understand present conditions it is imperative to understand what has taken place in the past. Students seem to express almost universal disdain for studying history, especially when it deals with race. Students will often make statements such as, "Why do we have to study about slavery? I wasn't there. I didn't have anything to do with it. Black people just need to get over it." If comments like these are made in a class, students might polarize and undo any progress made. African American students may feel a certain degree of shame, anger, and even a desire for revenge; others may view the occasion as an opportunity to exercise their racial pride and a time to state the case of African American resiliency, of their ability to survive against tremendous odds. The well-prepared instructor may want to remind students of the conduct clause in the syllabus and stress the importance of each student's right to his/her own position. Encouraging students to continue to be brave enough to speak their minds is also very important, because the only way the instructor can insure that the students learn as individuals and the class learns as a whole is to have them continue asking questions and seeking understanding.

Since each class has time restraints it is impossible to provide a comprehensive discussion of all the important historical events that have shaped race relations in this country. The instructor has to choose wisely. What follows is a list and a discussion of several landmark cases and decisions that teachers can draw upon. Paula S. Rothenberg's *Race, Class, & Gender in the United States* (1997) is a recent text well worth exploring for additional sources of inquiry and discussion. She includes a very thorough section entitled "How it Happened: Race and Gender Issues in U.S. Law" that contains 24 significant cases.

1. The United States Constitution, Article 1, Section 2.

The Three-Fifths Compromise. The Three-Fifths Compromise is a great starting place for students trying to understand the issue of race at the beginning of this American Republic. A review of the debates between the architects of the most important doctrine of our nation reveals the battle over whether or not slavery should exist in this new nation. The compromise that is reached sets forth a precedent that would continue until the passage of the Thirteenth Amendment. The rhetoric used by both sides in the debate reveals the flavor of the justifications and rationalizations for slavery as well as the ardent arguments against it. It might be effective to have students study some of these arguments and reenact them in class. Instructors who like this kind of group interaction could assign students to various roles like colonial delegates, members of the press, and various special interest groups, i.e., Negro freedmen, Native Americans, Southern plantation owners, and other relevant participants of the time. A good source of information for such a project is Adler's *The Annals of America* (1968).

2. The U.S. Census

One of the richest sources of information, past and present, is the United States Census Bureau, an almost inexhaustible source of possibilities when it comes to understanding the unique diversity of people in this country. For example, consider this analysis, researched by J. T. Lott (1993), President of Tamayo Lott Associates in Silver Spring, Maryland, of the changing identification systems used by the Census Bureau to classify people:

The first census of 1790 classified the population in terms of free white males, free white females, other persons (such as American Indians eligible for taxation, free blacks and persons of other races), and slaves. These categories divide the black population by civil status (slave or free). In 1820, the term "free colored persons" was introduced. The instruction for the 1860 Census stated: "Under heading 5, entitled 'Color' insert in all cases, when the slave is black, the letter B; when he or she is a mulatto, insert 'M.' The color of all slaves should be noted." The 1890 Census item stated: "Whether white, black, mulatto, quadroon, octoroon, Chinese, Japanese, or Indian." (Mulatto indicated one black parent; quadroon, one black grandparent; octoroon, one black great-grandparent.) In the 1900 Census the term race was added to color: "White, Black (Negro descent), Chinese, Japanese and Indian." In the 1950 Census, race replaced the term color, while neither term was used in 1960. In 1960, the item was: "Was this person White, Negro, American Indian, Japanese, Chinese, Filipino, Hawaiian, Aleut, Eskimo. . . . The 1970 Census provided detailed categorization for race (White, Negro or Black, American Indian, Japanese, Chinese, Filipino, Hawaiian, Korean and Other) and also asked about Hispanic "origin or descent." It was only in 1980 that the census used the term "ethnic origin."

This summary of census categories is helpful in understanding at least one aspect of our nation's changing opinion about race. Obviously the issue of slavery and mixed race individuals was a critical factor in the categorization of the U.S. population in the 18th and 19th centuries. The addition of the mulatto category under Blacks on the 1860 census forms indicates the numerical significance of mixed race individuals in the country at that time. The 1890 census form expands this division to include not only mulattoes, but quadroons and octoroons to meet the needs of an expanding "colored" population. In 1900 the census categories changed again dropping the degrees of blackness or whiteness while adding the term race as a modifier to the term color. This addition should not be surprising, given the social sentiments of that time. If further information is needed on the thinking of the time, students can research Social Darwinism, the Nativistic Movement, eugenics, and the Dillingham Commission Reports.

3. Dred Scott v. Sanford, 1857

In 1857 the Chief Justice of the U.S. Supreme Court wrote, in the Court's opinion, that:

They (the Negro) had for more than a century before been regarded as beings of an inferior order, and altogether unfit to associate with the white race, either in social or political relations; and so far inferior, that they had no rights which the white man was bound to respect; and that the negro [sic] might justly and lawfully be reduced to slavery for his benefit. He was bought and sold, and treated as an ordinary article of merchandise and traffic, whenever a profit could be made by it. This opinion was at that time fixed and universal in the civilized portion of the white race.

It is quite clear from this that many people in the United States, i.e., Dred Scott or any other African Americans, did not enjoy the same Constitutional rights as European Americans. Chief Justice Taney goes on to argue that, "there are two clauses in the Constitution which point directly and specifically to the negro [sic] race as a separate class of persons and show clearly that they were regarded as a portion of the people or citizens of the Government then formed" (Howard, 1857, pp. 9, 13-14, 15-17, 60). He is, of course, referring to the specifications that permitted the states to import slaves until 1808 if they so desired and the agreement among the states to respect the property (in this case the human chattel of slavery) of each state and to deliver this property up to appropriate authorities if found within their territories.

This is another powerful interpretation of the Constitution by the highest court of the land that clearly states the second-class status of African Americans. The instructor may want to explore with students the impact of this decision on both the Abolitionist movement during the time as well as the movement of some Southern states toward secession. The opening segment of the award winning teledocumentary series, the *Civil War*, is one source that demonstrates this point vividly. Another reliable source on these issues is *From Slavery to Freedom* by John Hope Franklin and Alfred Moss, Jr. now in its seventh edition (1994).

4. The Thirteenth, Fourteenth, and Fifteenth Amendments to the Constitution of the United States of America.

These amendments are extremely important to cover because of the changes they set forth in the treatment of African Americans by European Americans. Numerous works deal with the legal ramifications of these amendments, but one of the best is *The Constitution and Race* by D. E. Lively (1992). It provides clear summaries of the many cases citing these amendments as well as other pertinent legal issues related to race in the U.S.A.

5. Plessy v. Ferguson, 1896

The timing of the Plessy v. Ferguson decision makes it one of the most important cases of the post-Civil War era. Its significance at the end of the 19th century is that it set the stage for race relations throughout more than half of the 20th century. While most students may be vaguely aware of its significance, few will have examined the actual opinion or savored the court's thinking, and in a sense, society's thinking at that time. This case upheld the "separate but equal" doctrine and thus became the legal precedent for Jim Crow laws.

Part of Plessy's defense was an argument that his rights under the Fourteenth Amendment were violated as a result of a Louisiana statue that stated "all railway companies carrying passengers . . . in this state shall provide separate but equal accommodations for the white and colored races" (Plessy v. Ferguson, 1896). The Supreme Court supported this law and offered the following opinion.

The object of the amendment was undoubtedly to enforce the absolute equality of the two races before the law, but in the nature of things it could not have been intended to abolish distinctions based upon color, or to enforce social, as distinguished from political equality, or a commingling of the two races upon terms unsatisfactory to either. Laws permitting, and even requiring, their separation in places where they are liable to be brought into contact do not necessarily imply the inferiority of either race to the other, and have generally, if not universally, been recognized as within the competency of the state legislatures in the exercise of their police power." (Plessy v. Ferguson, 1896)

This interpretation clearly supports the states' right to distinguish between individuals on the basis of skin color in social situations, ranging from schooling to employment. The Louisiana statue goes on to say: "The power to assign to a particular coach obviously implies the power to determine to which race the passenger belongs, as well as the power to determine who, under the laws of the particular state, is to be deemed a white and who a colored person. . . ." (Plessy v. Ferguson, 1896)

Therefore, the state has the power not only to make decisions based on skin color but can also decide the race of an individual. The implications of this case are well documented in the segregation and discrimination of African Americans throughout the history of the 20th century. The *Eyes on the Prize* (Blackside, 1986) video documentary series can provide a rich source of vivid personal accounts of the struggle of African Americans against the institutionalization of the Jim Crow laws in the South.

An interesting example of the Federal government's right to name a person's race takes place every time a buyer in the U.S. fills out an application for a mortgage. The form one fills out for the loan requires the borrower to state race/national origin under a section referred to as "Information For Government Monitoring Purposes." The instructions for this section state:

> The following information is requested by the Federal Government for certain types of loans related to a dwelling, in order to monitor the Lender's compliance with equal credit opportunity, fair housing and home mortgage disclosure laws. You are not required to furnish this information but are encouraged to do so. The law provides that a Lender neither discriminate on the basis of this information, nor on whether you choose to furnish it. However, if you choose not to furnish the above information, under Federal regulations, this Lender is required to note race and sex on the basis of visual observation or surname. If you do not wish to furnish the above information, please check the box below. (Lender must review the above material to assure that the disclosures satisfy all requirements to which the Lender is subject under applicable state law for the particular type of loan applied for. (Universal Residential Loan Application, 1992).

It would seem from this statement that mortgage lenders must either have been trained to distinguish the racial characteristics of borrowers or that they possess some innate ability that will allow them to make these determinations accurately. If they have not been trained, they are probably relying on stereotypes to make their decisions. A person's surname is certainly not a valid indicator of race—nor is one's color. While this issue is not life threatening, it emphatically characterizes the ongoing race issue in this country.

Thus, in a nation of diverse ethnic, racial, and cultural backgrounds, we must continue to ask: Who has the right to name or define a person? Who should determine what a person should be labeled or called? If, in fact, a person traces his/her heritage through the European lines of the Irish, the African lines of West Africa, and the Native American lines of the Cherokee, what race should he/she be called? Often, when this question is raised in classrooms or workshops, the response is silence. Nobody wants to make the first move, yet almost everybody knows what the socially acceptable answer is in the United States of America.

The answer is, of course, **African American**. But why is this the correct or at least the socially acceptable answer? How did we learn it? The answer is certainly not based on any biological or genetic fact. It is based on a social definition derived by some form of agreement, legal or otherwise, by the people of the U.S.A. A person is African American, not necessarily because he/she chooses to be, but because the society demands it. If this person chooses to carry him/herself as a Native American but does not have legal documentation, he/she cannot enjoy the status of that heritage, but an African American needs no such documentation to be African American. Physical characteristics are enough. The person, if he/she chooses, can carry him/herself as an Irish American, but in all likelihood the only people who will believe this will be the individual's closest friends and family. It isn't that this triple heritage doesn't exist within this individual or millions of others in our country. It does. However, some lines of heritage are obviously more potent than others.

The Consequences of Racial Prejudice and Discrimination

Race has become an acceptable liability in U.S.A. life. The advantages of being European American here can be validated by numerous social indicators, including life expectancy, income per family or individual, and educational attainment, as well as by who is more likely to go to jail or to become a victim of a crime. The advantages of being European American, i.e., white, are so pervasive that most white people fail to even realize that they enjoy any advantage over the rest of the population in the country. Such is the power of socialization and the status-quo. Two of the most comprehensive texts available on the disparities within our society are Simpson and Yinger's *Racial and Cultural Minorities: An Analysis of Prejudice and Discrimination* (1985) and James M. Jones' *Prejudice and Racism* (1997). Both are easy to read, well organized, and contain a wealth of information teachers can incorporate into a study of racial prejudice and discrimination.

A. Dr. Molefi Asante of Temple University provides an example of the consequences of racism when he discusses children's need to be centered in an educational experience that provides a context in which they see themselves as whole, contributing persons. European American children experience this everyday. They are centered in an ocean of reminders about the greatness of Western Civilization, Europe, and the U.S.A. When one visits our great cities and travels their many streets and boulevards named after our Presidents and heroes or stands in front of their impressive buildings, statues, and monuments, little notice is given to the absence of African, Asian, Hispanic, or Native Americans who contributed to this country's greatness. In this macrocosm, what is there to center Native, African, Hispanic, and Asian American children? In their micro-world experiences, i.e., in school, what does a child see? Who is the school named after? What pictures hang on the wall? What artifacts are present in the building? In essence, whose culture is being celebrated? Whose culture is forgotten? Which children are being centered? The absence of a centering context for children of color is compounded through a curriculum that revels in Eurocentric accomplishments.

As Asante asserts, it is no wonder that European American children have higher self-esteem in these contexts than other children. If cultural scenes of importance reflect Eurocentric context cues, those individuals socialized to receive those cues will do so in a manner that gives them an advantage over other groups whose center is not reflected in the same manner. If history is being presented in ways that start your group in slavery and end it on welfare, or start your group as heathens and end it on reservations, or start your group as invited laborers and end up excluding it for almost 75 years after that labor is no longer needed, your group might have a problem understanding whether or not it can ever contribute in a meaningful way to this "white" society that obviously doesn't value "non-whites" as it does itself. (See Molefi Kete Asante's *Afrocentricity* [1998] for further information on these ideas).

B. Students often find it difficult to understand the pervasiveness of socialization in either their own lives or the lives of others. We are often blinded by our own ethnocentrism, making it hard for students to know what it's like to walk in another person's shoes. Socialization or enculturation provides the recipes or scripts that individuals have for interpreting and presenting the appropriate forms of behavior for any given situation. These scripts or recipes are learned by individuals throughout their lifetime (Adams, 1991), but the initial imprinting a person receives in childhood helps set the foundation for how that individual sees him/herself as well as how they think they are perceived by others in society. In a society that values the ethnic-racial culture of some groups over others, learning this difference begins early and is reinforced consistently through socialization.

A wonderful film adaptation of satirist Mark Twain's novel, *Pudd'nhead Wilson*, demonstrates the power of racial socialization. In the story, which takes place during the slave era, a mulatto nanny exchanges her child for the child of the plantation owner. The slave woman's child is, of course, more than half white, a quadroon, and his skin is as fair as the white child's skin. Consequently, the white child is raised as a slave while the black child is raised as the heir of a plantation owner. As you might expect, the black child grows up bright, articulate, and intelligent. He goes to college but later returns to his home and encounters his childhood friend with whom his mother had exchanged him at birth. This "boy" displays all the characteristics of the classic illiterate slave of the era. Through another twist of fate, the actions of the nanny are brought to light, and the roles of the two young men are reversed, with the African American being sold down river and the European American former fieldhand restored to the status of a Southern gentleman. However, the years of indoctrination are not easily reversed and the story ends with the latter character still being encumbered by the subordinate scripts he has learned so well. The story should provide plenty of discussion material as students explore its many implications.

Using Current Research

A. Analyzing current research like the ethnographic case study can be a very exciting method through which students explore racial issues. My research on Southeast Asian adolescent refugees (Adams, 1989) can provide some interesting examples on acculturation that can help students understand some of the difficulties of acculturation in the U.S.A. Many refugee students end up feeling "lost" or "isolated" in the early stages of their adaptation. This happens more frequently when they make heavy investments in trying to act "white." They often find that a "glass ceiling" limits just how much their peers and society will allow them to assimilate. Part of my study involved a series of interviews with a female Laotian high school student who made this kind of social investment. I will not forget the first time I met her. Her physical appearance was striking, with her trendy clothes, radical looking hair style, and her "down and cool" language. It would be hard to imagine a more acculturated first-generation Laotian adolescent. I looked forward to developing her as an ethnographic informant for my study because her English skills were so advanced.

As the months went by, she began to change. She was having trouble with the European American boys she dated because they seemed only to be interested in her physically. Her biggest disappointment came right before prom when her date for this event left her for a European American girl. This event, combined with other related social problems, including rejection by her Laotian peer group, who thought she was "acting too American," eventually led her to attempt suicide. The last time I saw her, she showed me the scars on her wrists. I suspect those physical scars have healed by now; the scars on her psyche are another matter.

B. Research by Ogbu (1978, 1987), Fordham (1980, 1988), Gibson (1988), Takaki (1994), and others suggests there exists a kind of social hierarchy of race-ethnicity in this country that places African American and other people of color in a castelike condition. Ogbu and others have discussed this phenomenon in detail and trace it to the decision to treat African Americans as chattel in the commerce of slavery. This condition and the subsequent rationalization and justification systems developed to support it have not lost their influence on how European Americans see themselves or the way they see any other group of people. All the players in this drama have learned their roles and play the game of superiority and subordination. Charles Lyons (1978) in a provocative article, entitled the "Colonial Mentality," discusses some of the rationalization and justification arguments.

C. Carlos Cortés, professor emeritus at the University of California at Riverside and a frequent keynote speaker and consultant, defines the **societal curriculum** as that, " . . . massive, ongoing, informal curriculum of family, peer groups, neighborhoods, churches, organizations, occupations, mass media, and other socializing forces that 'educate' all of us throughout our lives. Much of this informal education concerns ethnicity and ethnic groups" (1981, pp. 24-25). The pervasiveness of this curriculum reinforces and maintains the superordination of European Americans over Native, African, Asian, and Hispanic Americans through their day-to-day interactions in this country.

A good example of this societal curriculum of superordination-subordination was the prohibition against interracial marriage and the struggle necessary to end it. At one time or another 41 states had miscegenation laws. In the 1940s more than 30 states still prohibited interracial marriage. The final definitive decision was handed down in the Supreme Court case of Loving vs. The Commonwealth of Virginia. In 1992 this case celebrated its 25th anniversary. In an article that appeared in *The New York Times*, Mrs. Mildred J. Loving was interviewed about this landmark case by David Margolick (1992). He recounts

In the wee hours of one morning in July 1958, the quiet life that Mrs. Loving and her husband, Richard, enjoyed in this remote hamlet was shattered when three law officers opened the unlocked door of their bedroom and shined a flashlight on the couple. What they saw confirmed what they had been told: Mrs. Loving was black and Mr. Loving white, making their marriage illegal in Virginia. "What are you doing in bed with this lady?" Sheriff R. Garnett Brooks of Caroline County asked. Mr. Loving pointed to the wall where the couple had hung their marriage certificate, which was issued in the District of Columbia. "That's no good here," Sheriff Brooks replied. He charged the couple with unlawful cohabitation, carried them into nearby Bowling Green and threw them into the county jail. The county circuit judge, Leon M. Bazile sentenced the Lovings to a year in prison, telling them, "Almighty God created the races white, black, yellow, Malay,

301

and red, and he placed them on separate continents and but for the interference with his arrangement there would be no cause for such marriages." But the judge offered the Lovings a deal: they go free as long as they promised to steer clear of Virginia, at least as man and wife, for the next 25 years.

Over the next few years the Lovings exiled themselves to Washington, DC, but finally they made up their minds to fight the injustice the state of Virginia had imposed on them. It would take a long strenuous effort to resolve this issue at each level of the Virginia legal system all the way to the Virginia Supreme Court which upheld the lower courts' decisions. The issue was finally resolved in favor of the Lovings by the U.S. Supreme Court in June of 1967. At the time of the decision, 17 other states still enforced similar laws.

Conclusion

In this chapter I sought to provide instructors taking on the challenge of teaching about race some practical suggestions on strategies and issues. I am by no means providing exhaustive coverage of this complex and difficult subject. However, I do want to suggest the impact this issue has on U.S.A. society. As we prepare students for the 21st century, how we face the issue of race is likely to affect the quality of life, not only for our country but the world as well. Humankind will either learn to live in equality and equity or perish in our ethnocentrism. As educators we cannot let fear stop us from acting; that is exactly what has allowed the insidious nature of race to wreak havoc in our lives in the past and now. The question that must be asked and finally studied and answered by all teachers is, " What am I doing about it?"

References

Adams, J. Q. (1989). *Southeast Asian adolescent friendship preferences and functions in public high schools.* Dissertation Abstracts International.

Adams, J. Q. (1991). Understanding social interaction in the culturally diverse classroom. In J. Q. Adams, J. F. Niss, & C. Suarez (Eds.), *Multicultural education: Strategies for implementation in colleges and universities* (pp. 93-100). Macomb, IL: Western Illinois University Foundation.

Adler, M. J. (1968). *The annals of America. Volumes 1-18.* Chicago: Encyclopedia Britannica.

Allen, B. P., & Adams, J. Q. (1992). The concept 'race': Let's go back to the beginning. *Journal of Social Behavior and Personality, 7,* 163-168.

Asante, M. K. (1998). *Afrocentricity.* (2nd ed.). Philadelphia: Temple University Press.

Banks, J. A. (1996). *Teaching strategies for ethnic studies* (6th ed.). Boston: Allyn & Bacon.

Baker, J. R. (1974). *Race.* New York: Oxford University Press.

Coon, C. S. (1962). The origin of races. New York: Knopf.

Cortés, C. E. (1981). The societal curriculum: Implications for multi-ethnic education. In J. A. Banks & B. J. Shin (Eds.), *Education in the 80's: Multiethnic education.* Washington DC: National Education Association.

Cose, Ellis (1997). *Color-blind: Seeing beyond race in a race-obsessed world.* New York: Harper Collins Publishing.

Fordham, S., & Ogbu, J. U. (1980). Black students' school success: Coping with the "burden of acting white." *The Urban Review, 18,* 176-206.

Franklin, J. H., & Moss, Jr., A. A. (1994). *From slavery to freedom* (7th. ed.). New York: Knopf.

Gain, S. (1971). *Human races* (3rd ed.). Springfield, IL: Charles C. Thomas.

Gibson, M. A. (1988). *Accommodation without assimilation.* Ithaca: Cornell University Press.

Howard, B. J. (1857). Report of the decision of the Supreme Court of the United States in the case Dred Scott. Washington, DC.

Jensen, A. R. (1973). *Educability and group differences.* New York: Methuen.

Lively, D. E. (1992). *The constitution and race.* New York: Praegar.

Lott, J. T. (1993). Do United States racial/ethnic categories still fit? *Population Today, 21,* 6-9.

Lyons, C. (1978). The colonial mentality. In P. G. Altbach and G. P. Kelly (Eds.), *Education and colonialism* (pp. 181-201). New York: Longman.

Margolick, D. (1992, June 12). A mixed marriage's 25th anniversary of legality. *The New York Times.* Law, p. 1R.

McIntosh, P. (1988). *White Privilege and Male Privilege: A Personal Account of Coming to See Correspondences Through Work in Women's Studies.* Center for Research on Women. Wellesley College, Wellesley, MA.

Montagu, A. (1998). *Man's most dangerous myth: The fallacy of race* (6th ed.). New York: Altamira Press.

Montagu, A. (1999). *Race and IQ.* New York: Oxford University Press.

Ogbu, J. U. (1978). *Minority education and caste.* New York: Academic Press.

Ogbu, J. U. (1987). Variability in minority school performance: A problem in search of an explanation. *Anthropology and Education Quarterly, 18,* 312-344.

Olsson, J. (1997). *Detour spotting: For white anti-racists.* Hamburg, PA: Cultural Bridges.

Omi, Michael. (1997). Racial identity and the State: The dilemmas of classification. *Law & Inequality: A Journal of Theory and Practice, 15*(1), 7-23. (Department of Ethnic Studies, University of California, Berkeley, CA 94720-2306)

Plessy v. Ferguson, 163 U.S. 537 United States Reports: Cases Adjudged in the Supreme Court. New York: Banks & Brother, 1896.

Rothenberg, P. S. (1997). *Race, class, & gender in the United States* (4th ed.). New York: St. Martin's Press.

Simpson, G. E., & Yinger, J. M. (1985). *Racial and cultural minorities: An analysis of prejudice and discriminations* (5th ed.). New York: Plenum Press.

Shirts, G. (1999). *BaFa BaFa.* Del Mar, CA: Simulation Training Systems.

Shirts, G. (1999). *Star Power.* Del Mar, CA: Simulation Training Systems.

Tatum, B. D. (1992). Talking about race, learning about racism: The application of racial identity development theory in the classroom. *Harvard Educational Review, 62*(1), 1-24.

Twain, M. (1981). *Pudd'nhead Wilson.* New York: Bantam.

Universal Residential Loan Application. Fannie Mae Form 1003/rev. 10/92.

West, C. (1994). *Race matters.* New York: Vintage Books.

The world almanac and book of facts 1999 (1998). New York: Griffin Trade Paperback.

303

Internet Sources

American Demographics (www.demographics.com)
Central Intelligence Agency (www.odci.gov./cia/)
Federal Bureau of Investigation (www.fbi.gov/)
Population Reference Bureau (www.PRB.org)
United Nations (www.un.org)
United States Census Bureau (www.census.gov)

TEACHING ABOUT CULTURAL DIVERSITY: CHALLENGE AND RESPONSE AT A COMMUNITY COLLEGE

by
Bansrajh Mattai

For several years I have been thinking about two divergent philosophies which seem to yield answers to dominant questions in current educational thinking. The questions are: (1) what are the necessary and sufficient conditions for an education? and (2) what are the necessary and sufficient conditions for an education in a culturally diverse society? The first question presupposes an answer that defers to the value of education as an end in itself and is thus not shackled to a utilitarian philosophy. It proceeds from the thinking that to educate is to seek to raise the human mind above the concourse of the commonplace and mundane. This results in a host of enduring qualities such as the capacity to think freely, to distinguish between the rational and nonrational, and to be able to appreciate the cultural and moral achievements of mankind. The second argues that education must have a purpose outside itself, failing which, it loses its very reason for existence. It feeds on the pragmatic philosophy that recognizes that those who run educational institutions do so under the influence of political and/or religious patrimony, and are thus held accountable by what is of social worth over and beyond mere individual intellectual advancement and satisfaction.

Divergent as these two positions might seem, behind them both lies the unifying element of "empowerment"—a living, dynamic force that allows individuals to exercise significant, if not total, control over their destiny, to choose between alternatives, to participate actively in the historical process which they cannot truly escape. It is the lack of empowerment that makes people fatalistic, resigned to their lot, and doomed to perpetual questioning of their own worth as human beings without the necessary propensity toward engagement in the scheme of things so as to alleviate their condition. The point is made tellingly in several places in Marx's analysis of the notion of "false consciousness" and its consequences in creating the "alienated man." It is repeated in Durkheim's classic work on suicide in his consideration of the concept of "anomie." And in an earlier age the Bard of Avon, speaking to a similar, if not wholly analogous, theme, makes the ambitious Cassius suggest to his more stoical friend Brutus that it "is not in our stars, but in ourselves that we are underlings."

The facilitation of empowerment should be a matter of highest educational concern, especially in a society such as ours in which the philosophy of rugged individualism coupled with the almost inextricable link between wealth, power, and prestige has a way of disenfranchising large numbers of rural and urban poor, ethnic minorities, women, senior citizens, and people of color. For, while it is true that our society openly professes democratic principles as fundamental to all genuine human aspiration, the reality of American politics, as Michael Parenti (1987) so convincingly shows, is that such principles remain at the level of frozen abstractions when, either because of the lack of knowledge, or of sufficient financial resources to provide thereof, or because of the inability to influence others, people find the opportunity to participate well-nigh impossible.

In this essay I will share some thoughts on a program on Cultural Diversity in America in which I have been directly involved at Joliet Junior College since the fall of 1986. It accords a certain transcendence to the view that all education is empowerment, that there is no real antithesis between the education of the individual and the education of the citizen at the level of empowerment, and that courses in cultural diversity, if approached with genuine concern for the development of both the intellectual and the emotional sides of human nature, can greatly facilitate the process of empowerment, without which the individual, even or especially, in a democracy, is no more than an "underling".

Basic Assumptions

The Cultural Diversity in America course, focusing on ethnic and racial diversity, is founded on several assumptions, all of which derive from the incontrovertible fact of the pluralistic nature of American society. The *Harvard Encyclopedia of American Ethnic Groups* (1980) lists 119 ethnic groups, the overwhelming majority of which regard freedom of speech, political and religious persuasions, and the right to preserve aspects of their cultural identities as among America's greatest assets. Indeed, it is highly doubtful that the demographics of our society would be as they are had it not been for an almost worldwide recognition of this fact. In recognition of the additional fact that the future development of U.S. society depends to a considerable degree on the kind of education its citizens receive, a high degree of responsibility is placed on our institutions of learning to help promote awareness and understanding of the nature of America's cultural diversity and of the atmosphere of mutual tolerance that must underpin human relationships within it.

From the standpoint of an educational institution that espouses the philosophy and mission of the community college, the faculty and administration at Joliet Junior College, and especially the Department of Social and Behavioral Sciences, under whose aegis the course was initiated and is still run, were even more conscious of the need to recognize that the effectiveness of teachers lies in their ability to understand the complex racial and ethnic mix of the community being served, to come to terms with competing value systems, to cope with ever-increasing changes in our society, and to recognize their own needs as teachers and as individuals and to take steps to fulfill them.

Additionally, the college could not fail to appreciate:
- that exposure to the study of other cultures by all Americans from as early an age as possible is vital to a deeper and more discriminating appreciation of our own culture;
- that the study of different cultures, if pursued openly and objectively, can help individuals to make the leap from moral understanding to moral responsibility and obligation, which we see as a crucial aspect of a student's affective education; and
- that the study of cultural diversity in the U.S. can be seen as a valuable adjunct to studies aimed at providing students with a global perspective that defers to the reality of the world as becoming increasingly internationalized along economic, political, and cultural lines.

Background of the Course

At the inception of the Cultural Diversity in America course in the Spring of 1988, Joliet Junior College had a representation of 12.8% ethnic minority students (inclusive of Native Americans, African Americans, Asian Americans, Hispanic Americans, and a tiny fraction categorized as "other"). At the time of writing, this percentage had risen to 14.2%, and there is every indication that, with the changing demographics of the school district, even greater representations are likely. Among the European American majority themselves can be found students of diverse ethnic backgrounds (e.g. Poles, Lithuanians, Armenians, Greeks, Italians).

This information is provided in order to apprise the reader of the nature of the student population at Joliet Junior College rather than to suggest that the cultural diversity course is intended solely to address the needs of ethnic and racial minorities. Indeed, from the very beginning the message has been that learning about the nature of the pluralistic society in which we live has important social implications for the entire junior college student body, and we were so convinced of the importance of this message that I went out into the community to impress it upon the minds of teachers and administrators at the high school and grade school levels. Moreover, in discussions with people in leadership positions in education, a major concern was to urge widespread recognition of the need for participation in the drive to "multiculturalize" the curriculum. Historically, we have found such participation to be wanting, for the data indicated that the greatest interest in designing and implementing multicultural programs came from minority faculty and administrators. Joliet Junior College was no exception.

Efforts to sensitize some of our own faculty and administrators to the logic and terms of reference of the Cultural Diversity in America course translated into:

- enlisting the services of the media department to help disseminate information about the new program throughout the school;
- circulating to department heads material that spoke to the nature of the program, its general educational worth and its overall relevance in the context of the changing ethnic composition of the United States over the past 20 years, related demographic projections for the next decade and beyond, and global transformations currently taking place in the spheres of politics, commerce, and other aspects of social relations;
- addressing academic advisors and counselors on the eminent necessity to inform students about the value of such a program to their future careers in a pluralistic society characterized by high rates of occupational mobility; and
- drawing on the expertise of outside speakers of repute in the field of intercultural affairs (a) to stimulate less-than-interested faculty and administrators about the reciprocal benefits to be derived from an informed approach to race and ethnic relations in a society comprised of over 100 ethnic groups, and (b) to underline solid educational justifications for recognizing that an essential condition of learning is that teachers recognize how important it is for them to know their students as unique persons.

These measures had the overall effect of raising the level of consciousness of our school personnel to the urgency of implementing the program. In consequence, we had no difficulty recruiting the maximum of 35 students for our first class in January 1988. For the fall of 1988 we were able to offer two classes in Cultural Diversity in America and by the spring of 1989, three such classes. The demand for the course has not waned since, and we have continued to offer three classes per semester.

Course Goals

The goals set for the course are:

- to encourage students to develop a knowledge of opposing value-systems that must inevitably arise out of different constructions of reality by people who have originated from diverse cultural traditions and a knowledge of the manner in which these value-systems tend to influence individual and social behavioral patterns;

- to nurture a sense of the student's role as a person genuinely interested in other human beings who have historically made significant contributions to the economic, political, and social development of our nation;
- to help students develop a sense of what the philosopher Bertrand Russell liked to call "abstract sympathy," which obliges the individual to experience a sense of kinship with all people on the planet;
- to facilitate a good grasp of the fact that the human condition allows ample scope for healthy disagreement as to the effectiveness of the ways in which people of different cultures have sought to answer the basic problems of human existence as they relate to material comfort, love and human warmth, and spiritual and emotional satisfaction;
- to enable students to develop a historical perspective incorporating an understanding of the role of the United States in world affairs, and the role of students themselves in helping to shape the historical process, hopefully with a preference for "good" rather than "evil";
- to help students develop an appreciation of the notion of reciprocity which lies at the heart of all relationships that can be described as moral;
- to promote an understanding of the critical differences between equality, pure and simple, and equality of opportunity, and to encourage a philosophy that recognizes that, in whatever social structure people are involved, they should have the same opportunities to achieve their human fullness;
- to help students to develop an awareness not only of their own cultural heritage, but of the cultural and moral achievements of humankind;
- to enable students to gain insight into the manner in which language and culture form a seamless web and the ways language and thought are linked; and
- to enable students to gain some understanding of the effects of cultural differences on cognition and attainment.

To achieve these goals much depends, as in other courses, on the teachers' attitude towards those in their charge, to the material they wish to present, and to the manner of its presentation, but a great deal depends also upon the kind of students the class is able to attract. With respect to the latter, while we have continued to accord to our program a preeminent position in any liberal arts curriculum and thus deserving of a place in anyone's education, the course in Cultural Diversity in America at Joliet Junior College is optional, and, short of a dramatic turn of policy by the administration involving liberalization of the curriculum along multicultural lines, is likely to remain so for the foreseeable future. Historically, the course appears to have had its greatest attraction for those whose career focus is in nursing, teaching, or other caring professions. At any rate, after many semesters of offering Cultural Diversity in America, I can say with virtual certainty that, whoever the audience, the teacher's first encounter with the class is of the utmost importance in encouraging a sense of purpose larger than the acquisition of three hours of social science credit. Several imperatives are worthy of note in this regard.

- The teachers should demonstrate their intent and willingness to embrace the scientific approach of openness and humility before the facts, and to go where the evidence leads ever prepared to revise their views or to question received wisdom in the light of new information. This necessarily obliges them to establish early on in the program the critical distinction between fact and value, between "is" statements and "ought" statements, which in turn can be of considerable importance in underlining their own integrity as scholars and the primacy of facts in all decision making.

- With respect to the task in hand, the teachers' point of departure should be from the place where most students are, rather than from where they want them to be. This entails some understanding of the students' backgrounds in terms of the degree of their exposure in daily life or in their previous studies to people of ethnic backgrounds different from their own.

- The students should be made ready from the very outset of the program to confront moral dilemmas that might arise from the consideration of the full facts of a case— dilemmas that, against the ideals and principles of the U.S. Constitution, seem unavoidable in discussions of, say, the U.S. Government's treatment of Native Americans over the last century and a half, or of the rationale behind the Chinese Exclusion Act of 1883, or of the U.S. Supreme Court's decision to institute a poll tax, literacy tests, and residential qualifications with respect to voting rights of Black males under the Fifteenth Amendment, or again of the reasons offered for the internment of Japanese Americans in camps in the Southwest during World War II. Here there is much to commend an approach that eschews any semblance of imparting guilt, which in any case can hardly be justified, but defers instead to the principle that those who do not or cannot learn from the mistakes of history are condemned to repeat them, to use George Santayana's now classic dictum.

- Both teacher and student should be clear about the need for conceptual clarity with respect to basic terms such as minority, culture, integration, assimilation, pluralism, amalgamation, prejudice, discrimination, racism, ethnocentrism, cultural relativism, and bilingualism. In the absence of clarification of these terms, people can easily descend to talking at cross-purposes resulting in more harm than good.

- Students should be apprised of the fact that in the study of people of diverse cultures the education of feeling is as germane as the education of the intellect. No serious scholar in the general field of culture seems to be in disagreement with the principle that there is something gloriously original about looking at a culture from within rather than from without, or about the effectiveness of this means in promoting genuine cultural awareness and sensitivity. It is my conviction that the education of feeling is a valuable prerequisite for the development of empathy, a quality more often talked about than experienced, yet with great potential for enhancing the integrity of human reciprocal relationships.

- Students should be made aware that a course such as Cultural Diversity in America allows immense scope for the combined thrust of theory and practice.

- Students should be apprised of the value of a comparative approach to the study of different cultures in the United States—an approach that tends to reveal differences in socialization patterns, including linguistic codes and educational orientations that have crucial bearings on success and failure within our essentially middle-class insti- tutional structures—in order to critically assess how conditions can be altered to facil- itate greater participation by all in our democratic processes.

A Note on Course Content

Since it is hardly possible to deal with 119 ethnic groups over a period of a single semester, teachers of courses in cultural diversity which focus on racial and ethnic minorities, must be selective about the groups they consider, as well as the sequence, scope, and depth of treatment of each. However, in my experience, there does not appear to be any generally accepted criteria for making the selection. In some parts of the country where there are heavy concentrations of particular ethnic groups, e.g. Hispanics and Asians in the Southwest, African Americans and Poles in Chicago, and Puerto Ricans in New York City, it would seem appropriate to focus students' attention on the familiar cultures, but such focus need not be rigorously exclusionary, since this will miss the whole point about broadening the student's knowledge about ethnic diversity in the U.S.

At Joliet Junior College we have consistently adhered to the position taken several years ago that we should include the study of the ethnic heritages of the larger minorities such as Native Americans, African Americans, Hispanic Americans, and Asian Americans who together number approximately 22% of the nation's population. However, students are allowed to investigate groups outside these broad categories. This has resulted over the years in student contributions on the Amish, the Oneida, the Gypsies, the Arabs, the Pacific Islanders, and several Eastern European groups—all offering valuable opportunities for comparison and contrast.

Pedagogical Practice and Instructional Techniques

In terms of pedagogical practice, since the start of the Cultural Diversity course at Joliet Junior College, teaching strategies have included the lecture mode and group discussion as well as individual project-oriented activities. Several years of interaction with students at the community college level, where the open-door policy towards admission to most courses still holds, has convinced me that doses of sheer lecture are both appropriate and relevant in situations where pieces of factual knowledge are imperative to a discussion. The presumption that one can reasonably expect community college students to find the facts for themselves with proper direction is based more on benign hope than on the realities of the situation. My own experience bears out that many of those who come to the course in cultural diversity have neither the time nor the inclination to go after basic facts related to the demography, religion, geography, and nationality of the many groups they encounter. Thus, I find that when the lecture mode is used in moderation in, say, the organizing and structuring of facts and in conjunction with a standard text on racial and ethnic groups in the United States, students tend to develop a heightened awareness and confidence in getting involved in classroom discussion, which I see as vital to an appreciation of the subject matter.

Moreover, a judicious blend of lecturing with experiences drawn from the students' own backgrounds can be highly productive in terms of harnessing practice to theory. Theoretical perspectives on cultural diversity, models of integration, socioeconomic and political paradigms of power can assume added meaning and significance when set against students' personal constructs of reality. The process tends to generate affective/provocative responses that encourage healthy engagement of views which, in turn, can find expression in the most edifying anecdotes on all sides.

With respect to project-oriented activities, any number of possibilities emerges. It should be recognized that the study of diverse cultures in the U.S., as an academic exercise, is only now starting to gather momentum, and, accordingly, there is a large scope for original work even at the undergraduate level. Such work may range from investigation of the ethnic composition of a particular neighborhood or district, to focus on ethnic variations in family and kinship patterns or religion, to patterns of intergroup conflict and accommodation, to attitudes toward bilingual education. Such studies might employ any or all of the standard research techniques of sampling, case studies, participant observation, and planned experiments.

At Joliet Junior College all students in the course are required to conduct a case study (to be assessed as a major assignment), the goal of which is to become thoroughly acquainted with a member of an ethnic group other than their own with a strong emphasis on recognizing the affective benefits to be derived from such contact. Students are instructed in different interviewing techniques and are given a set of questions and strategies for eliciting focused and constructive answers. The questions are framed in such a way as to elicit answers relating to the subject's conception of himself or herself as a member of U.S. society at large, but, more importantly, to help the interviewer towards a firmer grasp of differences and similarities between dominant American attitudes and values and those of the subject. Points of focus include, among those mentioned above, individual ethnic commitment, intergroup contact, philosophies of education, teaching, and learning, comparisons and contrasts between life in the U.S. and in the mother country. The hope is that this activity will assist in the development of reciprocal relationships leading to greater sensitivity between interviewer and interviewee. Additionally, it is felt that such an activity affords the student facility in a method of communicating with others and promotes an attitude of openness, with a desire to learn about, and to relate to, rather than to be hastily judgmental about, others. Finally, the interview has the tangential benefit of training students in listening skills, but of listening so as to **hear** what is being said. The overall effect has been to transcend racial and ethnic consciousness and to see people as individuals in peculiarly human situations trying to work out solutions to the universal problems of human existence.

A most effective means of stimulating interest in the classroom is to draw on the experience of well-qualified outside speakers or of interested on-campus faculty and administrators of different cultural backgrounds to address the students. The serious teacher hardly needs convincing about the merits of having a well-informed speaker bring to life certain aspects of a culture that even the best textbook must, more often than not, leave to the imagination.

Other instructional techniques might include:

- the use of appropriate audio-visual aids such as filmstrips and videotapes treating themes on Black history and culture, arts and crafts of Native Americans, Eastern religious traditions, the "symbiotic" relationship between Puerto Rico and the United States, achievements of civilizations of Hispanic America, viz. Aztec, Inca, and Maya, the Greek and Roman legacy to western civilization, Eastern and Western attitudes to education and the work ethic;
- actively encouraging field trips to museums, temples, synagogues, mosques, archeological sites, and other places of cultural and historical interest by incorporating experiences in classroom projects.

The case for multicultural education as an integral part of the curriculum at all levels of the educational system has never been stronger. As the nations of the world move towards political, economic, and even ideological rapprochement, there is the lurking danger that the home-grown problems facing Americans will be drowned in the ensuing euphoria— problems that have their origins in injustice, cruelty, prejudicial attitudes, indifference to the sufferings of others, the inability to practice what is preached. It is my belief that courses that deal with this country's ethnic mosaic and the special contributions that each group has made to the American experience can be of considerable help in developing a certain sensitivity towards these problems. More importantly, such courses can help to elicit an ongoing commitment to **act** in recognition of the contributions of the various ethnic groups and in accordance with the principle of one nation in pursuit of justice and liberty for all.

If this sounds somewhat optimistic and perhaps even facile, the reader is invited to reconsider the extent to which an educator not merely responds to change, but initiates it. And in this respect we need to be venturesome, to accept challenges, and to take risks, with much hope, indeed, but with the prospect of rich rewards also. In the final analysis, if we are able to instill in the minds of those in our charge the habitual vision of truth, beauty, and goodness, and facility in pursuing these virtues, we will have succeeded in large measure in "empowering" them. The study of the culturally diverse, in my view, offers such a facility.

References

A nation at risk: The imperative for educational reform. (1983). Washington, DC: The National Commission on Excellence in Education.

A review of the development of standards regarding cultural pluralism: Considerations for teacher education institutions. (1981). Springfield, IL: Illinois State Board of Education.

Goals statement. (1980). Springfield, IL: Illinois State Board of Education.

Harvard encyclopedia of American ethnic groups. (1980). Cambridge, MA: Harvard University.

Parenti, M. (1987). Democracy for the few. New York: St. Martin.

COURSE ORGANIZATION AND THE CHALLENGES
OF STUDENTS' MULTIPLE INTELLIGENCES

by
Savario Mungo

Educators in higher education, much like educators at all levels, are concerned about being able to reach an increasingly diverse student population. Traditional tried and true methods do not seem to work anymore. Motivation to learn and to participate seems harder to instill in more and more of our students. Is this because diversity means a lowering of ability among the student population? Of course not. What we are facing in higher education is a challenge to relate our teaching styles and approaches more closely to the needs and characteristics of our students. This shift to a new paradigm, one in which we accept the idea that if students don't learn the way we teach, we should teach the way they learn, is difficult; it can also be challenging and exciting.

The movement to infuse multicultural concepts into our courses and to respond to diversity throughout our curriculum has provided us with an opportunity to use new approaches and strategies. If we use this opportunity, we will be able to relate more closely to a diverse student population and make the paradigm shift a reality. Faced with this challenge, many teachers, myself included, have looked to research on learning styles for direction. I have found the approach holding the greatest promise is based on Howard Gardner's multiple intelligence theory.

Multiple Intelligence Theory

The following quote from Gardner (1987) about his multiple intelligence theory indicates its usefulness:

It is of the utmost importance that we recognize and nurture all of the varied human intelligences, and all of the combinations of intelligences. We are different largely because we all have different combinations of intelligences. If we recognize this, I think we will have at least a better chance of dealing appropriately with the many problems that we face in the world. (p. 193)

Thus Gardner offers an underlying principle that allows us to clearly address student differences as we develop our strategies.

Gardner, in *Frames of Mind* (1983), provides a means of mapping the broad range of abilities humans possess by grouping these capabilities into seven comprehensive categories of intelligences:

1. Linguistic—the capacity to use words effectively, whether in speech or in writing;
2. Logical/Mathematical—the capacity to use numbers effectively and to reason well;
3. Spatial—the ability to perceive the visual-spatial world accurately and to perform transformations upon those perceptions;
4. Bodily/Kinesthetic—expertise in using one's whole body to express ideas and feelings and the facility to use one's hands to produce or transform things;
5. Musical—the capacity to perceive, transform, and express musical forms;

6. Interpersonal—the ability to perceive and make distinctions in the moods, intentions, motivations, and feelings of other people; and

7. Intrapersonal—self-knowledge and the ability to act adaptively on the basis of that knowledge.

According to Gardner, all people possess all seven intelligences, with some of them highly developed in a person, some of them less developed. Since most people can develop each intelligence to an adequate level of competency, we should not type individuals according to one or the other. The goal is to allow everyone to develop more fully all of their intelligences (Armstrong, 1994).

Assuming our students are probably highly developed in at least one of the seven intelligences and moderately developed in others does not, of course, mean we necessarily know which intelligences are stronger for which students. Our choice, therefore, is clear. In order to implement this theory, we need to develop strategies and approaches that address all of the seven intelligences, offering a variety of approaches to insure that every student, no matter what his or her strongest intelligence is, will be able to relate that intelligence to a class activity. Hopefully, each student, depending on the intelligence that is his or her strength, will be turned on by the activity addressing that strength and thus will be encouraged to use other intelligences in other activities and assignments. Though this theory cannot come to fruition overnight and demands ongoing development, it is possible to integrate strategies that address most of the seven intelligences for the major concepts or topics taught. If all seven cannot be addressed in a particular instance, they can all be addressed periodically throughout the course.

Although this may seem a difficult task, I know from experience that it can be done, having developed activities, assignments, and strategies for my classes over the past several years to address the diversity in my classrooms and having chosen Gardner's theory of multiple intelligences as a guide. I use activities that address most, if not all, of the seven intelligences for every major concept or topic I teach. The approach is two-fold. First, I organize each course so requirements, assignments, and assessment measures address the seven intelligences. In this way, all students have an opportunity to use their strength of intelligence, as well as to develop more fully their other intelligences. Second, I develop many specific activities and strategies within a course's major concepts and topics to relate to the seven intelligences.

Course Requirements, Assignments, and Activities

One of my major concerns is that course requirements reflect my attempt to understand and build on students' diversity. These requirements are developed around a variety of the seven intelligences so each student has the opportunity to experience initial success in at least one aspect of the course and thus be motivated to pursue success in others. The initial success can be in activities or assignments related to their strength of intelligence. Then, as they address other activities and assignments, they will be encouraged to participate more fully and to develop further additional intelligences with the result being a more positive and comprehensive learning experience.

The following examples of course requirements, activities, and strategies illustrate how this might work. Though individually they reflect what many educators already do, the combination of activities shows how the multiple intelligences approach to classroom diversity can be most effective.

Text Assignments

All students must be able to read and understand the texts used for a course. However, additional activities can not only enhance an understanding of the text, but also allow for the diversity of intelligences.

Chapter summaries. Ask students to complete and hand in a summary of each chapter, giving them a number of ways to do so, from summarizing the highlights to elaborating on the parts of the chapter they felt they learned most from. Require them to turn in the chapter summaries the day of the test on a particular chapter. This enables them to review their notes and the chapter in preparing for the test.

Chapter discussion groups. Divide the class into chapter discussion groups, with four or five students per group. The groups will stay together throughout the course. For each chapter, prior to the test on that chapter, have students hand in their summaries and then meet in their discussion groups to discuss the chapter. In each group have a recorder and a leader, roles that rotate each time the group meets. The recorder keeps track of the important issues discussed, and the leader keeps the discussion focused. At the end of the session each member of the group signs the recorder's notes, which are handed in to the instructor. The whole class then briefly discusses the issues raised in the small groups. Students who do not hand in a chapter summary can participate in the group discussion, but cannot sign the recorder's notes. Each person signing the recorder's notes receives points in addition to their chapter summary point total.

The discussions can be handled in a number of ways to add variety and interest to a class. For example, students can discuss what each found to be the most important aspects of the chapter or the instructor can offer questions for them to focus on. Cooperative learning strategies, such as JigSaw, can also be used. In this approach the instructor assigns a specific section of the chapter to each member of the discussion group. If, for example, there are four members in the discussion groups, the chapter is divided into four parts, with each student assigned a part. The students read their assigned section, write a summary of it, and make copies of it for each person in their group. Thus in each group, the students will get a summary of each part of the chapter. When the class arrives for the discussion, students from each group who read the first section will meet for about ten minutes to share what they have in their summaries. In these "expert" groups, students can add information to their own summaries if they missed an important point or concept. After these discussions, students return to their original chapter discussion groups and pass out their summary copies, verbally explaining anything gained from the expert group. At the end of the discussion, students hand in their chapter summaries.

Written tests on text readings. Although most tests follow a similar format, short answers and essays, variation can enhance student understanding and encourage them to study harder. In my own classes, the first chapter test is always open book. This allows students to understand the type of tests required on text assignments and encourages them to read the subsequent chapters with greater care and a better understanding of the expectations of the instructor.

If JigSaw is used to discuss a chapter, the test on that chapter can be done as a group assignment. Since members of the group were responsible for specific sections of the chapter, they should be responsible for the questions for their own section. Taking the test as a group allows each member to contribute answers to the section he or she reads and summarizes. The sharing and interaction experienced during this type of test enhances student collaboration and support for each other. It also forces students to face up to their responsibilities since they will be accountable for part of each group member's grade on the test.

Adherence to Diversity and Multiple Intelligences

Students who have difficulty reading the text and taking tests on those readings are allowed the opportunity to gain an understanding of the text not only through reading, but also through discussing the chapters with peers in groups, summarizing their ideas, listening to others explain what they learned from the text, and adding to their own summaries of important aspects of the readings. Taking the test on the first chapter with an open book approach removes the initial fear students have when faced with the unknown. Too often, a text reading assignment and the follow-up test on the readings primarily reward those with a strong linguistic intelligence strength. The above text activities address student diversity by allowing students to use, and be evaluated on, the results of engaging several different intelligences. The activities address interpersonal, intrapersonal, spatial, and mathematical/logical intelligences in addition to linguistic intelligence. This enables many students to gain an understanding of a chapter in the text while encouraging them to continue reading subsequent chapters and improve their linguistic intelligence.

Group Reports

All students are assigned a group presentation. The following structured approach has proven to be most successful. All students are given the opportunity to select from a series of topics to be covered in class and then are assigned to groups based on their choices. Groups of four or five are most effective when the following format and rules apply.
- Reports are to be in a semi-debate format, with students determining one or more current controversial aspects of the topic and researching the issues. Sides are chosen and students present their debate to the class in a very structured format. Not a debate in the sense that one side wins or loses, the success of the exercise is determined by how well the overall debate brings forth all the important aspects of the controversy. Thus each side helps and supports each other in finding material for arguments and rebuttals so a balanced presentation is possible. Students have the option of using any media, simulation, or other devices to make their points.
- Students are to use a minimum of four sources for their data and develop a bibliography for all class members.
- Students are to develop an outline of their topic and arguments for each member of the class, thus enabling the class to follow the report and to take notes as needed.
- The debate is to be followed by a question and answer (Q & A) period in which the class questions the presenters. Each presenter is to stay in character and on his or her particular side of the debate throughout the Q & A. The instructor can initiate the Q & A by raising particularly interesting questions for each side.

- Each student in the group is to submit an individual position paper on the topic as a whole.

In evaluating these group reports, I give group points in the following categories: opening and closing statements, bibliography, outline, and research. I give individual points for arguments, rebuttals, students' position papers, and the Q & A. Each student who is not part of a particular group report is required to complete a minimum of two article reviews related to the group topic and is able to participate in the Q & A period of the reports.

Adherence to Diversity and Multiple Intelligences

Too often group reports turn students off because they fear they will be stuck with a lower grade because only a group grade is given. In the format proposed, opportunities for both individual and group evaluations exist. In addition, students often have the concern that some members of the group will not pull their weight and thus will let the group down. Because multiple intelligences are addressed in this format, the potential for each student to be turned on by some aspect of the process will enable each student to contribute more fully. In the above structure, each of the multiple intelligences is addressed. The intrapersonal intelligence and linguistic intelligence is addressed throughout the report but particularly in the research, individual presentation, position paper assignment, and verbal report. Mathematical/logical and spatial intelligences are addressed in organizing and sequencing the report and in preparing the outlines. The kinesthetic and musical intelligences can be addressed as students use their creativity in developing their presentation to the class, and finally, the interpersonal intelligence is addressed during the group meetings leading up to the final preparation of the report. It is hoped some aspect of this assignment, from preparation to article reviews to Q & A, will address each student's strength of intelligence, and that each in collaboration with other group members, will have the opportunity to enhance and further develop his or her other intelligences.

Films/Videos

Since class presentations of short videos or excerpts from films to support a point or enhance a topic or concept are often extremely useful, I try to find at least one film or video related to as many class topics as possible. In addition to showing films and videos in class, I assign students films/videos to view at a media center outside of class. For each film viewed as part of the course students are asked to write a film review. Periodically, they use their chapter discussion groups as film discussion groups to discuss the films they have seen. The groups can either discuss what each found most useful in the films, or they can respond to questions posed by the instructor. Either way, students have an opportunity to share what they learned as well as to learn from those who saw the film differently.

Simulation/Games

As often as possible, I use simulations and games to make points important to the class topics. These are usually whole class activities, and many are either commercial games or simulations developed by the instructor.

Class Activities

Shorter than games and simulations, (usually 5-15 min.) numerous activities related to such topics as listening, verbalizing one's needs, and cross-cultural communication, as well as other topics related to specific class concepts, are available. I use these in conjunction with class topics or overall course development as often as possible. Most involve physical as well as verbal activity and require group interaction.

Assessment

If an instructor decides to use a variety of assignments and to initiate requirements such as those outlined above, each of the assignments must become part of the overall course evaluation. I assign points to each required assignment in the course, including quizzes, chapter summaries, article reviews, film reviews, discussion groups, oral reports, position papers, and attendance and participation. A student who does not do well in the quizzes has the opportunity to do well on the film reviews and in the discussion groups. Since each are worth points that are part of the overall course evaluation, students can gain points most easily in assignments related to their strength of intelligence and work on improving their performance on assignments related to their less developed intelligences. What should be avoided is basing the total evaluation of students primarily on the results of their performance on written tests that favor those with strong linguistic intelligence. If we teach to multiple intelligences, we must assess with those multiple intelligences in mind.

Adherence to Diversity and Multiple Intelligences

Using films and videos on a regular basis addresses the spatial intelligence of many students. In addition, by requiring film reviews and film discussion groups similar to those related to chapter texts, other intelligences such as linguistic, intrapersonal, interpersonal, and mathematical/logical are addressed. The use of simulations, games, and class exercises on a regular basis will allow students with strong spatial, bodily kinesthetic, and interpersonal intelligences to succeed. Instructors can effectively respond to student diversity if they combine media, activities, and discussions with readings and lectures. By combining activities that address multiple intelligences with assessments that reward success in a variety of intelligences, the potential for student involvement and learning will be greatly enhanced.

Classroom Climate

The above series of course structures, assignments, activities, and tests can be best implemented if a very open and positive classroom climate is created. To establish an environment in which students feel comfortable and safe in offering their opinions and debating issues with other class members and the instructor is a challenge for educators. No magic answer to attain this environment exists, but certain strategies that enable students to experience a level of comfort and trust do. The following are two ongoing activities I have used successfully to get students to risk participating and communicating. Whether these or similar activities are used, the point remains: in order to build on students' diversity and have them actively participate in class, a major effort must be made to create a comfortable and safe class climate.

Reaction Logs

An additional channel of communication between the class and the instructor, reaction logs are handed in by each class member at **every** class period beginning with the second meeting. These contain a student's reactions to either the previous class session, report, or activity or a reaction to any topic related to class content. They also provide an opportunity for students to comment on the discussion if they were unable to contribute in class, to ask questions they want the instructor to answer, or to critique the class structure, assignments, or their own progress. To be effective the instructor must read each one, answer every question, and comment on every log. They must be confidential, being read only by the student and the instructor, and must be returned promptly, that is, the next class day. Logs can be long or short, but they must be written. They are not graded, but are required.

This activity, since it is ongoing throughout the course, involves a commitment on the part of the instructor to read all of the logs before returning them to the students. After the first few logs are returned, students understand the purpose and, after reading the instructor's comments, are not intimidated by the assignment. What occurs is a very positive, ongoing discussion between the instructor and the majority of the students. Of course, some students will object to keeping a log and may not use it in the spirit intended. However, many students, not very verbal in class sessions, are grateful for a chance to communicate their ideas in this format. The practice establishes a good rapport and a level of trust, contributes to a positive class climate, and addresses student diversity. The reaction logs also provide an ongoing critique of various aspects of the course that the instructor can use in revising and upgrading the course.

Discussion Wheel

At the start of a course, either the first or second class period, divide the class into groups of six to eight students and distribute a discussion wheel to each group. Each discussion wheel consists of three paper discs of diminishing sizes, placed one on top of the other with the smallest on top, and attached through the center with a brad. Thus the three circles or discs are layered, with the smallest in front, the next largest in the middle, and the largest in the back. The inner disc is divided into eight sections, the middle disc is divided into four to six sections, and the outer disc is divided into six or eight sections. The inner disc sections are numbered one through eight. The names of individuals such as parents, friends, and relatives are written in the sections of the middle circle while words identifying general concepts, like anger, happiness, bias, prejudice, and wealth are written on the outer disc. An unlimited variety of options can be used.

When using the wheel, students are asked to pick a number from one to eight for themselves. A student in each group is given the discussion wheel upside down. He or she rotates the inner and middle discs without looking at them, then turns the disc over. Finding his or her number, the student matches the number with the closest section in the middle disc, for example, "friend," and with the closest section on the outer disc, for example, "anger." The student then shares with the group something in his or her life that is related to "friend" and "anger." These are brief sharings, only one or two minutes each. The disc is passed around the group, with each student again rotating the discs, turning it over, and proceeding as the first student.

After using an instructor disc a few times, the groups are given materials and asked to develop their own discs using any topic they wish. The instructor can develop additional discs based on these ideas or ask students to construct the discs for a subsequent discussion. This activity is done periodically throughout the course to provide the opportunity for student discussion of difficult topics in a non-intimidating, controlled environment. The discussion discs can, of course, include topics related to course content as well as interpersonal concerns.

In summary, I have found that establishing a positive class climate, developing activities to address student diversity, and incorporating a combination of assignments and approaches such as those I have described, allow students to strengthen their multiple intelligences. The result is more active, successful, and exciting classes for both students and instructor.

References

Armstrong, T. (1993). *Seven kinds of smart.* New York: Penguin Books.

Armstrong, T. (1994). *Multiple intelligences in the classroom.* Alexandria, VA: Association for Supervision and Curriculum Development.

Ballanca, J., Chapman, C., & Swartz, E. (1994). *Multiple assessment for multiple intelligences.* Palatine, IL: IRI/Skylight Publishers.

Campbell, C. (1993). *If the shoe fits . . . . How to develop multiple intelligences in the classroom.* Palatine, IL: IRI/Skylight Publishing.

Campbell, L., Campbell, B., & Dickinson, D. (1992). *Teaching and learning through multiple intelligences.* Seattle: New Horizons for Learning.

Gardner, H. (1983). *Frames of mind: The theory of multiple intelligences.* New York: Basic Books.

Gardner, H. (1987). Beyond I.Q.: Education and human development. *Harvard Educational Review, 57*(2), 187-193.

Gardner, H. (1993). Creating minds. New York: Basic Books.

Gardner, H. (1993). *Multiple intelligences: The theory in practice.* New York: Basic Books.

Lazear, D. (1991). *Seven ways of teaching.* Palatine, IL: IRI/Skylight Publishing.

Lazear, D. (1994). *Multiple intelligence approaches to assessment.* Tucson: Zephyr Press.

Lazear, D. (1994). *Seven pathways of learning.* Palatine, IL: IRI/Skylight Publishing.

THE USE OF EXPERIENTIAL LEARNING IN AN INTRODUCTORY MULTICULTURAL EDUCATION CLASS

by
Timothy R. McMahon, Nick Ippolito, Randall W. Maus, and Claire G. Williams

Introduction

Since the beginning of civilization, humankind has practiced the most basic form of learning—learning by doing. The earliest hunters and gatherers must have used this method to determine what foods were edible and which were poisonous; where the best hunting existed; and how to best start a fire and keep it burning. This form of learning is also described in the Chinese proverb: "Tell me and I will forget. Show me and I may remember. But, involve me and I will learn."

In this essay, the authors discuss the use of experiential learning in an undergraduate multicultural education course. We will explore the concept of experiential learning, describe how it was incorporated into the syllabus, and provide some examples of activities that were used in the course. For purposes of clarity, the generic "we" will be used to identify one or all of the authors.

Experiential Learning

Experiential learning has been defined simply as "learning through doing" (Luckner & Nadler, 1997, p. 3). Its roots in American education can be traced back to the writings of John Dewey (1938) and more recently to the work of David Kolb (1984). It has "grown in popularity over the past 20 years" and is "easier to experience than explain" (Luckner & Nadler, p. 5). While activities that utilize an experiential learning approach are numerous (e.g., Rohnke, 1992), the use of these methods in diversity education courses is just now becoming more common (see Adams, Bell, & Griffin, 1997).

In general, an experiential learning model or cycle follows a sequence of stages—experiencing, reflecting, generalizing, and applying. Once the applying stage is reached, the cycle begins all over again. Questions are used to process the experience and to help move students through the cycle. Examples of these questions are provided below with additional suggestions available from Gaw (1979).

Experiencing

In the Experiencing Stage, students (and teachers) do something. This could be anything from a structured simulation to watching a video. It doesn't necessarily involve physical activity but obviously the more actively engaged students are, the more connected they will be to it. Students enjoy being active in class—they want to be physically engaged if for no other reason than it makes the time go by faster.

Reflecting

In the Reflecting Stage, students share their observations about what happened during the experience. "What happened?" "What did you see, hear, feel, taste, smell?" The purpose of the Reflecting Stage is to gain a more complete picture of what took place during the experience. People see, hear, feel, taste, and smell different things. By sharing what they experienced, more things get noticed. An example that will ring true for most of us involves watching videos. No matter how many times you watch a video, you'll undoubtedly notice something new each time or someone else who is watching the same video will notice something that you didn't.

Generalizing

The Generalizing Stage asks the question "So what?" (Luckner & Nadler, 1997, p. 6). In this stage, students are asked to make connections between what they experienced and other aspects of the course or their lives: "Have any of you experienced something similar in your own life?" "What does this have to do with what we've been studying?" "What connections can you make between this experience and other issues in your life?" The Generalizing Stage helps students go beyond what they've just experienced and put it into a larger context. An example from a recent class involved the simulation "Star Power." The class completed the simulation and as the processing moved through the Reflecting Stage, one of the students commented "I can see where this train is heading!"

Applying

The Applying Stage completes the cycle and asks the question "Now what?" (Luckner & Nadler, 1997, p. 6). "How can you use this information?" "How might you apply this to a situation you're now facing?" "What effect might these new awarenesses have on your life?" This stage is critical if students are actually going to consider what impact the diversity course may have on their daily actions. It is also a reminder of how difficult this subject is for many students. At the end of one semester, a student wrote that she had learned a lot and had become more open to the concept of diversity but she knew that she was soon going home and that her family and significant other were not open to it. She doubted if she'd be able to continue her newfound attitudes in the face of these seemingly overwhelming odds.

Incorporating Experiential Learning into the Diversity Class

Introduction to the "Group Diversity" Course

"Group Diversity" is officially described as the "Study of cultural identities, values, and interaction of diverse groups. Among the concepts explored will be race, ethnicity, gender, class, sexual orientation, ableism, and age." A general education course that falls into the multicultural and cross-cultural studies category, the course is offered outside any specific department. Some sections are designated as "writing intensive" with a certain percentage of students' grades based on writing assignments (as opposed to objective tests or oral presentations). Enrollment varies each semester but most students sign up for the section under discussion because it is writing intensive. A few note they've heard good things about the primary instructor or the general approach taken in teaching the course. The class tends to be mostly sophomores and juniors with a very few first- and fourth-year students. Few students of color enroll in this section. The textbook used for the class and from which the questions for the mid-term and final examinations are taken is *Race, Class, and Gender: An Anthology* (Andersen & Collins, 1998).

Assumptions

This course is structured around a set of assumptions about students, learning, and teaching.
- Students want to learn.
- Students learn a great deal from each other. (Pascarella & Terranzini, 1991)
- Students learn best when they are physically and psychologically involved in the class. (Astin, 1984; Chickering & Gamson, 1991)
- Students will have a strong belief in knowledge they discover themselves. (Johnson & Johnson, 1994)
- Students will participate in class discussions and activities if the environment is safe and inviting and they find the topics and activities interesting.
- The role of teachers is to facilitate student learning by making the subject interesting.
- Students and teachers together shape the classroom environment.
- Students and teachers will learn from and teach each other.
- Students will be in the dualistic and multiplistic stages of cognitive development. (Perry, 1968)
- Most students will be in the early stages of racial identity development. (Cross, 1995; Helms, 1995)
- Learning about diversity involves both a cognitive and an affective process. (Adams, 1997)
- Learning about diversity involves increasing one's awareness, knowledge, and skills. (Pedersen, 1988)
- Teaching, especially about diversity, involves providing students with an environment that offers both challenge and support. (Sanford, 1966)

The First Class

The importance of the first class session cannot be overstated. Just as chaos and systems theory (Kellert, 1993) notes the "importance of initial conditions," the first class sets the stage for the rest of the semester. For that reason our first class is not typical. First we move all the traditionally aligned rows of chairs into one big circle—not an easy task with over thirty students and teachers—and then the instructors in the class provide a short introduction. Shifting gears, we pass out crayons and paper plates and students create nameplates. Students then introduce themselves by saying their name, major, hometown, and an interesting thing about themselves. (There are countless variations of this "who are you?" activity. We believe in starting as simply and with as little risk as possible.) We then ask three questions: How do we make this an outstanding class? What are your expectations of the instructors? What are your expectations of each other? These brainstormed ideas are put on the board, to which the instructors add their expectations of the students.

This notion of "shared ownership" in the class is not a new idea but sprung out of a conversation that our University President and Provost once had with new faculty. The new faculty were telling the President that he needed to "make students come to class." We listened for a while and then offered the comment that maybe we, as faculty, needed to make class so exciting and stimulating that students would want to come to class. The looks we received indicated that many in the group thought we must be from a different planet. Yet, this has become a part of every first class of every course that we teach. "How do we make this class so interesting, so wonderful, that you'll show up when it's pouring down rain, when it's freezing, or when it's sunny and beautiful?" Sometimes the looks that students give us indicate that they, too, think we must be from another world. This is obviously not business as usual.

The first class is also the time when we build the syllabus. "What do you want to learn?" "How do you learn best" "How should we evaluate what you've learned?" The process of gathering this information follows a format that we use throughout the semester:

- first students write their ideas down individually;
- then students talk about (process/discuss) these ideas in dyads or small groups;
- finally the whole class is brought back together as a large group and their ideas written (published) on the board.

This sequence works very well because it provides multiple opportunities for students to "compare notes" with their peers. They begin to realize there are ideas other than their own and these other ideas may even be better. It also prevents, or at least lessens, the number of students responding "I don't know" when asked for their ideas.

We also talk about our "expectations"—students of the instructors, students of each other, and instructors of students. The expectations that students have generated are provided in Figures 1, 2, and 3. While a few may not be feasible or appropriate, most are very reasonable and probably should be instructional goals for any course taught by any instructor.

Figure 1
Suggestions from students enrolled in course
on how to make this an outstanding class

Make it interesting	Treat students as equals	Teacher likes subject
Talk about anything	Relate material to everyday events	Open environment
Chance to develop leadership potential	Easy tests	Group work
Instructor goes out of way	Teacher told them what be on test	Learn from discussion
Teacher talks to you not down at you	Teacher approachable	All students equal
Not structured—different teaching methods	Group activities	Participation points
More sharing, less lecture	Lectures keep moving—vary topics	Current events
Real life/personal examples	Class discussion	Role playing/hands on
Grades reasonably	Non-comprehensive final	No group projects
Thought-provoking material		

Figure 2
Expectations of teachers by students

Know what you're talking about
Be fair
Cover lots of subjects
More insights instead of facts
Be prepared
Notify students if class cancelled
Listen to opinions of students

Encourage participation
Be organized
Enthusiastic
Be fair and nice
Create environment for sharing safely
Say sorry if make a mistake

Make it exciting
Know the students
Available for help
Speak slowly
Show up sober
Be fun

Figure 3
Expectations of classmates by students

Go to class
Give input
Participation
Foster safe, open environment
Be excited

Be on time
Give everyone a chance to speak
Honesty and respect
Be courteous

Be open minded
Communicate well
Be fun
Attend regularly

In answering the question, "What do you want to learn?" students have responded with three general comments: better understanding of people around us; better understanding of ourselves; and to be more open-minded—not a bad list of goals for any diversity-related course. The rest of the first class is spent with various activities designed to help students get to know each other as people.

Building Community

Building a community is a course goal and the main focus of the first two weeks of class. Chairs stay in a circle for the whole semester. It usually takes the students a couple weeks to realize this before they begin to rearrange the chairs as they arrive in class. A variety of name games are used at the beginning of class and students are asked to keep bringing and posting their nameplates so names can be associated with faces. This past year, the class was broken into small groups and digital pictures were taken of each group. These pictures were pasted into a word processing program and names placed appropriately. Color copies were provided for each student with the expectation that they learn the names of their classmates. A fun "quiz" during the third week of class showed almost everyone knew the names of their fellow students.

From the very first class students rearrange their chairs in a circle. Admittedly, thirty students and instructors make for a large circle but this has a really positive effect on the class. Students are always able to see all of their classmates whenever they speak. We are fortunate in having some students who are more than willing to take the initiative to speak up and get class discussions started. This is especially important at the beginning of the semester when many students feel a bit uneasy about sharing their ideas in the large group setting. Periodically throughout the semester, we have students change seats so they are forced to sit by different students. This became important when we realized they were sitting in the same seats, near the same peers, and breaking into small groups with generally the same people. Changing seats seems to create a positive environment in the class.

I was hesitant at first in the class because this is the first of its kind for me. I hate icebreakers but I now believe it was imperative we do that to create the right environment needed for this class. (Sophomore, Law Enforcement and Justice Administration major)

Class Assignments

Assignments are sequenced to move from a focus on the self to focus on "the other." In any diversity course, it is possible for majority students, especially young white men, to feel left out. We want to talk about all forms of diversity and, at the same time, to validate all students as individuals.

Weekly Journals

From the course syllabus: "Each Thursday, students will turn in their journals. In these journals, students will reflect on any experiences related to diversity that they have had recently. This could include, but is not limited to, something they experienced in their place of residence or in another class, something they read or watched on television, etc. The instructors will provide comments and return the journals the following Tuesday. Journals should be one to two pages in length each week and may be handwritten if legible. Students will receive from 0-1 point for each weekly entry. Late journals will not be accepted. The same graduate assistant will read your journal each week."

From a learning perspective, the journals are invaluable. From an experiential learning perspective they provide the mechanism to move students from the Experiencing Stage into the Reflecting Stage. They also provide a great starting point for classroom discussions that occur on the day the journals address a specific question, topic, or reaction to a class activity.

Personal Cultural Heritage Project

From the course syllabus: "In order to understand others different from ourselves, we must first develop a greater understanding of who we are and where we come from. To help in this process, students will write a paper analyzing their own cultural heritage. Topics to be covered include, but are not limited to, family background, racial/ethnic heritage, religious beliefs, sexual orientation, gender, and socioeconomic status. Students will describe their own heritage as completely as possible and discuss how their background has helped shape them as individuals and how they relate to others."

For many students this is an opportunity to explore their "roots." Some students take advantage of the situation and contact relatives to gather information about their ethnic heritage. For others the impact of their socioeconomic status is the major force that has shaped their lives. No matter what the focus of the paper, it validates the personal experiences of each student—something we find to be tremendously important in a class where the focus is typically on "the other." Making this assignment due fairly early in the semester helps the teachers find out more about students as individuals—especially about those who do not talk much in class.

Student Interview Report

From the course syllabus: "Students will interview at least two undergraduates who are members of a traditionally underrepresented population of which the student is not a member. Students will then prepare reports of their interviews, specifically noting the undergraduates' backgrounds, concerns, and issues related to college life."

Admittedly, this is a scary assignment for students, especially if they don't really know anyone who is "different" from them. For this reason, it is placed towards the end of the semester. It is also a very beneficial assignment for students because it attaches a human face, possibly for the first time, to the topics of the class. An additional assignment asks students to interview two members of the opposite gender. Since this assignment is probably less threatening it can precede the previous one and coincide ideally with the study of the gender differences section of the course.

Individual Projects

From the course syllabus: "Students will do two projects during the course of the semester. Each will be worth a maximum of five points and must be related to diversity (for example: a residence hall or university-sponsored diversity program or a show at the university art museum. Watching and reviewing videos cannot be used. After participating in the program, students will write a two-page paper with one page focusing on what they learned from their participation and one page focusing on how they can apply what they learned."

This assignment gets students out to events on campus they might otherwise ignore— in the residence halls, student union, and other areas in which programs occur. Benefits are both short and long term as students become more "involved" in college life (Astin, 1994) and discover another perspective or gather further information. Spring semester is always a time filled with wonderful Black History Month activities, Women's History Month events, and an annual International Bazaar that provides both cultural and culinary introductions to a wide array of peoples from around the globe. Having students write a reaction to these activities heightens their awareness and forces them to reflect on just what they might have learned from the experience. The International Bazaar becomes more than just food that "looked strange or weird." It turns into a metaphor for "different is not bad."

Class Activities

Rock Your World

From the course syllabus: "Students will sign up for a specific class period for which they will bring a favorite song on CD, cassette, music video, or film video. At the beginning of the class, the song will be played and the student will explain why the song is special or meaningful."

A colleague recently expanded this activity and now uses it in all the courses she teaches. Instead of using only music, students now have five minutes at the beginning of class to share something important about themselves in any appropriate format, including music, family pictures, and original poetry. During the course of the semester, each student receives an opportunity to make the short presentation.

We try to involve students in class activities as soon and as often as possible. One such activity is "Star Power" (©1993 by Simulation Training Systems)—a simulation that helps participants learn about how power can be used, abused, and maintained. While the experience of this commercial simulation is indeed powerful, it is in the processing afterwards that the bulk of the learning occurs. One student who would have probably described himself as having grown up with little power in his life became a tyrant when he obtained power in the simulation. Another student made a remark to the effect that "I saw what we were supposed to learn a long ways off." Still another student remarked that she gave up when faced with the overwhelming odds working against her gaining any power. The sharing of these ideas by students makes the experience more real for all participants. Without the processing students would only have a sense of what it's like to be in their particular station in life or, in this case, in the simulation. Those who don't have power learn from a peer how intoxicating it is to have power. Those who have the power get a sense of how corrupting it can be. This particular activity is one students tend to remember and comment on throughout the semester and in the final examination.

Another type of activity is much simpler. It involves children's puzzles—about one for every four to five students in the class. It helps that the puzzles are on the same theme, for example Pooh or Sesame Street. Before class, all puzzles are opened and the pieces mixed up between and among the boxes. The box covers are also switched. For the activity, the class is divided into groups of four to five students each and all the boxes are put in the center of the room. Students are told that the purpose of this activity is to get **all** the puzzles put together and that they need to do this in a safe manner. This activity is fun to watch as the students try to force-fit their pieces into the picture that appears on their particular box even though only some of the pieces actually are from that puzzle. Eventually people realize they all have to work together and get pieces from other groups. In one instance, the group that finished first began celebrating, having forgotten the goal of getting all the puzzles completed. The processing of this activity is great fun. Lots of interesting comments emerge about when people first noticed their puzzles might be different from that depicted on the box. Moving into the "generalizing" stage of the experiential learning cycle becomes fascinating. Comments like "don't judge a person by what's on the outside" and "what you see is not always what you get" were shared. In addition, the need for people to work together to accomplish the goal made what was a pretty simple activity into something with a bigger message.

All Process—No Content? And Other Issues of Concern

During one summer, we bumped into a faculty colleague who taught mathematics and was also a great ally and supporter of women's and other diversity-related issues. We noted that it would be fun to co-teach a section of Group Diversity. She said something we'll never forget: "Whenever I think about teaching one of those all process, no content classes, I break out in a cold sweat." Her comment was a reality check in two specific ways. First, many faculty assume any course that involves a lot of group activity and discussion must not have much content (usually a negative connotation on a college campus). Secondly, not everyone is comfortable teaching in an experientially focused manner.

Sutherland (1996) outlines possible problems in using experiential or active learning approaches in the classroom. A primary concern is the potential danger involved in garnering the disapproval of faculty peers, especially if this becomes connected to any form of evaluation process. The other area is the disapproval of students. Using an experiential learning approach in the classroom is often a new experience for students and, at least at first, seems strange. As noted above, a sophomore mentioned, "I was hesitant at first in the class because this is the first of its kind for me." While many students respond positively to the interaction with peers and learning from each other, some do not.

It is important, as Sutherland (1996) indicates, to provide students with the opportunity to give feedback on how the class is going for them. Periodically throughout the semester, we solicit feedback from students in the last five minutes of class by asking them to write answers to questions such as: "What is going well in class?" "What is not going well in class?" "What did you learn today?" and "What suggestions do you have to make class better?" These short "free writes" or "one-minute papers" (Angelo & Cross, 1993) are an easy method of obtaining immediate feedback from students. While the feedback may or may not lead to changes in how the class is taught, it provides information on how the class is being experienced by the students.

Students' Reactions

By far the most rewarding aspect of using experiential learning in the class is students' reactions. When asked "what are the good points of using this (experiential learning) approach?" the following comments were submitted.

The class discussion, group work, skits, etc . . . have been a real plus in really understanding the subjects. (Junior, Law Enforcement and Justice Administration major)

I think when you can be part of it then you know what it's like to be in someone else's shoes. (First-year student, Undecided major)

The class became close through an open atmosphere for learning. Participating in activities and listening to the true to life stories of my peers [h]as let me experience first hand learning. (First-year student, Political Science major)

I have learned the most from the students in here. (Sophomore, Marketing major)

The group activities make the class enjoyable while learning at the same time. (Sophomore, Law Enforcement and Justice Administration major)

Activities demonstrating what is it like to be oppressed. Open discussions. (Sophomore, Business major)

I have always been shy when it comes to talking in front of a class, but this class is very easy to speak to because of all the group discussion. (Sophomore, Business Management major)

The group involvement activities, the rapport building types of activities. Even if it's working in several different groups. This gives everyone a chance to be able to interact with everyone in the class. (Junior, Law Enforcement and Justice Administration major)

The structure of this class created a very open and honest environment that allowed for some excellent expression. Learning through participation has been very effective for me. (Junior, Law Enforcement and Justice Administration major)

Of course, things didn't always work out for the best, as indicated in the following comments from students to the question of "what has not worked well?"

I think when we break up into small groups [it] doesn't really work to[o] much. Sometimes it gets boring. (First-year student, Undecided major)

Too much small group talk, sometimes on big subjects you need facilitation. (Sophomore, Business major)

Even all the variety of activities meant to make students comfortable with each other didn't work for everyone.

Sometimes it's hard to talk to your neighbor. (Sophomore, Business Management major)

When asked for their overall evaluation of the class, the following comments were returned.

By far this is the best class that I have taken. I have learned so much from not only the teacher but my classmates. (Junior, Law Enforcement and Justice Administration Major)

I love this class. It's been a great experience for me, one that I'll never forget. (First-year student, Undecided major)

I think that this class has taught me a lot of things in a short amount of time. (First-year student, Political Science major)

Great. It is the only class I look forward to coming to. (Sophomore, Marketing major)

This class is great. I have learned a lot from the little activities rather than being talked at. (Sophomore, Business major)

I think this [is] good class to take because I have learned a lot about the people that surround me everyday. (Sophomore, Business Management major)

Overall impression of this class is that I am glad I was able to be part of this outstanding class. (Junior, Law Enforcement and Justice Administration major)

I really like coming to class every day, even if just sometimes it is to see what we will be doing today. (Junior, Law Enforcement and Justice Administration major)

They [the teachers] all made the environment safe to learn and never became too imposing or tending towards "we are the teachers you are the students" attitude. (Junior, Law Enforcement and Justice Administration major)

Conclusion

Using an experiential learning approach has proven to be successful in teaching an introductory multicultural education class. This approach encourages students to take responsibility for their own learning by physically and psychologically involving them in the class. It encourages students to make connections with each other, with the teachers, and with the course content. All of this makes learning more enjoyable—something that is of benefit to both students and teachers.

References

Adams, M. (1997). Pedagogical frameworks for social justice education. In M. Adams, L. Bell, & P. Griffin (Eds.), *Teaching for diversity and social justice: A sourcebook* (pp. 30-43). New York: Routledge.

Adams, M., Bell, L., & Griffin, P. (Eds.) (1997). *Teaching for diversity and social justice: A sourcebook.* New York: Routledge.

Andersen, M., & Collins, P. (1998). *Race, class, and gender: An anthology* (3rd ed.). Belmont, CA: Wadsworth.

Angelo, T., & Cross, P. (1993). *Classroom assessment techniques: A handbook for college teachers* (2nd ed.). San Francisco: Jossey-Bass.

Astin, A. (1984). Student involvement: A developmental theory for higher education. *Journal of College Student Personnel, 25,* 297-308.

Chickering, A., & Gamson, Z. (1991). *Applying the seven principles for good practice in undergraduate education.* New Directions for Teaching and Learning. no. 47. San Francisco: Jossey-Bass.

Cross, W. E. (1995). The psychology of nigrescence. In J. Ponterotto, J. Casas, L. Suzuki, & C. Alexander (Eds.), *Handbook of multicultural counseling* (pp. 93-122). Thousand Oaks, CA: Sage.

Dewey, J. (1938). *Experience and education.* New York: Collier Books.

Gaw, B. (1979). Processing questions: An aid to completing the learning cycle. In J. Pfeiffer & J. Jones (Eds.), *The 1979 annual handbook for group facilitators* (pp. 147-153). La Jolla, CA: University Associates.

Helms, J. (1995). An update of Helms's white and people of color racial identity models. In J. Ponterotto, J. Casas, L. Suzuki, & C. Alexander (Eds.). *Handbook of multicultural counseling* (pp. 181-198). Thousand Oaks, CA: Sage.

Johnson, D., & Johnson, F. (1994). *Joining together* (5th ed.). Boston: Allyn & Bacon.

Kellert. S. (1993). *In the wake of chaos.* Chicago: University of Chicago Press.

Kolb, D. (1984). *Experiential learning: Experience as the source of learning and development.* Englewood Cliffs, NJ: Prentice-Hall.

Luckner, J., & Nadler, R. (1997). *Processing the experience: Strategies to enhance and generalize learning* (2nd ed.). Dubuque, IA: Kendall/Hunt.

Pascarella, E., & Terenzini, P. (1991). *How college affects students: Findings and insights from twenty years of research.* San Francisco: Jossey-Bass.

Pedersen, P. (1988). *A handbook for developing multicultural awareness.* Alexandria, VA: American Association for Counseling and Development.

Perry, W. (1968). *Forms of intellectual and ethical development in the college years: A scheme.* New York: Holt, Rinehart, & Winston.

Rohnke, K. (1991). *The bottomless bag.* Dubuque, IA: Kendall/Hunt.

Sanford, N. (1966). *Self and society.* New York: Atherton.

Simulation Training Systems. (1993). Star Power.

Sutherland, T. (1996). Emerging issues in the discussion of active learning. In T. Sutherland & C. Bonwell (Eds.), *Using active learning in college classes: A range of options for faculty.* New Directions for Teaching and Learning, no. 67 (pp. 83-95). San Francisco: Jossey-Bass.

Resources

Association for Experiential Education
2305 Canyon Boulevard, Suite #100
Boulder, CO 80302
Phone: 303-440-8844
Fax: 303-440-9581
http://www.aee.org

Amherst Educational Publishing
PO Box 6000
Amherst, MA 01004-6000
Phone: 1-800-865-5549
http://www.amedpub.com
Publishes diversity educational and training materials including:
Diversity icebreakers: A guide for diversity training by S. Myers and J. Lambert
More diversity icebreakers: A trainer's guide by S. Myers and J. Lambert
50 activities for diversity training by J. Lambert and S. Myers
50 activities for managing cultural diversity by T. Dickerson-Jones

Intercultural Press
374 US Route One
PO Box 700
Yarmouth, ME 04096
Phone: 207-846-5168 or 800-370-2665 (within the U.S.)
Fax: 207-846-5181
http://www.interculturalpress.com
Publishes diversity educational and training materials including:
Experiential activities for intercultural learning edited by H. N. Seelye (Ed.).
A manual of structured experiences for cross-cultural learning by W. W. Weeks, P. B. Pedersen and R. W. Brislin (Eds.)

BEYOND VASCO DA GAMA:
UNLEARNING EUROCENTRIC PHALLACIES
IN THE CLASSROOM

by
Nada Elia

I was attempting to solve a crossword puzzle once when I came across a clue that struck me as unfathomable: "the first man who circled the southern tip of Africa." I left its space blank and moved on to the next line, hoping the empty squares would fill up as I completed the puzzle. But my roommate, who was looking over my shoulder, eagerly volunteered "Vasco da Gama." As an Arab in the United States, I have come to expect a lot of Eurocentric tunnel vision. But this was extreme in its presumption that not one of the millions of Africans, who for thousands of years had lived by the shores of southern Africa, could accomplish such an achievement until a Portuguese sailor showed them how.

As I wondered at how even highly intelligent Americans can accept such blatant false-hoods as facts, I was reminded of yet another incident that had puzzled me upon my arrival in the U.S. It was fall, the beginning of an academic year, and the end of the baseball season. During a class break, some students were discussing the World Series with the professor. I asked the professor, who seemed quite a sports fan, what countries were competing. "Canada and the U.S.," he said. Eager to learn new things—baseball not being a popular sport in the Middle East—I went on with more questions, about which countries had participated in the series and which had made the semi-finals. "Only Canada and the U.S. play in the World Series," the professor responded matter-of-factly. Oddly enough, in a doctoral program in comparative literature at a respectable American university, I was alone in finding it absurd that any competition involving only two countries should claim to be universal. But more so, I was acutely aware of the arrogance behind this claim.

Today, as a teacher fully committed to offering my students a multicultural education and primarily concerned with providing alternatives to Eurocentric views, I begin each of my courses with my crossword anecdote, or the World Series one. For the last four years, I have taught courses in world literature and postcolonial literature in Indiana and Illinois. My students have been primarily European Americans, who took my class because it is required of education majors. In a few years, they will likely be teachers themselves. This article does not address a teacher's need to recognize the diversity of students ever present in all classrooms, even the most seemingly homogeneous—for diversity is not only ethnic, but manifests itself in numerous ways, in, for example, different sexual orientations, religious upbringing or the lack of it, having experienced child neglect and/or abuse, growing up in a traditional family or the much more common "contemporary" one. Rather, I want to provide the teacher with some suggestions as to how to approach students required to take multi-cultural classes they have little initial interest in or much prejudiced resistance to.

Over the last few years, I have developed a few strategies that counter the resistance of students hostile to diversity, as well as encourage them to view a multicultural education as a plus, as a wealth of information that, far from seeking to replace the traditional canon, attempts instead to revive it, to infuse it with a vitality that spares it the fate of Greek tragedy: classic, epic, but falling short of addressing contemporary issues.

On the first day of class, I ask my students for the name of the first person to have circled the southern tip of Africa. Occasionally, a student will volunteer the infamous piece of information. If nobody does, I write it on the board: Vasco da Gama. Then I tell my students that he was Portuguese and give them the dates of his birth and death: 1469-1524 A.D. Hungry for information (or eager to secure their A) they write it all down. I go on to ask them if they can suggest any reasons as to why no African had been able to circle Africa's southern tip, though they had navigated those shores for thousands of years before the first Europeans arrived there. Of course, no one can provide a satisfactory answer. There isn't one; that Vasco da Gama should be the first simply doesn't make sense.

My approach may be deemed a little harsh for a first day of class, but it has been my experience that this reality check is extremely effective. If it were a student who provided the name Vasco da Gama—and more often than not that student is a crossword puzzle fan— I make sure that they do not feel foolish by pointing out that, according to numerous reference books, they are correct. Moreover, haven't all the rest of the students copied the data down without any questions? Then I ask my students to please cross out whatever notes they have taken, since my class requires critical thinking, not dictionary knowledge, and, as we have just seen, the two are frequently at odds. Critical thinking, I explain, does not always provide the answers, but it avoids incorrect answers. Thus we will never know who made the first lap around the Cape of Good Hope, but we do know it does not make sense that it should be a Portuguese sailor.

Moreover, I find it important to lay the ground rules in that first session: we are here to unlearn certain misinformation we have received, as much if not more than we hope to learn new material. And during the semester, when students are understandably frustrated at the lack of answers to some of the questions we raise, I can refer to this session and ask them "Do you want convenience? I can give you the 'Da Gama equivalent'. . . ." When I present lack of closure in these terms, they stop pressing for *the* correct answer. Indeed, da Gama has become one of my favorite historical examples, for he also allows me on that first day of class to introduce my students to the evils of racism (the denial of the humanity of Africans), sexism (Were there no women on Da Gama's ship? Why not?), and classism (Surely he had a whole crew to help him; why aren't they mentioned?). Da Gama also makes a good starting point for a discussion of European cultural hegemony and the numerous factors that contributed to the successful imposition of one paradigm over others.

Again, the importance of our first class must be emphasized, for it clearly establishes that the class allows, indeed favors, alternative modes of thinking. In a recent article, Linda Dittmar (1993) argues against leaving sensitive themes such as homosexual love till the end of a course. I agree with her, for the hegemonic discourse that has silenced these topics fully surrounds us, and the fourteen to sixteen weeks that make up a semester are barely sufficient for their discussion in a mature way. We should treat our students as adults. They are adults: they can drive a car, juggle credit cards, and, with very few exceptions, are of voting age. As I realize that the transition from sheltered home life to college campus is not easy, I help them recognize, or question, prejudices in a friendly environment.

One way I have found very effective in promoting individual thought is requiring students to formulate an opinion about the material they have just read. I require students to turn in, on the day we start discussing a new text, an index card with the following:

- three to five questions raised by the text;
- a page reference to a passage they would like discussed in class; and
- an opinion about the reading. Did they like it? Why or why not?

I emphasize to my students they will receive full credit for the index card, regardless of contents, the quality of their questions, or the positiveness of their response. Moreover, I stress that it is fully up to them to identify themselves, if they want to, when I answer their questions in class or read out their opinion. I identify them only in the case of the passage they would like to have us discuss together, since I then ask them to lead the discussion themselves. Whether it is because they indeed feel distance from the dominant discourse they would publicly express or because they are merely testing out alternatives or challenging assumptions, the students offer a rich array of responses that allow for lively debate.

The index cards are useful in many ways. They allow me to evaluate students' needs from the questions they ask and to prepare the next lesson accordingly. They give insight into the students' readings of texts. Through student-led discussion of the passage they have chosen—and quite frequently, two to three will choose the same passage, spontaneously creating group discussion—the learning experience becomes collaborative. Finally, students whose opinions would otherwise be underrepresented feel empowered when I read out their opinions. Here I do use my prerogative as a teacher in that I privilege original thoughts by sharing these with the rest of the class. In doing so, the traditionalists are not silenced, for they are, of course, entitled to respond, and most speakers of the hegemonic discourse feel safe speaking up.

A teacher communicates knowledge best when s/he successfully avoids alienating even the most resistant students, and humor plays an important role, helping in many instances to release tension. A few weeks into a course, as I feel my students weary of our politicized class, I tell them about the press conference I am calling next week, for I have a major announcement to make: I have discovered penicillin! Well, why not? Columbus discovered America, didn't he? Why can't I discover penicillin? Thus humor is not used to distract students from the seriousness of the matter at hand, but rather to present it to them in more acceptable ways, especially when their long-held beliefs are being shattered.

Despite my efforts to break classroom hierarchy, my students are ever aware that I am the authority, that I have special power in the classroom. When I am willing to show them that I, too, am quite fallible, they feel safer about acknowledging mistakes they have made. I tell them how readily I misjudged someone when I assumed that a man I had just met at a bar was drunk, simply because of his accent. He was an African American from a small town in Arkansas. Had I made a racist assumption? I meant no harm, but did I hurt him? Are we ever blameless?

It is easy to denounce racism. It is more challenging to do so without alienating European American students whose belief in a glorious heritage is shattered as they discover their ancestors, just like everybody else's, have at times murdered, pillaged, raped, stolen, and engaged in racial wars. When a student writes that s/he is ashamed of being white, it is essential to explain that shame and guilt can be paralyzing feelings or incitement to action, to change. Most are happy to know there is a positive way out. Yet I would in no way suggest my method is infallible. Very recently, I had a student who grew more angry at me, or the material I was presenting, with each class period and finally exploded during our discussion of the mistreatment of Native Americans by the Europeans. This student claimed that denouncing racism and sexism only aggravates these issues, and he argued that tolerance of others cannot be promoted through a discussion of past wrongdoings. Clearly, as a white male, he felt he had come under attack one time too many. Rather than turn this episode into a one-on-one confrontation between him and me, I asked the rest of the students if they in any way agreed with him. If that were the case, I would change my approach. Fortunately, the students came to my aid, as they explained to him the necessity of knowing how and why certain acts were wrong. Reassured, I was able to add that, just as with addictions or sexual abuse, one has to acknowledge the problem in order to treat it.

Because students learn in different ways, a combination of strategies is necessary when introducing them to concepts they have been trained to regard with suspicion, whether these concepts be feminism, anti-imperialism, or homosexuality. One simple yet effective way is to punctuate class handouts with empowering proverbs. Among my favorites are:

"Until the lions have their historians, tales of hunting will always glorify the hunter."

"The mind of a bigot is like the pupil of the eye: the more light you shine on it, the more it contracts."

"Freedom is merely privilege extended, unless enjoyed by one and all."

"Columbus didn't discover America, he invaded it."

I have included these on my syllabi or exams. You can ask students to contribute their own. One semester, our class started a racist/sexist/homophobic jokes bulletin board. This project was enlightening to those students for whom the prejudice was not evident, and who by the middle of the semester felt comfortable enough to inquire about how a joke was offensive. A bonus I had not anticipated was the broader audience this display reached, as other classes met in the same classroom and frequently commented on our clippings. Photocopies of the collage of some very prominent U.S. figures accompanied by the line "History has set the record a little too straight" never fails to affect students, as they realize that some of their heroes or role models were homosexual.

Students are also less likely to reject new concepts when they are presented to them not solely as the teacher's opinion, but as material of interest and validity to many of their classmates. Again, the index cards are helpful, since reading a positive student response to an alternative text makes the promoters and/or duplicators of the dominant discourse realize the diversity of opinions among their peers; the teacher's perspective is not singled out as that of a hostile authority to be resisted. This is especially helpful when the instructor is visibly other or when s/he openly acknowledges holding alternative views that are feminist, Marxist, or Afrocentric.

Some texts I have used in my classes have elicited very strong responses in my students. Two stand out at the top of a list of works that have sparked some of our best debates: Nawal al-Saadawi's *Woman at Point Zero* and Mehdi Charef's *Tea in the Harem*. The first is the narrative, defiant and unrepentant, of a prostitute on death row for killing her pimp. It is disturbing, as it confronts us with ugly aspects of life we would rather ignore. *Woman at Point Zero* also allows for a discussion of homosexuality, through hints that the prostitute may be lesbian, as well as for a critique of religion's role in the subjugation of women. The book does not contain a single passage that could be termed obscene even by the prudish. I generally also assign chapters from *Sex Works: Writings from Women in the Sex Industry*, which represents the views of COYOTE (Cast Off Your Old Tired Ethics) and WHISPER (Women Hurt in Systems of Prostitution Engaging in Resistance).

Tea in the Harem is the autobiography of a young immigrant in the Parisian housing projects. He writes of doing drugs, torching neighborhood cars, pimping, harassing a teacher, all before being jailed for taking a joyride in a stolen car. Written in street language, the text is explosive. I am ever surprised at how readily my students say they relate to this criminal. Like the prostitute in *Woman at Point Zero*, he is also a victim, pulling us into the gray zone where absolutes are questioned. One of my students, a senior in law enforcement, wrote me that he feels he will be a different, more understanding police officer now that he has taken my class.

To counter the resistance of students who believe sexism is a thing of the past or only present today in nonWestern cultures, no book has proven more helpful than Gerd Brantenberg's *Egalia's Daughters*. Through a humorous role reversal, this novel by a contemporary Norwegian novelist successfully denounces the continuing pervasive male dominance in modern European society. After reading it, my students no longer find it perfectly natural, and fair, that they should be called fresh**men** their first year at college, or that they should earn a **bachelor**'s degree, or a **master**'s or that, even if they choose to retain their names after marriage, they will still be carrying a man's name, their father's. Men who say they would readily change their baby's diaper at a restaurant have to reconsider when they realize most baby-changing facilities are in women's restrooms. Interestingly, it has been my experience and that of my friend and colleague, Loretta Kensinger (who first suggested the novel to me), that most women thoroughly enjoy the novel, while men find it extremely disturbing.

Another text that produces a divided reaction allowing for valuable classroom discussion is the play, *Trial of Dedan Kimathi*, by Ngugi wa Thiong'o and Micere Githae Mugo. In this case, the divide falls along racial lines, since African American students find it empowering, while European Americans criticize it for any number of reasons, including that it is a racist text, a charge that is definitely incorrect. The polarized responses to both of these selections allow for an enriching exchange of ideas. Another text, Buchi Emecheta's *Second Class Citizen*, tells of a Nigerian woman's successful struggle to overcome sexism at home as well as both sexism and racism in England. The response to this novel is generally unanimous, overwhelmingly positive, facilitating discussion of some of its underlying themes: domestic violence, marital rape, a woman's right to reproductive choice, mental emancipation.

These texts are but a few of a multitude of readily available, easily accessible titles that make the move away from a canon loaded with Eurocentric phallacies not only possible, but fun. Whether in women's studies classes or in general survey of literature courses, sociology courses or multicultural studies, we can and should assign them. We make a difference. We impact our students, who will impact others. Let us realize this potential for positive change by exposing our students to alternative texts, world views, and instructional methods.

References

Brantenberg, G. (1985). *Egalia's daughters*. (L. Mackay, Trans. In cooperation with Brantenberg). Seattle: Seal.

Charef, M. (1989). *Tea in the harem*. (E. Emery, Trans.). London: Serpent's Tail.

Dittmar, L. (1994). Conflict and resistance in the multicultural classroom. In J. Q. Adams & J. R. Welsch (Eds.), *Multicultural education: Strategies for implementation in colleges and universities*, Vol. 3. Macomb, IL: Illinois Staff and Curriculum Developers Association. (See this volume, pp. 235-244)

Emecheta, B. (1983). *Second class citizen*. New York: Braziller.

Saadawi, N. (1983). *Woman at point zero*. (S. Hetata, Trans.). London: Zed.

a Thiong'o N., & Mugo, M. G. (1976). *The trial of Dedan Kimathi*. London: Heinemann.

BUILDING CULTURAL BRIDGES:
A BOLD PROPOSAL FOR TEACHER EDUCATION

by
Geneva Gay

One of the most compelling features of current school demographics is the growing sociocultural gap between teachers and students. Although the percentage of citizens and students who are Hispanic, Asian, Indian, African American, poor, and limited English speaking is increasing significantly, the number of teachers from similar backgrounds is declining. This distribution has some major implications for the professional preparation of teachers and for how classroom instruction is conducted. The discussion that follows describes some of the specific demographic characteristics of students and teachers, explains some of the implications of these for teacher education, and offers some suggestions for how teacher preparation programs should be designed to respond to these demographic realities.

Student and Teacher Demographics

The percentage of students of color in U.S. schools has increased steadily since the 1960s. They now compose 30% of the total population of elementary and secondary schools. During the 1980s Hispanics and Asians/Pacific Islanders accounted for the greatest increases, by 44.7% and 116.4%, respectively (*The Condition of Education*, 1992). Although their percentages are not evenly distributed throughout the United States, the trend of increasing numbers of children of color in all school districts across the country is. Already, in at least 18 states and Washington, DC, between 30% and 96% of the public school students in grades K-12 are children of color (*Digest of Education Statistics*, 1992; *Education That Works*, 1990).

The increasing number of ethnically and culturally diverse students is attributable to two major factors—the relative youth of groups of color and their higher birthrates; and increased immigration from non-White, non-Western European countries in Asia, the Caribbean, Central and South America, Africa, and the Middle East. By the beginning of the 1990s, more than one third of Hispanics (39%) and African Americans (33%) were 18 years old or younger, compared to 25% of Anglos. Also, a greater proportion of the population of these groups fell within the prime childbearing years and produced a larger average number of children per family unit. The median ages of Hispanics, African Americans, and Anglos were 25.5, 27.3, and 33.1 years, respectively (*The Condition of Education*, 1992; *Statistical Abstract of the United States*, 1991).

During the 1980s, the pattern of immigration to the United States shifted radically from previous generations. People coming from Western European nations declined to a mere trickle, whereas those from other parts of the world, such as Southeast Asia, Central and South America, and the Caribbean, increased (*Statistical Abstract of the United States*, 1991). The reunification of Germany, the fall of the USSR, the democratization of Eastern European nations formerly under communist control, and political shifts in Arabic nations also are having a major impact on immigration patterns. As more people from these parts of the world arrive in the United States, even more strands of ethnic, religious, cultural, and language diversity are being added to the American mosaic. The overall impact of these demographic changes on U.S. society led *Time* magazine, in its April 9, 1990 cover story, to describe it as the "browning of America" (Henry, 1990).

Increasing levels of poverty are another salient characteristic of today's students. According to the latest statistics from the Bureau of the Census (*Statistical Abstract of the United States*, 1991), 38.4% of Hispanic and 44% of African American children under the age of 18 live in poverty. Rather than stabilizing or declining in the near future, these rates are expected to continue to increase.

The statistics on ethnic identity, immigration, and poverty among public school students have major ramifications for teacher education because there are direct correlations between these social descriptors and the educational opportunities and outcomes of different groups of students. Also, they are significant because the ethnic, racial, and cultural diversity among school teachers and administrators does not reflect similar trends.

Ethnic minorities now compose less than 15% of the teaching force, and less than 12% of school administrators. About 8.0% of all K-12 public school teachers are African Americans, 3.0% are Hispanics, 1.4% are Asians/Pacific Islanders, and 0.9% are American Indians/Native Alaskans (*Status of the American School Teacher*, 1992). Among public school principals and central office administrators there are 8.6% African Americans; 3.2% Hispanics; 1.1% American Indians, Eskimos, and Aleuts; and 0.6% Asians/Pacific Islanders (*The Condition of Education*, 1992; De La Rosa & Maw, 1990; *The Hispanic Population in the U.S.*, 1991)

Demographic Implications Greater than Numbers

A closer scrutiny of the demographics summarized above suggests that the problem is greater than the numbers and that the solution is more complex than merely recruiting teachers of color. There is a growing cultural and social distance between students and teachers that is creating an alarming schism in the instructional process. In addition to racial disparities, other key factors accounting for these widening gaps are residence, generation, gender, social class, experiential background, and education levels.

Many teachers simply do not have frames of reference and points of view similar to their ethnically and culturally different students because they live in different existential worlds. Whereas a growing percentage of students are poor and live in large urban areas, increasing numbers of teachers are middle class and reside in small- to medium-size suburban communities (*Statistical Abstract of the United States*, 1991; *Status of the American School Teacher*, 1992). Furthermore, there is not much mobility in the profession, which means that the teaching population is aging, and relatively few opportunities are available for significant numbers of new and younger individuals to enter the profession. The most recent summary of U.S. teachers compiled by the National Education Association (*Status of the American School Teacher*, 1992) indicates that their mean age is 42 years. Although 60% live within the boundaries of the school district where they are employed, only 37% live in the attendance area of the school where they teach. This percentage drops to 17.3 for schools in large systems, where the greater number of ethnically diverse and poor children are enrolled. The overwhelming majority of teachers continue to be Anglo (86.8%). More than 72% are female. By comparison, the student population in public schools is increasingly children of color.

Disparities in educational levels also contribute to the growing social distance between students and teachers. More and more teachers are achieving higher levels of education, whereas students of color and poverty are becoming less educated. Teachers with five years of college education and a master's degree, or its equivalent, are common throughout the country.

Another distancing phenomenon in who teaches and who is taught is that students are far more technologically adept than most teachers. Thus they are accustomed to high levels of multiple sensory stimulation and mediated information processing. These conditions are rather alien in most conventional classrooms, which tend to emphasize single sensory stimulation, similarity, passivity, and mental activities (Goodlad, 1984). These orientations and dispositions challenge the basic foundations of how teaching and learning are customarily organized and practiced. This challenge is apparent in the frustrations frequently voiced by teachers throughout the United States that they can no longer teach; they have to entertain. From the vantage point of students, many of them find it difficult to become personally invested in classroom learning because too often it lacks the "special effects" that characterize the dissemination of information they are accustomed to from constant exposure to technological media. Consequently, many of the assumptions, premises, programs, and strategies that have been used previously to teach students do not work any more. Therefore, radical changes must be made in how teacher preparation programs are conceived, designed, and implemented to meet these new challenges.

In classroom interactions, these sociocultural factors can become impenetrable obstacles to effective teaching and learning. The conduits or carriers of personal meaning in teaching and learning are examples, illustrations, vignettes, and scenarios. Understandably, teachers tend to select these from their own personal experiences and frames of reference. These examples, which are supposed to make subject matter and intellectual abstractions meaningful to culturally different students, often are irrelevant, too. The experiences, values, orientations, and perspectives of middle-class, highly educated, middle-aged Anglo teachers who live in small to mid-size suburban communities are very different from those of students who are poor, undereducated, racial and ethnic minorities, living in large urban areas. Yet establishing effective communication between students and teachers is imperative for academic success. Preparing teachers to connect meaningfully is the ultimate challenge of teacher education in an ethnically and culturally pluralistic and technologically complex world. Meeting this challenge requires reform in both the conceptual frameworks and substantive components of the preparation programs.

New Conceptual Frameworks Needed

In addition to the idea of **social distance**, there are several other behavioral science and multicultural education paradigms that offer some new and challenging directions for preparing teachers to work effectively with culturally diverse students and issues. Five are discussed here: cultural discontinuities, stress and anxiety, learned helplessness, situational competence, and cultural context teaching.

A growing body of behavioral science research and scholarship suggests that the burden of school failure does not rest on individual students and teachers but is nested in the lack of "fit" or syncretization between the cultural systems of schools and diverse groups. Spindler (1987), and other contributing authors to *Education and Cultural Process*, refer to this phenomenon variously as **cultural incompatibilities, cultural discontinuities,** and **cultural mismatches.** They and others (Gibbs, Huang, & Associates, 1989; Kochman, 1981; Shade, 1989; Trueba, Guthrie, & Au, 1981) agree that many of these mismatches occur at the level of procedures rather than substance. That is, culturally diverse students often have difficulties succeeding in school because **how** they go about learning is incompatible with school expectations and norms, not because they lack desire, motivation, aspiration, or academic potential. Opportunities to participate in the substantive components of teaching and learning frequently are a condition of the extent to which students conform to the "correct procedures and social protocols" (Holliday, 1985) of teaching. Failure to master these virtually ensures academic failure as well.

Some of the most crucial cultural discontinuities in classrooms occur in the areas of cultural values, patterns of communication and cognitive processing, task performance or work habits, self-presentation styles, and approaches to problem solving. That many of these incompatibilities happen without deliberate and conscious intent does not distract from their importance. If anything, this increases their significance as obstacles to successful teaching and learning in culturally pluralistic classrooms and as variables to be targeted for inclusion in multicultural teacher preparation programs.

Living and functioning effectively in culturally pluralistic classrooms can be highly stress provoking for both students and teachers. Trying to negotiate two or more different cultural systems can take psychoemotional priority over attending to academic tasks. **Stress and anxiety** correlate inversely with task performance. As psychoemotional stress levels increase in culturally pluralistic classrooms, teaching and learning task performance declines, thereby reducing the overall quality of academic efforts and achievement outcomes (Beeman, 1978; Gaudry & Spielberger, 1971). Teachers spend inordinate amounts of time on classroom control and maintaining the Anglocentric cultural hegemonic status quo. Culturally different students spend much of their psychoemotional and mental resources defending themselves from attacks on their psychic sense of well-being. Many find themselves in what Boykin (1986) calls a "triple quandary," having to negotiate simultaneously in three often disparate realms of experience: the mainstream school culture, their natal ethnic cultures, and their status as members of oppressed, powerless, and unvalued minority groups.

These conditions do not create "safe and supportive" environments for learning, one of the commonly accepted requirements for effective schooling. Instead, the result is classroom climates charged with adversarial opposition, distrust, hostility, and heightened levels of discomfort and tension. Neither students nor teachers can function at their best under these circumstances. Thus being able to identify stress-provoking factors in cross-cultural instructional interactions and knowing how to alleviate them can be a vital way to improve the overall quality of teaching in pluralistic classrooms.

An assumption held by many teachers is that children from certain ethnic groups and social classes are "universally disadvantaged or incompetent" because they do not do well on school tasks. These teachers further assume that the normative ways of doing things in school, whether they deal with social adaptation or academic issues, are the only "correct" and acceptable ones. Research conducted by cultural anthropologists, social psychologists, ethnographers, and sociolinguists (Boggs, Watson-Gegeo, & McMillen, 1985; Florio & Schultz, 1979; Greenbaum, 1985; Holliday, 1985; Kochman, 1981) indicate that ethnically and socially diverse students are very capable in their own cultural communities and social contexts. But these skills do not necessarily transfer to schools. A case in point is African American youths who are verbally adept, creative, imaginative, and fluent among other African Americans but appear inarticulate and unthinking in the classroom. The Kamahameha Early Education Program (KEEP) demonstrates the positive benefits of modifying the schooling process to incorporate the social competencies native Hawaiian children exhibit in their homes and cultural communities (Au & Jordan, 1981; Boggs, Watson-Gegeo, & McMillen, 1985).

Furthermore, all individuals are not equally capable in all intellectual areas. Some are artistic; others are more scientific, mechanical, literary, or musical. Gardner (1983) reaffirms this point in his work on multiple intelligences, and Barbe and Swassing (1979) explain the merits of teaching to different students' modality strengths. But teachers frequently do not extend this principle to functioning in different cultural systems. They assume that deficiency in one area extends to all others. Thus children who are poor and from racial minority groups become "culturally deprived," "at risk," "learning disabled," and "socially maladaptive," and **all** of their educational experiences are so affected. Children with limited English proficiencies are too often assumed also to have limited intellectual potential in mathematics, science, computers, and critical thinking. These orientations need to be replaced with ones that emphasize **situational competence** and the understanding that all students are competent in some things within certain environments. The challenge is for teachers to determine what individual strengths and cultural competencies different students bring to the classroom and to design learning experiences to capitalize on them.

Irrespective of their ethnic identity, socioeconomic status, gender, or cultural background, most children begin school eager to demonstrate their abilities and excited about engaging in new learnings, experiences, and interactions. However small the rest of the world might think their achievements are, these youngsters see them as major accomplishments. They do not focus their energies on what they do not have and cannot do; they naturally take great pride in showing off what they do have and can do. They have the dispositions and perspectives on their own experiences that Giovanni (1970) praised in the poem, "Nikka Rosa," while she also lamented these strengths being ignored or abused by those who do not understand them. Giovanni explains that what she remembers most about her childhood is self-pride, a strong sense of accomplishment, love, and happiness, not the constraints of poverty that others outside her social network feel define her essence.

These positive perceptions of personal competence begin to erode for many culturally different students shortly after they start their formal schooling. A persistent message is sent to them, in innumerable ways, of all the things they do not have and cannot do. The longer they stay in school, the more persuasive this message becomes. They become helpless, insecure, and incompetent. This concept of **learned helplessness** is crucial to understanding the plight of these students in schools and developing teacher attitudes and behaviors to avoid its perpetuation.

Basic principles of learning (Gagne, 1985) suggest that students are more likely to master new learnings when they build on previous learnings. These principles apply to the content to be learned, as well as to the structures, conditions, and environments under which learning occurs. Ecological psychologists have found that setting, environment, and climate are important factors in fostering desired behavior (Shade, 1989). Thus students who are accustomed to work being framed in informal social relations and group structures outside school will perform better if this tradition is continued in the classroom, rather than in formal, highly competitive, and individualistic situations.

This continuity can be achieved by doing cultural context teaching. That is, placing the mechanics and technical components of teaching and learning into the cultural frameworks of various ethnic, racial, and social groups. Stated somewhat differently, cultural context teaching is synchronizing various cultural styles of teaching and learning and creating culturally compatible classrooms that provide genuine invitations and opportunities for all students to engage maximally in academic pursuits without any one group being unduly advantaged or penalized (Barbe & Swassing, 1989; Shade, 1989).

Cultural context teaching is somewhat analogous to **segmented marketing** in business and industry. As the United States evolved from a factory-driven to consumer-driven economy, corporations moved rapidly from total reliance on mass media advertising to marketing strategies designed for specifically targeted segments of the population. The shift involves identifying the values, institutions, connections, concerns, experiences, and motivations of key consumer segments; affiliating with esteemed individuals, organizations, and activities that embody these features to enter into the "circles of trust" of different consumer groups; and packaging products and services to match the lifestyles of the various groups (Swenson, 1990). The merits of these strategies are readily apparent—"increased consideration translates into increased sales" (Swenson, 1990, p. 12).

Educational institutions are very susceptible to the opinions of business and industry. They have a long tradition of borrowing models from the corporate world and using economic reasoning to justify program priorities. Education, like other consumer goods and services, must be marketed effectively if it is to "sell" and succeed. Just as mass, homogeneous advertising is obsolete in the economic marketplace, so is it in the educational marketplace.

The questions now are: a) What knowledge and skills do teachers need to acquire to respond to the practical implications of **consumer-segmented teaching** and other paradigms for understanding cultural pluralism in the classroom? and b) How should teacher preparation programs be redesigned to address these needs?

Teachers as Cultural Brokers

No one should be allowed to graduate from a teacher certification program or be licensed to teach without being well grounded in how the dynamic of cultural conditioning operates in teaching and learning. To achieve this goal, the preparation programs should be designed to teach teachers how to be **cultural brokers** (Gentemann & Whitehead, 1983) in pluralistic classrooms and to be competent in **cultural context teaching** (e.g., **segmented marketing of pedagogy**).

A cultural broker is one who thoroughly understands different cultural systems, is able to interpret cultural symbols from one frame of reference to another, can mediate cultural incompatibilities, and knows how to build bridges or establish linkages across cultures that facilitate the instructional process. Cultural brokers translate expressive cultural behaviors into pedagogical implications and actions. They model maneuvers within and negotiations among multiple cultural systems without compromising the integrity of any. They provide mechanisms for establishing continuity between ethnically and socially diverse cultures and mainstream school culture. Cultural brokers are **bicultural actors** who are able to straddle or syncretize different cultural systems and integrate elements of ethnic cultures into classroom procedures, programs, and practices (Gentemann & Whitehead, 1983). How they function epitomizes cultural context teaching at the levels of interpersonal interactions with students, pedagogical strategies employed in the classroom, and the infusion of multiculturalism throughout the entire instructional process.

Several skills are necessary for teachers to become cultural brokers. These can be classified as acquiring cultural knowledge, becoming change agents, and translating cultural knowledge into pedagogical strategies. They should form the substantive core of all teacher preparation programs.

Acquiring Cultural Knowledge

This component of preparing teachers to be cultural brokers should have three aspects: learning factual information about the specific characteristics of different ethnic and cultural groups, understanding the pedagogical implications of these cultural characteristics, and developing a philosophy for cultural context teaching. The students enrolled in the preparation programs should declare a cultural or ethnic group for concentrated study. They also may choose more than one group to concentrate on with the understanding that this choice will extend the time they spend in the preparation program. When they finish the program, the graduates will have a culturally diverse area of specialization (e.g., African Americans, Mexican Americans, children of poverty), as well as a subject matter major and endorsement.

Knowledge about cultural diversity should be acquired through two primary means: studying the accumulated research and scholarship on different ethnic and cultural groups and first-hand experiences gained from participatory observations in various cultural communities. Both of these should be in-depth experiences, guided by the methodologies, orientations, conceptual frameworks, and knowledge funds generated by behavioral scientists, ethnic studies scholars, and expressive artists (such as cultural anthropologists, social psychologists, sociolinguists, ethnomusicologists, ethnographers, cultural artists, and literary authors). College of Education faculties will need to establish previously unexplored instructional partnerships with some university divisions and scholars. These partnerships in search of accurate and authentic knowledge about cultural patterns and functions are as essential as the more traditional ones between educationists and social scientists designed to increase mastery of the subject matter taught in schools.

Some dimensions of culture are more applicable than others to understanding and mediating cultural conflicts in pluralistic classrooms. These include cultural values, relational patterns, learning styles and work habits, communication styles, rewards and punishments, social etiquette and decorum, cultural ethos, self-presentation styles, and patterns of ethnic identification and affiliation. Students enrolled in teacher education programs should be expected to take relevant behavioral science courses to learn specific content about each of these cultural components for specific ethnic groups. They may take courses in ethnic literature, cultural values, folklore, family, art and aesthetics, celebrations and ceremonies, customs and traditions, and developmental psychology.

The cultural content courses should be complemented with education seminars that have three primary purposes. The first is the extrapolation of pedagogical principles and practices embedded in the cultural content. Seminars should be sequenced so that students' enrollment in the content courses and the seminars coincide with each other or follow closely thereafter. The courses could even be team taught by behavioral scientists and educationists working together. A second component of the seminars is a field-based practicum in which students spend concentrated periods of time in culturally pluralistic school sites. During these experiences, students will function as participant observers to document how the cultural characteristics they are studying are expressed in actual classroom settings and interactions. The third element of the seminars should be the development of students' philosophies for cultural context teaching. The emphasis here is on developing an understanding and appreciation of cultural pluralism in the classroom as a vital, creative, and enriching phenomenon, as well as its potential for transforming the quality of schooling for students from historically disenfranchised groups. The conceptual paradigms discussed earlier should be the foundation of this philosophy.

Becoming Change Agents

To be effective cultural brokers and cultural context teachers, students in teacher education programs must be taught how to be agents. This role requires a commitment to institutional transformation and developing skills for incorporating cultural diversity into the normative operations of schools and classrooms. A four-step process should constitute this aspect of teacher education.

First, teacher education students should be taught skills of critical analysis and self-reflection. These skills will help them learn to analyze systematically the structures and procedures in schools and classrooms and their own habitual ways of behaving in institutional settings from various cultural vantage points; to identify points of conflict between the culture of the school and different ethnic groups; and to determine which of these offer the best and the worst opportunities for negotiation and change to serve the academic needs of culturally different students better.

Second, education students should be taught how to deconstruct mainstream hegemonic assumptions, values, and beliefs embedded in the normative structures and procedures of conventional classroom teaching. This requires a thorough understanding of how cultural values shape classroom policies, procedures, and practices; an awareness of the points in the instructional process that are most susceptible to cultural conflict; and the ability to discern those structural components that are most significant to incorporating cultural pluralism into routine classroom procedures.

Commitments to making teaching more culturally relevant need to be grounded in principles of organizational behavior and change (e.g., Belasco, 1990; Bowditch & Buono, 1985; Meltzer & Nord, 1980; Robbins, 1991). Many teacher education students recognize the need for change and have strong affinities for making their classroom teaching more culturally sensitive. But they do not know how to anchor it in a realistic and reliable operational framework. They seem to believe that desire alone is sufficient to bring about change. In the long run, this naïveté is a serious obstacle to real change. Students must understand the organizational culture, climate, and psychology of schools; why schools are self-perpetuating institutions; obstacles to change; cooperative strategies for planned change; and techniques to initiate and sustain change.

An integral feature of success as cultural brokers is being able to relate well to students from culturally, ethnically, and racially diverse backgrounds. Therefore, a fourth part of becoming effective change agents is developing competencies in cross-cultural communications and multicultural counseling. Both of these fields of research and scholarship have rich data bases from which students can acquire conceptual skills and practical techniques. The emphasis should be on sociolinguistic and paralinguistic communication components (Cazden, John, & Hymes, 1985; Greenbaum, 1985; Hall, 1981; Kochman, 1981; Smitherman, 1977; Trueba, Guthrie, & Au, 1981). In some instances, language studies and principles of bilingual education and second language learning are also appropriate. Techniques of cross-cultural counseling are important because teachers need to know how to help students deal with the stress and strain of living and functioning in culturally pluralistic settings. Some of the specific associated needs are style shifting across cultures, self-declaration for different ethnic group members, dealing with interracial and interethnic group hostilities, editing cultural nuances out of public behaviors, and coping with traumas and anxieties related to functions in cross-cultural settings (Beeman, 1978; Schofield, 1982; Spencer, Brookins, & Allen, 1985).

Translating Knowledge into Practice

Finally, teacher education programs should provide ample opportunities for students to engage in supervised practice doing cultural context teaching and being cultural brokers in actual classroom settings. Through a combination of classroom simulations, sample demonstrations, media protocols, case studies, and field experiences, students should develop skills in diagnosing teaching and learning styles, matching teaching styles with learning styles, creating inviting classroom climates (Purkey, 1978), using culturally sensitive assessment tools and techniques, and integrating culturally diverse content into subject matter curricula. These action strategies will need to be accompanied by corresponding changes in beliefs about what knowledge is of greatest worth for citizenship in a pluralistic world and what are the best ways it can be acquired for students from different ethnic, cultural, racial, and social backgrounds. The overriding principles should be the cultural contextuality of teaching and learning and using alternative pedagogical means to achieve common learning outcomes.

All teacher education students also should be expected to participate in a cultural brokerage internship before completing their preparation program. This internship should take place in actual classroom settings and provide opportunities to practice all of the skills involved in being a cultural broker. It is to be a complement to, not a replacement for, the traditional student teaching experience. The duration of the experience should be long enough for the students to get a sampling of the wide variety of issues and challenges involved in the institutional culture of schools. The internship should be carefully monitored and assessed by experienced classroom teachers or university professors. Successful completion should be a condition of graduating from the teacher preparation program and receiving a license to teach.

Conclusion

The plight of many culturally different students in U.S. public schools is chronic and critical. Because teachers play a central role in resolving it, their preparation must be a prime target of reform. This need is becoming even more imperative, given shifts in school demographics that show rapid increases in the numbers of children who are poor, limited English speakers, immigrants, and members of ethnic groups of color, as well as a decline in teachers from similar backgrounds. The resulting social distance can be an impenetrable obstacle to effective teaching and learning.

Generic teacher education programs that are supposed to prepare teachers to function well in all types of school communities are no longer viable. Instead, preparation must be population based and contextually specific. Nor can participation in multicultural learning experiences be left to choice and chance—it must be mandatory and carefully planned. The best way to translate these ideas into practice is preparation programs that emphasize developing skills in cultural context teaching and how to be cultural brokers in pluralistic classrooms. The essence of these strategies is affirming the cultures of diverse students, establishing continuity and building bridges across different cultural systems, creating supportive classroom climates where diverse students feel welcome and valued, and replacing cultural hegemonic pedagogy with one that models cultural pluralism without hierarchy. Mastering the skills necessary for cultural brokering and cultural context teaching may require longer time in preparation. But it is time well spent, and long-range payoffs are more than worth the relative short-term investments.

Preparing teachers to work better with culturally different students and communities demands action now. Conventional approaches to teacher education must be decentered and transformed at their most fundamental core if teachers are to be maximally prepared to teach students of the 21st century who will be increasingly racially, culturally, ethnically, socially, and linguistically pluralistic.

References

Au, K. H. P., & Jordan, C. (1981). Teaching reading to Hawaiian children: Finding a culturally appropriate solution. In H. T. Trueba, G. P. Guthrie, & K. H. P. Au (Eds.), *Culture and the bilingual classroom: Studies in classroom ethnography* (pp. 139-152). Rowley, MA: Newbury House.

Barbe, W. B., & Swassing, R. H. (1979). *Teaching through modality strengths: Concepts and practice*. Columbus, OH: Zaner-Bloser.

Beeman, P. N. (1978). *School stress and anxiety: Theory, research, and intervention*. New York: Human Sciences Press.

Belasco, J. A. (1990). *Teaching the elephant to dance: Empowering change in your organization*. New York: Crown.

Boggs, S. T., Watson-Gegeo, K., & McMillen, G. (1985). *Speaking, relating, and learning: A study of Hawaiian children at home and at school*. Norwood, NJ: Ablex.

Bowditch, J. L., & Buono, A. T. (1985). *A primer on organizational behavior*. New York: Wiley.

Boykin, A. W. (1986). The triple quandary and the schooling of Afro-American children. In U. Neisser (Ed.), *The school achievement of minority children: New perspectives* (pp. 57-92). Hillsdale, NJ: Lawrence Erlbaum.

Cazden, C. B., John, V. P., & Hymes, D. (Eds.). (1985). *Functions of language in the classroom*. Prospect Heights, IL: Waveland.

The condition of education. (1992). Washington, DC: U.S. Department of Education, National Center for Education Statistics, Office of Educational Research and Information.

De La Rosa, D., & Maw, C. E. (1990). *Hispanic education: A statistical portrait.* Washington, DC: National Council of La Raza.

Digest of education statistics, 1991. (1992). Washington, DC: U.S. Department of Education, Office of Education Research and Improvement, Center for Educational Statistics.

Education that works: An action plan for the education of minorities. (1990). Cambridge, MA: MIT, Quality Education for Minorities Project.

Florio, S., & Shultz, J. (1979). Social competence at home and at school. *Theory into Practice, 18*, 234-243.

Gagne, R. M. (1985). *The conditions of learning and theory of instruction* (4th ed.). New York: Holt, Rinehart & Winston.

Gardner, H. (1983). *Frames of mind: The theory of multiple intelligences.* New York: Basic Books.

Gaudry, E., & Spielberger, C. D. (1971). *Anxiety and educational achievement.* New York: Wiley.

Gentemann, K. M., & Whitehead, T. L. (1983). The cultural broker concept in bicultural education. *Journal of Negro Education, 54*, 118-129.

Gibbs, J. T., Huang, L. N., & Associates (1989). *Children of color: Psychological interventions with minority youth.* San Francisco: Jossey-Bass.

Giovanni, N. (1970). *Black feeling, Black talk and Black judgment.* New York: William Morrow.

Goodlad, J. I. (1984). *A place called school: Prospects for the future.* New York: McGraw-Hill.

Greenbaum, P. E. (1985). Nonverbal differences in communication style between American Indian and Anglo elementary classrooms. *American Educational Research Journal, 22*, 101-115.

Hall, E. T. (1981). *The silent language.* New York: Anchor.

Henry, W. A., III. (1990, April 9). Beyond the melting pot. *Time*, pp. 28-31.

The Hispanic population in the U.S. (1991, March). (Current Population Reports, Series P-20, No. 455). Washington, DC: U.S. Department of the Census.

Holliday, B. G. (1985). Towards a model of teacher-child transactional processes affecting Black children's academic achievement. In M. B. Spencer, G. K. Brookins, & W. R. Allen (Eds.), *Beginnings: The social and affective development of Black children* (pp. 117-130). Hillsdale, NJ: Lawrence Erlbaum.

Kochman, T. (1981). *Black and White styles in conflict.* Chicago: University of Chicago Press.

Meltzer, H., & Nord, W. R. (1980). *Making organizations humane and productive: A handbook for practitioners.* New York: Wiley.

Purkey, W. W. (1978). *Inviting school success: A self-concept approach to teaching and learning.* Belmont, CA: Wadsworth.

Robbins, S. P. (1991). *Organizational change: Concepts, controversies and applications.* Englewood Cliffs, NJ: Prentice-Hall.

Schofield, J. W. (1982). *Black and White in school: Trust, tension, or tolerance.* New York: Praeger.

Shade, B. J. R. (Ed.). (1989). *Culture, style and the educative process.* Springfield, IL: Charles C. Thomas.

Smitherman, G. (1977). *Talkin' and testifyin': The language of Black America.* Boston: Houghton Mifflin.

Spencer, M. B., Brookins, G. K., & Allen, W. R. (Eds.). (1985). *Beginnings: The social and affective development of Black children.* Hillsdale, NJ: Lawrence Erlbaum.

Spindler, G. D. (Ed.). (1987). *Education and cultural process: Anthropological perspectives.* Prospect Heights, IL: Waveland.

Statistical abstract of the United States (111th ed.). (1991). Washington, DC: Department of Commerce, Bureau of the Census.

Status of the American school teacher 1990-1991. (1992). Washington, DC: National Education Association, Research Division.

Swenson, C. A. (1990). *Selling to a segmented market: The lifestyle approach.* New York: Quorum.

Trueba, H. T., Guthrie, G. P., & Au, K. H. P. (1981). *Culture and the bilingual classroom: Studies in classroom ethnography.* Rowley, MA: Newbury House.

TEACHING AND LEARNING WITH CULTURALLY DIVERSE STUDENTS: A TEACHER PREPARATION COURSE AT A COMPREHENSIVE PUBLIC UNIVERSITY

by

Mario Yepes-Baraya

This article will identify and discuss instructional strategies for multicultural education at the college level, making reference to and using examples from Multicultural Education: Teaching and Learning with Culturally Diverse Students, an introductory, junior-level course I (Yepes-Baraya, 1990) developed in the context of the State University of New York College at Fredonia's teacher education program.

Even though the examples of instructional strategies that will be presented correspond to an education course, many, if not all, of these strategies can be used in social sciences courses, in the humanities, and in other disciplines.

Instructional Objectives for Multicultural Education

Before one can appropriately address the issue of instructional strategies, one must consider the aims of instruction and, more specifically, the learning objectives for a given course (Romiszowski, 1984). Virtually all college courses in education, social sciences, and the humanities encompass objectives in the cognitive and affective domains (Bloom & Krathwohl, 1972; Krathwohl, Bloom & Masia, 1972). Moreover, most college instructors agree that learners should be expected to go beyond the information given in the course and develop both cognitive and affective skills needed to function in an increasingly complex world.

Cognitive skills are those skills resulting from the manipulation of information and application of information in new situations. Examples of cognitive skills in high demand are decision making, problem solving, and critical thinking. Affective skills are those skills dealing with self-knowledge and interpersonal communication, and the degree of one's awareness of one's own attitudes and conditioned habits. Examples of affective skills are personal control skills and developing a value system congruent with one's personal and professional behavior. In addition to the cognitive and affective domains, multicultural education courses are likely to have a component requiring the development of what Romiszowski (1984) has labeled "interactive skills." These are skills one exercises in interpersonal communication and dealings with others. Examples of interactive skills are listening, leadership, supervision and persuasion.

Essentially, for each one of the cognitive, affective, and interactive domains, instructors can develop knowledge objectives and skills objectives. Knowledge objectives are needed to provide the conceptual foundation and in-depth understanding of the subject matter and the skills objectives are needed to guide learners and instructors in the acquisition, development, and mastery of skills required for professional competency.

Given the cognitive, affective, and interactive domains and the distinction between knowledge objectives and skills objectives, it is pertinent to ask how these domains and types of objectives are represented in multicultural education courses at the college level.

Table 1 lists the objectives for the introductory multicultural education course used as a basis for this article. For this particular course there is a knowledge base for the cognitive, affective, and interactive domains consisting of ten knowledge objectives. In addition, there are ten skill objectives, some of which pertain primarily to each of the cognitive, affective, or interactive domains.

Since multicultural education is a philosophy for education that (1) questions prevailing attitudes toward minorities and other groups that remain outside the American mainstream, and (2) aims to foster understanding, respect, and appreciation of these groups, their cultural heritage and their contributions, it is appropriate to assume that, generally, multicultural education courses at the college level will have a large proportion of affective and interactive objectives in addition to the cognitive objectives more commonly found in other college courses. Moreover, because multicultural education is concerned with bringing about changes in society to eliminate existing poverty, discrimination, and oppression (Sleeter & Grant, 1988), it has to consider the need to develop learners' skills—cognitive, affective, and interactive—to effect these changes.

Table 1
Course objectives for
multicultural education: teaching and learning with
culturally diverse students*

KNOWLEDGE OBJECTIVES for the cognitive, affective, and interactive domains

---

1. The need for multicultural education, its historical development, goals, and processes.
2. The patterns of perception and thinking, assumptions, values, and cultural norms of American mainstream society and America's major ethnic and racial minority groups.
3. The cultural experience, contemporary and historical, and the contributions of America's major ethnic and racial minority groups.
4. Developmental considerations affecting teaching and learning in children.
5. Children's responses to racial, cultural, and socioeconomic differences.
6. Assessment criteria and procedures necessary to introduce a multicultural perspective in the classroom.
7. Criteria and elements required to create a culturally diverse learning environment.
8. Criteria and guidelines to help children understand themselves and others and to promote cooperative relationships.
9. The philosophy and theory concerning bilingual education.
10. Criteria and guidelines to establish communication and obtain involvement of parents and extended families.

SKILLS OBJECTIVES for the cognitive domain

---

11. Develop a rationale or model for the development and implementation of a curriculum reflective of the cultural pluralism of contemporary American society, and make reference to historical, cultural, demographic, and socioeconomic factors, as well as the status and school achievement of America's major ethnic and racial minority groups.

SKILLS OBJECTIVES for the affective domain

12. Develop awareness of the value of multicultural education.
13. Maintain and expand identification with and pride in one's mother culture.
14. Recognize similarities and differences between American mainstream culture and America's major minority cultures.
15. Recognize and accept languages other than English.
16. Recognize and accept differences in social structure, including familial organization and patterns of authority, and their implications for education.

SKILLS OBJECTIVES for the interactive domain

17. Demonstrate skills for effective participation and utilization of community resources, including parents and extended families.
18. Analyze, critique, and identify possible cultural or racial biases in an existing educational environment, including the physical setting, curricula, materials, and methods of discussion, testing, and assessment.
19. Acquire, evaluate, adapt, and develop instructional materials appropriate for the culturally diverse classroom.
20. Design, develop, and implement an instructional module or unit that is appropriate for the culturally diverse classroom.

*Adapted from Yepes-Baraya (1990).

Matching Activities to Objectives

Instructional designers attempt to match instructional activities to instructional objectives. They ask questions such as: What are the most effective ways to promote learning? What should be the instructor's role(s)? What should be the learner's role(s)? How does one know when learning has occurred? Instructional designers are aware that the process of learning shapes the product(s) of learning and that if one is not careful, the most noble educational ends can be subverted by inappropriately chosen means.

Wegenast, et al. (1985) provide a simple but useful framework for selecting instructional activities to effect cognitive, affective, and operative change. The terms cognitive and affective as used here have similar meanings to those used in the previous section when referring to the **knowledge** component of the cognitive and affective domains. The term operative, on the other hand, refers to the development of new skills and behaviors regardless of the domain considered. According to this framework, and as shown in Table 2, certain instructional activities are appropriate if only cognitive change is desired; other activities are more suitable to bring about affective change. Still others have proven effective in bringing about operative change. It is also apparent in going from cognitive to operative change that (1) learners have greater involvement in and greater control of their learning, (2) the instructor's role becomes less intrusive, and (3) the content of learning depends less on abstract material and more on direct experience.

Table 2
Learning activities types and change desired*

LECTURE	DISCUSSION	SIMULATION	EXPERIENCE
Lecture	Panel discussion	Case study	Ethnography
Mini-lecture	Brainstorming	Role play	Internship
Self-instruction	Forced choice	Simulation	Project
	Suited for COGNITIVE Change	Suited for AFFECTIVE Change	Suited for OPERATIVE Change

*Adapted from Wegenast, et al. (1985).

Instructional Strategies

Above and beyond the instructional activities already discussed, when developing a new course it is important to develop general strategies to serve as guides for making instructional decisions. Some of the instructional strategies presented below are well documented in the growing multicultural education literature and/or the instructional design literature, while others are a product of my experience.

Become aware of your own attitudes and values relative to cultural diversity and pluralism (Ramsey, 1987). Although this is not considered a strategy *per se*, it is worthwhile discussing here because of its obvious impact on instructor-learner interaction. In a course like multicultural education, knowledge alone does not guarantee instructional effectiveness. The instructor's behavior, verbal and nonverbal, should reflect the respect, acceptance, and appreciation of cultural diversity in a wide range of manifestations. This attitude is important in all cases, but particularly when the learners themselves constitute a culturally diverse group. Perception of the instructor as unfair, disrespectful, biased, or intolerant is likely to diminish credibility and teaching effectiveness. The expectation is not for instructors to be free of bias—no one is—but rather to become aware of their own shortcomings and gradually come to adopt a more sensitive perspective.

Become knowledgeable about your community. This strategy is important for primary and secondary instructors (Ramsey, 1987), and just as important for college instructors. Knowledge of the community refers to the college community and the community at large. All communities have resources for multicultural education that would go untapped if instructors were not aware of their existence. Some of the most obvious resources are those found in libraries and media centers. The identification of relevant books, journals, and technology-based materials is a necessary step in the development of multicultural education courses and programs. Because multicultural education feeds off disciplines like history, sociology, anthropology, political science, psychology, and the humanities, in addition to the growing education literature, the task of identifying these resources may appear onerous at first, but it should be regarded as ongoing and part of one's professional development.

Another community resource worth learning about is its people. In every community there are a variety of ethnic, racial, and socioeconomic groups. Most of these groups are readily identifiable, either by their location within the community or by the social, cultural, or religious organizations to which they belong. Representatives of these groups are often happy to host visitors or to make presentations to share their unique perspectives and particular experiences.

A third and most important community resource for multicultural education, especially for teacher education programs, is the public schools. It is my experience that colleges and universities often fail to develop a working relationship with those public schools in their communities that have large culturally diverse populations. With school-college partnerships becoming increasingly common (Maeroff, 1983; Gaudiani & Burnett, 1986), the potential to embark on mutually beneficial projects is substantial. Not only can college instructors become knowledgeable in this way about multicultural education curriculum materials and instructional activities (or lack thereof), but they can also explore the possibility of placing their own students in these schools for field experiences with culturally diverse students or for conducting research on instruction, assessment, administration, or community involvement issues.

Encourage student involvement and diversity of perspectives. As discussed earlier, multicultural education is concerned with cognitive, affective, and operative change on the part of the learner, as well as with the effective development of skills required for living, learning, and working in a pluralistic society. Therefore, student involvement in learning is indispensable if such changes are to occur. Lectures and instructor-centered instructional activities should be balanced with student-centered activities and with activities that require learners to actively interact with culturally diverse groups. Following is a brief discussion of the role that different instructional activities have in multicultural education, relative to their potential for effecting the desired changes.

Lectures and Mini-Lectures. Lectures are instructor-centered activities and, as such, do not encourage a high level of learner participation. There is room, however, in multicultural education, as in many other college courses, for lectures in order to provide information that otherwise would not be readily available to learners. Instructors who rely excessively on lectures should make it a point to give mini-lectures instead of lectures. Mini-lectures can range anywhere from five to fifteen minutes, and require that instructors prepare their material very carefully. The remaining time can be devoted to activities that allow for greater learner input.

Reading Assignments and Written Responses. This self-instructional activity that, like lecturing, aims primarily at producing cognitive change. Unlike lecturing, this activity provides greater learner involvement and greater potential for affective change. The requested response to the assigned reading may vary: it may be a summary of the reading, a personal reaction, or a request to consult additional sources. In addition to helping learners be better prepared for class, written responses can be made part of a journal that learners keep throughout the course which reflects their cognitive and affective change. Moreover, in large classes where one-on-one communication is difficult, instructors can collect journals at random and provide individualized feedback to learners.

Class Discussions. Learners may be asked to prepare for a discussion based on a reading assignment or research project, or they may be encouraged to generate ideas and discussion in response to issues or questions raised by other learners or the instructors themselves. The instructor's role is to facilitate and moderate the discussion, to clarify concepts as needed, to ask thought-provoking questions, and to encourage self-expression and creative thinking. Discussion of ideas is essential in multicultural education as a tool, for example, to increase awareness of one's own biases and prejudices, or to help learners recognize similarities and differences among culturally or racially diverse groups. By asking questions in the Socratic fashion, instructors can model for learners the thinking processes required to elucidate complex issues.

Presentations by Members of Culturally Diverse Groups. Such presentations are particularly effective, especially in settings where most learners come from similar cultural backgrounds. When planning these presentations, instructors should clearly communicate their instructional objectives and expectations to their prospective guest speakers. In order to prevent stereotyping, instructors should also make it clear to their students that guest speakers can only convey their ideas, feelings, and opinions as individuals and are not the spokespersons for the groups they represent.

Research Projects and Student Presentations. These can be excellent vehicles for affective, as well as operative change. For example, in order to maintain and expand their identification with their mother culture, learners can be asked to research their own backgrounds and/or family histories and present their findings to the class. Student presentations can be followed with class discussions or with other presentations in such a way that two or more groups can be compared and contrasted along several dimensions.

Field Experiences. In the case of teacher education programs with a strong commitment to multiculturalism, there is a wide range of field experiences available. Ideally, learners should come in direct contact with individuals from culturally diverse backgrounds both inside and outside the classroom. Classroom and community observations, attendance at ethnic and cultural events, ethnographic studies, and tutorial instruction are some possibilities. In homogeneous communities that are geographically isolated, special arrangements need to be made. One such arrangement is the establishment of student exchange programs, where learners are immersed in a different culture. If well-coordinated, these programs have the potential of bridging the gap between ethnic, racial, linguistic, and socioeconomic groups; fostering cross-cultural communication skills; and enhancing future teachers' effectiveness inside and outside the school. The successful implementation of these programs requires collaboration among colleges and universities, school districts, and host families.

A Final Word

The decade of the nineties began with a renewed interest in multiculturalism both domestically and abroad. In the United States a lively discussion has followed the abandonment of the idea of the melting pot and the search for alternatives to forge a national identity for the next century. While there is recognition and ample support for the notion of equal rights for all people regardless of race, gender, socioeconomic status, disability, or national origin, there is no consensus on how to achieve this ideal. It is clear, however, that the education sector has a key role to play in preparing today's children and tomorrow's citizens to live and work in a pluralistic world.

Higher education has been quick to respond to the challenges of multiculturalism: new course offerings, new faculty and staff development programs, new research initiatives, and new ventures with inner city schools are examples of the activities and events occurring across the country. How can one assess whether or not these developments are having the intended effect? In most cases, appropriate monitoring and evaluation, as well as research conducted by independent parties, would appear to be indicated.

In the case of instruction with a multicultural perspective, my recommendations for increased teaching effectiveness include: first, that instructors do a self-assessment of their motivation and commitment to teach with a multicultural perspective; second, that instructors become knowledgeable about different resources available for multicultural education in their own communities; third, that instructors match instructional strategies to instructional objectives in order to effect the desired learning; fourth, that instructors balance lecturing with other instructional activities that foster learner involvement in direct experiences with culturally diverse populations. These recommendations should help us go beyond the "business-as-usual" approach to multicultural education that is still prevalent in higher education.

References

Banks, J. A. (1981). *Multiethnic education: Theory and practice*. Boston: Allyn & Bacon.

Bloom, B. S., & Krathwohl, D. R. (1972). *Taxonomy of educational objectives, handbook I: Cognitive domain*. New York: Longman.

Gaudiani, C. & Burnett, D. (1986). *Academic alliances: A new approach to school-college collaboration*. Washington, DC: American Association for Higher Education.

Krathwohl, D. R., Bloom, B. S., & Masia, B. B. (1972). *Taxonomy of educational objectives, handbook II: Affective domain*. London: Longman.

Maeroff, G. (1983). *School and college partnerships in education*. Princeton, NJ: The Carnegie Foundation for the Advancement of Teaching.

Ramsey, P. G. (1987). *Teaching and learning in a diverse world: Multicultural education for young children*. New York: Teachers College, Columbia University.

Romiszowski, A. J. (1984). *Designing instructional systems: Decision making in course planning and curriculum design*. London: Kogan Page.

Sleeter, C. E., & Grant, C. A. (1988). *Making choices for multicultural education: Five approaches to race, class, and gender*. Columbus, OH: Merrill.

Wegenast, D. P., et al. (1985). *Curriculum, instruction, and evaluation design: A training program for staff development personnel*. Buffalo: State University of New York College at Buffalo.

Yepes-Baraya. M. (1990, Fall). "Multicultural education: Teaching and learning with culturally diverse students." Unpublished course syllabus. Fredonia, NY: State University of New York College at Fredonia.

TRAINING EARLY CHILDHOOD TEACHERS TO COUNTER INDIRECT INFLUENCES ON YOUNG CHILDREN'S ATTITUDES TOWARD DIVERSITY

by
Jeanne B. Morris

As the 21st century approaches, America is unparalleled in its diversity, reflecting predictions that by the year 2000, minorities would account for an ever-increasing percent of the total population (Illinois Board of Regents, 1991). Schools mirror the society. Culture and diversity are terms that have become a part of today's educational jargon so it is expected that the nation's schools will be major players in the destruction of cultural barriers to bring harmony and accord. In the "6th Annual State of American Education Address." Secretary of Education Richard Riley (1999) cited the following as one of five dynamics transforming American education: "With one out of five children living in poverty and growing diversity, the makeup of the classroom is requiring teachers to broaden their skills."

Although there have been improvements in the status of cultural relationships, the results of classic research indicate the need for continued modification in the development of racial attitudes. Children in America's school now experience and will increasingly experience demographic transformations that will have tremendous effects on their lives. For all children, living with and embracing such a challenge requires pluralistic mindsets and abilities to communicate across cultures. Therefore it is imperative that all children come to know and celebrate their own family heritage with pride as they develop appreciation and respect for the cultural backgrounds and uniqueness of others (Gordon & Brown, 1996).

The most effective professionals who will provide services to young children in the next century must first clarify their dispositions toward diversity to enable authentic responses to the challenges of the increased heterogeneity of schools. Teachers are foremost among these professionals. In our projected world, teachers for whom responding to cultural diversity remains a dilemma will be confused and disoriented. Consequently, the children they teach may be confused and disoriented. Both these teachers and children are likely to wander with unrealistic and unacceptable perceptions through a pluralistic world. They will be in a world of distrust and suspicion—a world of wonderment which could be likened to that in Lewis Carroll's classic tale. In *Alice in Wonderland,* Carroll illustrated typical reactions to divergent aspects of a society. As Alice traveled through a world quite unlike the one to which she was accustomed, all rules of perception and behavior she had come to know were turned inside out **and** upside down (Cushner, McClelland, & Safford, 1992). So it can be for teachers and students whose perceptions cannot and do not respond to the realities of a culturally diverse world.

Rejection based on unfounded perceptions is the end result of prejudice and is destructive. In *Teaching Young Children in Multicultural Classrooms*, de Melendez and Ostertag (1999) suggest that prejudice has caused more destruction in the world than any war and that prejudice flourishes in environments that tolerate or encourage negative perceptions of others based on false, misleading, or inadequate knowledge (p. 67). Researchers, practitioners, and parents agree the family is the first and prime socializer, but learning additional ways of behaving and interacting, the socialization of young children into the larger society, is an appropriate goal for early childhood education. Teachers' credible knowledge of and positive attitudes toward diversity and choice of experiences that promote appreciation of cultural diversity are foundations of climates of acceptance for all children.

Teachers are catalysts of transformation who can convey and promote attentiveness to, appreciation of, and respect for cultural diversity. Several years ago The Illinois Regency Task Force on Teacher Education (1991) directed attention to the recruitment of minority teachers. It suggested that distinct efforts be made to increase the number of minorities enrolled in and graduating from teacher education programs as well as the number of minorities who apply for and accept teaching positions (p. 2). The summary and conclusions of the Task Force remain relevant today. Yet, while teachers who are members of minority ethnic groups are often effective motivators of content as well as positive role models for ethnic minority students, all teachers represent cultural groups. In addition, there is no assurance that there will be sufficient numbers of minority teachers for the 21st century work force. While the recruitment and training of minority teacher education candidates is imperative, so is the increase in training non-minority teachers in knowledge of and appreciation for the histories and cultures of all groups of society (p. 3). Persistent progress in these areas is more critical than ever.

The availability of appropriately trained personnel and continued in-service opportunities is a recommendation that underscores the essential role of culturally proficient teachers, a position supported in the National Council for the Social Sciences Task Force Report on Ethnic Studies Curriculum Guide (1992). This report underscored the importance of effective 21st century pre-service and in-service teachers who have examined their own perceptions, biases, and behaviors related to cultural diversity. These are the teachers who will be best prepared to guide learners to explore attitudes and feelings about their ethnicity and the ethnicity of others. Early childhood classrooms that best promote cross-cultural understanding are those in which teachers lead each young student to embrace diversity. Channeling social transformation thrives in special settings conducive to the children's dreaming and fantasizing, and to skill building and socialization (de Melendez & Ostertag, 1997, p. 7).

Early childhood teachers who can best promote cross-cultural understanding must also have understanding of the realities of multicultural/intercultural classrooms. Without genuine understanding by responsible educators, cultural diversity has been and will continue to be threatening to some, disconcerting to others. It is also clear that very early in the intercultural settings, and with multicultural curricula, some teachers may experience intense feelings. These teachers can and must be helped to anticipate, understand, and accommodate typical as well as idiosyncratic reactions and thus cope with potentially stressful situations in positive ways (Cushner, et al, 1992, p. 44).

There have been efforts to purge the U.S. society of bigotry, intolerance, racism, and prejudice through planned and/or forced legislation, elimination of discriminatory practices, cultural interaction, and communication of information and insights regarding cultural groups. These endeavors have resulted in changes in attitudes and perceptions at a pace that has been at times painfully slow and sometimes unexpectedly accelerated. Yet, such endeavors are constantly necessary and seemingly endless.

While it is impossible to control all the factors that shape children's attitudes toward diversity, positive experiences in the early years can counteract the development of negative attitudes. Teachers must be those who are sensitive to differences among and between people,

360

who have unambiguous understanding of cultural diversity, and those who have depth of knowledge of the processes through which favorable perceptions of diversity are developed and nurtured and unfavorable ones neutralized. Early childhood teachers of the future must have a commitment to and demonstrated skills through which the compelling challenges of education that is multicultural are met. Multicultural education must be seen to embrace the whole of humankind. Goodlad (1986) recognized more that a decade ago that the maturing of multicultural education presents opportunities to assist humans to live together in understanding, appreciation, and peace. Action cannot be postponed.

As early childhood teachers are prepared to meet the challenge, teacher trainers must help teacher candidates to look through and beyond any narrowly internalized attitudes about cultural diversity to reach a level of consciousness to effectively dispel and correct impressions created by myths, stereotypes, and environmental symbolism. This level of consciousness is essential for teachers in multicultural classrooms who must be conduits for the clarification of facts and interpretations related to the cultural identification of those not of the mainstream culture and for the development of effective multicultural experiences for all. Teachers who are culturally skilled are essential in early childhood education for they are the first within the educational system to respond to the changing demographic profile of our nation.

Teaching in the future will require not only training in instructional content for classrooms which reflects ethnic diversity but adjustment of habitual ways of interacting to provide education that is appropriate and relevant for all young citizens. It is essential that future teachers understand early in their training programs that changes begin with teachers and their ability to effect changes in others (Cushner, et al., 1992). This assessment is congruent with one of the most potent goals of schooling: to dispel ignorance.

There are no clearer descriptions of 21st century culturally skilled teachers than those by Stills in 1988 who wrote that culturally skilled teachers are those who:

- have moved from being culturally unaware to being culturally defined with acknowledgment of the impact of self values on diverse students;
- have an understanding of the society's socio-political systems and treatment of culturally diverse populations;
- are comfortable with differences that exist between teachers and students in terms of race and beliefs;
- are sensitive to circumstances that may dictate references to culture or race by a member of a student's culture/race;
- possess knowledge of the particular group(s) with whom they are working; and have the ability to generate and send a variety of verbal and nonverbal responses appropriately and accurately. (pp. 17-18)

As we plan for the future, there must be efforts to ensure that all young children will be guided by teachers who can facilitate and support the realization of student potential through an unabridged understanding of all that cultural identification implies. Therefore,

Effective early childhood teachers in the 21st century and beyond will be those who have a clear understanding of the origins of cultural identification.

Everyone, every environment has a culture that influences thoughts, feelings, and actions. Teachers' knowledge and appreciation of the sources and power of cultural orientation must consciously and continuously direct efforts to blend the cultures of home and school beginning with the cultural orientation each child brings to the learning environment. Despite the radical changes that have taken place within this country in recent decades, the family remains the most influential part of the socialization network. It is in the family that cultural identity materializes. Cultural cognition, awareness of one's own culture as unique and distinct from other cultures, and cultural identification (shared values, behavioral patterns, and traits without particular awareness of their distinctiveness from other cultures), develop within the context of the family (Banks & Banks, 1989). Traditions and beliefs shared and valued by family and others in the child's cultural group are significant and must be respected and not judged worthy or unworthy, only different one from the other.

All children share parts of the school culture but some children enter the learning environment sharing more of that culture than other children.

It remains true that when "school ways" are different from "home ways," children have to learn to respond to different expectations. Some may have to learn to use different linguistic codes, to function according to unfamiliar behavioral patterns, and, perhaps, to achieve satisfaction in new ways. For these children the world of school may be quite unlike the worlds to which they have become accustomed. As Alice had to adjust in her trip through Wonderland, there will have to be adjustments to dissimilarities between the world of home and the world of school. Teachers who have clarified their perceptions of cultural diversity can respond appropriately to dissimilar linguistic codes, behavioral patterns, and distinct values and customs since they understand the cultural mores brought to the classroom by children from diverse backgrounds and can use those as advantages to develop effective instructional strategies (Gollnick & Chinn, 1986). The circumstances under which cultural distinctiveness flourishes or is humbled is eminently dependent on teacher knowledge, appreciation, and acceptance of diversity.

In the educational environment, teachers are the primary influencers of children's development through directly or indirectly controlling all that occurs in classrooms.

Teachers are the significant adults and role models beyond family units and are vehicles for the acceptance and/or rejection of every child. There is evidence of strong support for child-responsive environments in which all children have opportunities to grow and develop to their full potentials. Knowledge of the cultural backgrounds of young children is as important to developing effective instructional strategies as knowledge of their physical and mental capabilities. When teachers are sensitive to the cultural orientation of each child, learners in child-responsive environments can freely construct knowledge of the world guided through their own experiences so that they all contribute to and profit from fulfillment of the American Dream.

Beginning with the 21st century, effective early childhood teachers must have a clear understanding of the processes through which unfavorable perceptions of diversity are developed.

It is a fairly common notion that young children are eager to accept any person regardless of race or nationality and that most negative attitudes toward diversity are learned. The perceptions conveyed by the Rodgers and Hammerstein lyrics, "Carefully Taught" from *South Pacific,* suggest that children's attitudes toward the racially different are innately positive.

You've got to be taught to fear and hate
Before you're six or seven or eight.
You've got to be carefully taught.

These lyrics hypothesize that as long as adults do not actively indoctrinate racist attitudes, children will grow up without prejudice. Since the early part of the century, social scientists have been well aware that children as young as three years of age are able to differentiate human physical characteristics such as skin color. In addition, from the age of five, children also assign attributes to others based on their skin color, associating black with negative value, white with positive value (Cushner, et al., 1992, p. 156). Many children are taught to dislike, mistrust, reject, or stereotype people with diverse characteristics like members of racial groups, yet convincing evidence across cultures indicates young children absorb negative and positive meanings about diversity even when those meanings are never communicated directly (Morris, 1981). Concepts inherent in the environment are internalized and become powerful determinants of attitudes and behaviors.

The results of research on the influence of environmental stimuli strongly suggest that young children are capable of discriminating among stimuli which adults employ for racial classification. For example, languages transmit dynamic messages through symbolism, color connotations, analogies, and similes. Cross-cultural research on the development of attitudes toward racial characteristics has demonstrated that children positively evaluate objects and people on the basis of color connotations, especially black and white (Adams & Osgood, 1973; Williams, Bosswell, & Best, 1975; Best, Naylor, & Williams, 1975). In many cultures white is associated with goodness and purity, black with evil and death. In addition, there are the typical references to "black as sin" and "pure as driven snow," the black sheep of the family, black and ominous clouds, and calamitous events such as blackballing or blacklisting. Young children's internalization of these meanings was established in classic studies of the affective meanings of color in 23 language cultures in Europe, Asia, and the Americas (Adams & Osgood, 1973). These researchers found that young children consistently rated white positively and black negatively. Further, three-to-five year old children's responses to specific questions, spontaneous verbalizations, and awareness indices were insightful. White children made more positive comments in more favorable affect-laden terms and fewer negative comments about their skin color than black children; black children tended to be less favorable about their skin color than white children. Present-day demographics and efforts in multicultural education suggest the need for current research similar to that conducted by Adams, Osgood, Williams, Best, and Naylor.

A summary of the 1988 findings on the formation of prejudice in children provides the basis for guidelines in developing programs for young children:

(1) children learn prejudice from observing the behaviors of others;
(2) children learn prejudice as a survival technique when excluding or including others is considered the proper thing to do;
(3) prejudice may be actively created and stereotypes reinforced through children's exposure to media; and

(4) exposure to rigid orthodox or fundamentalist religious attitudes and practices may contribute to beliefs that all other doctrines are at best "wrong" as are the individuals who believe in them. (Cushner, et al., 1992, p. 263).

Research has shown that during the early childhood years children become increasingly aware of the ways people differ, especially in appearance. The growth of logic and the ability to place objects and things into categories enable children to classify people according to racial categories, unintentionally setting foundations for prejudice. Abundant evidence supports conclusions that children's negative attitudes about diversity result from indirect influences as well as adult teaching. In the 21st century teachers of young children must comprehend and embrace the processes through which favorable perceptions of diversity can be developed and nurtured.

One of the most essential tasks of schooling is the creation of caring and growth-producing environments for learners. The quality of relationships within school environments is highly invested in what teachers say and do. Barth and Manning (1993) noted that the attitudes of teachers also influence the effectiveness of multicultural education. Each child is a unique individual and teachers' responses to children's emerging needs shape perceptions and behaviors. "When teachers personalize education, they ensure that children are ready to learn, and feel good about themselves, and are healthy," says Marian Edelmann, President of the Children's Defense Fund (1990). Personalizing education includes efforts to listen to, direct the interests of, and convey concern for students both inside and outside of school. Teacher behaviors toward each child signal if the classroom is a safe and trust-worthy place, build or prevent feelings of confidence to explore and develop new skills and understandings, foster or inhibit anxieties and uncertainties, and influence how children learn to relate to others.

There is no question about the effects of direct and indirect influences on the development of negative attitudes toward diversity. Fortunately, the minds of young children are sufficiently receptive to positive teaching they can modify unfavorable and often detrimental impressions. The effects of positive experiences on the development of attitudes toward racial diversity have been clearly demonstrated using black studies curriculum with young black and white children in different settings. Results indicate significant positive changes in the attitudes of whites towards blacks and significant positive modification of the self-concepts of young black children (Andrews, 1971). We can expect strategies that were effective in times when cultural diversity was not an openly accepted or discussed concept will be even more useful in contemporary classrooms.

Experiences that promote the acquisition of positive concepts of racial diversity must be provided in the early years as our schools are populated by greater percentages of minority learners. Their positions as significant adults in the lives of children mean that early childhood teachers have a vital responsibility and unparalleled opportunities to provide experiences that promote the acquisition of positive concepts of racial diversity. With exposure to positive experiences, children are less likely to become casualties of indirect influences that can be translated into rigid prejudices and meager self-regard. Early childhood teachers' identification and use of meaningful curriculum activities, careful selection of experiences and recognition, and valuing diversity are crucial (Morris, 1983, p. 88). When these conditions are satisfied, every child benefits regardless of his or her cultural orientation. When these conditions are satisfied, every child benefits regardless of the point in time.

Successful early childhood multicultural education requires that teachers plan and organize activities and experiences carefully, supported by carefully selected instructional materials and resources so that new information and concepts are catalysts for attitude formation and modification. Activities that help children to understand the humanness of each individual are especially important. People throughout the world share the same biological and social needs that are satisfied through specific cultural values, customs, and beliefs. Acceptance of diversity is promoted when explorations of the different responses to human conditions are presented in positive climates as differences not deficiencies. The perceptions of all children can be enlarged as they realize that we are all more alike than different. Experiences that help children to know and appreciate the customs and history of cultural groups can lead to deep and meaningful levels of understanding for **all** children. Carefully chosen teacher techniques and activities can prevent overgeneralizations and assumptions about culture and the degrees of cultural attachment among individuals.

For several decades a range of approaches has been used to introduce ethnic content into the curriculum of our public schools. Inclusive approaches to multicultural education aim to incorporate multicultural content in all subject areas for all learners using the diversity characteristic of our national population as the source of that content. Such an approach is preferable to the prevalent mainstream-centered curriculum. Banks (1991, 1993, 1995) offers four viable approaches he describes as the contribution, the additive, the transformation, and the social action approaches. All are empirically based. Sleeter and Grant (1994) describe five multicultural approaches from which educators might chose: teaching the exceptional and culturally different, human relations, single group studies, multicultural, and education that is multicultural and socially reconstructive.

The diverse characteristics of U.S. society have increased. Public interest in diversity issues has increased. As early childhood teachers enter the new millennium, their realization of the responsibilities toward children is heightened. They understand that multicultural understandings form the basis for a humane education with a high probability of educating students to participate in creating a truly democratic society that contributes to world harmony (Tiedt & Tiedt, 1990). Early childhood teachers in the 21st century and beyond must lead the way so that the compelling dream of Martin Luther King is fulfilled for every child in every classroom in America. de Melendez and Ostertag indicate what is needed in building a strong and prosperous nation. They address in particular the early childhood practitioner when they note multicultural efforts in education are still young: **"Although much has been accomplished, many areas still require reform as our society grows more diverse. Many chapters remain to be written. Which one will you begin?"** (p 175).

References

Adams, C. M., & Osgood, C. E. (1973). A cross-cultural study of the affective meaning of color. *Journal of Cross-Cultural Psychology, 4,* 135-136.

Andrews, P. (1971). *Effectiveness of Afro-American studies on the racial attitudes of young black children.* Unpublished doctoral dissertation, University of Illinois, Urbana-Champaign.

Banks, J. A. (1979). *Teaching strategies for ethnic studies* (2nd ed.). Boston: Allyn & Bacon.

Banks, J. A. (1991). Multicultural education: Its effects on students' racial and gender role attitudes. In J. P. Shaver (Ed.), *Handbook of research on social studies and teaching and learning* (pp. 459-469). New York: Macmillan.

Banks, J. A. (1993). The canon debate, knowledge construction, and multicultural education. *Educational Researcher, 22*(5), 4-14.

Banks, J. A. (1996b). Multicultural education: Its effects on students' racial and gender role attitudes. In J. A. Banks & C. A. M. Banks, (Eds.), *Handbook of research on multicultural education* (pp. 617-627). New York: Macmillan.

Banks, J. A., & Banks, C. A. (1989). *Multicultural education: Issues and perspectives.* Boston: Allyn & Bacon.

Barth, L., & Manning, M. L. (1992). *Multicultural education of children and adolescents.* Boston: Allyn & Bacon.

Best, D., Naylor, A., & Williams, J. (1975). Extension of color research to young French and Italian children. *Journal of Cross-Cultural Research, 6,* 390-405.

Cushner, K., McClelland, A., & Safford, P. (1992). *Human diversity in education: An integrative approach.* New York: McGraw-Hill.

de Melendez, W., & Ostertag, V. (1997). *Teaching young children in multicultural classrooms.* New York: Delmar Publishers.

Edelmann, M. (1990). *KIDNET.* Florida Children's Forum. www.kidnetflorida.org

Goodlad, J. (1986). Speech delivered at the Center for Educational Renewal, University of Washington, Seattle, WA.

Gollnick, D., & Chinn, P. (1983). *Multicultural education in a pluralistic society.* St. Louis: Mosby Company.

Gordon, A., & Browne, K. (1996). *Guiding young children in a diverse society.* Boston: Allyn & Bacon.

Illinois Board of Regents. (1991). *Report of the Regency System Task Force on Teacher Education.* Springfield, IL: Author.

King, C. S. (1983). The words of Martin Luther King, Jr. New York: New Market Press.

Morris, J. B. (1981, January). Indirect influences on the development of children's racial attitudes. *Educational Leadership, 38*(4), 286-287.

Morris, J. B. (1983). Classroom methods and materials. In O. Saracho & B. Spodek (Eds.), *The multicultural experience in early childhood education* (pp. 77-90). Washington, DC: The National Association for the Education of Young Children.

National Council for the Social Sciences. (1991). *Curriculum Guidelines for Multicultural Education.* Washington, DC: Author.

Riley, R. (1999, February 16). New Challenges, a New Resolve: Moving America into the 21st Century. Sixth Annual State of American Education Address. Long Beach: California State University.

Sleeter, C. W., & Grant, C. A. (1994). *Making choices for multicultural education* (2nd ed.). New York: Merrill.

Stills, A. B. (1988). The development of multicultural environments within the school. In C. A. Heid (Ed.), *Multicultural education: Knowledge and perceptions* (pp. 18-22). Bloomington: Indiana University Center for Urban and Multicultural Education.

Teidt, P. L., & Teidt, M. (1990). *Multicultural teaching: A handbook of activities, information, and resources.* Boston: Allyn & Bacon.

Valdez, A. 1999. *Learning in living color.* Boston: Allyn & Bacon.

Williams, J. E., Bosswell, A., & Best, D. (1975, June). Evaluative responses of preschoolers to the colors black and white. *Child Development, 46*(2), 501-581.

EDUCATING ASIAN AMERICAN STUDENTS: PAST, PRESENT, AND FUTURE

by
Ming-Gon John Lian

Asian American children are one of the fastest-growing populations in U.S. schools. Between 1991 and 1996, Asian Americans in the United States increased by 28.9 percent, compared to 25.3 percent Hispanics/Latinos, 9.5 percent African Americans, and 2.9 percent Caucasians (see Table 1). It is predicted that, by the year 2050, the number of Asian Americans will increase from the current 3.7 percent to 10 percent, or 40 million, of the nation's total population (Chan, 1998).

Table 1
Increase in racial/ethnic populations (1991–1996)

	1991	July, 1996	Increase 1991–1996
African Americans	30,600,000	33,500,000	9.5%
Asian Americans	7,550,000	9,700,000	28.9%
Caucasians	188,500,000	194,000,000	2.9%
Hispanics/Latinos	22,500,000	28,200,000	25.3%
Total	231,900,000	265,284,000	14.4%

Source: U.S. Census Bureau (1997a).

Ong and Hee (1993) reported that there were three million Asian/Pacific American students in U.S. schools. They predicted that the number of these students may be increased to twenty million by the year 2020. Though Asian/Pacific Americans are frequently identified as a unified group, Asian ethnic groups vary greatly in culture, language and experience (Lian & Poon-McBrayer, 1997). Actually, members in the Asian American population may represent diverse familial and cultural backgrounds, including those from Bangladesh, Cambodia, China, Hong Kong, Cambodia, India, Indonesia, Japan, Korea, Laos, Malaysia, Pakistan, Sri Lanka, Taiwan, Thailand, the Philippines, Vietnam, and many other Asian countries and areas. A broader classification of the Asian American population also includes the Pacific Islanders from Guam, Hawaii, Micronesia, Okinawa, Polynesia, Saipan, Samoa, Tonga, and other islands in the Pacific Ocean (Lian, 1995; U.S. Census Bureau, 1997a).

Asian Americans were previously referred to as "Orientals," a term that may critically disadvantage Asian American children. Through the years, a stereotype of the "Orientals" has existed. Some people, for example, may still relate Chinese Americans to illegal aliens, slanted eyes, chopsuey or chowmein-style ethnic foods, and funny speaking mannerisms, thinking of them as different from persons of "the Western World." As a result, Asian American children in the school may suffer from cultural and social discrimination and racism (Luke, 1987).

"Asian American" is a preferred term, originating during the last ten to twenty years. Just like African Americans, European Americans, Latin Americans, and Native Americans, many persons with Asian descent are also Americans. Chinese Americans, Filipino Americans, Indian Americans, Indonesian Americans, Japanese Americans, Korean Americans, Malaysian Americans, Thai Americans, Urdu Americans, and Vietnamese Americans represent subpopulations of Asian Americans.

Characteristics of Asian American Students

Asian American students may include children and youth who have recently immigrated to the United States as well as those who were born or raised in this country and are second, third, fourth, or fifth generation. Some Asian American students may have limited-English-proficiency (LEP) or speak English as a second language (ESL), while others may speak only English. Some children may speak only one of numerous Asian languages, while others may be bilingual, trilingual, or multilingual (e.g., English, Vietnamese, and French). Even students who speak the same Asian language may use different dialects (e.g., Mandarin Chinese, Cantonese, Shanghainese and Taiwanese). Any of these linguistic factors could add to the complicated multicultural experience of school-age Asian American children.

Hu-DeHart (1999) points out that, in the next decade, more students will come from biracial (e.g., Asian American and Latino) or multiracial (e.g., African American, Pacific American, and Native American) families and cultural backgrounds. Another group of Asian American students are children who were adopted from Asian countries, such as China and Korea, by their African American, Asian American, Caucasian, or Hispanic/Latino parents. In 1993, 89 Chinese infants were brought to the U.S. by their adopting families. The number of adoptions went up to 4,000 in 1998.

For many years, Asian Americans were ignored in U.S. literature on ethnic relations, resulting in the general public knowing very little about this population. Wakabayashi (1977) describes Asian Americans as the "least acknowledged of the national minorities" (p. 430). Many Americans developed their awareness and knowledge of Asian Americans based on false or stereotypic information eventually leading to prejudice, negative attitudes and discriminatory responses. Kim (1993) points out that, in the mid-19th to the mid-20th century, Asian Americans were often perceived to be "unassimilable," "inscrutable," "cunning," or "filthy." Because of the *exclusion legislation* enacted in 1882, most Asian Americans were not allowed to become U.S. citizens until 1952. Even today, Asian American children may be perceived by their teachers or peers in schools as foreigners or refugees (Cheng, Ima, & Labovitz, 1994) and many Asian Americans who are U.S. citizens are asked about their nationality or when they plan to "go back."

Since the 1960s, a new stereotypic image of Asian Americans has developed. Asian Americans are now often classified as diligent, hard-working, and high educational and economic achievers. Such overgeneralizations cause the public to overlook hidden issues and concerns among this population including poverty, limited health care, family violence, child abuse and neglect, and increased school failure and dropouts among Asian American children. As Sadker and Sadker (1994) indicate,

Despite outstanding accomplishments, the statistics hide problems that many of the new immigrants from Southeast Asia and Pacific Islands face. Cultural conflict, patterns of discrimination, lower educational achievement, and the diversity of the Asian/Pacific Americans are all hidden by the title "model minority." (p. 411)

Similar situations occur in the classroom setting, as Pang (1997) suggests:

… [Asian/Pacific American] students are often overlooked or misunderstood in schools. Many teachers do not feel pressured to attend to the needs of APA children since they are not discipline problems and do not seem to need special attention; however, many students may feel invisible and forgotten. Many APA students are seen and never heard. It happens in the classrooms of the best teachers and in classrooms where teachers have little interest in their students. (p. 149)

Chen (1989) expresses a concern about the lower self-concept which may exist among general Asian American students. He lists a number of positive characteristics of Asian American students, including bilingual and bicultural experiences, a long cultural history, respect within the culture for each other, strong family bonding, assertiveness, trustworthiness, high expectations, industriousness, a strong work ethic and moral values, flexibility, and adaptability. For example, Asian American students tend to be described as having "inner strength"—being flexible and able to bend but hard to break, especially during hardships. However, he worries that low self-concepts among Asian American students still exist.

Lian (1992) contends that the "melting pot" concept tends to force culturally and linguistically diverse students to assume Caucasian culture and language are priorities for learning and living. If the student does not learn well, he or she may be labeled a slow learner or even removed from the mainstream classroom. Such students may thus have lower self-esteem and expectations for educational achievement.

Leung (1990) indicates six major concerns related to educating Asian American students: physical differences, linguistic differences, culture-based differences, acculturation dilemmas (adjustment problems), identity crises, and uninformed and insensitive significant others. According to Leung, an example is provided when Asian American students speak their native language at school and other children laugh. It is not unusual for a child in this situation to say, "Mom, don't speak Chinese! It's embarrassing."

Like adults, students in the schools may face cultural differences and conflicts between the Asian American community and other ethnic populations. Lian and Poon-McBrayer (1998) suggest "Asian American youth may struggle with a number of issues such as racism and conflicts with traditional values" (p. 18). In a study by Poon-McBrayer (1996), teachers overwhelmingly reported that students from Asian American families tend to concentrate more on academic subject matter in school than do their nonAsian peers. However, Feldman and Rosenthal (1990) note that Asian American youth may often be torn by pressures associated with demands to conform to diametrical values: the Western notion of individualism and the traditional Asian value of collectivism. According to Rick and Forward (1992), Asian youth perceive themselves to be less connected to parental value systems as they become more acclimated to U.S. norms. This phenomenon is logically more apparent between the first-generation immigrant parents and the U.S.-born, second-generation youth. Cultural conflicts and linguistic differences between these parents and youth are more frequently found and severe than if the parents themselves were also U.S.-born. Other variables that may affect the severity of conflicts and differences between Asian parents and youth include the education of parents, where they received their education, parents' length of stay in the U.S., and their level of acculturation.

In U.S. schools, maintaining eye contact with the teacher during instructional activities is emphasized whereas Asian American students are told at home that it is rude to stare at or to look into the eyes of an adult whom they respect (Lian, 1995). Direct eye contact may give Asian American parents or teachers the impression that the child disagrees or wants to argue with them, or is showing disrespect toward them. Such a response, from an adult perspective, represents a serious behavioral problem. At the same time, teachers may find that Asian American students show politeness by standing while parents, teachers, or elderly persons sit and by remaining quiet or silent when adults are talking.

Asian American children may exhibit learning and response patterns that appear to be unusual in U.S. schools. In the classroom, Asian American children may feel more comfortable answering a yes-no question instead of an open-ended question. Also, in addition to "yes" and "no" answers, children may select the third choice—silence, which may mean yes, no, agree, disagree, no answer, no comment, didn't understand the question, or waiting for the answer to come up by itself (e.g., the teacher or other children eventually will answer the question). Heward and Orlansky (1992) state that "the toughest thing a teacher of Asian students must deal with is the silence; its reasons are complex" (p. 510).

Instead of showing and telling, an Asian American child in the classroom may define "sharing" as listening quietly. In addition, teachers may observe that Asian American children find it difficult to talk about their own achievement, to ask for or offer help, to ask questions in class, to answer a teacher's questions, or to express their own opinion (Brower, 1983). Teachers should avoid the conclusion that Asian American children are less active in classroom learning activities. This is especially true for a new, non- or limited-English-speaking child who may exhibit a great deal of silence in class.

Asian American children may show another type of passive resistance. When an Asian American child is selected to represent his or her class in an activity, the child may feel that his or her friends are more deserving of the honor and decline. This passive resistance should not be interpreted as a lack of willingness to volunteer.

A general autonomy issue also exists among Asian American children. Research indicates that Asian American children may take a few more years than European American children to become independent. Asian American parents may provide their children with extensive care, which often means doing as many nonacademic chores for them as possible. Asian American children may also rely heavily on adults for decision making. Asian American parents may expect their child's major responsibility in school to be to concentrate on academics, to study and to get good grades.

Uniqueness in Educating Asian American Children

Asian American students have unique cultural and linguistic backgrounds. Families of these students have special traditions and values affecting their daily life, including education. Members of Asian American families generally have a strong respect for parents, the elderly, teachers, scholars, tradition, and the educational system, thinking of them as authorities. Asian American children are usually taught to be obedient and cooperative, to be dependent at home and in school, and to express unconditional loyalty to their ethnic community. As Barrett-Schuler (1997) notes,

In sharp contrast to the Western emphasis on the individual, collectivist societies predominate in Asia. Individualism is viewed rather negatively in countries such as China and Japan. They have hierarchy-sensitive traditions with collectivist mentalities. (p. 165)

Education, in the eyes of Asian American parents, is of extremely high value and is perceived to be the vehicle for upward mobility. Heward and Olansky (1992) describe the influence of such a perception of education:

For many years, teachers and scholars have been revered in China and other Asian countries. For parents influenced by their traditional cultural heritage, no sacrifice is too great to obtain a good education for their children. From the child's view point, scholastic achievement is the highest tribute one could bring to his or her parents and family. . . . This philosophy and work ethic has helped many Asian American students excel in schools. (p. 507)

Most Asian American parents and families value and support the education of their children. In fact, Chen (1989) identifies Chinese parental support and commitment as two of the major strengths and assets in the education of Chinese American children. However, educators need to be aware of the incongruencies between nonAsian teachers' expectations and Asian American parents' expectations (Cheng, 1987). In U.S. schools, students are encouraged by teachers to participate actively in classroom discussion and activities, while Asian American students may be told by their parents to "behave," i.e., to be quiet and obedient at school. Students may be encouraged by nonAsian teachers to be creative, while Asian American parents may think that students should be told what to do. In U.S. schools, students learn through inquiry and debate, while Asian American students may prefer to study and place their trust in what the teacher says and what is written in the textbooks, i.e., to learn through memorization. NonAsian teachers may believe Asian American students generally do well on their own, while Asian American parents may think the teacher's role is to teach and the student's job is to "study." In a U.S. school, critical thinking and analytical thinking are perceived to be important, while Asian American parents may believe that it is more important to learn the existing facts. Students' creativity and fantasies are encouraged by nonAsian teachers, while Asian American parents may perceive factual information to be much more important than imagination. Problem-solving skills are emphasized in U.S. schools, while Asian American parents may want their children to be taught the exact steps required to solve problems. In U.S. classrooms, students need to ask questions, while Asian American parents and their children may try not to ask questions, thinking that teachers should not be challenged. The teacher may think of reading as a way of discovering, while Asian American parents may think of reading as the decoding of information and facts.

Many Asian Americans believe and follow the thoughts of Confucianism, Buddhism, and/or Christianity, in which moral behaviors and a sense of forgiveness are strictly emphasized. Asian Americans also tend to rely on the *Yin-Yang philosophy*. Yin-Yang means a contrast between two extremes such as darkness and brightness, femininity and masculinity, interior and exterior, fast pace and slow pace, and happiness and sadness. Asian Americans tend to seek harmony and equilibrium between two distinct phenomena, feelings, or theories (Chan, 1998). In other words, Asians Americans may avoid either extreme or criticism of the opposite point of view. They may try to stay at the neutral-point in a controversial issue and attempt to make both sides in an argument happy—to avoid competition, conflict, and the related debate, and to work out a compromise. Asian Americans try to avoid conflict with nature. Many tend to accept their fate and do nothing to change it or create a "new" fate. This contrasts with the fighting-for-rights effort prevalent in the United States.

While differences between the Asian American culture and the majority culture may create educational obstacles, Asian American traditions and values significantly contribute to diversity in U.S. schools and society. Heward and Orlansky (1992) state that a great strength of the United States is cultural diversity. Our society is made up of immigrants from many lands, and we have all benefited from the contributions of the many ethnic groups. It is the educators' responsibility to attend to the Asian American heritage and the unique educational needs of children from the Asian American population.

Parents of Asian American Children

Asian American parents play a significant role in the education of their children. Most parents of Asian American children tend to treasure education and respect teachers and scholars highly, expecting high standards and academic achievement from educators. A Thai American parent, for example, may want his or her child to be educated to become an "ideal student" with the following traits (Sriratana, 1995):

1. values
   - to be well-rounded and honest,
   - to have confidence,
   - to be trustworthy and have integrity,
   - to have courage and dare to attempt difficult tasks and challenges,
   - to be peaceful, calm, and serene when dealing with conflict, and to be self-reliant and well-disciplined;
2. giving
   - to be dependable and loyal to family,
   - to respect life, property, and nature,
   - to love friends and neighbors,
   - to be sensitive to others' needs and feelings and to be unselfish,
   - to be kind and friendly, and
   - to act with justice and mercy.

However, Asian American families are generally reluctant to convey their expectations to teachers. Dao (1994), for example, reports that

> Hmong, Cambodian and Lao parents tend not to speak up . . . because of a cultural politeness and respect toward the professional, who is seen as the expert. They don't want to insult him or her by asking too much—even though they have a right and even though the question or observation might help the professional. (p. 15)

This may lead to a reluctance to indicate when they need help. For instance, advocacy may be difficult for Asian American families to understand and engage in for a person with disabilities.

Asian American parents may also be unaware of how to participate actively in PTO or other school activities. Instead of concluding these parents are less willing to volunteer for school activities, it may be more appropriate to assume that they need more time to get acquainted or become comfortable with the U.S. school system, or that they might need to be informed or provided with information and opportunities before they become active volunteers to support school programs.

In the Asian American community, there is also general concern for "face." To challenge the educational system may not be acceptable because it causes trouble and, even worse, causes school administrators and teachers to lose "face." Parents and other family members may apologize repeatedly, worrying that they have bothered the school too much if they make requests for services.

Dao (1994) lists potential barriers that may prevent Southeast Asian American parents from accessing services:

- fear of persecution as a result of the experience in the war against the communists in Vietnam, Laos, and Cambodia;
- self-reliance which may cause Asian American families to be the main caregivers of children with special education needs, to solve educational problems, and to fulfill needs within the families;
- limited English proficiency which may slow the assessment process and cause a delay of service;
- a tendency to trust the psychoeducational system and authority and not to question;
- a perception and expectation based on a disabling condition, e.g., feeling of guilt;
- lack of training and experience in evaluating their child's progress and achievement;
- cultural and custom differences, e.g., trying not to be demanding, not to advocate, or to avoid court actions; and
- general misunderstanding on the part of the Asian American families.

Asian American parents may have different perceptions of a child's failure in school. Lynch (1994) identifies three educational failure paradigms perceived by Asian American parents:

1. *child deficit orientation* (the medical model)—the cause of failure resides within the child's physical body.
2. *environmental deficit orientation* (the behavioral model)—since behavior is learned, children fail as a result of inappropriate or inadequate environmental circumstances in which to learn;
3. *contextual or sociological paradigm*—learning and behavioral problems are not a result of within-child deficits or environmental inadequacies, but the product of inappropriate child-environment interactions.

Asian American parents may also misunderstand English-as-a-second-language (ESL) programs, or other educational support systems for limited-English-proficient (LEP) students, thinking that the ESL program is a type of special education program for slow learners and, thus, shameful for their children to be involved in. In addition, parents may be concerned their children are missing classes in other subject areas because of the pull-out for ESL instruction. Actually, ESL programs provide significant benefits for LEP students through individualized assistance to enhance their English language skills (San, 1992).

Professionals must be sensitive to each family's values and not judge the family based upon social status—poor or rich, educated or not. Nor should they assume the family knows the law or the educational system. Lian and Aloia (1994) recommend teachers utilize internal and external resources to support parents with specific needs related to the education of their children. Significant *internal resources* of parents include the degree of perceived control of the parenting situation, the extended family, parental relationships, health, energy, morale, and spiritual perspectives, problem-solving skills, and available financial and related resources. School personnel may also utilize *external resources* of parents, such as friends, neighbors, professionals, and community agencies and organizations, to meet parental concerns and fulfill their need to see their children successfully involved in the school program.

Suggestions for Teachers

When teaching and learning in a culturally and linguistically diverse environment, teachers and students should try not only to prevent stereotypes and prejudice, but they should also utilize more appropriate and less restrictive approaches in their teaching and learning activities (Lian 1990). Three different approaches may be implemented when teachers and culturally and linguistically diverse children interact with each other—aggressive, assertive, and passive.

The *aggressive approach* tends to be used by teachers and students who consider certain things only to be for themselves. For example, an aggressive teacher may view a culturally and linguistically diverse student as a burden on the class or a mismatch with other students. The teacher may determine that this student should "go back to where he or she belongs" or that the student deserves a lower grade in classroom evaluations. An aggressive nonAsian student may perceive Asian American students to be followers instead of leaders. Other aggressive stances to be made by some members of the nonAsian populations are expressed in statements such as: "Orientals are not good at sanitation," "They are always late for their appointments," and "They speak broken English or 'Chinglish'." Asian American students and their parents may also be aggressive. For example, parents might tell their children who are attacked by nonAsian peers that, "The only way for you to survive in this country is to fight back."

The *passive approach* is the opposite of the aggressive approach. A passive teacher or student may decide there is no need to deal with the issue because "everything is going to be all right." Persons using a passive approach may think totally for others, blame themselves, and "swallow" the complaint or the unfair situation.

The *assertive approach* represents an effort to consider both sides—one's own and that of one's counterpart. Persons utilizing the assertive approach may conduct rational thinking and find the balance point to understand and handle issues. They engage in a thoughtful evaluation of the situation, find each individual's needs and concerns, and fulfill as many personal and group goals as possible.

The following are general suggestions for teaching Asian American students.

Accept Asian American students as they are. A teacher needs to understand, accept, and appreciate students who are from Asian American cultural and linguistic backgrounds. Efforts must be made to develop an awareness of these students' specific needs, learning styles, and response patterns. Teachers must let the students work at their own pace and assure that major learning objectives are mastered. The major concepts children are to learn may be presented in different ways and then followed by the teacher giving repeated review. Teachers should avoid frustration, while encouraging students to think things out instead of supplying answers too quickly. Overall, teachers need to create learning environments which fit the students and not simply to ask the students to fit the school.

Strive to achieve unbiased assessment. Asian American students may be at-risk for socially, culturally, and linguistically biased assessment, educational placement, and instructional activities that may lead to misunderstandings, fewer opportunities, and lower expectations. School administrators and teachers need to help these students by providing opportunities to learn and achieve their maximum potential. Cheng (1991) suggests Asian American students be observed over time by the teacher in multiple contexts with various interactants to obtain a better understanding of their response patterns to different individuals and situations. Maker, Nielson, and Rogers (1994) suggest the use of the approaches of *multiple intelligence assessment* to prevent underestimating culturally and linguistically diverse children's giftedness and problem-solving abilities. A *portfolio assessment* system is highly recommended for limited-English-proficient students. Examples of various types of student work, such as art work, creative writing, math exercises, and book reports completed at different times, are collected to provide a more reliable evaluation of their ability, performance, and learning progress.

Promote meaningful communication. Teachers of new Asian American students should enunciate clearly, avoid speaking too quickly or too slowly, and use gestures to reinforce oral language, but not to replace it. Teachers should not introduce too much new information in one sentence; they should write on the chalk board or paper frequently to reinforce key terms and concepts. Also, the experiences they incorporate into lessons should be familiar to the students. Teachers should start out by asking yes-no questions and work up to "wh" questions (i.e., what, when, where, why, and how). Teachers should not assume a "yes" necessarily means the student has understood. They should praise the student's efforts and model the correct forms in both written and oral language.

In addition, meaningful communication should be facilitated between Asian American students and their parents, so they can reach consensus on appropriate value systems and mutual expectations (Lian, 1995; *The World Journal*, 1997). As indicated by Lian and Poon-McBrayer (1997), "The fact that more than half of the youth expressed a wish for parents to listen to them and trust them more while 90% of parents expressed that they trusted their children may confirm the need for better communication" (p. 20).

Develop new curricula. Kim (1993) suggests teachers should develop new curricula that will focus on life experiences of Asian Americans and their structural position in the United States. Major issues, such as immigration patterns, ethnic diversity among Asian American groups, socioeconomic diversity within groups, high and low educational achievement, experiences of discrimination and civil rights violations, and the complexity of family life, should be addressed.

Many local schools are still at the stage of emphasizing Asian foods and festivals as the major elements of Asian culture to which students are exposed. The multicultural education curriculum should include in-depth discussion of Asian families' traditions and values. It should help all students to develop more positive attitudes toward diverse cultural, racial, ethnic, and religious groups and to consider the perspectives of other groups (Banks, 1989).

Promote cooperative learning. Children learn quickly and effectively from each other. Teachers need to facilitate opportunities and encourage learning through cooperation. Cooperative learning assignments start with concrete and simple game-oriented projects. In such projects, an Asian American student will have the chance to take a role in which he or she feels competent and comfortable. Gradually, the teacher can move onto more complicated and abstract projects through which an Asian American student can increase his or her participation, contribution, and leadership.

Adopt collaborative teaching. Sadker and Sadker (1994) suggest that teaching be done in collaboration with other educators. Contemporary schools are more complicated than ever before, dealing with such issues as bilingual and multilingual special education services, limited English proficiency, low self-esteem, family crises, and poverty. A teacher cannot stand alone. He or she needs to be assisted and supported by experienced educators and professionals from various disciplines, for example, social work, counseling, nursing, and teacher education (Farra, Klitzkie, & Bretania-Schafer, 1994).

Summary

Asian American children are a special group of learners who bring unique cultural and linguistic backgrounds to U.S. schools. They have special traditions and values as well as learning styles which may significantly enrich school programs and society in general. These students may also have unique educational needs. Teachers of Asian American students will need to understand each individual student's attributes and learn to implement instructional strategies and contents which provide the optimal benefits and educational outcomes for these special learners.

References

Banks, J. A. (1989). Multicultural education: Characteristics and goals. In J. A. Banks & C. A. M. Banks (Eds.), *Multicultural Education: Issues and Perspectives* (pp. 2-26). Boston: Allyn & Bacon.

Barrett-Schuler, B. (1997). Module for Asian studies: The impact of culture on business behavior. In J. Q. Adams & J. R. Welsch (Eds.), *Multicultural prism: Voices from the field* (vol. 3) (pp. 159-177). Macomb, IL: Illinois Staff and Curriculum Developers Association.

Brower, I. C. (1983). Counseling Vietnamese. In D. R. Atkinson, G. Morten & D. W. Sue (Eds.), *Counseling American Minorities* (2nd ed.) (pp. 107-121): Dubuque, IA: William C. Brown.

Chan, S. (1998). Families with Asian roots. In E. W. Lynch & M. J. Hanson (Eds.), *Developing cross-cultural competence* (2nd ed.) (pp. 252-343). Baltimore, MD: Paul H. Brookes.

Chen, V. L. (1989). Know thyself: Self-concept of Chinese American youths. *Asian Week*, 8-9.

Cheng, L. L. (1987). *Assessing Asian language performance: Guidelines for evaluating limited English-proficient students.* Rockville, MD: Aspen Publishers.

Cheng, L. L. (1991). *Assessing Asian language performance: Guidelines for evaluating LEP students* (2nd ed.). Oceanside, CA: Academic Communication Associates.

Cheng, L. L., Ima, K., & Labovitz, G. (1994). Assessment of Asian and Pacific Islander students for gifted programs. In S. B. Garcia (Ed.). *Addressing cultural and linguistic diversity in special education* (pp. 30-45). Reston, VA: Council for Exceptional Children.

Dao, X. (1994, Winter/Spring). More Southeast Asian parents overcoming barriers to service. *Pacesetter,* 15.

Farra, H. E., Klitzkie, L. P., & Bretania-Schafer, N. (1994). Limited English proficient, bilingual, and multicultural special education students: Implications for teacher education and service delivery. *International Journal of Special Education, 9*(2), 128-134.

Feldman, S.S., & Rosenthal, D.A. (1990). The acculturation of autonomy expectations in Chinese high schoolers residing in two western nations. *International Journal of Psychology, 25,* 259-281.

Heward, W. L., & Orlansky, M. D. (1992). *Exceptional children: An introductory survey of special education* (3rd ed.). Columbus, OH: Merrill.

Hu-DeHart, E. (1999, April 20). *How to recruit and retain Asian American students at American colleges and universities.* Keynote speech at the MECCPAC Workshop, Illinois State University, Normal, IL.

Kim, S. (1993). Understanding Asian Americans: A new perspective. In J. Q. Adams & J. R. Welsch (Eds.), *Multicultural Education: Strategies for Implementation in Colleges and Universities* (pp. 83-91). Macomb, IL: Illinois Staff and Curriculum Developers Association. [See this volume, pp. 145-156 for a revision of this essay.]

Leung, E. K. (1990). Early risk: Transition from culturally/linguistically diverse homes to formal schooling. *The Journal of Educational Issues of Language Minority Students, 7,* 35-49.

Lian, M-G. J. (1990). Enhancing ethnic/cultural minority involvement. *TASH Newsletter, 16*(5), 1-2.

Lian, M-G. J. (1992). *Project TCLDSD: Teaching culturally and linguistically diverse students with disabilities.* Unpublished software program, Illinois State University, Normal, IL.

Lian, M-G. J. (1995, September). Education of Chinese-American students: Trends, issues, and recommendations. In A.M. Hue, C. Hwang, J. Huang & S. Peng (Eds.), *The 3rd annual national conference program proceedings of the Chinese-American educational research and development association* (pp. 155- 169). Chicago: Chinese-American Educational Research and Development Association.

Lian, M-G. J., & Aloia, G. (1994). Parental responses, roles, and responsibilities. In S. Alper, P. J. Schloss, & C. N. Schloss (Eds.), *Families of persons with disabilities: Consultation and advocacy* (pp. 51-93). Boston: Allyn & Bacon.

Lian, M-G.J., & Poon-McBrayer, K. F. (1998, June). General perceptions of school and home among Asian American students and their parents. *New Wave—Educational Research and Development, 3*(3), 18-20.

Luke, B. S. (1987). *An Asian American perspective.* Seattle, WA: REACH Center for Multi-cultural and Global Education.

Lynch, J. (1994). *Provision for children with special educational needs in the Asia region.* Washington, DC: World Bank.

Maker, C. J., Nielson, A. B., & Rogers, J. A. (1994). Giftedness, diversity, and problem-solving. *Teaching Exceptional Children, 27*(1), 4-17.

Ong, N. T., & Hee, S. (1993). The growth of the Asian Pacific American population: Twenty million in 2020. In *The state of Asian Pacific America: A public policy report: Policy issues to the year 2020.* Los Angeles: LEAP Asian Pacific American Public Policy Institute and UCLA Asian American Studies Center.

Pang, V. O. (1997). Caring for the whole child: Asian Pacific American students. In J. J. Irvine (Ed.), *Critical knowledge for diverse teachers and learners* (pp. 149-189). Washington, DC: American Association of Colleges for Teacher Education.

Poon-McBrayer, K. F. (1996). Profiles of Asian American students with learning disabilities. *Dissertation Abstracts International, 58*(01), 65. (University Microfilms No. 9719430)

Rick, K., & Forward, J. (1992). Acculturation and perceived intergenerational differences among youth. *Journal of Cross-Cultural Psychology, 23*(1), 85-94.

Sadker, M. P., & Sadker, D. M. (1994). *Teachers, schools, and society* (3rd ed.). New York: McGraw-Hill.

San. (1992, June 14). Don't misunderstand ESL. *The World Journal, 25*.

Sriratana, P. (1995). *Education in Thailand: Past, present and future*. Paper presented at the Thailand Culture and Heritage Night, Illinois State University, Normal, IL.

The World Journal. (1997, July 23). How much do parents understand their children? Author, B1.

U.S. Census Bureau. (1997a). *Statistical abstract of the United States* (117th ed.). Washington, DC: U.S. Government Printing Office.

U.S. Census Bureau. (1997b, March). *The Asian and Pacific Islander population in the United States* (Document #P20-512). Washington, DC: U.S. Government Printing Office.

Wakabayashi, R. (1997). Unique problems of handicapped Asian Americans. In *The White House conference on handicapped individuals* (vol. 1) (pp. 429-432). Washington, DC: U.S. Government Printing Office.

CLIMATE, CO-CURRICULAR ACTIVITIES, AND ASSESSMENT

DIVERSITY AND MULTICULTURALISM ON THE CAMPUS: HOW ARE STUDENTS AFFECTED?

by
Alexander W. Astin

Amidst debates over multiculturalism, diversity, and political correctness by academics and the news media, claims and counterclaims about the dangers and benefits of multiculturalism have abounded, but so far little hard evidence has been produced to support any of these claims. Most of the "evidence" injected into the debate thus far is of a purely anecdotal nature, with the veracity of the ancedotes cited by critics on one side of the argument usually disputed by critics on the other side.

As a political animal, I might have certain strong views about multiculturalism—whether it is a good or a bad idea—but as an educator and a researcher, my most important question about multiculturalism and diversity is how students are affected by campus policies and practices. I recently had the opportunity to examine this question empirically in a major national study of undergraduates attending 217 four-year colleges and universities. Published this year [1993], the study involved 82 outcome measures on 25,000 students who entered college as freshmen in the fall of 1985 and were followed up four years later in 1989. It also included data that enabled us to determine how much each institution emphasized diversity and multiculturalism, and measures of each individual student's direct experience with diversity and multiculturalism.

The following analysis of this study addresses several pertinent questions: How are students' values and beliefs about other races and cultures affected by their institutions' policies on diversity and multiculturalism? What difference does it make in students' attitudes and behavior when their professors emphasize diversity issues in the classroom or in their research? How are students' academic progress and values affected by direct involvement in "diversity" experiences?

Method

The basic purpose of this research project was to determine how various student outcomes are affected by environments. The larger study of student development, which provides the data for the findings reported here, included 82 different student outcome measures covering a wide range of cognitive and affective development: attitudes, values, beliefs, aspirations, and career plans, as well as measures of undergraduate achievement and degree completion and scores on nationally standardized tests such as the GRE, MCAT, and LSAT. Since many of these outcomes were pre-tested when the students entered college as freshmen and post-tested four years later, we can determine how students actually changed during the four years. The study also incorporated more than 190 measures of the students' environmental experiences, including characteristics of the curriculum, faculty, and student peer group (for details, see Astin, 1993). Of particular relevance to this article are seven environmental measures reflecting a) the institution's and its faculty's policies on diversity issues and b) the student's direct experience with diversity and multiculturalism at the institution. Given the centrality of these seven environmental measures to the issue of diversity on campus, more detailed discussion of each is in order.

Measures of Diversity/Multiculturalism

The study incorporated three types of environmental measures relating to issues of diversity or multiculturalism: Institutional Diversity Emphasis, Faculty Diversity Emphasis, and Student Diversity Experiences (five measures).

The first two measures are based on the responses of the faculty at each of the 217 institutions to an extensive questionnaire administered during the 1989-90 academic year. The mean faculty responses to a large number of questionnaire items were computed and then factor analyzed in order to identify clusters of items that "go together" as determined by the patterns of faculty responses. Environmental measures for any institution were then obtained by averaging the responses of its faculty separately for each cluster of questions. Institutional Diversity Emphasis, for example, reflects the extent to which faculty believe that their institution is committed to each of the following five goals:

1. to increase the number of minority faculty;
2. to increase the number of minority students;
3. to create a diverse multicultural environment;
4. to increase the number of women faculty;
5. to develop an appreciation for multiculturalism.

By looking at the faculty's perception of the degree of institutional emphasis on diversity and multiculturalism, as one might guess, a considerable variation emerges among the 217 institutions in their degree of emphasis on diversity.

Faculty Diversity Emphasis is defined in terms of four other questionnaire items, which also were shown by the factor analyses to produce similar response patterns:

1. instructional technique that incorporates readings on women and gender issues;
2. instructional technique that incorporates readings on racial and ethnic issues;
3. research or writing focused on women or gender;
4. research or writing focused on racial or ethnic minorities.

Note that Faculty Diversity Emphasis is based on the faculty's own scholarly and pedagogical practices, while Institutional Diversity Emphasis reflects the faculty's perceptions of the overall institutional climate. The latter measure presumably reflects not only faculty values and behavior, but also the policies of the administration and possibly even the trustees. As would be expected, these two environmental measures are substantially correlated ($r = .55$), which means simply that faculty who emphasize diversity issues in their teaching and research are likely to be found in institutions that also emphasize diversity and multiculturalism in their admissions and hiring policies. However, the fact that the correlation is far from perfect indicates that there are some institutions where the institutional emphasis on diversity is strong but where the faculty do not emphasize diversity issues in their teaching or research and, conversely, some institutions where the reverse pattern occurs. The two measures, in other words, are not completely interchangeable.

Student Diversity Experiences were measured in terms of five items from the follow-up questionnaire completed by the 25,000 students during the 1989-90 academic year. Each of these items is treated separately in the analysis:

1. took ethnic studies courses;
2. took women's studies courses;

3. attended racial/cultural awareness workshops;
4. discussed racial or ethnic issues;
5. socialized with someone from another racial/ethnic group.

Analysis of Environmental Effects

The method used for analyzing the effects of these seven environmental variables on the 82 student outcomes has been described in detail in earlier works (Astin, 1991, 1993). Pre-tests and other entering student characteristics assessed in 1985 are controlled first by means of stepwise regression analyses, after which the possible effects of environmental variables are examined. Basically, the analyses are designed to "match" students statistically in terms of their entering characteristics before evaluating the effects of environmental variables on the outcome measures obtained four years later. In effect, this method attempts to determine whether students change differently under differing environmental circumstances.

Before discussing the specific findings from these analyses, it should be mentioned that 26 of the 82 outcome measures were specifically identified as directly relevant to the goals of general education as spelled out in the considerable literature on this subject (Astin, 1992). These 26 goals include a variety of cognitive and academic outcomes, as well as completion of the baccalaureate degree, interest in and enrollment in graduate study, and several value and attitudinal measures. In reporting the findings, I pay special attention to these 26 measures because one of the critical policy questions is whether or not the overall goals of general education are facilitated by emphasizing diversity and multiculturalism.

Institutional Diversity Emphasis

The effects of Institutional Diversity Emphasis are of some practical as well as theoretical interest, since the factors that make up this environment measure are presumably under the direct control of the institution. Its strongest positive effects are on two outcomes: cultural awareness and commitment to promoting racial understanding. Cultural awareness is one of the developmental outcomes that was identified as particularly relevant to the goals of most general education programs. It is based on the students' estimate of how much their undergraduate experience has enhanced their understanding and appreciation of other races and cultures. The fact that a strong emphasis on diversity enhances the students' commitment to promoting racial understanding is of special interest, given that some critics have alleged that emphasizing issues of race and multiculturalism tends to exacerbate racial tensions on the campus. Quite the opposite seems to be the case.

Emphasizing diversity also has positive effects on several measures of student satisfaction with the college experience: overall satisfaction, as well as satisfaction with student life, opportunities to take interdisciplinary courses, facilities, and the quality of instruction. Institutional Diversity Emphasis also has positive effects on political liberalism, libertarianism, and participation in student protests.

Consistent with its positive effect on the students' personal commitment to promoting racial understanding, Institutional Diversity Emphasis has a negative effect on the belief that racial discrimination is no longer a problem in America. It also has negative effects on the students' chances of joining a social fraternity or sorority, or getting married while in

383

college, and on the belief that the chief benefit of college is to increase earning power. This last measure is another outcome judged as relevant to the goals of most general education programs, since such programs would hopefully weaken the students' tendency to see liberal learning in strictly instrumental or monetary terms.

What, then, are the consequences for students who are associated with a strong institutional emphasis on issues of diversity and multiculturalism? If one were to attach values to the outcomes just discussed, emphasizing diversity appears to have uniformly positive effects, not only on those outcomes that are relevant to the goals of general education—heightened cultural awareness and satisfaction and reduced materialism—but also on the students' commitment to promoting racial understanding. The positive effect on political liberalism could be judged as either a plus or minus, given one's own political preferences. The same goes for participation in campus protests, which might be considered by some as a negative outcome. However, to render such a judgment, it is first necessary to determine what effects protest participation itself has on the students' subsequent development. This issue will be addressed shortly.

Faculty Diversity Emphasis

Faculty Diversity Emphasis produces a pattern of effects that is very similar to the pattern associated with Institutional Diversity Emphasis. The strongest positive effects are on cultural awareness and overall satisfaction with the college experience. Faculty Diversity Emphasis also had a positive effect on the students' chances of voting in the 1988 presidential election. This item was included as a measure of "citizenship," another of the 26 outcomes that were included among the goals of general education.

That Faculty Diversity Emphasis and Institutional Diversity Emphasis produce very similar patterns of effects does not mean that these two measures are entirely redundant. Both measures, for example, produced independent effects on cultural awareness, overall satisfaction, and participation in campus protests. By "independent," we mean that the faculty's focus on diversity issues contributes to these outcomes over and above the contribution of the overall institutional emphasis.

Direct Student Experience with Diversity

Let us now consider the effects of individual Student Diversity Experiences. Even though these "effects" were obtained only after all student input and faculty environmental measures were controlled for, the fact that the student experiences occurred after the student actually enrolled in college requires that we interpret these effects with caution. Even so, the pattern and results are very interesting.

Critics of political correctness have focused much of their attack on efforts to diversify the curriculum. Our data base included two items bearing on this issue: the number of ethnic studies courses and the number of women's studies courses taken by the students during their undergraduate years. These two measures produced almost identical patterns of effects on student outcomes. The strongest positive effects were on cultural awareness and commitment to promoting racial understanding, as well as a commitment to helping clean up the environment. There were also weaker, but still significant, positive effects on participation in campus protests, political liberalism, listening ability, foreign language skills, and attendance at recitals and concerts. Only one outcome was negatively associated with taking ethnic or women's studies courses: the belief that racial discrimination is no longer a problem in America. Once again, taking ethnic studies or women's studies courses is associated with a wide range of generally positive outcomes rather than alienating students of different races from each other.

Another controversial issue concerns whether the campus administration should sponsor "cultural awareness" workshops designed to enhance racial/cultural understanding among students from different backgrounds. A large number of outcomes are significantly associated with attending such workshops: commitment to promoting racial understanding, participating in campus demonstrations, cultural awareness, and social activism. Of particular interest is that participation in such workshops is positively associated with undergraduate retention (completion of the bachelor's degree) as well as with six different measures of satisfaction with various aspects of the undergraduate experience and six different measures of academic development (critical thinking, general knowledge, public speaking ability, listening ability, writing ability, and preparation for graduate school). Participation in racial/cultural awareness workshops has negative effects on materialistic values and on two beliefs: that racial discrimination is no longer a problem and that the individual can do little to change society. This last item was included among our 82 outcomes as a measure of "empowerment," the student's sense that he or she can actually make a difference through individual effort and dedication. In effect, participating in such workshops appears to strengthen a student's sense of personal empowerment to effect societal change.

Another item from the list of individual Student Diversity Experiences was the frequency with which the student socialized with persons from different racial/ethnic groups. While this experience has its strongest positive effects on cultural awareness and commitment to promoting racial understanding, it also has significant positive associations with commitment to helping clean up the environment, attending recitals and concerts, and—most importantly—with practically all measures of the student's academic development and satisfaction with college. It has negative associations with the beliefs that racial discrimination is no longer a problem in America and that the individual can do little to change society. It is of some interest to note that socializing with persons from different racial/ethnic groups, in contrast to most of the other diversity experiences discussed so far, does not have positive effects either on political liberalism or on participation in campus protests.

Interestingly enough, the largest number of positive effects was associated with the frequency with which students discussed racial/ethnic issues during their undergraduate years. As would be expected, the strongest effects are on commitment to promoting racial understanding and cultural awareness. This item showed other positive and negative effects that closely follow the pattern associated with the other diversity variables. However, one of the strongest effects not found for most of these other diversity variables is the positive impact on the student's commitment to developing a meaningful philosophy of life. This value, which was also included among the 26 goals of general or liberal education, is what we call our "existential" value question. It was the most popular value question on surveys that we conducted in the early 1970s, but its importance to students has since dropped precipitously. That frequent discussions of racial/ethnic issues should appear to strengthen students' commitment to developing a philosophy of life is interesting and provocative. Could it be that issues of race, culture, and ethnicity represent promising curricular subject matter for confronting some of the existential dilemmas that many contemporary students seem to be avoiding?

Effects of Campus Activism

Since emphasizing diversity on the campus seems to enhance the likelihood that students will engage in some kind of protest activity during their undergraduate years, it is important to ask how activism itself affects the student's development. The strongest positive associations are with political liberalism, cultural awareness, and commitment to promoting racial understanding. In other words, individual participation in campus protest activities does not, as some critics would have us believe, serve to alienate students from each other. On the contrary, it seems to strengthen students' sense of cultural awareness and appreciation and to reinforce their commitment to promoting greater understanding between the races. Campus protest participation is also associated with strengthened commitment to helping clean up the environment and developing a meaningful philosophy of life, growth in artistic interests and leadership abilities, aspirations for advanced degrees, and increased chances of voting in a presidential election. Participating in campus protests is negatively associated with materialistic values and the beliefs that racial discrimination is no longer a problem and that the individual can do little to change society. About the only outcome associated with protest participation that might be considered negative is a positive effect on the student's degree of hedonism (defined in this study as drinking beer, smoking cigarettes, and staying up all night). Hedonism, it should be stressed, was not affected one way or the other by any of the environmental diversity measures or individual Student Diversity Experiences.

In short, participation in campus protest activities is associated with a pattern of outcomes that is quite similar to the pattern associated with diversity activities, with the exception of its positive effects on hedonism, voting in a presidential election, artistic inclination, leadership, and aspiration for advanced degrees.

Reflections

Through these analyses I have attempted to shed some new light on the heated debate over political correctness and multiculturalism on college campuses by seeking some empirical answers to the following questions: Does emphasizing or not emphasizing diversity issues have any real consequences for students? How are students actually affected by some of the policies and practices that conservative critics find so objectionable? The findings present a clear-cut pattern: emphasizing diversity either as a matter of institutional policy or in faculty research and teaching, as well as providing students with curricular and extracurricular opportunities to confront racial and multicultural issues, are all associated with widespread beneficial effects on a student's cognitive and affective development. In particular, such policies and experiences are associated with greater self-reported gains in cognitive and affective development (especially increased cultural awareness), with increased satisfaction in most areas of the college experience, and with increased commitment to promoting racial understanding. Emphasizing diversity and multiculturalism is also associated with increased commitment to environmental issues and with several other positive outcomes: leadership, participation in cultural activities, citizenship, commitment to developing a meaningful philosophy of life, and reduced materialistic values. If we confine our analyses just to outcomes that are relevant to the goals of most general education programs, the effects of emphasizing multiculturalism and diversity appear to be uniformly positive.

Perhaps the only outcome consistently associated with diversity variables that might be considered "negative" is the positive effect on participation in student protests. While protest activities are often seen by some faculty, and especially by campus administrators, as a nuisance or possibly even as detrimental to campus order and tranquility, engaging in such protests seems to be associated with generally positive outcomes for the individual student participating. It is also true that an emphasis on multiculturalism is associated with increases in the student's political liberalism, but how one chooses to value such an effect would depend on one's political orientation.

While these findings provide strong evidence supporting campus attempts to emphasize issues of diversity and multiculturalism, there are other aspects of the PC debate which we have not directly addressed in this study. One particularly touchy issue is speech codes. Perhaps the most bizarre and ironic aspect of the PC debate is that, when it comes to speech codes, people at the extremes of the political spectrum seem to have switched sides. Those on the left who have supported codes that outlaw racist and other forms of hateful speech and conduct on the campus come from the same political camp that has always championed first amendment rights and supported the dismantling of *in loco parentis*. At the same time, those on the political right who have, with the help of the news media, promoted the PC issue, come from a political perspective that has regularly advocated censorship in speech, writing, and the arts and that has endorsed restrictive codes of student conduct on the campus.

Ironically, the PC debate has once again underscored the critical importance of academic freedom and tenure in academia. Tenure, lest we forget, was established primarily to protect academic freedom. I am a living example of the necessity for tenure, since some of what I have to say in my writing and speechmaking does not fall on receptive ears in my own university. While I like to think of myself as a free thinker, there is a serious question in my mind as to whether I might be much more circumspect in what I say and do if there were no academic freedom and tenure. I might even be in a different line of research.

That emphasizing multiculturalism and diversity reinforces political liberalism on the campus, should come as no surprise. Nor should academics necessarily feel defensive or apologetic about such effects. The very values and traditions of academia naturally attract people of a liberal persuasion. An environment that places a high value on teaching, learning, discovery, artistic expression, independence of thought, critical thinking and freedom of speech and expression naturally tends to attract such people, since these are values that have traditionally been very important to people from the left. In the same way, the corporate and military worlds have tended to attract people from the right because business and the military have traditionally placed a high value on power, control, hierarchy, authority, capitalism, free enterprise, and making money.

Academics should more openly acknowledge that the PC critics are right when they claim that the expression of right-wing viewpoints is not warmly received in a liberal campus climate. What the PC critics themselves fail to do, however, is to make any distinction between the right to express a particular point of view and the right to have others agree with it. There is no such thing as a "right" to expect agreement. As a matter of fact, liberal academics don't even agree with each other on matters like speech codes and curricular reform. If the PC critics want people to agree with them, then they should look, instead, into conservative politics, corporate business, fundamentalist religion, or the military.

Despite the liberal leanings of most faculties, I would submit that in academia there is still far more tolerance shown for the expression of deviant viewpoints than in any other social institution. In other words, an employee in business, government, or the military has much less freedom of expression—especially when it comes to expressing deviant political viewpoints—than does an employee in academia. And this is as it should be. This is our tradition, our strength.

One thing that we tend to forget about academic freedom is that it is not merely an end in itself but that it has a larger purpose: the pursuit of truth. The link between academic freedom and the pursuit of knowledge is often overlooked in the PC debate, but the underlying logic is really very simple: the quickest and surest way to the truth is to encourage the expression of diverse points of view and to promote active discussion and debate of these different views. This is really what academic freedom is all about.

Related Readings

Astin, A. W. (1991). *Assessment for excellence: The philosophy and practice of assessment and evaluation in higher education.* Phoenix: Oryx.

Astin, A. W. (1992, Fall). What matters in general education: Provocative finding from a national study of student outcomes. *Perspectives, 22*(1), 23-46.

Astin, A. W. (1993). *What matters in college? Four critical years revisited.* San Francisco: Jossey-Bass.

ASSESSING THE IMPACT OF MULTICULTURAL CURRICULUM INITIATIVES IN COLLEGES AND UNIVERSITIES: RECENT ADVANCES

by
Patricia L. Francis

There is an urgent need for the issues, problems, successes, and failures important to the implementation of education that is multicultural to be objectively and systematically analyzed and discussed.

Grant, 1992, pp. 436-437

Over the last thirty years, education at the primary and secondary levels increasingly has reflected and promoted a multicultural perspective. This perspective, compared to earlier, "Anglo-conformity" models (Gordon, 1964), strives to enhance students' understanding of diversity and their knowledge of groups whose contributions to society generally have been ignored.

Similar changes have occurred at the college and university level, where attempts to integrate multicultural perspectives are frequently termed "curriculum transformation" or "curriculum infusion." Noting the proliferation of curriculum transformation projects implemented in the past decade (Michael & Thompson, 1995), authors have commented in particular on the great variety characterizing these efforts, which range from the development of a single course (White, 1994) to the transformation of entire academic programs (Wang, 1998). Similarly, there is no common philosophy underlying these efforts, although they do assume that education traditionally has stressed dominant group experiences and excluded the experiences of subordinate groups. Therefore, one goal of all curriculum transformation efforts is to challenge this exclusionary approach and produce a "reconstructed curriculum based on knowledge that refuses to privilege one group's experiences over another" (Collins, 1991, p. 368).

The present chapter reviews published assessment information from multicultural curriculum initiatives in our nation's colleges and universities. It is of special interest how this area of endeavor has progressed since Francis (1993) conducted a similar review six years ago. At that time, this author reached the following conclusions: 1) systematic assessment was the exception rather than the rule, with most available information descriptive and not evaluative; 2) most of the evaluative information that did exist had been produced in work on gender studies, as opposed to efforts to infuse issues related to race and ethnicity; and, 3) available data suggested that curriculum transformation efforts had generally benefitted faculty and students alike, using a relatively wide range of measures. The present chapter will test the current validity of these conclusions, based on a comprehensive search of the literature from 1993 to 1998. A related question involves the extent to which assessment of multicultural curriculum initiatives has become more sophisticated methodologically. That is, if there was an increase in the quantity of assessment activity during the time in question, was there also a corresponding increase in the quality of this activity? Evidence for such qualitative advances would include at the minimum increased concern regarding the reliability and validity of measures being utilized, the use of control or comparison groups, the employment of pre-test/post-test designs and longitudinal designs, and the utilization of more complex statistical techniques such as factor analysis or principal components analysis (Myers & Wells, 1995).

Assessing Multicultural Curriculum Initiatives in Higher Education: A Current Appraisal

In what is now viewed as a classic article on feminist approaches to evaluation in higher education, Tetreault (1985) lamented the lack of evaluative data emanating from projects to integrate gender issues into the college curriculum. To some extent, this situation reflected the overall status of assessment in higher education at that time. As Gray (1997) notes, however, within the last ten to fifteen years there has been "relentless" pressure for colleges and universities to carry out assessment activities, not because educational institutions are not efficient or effective enough, but because all organizations can improve their practices.

It may be especially important for those committed to multicultural education to contribute to higher education's current climate of accountability. That is, at a time when critics freely distort multiculturalism as political correctness (Cheney, 1992), curriculum transformation efforts that are not evaluated systematically may become increasingly more difficult for colleges to justify and, ultimately, to support. In short, assessment provides an excellent opportunity to demonstrate the value of these efforts to a liberal arts education and thus ensure their continued place in the curriculum.

The present section reviews available assessment information on curriculum transformation efforts at both the course and program levels. While there is an emphasis on research published since 1993, earlier studies are included if they were especially well done or if they played an important role overall in the multicultural evaluation literature. An effort was made to choose studies that are representative of the transformation literature, and which incorporate a wide range of measures, both quantitative and qualitative. Generally, these measures have focused on students' attitudes toward course or program content, changes in students' personal and skill development resulting from enrollment in courses or programs with multicultural perspectives, the attitudes of faculty who teach these courses, and students' evaluations of faculty and teaching effectiveness in these programs.

Assessment of Individual Courses

In one extensive study of students' attitudes, Hartung (1990) compared the reactions of students to required ethnic studies and women's studies courses with their reactions to other required general education courses. The results showed that, overall, ethnic studies and women's studies courses received the second most positive ranking. Instructors in these courses, however, received a relatively high proportion of personalized, negative comments (e.g., "man-hater," "reverse racist"), leading Hartung to conclude that ethnic studies and women's studies instructors are evaluated on dimensions other than teaching ability.

More recently, White (1994) provided a detailed analysis of students' evaluations of a course entitled the Psychology of Oppression. This course was designed specifically to demonstrate the effectiveness of an alternative approach to teaching about diversity, one which emphasized the social construction of race and gender, the ways these constructs are used as criteria for determining which groups will succeed, and theories of social change and liberation. White reported on two waves of assessment data, which indicated that students were extremely positive in their evaluations of course content, materials, and assignments and of class discussions.

Some intriguing information has been provided regarding the long-term impact of a course taught in the early 1970s at the University of North Florida entitled "Human Conflict in Black and White" (Kranz & Lund, 1998; Lund, Kranz, & Porter, 1998). Requirements for this course included small group discussions of racial issues, readings about race, personal journals about relevant experiences, and a live-in seven-day home stay with a family of another race. Retrospective studies conducted twenty years later found that students reported this course to be one of the most meaningful of their educational career, having a "notable, lasting impact" on their lives. In addition, subjects strongly recommended that similar courses be taught today, perhaps beginning at the high school level.

Investigators have also shown substantial interest in changes in students' personal development as a result of enrollment in multicultural courses, with much of this information provided from evaluations of gender studies courses. Bargad and Hyde (1991) developed the Feminist Identity Development Scale (FIDS) to assess individuals' conceptions of feminism and of themselves as feminists, and administered it to female students enrolled in women's studies courses. Compared to control subjects, these students reported more positive attitudes toward feminism and were more likely to view themselves as feminists after taking these courses. Taking a different approach, Pence (1992) developed the Attitudes Toward Men Scale (AMS) and administered it to women enrolled in women's studies courses using a pre-test/post-test design. These females showed a significant increase in their acceptance of nontraditional masculine behaviors in men as well as in positive attitudes toward men generally. According to Pence, these results dispel the idea that women's studies courses promote negative attitudes toward men, an argument that has been used by critics to marginalize these classes.

The positive impact of a women's studies curriculum is not limited to female students. Stake and Gerner (1987) reported that both men and women enrolled in women's studies courses showed significant positive changes in self-esteem scores as well as higher job motivation and certainty compared to students enrolled in non-women's studies classes. More recently, Stake, Roades, Rose, Ellis, and West (1994) evaluated the extent to which the women's studies curriculum promotes heightened feminist activism. Using a pre-test/post-test design, these authors compared male and female students enrolled in women's studies courses with two other groups, one in which the students were taking courses not affiliated with the women's studies program and one in which the students were taking courses from women's studies faculty but outside of the women's studies program. Using self-report measures, Stake et al. found that both males and females enrolled in the women's studies courses demonstrated greater participation in feminist activities compared to the other groups. A follow-up study by Stake and Rose (1994) with this same sample found that these differences were maintained up to nine months following completion of the courses.

Program Assessment

Since the early 1980s, numerous curriculum projects have been implemented in an effort to integrate multicultural issues at the program level. In one noteworthy early report, Schmitz (1984) described measures used in evaluating a gender integration project at Montana State University as well as the Northern Rockies Program on Women in the Curriculum, a consortium project. These measures included pre- and post-tests of students' perceptions of course content on women's issues, attitude changes in participating faculty compared to controls using the Attitudes Toward Women Scale (AWS) (Spence & Helmreich, 1972), classroom behaviors (e.g., modifications in language), self-reported increases in consciousness by faculty, and increased research activity by faculty on women's and gender issues. One year later, Schmitz, Dinnerstein and Mairs (1985) reported evaluative information obtained from these projects as well as from a transformation project at the University of Arizona. According to Schmitz et al., students reported an increase in content on women in target courses as well as a decrease in misconceptions about women. Further, faculty project participants demonstrated significant positive changes in AWS scores compared to controls, increased communication between faculty and administrators interested in women's scholarship, and greater awareness of gender bias in higher education.

More recently, Wang (1998) reported on the effectiveness of a multicultural curriculum developed for genetic counselor education intended to increase multicultural counseling competence. Using the Multicultural Awareness-Knowledge-Skills Survey, Wang found that 62 students enrolled in the program demonstrated significant gains in cross-cultural competence. Further, trend analyses measuring the longitudinal impact of the curriculum on multicultural competence were significant and positive.

To date, the most comprehensive assessment of curriculum transformation efforts at the program level has occurred through a FIPSE-supported project entitled "The Courage to Question: Women's Studies and Student Learning" (Musil, 1992a, 1992b). This project, which involved seven women's studies programs across a three-year period, was unique in that it was based on non-traditional notions of assessment. These ideas have best been presented by Shapiro (1988), who argues that traditional assessment is insufficiently eclectic and too inflexible to be useful in evaluating multicultural curricula. She notes that traditional assessment erroneously assumes that evaluation is a neutral process, is often based on exclusionary sampling techniques, and relies excessively on quantitative data. Instead, Shapiro proposes a system of "participatory" evaluation, in which evaluators make an effort to establish trust with those being evaluated, to include anyone who wants to provide feedback, and to use a mixture of quantitative and qualitative techniques. Shapiro's ideas correspond closely to Worell's (1996) notions about feminist research, which Worell advocates as an alternative to more conventional methodologies. According to Worell, feminist research poses a challenge to traditional scientific inquiry, with its emphasis on the lives and experiences of women; its inherent attention to language, asymmetrical power arrangements, and gender as an essential category of analysis; and its promotion of social action and societal change.

The assessment procedures utilized in the "Courage to Question" project are summarized in Musil (1992b), while its results can be found in Musil (1992a). It is far beyond the scope of this chapter to summarize these reports, but it should be noted that a thorough mix of assessment procedures was used. Qualitative data were collected through ethnographic techniques, transcripts and observations of class discussion, textual analysis, portfolios, and student/faculty interviews, while quantitative procedures were utilized in collecting information such as course/program enrollments and students' course-teacher evaluations. Also, while results varied across campuses, the evaluations showed generally that the women's studies programs were contributing significantly and positively to the participating campuses.

Assessment of Faculty and Teaching Effectiveness

A final issue to be addressed in this section involves students' evaluations of faculty members who teach courses from a multicultural perspective. Despite the negative findings reported above by Hartung (1990), these evaluations for the most part are highly positive. Capuzza (1992), in evaluating a communications studies course which integrated gender, race, and class issues, found that students especially enjoyed the course's atmosphere of tolerance and the opportunity to discuss personal experiences. Stake and Gerner (1987) suggest that students in women's studies courses benefit in particular from the more process-oriented techniques (e.g., student participation, egalitarian faculty-student relationships) that these instructors tend to use, a suggestion that is corroborated by evaluations of faculty who teach these courses. For example, Brown (1992) surveyed over 200 women's studies instructors and found that they attempted to provide a more democratic classroom atmo-sphere, grant more authority to students, encourage class participation, and lecture less in these classes. More recently, Okazaki (1998) presented a set of pedagogical approaches for teaching gender issues in Asian American psychology courses. According to this author, it is necessary for instructors in these kinds of classes to use multimedia resources and inter-disciplinary approaches to promote critical thinking about the complex interactions that exist between ethnicity and race, especially as they take place within larger social, political, and economic contexts. McLeod (1996), reviewing challenges facing teachers in multicul-tural classrooms at the community college level, concluded that multicultural curricula can be implemented most effectively through techniques such as literature-based instruction, thematic units, project-based learning, and alternative evaluation methods.

These findings support the notion that courses that infuse multicultural content are likely to be characterized by somewhat specialized pedagogical approaches compared to more traditional classes. As one specific example, Junn, Morton, and Yee (1995) reported on the effects of an in-class activity entitled the "gibberish" exercise, which had students selecting their membership to a dominant and non-dominant mythical culture and then participating in role playing and small group discussions. Cognitive, affective and behavioral measures were used to assess the effectiveness of the exercise. Overall, subjects reported becoming more sensitized to, appreciative of, and empathic toward other ethnic groups, especially those who are non-English-speaking. In another study, Young (1997) discussed the need to move toward teaching strategies that empower students in multicultural education courses, and described a cooperative learning method of student assessment based on an empow-erment model.

Summary

Since 1993 the literature on the implementation of multicultural education efforts at the college and university level has increasingly reflected researchers' attempts to evaluate the impact of these efforts, using a relatively wide range of measures. Overall, evidence for this impact is most clear in two areas of investigation. First, students respond very positively to the content of courses that incorporate multicultural perspectives as well as to the faculty who teach these classes. Second, faculty members themselves report overwhelmingly that they enjoy teaching these courses. A related conclusion is that these faculty tend to use somewhat specialized pedagogical techniques, a fact some authors use to help explain students' favorable perceptions of these instructors (e.g., Stake & Gerner, 1987).

In addition to this increase in assessment activity, there have been advances in the quality of evaluations of multicultural curriculum initiatives, with researchers routinely using pre-test/post-test designs (e.g., Stake et al., 1994) and providing follow-up data on course and program effectiveness through the utilization of longitudinal designs (e.g., Kranz & Lund, 1998; Lund et al., 1998; Stake & Rose, 1994). A critical methodological shortcoming continues to be the use of non-random samples, especially when coupled with researchers' general failure to employ control or comparison groups (e.g., Junn et al., 1995). Unfortunately, many of the positive outcomes attributed to multicultural education to this point may actually reflect the fact that students included in these studies elected to be in the courses or programs being evaluated and, therefore, were likely predisposed to react favorably to the curriculum and instructors. Stake et al.'s (1994) use of comparison groups would be a good model for future researchers who want to alleviate this problem.

Another key methodological shortcoming is investigators' continued reliance on non-standardized, self-report measures (e.g., Stake et al., 1994) or even subjects' retrospective accounts (e.g., Kranz & Lund, 1998; Lund et al., 1998). There are signs that researchers are becoming more concerned with the development of reliable and valid measures to document multicultural course and program effectiveness. Ponterotto, Baluch, Greig, and Rivera (1998) described the development and initial score validation of the 20-item Teacher Multicultural Attitude Survey, a self-report inventory of teachers' multicultural awareness and sensitivity. Using principal components analysis, the authors demonstrated the existence of a global factor of multicultural awareness, and construct validity was established through convergent correlations with related instruments. In addition, multiple measures of internal consistency and a test-retest stability assessment indicated satisfactory levels of score reliability. Marshall (1996) also reports on the use of factor analysis in developing a scale to measure pre-service teachers' concerns about working with diverse student populations.

McClellan, Cogdal, Lease, and Londono-McConnell (1996) undertook an especially ambitious task with the development of the Multicultural Assessment of Campus Programming (MAC-P), designed to assess campus climate, institutional valuing of diversity, majority-minority student group relations, collaborative sponsoring of campus programs, accessibility, and the effects of multicultural programming. This 42-item instrument was completed twice by 80 undergraduates, with one month passing between testings. In a second study, 167 college faculty and staff and 1,328 students completed the MAC-P, and factor analyses of scores revealed six distinct factors: institutional responsiveness, student relations, cultural accessibility, diversity recognition, students' cultural integration, and cultural sensitivity. Overall, McClellan et al. concluded that the MAC-P had acceptable reliability and validity.

Conclusions

Compared to the conclusions reached by Francis (1993), the preceding review reveals the following: 1) most articles published since 1993 on efforts to infuse the curriculum in higher education with issues related to diversity include at least some evaluative information regarding the effectiveness of those efforts; 2) much of this more recent evaluative information has been derived from attempts to integrate information related to race and ethnicity, although assessment at the program level continues to be dominated by major gender integration projects; and, 3) data yielded by these evaluations indicate that multicultural curriculum initiatives in colleges and universities continue to exert a positive impact on students and faculty alike, especially with respect to attitude measures.

Of additional interest to the present article, investigators' approach to evaluating the effectiveness of these initiatives has become more sophisticated from a methodological viewpoint, although there remains significant room for improvement. Overall, this area of investigation might benefit in particular from the general emphasis that exists currently in higher education on student learning outcomes as an index of program effectiveness (Gardiner, 1994). That is, while it is important to demonstrate that exposure to multicultural education is perceived positively and produces beneficial changes in individuals' personal and social development, it would seem even more valuable to show that multicultural curriculum initiatives foster a student's intellectual, cognitive, and skill development. Few investigators to this point, however, have included such measures in their attempts to demonstrate the effectiveness of these initiatives in higher education.

To conclude, the present review reveals that the evaluation of multicultural curriculum initiatives has become more sophisticated methodologically over the past six years, as would be expected for any active research area. Such continued progress is necessary in order to demonstrate the value of these courses and programs to the liberal arts curriculum. Still, consistent with arguments made by Tetreault (1985), Shapiro (1988), and Worell (1996), it is not desirable that the evaluation of multicultural curriculum initiatives approximate traditional assessment or research practices too closely. Instead, the nature of multicultural education itself requires evaluative approaches that are more flexible, inclusive of different methods and measures, and based on the knowledge that scientific inquiry is far from "value free." As a final comment, the assessment of multicultural curriculum initiatives need not be an overwhelming task. In fact, educators can build evaluation into these initiatives with relative ease, by attending carefully from the outset to course or program objectives, strategies for meeting those objectives, and ways of measuring outcomes. In this way, those engaged in infusing multicultural perspectives into the curriculum can continue to prove what they know intuitively and have already demonstrated to themselves: this work significantly and positively transforms the college curriculum and is also highly beneficial to the classroom and campus climate in general.

References

Bargad, A., & Hyde, J. S. (1991). Women's studies: A study of feminist identity development in women. *Psychology of Women Quarterly, 15*, 181-201.

Brown, J. (1992). Theory or practice—What exactly is feminist pedagogy? *Journal of General Education, 41*, 51-63.

Capuzza, J. (1992). Why good intentions aren't good enough: Reflections and suggestions for curriculum inclusion. *SUNY at Plattsburgh's Faculty Forum, 18*, 14-17.

Cheney, L. V. (1992). Beware the PC police. *Executive Educator, 14*, 31-34.

Collins, P. H. (1991). On our own terms: Self-defined standpoints and curriculum transformation. *National Women's Studies Association Journal, 3*, 367-381.

Francis, P. L. (1993). Assessing the effectiveness of multicultural curriculum initiatives in higher education: Proving the self-evident. In J. Q. Adams & J. R. Welsch (Eds.), *Multicultural education: Strategies for implementation in colleges and universities: Vol. 3* (pp. 101-109). Macomb, IL: Illinois Staff and Curriculum Developers Association.

Gardiner, L. F. (1994). *Redesigning higher education: Producing dramatic gains in student learning*. Report No. 7. Washington, DC: Graduate School of Education and Human Development, The George Washington University.

Gordon, M. M. (1964). *Assimilation in American life: The role of race, religion and national origins*. New York: Oxford University Press.

Grant, C. A. (Ed.) (1992). *Research and multicultural education: From the margins to the mainstream*. London: The Falmer Press.

Gray, P. J. (1997). Viewing assessment as innovation: Leadership and the change process. In P. J. Gray & T. W. Banta (Eds.), *The campus-level impact of assessment: Progress, problems, and possibilities*. San Francisco: Jossey-Bass.

Hartung, B. (1990). Selective rejection: How students perceive women's studies teachers. *National Women's Studies Association Journal, 2*, 254-263.

Junn, E. N., Morton, K. R., & Yee, I. (1995). The "Gibberish" exercise: Facilitating empathetic multicultural awareness. *Journal of Instructional Psychology, 22*, 324-329.

Kranz, P. L., & Lund, N. L. (1998). Design of a race relations course. *Journal of Instructional Psychology, 25*, 271-276.

Lund, N. L., Kranz, P. L., & Porter, A. J. (1998). Journeys inward and outward: A class in racial understanding. *Journal of Instructional Psychology, 25*, 122-129.

Marshall, P. L. (1996). Multicultural teaching concerns: New dimensions in the area of teacher concerns research? *The Journal of Educational Research, 89*, 371-379.

McClellan, S. A., Cogdal, P. A., Lease, S. H., & Londono-McConnell, A. (1996). Development of the Multicultural Assessment of Campus Programming (MAC-P) Questionnaire. *Measurement and Evaluation in Counseling and Development, 29*, 86-89.

McLeod, D. (1996). Instructional strategies in the multicultural classroom. *Community College Journal of Research and Practice, 20*, 65-73.

Michael, S. O., & Thompson, M. D. (1995). Multiculturalism in higher education: Transcending the familiar zone. *Journal for Higher Education Management, 11*, 31-48.

Musil, C. M. (Ed.). (1992a). *The courage to question: Women's studies and student learning*. Washington, DC: Association of American Colleges.

Musil, C. M. (Ed.) (1992b). *Students at the center: Feminist assessment*. Washington, DC: Association of American Colleges.

Myers, J. L., & Well, A. D. (1995). *Research design and statistical analysis*. Hillsdale, NJ: Lawrence Erlbaum.

Okazaki, S. (1998). Teaching gender issues in Asian American psychology: A pedagogical framework. *Psychology of Women Quarterly, 22,* 33-52.

Pence, D. (1992). A women's studies course: Its impact on women's attitudes toward men and masculinity. *National Women's Studies Association Journal, 4*, 321-335.

Ponterotto, J. G., Baluch, S., Greig, T., & Rivera, L. (1998). Development and initial score validation of the Teacher Multicultural Attitude Survey. *Educational and Psychological Measurement, 58*, 1002-1016.

Schmitz, B. (1984). Project on women in the curriculum: Montana State University. In B. Spanier, A. Bloom, & D. Bordviak (Eds.), *Towards a balanced curriculum: A sourcebook for initiating gender integration projects* (pp. 80-90). Cambridge, MA: Schenkman.

Schmitz, B., Dinnerstein, M., & Mairs, N. (1985). Initiating a curriculum integration project: Lessons from the campus and the region. In M. R. Schuster & S. R. Van Dyne (Eds.),

Women's place in the academy: Transforming the liberal arts curriculum (pp. 116-129). Totowa, NJ: Rowman & Allanheld.

Shapiro, J. P. (1988). Participatory evaluation: Towards a transformation of assessment for women's studies programs and projects. *Educational Evaluation and Policy Analysis*, *10*, 191- 199.

Spence, J. T., & Helmreich, R. (1972). The Attitude Toward Women Scale: An objective instrument to measure attitudes toward the rights and roles of women in contemporary society. Abstracted in JSAS *Catalog of Selected Documents in Psychology, 2,* 66.

Stake, J. E., & Gerner, M. A. (1987). The women's studies experience: Personal and professional gains for women and men. *Psychology of Women Quarterly*, *11*, 277-284.

Stake, J. E., Roades, L., Rose, S., Ellis, L., & West, C. (1994). The women's studies experience: Impetus for feminist activism. *Psychology of Women Quarterly*, *18*, 17-24.

Stake, J., E., & Rose, S. (1994). The long-term impact of women's studies on students' personal lives and political activism. *Psychology of Women Quarterly*, *18*, 403-412.

Tetreault, M. K. T. (1985). Feminist phase theory: An experience-derived evaluation model. *Journal of Higher Education*, *56*, 363-384.

Wang, V. O. (1998). Curriculum evaluation and assessment of multicultural genetic counselor education. *Journal of Genetic Counseling*, *7*, 87-111.

White, A. M. (1994). A course in the psychology of oppression: A different approach to teaching about diversity. *Teaching of Psychology*, *21*, 17-23.

Worell, J. (1996). Opening doors to feminist research. *Psychology of Women Quarterly*, *20*, 469- 485.

Young, R. L. (1997). Toward an empowering multicultural assessment technique. *Teacher Education Quarterly*, *24*, 21-27.

WHERE DO STUDENTS OF COLOR EARN DOCTORATES IN EDUCATION?: THE "TOP 25" COLLEGES AND SCHOOLS OF EDUCATION

by
Stafford Hood and Donald Freeman

Although African Americans and other students of color have sought graduate degrees in education more often than in any other academic field, non-white students are consistently underrepresented in the proportions of doctoral degrees awarded in education (National Research Council, 1976-1988). During academic year 1989-90, for example, only 518 African Americans, 161 Hispanics, 95 Asian Americans/Pacific Islanders, and 38 American Indians/Alaskan Natives earned doctorates in education (National Center for Education Statistics, 1992b). The 812 individuals in this group represented only about 11.7% of all of the doctorates awarded in education during that academic year.

Discussions of efforts to attract more students of color to academic careers are typically cast in terms of supply and demand (Quality Education for Minorities Project, 1990). Early work in this field focused on the recruitment and retention of African American graduate students (Pruitt, 1985; Thomas, Mingle, & McPartland, 1981), faculty (Epps, 1989; Moore & Wagstaff, 1974), and other delineated conditions that tend to limit the supply of African Americans at both levels. Given the limited supply of doctoral recipients of color in education and other fields (Thomas, 1987, 1992; Trent, 1991), it is not surprising that professors of color are grossly underrepresented on university faculties across all academic disciplines (Blackwell, 1987; Bowen & Schuster, 1986; Jackson, 1991; Moore, 1988; Moore & Wagstaff, 1974). Although the field of education can generally claim to have the highest levels of racial representation, a severe shortage of faculty of color exists in colleges and schools of education throughout the United States (National Center on Postsecondary Education, 1990). This shortage is particularly acute in the nation's elite research universities (Schneider, Brown, Denny, Mathis, & Schmidt, 1984).

Two general areas of concern that are directly related to these racial representation issues prompted the present investigation. First, we wanted to know which universities have been the most successful in preparing students of color for leadership positions in education in general. That is, which schools or colleges of education are most likely to have prepared those doctoral recipients of color who have chosen to work in our nation's public schools or in other applied settings? Second, we wanted to know which schools and colleges of education have been most successful in preparing students of color for leadership positions in educational research and development.

In addressing the first question, we adopted an analysis strategy similar to that used by Cooper and Borden (1994) to generate a list of the 100 universities (the "Top 100") that have conferred the highest number of doctoral degrees to racial minorities across all academic disciplines. As an extension of that approach, we narrowed our focus to the field of education and began our analyses by determining which institutions have awarded the highest numbers of doctoral degrees in education to students of color during each of four academic years: 1984-85, 1989-90, 1990-91, and 1991-92. We also determined which colleges and schools of education have been most successful in achieving this goal across the three most recent years for which these data were available: 1989-1992. Our goal was to identify the 25 institutions that headed each of these lists. To circumvent the issue of ties, we varied the actual numbers of colleges and schools of education that were included on this "Top 25" list from one year to another. The number of universities identified ranges from 23 institutions in 1991-92 to 25 institutions in 1984-85 and 1989-90, while 26 universities headed the list for the three most recent years, 1989 to 1992.

Our first set of research questions centered on the "Top 25" lists. They were as follows:

- Do the top 25 universities account for a significant proportion of all of the doctoral degrees in education that were awarded to students of color?
- Was minority doctoral production at these universities stable from one year to the next?
- Do the top 25 lists feature proportional representations of institutions from different regions of the country?
- Do the lists include a reasonable representation of elite research universities?

To determine which institutions have been most successful in preparing students of color for leadership positions in educational research and development, our attention shifted to colleges and schools of education at the nation's major research institutions. As Jackson (1991) and others have noted, students of color are often reluctant to enroll in graduate programs at major research universities because the campus climate and opportunities to develop satisfactory relationships with faculty are viewed as problematic. As a result, many doctoral recipients of color do not have the opportunity to participate in the social networks that typically prevail within and among elite research institutions. These social networks may provide opportunities to participate in externally funded research projects, to co-author research papers and publications with faculty, to establish personal contacts with other prominent researchers nationwide, and to participate in other forms of mentoring in research (Jackson, 1991; Padilla, 1994; Schneider, 1984). Because those who have functioned in social networks such as these have a competitive edge over those who have not, and because graduation from an elite research university is often a prerequisite for employment in other institutions of this type, the pool of candidates of color who can assume leadership positions in educational research and development may be severely restricted (Hood & Hood, 1993).

Thus, our second set of research questions centered on the number of doctorates in education awarded to students of color by the leading educational research institutions. They were:

- Which of the leading educational research universities have been the most successful in awarding doctorates in education to students of color?
- What proportion of those students of color who have earned doctorates in education have graduated from these major research institutions?
- Do the records of success in awarding doctorates in education vary among major research institutions located in different regions of the country?
- How does the proportion of doctoral recipients of color who earned their degrees from prestigious education research universities compare with the corresponding statistic for colleges and schools of education that ranked lower in academic productivity?

Method

Data Source

The graduation rates reported in this analysis were derived from surveys conducted by the U.S. Department of Education. These surveys asked representatives of the postsecondary institutions that participated in the Integrated Postsecondary Education Data System (IPEDS) to report the number of academic degrees they awarded to various subgroups of students in a given academic year. IPEDS surveys were conducted during each of the four academic years considered for the present investigation: 1984-85, 1989-90, 1990-91, and 1991-92. Although the incidence of missing data for graduates of doctoral programs was relatively rare, it is important to recognize that the frequencies reported throughout this analysis may underestimate the actual numbers of doctorates earned by students of color to at least some degree. This issue was especially problematic in 1990-91, when usable data were not available for four relatively large and prestigious institutions: the University of California-Los Angeles, Harvard University, New York University, and Stanford University.

Data Analyses

The analyses that serve as the focus of this report were derived from printouts of IPEDS data summarized in cross-tabulations depicting the number of students earning doctorates in education in a given academic year by individual institutions, states, gender, race, and ethnicity. Six categories of race/ethnicity were reported: nonresident alien, non-Hispanic White, non-Hispanic Black, Hispanic, Asian/Pacific Islander, and American Indian/Alaskan Native. Because this investigation focused on the preparation of students of color for leadership positions in our nation's public schools and universities, the data for nonresident aliens were not included in any of the analyses that were conducted.

The initial phase of data analysis focused on efforts to identify the institutions that awarded the highest numbers of doctorates in education to students of color during each of the four academic years that were considered. A list of the "Top 25" institutions for 1984-85 is presented in Table 1 as an illustration of the results of these analyses. Comparable tables were also prepared for 1989-90, 1990-91, and 1991-92.[1] Data from the three most recent IPEDS surveys were then combined and a list of the 26 institutions that awarded the most doctorates in education to students of color during the three-year period from 1989 to 1992 was compiled.

The second phase of the data analysis centered on the minority doctoral production rates of the leading research institutions. A precondition for conducting these analyses was the identification of the colleges and schools of education (CSEs) that constitute the leading educational research institutions in the United States. In this case, a choice had to be made between the results of two recent national surveys of colleges and schools of education: one conducted by two professors from the University of Illinois that identified the "most productive" colleges of education (West & Rhee, 1995); and the other a survey published by *U.S. News & World Report*, which identified America's "best graduate schools for education and other disciplines ("America's Best Graduate Schools," 1995).

Table 1
Doctorates in education awarded to students of color in 1984-85:
the "Top 25" institutions

	State	AA	AI/AN	A/PI	H	Total minority	% of all grads
Columbia U.	NY	20	0	5	1	26	18.2%
Temple U.	PA	16	0	4	5	25	16.7%
Nova U.	FL	20	0	0	2	22	16.5%
Clark Atlanta U.	GA	21	0	0	0	21	91.3%
Kansas State U.	KS	14	0	4	1	19	24.1%
U. of Massachusetts—Amherst	MA	11	0	0	7	18	20.2%
Florida State U.	FL	15	0	0	2	17	23.6%
U. of Michigan	MI	12	0	0	3	15	17.9%
Southern Illinois U.—Carbondale	IL	10	0	3	1	14	19.2%
U. of Texas—Austin	TX	1	1	1	11	14	14.1%
George Washington U.	DC	11	0	1	1	13	35.1%
Michigan State U.	MI	8	0	2	3	13	10.9%
U. of Pittsburgh (main campus)	PA	12	0	1	0	13	9.3%
Wayne State U.	MI	11	0	0	1	12	26.1%
Pennsylvania State U. (main campus)	PA	2	1	0	9	12	14.6%
East Texas State U.	TX	6	1	0	4	11	20.0%
Vanderbilt U.	TN	10	0	0	1	11	13.4%
Georgia State U.	GA	11	0	0	0	11	11.7%
Ohio State U. (main campus)	OH	8	1	2	0	11	10.8%
Fordham U.	NY	7	0	0	3	10	17.9%
U. of Alabama	AL	10	0	0	0	10	14.7%
U. of Nebraska	NE	5	0	2	3	10	14.3%
U. of Maryland—College Park	MD	9	0	0	1	10	8.3%
Harvard U.	MA	3	1	2	3	9	14.8%
U. of Wisconsin	WI	4	1	0	4	9	10.3%
Totals for top 25 institutions		257	6	27	66	356	16.5%
Totals for other institutions (n=158)		242	37	46	85	410	10.2%
Combined totals (n=183)		499	43	73	151	766	12.4%

Note: Nonresident aliens were not included in this or any of the other analyses considered in this report.
Subgroups: AA=African American; AI/AN=American Indian/Alaskan Native; A/PI=Asian/Pacific Islander; H=Hispanic.

The choice was relatively straightforward. The West and Rhee survey identified 31 colleges and schools of education that have ranked highest in academic productivity in recent years. These rankings were based on multiple indicators of academic productivity including: (a) the number of articles and documents published by each institution's faculty in the Educational Resources Information Center (ERIC) database from 1983 to mid-1990, (b) the number of citations of faculty publications from 1972 to mid-1990, (c) the number of faculty who served as editors of prestigious professional journals in 1979 and 1989, (d) the level of external funding the school or college received during the 1989-90 academic year, and

(e) the number of doctoral graduates of these institutions who have joined the faculties of other elite research institutions. By contrast, the *U.S. News & World Report* ratings were based on independent rankings of each institution across four different categories: student selectivity, faculty resources, research activity, and institutional reputation among deans, university faculty, and school district superintendents. The indicators of research activity in this latter survey were limited to: (a) the total level of external funding received by each institution in 1994, and (b) that total divided by the number of faculty members engaged in research. The West and Rhee survey considered a wider range of indices of academic productivity than did the *U.S. News & World Report* rankings and was not confounded with other measures that are not directly related to research or academic productivity such as student selectivity and reputations among educators. Thus, the results of West and Rhee's analyses were used in our identification of the leading education research universities. Nevertheless, some of the data from the *U.S. News & World Report* analysis was considered in our presentation of findings.

In the second phase of the data analysis, the number of doctorates awarded to students of color for the three years from 1989 to 1992 was determined for each of the 31 CSEs that ranked highest in academic productivity in West and Rhee's survey. Analyses contrasting the levels of success of these units in recruiting and retaining advanced graduate students of color were also conducted. However, these analyses are limited because data on the actual number of students of color who were recruited, applied, admitted, and subsequently graduated from each of the reported CSEs were not available to the researchers.

Results

How Many Doctorates in Education Were Awarded to Students of Color?

Table 2
Number of doctorates in education awarded to students of color
(1984-85, 1989-90, 1990-91, 1991-92)

	Number of institutions reporting	AA	AI/AN	A/PI	H	W	Minority totals	% of all grads
1984-85	183	499	43	73	151	5,431	766	12.4%
		(8.1%)	(0.7%)	(1.2%)	(2.4%)	(87.6%)		
1989-90	170	495	37	95	143	5,010	770	13.3%
1990-91	188	455	35	122	141	5,086	753	12.9%
1991-92	196	492	32	99	182	5,457	805	12.9%
Totals, 1989–92		1,442	104	316	466	20,984	2,328	13.0%
		(8.1%)	(0.6%)	(1.8%)	(2.6%)	(87.0%)		

Note: Nonresident aliens were not included in this or any of the other analyses considered in this report.
Subgroups: AA=African American; AI/AN=American Indian/Alaskan Native; A/PI=Asian/Pacific Islander; H=Hispanic.

The total numbers of doctorates in education earned by students of color during the years in question are summarized in Table 2. As noted earlier, these statistics may represent somewhat conservative estimates of the actual number of doctoral recipients of color in a given year. Nevertheless, they suggest that the total numbers of doctorates in education earned by students of color were fairly stable from one year to the next. The same was true of the proportions of doctorates earned by members of each of the four non-white subgroups. From 1989 to 1992, for example, at least 1,442 African Americans, 466 Hispanics, 316 Asian Americans/Pacific Islanders, and 104 American Indians/Alaskan Natives earned doctorates in education. These 2,328 individuals accounted for about 13% of all doctorates in education attained during that three-year period, with the respective groups accounting for 8.1%, 2.6%, 1.8%, and 0.6% of the total number of doctorates in education awarded.

Which Universities Awarded the Most Doctorates in Education to Students of Color?

The 25 universities that awarded the most doctorates in education to students of color in 1984-85 are listed in Table 1. The 26 universities that headed the list of minority doctorates in education during the three-year period from 1989 to 1992 are presented in Table 3. Fifteen of the universities that ranked in the "Top 26" list from 1989 to 1992 also ranked on the "Top 25" list in 1984-85.[2] Thus, the records of success in the recruitment and retention of advanced graduate students of color for this subset of 15 universities are shown to have spanned a period of at least eight years. Other universities that were included on at least one of the Top 25 lists for each of the four academic years were the University of Alabama (1984-85), the University of California-Los Angeles (1991-92), East Texas State University (1984-85), George Washington University (1984-85 and 1991-92), Georgia State University (1984-85), the University of Hawaii-Manoa (1990-91), the University of Houston (1989-90), Iowa State University (1991-92), Kansas State University (1984-85 and 1990-91), the University of Miami (1991-92), the University of Michigan (1984-85), Michigan State University (1984-85), the University of Nebraska (1984-85), New York University (1989-90 and 1991-92; the data for 1990-91 were missing), the University of North Texas (1990-91), Pepperdine University (1991-92), Rutgers University (1989-90), Southern Illinois University (1989-90), and historically Black Tennessee State University (1990-91 and 1991-92).

Proportions of Doctorates Earned. As the data presented in Table 1 indicate, 356 students of color earned doctorates in education from the Top 25 universities in 1984-85. This number represents 46.5% of the 766 doctorates in education earned by racial/ethnic minority students during that academic year. The corresponding percentages for the other three academic years were 54.5% for the Top 25 universities in 1989-90, 50.7% for the Top 24 universities in 1990-91, and 45.1% for the Top 23 universities in 1991-92. In other words, a relatively small subset of from 23 to 25 universities accounted for about one-half of all of the doctorates in education that were awarded to students of color for each year.

Table 3
Doctorates in education awarded to students of color from 1989 to 1992:
the "Top 26" institutions

		Subgroups						Totals by years		
	State	AA	AI/AN	A/PI	H	Totals	% all grads	89-90	90-91	91-92	84-85
Nova U.	FL	80	3	31	12	126	19%	42*	47*	37*	22*
Columbia U.[a]	NY	75	2	21	25	123	23%	44*	44*	35*	26*
Clark Atlanta U.	GA	78	0	0	0	78	98%	45*	14*	19*	21*
U. of Massachusetts— Amherst	MA	43	1	3	30	77	22%	27*	23*	27*	18*
U. of Maryland— College Park[a]	MD	44	1	3	4	52	15%	18*	15*	19*	10*
Wayne State U.	MI	31	2	2	9	44	18%	10*	24*	10*	12*
Temple U.	PA	26	0	7	7	40	11%	14*	13*	13*	25*
Fordham U.	NY	12	0	2	24	38	30%	7	11*	20*	10*
Florida State U.[a]	FL	25	1	2	9	37	17%	10*	12*	15*	17*
Vanderbilt U.[a]	TN	33	1	0	2	36	16%	19*	3	14*	11*
U. of New Mexico	NM	4	1	2	28	35	25%	8	10*	10*	6
U. of Illinois—Urbana[a]	IL	20	2	6	7	35	14%	14*	8	13*	5
Texas Southern U.	TX	34	0	0	0	34	81%	15*	7	12*	8
Ohio State U.[a]	OH	26	0	5	3	34	11%	10*	12*	12*	11*
U. of Texas—Austin[a]	TX	8	1	2	23	34	10%	12*	14*	8	14*
U. of San Francisco	CA	16	0	9	8	33	17%	13*	12*	8	7
Pennsylvania State U.[a]	PA	13	7	2	10	32	15%	14*	12*	6	12*
Harvard U.[a]	MA	10	1	7	10	28	21%	22*	?	6	9*
U. of Pittsburgh[a]	PA	23	0	4	1	28	11%	11*	9*	8	13*
U. of South Carolina	SC	25	1	0	1	27	69%	13*	14*	0	?
U. of Wisconsin[a]	WI	10	3	5	9	27	12%	8	11*	8	9*
Northern Illinois U.	IL	15	0	5	7	27	13%	7	10*	10*	3
Texas A&M	TX	10	1	1	14	26	12%	9*	10*	7	2
Seattle U.	WA	24	0	0	1	25	38%	2	2	21*	1
Loyola U. of Chicago	IL	18	0	4	3	25	17%	10*	10*	5	6
Virginia Polytechnic Institute[a]	VA	23	0	1	1	25	13%	8	12*	5	7
Totals: top 26 institutions		726	28	124	248	1,126	18.5%				
Totals: all institutions		1,442	104	316	466	2,328	13.0%				
% of all minority doctorates from 1989 to 1992		50.3%	26.9%	39.2%	53.2%	48.4%					

*Institutions ranked among the top 25 universities in the number of minority doctorates in education awarded that year

[a]Universities ranked among the top 31 colleges of education in academic productivity by West and Rhee (1955) (see Table IV)

? = missing data

The numbers of doctoral recipients of color who completed their graduate studies at one of the Top 26 universities during the three-year period from 1989 to 1992 are also summarized in Table 3. As these data indicate, 1,126 students of color earned doctorates in education during this three-year period at one of the 26 universities cited on this list. This figure represents nearly one- half (48.4%) of the total number of doctorates in education earned by students of color from 1989 to 1992 ($n = 2,328$). This subset of 26 universities also accounts for slightly more than one- half of all doctorates in education awarded to African Americans (50.3%) and Hispanics (53.2%) during those three years.

Consistency Across Years. A total of 46 universities qualified for one or more of the Top 25 lists for the four academic years considered in these analyses. As shown by the asterisks in the column labeled "Totals by Years" in Table 3, 9 universities qualified for all four of the lists, 5 appeared on three of the lists, and 10 qualified for two of the lists. Thus, 24 universities ranked among the Top 25 institutions in numbers of doctorates in education awarded to students of color for at least two of the four academic years that were considered, while 22 institutions qualified for only one of the four lists.

Regional Contrasts. As a closer review of the data in Table 3 confirms, more than one-third of the 26 institutions that ranked highest in numbers of doctorates in education awarded to students of color during the three-year period from 1989 to 1992 were located in states east of the Mississippi River ($n = 9$). By contrast, only 6 of the 26 universities on this list were located west of the Mississippi, including four universities in Texas. Moreover, although three Pacific Athletic Conference (PAC-10) universities ranked among the top 25 institutions on Cooper and Borden's (1994) list of the 100 universities that conferred the most doctoral degrees to students of color across all academic disciplines in 1990-91, none of the colleges or schools of education in this conference qualified for our Top 26 list of institutions awarding doctorates in education to students of color from 1989 to 1992.

Representation of the Major Research Universities. As shown in Table 3, the Top 26 list for the three-year period from 1989 to 1992 includes elite research universities as well as other four-year institutions that are not generally recognized for their research productivity. The same is true for the Top 25 lists for each of the four academic years. Those universities that were included in both West and Rhee's (1995) list of the 31 most academically productive colleges of education in the United States and on our list of the top 26 U.S. universities that awarded the highest numbers of doctorates in education to students of color from 1989 to 1992 are noted in the first column of Table 3. As the table indicates, a total of 12 universities had the distinction of being included on both lists.

How Many Students of Color Earned Doctorates from the Most Academically Productive Colleges/Schools of Education?

Variations in Levels of Success in Awarding Doctorates in Education to Students of Color. Data summarized in Table 4 describe the number of doctorates in education awarded to students of color by each of the 31 North American CSEs that ranked highest in academic productivity in West and Rhee's (1995) survey. As these graduation data indicate, considerable variation exists in the total number of doctorates in education earned by students of color during the three years from 1989 to 1992. Only about one-fourth of these 31 CSEs awarded doctorates to more than 25 students of color during this three-year period. One of these institutions, Columbia Teachers College, located in New York City, granted a total of

123 doctorates in education to non-white students and easily outdistanced all of the other leading education research universities in this regard. At the other end of the continuum, five of the institutions on this list awarded fewer than 10 doctorates in education to students of color during the same three-year period. The final column of Table 4 reports the total amount of publicly and privately funded research dollars (in millions) that were administered by each of these institutions in 1994, according to the *U.S. News & World Report* analysis. These data reveal that the median level of research funds distributed to each of these 31 research institutions in 1994 was $5.65 million.

Proportions of Doctorates Earned. The wide variation in the number of graduate students enrolled at each of the leading research institutions suggested the importance of determining the proportions of doctorates awarded to students of color at each university. Here again, considerable variation was found by institutional category. In 6 of the 31 CSEs with distinguished records of academic productivity, more than 15% of all doctorates were awarded to students of color during the three-year period from 1989 to 1992. By contrast, students of color accounted for less than 10% of all doctorates in education awarded by 10 of the 31 elite education research universities during this same period.

Contrasts Between Graduation Rates at Major Research Universities and Other Institutions. During the three years from 1989 to 1992, a total of 745 students of color earned doctorates in education from one of the 31 academically productive CSEs listed in Table 4—an average of about 250 students per year. These individuals represented 12.2% of the 6,127 doctorates in education awarded by this subset of universities during this period of time. During this same period, 1,583 students of color earned doctorates in education from CSEs within the IPEDS system (*n* = approximately 155 institutions each year) that ranked lower in academic productivity. These individuals accounted for 13.5% of the 11,760 doctorates in education awarded by this larger subset of institutions. Therefore, the proportion of doctorates awarded to students of color by the 31 CSEs that ranked highest in academic productivity was lower than that of CSEs with less distinguished records of research productivity (12.2% compared to 13.5%).

Viewed from a different perspective, the 745 students of color who completed their doctorates in education at one of the 31 colleges and schools of education listed in Table 4 represent 32.0% of the 2,328 doctorates in education awarded to students of color nationwide from 1989 to 1992, including 30.9% of all doctorates earned by African Americans, 33.7% of all doctorates awarded to American Indians/Alaskan Natives, 32.6% of all doctorates earned by Asian Americans/Pacific Islanders, and 34.8% of all doctorates awarded to Hispanics. The consistency of these proportions from one racial/ethnic subgroup to another is striking. Collectively, these statistics suggest that approximately one-third of all students within each of these four subgroups who received doctorates in education from 1989 to 1992 earned their degrees from one of the 31 most academically productive CSEs in the country.

Regional Contrasts. As a closer analysis of the data presented in Table 4 confirms, significant differences exist in minority graduation rates among major research institutions located in different regions of the country. Consider, for example, the contrast between the eight midwestern universities of the Big 10 Conference that were included on West and Rhee's (1995) list and the six PAC-10 universities that were also included on this list. The mean number of doctorates awarded to students of color from 1989 to 1992 by these two subsets of universities are summarized in Table 5.

Table 4
Doctorates in education awarded to students of color
from 1989 to 1992 by the 31 colleges and schools of education
ranked highest in academic productivity by West and Rhee (1995)

	Rankings AP vs. US[a]	AA	AI/AN	A/PI	H	Totals	% all grads	1994 research funds[b]
U. of Wisconsin—Madison	1–5	10	3	5	9	27	12.0%	$10.9
U. of Illinois (main campus)	2–7.5	20	2	6	7	35	14.2%	$7.3
Ohio State U.	3–9	26	0	5	3	34	11.2%	$15.4
Stanford U.[c]	4–2	5	2	3	4	14	22.2%	$7.4
U. of Minnesota—Twin Cities	5–25.5	10	4	2	7	23	7.8%	$11.0
Indiana U.—Bloomington	6–13	7	0	4	3	14	7.2%	$2.4
Michigan State U.	7–7.5	13	0	1	1	15	6.7%	$13.3
Columbia Teachers College	8–4	75	2	21	25	123	23.1%	$11.5
U. of Georgia	9–15	9	0	2	4	15	4.9%	$14.5
Pennsylvania State U.— University Park	10–25.5	13	7	2	10	32	14.8%	$4.6
U. of Maryland—College Park	11–21	44	1	3	4	52	15.0%	$7.0
U. of Texas—Austin	12–27	8	1	2	23	34	10.0%	$1.2
U. of Michigan—Ann Arbor	13–22	8	1	2	2	13	13.1%	$2.3
Arizona State U. (main campus)	14–47	4	4	5	7	20	13.8%	$3.3
U. of California—Los Angeles	15–10.5	6	0	6	6	18	18.2%	$8.0
U. of Washington	16–18	3	1	4	1	9	9.9%	$5.7
U. of California—Berkeley	17–3	5	3	3	4	15	14.7%	$14.0
U. of Chicago	18–19	7	0	1	1	9	12.2%	$3.3
Harvard U.[c]	19–1	10	1	7	10	28	20.9%	$7.1
U. of Virginia	20–13.5	13	0	2	1	16	8.1%	$4.4
Vanderbilt U. (Peabody College)	21–6	33	1	0	2	36	16.0%	$16.8
U. of North Carolina—Chapel Hill	22–32	15	0	1	2	18	12.4%	$1.4
U. of Florida	23–36	8	1	1	6	16	11.9%	$2.9
Florida State U.	24–30	25	1	2	9	37	17.1%	$6.2
Syracuse U.	25–28	3	0	0	0	3	2.9%	$5.6
U. of Arizona	26.5–35	3	0	2	8	13	12.0%	$4.0
U. of Nebraska—Lincoln	26.5–48	6	0	4	0	10	4.8%	$2.4
Virginia Polytechnic Institute	28–>50	23	0	1	1	25	12.7%	?
State U. of New York—Buffalo	29.5–39	6	0	1	1	8	8.3%	$1.9
U. of Missouri—Columbia	29.5–34	4	0	1	0	5	2.5%	$5.3
U. of Pittsburgh (main campus)	31–44	23	0	4	1	28	10.9%	$3.8
Totals for the 31 AP institutions		445	35	103	162	745	12.2%	
Totals for all institutions		1,442	104	316	466	2,328	13.0%	
% of all doctorates awarded by the 31 AP institutions		30.9%	33.7%	32.6%	34.8%	32.0%		

Notes:
[a]AP = rankings of academic productivity derived from West and Rhee (1995); US = *U.S. News & World Report* rankings of graduate schools of education.
[b]Data in this column were taken from the *U.S. News & World Report* analysis and represent total dollars in research grants awarded to each institution during the 1994-95 academic year (in millions).
[c]Data for 1990-91 were missing for these universities; numbers therefore represent totals for two rather than three years.
? = missing data

As the data in Table 5 indicate, the graduation rates for students of color were roughly equal across the eight universities of the Big 10 and the six of the PAC-10 (with means of 3.0 and 2.9 graduates of color per institution, respectively). Given the racial/ethnic differences in demographics across the two regions of the country that these two conferences represent, it is not surprising that the universities in the Big 10 were more successful than their PAC-10 counterparts in recruiting and retaining African Americans graduate students. What is surprising, however, is that the universities in the Big 10 were nearly as successful as the PAC-10 institutions in recruiting and retaining American Indian and Hispanic graduate students. Likewise, although the PAC-10 research universities were more successful in recruiting and retaining Asian Americans, the difference in graduation rates among CSEs in the two conferences was not as large as we expected.

Table 5
Mean number of doctorates in education awarded to students of color
in Big 10 and PAC-10, 1989–92*

Conference	African Americans	American Indians	Asian Americans	Hispanics	Total
Big 10 (n=8)	13.4	2.1	3.4	5.3	24.2
PAC-10 (n=6)	5.3	1.8	4.6	5.8	17.5

*The means for the PAC-10 schools are adjusted to include interpolations of missing data for the 1990-91 academic year from the University of California–Los Angeles and Stanford University.

Discussion

Interpretations of the results of this investigation are likely to vary from one reader to the next; however, our findings should be meaningful in one way or another to nearly all stakeholders in education. For example, when viewed from one perspective, these results should provide a better understanding of why the number of applicants of color for faculty positions at major educational research institutions is typically meager. As noted earlier, faculty search committees at such universities are likely to view persons who received their doctoral degrees from comparable institutions as the most viable candidates for faculty positions. Moore (1988) takes this line of reasoning one step further by contending that faculty members of search committees function as gatekeepers for the "ruling class" of educational elites at these predominantly white institutions and may pose a significant barrier to the selection and hiring of faculty of color. Given these conditions and the findings of this investigation, which suggest that only about 250 students of color complete their doctorates at the 31 most prestigious educational research institutions each year, it is evident that the national pool of viable applicants of color for faculty positions at major education research institutions is severely restricted. The size of this pool is further reduced because students of color who complete their doctorates at major research universities may be more likely than their white counterparts to accept non-university positions such as school- or district-level administrative assignments in public schools or positions in state departments of education (Brown, 1988). Given these and other conditions such as the uneven distribution of doctoral recipients of color across specialty areas within education, the national pool of qualified applicants of color in some educational fields—for example, educational measurement and statistics—may be minuscule (Hood & Freeman, 1995).

This self-perpetuating cycle is not likely to be broken until the graduate faculties at most major educational research universities become more aggressive in recruiting and retaining students of color in their doctoral programs. Steps must also be taken to improve the professional lives of untenured faculty of color at the most prestigious research institutions so that these positions will become more appealing to doctoral recipients of color who have earned their degrees from comparable institutions. Moreover, faculty search committees at these institutions must also begin to take more deliberate steps to encourage qualified doctoral recipients of color working in non-university settings to apply for the university-based faculty positions they are trying to fill.

Shifting to a different area of concern, the findings of these analyses might also serve as a springboard for further research related to issues of minority representation in education. These results could provide the logistical foundation for a variety of research investigations in this field. Future studies might address questions such as the following:

- Why have some of the CSEs identified in this study been very successful in recruiting and retaining doctoral students of color while others have not?
- Why have the graduation rates for students of color seeking doctorates in education been considerably higher for universities located in the East and throughout the Midwest than for universities located in the West?
- Why have minority graduation rates been lower at prestigious education research universities than at universities that rank lower in academic productivity?
- Would an in-depth analysis of a university (or universities) that has established a noteworthy record of success in recruiting and retaining doctoral students of color shed additional light on this issue? (A comprehensive study of the recruitment and retention practices of Columbia Teachers College might prove to be especially fruitful in this regard.)
- In what ways, if any, have the career paths of students of color who earned doctorates in education from one of the major education research universities differed from those of their white counterparts and from minority doctoral recipients who earned their degrees from one of the other colleges or schools of education listed in Table 3?

Further, university professors and administrators might use the results of our analyses to compare their institution's success in preparing students of color for leadership positions in education with that of other colleges and schools of education nationwide. Faculties in universities that have enjoyed high levels of success in this regard should welcome the results of this investigation and view them as a recognition of their noteworthy accomplishments. Consider, for example, the record of success Columbia Teachers College (CTC) has established in recruiting and retaining minority doctoral students in education. Bear in mind that CTC ranked eighth in academic productivity among all of the North American CSEs surveyed by West and Rhee (1995), and fourth in the *U.S. News & World Report* (1995) listing of "America's Best Graduate Schools" of education. Notwithstanding, during the three-year period from 1989 to 1992, a total of 123 students of color earned doctorates in education from this prestigious institution. This number (a) was more than double that of the academically productive university that ranked second in the number of doctoral recipients of color from 1989 to 1992—namely, the University of Maryland-College Park ($n = 52$ doctorates in education); (b) accounted for more than 5% of all of the doctorates in education awarded to students of color nationwide from 1989 to 1992, including 5.2% of all African Americans, 6.6% of all Asian Americans, and 5.4% of all Hispanics; and (c) accounted for a higher percentage of all doctorates in education awarded to students of color from 1989 to 1992 than the six most academically productive institutions in the PAC-10 combined (5.3% compared to 4.5%). Indeed, Columbia Teachers College ranked first among CSEs in the number of its students of color who earned doctorates in education during the 1984-85 academic year, the earliest of the four years considered in these analyses (see Table 1). Simply stated, for at least eight years, this institution's distinguished record of success in recruiting and retaining doctoral candidates of color in education was unchallenged by any other prestigious university in the country.

Other academically productive universities that may have assumed significant roles in the preparation of leaders of color in education during the three-year period from 1989 to 1992 include the University of Maryland-College Park, Florida State University, Vanderbilt University's Peabody College, the University of Illinois at Champaign-Urbana, the University of Texas-Austin, Ohio State University, and Pennsylvania State University-University Park (see Table 4). These and the other institutions listed in the Top 26 list summarized in Table 3 assumed comparable roles in the preparation of educational leaders of color for our nation's public schools and schools and colleges of education.

At the other end of the continuum, the results of this investigation also provide reason to believe that the graduate faculties of most CSEs are content to take a reactive stance rather than a proactive one with respect to minority recruitment and retention at the doctoral level—whereby qualified candidates of color may be admitted if—and only if—they take the initiative to apply. The results of this analysis of doctorates in education awarded to students of color across the 31 most academically productive CSEs are especially problematic in this regard. As our results indicate, the proportion of students of color who earned doctorates in education from these prestigious universities from 1989 to 1992 was lower than the corresponding statistic for less prestigious universities (12.2% compared to 13.5%). This finding seems to support Jackson's (1991) contention that students of color often view the campus climates of major research universities as problematic. Thus, faculties of major research institutions should be challenged to examine the psychological climate of their colleges or schools of education and the forms of personal and academic support their institutions provide for advanced graduate students in education.

The findings of the present study should also challenge the graduate faculties at most of these institutions to explain why their records of success in recruiting and retaining doctoral students in education lag behind the national norm. Our own informal interactions with graduate faculty from a number of different educational research institutions suggest that shortcomings in this area are often attributed to one or more of the following reasons: (a) the lack of sufficient funds directed toward this effort that would enable these institutions to become competitive with other universities that are also trying to recruit qualified students of color, (b) the undesirable geographical locations of the low-minority institutions, (c) the lack of a large enough pool of qualified minority candidates in the state or region in which these institutions are located, and/or (d) the limited presence of faculty of color in their colleges or schools of education. Although these 31 academically productive institutions appear to have ample funds from research grants to make them competitive with other universities in this regard, when Columbia Teachers College is posed as a counter example,

411

most of them are hard pressed to provide convincing evidence that CTC is better positioned on all (or even most) of these variables.

Conclusion

The results of this investigation support those who contend that the differential levels of success in recruiting and retaining doctoral students of color in education are more closely related to the level and consistency of institutional commitment to this goal than to the combined effects of differences in available funds, geographical locations, accessible pools of qualified minority applicants, or numbers of faculty of color. Collectively, our findings seem to indicate that the graduate faculties of most major educational research institutions have adopted a passive rather than an assertive stance when it comes to preparing increasing numbers of students of color for leadership positions in educational research and development. This is true even in the present era, in which the ever-increasing levels of racial and cultural diversity in our nation's public schools and universities have become obvious to just about everyone.

Based on our reading of the data, more than a few of our colleagues at elite CSEs seem to lack a strong and consistent commitment to the production of students of color for faculty positions. Yet, we find it hard to accept that the success of Columbia Teachers College cannot be reasonably duplicated by more of its peer institutions. We urge faculties at these CSEs to take a close, critical look at their recruitment and retention practices relative to students of color. Their goal should be to establish noteworthy rather than questionable records of success in this regard.

Endnotes

[1]These tables are available upon request from the authors.

[2]The 1984-85 graduation rates for each of the Top 26 institutions are starred in the last column of Table 3 (labeled "89-90").

References

America's best graduate schools. (1995, March 20). *US. News & World Report* (Special Supplement).

Blackwell, J. E. (1987). *Mainstreaming outsiders: The production of Black professionals.* Dix Hills, NY: General Hall.

Bowen, H., & Schuster, J. (1986). *American professors: A national resource imperiled.* New York: Oxford University Press.

Brown, S. V. (1988). *Increasing minority faculty: An elusive goal.* Princeton, NJ: Educational Testing Service.

Cooper, A., & Borden, V. (1994, May 19). Top 100 degree producers. *Black Issues in Higher Education, 11*(6), 49-87.

Epps, E. G. (1989). Academic culture and the minority professor. *Academe, 36*(5), 23-26.

Hood, S., & Freeman, D. (1995, April). Breaking the tradition: Increasing the production of doctoral recipients of color in research methodology, educational measurement, and statistics. Paper presented at the annual meeting of the American Educational Research Association, San Francisco.

Hood, S., & Hood, D. W. (1993, April). The production of minority teachers and faculty: Are colleges of education at major research universities pulling their weight? Paper presented at the annual meeting of the American Educational Research Association, Atlanta, GA.

Jackson, K. (1991). Black faculty in academia. In P. C. Altbach & K. Lomotey (Eds.), *The racial crisis in American higher education* (pp. 135-148). Albany, NY: State University of New York.

Moore, W. (1988). Black faculty in White colleges: A dream deferred. *Educational Researcher, 17,* 117-121.

Moore, W., & Wagstaff, L. H. (1974). *Black educators in White colleges.* San Francisco, CA: Jossey-Bass.

National Center for Education Statistics (NCES). (1992a, January). *Characteristics of doctorate recipients: 1979, 1984, and 1989* (NCES Report 91-384). Washington, DC: U.S. Department of Education, Office of Educational Research and Improvement.

National Center for Education Statistics, (1992b, May). *Race/ethnicity trends in degrees conferred by institutions of higher education: 1980-81 through 1989-90* (NCES Report 92-039). Washington, DC: U.S. Department of Education, Office of Educational Research and Improvement.

National Center on Postsecondary Education. (1990). *Faculty in higher education institutions, 1988.* Washington, DC: U.S. Department of Education, Office of Educational Research and Improvement.

National Research Council. (1976-1988). *Doctorate recipients from United States universities.* Washington, DC: National Academy Press.

Padilla, A. M. (1994). Ethnic minority scholars, research, and mentoring: Current and future issues. *Educational Researcher, 23,* 24-27.

Pruitt, A. S. (1985). Discrimination in recruitment, admission, and retention of minority graduate students. *Journal of Negro Education, 54(4),* 526-536.

Quality Education for Minorities Project. (1990). *Education that works: An action plan for the education of minorities.* Cambridge: Massachusetts Institute of Technology, Quality Education for Minorities Project.

Schneider, B. (1984). Graduate programs in schools of education: Facing tomorrow, today. In M. Pelezar & L. Solomon (Eds.), *Keeping graduate programs responsive to national needs* (pp. 57- 63). San Francisco: Jossey-Bass.

Schneider, B., Brown, L., Denny, T., Mathis, C., & Schmidt, W. (1984). The deans' perspective: Challenges to perceptions of status of schools of education. *Phi Delta Kappan, 65,* 617-630.

Thomas, G. E. (1987). Black students in U.S. graduate and professional schools in the 1980s: A national and institutional assessment. *Harvard Educational Review, 57(3),* 261-282.

Thomas, G. E. (1992). Participation and degree attainment of African American and Latino students in graduate education relative to other racial and ethnic groups: An update from Office of Civil Rights data. *Harvard Educational Review, 62(1),* 45-65.

Thomas, G. E., Mingle, J. R., & McPartland, J. M. (1981). Recent trends in racial enrollment, segregation, and degree attainment in higher education. In G. D. Thomas (Ed.), *Black students in higher education* (pp. 107-125). Westport, CT: Greenwood Press.

Trent, W. T. (1991). Focus on equity: Race and gender differences in degree attainment, 1975-76 to 1980-81. In W. Allen, E. Epps, & N. Haniff (Eds.), *Colleges in Black and White: African American students in predominantly White and historically Black public universities* (pp. 41-60). Albany, NY: State University of New York Press.

West, C. K., & Rhee, Y. (1995). Ranking departments or sites within colleges of education using multiple standards: Departmental and individual productivity. *Contemporary Educational Psychology, 20,* 151-171.

A STUDY OF THE CAMPUS CLIMATE: METHODOLOGY AND RESULTS

by
Catherine A. Riordan[1]

Reflections on Stimulating Change

The following article summarizes a study of the campus climate we did about ten years ago. When I contemplated doing a retrospective on it, I looked for evidence of its impact on our institution. Although the study and various reports emanating from it were discussed widely on campus, there were no big splashes—no obvious changes in policy, no big increases in the diversity of the student body or faculty, no new appointments or programs clearly stimulated by our efforts, and no "heads rolled." My initial reaction was to question if the study had been a failure or a waste of time. Had it just been a way of placating a few individuals, creating busywork in the absence of substantive change? Since our study there has been another campus-wide survey regarding the climate (Meinholdt & Murray, in press; Murray, Meinholdt & Bergmann, in press), and a committee appointed by the Chancellor to address issues related to the climate for underrepresented groups. Were these activities merely busywork too? Exercises in futility? Substitutes for action?

As I began to map out a retrospective commentary lamenting the absence of the big splashes, I started to think of big splashes that had occurred around that time. Some of those are still in place, but some—the ones probably most closely aligned with the climate study—are not. Perceived by some as top down initiatives, they faded with changes in administration. Thus, even if I had been able to identify some big splashes it would not have meant the study was necessarily a success in the long run.

Research in organizational development and change over the ten years since we did this study has focused on the distinction between **episodic** and **continuous** change in organizations (see Weick & Quinn, 1990). Episodic change occurs in distinct periods, when attempts are made to bring an otherwise static organization into alignment with new environmental demands. Theoretically, episodic change is necessitated because an organization has failed to achieve the more desirable condition: continuous adaptation. Episodic change is a response to a failure to adapt over time. It is often strategic, planned, top down, and disruptive because it **replaces** rather than **changes** existing activities (Mintzberg & Westley, 1992).

Continuous change, on the other hand, emerges more slowly, in smaller, much more frequent adaptations to the environment. Continuous change can be easier to sustain in the long run because new practices are not substituted for the old, but new practices gradually evolve from current practices being modified. These continuous change processes are viewed as the ideal form of change because they imply an alert organization that attempts to closely map and respond to the continuously fluctuating demands placed on it. Change becomes accepted as an ongoing, daily event. Organizations do not have to be startled into change. Instead, they are reinterpreting, rebalancing, and reorganizing all the time. Continuous change creates more adaptive organizations that are more likely to be successful in the long run.

The backlash against affirmative action and some other diversity programs can be viewed as an instance of a reaction against attempts to force episodic changes in organizations. In

415

most applications, affirmative action is viewed as top down. Because it is viewed as being forced on the organization, sometimes even the supporters of the basic principles end up objecting to the implementation of specific policies. Yet, despite the objections, affirmative action programs have been shown to be effective in increasing the representation of previously underrepresented groups. To stimulate the internalized, long-range change among individuals and organizations that make affirmative action programs unnecessary, however, additional strategies that support continuous change are needed. In the area of cultural diversity, continuous change rather than episodic change is a sign of success. Episodic change happens when organizations do not change. Continuous change reflects a learning organization, an ongoing process. It would be nice to think we were at a place in this country where most organizations recognized they must be involved in a continuous change process regarding the climate for underrepresented groups.

An essential ingredient for continuous change is discourse, especially "everyday conversation" (Dixon, 1997). Organizational members must be engaged in dialogues, hearing new perspectives, sharing their own, and testing new understandings as they assimilate day-to-day events. Stories need to evolve in which new values and practices are interwoven and used to interpret the future. These discourse processes were stimulated by our climate study. The open forums brought folks from very different backgrounds and status together to discuss their perspectives on common events. They found that often their perspectives diverged when convergence had been assumed—especially by those in "majority" groups, including campus leaders. The open sessions called for people to discuss issues they usually avoided. The richness of the anecdotes made aspects of the climate come alive in ways that would have been very difficult to do otherwise. The anecdotes were shared informally, in formal written and oral summaries, and even developed into case studies used in campus-wide training. The subsequent surveys of alumni conducted as part of the climate study also provided anecdotes and evaluative data from individuals who now were professionals and so had credibility they might not have had as students. Summaries of the survey data, and presentations based on it were a springboard for those wanting to prompt formal institutional change. In sum, the study engaged people in exchanges about topics they would have otherwise avoided. It gave them salient, meaningful, personal narratives and divergent perspectives they could integrate with their own world views.

In this light I now look at the climate study we did as a success. Much evidence indicates it stimulated dialogue. The small scale specific remedies recommended were all implemented in one way or another. No big splashes occurred that would boost the ego of developers or make its effectiveness easy to quantify, but it seems very likely from what we are learning about change, that it might have been an important ingredient in fostering long-range continuous change.

> A concern with "changing" means greater appreciation that change is never off, that its chains of causality are longer and less determinant than we anticipated, and that whether one's viewpoint is global or local makes a difference in the change that will be observed, the inertias that will be discovered, and the size of accomplishments that will have been celebrated (Weick & Quinn, 1999, p. 382).

Thus, I don't think our and subsequent climate studies or committees have been busywork, futile or a waste of time. Conducting a study that stimulates discussion and collects and shares perceptions of various groups is still valid and could have benefit in a wide variety of educational settings.

The Study

A serious shortage of engineers and other technically trained professionals has been projected to occur in the United States prior to the turn of the century. Yet, there has been a recent decline in the number of engineering degrees awarded in the United States (Ellis, 1992). Moreover, while 53% of students in college are female and 14% are African American, Native American, or Hispanic, in the field of engineering, only 16% of graduates are female and 8% are from the aforementioned minority groups.[2] If this disparity alone were eliminated, i.e., these groups entered and completed engineering degrees at the same rate European American males did, significant progress would be made toward addressing the projected shortfall in technical professionals. Eliminating this disparity between the numbers of European American males and others interested in engineering will become even more important as the proportion of college students who are female and minority grows relative to the proportion who are European American males. A recent study by Ellis (1992), the Director of Manpower Studies for American Association of Engineering Societies, shows that in fact slight increases in the proportion of females and minorities pursuing engineering degrees has occurred over the past two years.

Engineering schools around the country are trying to figure out how to attract and keep even more students in engineering, particularly minority and female students. A key factor in both retention and recruiting is the campus climate. "Campus climate embraces the culture, habits, decisions, practices, and policies that make up campus life. It is the sum total of the daily environment, and central to the 'comfort factor' that minority students, faculty, staff and administrators experience on campus" (American Council on Education, 1989, p. 113). A good climate can facilitate success. A poor climate can lead to difficulty attracting and retaining new students from diverse backgrounds. In fact, a poor climate can diminish the learning of all students. Moreover, intense racial conflict, triggered by relatively minor incidents, is more likely to occur on campuses with a poor climate.

This paper summarizes a study of the campus climate at a midwestern technological university. Beyond determining the climate, another key objective of this study was to educate the greater campus community in a nonthreatening and persuasive way about the experience of minority students, staff, and faculty who come from ethnically diverse backgrounds. A committee conducted the study. This approach had advantages in gaining participation in the study and acceptance of the results and recommendations. The methodology is outlined below so that it might be considered for implementation elsewhere. The results are also summarized at length so they might contribute to our understanding of the experience of ethnically diverse students at traditionally white institutions. They reveal divergent perceptions of the climate by students based on their ethnicity. They converge with other studies pointing to the critical role faculty play in the retention of minority engineering students, particularly African American students.

Objectives

In 1988, the University of Missouri-Rolla (UMR) Equal Employment Opportunity/Affirmative Action Advisory Committee (AAAC), with the strong support of the Chancellor, undertook a study of the campus climate for minorities. A campus-level committee reporting to the Chancellor and comprised of key vice chancellors and directors, eight students and five faculty members, the AAAC is chaired by the Affirmative Action Officer.[3] The objectives of the committee's study were to "1) assess the climate for minorities; 2) increase the campus awareness of, sensitivity to, and discussion of, the climate for minorities; 3) identify changes that should be made to improve the climate; and 4) suggest means of accomplishing those changes."

Student Demographics

During the time the climate study was conducted, there were just over 4800 students on campus, 86% of them enrolled as undergraduates. UMR is like many engineering schools: a traditionally white male institution. During the time of the study, no other group comprised more than 5% of the student body.

During the 1988-89 academic year, plans were made for the study, and selected individuals were interviewed by the committee concerning their experiences as minorities on the UMR campus. Plans for the second year were to conduct a survey of African American alumni and coordinate a series of open forums on campus for the discussion of the campus climate. The third year was for committee deliberation and the formulation of recommendations. The final report (Riordan, 1991) was circulated widely on campus and in the university system and was mailed to interested groups of UMR alumni.[4] The focus of this report is the results of our data-gathering activities—a series of campus forums and an alumni survey to assess the climate for minority students.

Forums on Campus Climate for Minorities

Open forums were scheduled for afternoons and were open to all staff, students, faculty, and administrators. They were widely advertised; printed publicity mentioned the opportunity to submit questions anonymously beforehand in boxes placed around campus. Each forum began with a structured presentation, led by student, faculty, or staff facilitators, followed by an open discussion. Introductory presentations dealt with topics like: what it is like to be different; what if offices dealing with minority students became "mini universities" handling virtually all functions relative to minority students; and what were individuals' earliest experiences of racism. Ground rules for the discussions were outlined: speakers had to be recognized by a moderator before speaking, and individuals not present were not to be criticized by name.

Classroom Climate

With respect to the climate in classrooms, a number of themes emerged. First, some minority students seemed hesitant to approach professors because they questioned the support faculty members would extend to minority students. Students also mentioned some professors being inhospitable to them during their office hours. Students perceived this as possible evidence of racism. Some faculty and administrators in attendance suggested that those faculty members might be treating all students that way.

A common complaint by minority students was that faculty had low expectations for their performance. Students felt this was revealed when a faculty member was quick to jump to the conclusion a minority student had cheated; seemed too surprised when the minority student performed well; or was very curious about where the student had gone to high school as if somehow he or she was better prepared academically than the faculty member had expected. Some students felt faculty members were unwilling to answer their questions in class and assumed the professors didn't have the confidence minority students could understand the material with a quick explanation. A number of students reported feeling professors—and other students—were more closely scrutinizing their behavior which made them feel uneasy.

Some students spoke about how they coped with these perceptions. They felt they needed to do better than other students in order to be accepted and to disconfirm instructors' low expectancy for their academic performance. Moreover, a number of students seemed to feel a need to prove they could succeed without any help; they could make it on their own and didn't need anyone else's help, especially that of a teacher who doubted their ability.

Being the only African American (or female) in a class or lab was raised as a concern a number of times. Students in this situation reported feeling conspicuous and isolated. They had difficulty forming relationships with other students and even knowing where to sit in such classes.

Climate Outside the Classroom

With respect to the overall climate on campus, the issues of racial polarization and the realities of "feeling different" arose. Reactions to racial polarization and segregation differed roughly along racial lines. Minority students saw obstacles and non-minority students saw few real problems.

A number of white students voiced their opinion that many of the concerns being raised by the black students were exaggerated and might be only in their minds. For example, they told a black female who felt uncomfortable when visiting her lab partner in his white fraternity house that everyone felt uncomfortable going into a fraternity house unless they were a member of, or frequently visited, that fraternity. Often, they said, the discomfort is in the mind of the person, not the result of how others are treating them.

There seemed to be an underlying feeling among many white students that simply acknowledging or talking about differences could not better race relations. "If you think you are different then you are doomed to be by yourself or with your own little group. I think that is your own problem. I don't think it is all the majority's fault. I don't think they should breed more minorities so you will have more friends and kill off all the majorities so that it is even."

A number of comments by white students said the minorities needed to become more like the majority. Others felt that the people in the room were not the ones with the problem: it was people not in attendance. This was countered with, "The people who are here do need to be here because they are learning and then they can help someone else understand."

Another concern raised had to do with campus programming and student organizations. A number of students complained that programming by the student groups did not target interests of the minority community. Furthermore, they felt most student organizations and campus functions were largely segregated.

Finally, there was also a discussion of affirmative action. A student in attendance eloquently clarified some of its history and purposes. Other comments clearly reflected the backlash against affirmative action: "Once you get on the defensive, you can't get anything accomplished for a better cause. A lot of laws today are making people get on the defensive."

Summary of the Findings

The predominantly white faculty, staff, and student body, as well as experiences gained with segregation and discrimination in the larger society, fostered doubt in the minority students' minds that made them ready to interpret even ambiguous situations as evidence of prejudice. Additionally they reported feeling instructors' perceptions of their ability were low and some minority students reported adopting avoidance or overcompensation as strategies to deal with the perceived prejudice.

A salient impression was the divergence along racial lines of the perceptions of the climate and desirable remedies. Minorities thought the climate was chillier for them than did non-minorities. Minorities saw discussion and action as remedies while many non-minorities felt such an approach would only heighten tensions.

Survey of African American Alumni

Methodology

The purpose of the survey was to assess African American alumni perceptions of the social and academic climate during the time they attended college and their current reflections on those years given the benefit of their broader range of experience. African Americans were selected because there had been more African American graduates than other minority graduates, yet they were still the most underrepresented group. Three hundred surveys were bulk-mailed in May 1989. A second mailing in June yielded an overall return rate of 38% which was considered adequate. A randomly selected comparison group of non-minority alumni, matched by major and year of graduation, was obtained and a similar survey mailed. Responses for most of the survey items can be seen in Figure 1. Items with an asterisk are ones for which differences between African Americans and non-minorities differed significantly according to an analysis of variance.

Figure 1
Results of alumni survey

Academic ability	African-American	Non-minority
Did you feel academically isolated at UMR?	2.86	2.42
Did you feel the course work at UMR was unnecessarily difficult?	2.70	2.65
Did you feel academically prepared?*	2.59	3.83
Did your instructors doubt your ability to succeed at UMR?*	3.83	2.58

Social support and environment	African-American	Non-minority
Compared to your present work environment, how would you rate the social environment at UMR?*	2.32	2.97
Compared to other universities, how would you rate the social environment at UMR?*	1.76	2.63
Did you feel socially isolated at UMR?*	3.17	2.02
Based on your experiences at UMR, how would you rate the social environment?*	2.07	2.70
How supportive were the faculty at UMR?*	2.70	3.50
How supportive were the staff at UMR?	3.22	3.58

Long-range effects	African-American	Non-minority
What effect did UMR have on your self-confidence?	3.51	3.80
Do you recommend UMR to young people as a good place to go?*	3.49	4.23

Overall Evaluation of Campus

When alumni gave their general reactions to the campus, their views were very positive. Alumni felt that overall their college experience had had a somewhat positive effect on their self-confidence; this was equally true for African American and non-minority alumni. Comments throughout the surveys suggested alumni felt proud of their success in having met the challenges—particularly the academic challenges. This may be the factor that produced the positive impact on their self-confidence they attribute to their college experience.

When asked whether they recommend this university to young people as a good place to go to school, the response was also quite positive. African American alumni, who were less likely to recommend it, still were more likely to say they would recommend it than not.

Specific Evaluations

In general, African American alumni views of the campus were not as positive as those of the non-minority alumni, although, some of these differences were not large enough to be considered statistically reliable. One large difference was African American alumni perceived that instructors doubted their ability more than the ability of majority students in their classes. Also, African American students themselves felt they were less well prepared academically than other students.

Alumni did not see the faculty and staff as a whole as being particularly supportive or unsupportive. African American alumni perceived faculty had been significantly less supportive than did non-minority alumni. Comments from the forums and written comments from the surveys suggest that many African American students had had bad experiences with one or two faculty, and possibly no very good relationships to balance those out.

Although alumni rated various aspects of the social environment fairly low, we have been told by some consultants our students' views of the social environment are actually quite positive according to national standards (Dehne, 1990). Nevertheless, African American alumni's responses were significantly lower on each dimension than were those of non-minorities. They felt more socially isolated and felt their current work environments and environments at other universities were more supportive of minorities.

What Makes a Good Professor?

Respondents also described the important characteristics of a really good professor. Their answers dealt largely with professor characteristics that would foster the development of relationships with students rather than particular teaching styles or activities. Over half of the comments (53%) mentioned a sensitive, caring attitude on the part of the instructor. Also mentioned were knowledge of the subject taught and its real world applications (34%), fairness and a lack of prejudice (29%), availability outside of class (27%), good communication skills (21%), enthusiasm or dedication (21%), providing a challenge for students (8%), and being organized (7%). Responses given by non-minority alumni focused almost exclusively on content knowledge (67%) and organization (42%) as traits making a good professor.

Advice for Current Students

When asked to give a few bits of unsolicited advice to current African American students at UMR, alumni emphasized the importance of studying hard (40%) and being persistent (38%). Some alumni also recommended getting involved in a number of campus organizations or activities—especially non-minority activities—to learn interpersonal skills important for the working world (19%). With equal frequency (18%), current students were advised to get involved in study groups and to help support each other. Eighteen percent of the respondents told students that they would have to endure a tough time because of the social environment in Rolla. Finally, students were advised to seek help when they needed it, to be persistent in getting it, and not to stand for rebuffs.

Advice for Faculty and Administration

Alumni were also asked to give a few bits of unsolicited advice to faculty and administrators. Over half of the comments (51%) asked faculty and administrators to stop discriminatory treatment of one kind or another. They wanted all students to be treated fairly, equally, the same, or without regard to color. One alum said, "Don't assume all black students are lazy because you had one ten years ago. You would not lump white students together like that."

Forty-three percent asked faculty and administrators to take a more active role in encouraging and helping minority students. A few of the specific recommendations offered were developing personal relationships with minority students, showing concern, talking to minority students, and involving them in classroom discussions and leadership roles. Sixteen percent of the responses mentioned improving the social environment and making it supportive of a diverse student body. Only nine percent of the responses mentioned the need to diversify the faculty.

Summary of the Findings

When we looked at the study results, we were somewhat reassured that the problems minority students were facing at this university were no worse than ones minorities often report at traditionally European American institutions (Altbach, 1990; Astin & Cross, 1981; McBay, 1986). In fact, there were fewer incidents of overt racism on the UMR campus than on many other campuses (Racism on Campus, 1989).

On the other hand, the study revealed many areas where there was significant room for improvement. Faculty-student relationships were not as strong as we would like them to be. These relationships are essential to reducing attrition which is at alarming levels among African Americans in engineering programs across the country. Our study suggested three reasons why faculty-student relations may be poor. First, the problem with low expectancies among some faculty is very salient to students. Having had a few experiences with poorly performing minorities in the past and generalizing those to all minorities and assuming that African American students have attended inner city schools, and that those schools are all of inferior quality, seem to be the key contributors to low expectancies. If faculty members had closer relationships with minority students, they could learn the abilities and backgrounds of minority students as individuals. This would help to minimize racially biased expectancies.

A second feature leading to poor faculty-student relationships may be the minority student being insecure about his or her chances for success because there are not enough examples of minorities who have succeeded at this university—either as graduates, faculty, or staff. This insecurity may lead minority students to exaggerate the negativity of certain interactions, attribute the cause to racism, or even worse, start to doubt their own ability (Hewitt & Seymour, 1992). They may withdraw because there is little one can do to "cure" a racist, or if they have begun to doubt their own ability, they may withdraw in an attempt to hide suspected inadequacies. Many examples of this withdrawal came out during the forums. Students described faculty members who were rude or hostile when students stopped by their offices. There are many nonracial reasons for this type of behavior on the part of faculty members. However, minority students may not ever learn what these are. The pattern of withdrawing and developing an "I'll show you attitude" makes it unlikely they would ever get an apology, learn the reason for the rudeness, or get to know the professors better so the outburst is seen as a fluke. In this way relations with that professor may never improve. Because the students carry the persistent worry that a professor acted rudely out of prejudice, the withdrawal may generalize to interactions with other professors.

The final aspect of faculty-student relationships contributing to minority students' perceptions that faculty are less supportive of them may be that minority alumni in our study placed much more importance on socio-emotional qualities (sensitivity, fairness) of the professors than did non-minority alumni. Non-minorities were more likely to evaluate faculty on content-related features (knowledge, organization). Given these divergent preferences, it may mean that minority students have higher standards for the nature of the relationships they want to have with their professors. Other studies of minorities at traditionally European American institutions have shown that minority students are less likely to have close relationships with faculty: they wanted closer relationships, yet they were less likely to have them.

Committee Recommendations

Recommendations for how to improve the climate clearly emerged from the study. This made deliberation by the committee fairly easy. The recommendations made to the campus are summarized in Table I. The committee also made plans for the actions it should take the next year. Many of the recommendations were already being implemented by the time the final report of this study was made because individuals responsible for those activities were committee members and had been convinced of the need for action as a result of participating in the study. Recommendations implemented most quickly were those that could be "added on" to an ongoing activity: adding diversity to new student and staff training, assigning minority students to classes in a different way, diversifying campus programming. New activities, like bringing off-campus experts to run full-day diversity workshops, have not been widely implemented.

Table 1. Recommendations and Plans Based on Results of Climate Study

Recommendations to the Campus

- Cluster Minority Students in Freshmen Classes
- Educate on Diversity
- Encourage Mentoring of Minority and Female Faculty and Staff
- Further Diversify Participation in Student Activities
- Improve Efforts to Recruit and Retain Minority Faculty and Staff
- Continue Implementation of Retention Committee Report

- Disseminate Information Acquired Through Forums
- Host Monthly Luncheon Series Focusing on Ethnicity and Gender
- Conduct Study of Images the Campus is Communicating to Campus Visitors
- Contribute Articles and Letters to the Student Newsletter
- Nominate Individuals for Standing Campus Awards Based on Their Contributions to Diversity

Evaluation

Overall, we felt this study was useful primarily because it helped to educate the campus community about diverging perceptions of the climate. Minority students and alumni clearly told us there were aspects of campus climate that were impeding their success and making them uncomfortable. Recommendations were made and adopted. Whether actions will have any significant impact on faculty-student relationships and student retention has yet to be seen. The results of our study indicate faculty play a key role in minority students' perceptions of the climate and that there is room for improvement. The faculty who participated in the campus forums and the AAAC now have a better understanding of the importance of their relationships with students and how relationships with faculty can go awry.

Unfortunately, not all faculty participated. Some senior faculty members in particular were very threatened by the complaints of students and the actions recommended by the committee. However, these senior faculty members, in the process of voicing their concerns drew in other faculty who had not previously been part of the discussion of the divergent perceptions and how faculty-student relationships might be improved. Thus, while these senior faculty members were not supporters of the committee's actions, they were part of the change process. Overall, the AAAC has laid the groundwork by identifying perceptions of the climate and building a broad-based consensus for change. We hope this will make subsequent efforts to address concerns of minority students easier and more fruitful.

Endnotes

[1]Thanks go to all members of the AAAC during 1988-1991, especially Carol Heddinghaus for her assistance coding the data, to Ginny Maedgen for preparing the original report, to Marcy Scott for preparing this report, to the most active committee members, Sema Alptekin, Becky Edwards, Robert Graff, Glen Haddock, Floyd Harris, Sam Hutson III, Sharon Irwin, Regina Jacobs, Torrance Jones, Chris Koubdje, Robert Lewis, Yolanda Luster, Kathleen Mahoney, Jason Mathis, Phyllis McCoy, John Molchan, Daopu Numbere, Wendell Ogrosky, John Park, Marilyn Peebles, Luke Peterson, Robert Phillips, Mark Potrafka, Juana Sanchez, Mike Schmid, David Tepen, and student leaders who served as moderators for the forums, Eugene Bae, Michael Tolbert, and Tamiko Youngblood.

I want to thank the editors of this volume for their wisdom and advice.

Preparation of this report was supported in part by a Missouri Youth Initiative Fellowship sponsored by the Kellogg Foundation.

[2]In conceptualizing and carrying out the study, the term "minority" was used. I have continued to use the term throughout this report for a number of reasons. The primary purpose

of the study was to make the campus aware that students, whose backgrounds were demographically different from those of the majority of the faculty and student body, had perceptions of the climate that differed from those of the majority. In this sense, the study focused on "non-white" students, i.e., students defined not by their individual character-istics or the particular ethnic group with which they identified, but by the fact that they were not members of the majority group.

In reality the minority population of this university is largely African American and Asian. However, we did not distinguish between ethnic groups during the course of the study. Consequently, another reason I chose to use the term minority, with all of its limita-tions, is that it most accurately reflects the terminology, the perspective, and the under-standing we had at the time of the study.

We could have used different terminology when conducting the study. However, to further our objective of letting most people on the campus hear first hand that students of color often have perspectives on the climate that are very different from their own, we needed to help those students feel comfortable sharing their perspectives. This university is like most other predominantly engineering schools—there are relatively few African Americans, Native Americans and Hispanics. We were convinced in planning this study that students asked to share their perspectives would feel more comfortable if they perceived a "safety in numbers." This fact was borne out during the open forums in which it was not until persons of color constituted the majority of participants that many felt comfortable being frank about their experiences. Dividing these students into smaller groups could have eliminated the safety they felt.

[3]The author was Affirmative Action Officer during the time of the study.

[4]Copies of a longer report of this study, including specifics of the methodology can be obtained from Catherine A. Riordan, Management Systems, University of Missouri Rolla, Rolla, MO 65401.

References

Altbach, P. G. (1990). The racial dilemma in American higher education. *Journal for Higher Education Management, 5*(2), 3-17.

Astin, H. S., & Cross, H. (1981). Black students in black and white institutions. In G. E. Thomas (Ed.), *Black students in higher education* (pp. 30-45). Westport, CT: Greenwood Press.

Dehne, G., & Associates. (1990, November). *Institutional admissions audit.* Rolla: University of Missouri-Rolla.

Dixon, N. M. (1997). The hallways of learning. *Organizational Dynamics, 25,* 23-24.

Ellis, R. A. (1992, February). Degrees '91: A mixed report. *ASEE Prism,* 30-32.

Green, M. F (Ed.). (1989). *Minorities on campus: A handbook for enhancing diversity,* Washington, DC: American Council on Education.

Hewitt, N. M., & Seymour, E. (1992, February). A long, discouraging climb. *ASEE Prism,* 24- 28.

Kanter, R. (1980). *A Tale of 0.* Cambridge, MA: Goodmeasure Associates.

McBay, S. H. (1986). The racial climate on the MIT campus: A report of the minority student issues group. Cambridge: Massachusetts Institute of Technology.

Meinholdt, C., & Murray, S. L. (in press). Why aren't there more women engineers? *Journal of Women and Minorities in Science and Engineering, 5.*

Mintzberg, H., & Westley, F. (1992). Cycles of organizational change. *Strategic Management Journal, 13,* 39-59.

Murray, S. L., Meinholdt, C., Bergmann, L. S. (in press). Addressing gender issues in the engineering classroom. *The Feminist Teacher.*

Payne, J. (1989, September-October). Hidden messages in the pursuit of equality. *Academe,* 19-22.

Black Issues in Higher Education. (1989). Racism on campus. Teleconference.

Riordan, C. A. (1991). *The campus climate for minorities at the University of Missouri-Rolla.* Rolla, MO: University of Missouri-Rolla.

Weick, K. E., & Quinn, R. E. (1999). Organizational change and development. *Annual Review of Psychology, 50,* 361-386.

THE DIVERSITY CONTINUUM: ENHANCING STUDENT INTEREST AND ACCESS, CREATING A STAYING ENVIRONMENT, AND PREPARING STUDENTS FOR TRANSITION

by
Karen A. Myers, Robert Caruso, and Nancy A. Birk

In this essay, we attempt to take a longitudinal view of diversity by looking at a continuum of models designed to improve student interest in and access to higher education, create a "staying environment" which promotes student persistence, and facilitate the transition of students to the world of graduate study and/or employment. Reasons for implementing such programs clearly are as varied as the institutions themselves but are generally related to institutional mission, altruism, and economics.

Institutional mission statements which embrace diversity as part of the ethos of the institution prompt many initiatives. This thrust may be related to enhancing the learning environment through multiculturalism, maintaining or increasing enrollments by reaching typically underrepresented student populations, preparing students for work in a diverse employment setting, and, in some cases, overcoming egregious historical discrimination practices at the institution.

"It's the right thing to do." "It's morally correct." "We need to be sensitive to the welfare of our minority students." These are all common expressions used to justify improvements. Professionals in student affairs, for example, are typically guided by a philosophy which respects the worth, dignity, and uniqueness of individuals. Individuals are viewed as "proactive" beings in the process of developing, changing, and growing. The professional's role is to support the individual and help shape the environment to guarantee a dynamic, growth-producing climate for learning and living. Assisting minority students is in many ways an expression of this philosophy.

Supporting traditionally underrepresented students can also have clear economic benefits since students contribute to the economic strength of an institutional community and graduates become part of an educated work force that contributes to increased productivity. As businesses, educational institutions, and governmental agencies attempt to meet their goals, given current and projected demographics, creating multicultural employment settings is critically important not only by insuring their economic success but also because placing more trained people in the work force increases the tax base, expands contributions to the social security system, and insures that all Americans can live comfortably into their retirement years.

We believe that colleges and universities interested in achieving a diverse student body must:

- actively seek opportunities for collaboration with elementary schools, middle schools, and junior high schools as well as explore more traditional linkages with secondary schools—all with the primary goal of raising student aspirations;
- mobilize the resources of the campus and the community to help foster a caring environment which supports the primacy of learning and academic achievement;
- work with families to foster a supportive home atmosphere that is conducive to successful participation in postsecondary education; and

- prepare students for life after the institution through programs and services which encourage graduate school enrollment and/or facilitate effectiveness in employment settings.

Although there are many outstanding examples of minority recruitment and retention activities in our nation's colleges and universities, too often institutional efforts may be characterized as fragmented or shortsighted. Among the weaknesses which often stand out are:

- lack of ownership of the problem of student persistence by all members of the institutional community;
- failure to endorse diversity, equity, and justice as institutional priorities;
- lack of appreciation of the importance of reaching students at an early age to elevate aspirations and promote interest in furthering their education;
- lack of collaboration with families and guardians well known to play a major role in the education of their children and in their college participation rates;
- lack of appropriate services and programs to support students once they are enrolled despite vigorous recruitment efforts;
- poor connections with the minority community in the service area of the institution and lack of sensitivity among some businesses, agencies, and community groups to the needs of minority students; and
- lack of minority faculty, administrative, and staff role models, coupled with majority staff unwilling to invest time and energy to insure minority student success.

Throughout this essay we describe models which address the issues of student access and achievement and attempt to overcome many of these weaknesses.

Early Awareness Programs: The Beginning of the Diversity Continuum

While the latter half of the 1980s and the early 1990s was a period of diminished college attendance for minorities, in the past five years the number of African American, Hispanic, Asian, and Native American students receiving college degrees has soared (Chenoweth, 1998b). This is undeniably good news. However, the proportion of minority students attending four-year public institutions in 1997 was only 23.2% of the total college student population. In Missouri, however, that figure is even lower—approximately 13% (*The Chronicle Almanac*, 1997). The rate of incarceration of minorities is increasing faster than the rate of minorities receiving college degrees (Chenoweth, 1998b). Moreover, few minority students are preparing for teaching or science careers; fewer still are preparing for leadership roles.

Neither the interest in nor the aptitude for a college education occurs suddenly upon the completion of high school. A foundation for developing student potential should begin early and continue throughout the K-12 educational experience, as large numbers of minority students are lost at each level of schooling. Exposure to higher education must occur long before college matriculation if students are to see it as viable and that through higher education their social and economic well-being will be improved.

A wide variety of programs exist that are designed to expose young students to higher education. Such programs vary by institution, but many offer mentoring as a way to connect elementary and secondary students with individuals in higher education or industry. The underlying goal of these efforts is to expose students to the culture and ultimately the benefits of higher education. As young students have positive experiences through such programs, higher education becomes a real possibility for them. As a result, the importance of current academic pursuits and the clarification of life goals are highlighted.

Talent Search

Across the country many institutions participate in Talent Search, one component of the TRIO programs established under Title IV of the Higher Education Act of 1965. This program serves young people in grades six through twelve, offering counseling, information about college admissions requirements, and scholarships and financial aid. This early intervention program helps young students better understand their educational opportunities and currently serves over a quarter of a million individuals. At Western Carolina University, this program has served approximately 900 students each year for almost twenty years.

Connecticut Pre-Engineering Program (CPEP)

Sponsored by the University of New Haven, this program is designed to generate interest in careers in engineering on the part of seventh- and eighth-grade students in the area. Initiated ten years ago, the program targets low-income minority and female students, primarily from the inner city, who show academic promise and who are interested in technology and engineering. Faculty at New Haven work collaboratively with the secondary school staff to provide a summer institute in which students are given instruction in academic areas as well as in self-esteem building and communication skills. Participants enjoy field trips and design science projects. CPEP Day is held each year during which students participate in a variety of scientific contests, such as creating a solar car. Activities take place during the academic year as well, after school and on Saturdays.

Stevens Institute of Technology and the NASA Pilot Telementoring Project

Launched in the spring of 1997, this project pairs NASA engineers and scientists with eighth- and ninth-grade Hispanic students in New Jersey. The NASA mentors, whose backgrounds are also primarily Hispanic, work closely with the students via the Internet to encourage interest in science. Using desktop videoconferencing, students and mentors proceed through a structured curriculum on meteorology. Students are strongly encouraged to take questions and concerns to their mentors via e-mail (Mellander & Mellander, 1998).

Minority Early Awareness Program Project

This project was initiated several years ago by Western Illinois University in partnership with Beethoven School in an effort to connect minority students in seventh and eighth grades with minority college students. The college students guide the Beethoven students through recreational events as well as academic programs and social gatherings.

Minority Teacher Incentive Program

Begun as a co-sponsored initiative in the spring of 1992 by the WIU College of Education and the Office of Academic Orientation, this program is designed to encourage minority students of middle school through high school to consider education as a career and develop skills that will facilitate success in higher education. Students spend time on the WIU campus meeting with minority college student mentors, attending workshops and "ice breaker" activities.

Many programs are in place which focus on improving the academic skills of students who are interested in attending college, particularly students who are among the first generation in their families to pursue higher education. Family members, whose influence on students is considerable, may not value higher education, thus producing a home environment that is not conducive to a successful college experience, leading to a greater drop-out risk (*The Chronicle of Higher Education*, 1999). It is important to recognize the significant role family attitudes play in student success. Programs emphasizing skill acquisition or enhancement must also incorporate support structures to assist students in overcoming some of the fears they and their families might have about college. This emphasis includes information about the culture of college life as well as academic expectations and demands.

First-Generation Student Success Program

Part of a three-year study beginning in 1996 at the University of LaVerne in California, this program works with first-generation college students and their families to help them negotiate the admissions process and to provide support through the first two years of college. About 55 Latino students participate in the program and are linked with a mentor. Students attend a series of workshops and also receive a $1,000 scholarship. Results from the first year indicate an 86% retention rate, compared to 75% in the general student population. The program is designed to teach students and their families the "ins and outs" of college attendance and to give support as families experience the adjustment of having a child go to college. It was implemented to ease the struggle many minority students experience between the demands of family life and college (*The Chronicle of Higher Education*, 1999).

Upward Bound

Another of the original TRIO programs, Upward Bound helps young people prepare for college through instruction in literature, composition, foreign languages, mathematics, and science on college campuses after school, on Saturdays, and during the summer. At Southeast Missouri State University, 50 ninth- through twelfth-grade students participate in a six-week summer course that emphasizes academic abilities as well as time management and study skills. The goal of the program is to promote student success, laying the foundation for a positive college experience. Upward Bound has been a presence on the Southeast campus for five years, primarily serving minority students from eight schools in the area. Students also enjoy recreational and cultural experiences as part of the program.

Pre-Admission Education Program (PREP)

This program is a partnership between Southeast Missouri State University and Three Rivers Community College in Missouri designed for students who do not qualify for admission to Southeast. Candidates are recent high school graduates in the surrounding area who do not meet Southeast admissions requirements based on ACT scores. Those selected are admitted to Three Rivers and enroll in 34 hours of coursework on the Southeast campus for one academic year. Students must achieve at least a 2.0 GPA, at which time they are granted regular admission to Southeast. In addition to academic enhancement skills, students receive assistance with time management, test taking, reading for comprehension, and general college survival skills. Students in the Fall 1998 cohort demonstrated gains in information processing, use of study aids, motivation, and time management, as well as a significant reduction in academic anxiety. Student comments about the program are extremely positive, indicating that it made college accessible to them.

UCLA Feeder Program

In a collaborative effort between the University of California-Los Angeles (UCLA) and the Los Angeles school district, tenth- and eleventh-grade students in a Los Angeles magnet school have been given the opportunity to complete as much as forty-three hours of college credit by the time they graduate from high school. There is no charge for tuition. Students, who are primarily non-Native speakers of English, find that the program gives them an edge in admission to UCLA, whose admission competition is growing fierce. The program differs from many other pre-matriculation models in that the students are largely involved in their honors programs and must have a 3.0 grade point average to participate. The program began in the fall semester of 1998 and is expected to offset the sharp declines in minority student enrollment experienced by UCLA recently (Chiang, 1998).

Summary

Early awareness programs provide students, both minority and non-minority, with an introduction to the world of higher education. The programs attempt to plant the positive seeds of high aspirations and help young people realize that they can attend college if they have the desire and willingness to do so. Families, too, are made aware that college careers can become a reality for their children. The availability, accessibility, and affordability of post-secondary education is emphasized and encouraged. The dissemination of information along with the campus experiences provided by these programs tend to have a "ripple effect" on parents, families, and friends of the young participants; thus, the message emphasizing the importance of higher education spreads. Longitudinal tracking of students through the point of college matriculation serves as an important determinant of program success.

University students and staff involved in the early intervention programs benefit in significant ways. Mentoring youngsters, educating them about academic and campus life, and virtually opening young people's eyes and minds to a new world is an enjoyable, rewarding experience for university volunteers. Just as important is the opportunity for the development of leadership skills among staff and student mentors through activities such as goal setting, assessment, instruction, consultation, environmental management, and evaluation.

Programs for New and Continuing Students: Creating a "Staying Environment"

These models encompass a wide range of activities directed toward orienting students to the campus environment, supporting them as they begin their studies, and encouraging students to persist to graduation or to the completion of their planned program of study. Among the many retention principles inherent in strong orientation and new-student programs enumerated by Mann (1986) are:

- creating a balanced program which incorporates not only the goals of the institution to disseminate and collect student information but also allows students opportunities for personal development;
- developing students' responsibility for their own actions and for reading and following directions;
- utilizing effective faculty and staff members to achieve optimum contact time with students;
- establishing an effective student orientation leadership staff through careful selection, training, and professional staff supervision, and using these student leaders to help implement the program; and
- reaching parents, guardians, and significant others as part of the overall orientation and retention effort.

Programs aimed toward creating a "staying environment" for minority students represent the second part of the diversity continuum. Cognitive and noncognitive factors related to minority student success must be addressed and incorporated into these retention/persistence models if they are to succeed. Programs which combine the resources of academic affairs and student services professionals have the capacity for broad-based, significant impacts on traditionally underrepresented students. As Tinto (1979) strongly suggested in his student retention model, persistence is directly correlated to the degree of integration students achieve within both the academic and social systems of an institution.

Mentoring Programs

Mentoring is increasingly recognized as an effective tool in retaining students, particularly students of color. A wide variety of such programs exists whose goal is to provide students with a vital connection to the institution. Mentors may simply be a resource, someone who provides information, or they may play a more intrusive role, being a significant part of the student experience.

Southeast Friends

Begun in the early 1990s at Southeast Missouri State University, the program was billed as "Project Retention" and was an intrusive method of contacting all first-year students to check on their satisfaction with college life. Although not specifically geared toward minority students, the concept underlying the program was to provide a support network for those students who might be "at-risk" for dropping out. In the fall semester of 1997, the program was retitled, "Adopt-A-Student" and faculty and staff were recruited to serve as mentors to individual students. The following year, the program was again renamed, adopting the "Southeast Friends" moniker. As before, faculty and staff served as mentors to new students, contacting them periodically to check on their academic and social adjustment to college. While successful, the program could only reach a limited number of new students. To address this concern, New Student Programs worked with Computer Services to create a listserv of new students in the spring semester of 1999. E-mail messages are sent to new students on a regular basis, providing information about college success skills, as well as special events on campus. Students are encouraged to reply with questions or concerns. A mentor is assigned to any student who replies and/or gives any indication of being at risk.

Minority Mentor Program

Sponsored by Minority Student Programs, eligible minority students at Southeast Missouri State University are placed in two-year workshops in various on-campus offices and have a mentoring relationship with their supervisors. These are students who show academic promise but whose ACT scores are such that other scholarships are not available to them. Academic achievement is emphasized, as is co-curricular involvement. In order to provide a holistic educational experience, students in the program are required to live on campus. Mentors meet regularly with the participants to discuss not only academic progress, but also other areas of students' lives that might impact the college experience.

Project C.A.R.E.

Project C.A.R.E. (Committed to African-American Retention in Education) is a combination of programs seeking to improve the academic performance and retention of Western Carolina University's African American student population. Project C.A.R.E. is a unique collaboration between the Offices for Student Affairs and Academic Services.

Peer Mentor Program

Minority Student Programs at Southeast Missouri State University sponsors this program to assist first-year minority students in their transition to college life. The goal of the program is to improve minority student retention and graduation rates. Upper-class students who have demonstrated academic achievement and leadership abilities serve as mentors to first-year minority students. Mentors meet with students several times each month, acquaint students with campus resources and services, assist new students in understanding the University's structure, invite new students to attend cultural and educational events, and challenge new students to be academically competitive and to assume leadership roles on campus. Mentors are trained to be non-judgmental and open, making appropriate referrals when necessary. More than half of the University's new minority students participate in the program, which was initiated in the mid-1990s.

Partnership for Progress

Begun several years ago, this program was begun as a collaborative effort at Western Illinois University by the Enrollment Management Office, Student Multicultural Services Office, and the Minority Student Retention Task Force. The program pairs selected incoming minority students with members of the faculty and administration on a one-to-one basis to develop a "helping network" for minority students and insure that they quickly become comfortable within the university environment.

Let the Dialogue Begin

Developed through the Student Multicultural Services Office at Western Illinois University several years ago, this program links specially trained undergraduate minority leaders with incoming minority students and stimulates relationship-building with teaching faculty and staff. Upper-level students serve as peer advisors, assisting students in understanding academic expectations, social opportunities, sources of assistance, and strategies for success.

Beyond Mentoring

While mentoring programs are crucial in terms of providing a connection to higher education institutions, other services exist to support students academically. Such programs vary greatly in the populations served, but many target minority students, first-generation college students, and students with learning or physical disabilities. Others may not target specific student populations, but have as their goals helping students learn to cope with college, build self-esteem, become integrated academically, and develop a connection with the university, all important predictors of college student success for diverse student populations (Zea, Reisen, Beil, & Caplan, 1997).

Student Support Services

One component of the TRIO program, Student Support Services works with 200 students each year at Southeast Missouri State University. To participate, students must either be a first-generation college student, be eligible for financial assistance, or provide documentation of a disability. The goal of the program is to increase the retention and graduation rates of students by providing tutoring, academic and study skills workshops, cultural activities, financial aid information, mid-semester grade checks, personal counseling, graduate school assistance, and academic advising. This nationwide program serves students at over 700 colleges and universities.

Exploring Transfer

In the mid-1980s, Vassar College began to reach out to neighboring community colleges, encouraging promising students to transfer upon completion of the associate's degree. The students, primarily older minority individuals, were required to be hard-working academic achievers, many of whom enrolled in college to enhance their job opportunities. As of 1996, 399 community college students had completed the program, having become first-rank scholars. The students and faculty are enthusiastic about the program, emphasizing the positive experiences associated with different cultural and educational environments (Chenoweth, 1998b).

Minority Student Retention Task Force

Composed of a cross-section of Western Illinois University personnel interested in minority student achievement, the Minority Student Retention Task Force brings together professionals from both academic affairs and student services. The principal objective of the task force is to provide an ongoing forum for the discussion of policies and programs which encourage minority student persistence.

Early Academic Warning System

This system provides mid-term reports to students who are performing below satisfactory levels. The reports are based on grades faculty members voluntarily submit each semester. A letter is sent to each student by the Assistant Vice President for Enrollment Management providing information about the importance and meaning of early-warning grades and encouraging students to take advantage of several academically oriented outreach workshops.

Minority Achievement Program

This program was developed in an effort to attract and retain minority students with high academic promise. Coordinated by the Student Multicultural Services Office at Western Illinois University, the program encourages academic achievement among minority students, offering financial incentives to participants.

The Scholastic Career Advancement Network

Initiated by the Student Multicultural Services Office at Western Illinois University, this resource provides information of interest to minority students on undergraduate research, internships, graduate assistantships/fellowships, and other academic career development opportunities.

University 103: Learning Strategies

Students eligible for Student Support Services at Sonoma State University may take this course, which is designed to enhance academic success in reading, mathematics, science, and writing. Developed from a series of workshops, this course offers a continuum of support services, including individual, small group, and classroom instruction (Highhouse, Fraser, & Freund, 1996).

GC110: Principles of Personal Adjustment

This three-credit-hour course is offered at Southeast Missouri State University to students with fewer than 45 credit hours. Although academic success strategies are emphasized, the focus also includes topics such as time and money management, relationships, and drug and alcohol use. Such subjects are pertinent to students and have a significant impact on student success.

Student involvement and commitment to higher education are significant contributors to a successful college experience (Astin, 1977; Tinto, 1987). In this era of accountability, institutions of higher learning must focus on the factors that help retain students. Research indicates that when new students feel strong institutional commitment, particularly during the first eight weeks, they are more likely to re-enroll for subsequent semesters (Miles & Berger, 1997). Many institutions across the country are implementing programs to promote student involvement, particularly among students of color.

First-year Learning Team (FLighT) Program

In the fall semester of 1997, the FLighT Program, sponsored by New Student Programs, was implemented at Southeast Missouri State University for first-year students in an effort to foster student involvement and commitment. Cohorts of 25 students were co-enrolled in three general education classes linked by a theme or area of interest. Most of the participants lived on campus and were housed in a common residential hall. Results from the first year were extremely positive, showing high levels of student involvement on campus. The few students who did not return for their second year were contacted by New Student Programs; all of them cited personal reasons for not re-enrolling, emphasizing their positive feelings for the university. The program is in its second year and funding has been obtained for at least two more years.

Leadership in Diversity

Sponsored by Residence Life and Minority Student Programs at Southeast Missouri State University, this program recognizes and celebrates diversity on campus. A wide variety of individuals have been housed together on a common floor and work with Community Advisors trained to promote diversity and multicultural understanding. The program is in its second year and is a positive experience for students and staff alike.

Outreach Programs

A racial misunderstanding at Cornell University prompted administrators and students to develop a series of programs designed to educate students about diversity and multiculturalism. Based in the residential housing division, the programs are intended to increase interaction and multicultural understanding among students. Cornell's ten theme residence halls will increase their educational efforts for students, focusing particularly on those students who do not live in a residence hall. Funds have been made available to student groups to develop projects that will spur interaction among students (Roach, 1997).

Developmental Advising

The final model under discussion in this section is academic advising. No longer viewed as a routine, prescriptive activity, academic advising may now be viewed as developmental or even intrusive. Such a concept implies deliberate, structured intervention at the first indication of academic or personal difficulty in order to motivate the student to identify the problem and seek assistance. Research indicates that students prefer the developmental approach and that it leads to higher retention and graduation rates (Bernhardt, 1997). Within such a paradigm, the focus is on potential rather than limitation, achievement and personal growth rather than the simple acquisition of credits. The advisor-student relationship is collaborative. Many institutions are beginning to recognize the benefits of developmental advising, incorporating the paradigm into existing programs or introducing it as an entirely new experience for students.

Developmental advising programs are incorporated into many programs already discussed such as the TRIO Programs, Early Academic Warning Systems, and the Minority Mentor Program. Student Support Services in particular places a strong emphasis on integrated, intrusive academic advising, utilizing the services of degreed professional counselors/advisors who are current on the latest academic and legislative mandates that affect students in the program. Developmental advising should encourage personal growth and development in areas of decision making, personal responsibility, critical thinking, life skills (e.g., time management, stress management, financial management), and problem solving. Students are empowered to assume responsibility for their own academic progress, working collaboratively with advisors to focus on abilities. While many faculty advisors, limited in the time they may spend with students, appear to prefer the more traditional prescriptive advising methods, the developmental approach is appealing to students. Moreover, this approach has the added benefit of enhancing retention and graduation rates (Bernhardt, 1997). Further research indicates that the climate of an institution can be critical to the retention of its students of color. Zea et al. (1997) found that academic achievement has a stronger impact on the commitment of minority students than on nonminority students. Social integration is a significant factor as well. Given that, it is crucial that students take charge of their lives on campus through developmental advising.

Transition Programs: The End of the Diversity Continuum

According to John Gardner, Vice Chancellor for Continuing Education at the University of South Carolina, "the Freshman Year Experience is about transition, specifically those critical transitional experiences common to college freshmen. But college involves another equally important transition from college to post-college situations of work, marriage, parenting, community and national service, and leadership" (*Freshman Year Experience Newsletter*, 1989, p.4). Educators are beginning to recognize the need for transitional activities aimed at both students contemplating graduate studies and those preparing to enter the workplace. Input from the general public as well as from college governing boards indicates that undergraduate students need to be better prepared for both transitions.

The whole area of senior-year experiences will continue to grow as more institutions recognize that not only do incoming students face major transitional challenges but that juniors and seniors also must be supported in their transitions from the institution. Such programs indicate that an institution offers a caring environment for all students and provides for the special challenges related to each academic level.

The Senior Year Experience and Capstone Courses

Developed by the University of South Carolina, the Senior Year Experience is not simply a course, but rather a philosophy. It refers to the total experience of seniors inside and outside the classroom, as provided by the faculty, student affairs officers, academic administrators, and seniors themselves. The Senior Year Experience focuses on efforts to help seniors make meaning of the senior experience, bringing closure, connectedness, integration, and reflection to the diverse set of activities they have experienced as undergraduates. It is a last concluding effort on the part of the institution to help students graduate with the kinds of skills they will need to be successful in the work force or in graduate school. The capstone course offers seniors an opportunity to reflect on the outcomes of their major, to enhance their research skills, to consider the issues related to the transition from the university to post-collegiate life, and to develop further written and oral communication. At South Carolina, students may enroll in University 401: Senior Capstone Experience for variable credit. Other institutions, such as Southeast Missouri State University, also recognize the value of the senior year experience and are in the process of designing capstone courses for a variety of majors.

Career Development

According to data obtained from the 1998 Cooperative Institutional Research Program (CIRP), students cite "getting a good job" as their main motivation for attending college, a trend that has been noted for the past few years. Because a good job is an important objective, students must be proactive in planning their career development. At Southeast Missouri State University, the Career Services office has developed a comprehensive career development model and strongly encourages students to register in their first year to begin identifying career goals. Students use a computer program, FOCUS II, to explore career options related to academic majors. A course for first- and second-year students, GC231 Career/Life Planning, is available for credit to help further clarify goals. Career Services urges students to become involved in campus organizations to develop confidence, leadership abilities, communication skills, and an appreciation of diversity. As students progress through their academic programs, Career Services assists them in obtaining internships to gain "hands-on" experience, as well as helping students write resumes, cover letters, and do mock interviews. A course in job search techniques, GC431 Job Search Strategies, is open to seniors, who also receive information on graduate school selection and admissions procedures. Special events are held each year, including career and internship fairs, on-campus interviews with employers, and a minority career exploration dinner. All services are provided at no cost to students.

Diversity Continuum and the Hispanic Program for Educational Advancement

The Hispanic Program for Educational Advancement (HPEA) represents many of the best features of the diversity continuum discussed throughout this essay. The program has the capacity for early awareness activities, student recruitment and retention initiatives, and student transitional support.

Initiated in 1990 as a collaborative effort between Western Illinois University and Black Hawk College in Illinois, the HPEA is a multipurpose educational program geared toward the Hispanic community in the Quad Cities area. In recent years, the program has expanded to Sauk Valley College and community colleges in the greater Chicago area. Among the program's goals are increasing student post-secondary access, retention, and graduation rates; strengthening student motivation to seek academic success and degree completion at a college or university; and raising the awareness of the Hispanic community about higher education. The program's bilingual staff offers educational information, financial aid resources, tutoring, day-care for children, career planning assistance, and cultural programs.

The HPEA works closely with the public school system and community to raise student aspirations through awareness programs, educational materials, and an ongoing academic talent search. An attempt is made to establish strong relationships with the Hispanic community in the service area of the participating higher education institutions to develop a campus-community connection which encourages academic achievement. Finally, the program incorporates both academic and co-curricular activities designed to enhance the learning environment and encourages student persistence and graduation.

Implementing such comprehensive programs or those we have described earlier will move institutions toward their diversity goals. The diversity continuum can become a reality at many institutions through leadership that emphasizes vision, commitment, and creativity.

References

Astin, A. W. (1977). *Four critical years: Effects of college on beliefs, attitudes, and knowledge.* San Francisco: Jossey-Bass.

Bernhardt, J. J. (1997, Winter). Comprehensive academic advising increases student retention, graduation, and transfer in post-secondary TRIO programs. *Journal of the National Council of Educational Opportunity Associations,* 14-18.

Chenoweth, K. (1998a, February 19). The new faces of Vassar. *Black Issues in Higher Education, 14*(26), 22-23.

Chenoweth, K. (1998b, July 6). The surging degree wave. *Black Issues in Higher Education, 15*(10), 20-23.

Chiang, S. (1998). UCLA feeder program takes sting out of anti-affirmative action policies. *Black Issues in Higher Education, 15,* 12-13.

The Chronicle of Higher Education Almanac. (1997, August 29).

Cooperative Institutional Research Program (1998). *The CIRP Freshman Survey.* Los Angeles, CA: University of California at Los Angeles, Higher Education Research Institute.

Highhouse, Y., Fraser, K., & Freund, C. (1996, June). Learning-to-learn: Specialists collaborate to teach success. *Journal of the National Council of Educational Opportunity Associations,* 9-12.

Mann, B. A. (1986). Retention principles for new student orientation programs. In *Student services: Enhancing student life* (pp. 85-92). Chapel Hill: The University of North Carolina General Administration.

Mellander, N., & Mellander, G. (1998). Telementoring the young: One-on-one, Q&A, and subject data on tap. *The Hispanic Outlook, 9,* 20-22.

Miles, J. F., & Berger, J. B. (1997). A modified model of college student persistence: Exploring the relationship between Astin's theory of involvement and Tinto's theory of student departure. *Journal of College Student Development, 38,* 387-399.

Roach, R. (1997, September 4). Spurring interaction. *Black Issues in Higher Education, 14,* 15.

The senior year experience: An interview with John Gardner. (1989). *The Freshman Year Experience Newsletter,* pp. 4-5. University of South Carolina.

Tinto, J. V. (1979). Dropout from higher education: A theoretical synthesis of recent research. *Journal of Educational Research, 45,* 89-125.

Tinto, J. V. (1987). *Leaving college: Rethinking the causes and cures of student attrition.* Chicago: University of Chicago Press.

To help Latino students, a college looks to parents. (1999, January 15). *The Chronicle of Higher Education,* pp. A43-A44.

Zea, M. C., Reisen, C. A., Beil, C., & Caplan, R. D. (1997). Predicting intention to remain in college among ethnic minority and nonminority students. *Journal of Social Psychology, 137,* 149-161.

MULTICULTURAL PERSPECTIVES IN COUNSELING

by

Edward Johnson, Linda S. Aguilar, and Vera Mitrovich

The concept of multicultural counseling, though not new by any means, was given a formal beginning in this country over 30 years ago when the American Personnel and Guidance Association (now called the American Counseling Association) formed its Human Rights Commission in 1965 (Burn, 1992). In the midst of a decade focusing on civil rights for minority groups, and a growing effort on the part of those groups to maintain their cultural identities, it was decided by this professional counseling organization that the needs of all individuals should be considered and assessed. In 1973 ethical guidelines for the profession were endorsed by the American Psychological Association (Casas, Ponterotto, & Gutierrez, 1986). Although many saw these beginnings as more rhetoric than action, recently momentum supporting the validity and necessity of multiculturalizing the mental health field has been building. Indeed, the future will force the issue. The population is changing, shifting away from a single, dominant majority group. This country is fast becoming more pluralistic, and the sheer numbers of minorities are growing too large to ignore (Ancis, 1998; Sue, 1992; Ibrahim, 1991).

The multicultural counseling movement and its impetus toward more sensitivity for all groups has contributed to the counseling profession's awareness of the factors that influence a client's processing of past experiences. Thoughts, feelings, behaviors, and spirituality of clients are strategic elements for counselors to consider in the counseling session (Weinrach & Thomas, 1998). Currently attempts to address this issue are already in place. The professional organizations (such as American Psychological Association and American Counseling Association) have set ethical standards and guidelines concerning the treatment of all individuals with regard to diversity, as a way of influencing their members and the profession as a whole (Burn, 1992). Affiliate organizations specializing in multicultural concerns, development, and professional growth have blossomed in the past 20 years, setting their own, more inclusive ethical standards of practice and encouraging their peers to adapt them (Arredondo, 1998). Accrediting boards have mandated that counselor training programs include course work in this area (Midgette & Meggert, 1991). There has also been a significant increase in the number of studies on various aspects of multicultural counseling, accompanied by a growing body of literature to provide awareness and ongoing opportunities for new therapists and those already in the field to learn more (Pack-Brown, 1999; Parker, Moore, & Neimeyer, 1998; Merchant & Dupuy, 1996; Sue, Arredondo, & McDavis, 1992; Burn, 1992; Ibrahim, 1991).

Several important developments in the movement toward multiculturalizing the field of counseling have occurred. Initially, there was a real need for people to become aware of the influence of culture on thought processes and behavior since most counseling theories were based on European American, middle-class values and beliefs. Therapists did not take into account that these theories were often foreign and discriminatory toward clients who were of low socioeconomic status or who came from other cultural groups (Sue, 1981). Scholars and concerned professionals in the field began to publish articles calling on their colleagues to recognize, respect, and value the fact that all people are not the same. In response, courses were designed to educate both new and experienced counselors about people from other cultures. A lot of attention was given to describing various characteristics of certain groups, and how to "handle" them. Though these courses had the altruistic goal of increasing awareness and sensitivity to others, they often resulted in stereotyping the very groups they were intending to help (Speight, Myers, Cox, & Highlen, 1991).

Increasing the counselor's awareness of the differences in clients of other cultures is an important first step, but awareness alone is not enough. Much of the criticism aimed at the early attempts of helping professionals to be more concerned with the cross-cultural implications of counseling was that they focused on "exotic" groups, and acted as if only certain clients had ethnicity or a specific culture, while ignoring the obvious culture bias of the counselor (Jackson & Meadows, 1991). It was as though the European model of therapy was an absolute, administered by a values free/culture free therapist. Client differences were seen as deficiencies that needed to be changed, corrected, and brought into line with "normal" people living in this country. Small wonder then that many studies found that minorities underused available counseling services, either not seeking professional help at all or terminating early (Pedersen, 1987).

A new paradigm was needed if the profession was going to serve the entire population, not just those of European descent. Counselors had to examine themselves and their own biases as part of this shift in thinking. Pedersen (1988) identified three important factors indicative of competence as a multicultural counselor: awareness, knowledge, and skill development. These areas correspond with those recommended in the literature as being significant in the training of effective cross-cultural counselors (Arredondo, 1999; Midgette & Meggert, 1991). To elaborate, awareness includes not only recognition of differences and the influences of and between cultures, but also self-awareness. The therapist must be sensitive to and comfortable with his/her own culture, attitudes, beliefs, values, biases, and the role they play in any interaction with the client. Knowledge is a crucial part of competence and is broadly interpreted here. Facts and information about other cultures, gained through study and life experiences, the history and sociology of the people, and awareness of institutional barriers for minorities are combined with knowledge of counseling theories and techniques in general. Knowledge also includes being cognizant of one's own cultural socialization and its influence on attitudes and beliefs. Skill development is a process learned through application. It leads to more effective communication and the ability to interact with those from other cultures. It includes being able to accurately and appropriately send and receive nonverbal signals as well as interpret verbal messages. The skilled counselor actively seeks to develop a non-racist identity, engages in interaction with those who are different, and uses appropriate counseling techniques for each client (Arredondo, 1999; Midgette & Meggert, 1991; McRae & Johnson, 1991).

In the early development of the multicultural counseling movement many thought developing this type of competence might be a formidable task for the average practitioner. Researchers postulated that clients were better served when they were matched with a culturally similar counselor (Dillard, 1983). Several studies mentioned by Sue (1981) conducted primarily with African American subjects indicated that this might be true. However, he also cited a number of contrasting reports that concluded other factors such as belief similarity, counselor style, experience, sex, and type of problems may be equally important. In a similar literature review Pedersen (1988) expanded on these findings. Previous studies were criticized for failing to take into consideration variables such as socioeconomic status, a more likely predictor of a person's ability or desire to seek professional help. Other factors which may negatively impact the success of a culturally matched counselor-client alliance are the lack of respect shown to therapists from some ethnic groups; the perception that the therapist has forsaken his/her own culture and now is too identified with the dominant culture and its institutions, therefore creating a lack of trust; jealousy of what the therapist has achieved; or reluctance on the part of the therapist to identify effectively with the client because he or she is a reminder of the therapist's own past.

Yet another argument against the idea of cultural matching is that people cannot be neatly categorized into one group or another (Speight, et al., 1991). Pedersen (1988) introduces a triad model with two counselors, one similar and one dissimilar to the client's culture as a solution to the debate. He cites several sources that describe situations where another professional has worked collaboratively in the counseling process to achieve successful outcomes. Pedersen's triad model has been successfully adapted as an effective training technique for new counselors (Parker, Moore, & Neimeyer, 1998).

From the beginning there has also been a controversy in the literature over whether to interpret the concept of multiculturalism broadly and apply it to all groups, or to keep a more traditional definition of culture. It is currently popular for courses on diversity to deal with a wide range and scope of differences including along with ethnicity other variables such as age, gender, sexual orientation, ability, and social class (Adams, 1997). If that approach is used, "the construct multicultural becomes generic to all counseling relationships" (Pedersen, 1991). Every experience with another person will include a variety of differences because all humans have unique characteristics that stem from their individual backgrounds, values, beliefs, etc. (Ivy & Ivy, 1997; Adams, 1991; Speight, et al., 1991). However, most authors, after acknowledging the broad definition of culture, choose to limit their study to the more narrow interpretation. Pedersen (1991), cited the work of R.W. Brislin, who describes seven indicators that separate culture from individual differences: (1) cultural aspects are part of a group of people's way of life; (2) they include ideas passed from one generation to the next; (3) the group's common experiences instill values in the children; (4) children are socialized into adults through a cultural process; (5) beliefs and practices are consistently maintained; (6) traditions and practices are stable even though everything doesn't always go right; (7) people feel disoriented, helpless and out of control when cultural patterns are changed.

From this frame of reference much attention has been given to studying specific racial and ethnic groups as a way of understanding their culture (Sue, 1981; Dillard, 1983; Samuda & Wolfgang, 1985; Axelson, 1985; Pedersen, 1987; Speight, et al.,1991; Adams, 1997). Inherent in this study, though, is the criticism mentioned earlier that learning about a culture is not always sufficient. Another problem is the difficulty or impossibility of learning about all the cultures of all the clients one might encounter. As a factor for consideration, Weinrach and Thomas (1998) recognize that it is almost impossible to know exactly where a client is located in the acculturation process. Because the U.S. population is becoming diversified at a rapid rate, younger members of immigrant families want to enter into the American culture as quickly as possible so as not to feel isolated from the rest of their new peers. The elders are not so anxious to do the same. Even those who have lived in this country for generations have differing levels of acculturation. Lee (1991) suggests that an operational definition of multicultural counseling is "an intervention process that places equal emphasis on the racial and ethnic impressions of both counselor and client." This definition seems to bridge the gap between looking at culture as a specific entity, separate for each group, and the more universal emphasis.

A fourth area of attention in the literature is the type of counseling theory that works best in a multicultural context. Vontress (in Samuda & Wolfgang, 1985) proposed four criteria to evaluate a theory's usefulness in multicultural counseling. One must first consider its assumptions about human nature. Are people free agents? Are they "blank slates" at birth, influenced by genetics or the environment? Are people predetermined to be one way or another? What shapes the person? Next, a theory must address the significance of culture on a person's thoughts and behaviors. Do universal behaviors and ways of thinking exist? How much does nationality influence behavior? Is affiliation with a subgroup more influential than nationality? Are individual differences more significant than cultural differences? A third area to consider is the concept of normal or abnormal behavior. Is the cultural context the determinant of acceptable behaviors? What happens when a person moves to another country? Finally, one must consider the methodology of therapy using a particular theory. How does a counselor intervene with a culturally different client?

The major theories have been categorized by Vontress as psychoanalytical, rational, behavioristic, humanistic, and existential. Each was rated according to the four criteria listed above. Psychoanalytical approaches did not fare well in their adaptability for use in multicultural settings. So much of the methodology consists of the therapist interpreting the client's unconscious or subconscious motivations and conflicts; it would be almost impossible for a therapist not to impose his/her own cultural biases onto the client. Rational approaches rely on the idea that the individual is responsible for his/her own thoughts, beliefs, and such and, therefore, can change behaviors by intellectually deciding to do so. Counseling interventions are highly cognitive and stress a person's ability to take charge of his/her life. This, of course, is a Western oriented philosophy incompatible with many other cultures.

Behaviorism rests on the foundation that all behavior is shaped by societal forces which reward or punish, thereby reinforcing a behavior or extinguishing it. In a multicultural setting it would have to be determined what kind of changes were needed or wanted, according to which set of standards. The humanistic approaches rely on the counselor-client alliance to help the client activate his/her inner resources. A competent, highly skilled counselor could perhaps form the type of genuine, empathic relationship this theory proposes as necessary to effect change; however, the lack of directiveness could be interpreted by clients of another culture as indifference. Also, a client from an oppressed minority may not have access to the same type of resources as a majority counselor and may desire more than empathy.

Existentialism is a philosophy more than a counseling theory in that it contains no specific techniques. It views humans in a holistic way that stresses people's commonalities over their differences, and focuses on the counselor-client alliance to explore the client's inner needs and to discover ways to fulfill them. Since existentialists believe that all of life is filled with struggles, tensions, and conflict, they do not look for the cause of maladaptive behaviors or try to say what constitutes mental illness. Instead, they strive for harmony with nature, self, and others, a philosophy compatible with multiculturalism (Samuda & Wolfgang, 1985).

Given the limitations of the major theories just described, many speculate that multicultural counseling in itself will become a whole new paradigm, a new "fourth force" that will shape the field in the same way that behaviorism and humanism have (Pedersen, 1988, 1991; Midgette & Meggert, 1991). This conceptual shift brings with it a complete change in the philosophy of the nature and purpose of counseling and necessitates a new worldview. Worldview, defined as the assumptions one holds about the world, or the individual's perceptions about his/her relationship to the rest of the world (Ibrahim, 1991), is a very culturally bound concept that effects the way people behave, make decisions, solve problems, and relate (Jackson & Meadows, 1991). However, "[T]he traditional counselor role has been founded on what can be described as a psychological worldview," (Cottone, 1991), the basis of which is the study of the individual.

The assumption everything exists within the individual is a common thread that links and limits current counseling theories (Sue, Ivey, & Pedersen, 1996). Other shared assumptions include linear thinking, such as A causes B; subject-object dualism, or the separation between the observer and what is being observed; determinism, i.e., everything has a cause; and absolutism, or the thinking that a reality exists outside the subjective realm (Cottone, 1991). Other aspects of a Western worldview posited by traditional counselors are the belief that acquiring objects has the highest value; knowledge is external and is based on counting and measuring; logic is linear; and self worth and identity are based on things that exist outside of the person, for example, possessions, status, appearance (Jackson & Meadows, 1991). Although these views have dominated the field in the past, they are being challenged by the multicultural counselors.

Cottone (1991) summarized the systemic worldview and its implications for counseling. The fundamental premises include: (1) relationships form the basis of study; (2) relationships isolated for study are to be understood relative to the observer and his/her frame of reference; (3) circular causality exists only within the context of the system; and (4) social relationships form the basis for therapeutic change. With this view the counselor does not look at the individual to find the problem, but rather, sees the larger context of the entire system. The role of the counselor becomes one of helping the client assess which relationships will have positive impact and which will not. The counselor becomes a facilitator to help the client access the system that will be most beneficial to the client. To do this effectively the counselor must be knowledgeable about the cultural system he/she represents as well as the cultural system of the client. Lee (1991) saw a similar role for the counselor as an advocate for clients, helping them to empower themselves to break down social and institutional barriers which keep them from achieving their highest goals. D'Andrea (1999) reports that his work with African American clients was enhanced by his ability to be an advocate, since clients' psychological sense of well being is often linked to their environment.

This shift in worldview and the role of the counselor has not come without dissension. Some consider becoming overly involved in projects and services that typically fall into the realm of social workers, public health administrators, and community outreach groups to be a misdirection of a counselor's time and resources that takes away from his/her primary function (Weinrach & Thomas, 1998). Patterson (1996) supports a more traditional view of counseling based on the belief that people are more similar than different. He maintains that true counseling is that which uses the Western oriented theories with the goal of teaching the client to be independent, responsible, and able to solve his/her own problems. The counselor need not become "a chameleon who changes styles, techniques, and methods to meet the presumed characteristics of clients from varying cultures and groups" (p. 230). Culture is one of many variables that each client brings to the sessions, but to emphasize it above the others is unnecessary and may deter the therapeutic process. Patterson sees a danger in counselors creating self-fulfilling prophecies by having expectations about clients from certain groups. Another criticism raised by Weinrach and Thomas (1998) is that the multicultural counseling movement has failed to produce any viable theories to replace those deemed inappropriate. They challenge those in the movement to provide clear and specific interventions and examples of diversity-sensitive counseling on videotape for trainees to observe, and to demonstrate the differences in their approach by contrasting it to other approaches in the same manner that Carl Rogers (using a client-centered orientation), Fritz Perls (using Gestalt), and Albert Ellis (using rational-emotive therapy) did with their client Gloria in the 1960s.

Perhaps the reason for the lack of a clearly defined multicultural counseling theory is that most experts in the field choose to be eclectic in their approach. They do not discard current and traditional theories, but utilize the best strategies and techniques from each, such as unconditional positive regard and empathy from client centered therapy, and goal setting, active participation, and role playing from the cognitive and behavioral approaches. Rather than seeing themselves as a chameleon, these counselors choose to "match" their clients in order to increase client trust and be more effective (Ramirez, 1999). "Multiculturalism is more than an emphasis on techniques; the focus must always be on competence in an effective therapeutic relationship, which will be assessed differently in each cultural context" (Pedersen, 1996, p. 236).

What the multicultural counseling movement **has** brought to the field is a wealth of literature on identity development models. At first the emphasis was on the identity development of clients. Sue's (1981) well known theory of cultural development is based on his research of worldviews. Within his model, identity is defined in terms of a person's perceptions of how much control he/she can exert over his/her environment and how much a person can make real changes in life. Other identity development models that serve cultural or ethnic minorities include Bank's five stages, Atkinson's Minority Identity Development Model, and Cross' Black Identity Model. They all include a process in which individuals from an oppressed group go through a series of stages. Beginning with lack of awareness or denial of oppression, they move on to question their culture, becoming immersed in it and identifying only with it, then recognizing the devalued sense of self and limitations of identifying only with oppression, and finally reaching some type of integration (Myers, et al., 1991). Critics of these models point out that they are an outgrowth of a particular period such as the civil rights movement or the women's movement, and may represent characteristics of a specific time rather than a universal process. They also do not address the identity development of persons with more than one kind of oppression (such as an African American female with a disability) or biracial individuals who have more than one cultural orientation (Myers, et al., 1991).

Myers et al. (1991) present an interesting model of spiritual and identity development based on the African conceptual system. This system is different from the European worldview discussed earlier in its emphasis on the spiritual as well as material. In this belief system interpersonal relationships are primary, and knowledge is based on self-knowledge. Human and spiritual networks are interrelated, and the union of opposites is the basis for logic. Identity and self-worth come from within (Jackson & Meadows, 1991). The individual's spiritual dimension has been basically ignored by western psychology, but is recognized by other cultures as being the very core of the person. In such cultures, the development of a person's spiritual awareness is an essential part of identity and of a person's knowing him/herself more fully.

448

Myers et al. (1991) reviewed the stages of faith identified by Fowler and subsequently combined them with their research into optimal theory, which offers a holistic view of individuals (Speight, et al., 1991). The process of knowing oneself includes all aspects of being, such as age, gender, ethnicity, size, and does not necessitate gaining more information as much as gaining a deeper, truer understanding of oneself. With this in mind Myers et al. (1991) developed a model called Optimal Theory Applied to Identity Development (OTAID). Like the other models this has stages of development, but rather than a linear sequence, the authors perceive these stages as forming an upward, expanding spiral. People are continuously evolving as they interact with others in the society around them and increase their self-knowledge. At times they may be on a parallel level, although progress has been made toward the next stage. They may never go through all of the stages, nor is there a prescribed amount of time that should be spent at any one stage. The person is on a journey of self-discovery that leads from a narrow perspective of seeing life in segments to being able to perceive one's life as a total entity.

The journey begins with Phase 0, or an "Absence of Conscious Awareness." This is the stage of an infant who still does not perceive him/herself as a separate individual and accepts life just as it is without judgment or concern. Phase 1 is "Individuation." The person in this stage views him/herself from one perspective, usually based on values and beliefs held by his/her family. The individual does not reflect on how he/she is perceived by others or believe it is any different than the way he/she sees him/herself. Egocentric and ethnocentric describe someone in this stage.

Phase 2 is a state of "Dissonance." The person here begins to reflect on who he/she is while developing an awareness that not everyone is valued equally in society. Experiences with prejudice and discrimination cause a negative self-image that clashes with the original concept of self and leads to feelings of anger, confusion, insecurity, and isolation.

During Phase 3, "Immersion," the individual begins to identify totally with people of a similar culture or group and experiences a strong bond and sense of belonging with the group. Learning more about the history, contributions, and culture of the group becomes exciting and results in an increase of self-awareness and appreciation for aspects of oneself that may have been devalued before. A lack of trust, anger, and other negative feelings are expressed toward the larger society and an " us-them" attitude may be prevalent.

In Phase 4, "Internalization," the person accepts him/herself fully and can be more tolerant of others who do not pose a threat to his/her well being. This person is confident and comfortable with people from other groups because of a sense of security within.

Phase 5 is "Integration," during which the person begins to make a conceptual shift to a more universal worldview. Being fully comfortable with themselves, people in this stage can make the transition to valuing others not on external criteria, but because they are a part of humanity. They are able to see others as individuals who can be oppressed in a variety of ways regardless of their culture or ethnicity. People in this phase may form friendships and alliances with those representing many groups.

Phase 6 is the "Transformation" stage. The person has integrated all aspects of the cycle of life. Everything is interrelated and interdependent; a spiritual awareness allows one to move beyond external circumstances to see that everyone has value and contributes something to the world. People in this stage have learned to accept those who lack knowledge and to believe that most people are doing the best they can, given their level of awareness and understanding. People in this stage see that good can even come from negative experiences (Myers, et al., 1991).

The authors demonstrate how the stages can be used in counseling situations such as working with crime victims. They discuss the way victimization is perceived using current suboptimal worldviews and contrast that with the optimal worldview. The current way of thinking directly links victimization and shame. Often victims are even blamed, as though some deficiency on their part made them capable of being victimized. Because being a victim shows a lack of power, the person is further devalued. If a person's self worth is a product of other people's perceptions and based on external criteria, as it is in Western oriented thinking, the victim is not highly esteemed.

From the optimal perspective, victims can use the negative experience to learn and become stronger. Their sense of self worth is never in question; rather the perpetrator is seen as being at a lower state of development. People in phases 1 to 4 will often view the crime and their own victimization in a suboptimal way. For example, if victims are in the individuation phase, the crime may be attributed to some personal limitation. They may take the blame for doing or not doing something. Persons in the dissonance phase might see the crime as an act of discrimination or believe negative things will happen because they belong to a certain group. They may feel anger or depression as a result. In the immersion phase victims will often blame the system for creating the circumstances that led to the crime and will react with extreme anger, using the crime to show how discriminated against and oppressed they are. Victims in the internalization phase may blame societal factors, but will also see the crime as being perpetrated by an individual. They will focus more on seeing the perpetrator punished for the crime.

For those who have reached the integration stage, acts of violence are not viewed as displays of power. Victims feel no blame or shame, nor do they differentiate their response based on what group the perpetrator is from. At the final stage, transformation, victims, while experiencing natural feelings of pain and outrage, will not be oppressed by the crime. They will try to find something to be learned from the experience (Myers, et al., 1991). Using this model, the counselor must be aware of his/her own stage of identity development as well as that of the client. Helping a person grow toward greater understanding is the goal, one that must be an ongoing process for both members of the cross-cultural exchange.

In more recent years the focus of identity development has shifted to that of the counselor. Although the counseling field in the United States continues to be dominated numerically by Americans of European descent, little initial attention was given to helping them understand their own, White identity, even though the attitudes, beliefs, and understandings of the counselor were recognized as an important factor in the therapeutic alliance. That void has been filled by a wealth of studies and publications about White racial identity. In these studies attention is given to helping new and experienced counselors perform the kinds of self-assessment needed to discover their own stage of development.

Some of the most prevalent models in the literature include the stages of White racial identity developed by Helms (Pack-Brown, 1999; Kiselica, 1998; Richardson & Molinaro, 1996). The Contact stage describes individuals who are vaguely aware of their own Whiteness, but typically do not consider themselves as "racial beings." They may advocate a "color blind" approach where all people are treated the same regardless of race or ethnicity and do not accept the notion of White privilege. Counselors in this stage may have difficulty showing empathy or understanding for client issues that stem from institutionalized racism and may not be able to perceive the client's reality (Richardson & Molinaro, 1996).

Counselors in the Disintegration stage "see themselves as White and acknowledge the existence of discrimination and prejudice. However, as White persons belonging to a racial group known as the 'oppressor,' they often feel (a) guilty when racial differences emerge and (b) disoriented and anxious when seemingly unresolvable moral dilemmas force them to choose between loyalty to the White race and humanism" (Pack-Brown, p. 89). They may be ambivalent about fighting or confronting racism in the presence of other Whites.

In the Reintegration stage the counselor consciously or unconsciously, believes in the superiority of Whites and, therefore, may attribute clients' problems to innate deficiencies. The counselor may be unable to develop a suitable therapeutic relationship or may be impatient with the issues of perceived discrimination and racism. Denial of his/her own racism occurs because he/she lacks the ability to maintain an objective understanding of the systemic, historical, and on-going nature of racism. Counselors in any of the first three stages may be ineffective when working with clients of other racial/ethnic cultural groups (Pack-Brown, 1999; Richardson & Molinaro, 1996).

A Pseudo-independent stage counselor is consciously trying to overcome racism, but may find him/herself slipping back to familiar behaviors, fears, and attitudes. This is disconcerting because he/she genuinely wants to help. However, he/she may still believe that clients would be better off if they would adopt traditional European-American values, behaviors, ways of thinking and problem solving. This may still limit their effectiveness in assisting diverse clients to develop resources within their own culture.

By the time a person reaches the Immersion/emersion stage, he/she is comfortable with his/her own White identity. This counselor feels professionally and personally obligated to be educated and informed about other cultures and culturally appropriate interventions which may seem foreign to the mainstream counselor. He/she becomes an advocate for clients and can establish the type of therapeutic rapport that is genuine.

The final stage is Autonomy, which is a total commitment to racial/cultural integration on a personal as well as a professional level. White privilege is renounced, and oppression of others is regarded as unconscionable. The autonomous counselor seeks to use culturally appropriate principles as a guiding force in interactions with clients of all cultural backgrounds (Pack-Brown, 1999; Richardson & Molinaro, 1996).

The training processes for new counselors is a major concern for those in the profession. What theories, techniques, and experiences will help them develop the skills necessary to work with people in a society growing more diverse every year? Currently, most students entering the field have exposure to the concepts of pluralism through a course on the subject. Added to their regular curriculum, this is a convenient and cost effective way for university programs to fulfill their certification requirements (Locke & Kiselica, 1999; D'Andrea, Daniels & Heck, 1991). However, it does not facilitate acquiring the necessary knowledge and skills recommended for competence. Ponterotto (1996) describes several models of multicultural training that have been designed to promote: (a) self-knowledge, especially an awareness of one's own cultural biases; (b) knowledge about the status and cultures of different cultural groups; (c) skills to make culturally appropriate interventions, including a readiness to use alternative counseling strategies that better match the cultures of clients than do traditional counseling strategies; and (d) actual experiences in counseling culturally different clients.

Training programs that include exposure to and actual experience working with clients from a variety of cultural backgrounds are generally preferred over those using the course alone approach. Even role playing helps to increase awareness of the student counselor's own culture as well as his/her sensitivity to other cultures (McRae & Johnson, 1991). Kiselica (1998) notes that training programs for new counselors must assist the "trainees to process the intensely personal experiences and changes that are prompted by multicultural training and counseling" (p. 6). Multicultural training, especially when it confronts White racism and privilege, can be unsettling and anxiety provoking because it requires sincere self-examination, which is often painful.

Teaching about racism and White racial identity are major thrusts in many multicultural counseling courses (Arredondo, 1999; Parker, Moore & Neimeyer, 1998; Richardson & Molinaro, 1996). Racism is usually recognized as existing on three levels: individual, the personal beliefs about the inferiority of a particular group or groups; institutional, the public imposition of laws and practices that discriminate against a group or groups; and cultural, the belief that certain cultures are deficient or invisible (Locke & Kiselica, 1999; Pack-Brown, 1999). Counselors need to guard against all three.

A final, important element in any training program is the level of competence and multicultural expertise of those doing the training. In their article challenging counselor educators, Midgette and Meggert (1991) focus on the attitudes and beliefs of faculty. Many professors in colleges and universities are themselves products of racist and monocultural educational systems. The authors suggest that the entire faculty needs to address the issue of multicultural awareness.

People in leadership and teaching positions need to assess their own openness to change and their practices to ensure they are, indeed, practicing what they preach. In order to truly educate new counselors in a multicultural way, a systematic change that permeates the entire training program is needed. Elements of such a program include the infusion of multicultural content into every course and the hiring of faculty members from a variety of cultures to provide mentors and role models as well as to present different views. Clinical experiences that give students a wide range of exposure to clients of diverse backgrounds, an emphasis on research that includes multicultural perspectives, ongoing staff development for current faculty, and advanced course work to help students achieve a greater level of comfort in a variety of counseling tasks with members of other groups are also foundational in this systematic change (Kiselica, 1998; Midgette & Meggert, 1991).

Because "[culture] will influence a client whether the counselor chooses to be aware of it or not" (Pedersen, 1988), the counselor must give due consideration to the importance of culture in the counseling process. Since the facilitation of constructive change or gain in client behavior is a major goal in counseling theory, the fully functional counselor will need to develop and employ creative ways of applying counseling methodology. While all scientific counseling theories are useful, all have unique limitations in a multicultural context. The counselor must develop a broad framework and integrate ideas and approaches from a variety of sources. For counselors who work in the schools this has never been more critical than now.

The 1990 U.S. Census revealed some very radical demographic changes in the population. The 2000 census will reveal even more. Counselors and teachers are encountering these changes in their schools throughout the country. In California, for example, the number of students classified as "white, non-Hispanic" has already dropped below 50%

enrollment. One in every four students in California live in a home in which English is not spoken as a first language and one in every six students is foreign born (Sue, 1992). Increasingly, working with students from different cultural backgrounds will become the norm rather than the exception. Projections for the next twenty years indicate that racial and ethnic minority students will become a numerical majority (Sue, 1992). Educational institutions are most likely to be the first affected by the shifts in student populations. However, most of the education in the United States is based on European philosophies that are highly individualistic and have a very competitive structure for evaluation. Many ethnic group members value cooperation rather than competition and the needs of the group rather than the needs of the individual. Thus, the inherent value structure of many ethnic students conflicts directly with the basic structure of education in the U.S.

Sometimes teachers or counselors who have been in the profession for many years see no reason to adjust their methods or attitudes in order to adopt a more multicultural perspective. This is especially true in communities with predominantly European American populations. The few students they encounter that come from another cultural or ethnic group may be fairly well assimilated into the common culture of the town. These instructors see no reason to fix something that isn't broken, so they use the same ways to educate students that they have used for years. The only problem with such a philosophy is the world around these communities is rapidly changing. It is unlikely every one of their students will remain isolated in them. As the students move on and out they will be forced to deal with diversity. Will they have the skills to do so?

With the increase in technology bringing the world closer together and with the demographic trends of this country changing dramatically, educators can no longer avoid the issues of multiculturalism. One of the goals of education is to prepare students for the rest of their lives. How prepared are today's students to live and work with all the kinds of people they will encounter now and in the next century? How prepared are their counselors and teachers to show them the way? Counselors who wish to be effective may have to unlearn and relearn some concepts and consider different ways of viewing the world. Faculty and administrators in institutions of higher learning will have to give more than lip service to the growing need to educate professionals who are truly equipped to work in a multicultural society.

References

Adams, J. Q. (1991). Understanding social interaction in culturally diverse settings. In J. Q. Adams, J. F. Niss, & C. Suarez (Eds.), *Multicultural education: Strategies for implementation in colleges and universities* (pp. 93-100). Macomb, IL: Western Illinois University Foundation.

Adams, J. Q. (1997). *Dealing with diversity teleclass study guide.* Dubuque, IA: Kendall/Hunt Publishing Company.

Ancis, J. R. (1998, Spring). Cultural competency training at a distance: Challenges and strategies. *Journal of Counseling and Development, 76,* 134-143

Arredondo, P. (1998, July). Ethical practice from a multicultural and diversity perspective. *Counseling Today,* 16.

Arredondo, P. (1999, Winter). Multicultural counseling competencies as tools to address oppression and racism. *Journal of Counseling and Development, 77,* 102-108.

Axelson, J. A. (1985). *Counseling and development in a multicultural society.* Monterey, CA: Brooks/Cole.

Burn, D. (1992, May/June). Ethical implications in cross-cultural counseling and training. *Journal of Counseling and Development, 70,* 578-583.

Casas, J. M., Ponterotto, J. G., & Gutierrez, J. M. (1986). An ethical indictment of counseling research and training: The cross-cultural perspective. *Journal of Counseling and Development, 64,* 347-349.

Cottone, R. R. (1991, May/June). Counselor roles according to two counseling worldviews. *Journal of Counseling and Development, 69,* 398-401.

D'Andrea, M. (1998, November). When White counselors work with African American clients: Some notes from the field. *Counseling Today,* 26-27.

D'Andrea, M., Daniels, J., & Heck, R. (1991, September/October). Evaluating the impact of multicultural counseling training. *Journal of Counseling and Development, 70,* 143-150.

Dillard, J. M. (1983). *Multicultural counseling.* Chicago: Nelson-Hall.

Ibrahim, F. A. (1991, September/October). Contribution of cultural worldview to generic counseling and development. *Journal of Counseling and Development, 70,* 13-19.

Ivey, M. B., & Ivey, A. E. (1997, April). And now we begin. *Counseling Today,* 40-42.

Jackson, A. P., & Meadows, F. B., Jr. (1991, September/October). Getting to the bottom to understand the top. *Journal of Counseling and Development, 70,* 72-76.

Kiselica, M. S. (1998, January). Preparing for the challenges and joys of multiculturalism. *The Counseling Psychologist, 26(1),* 5-22.

Lee, C. C. (1991, January/February). Empowerment in counseling: A multicultural perspective. *Journal of Counseling and Development, 69,* 229-230.

Locke, D. C., & Kiselica, M. S. (1999, Winter). Pedagogy of possibilities: Teaching about racism in multicultural counseling courses. *Journal of Counseling and Development, 77,* 80-86.

McRae, M. B., & Johnson, S. D., Jr. (1991, September/October). Toward training for competence in multicultural counselor education. *Journal of Counseling and Development, 70,* 131-135.

Merchant, N., & Dupuy, P. (1996, July/August). Multicultural counseling and qualitative research: Shared worldview and skills. *Journal of Counseling and Development, 74,* 537-541.

Midgette, T. E., & Meggert, S. S. (1991, September/October). Multicultural counseling instruction: a challenge for faculties in the 21st century. *Journal of Counseling and Development, 70,* 136-141.

Myers, L. J., Speight, S. L., Highlen, P. S., Cox, C. I., Reynolds, A. L., Adams, E. M., & Hanley, C. P. (1991, September/October). Identity development and worldview: Toward an optimal conceptualization. *Journal of Counseling and Development, 70,* 54-63.

Pack-Brown, S. P. (1999, Winter). Racism and White counselor training: Influence of White racial identity theory and research. *Journal of Counseling and Development, 77,* 87-92.

Parker, W. M., Moore, M. A., & Neimeyer, G. J. (1998, Summer). Altering White racial identity and interracial comfort through multicultural training. *Journal of Counseling and Development, 76.* 302-310.

Patterson, C. H. (1996, January/February). Multicultural counseling: From diversity to university. *Journal of Counseling and Development, 74,* 227- 231

Pedersen, P. (1987). *Handbook of cross-cultural counseling and therapy.* New York: Praeger.

Pedersen, P. (1988). *A handbook for developing multicultural awareness.* Alexandria, VA: American Association for Counseling and Development.

Pedersen, P. (1990, May/June). The constructs of complexity and balance in multicultural counseling theory and practice. *Journal of Counseling and Development, 68,* 550-554.

Pedersen, P. (1991, September/October). Multiculturalism as a generic approach to counseling. *Journal of Counseling and Development, 70,* 6-12.

Pedersen, P. (1996, January/February). The importance of both similarities and differences in multicultural counseling: Reaction to C. H. Patterson. *Journal of Counseling and Development, 74,* 236-237.

Ponterotto, J. G. (1996). Multicultural counseling in the twenty-first century. *The Counseling Psychologist, 24,* 259-268.

Ramirez III, M. (1999). *Multicultural psychotherapy.* Boston: Allyn & Bacon.

Richardson, T. Q., & Molinaro, K. L. (1996, January/February). White counselor self-awareness: A prerequisite for developing multicultural competence. *Journal of Counseling and Development, 74,* 238-242.

Samuda, R. J., & Wolfgang, A. (1985). *Intercultural counseling and assessment: Global perspectives.* Lewiston, NY: C. J. Hogrefe.

Speight, S. L., Myers, L. J., Cox, C. I., & Highlen, P. S. (1991, September/October). A redefinition of multicultural counseling. *Journal of Counseling and Development, 70,* 29-36.

Sue, D. W. (1981). *Counseling the culturally different.* New York: John Wiley.

Sue, D. W. (1992, March/April). The diversification of the United States. *Journal of Counseling and Development, 70,* 477-483.

Sue, D. W., Arredondo, P., & McDavis, R. (1992, March/April). Multicultural counseling competencies and standards: A call to the profession. *Journal of Counseling and Development, 70,* 136-141.

Sue, D. W., Ivey, A. E., & Pedersen, P. (1996). *A theory of multicultural counseling and therapy.* Pacific Grove, CA: Brooks/Cole.

Weinrach, S. G., & Thomas, K. R. (1998, Spring). Diversity-sensitive counseling today: A postmodern clash of values. *Journal of Counseling and Development. 76,* 115-122.

FACULTY DEVELOPMENT PROGRAMS IN SUPPORT OF MULTICULTURAL EDUCATION

by
Emily C. Wadsworth

Because they work with faculty, faculty development programs can do much to create a campus culture that appreciates cultural diversity and ensures the success of all students.[1] Faculty lie at the center of the educational process. They can provide classrooms that are safe environments in which students are challenged to grow and develop intellectually. Outside the classroom faculty members can encourage student growth and development through mentoring.

Faculty development activities can be costly or inexpensive. The difference in cost is often the difference between using internal volunteer resources and using outside paid experts and consultants. If you are starting a new faculty development program or if you are starting a new faculty development emphasis on multicultural education, you may want to survey the faculty and other professional staff to identify those who have research interests or expertise in areas that relate to multicultural education. These persons are good candidates for an advisory committee, sources of expertise for workshops for other faculty, and sources of support for multicultural education in general.

Supporting the Selection of a Culturally Diverse Faculty

It is important that newly hired faculty are multiethnic and committed to working with multiethnic students. Faculty development programs can work with department chairs to make sure that the entire hiring process conveys the institution's commitment to cultural diversity. Advertisements should specifically invite women and minorities to apply and should be placed in publications they are likely to read. Some institutions reward departments who hire culturally diverse faculty and staff by providing temporary or permanent extra resources to those departments. The interview process should include questions intended to elicit the candidate's attitude toward cultural diversity in the classroom, on campus, in the curriculum, and in research. Many institutions require a lecture in the candidate's area of expertise. Faculty development programs might encourage departments to substitute a simulated teaching demonstration with the search committee serving as a culturally diverse class. Another option is to create vignettes that represent cultural issues in the classroom and ask candidates how they would respond.

Building Commitment Among New Faculty

Orientations are an opportunity for all representatives of the institution to convey their commitment to cultural diversity in all of their exchanges, both formal and informal, with new faculty members. Eison and Hill (1990) describe various workshop models for new faculty and provide a list of suggestions to ensure success. Welch, Solkoff, Schimpfhauser, and Henderson (1988) describe in detail a specific new faculty orientation at the University of Buffalo. These models could be used in support of multicultural education by inserting diversity as the theme of the orientation. Fink's (1990) annotated bibliography is a good resource for identifying research on the concerns of new faculty. New faculty orientations should be designed to meet those needs as well as to promote multicultural education.

New faculty can be made to feel welcome by providing them with a pleasant work environment and a thorough introduction to the institution and surrounding community. In addition to information about navigating the institution, new faculty will want specific information about the community (e.g., what kind of housing is available at what price, what cultural activities are available, what are the best restaurants). Here, the key is to brainstorm what you would want to know about an institution and a community that was entirely new to you. It is especially important that institutions located in predominately white communities with little diversity among the faculty be attentive to this area if they wish to hire and retain a diverse faculty. Faculty development programs should make every effort to use current faculty with diverse backgrounds as the source of information about the community and the institution.

One of the most effective ways to emphasize cultural diversity is to have a culturally diverse faculty. They must be retained if the faculty is to become truly culturally diverse. Mentoring programs for women and minorities can do much to assure that traditionally underrepresented faculty feel welcome in the institution and that they clearly understand what the institution expects of them in the retention, promotion, and tenure process. Hall and Sandler (1983) describe factors to consider in designing such a mentoring program. Boice and Turner (1989) describe a mentoring program at California State University at Long Beach. Additionally, the institution may want to provide special opportunities for women and minority faculty to meet in homogeneous groups to share concerns and perceptions and promote networking.

Faculty development can promote cultural diversity in faculty research by providing extra travel funds for faculty who pursue culturally diverse projects. Faculty development programs can also bring faculty together across disciplines to do interdisciplinary research on multicultural education and related subjects.

Many faculty development activities appeal to the human side of faculty members, engaging their needs for companionship and intellectual stimulation. One thinks of ethnic dining (potluck lunches or dinners, restaurants), films, book groups, dance, music, theater. By weaving together social opportunities, intellectual stimulation, and cultural diversity, faculty will become more culturally aware while meeting other important needs.

Developing New Teaching Strategies

Most faculty teach the way they were taught, particularly the way they were taught in graduate school with an emphasis on the printed word and lecture. Faculty development programs can provide faculty with opportunities to learn what culturally diverse students find most helpful to the learning process. Culturally diverse panels of students talking about their experiences at the institution, videotapes demonstrating the effect of faculty comments on culturally diverse students, and articles in newsletters can all help to broaden the faculty member's awareness of the interplay of teaching, learning, and cultural diversity. Faculty development programs can generate awareness of and interest in multicultural education by sponsoring an annual colloquium on multicultural education. See Ferren (1989) for a colloquia model. Institutions with sufficient resources will want to provide travel funds for faculty to attend conferences on multicultural education.

Faculty development programs can promote a culturally diverse curriculum using a variety of possible strategies: working with an interdisciplinary group of faculty, working with a single department, sponsoring university-wide lectures on multicultural education given by culturally diverse faculty and visiting experts. Aiken, Anderson, Dinnerstein, Lensink, and MacCorquodale (1987) describe a feminist curriculum integration project funded by the NEH at the University of Arizona. The women's studies faculty conducted interdisciplinary seminars in feminist thought and pedagogy for ten senior faculty members in each of four years. Bloomfield College in Bloomfield, New Jersey, and Southern Illinois University have conducted similar curriculum integration projects.

Stark, Lowther, Ryan, Bomotti, and Genthon (1990), in a survey of faculty teaching introductory courses at 97 colleges across the country, found that the most important influences on faculty course planning are the disciplinary construct and disciplinary colleagues. Thus, one might choose to work with an entire department in assessing and revising their curriculum. Hruska (1983) describes three models for consultation with individual departments.

Assessing Commitment to Diversity

Faculty development programs can conduct exit interviews with culturally diverse students and faculty to assess their impressions of the institution's commitment to cultural diversity and the areas in which it needs to be improved. Faculty development can also conduct focused group interviews with culturally diverse students and faculty who describe their perceptions of the atmosphere on campus. The conclusions drawn from these interviews can be made available to faculty in workshops and newsletters. Often such information will serve as an impetus for faculty to change negative behaviors that contribute to an unhealthy atmosphere.

Information about student perceptions of the classroom can also be used in workshops to help faculty alter their teaching strategies and create classrooms that are user-friendly for culturally diverse students. Changing faculty teaching behaviors can also be approached through individual consultation. Larger institutions and more mature faculty development programs often include one or more instructional specialists who work with individual faculty or groups of faculty to improve their teaching. On smaller campuses, faculty development programs can train faculty to help each other through peer consultation (Sweeney & Grasha, 1979).

Sensitivity to cultural diversity as a requirement of the regular retention, promotion, and tenure process is a powerful method of ensuring institutional commitment. At the least, student course evaluations should include questions that reveal the faculty member's attitude toward culturally diverse students and the amount of emphasis on diversity contained in the course content. The Women's Studies Student Course Evaluation form at Northeastern Illinois University includes questions about students' perceptions of the inclusion of gender and ethnic diversity in the course content and students' perceptions of the faculty member's attitudes toward diverse students. Evaluation criteria should include demonstration of sensitivity to culturally diverse students and broadly inclusive content as a requirement for retention, promotion, and tenure.

Keeping Faculty Informed

Faculty are busy professionals who teach, engage in research, and serve on university committees. Anything that faculty development programs can do to save time for faculty while bringing the message of cultural diversity has a good chance of being successful. Regular, short, scholarly, practical newsletters that focus on issues of cultural diversity are likely to be read and heeded. Faculty developers are also busy and might be wise to initiate a consortial arrangement with other institutions to spread the work of producing such a newsletter. Professional and Organizational Development Network in Higher Education does just this with *Teaching Excellence*, a one-sheet newsletter on issues in higher education to which institutions may subscribe at a modest fee and reproduce for their faculties. Faculty development programs might work with the library to produce annual or semi-annual annotated bibliographies on multicultural education, effective teaching strategies for culturally diverse classrooms, and discipline-specific research on multicultural pedagogy and curriculum.

Summary

Promoting multicultural education through faculty development programs is primarily a matter of weaving the theme of cultural diversity through all of the activities of the faculty development program. Faculty want to be successful teachers and researchers. Showing them how they can be more successful by becoming sensitive to cultural diversity is likely to engage their attention and persuade them to begin changing their behaviors and designing inclusive curricula.

Endnote

[1]Faculty development programs focus on faculty members as teachers, scholars, professionals, and persons. They provide consultation and workshops on teaching; assistance in career planning, grant writing, publishing, and a wide range of skills expected of faculty members as professionals; personal support through wellness programs, stress and time management, assertiveness training, and a host of other programs which address the individual's well-being. Beginning programs are often run by faculty committees or a professional advised by faculty committees. Larger institutions and older programs frequently have centers administratively located under the Office of Academic Services (Adapted from *An Informational Brochure about Faculty, Instructional, and Organizational Development*).

The most common methods of providing faculty development services are workshops, individual consultation, and grants of time and/or money to faculty to work on projects. The professional organization centrally concerned with faculty development in higher education is the Professional and Organizational Development Network in Higher Education (POD). Any institution that has a faculty development program or anticipates starting one to support multicultural education should make sure that at least one faculty member or one administration and professional staff person belongs to POD. Information about POD can be obtained by contacting Dr. David Graf, Director/Administrative Services, POD, Valdosta State University, Valdosta, GA 31698-0840 (podnet@valdosta.edu).

References

Aiken, S., Anderson, K., Dinnerstein, M., Lensink, J., & MacCorquodale, P. (1987). Trying transformations: Curriculum integration and the problem of resistance. *Signs: Journal of Women in Culture and Society, 12*(2), 255-275.

Boice, R., and Turner, J. (1989). The FIPSE-CSULB mentoring project for new faculty. *To Improve the Academy, 8,* 117-139.

Eison, J., & Hill, H. (1990). Creating workshops for new faculty. *The Journal of Staff, Program, and Organization Development, 8*(4), 223-234.

Ferren, A. (1989). Faculty development can change the culture of a college. *To Improve the Academy, 8,* 101-116.

Fink, L. (1990). New faculty members: The professorate of tomorrow. *The Journal of Staff, Program, and Organization Development, 8*(4), 235-245.

Hall, R., & Sandler, B. (1983). *Academic mentoring for women students and faculty: A new look at an old way to get ahead.* Washington, DC: Project on the Status and Education of Women, Association of American Colleges.

Hruska, S. (1983). Improving academic departments. *To Improve the Academy, 2,* 97-107.

Stark, J., Lowther, M., Ryan, P., Bomotti, S., & Genthon, M. (1990). *Planning introductory college courses: Influences on college faculty.* Ann Arbor, MI: National Center for Research to Improve Postsecondary Teaching and Learning.

Sweeney, J., & Grasha, A. (1979). Improving teaching through faculty development triads. *Educational Technology, 19*(2), 54-57.

Welch, C., Solkoff, N., Schimpfhauser, F., & Henderson, N. (1988). The University of Buffalo program for new faculty. In E. Wadsworth (Ed.), *Professional and organizational development in higher education: A handbook for new practitioners.* Stillwater, OK: New Forums Press.

Resources

On Development

Eble, K. E., & McKeachie, W. (1985). *Improving undergraduate education through faculty development.* San Francisco: Jossey-Bass.

Menges, R. J., & Mathis, B. C. (1989). *Key Resources on teaching, learning, curriculum and faculty development.* San Francisco: Jossey-Bass.

Wadsworth, E. C. (Ed.). (1988). *Professional and organizational development in higher education: A handbook for new practitioners.* Stillwater, OK: New Forums Press.

On Teaching

Fuhrmann, B. S., & Grasha, A. F. (1983). *A practical handbook for college teachers.* Boston: Little, Brown.

McKeachie, W. (1999). *Teaching tips: A guide for the beginning college teacher* (10th ed.). Boston: Houghton Mifflin.

Menges, R. J., & Svinicki, M. D. (Eds.). (1991). *College teaching: from theory to practice.* San Francisco: Jossey-Bass.

Tiedt, P. L., & Tiedt, I. M. (1986). *Multicultural teaching: A handbook of activities, information, and resources* (2nd ed.). Boston: Allyn & Bacon.

Report Series

To Improve the Academy, series available from the POD Network. Multiple volumes available from New Forums Press, Stillwater, OK.

New Directions in Teaching and Learning, series from Jossey-Bass Publishers, San Francisco, CA.

ASHE/ERIC report series available from the Association for the Study of Higher Education, Educational Administration, Texas A & M University, College Station, TX.

Publications from the National Center for Research to Improve Postsecondary Teaching and Learning, School of Education, University of Michigan, Ann Arbor, MI.

The Journal of Staff, Program & Organization Development, journal available from New Forums Press, Stillwater, OK.

College Teaching, journal available from HELDREF Publisher, Washington, DC.

Teaching Excellence, newsletter series available from POD Network.

The Teaching Professor, newsletter available from Magna Publications, 1718 Dryden Dr., Madison, WI, 53704-3006.

MOVING TOWARD JUSTICE, EQUITY, AND DIVERSITY: A CASE STUDY

by
Janice R. Welsch

In February 1912, *The English Journal* published an editorial under the guise of "A New Fable of Bidpai" (Hosic, pp. 122-123) in which a sandpiper approaches a great forest where he hopes to learn nest building.[1] Stopped by a woodpecker who questions him about his readiness for admission, the sandpiper quickly learns that he is not ready with the answers since the questions assume familiarity with the forest, an environment entirely new to him. Unsympathetic, the woodpecker dismisses him, refusing to examine him on what he knows about marshes, fens, and the sands where sandpipers build their nests. Fortunately, as he leaves, he consults a wise owl, who deftly teaches him the woodpecker's examination repertoire, and the sandpiper, presenting himself to the woodpecker the next day, breezes through the admission exam.

We might wonder who the editor was targeting when he wrote this fable or we might be struck by its appropriateness over eighty years after its publication. When rebutting the sandpiper the woodpecker takes a disconcertingly familiar position, assuming whatever the sandpiper knows is inferior to what forest inhabitants know and refusing even to listen to him, much less learn from him. The woodpecker's stance is remarkably similar to that of some traditionalists within the academy today who, assuming the superiority of the established curriculum, refuse to adjust their course content or their teaching methods to the needs of a changing student. The owl's solution to the problem, however, is questionable. Learning to play the game works in as much as it gains the sandpiper admission, but do we want learning reduced to a game? Who is fooling whom in the process? How much is gained and by whom? Obviously, answers to these questions will vary in individual cases, but given the increasingly diverse student populations entering college and the critical thinking that is one of the goals of education, recognizing and building on students' strengths, even when this entails revising course content and adapting new teaching strategies, seems a more effective approach.

Expecting faculty to change what and how we teach in order to reach the diverse students in our classrooms and laboratories is not expecting too much; we are continually doing so. As James Schultz (1988), writing for the Modern Language Association Committee on Academic Freedom, decisively stated in *Profession 88* when addressing the issue of canons: "Values always change, knowledge is always in flux, and learning requires active engagement. . . . Both [standards of value and of knowledge] are subject to history" (p. 66). The kinds of change and the rapidity with which we are being asked to change as we exit the 20th and enter the 21st century, however, may be daunting to some. The challenge is not exclusively a faculty challenge. College and university administrators must support faculty as we prepare for more culturally diverse course content and classes, and the entire campus community must share responsibility for insuring a climate that supports diversity.

Avenues of possible administrative support are numerous and have been explored in two early volumes of *Multicultural Education: Strategies for Implementation in Colleges and Universities* by Floyd and Thurmon, (1991), Wadsworth (1991), Kayes (1992), Felder (1992), and Floyd and Batsche (1992). As several of these authors point out, Faculty Development is among the university offices that can link administration and faculty in an effective alliance to make the changes in curriculum and pedagogy a diverse student population demands (Wadsworth, 1991; Felder, 1992; Floyd & Batsche, 1992). I would like to expand on the potential of this alliance using the Western Illinois University (WIU) experience as an example.

As Felder (1992) has pointed out, "faculty must provide the major thrust for multicultural education [but] administration . . . must be supportive" (pp. 96-97). WIU administrators have been supportive in multiple ways. Recent Presidents, for instance, have made "the development of diversity, equity, and justice in the campus community . . . an integral part of the university planning process" (Wagoner, 1989, p. 8; FY 2000 Priorities Statement, 1998) and have backed this commitment by action and advocacy. Besides frequently and unequivocally stressing to administrators, faculty, staff, and students the importance of fostering a hospitable environment that promotes the academic and social growth of all students (Planning Statement, 1990), they have facilitated the organization of a state multicultural conference and an on-campus diversity workshop for administrators. They have seen to the adoption of sexual harassment and racial and ethnic harassment policies and have supported Affirmative Action administrative internships, a doctoral scholars program, and the implementation of multicultural initiatives by student services personnel and by faculty.

Other WIU administrative offices, including those of the Provost and the Vice President of Student Services, and university committees, such as the Faculty Senate and the Council on Curricular Programs and Instruction (CCPI), have also endorsed multicultural activities and processes. For example, the Faculty Senate and the Provost approved a recommendation that the University "provide faculty with the means and opportunity to extend their knowledge of multicultural contributions to [their] disciplines" and assist them "in . . . incorporating into the curriculum the body of knowledge available on multicultural . . . contributions to the . . . disciplines" (Faculty Senate Agenda, 1988). Faculty Development has helped implement this and other diversity programs, the President and the Provost having designated the unit one that should help faculty revise the curriculum to reflect multicultural perspectives. By appointing a multicultural curriculum associate, awarding mini-grants for innovative course development and revision proposals, and funding seminars and workshops that focus on diversity issues, the Office of the Provost has given Faculty Development the means to assist faculty, has in effect provided the seeds necessary for the growth of multicultural thinking and sensitivity on campus.

With the appointment of the first multicultural curriculum associate, a variety of specific programs began to take shape. Working with a small group of faculty already looking for ways to integrate multicultural perspectives into the curriculum, the associate asked deans and chairs to nominate individuals who could become the nucleus of a cultural diversity cadre. Other faculty who had indicated an interest in multicultural education were also invited to join the Cadre. Initially designated the Cultural Diversity Curriculum Development Cadre (CDCDC), the name was changed to the Cultural Diversity Cadre (CDC) when the group realized its membership and focus had grown beyond faculty and narrowly defined curricular issues. As it has evolved, Cadre membership has broadened to include academic support staff, civil service personnel, administrators, and students as well as all interested faculty, while the Cadre's concerns now encompass campus climate and multicultural communication across the university as well as course content and teacher/student interaction. New members continue to be recruited at each CDC-sponsored event and are asked to help define the Cadre's focus and priorities.

Its link with Faculty Development has been a critical aspect of the Cadre's success since that office has supported the Cadre's programs via its funds, office staff, and newsletter. Led by the multicultural associate, who is given reassigned time (the equivalent of one course off) to facilitate Faculty Development's diversity programs, the Cadre has been able to count on the associate, assisted by a secretary and student workers, to coordinate and publicize its activities, including its series of presentations by national leaders in multicultural education; its in-house workshops, forums, and panel discussions; its course development initiatives; its let's-get-acquainted dinners; and the annual Dealing with Difference Summer Institutes which have superseded its earlier cultural diversity retreats. Besides funding the associate's reassigned time, Faculty Development has provided money for speaker honorariums, for print and audio-visual materials, for conference travel, and for program publicity. Through its newsletters, the multicultural associate has been able to discuss CDC activities and publish its calendar of events.

The Faculty Development-Cadre link has allowed Faculty Development to reach more of the campus community than it could with the multicultural associate working alone. Several Cadre committees have been particularly effective. The Student Study Group, for example, helped prepare the "Dealing with Differences" component of a one-credit-hour orientation course for new students. Built around a short video, "Facing Difference: Living Together on Campus," the package includes an outline, glossary, bibliography, set of discussion questions, and a variety of exercises and activities. The Colloquia Committee organized a number of programs including a video-discussion series on "Political Correctness: Trend or Mission?," a forum on the addition of a multicultural studies category to the General Education curriculum, and panels on "American History from the Native American Perspective" and "South Central L.A.: One Year Later." The Colloquia Committee also led a series of panels and discussions on intercultural communication for civil service employees.

A third CDC committee formed specifically to develop a multicultural course that would focus directly on issues of race/ethnicity, gender, class, sexual orientation, ableism, and age. Group Diversity (University 210) is the result of the committee's cooperative effort. The course is an important element of the newly approved Multicultural and Cross-cultural Studies category of the revised General Education curriculum. Committee members not only created the course; they also saw it through the approval process and became major proponents of the new Multicultural Studies category, helping to define the category and working with members of the Faculty Senate for its approval. Since its approval in 1991, several Cadre members have taught Group Diversity regularly while others, just as regularly, have made guest presentations on specific topics in various sections of the course.

Another curriculum related task addressed initially by Cadre members was the preparation of material to help faculty take into account multicultural scholarship and perspectives when developing new courses. Working with CCPI, members provided information about James Banks' "Approaches for the Integration of Ethnic Content" and for gender balance in courses (Banks & Banks, 1989) as well as criteria for evaluating course texts to insure multicultural representation. The information is important to faculty since, when preparing new course requests, they are specifically asked what they have done to insure the "course has been developed with an awareness of the place and contributions of women and minorities within the discipline."

Besides working through committees, individual members have contributed to the Cadre in a variety of ways: by compiling periodic multicultural bibliographies based on WIU library acquisitions; by organizing dinners—potluck or local restaurant—so CDC members from across campus can become better acquainted; by setting up a faculty collaborative learning support group; and by participating in or leading workshops and panels on campus as well as at state and national conferences. Several members have coordinated the publication of *Multicultural Connections* as a special section of the *Western Courier*, the WIU student newspaper. The supplement covers academic and student services activities that promote intercultural communication and cooperation. CDC members have met regularly to assess the work of the Cadre, to discuss relevant campus situations and issues, to share information, and to explore appropriate new initiatives. Cadre members have also met with nationally known multicultural educators (among them James Banks, Professor of Education at the University of Washington and author of many ground-breaking multicultural texts; Suzanne Pharr, civil rights activist and author of *Homophobia, A Weapon of Sexism*; Betty Schmitz, coordinator of curriculum transformation projects throughout the country; and Troy Duster, Director of the Institute for the Study of Social Change at the University of California-Berkeley) to discuss the multicultural challenges we face in our classrooms and offices.

Faculty Development and the Cadre have sponsored or co-sponsored (with Student Residential Programs, the Office of Multicultural and Special Services, the Women's Center, Casa Latina, and student groups including Hillel and the Bisexual, Gay, Lesbian and Friends Association) campus visits by a number of people versed in diversity issues. At times these speakers have made presentations to large general audiences on topics including "Ethnic Relations"; "Diversity in Higher Education: Can We Elevate the Dialogue and Address the Experience?"; and "Women and Politics: Past, Present, Future." At other times educators were brought in to interact more specifically with CDC members (though invitations have always been extended to the entire campus community) and to focus on particular multicultural communication or curricular questions. Thus, in all-day or half-day workshops, we have focused on such topics as "The Pedagogy of Prejudice and Discrimination: Teaching vs. Preaching"; "Curricular Reform in General Education"; "Teaching Diversity through Literature and Writing"; "Communicating Cross-Culturally"; and "Differences in Cultural Frames of Reference."

Several of these workshops have taken place during annual Cultural Diversity Cadre retreats. The retreats, in place for three years, and scheduled immediately following the spring semester, gave Cadre members, other interested WIU faculty and staff, and Illinois Staff and Curriculum Developers Association (ISCDA) members, an opportunity to study multicultural issues from a variety of perspectives. In addition to the topics mentioned above, retreat workshops included "Achieving Instructional Excellence While Enhancing Diversity"; "Discipline-specific Multicultural Course Development"; "Voluntary and Involuntary Immigration: Reverberations in Higher Education"; "Ethnic Identity: Developmental Stages"; and "Teaching the 'Other.'" The retreats offered all participants opportunities to increase their knowledge about multicultural education and to discuss questions about implementing multicultural goals within their office or classroom; they also gave CDC members a chance to propose strategies and activities for the next academic year.

466

Another focus of Faculty Development and the CDC has been multicultural instruction within specific departments. Initially members of the Cadre steering committee met with the chairs and program directors of various departments to determine how faculty were addressing multicultural issues in their course content and through their teaching methods. Among the departments visited were chemistry, physics, psychology, mathematics, and English and journalism, but very quickly programs in the latter two departments were emphasized because they serve such a large number of students taking basic curriculum courses and because a narrower, more concentrated effort seemed more feasible than the broader approach.

With the support of the College of Arts and Sciences dean, meetings with the chairs and representative faculty were held to discuss the faculty's multicultural awareness and commitment as well as specific initiatives the departments and individual faculty could take to strengthen both the multicultural content of their basic math and writing courses and the pedagogical strategies necessary to reach increasingly diverse classes. Subsequently, some CDC programs, including co-sponsored workshops on "Women in American Mathematics" and "Students at Risk in Mathematics," as well as the 1991 retreat workshops, were planned specifically with the mathematics and writing faculties in mind. In addition, beginning-of-the-semester multicultural workshops for graduate students assigned as tutors to the Writing Center, the math help centers, and the Office of Academic Services (OAS) were begun with OAS.

While most of the Faculty Development and CDC multicultural activities have been funded by and directed toward WIU, one of the first was conceived as a collaborative effort with several other Illinois colleges and universities. Planned as a FIPSE (Fund for the Improvement of Post-Secondary Education) project but not funded on that level, the proposal was rewritten and submitted to the Illinois Board of Higher Education (IBHE) for a Higher Education Cooperation Act (HECA) grant. The project's primary goal is clear from its title— Expanding Cultural Diversity in the Curriculum and in the Classroom—and includes: 1) the creation of greater "statewide recognition of the importance of diversity"; 2) the development of a handbook for college and university faculty and staff to help them implement multicultural curriculum and instructional initiatives; and 3) the preparation of a long-term, comprehensive plan for increasing the appreciation of diversity and improving the instruction of our diverse student populations (Planning & Status Determination Committee, 1991, p. 136). "Multicultural Education: A Rationale for Development and Implementation" lays out this plan and was completed and sent to the IBHE in 1991 (See Planning & Status, pp. 137-38). This book, the earlier volumes of *Multicultural Education* and *Multicultural Prism: Voices from the Field*, an annotated bibliography of print and audiovisual resources, a videotape complementing the first *Multicultural Prism* and focusing on Faculty Development's role in multicultural education, and a CD-ROM covering multicultural curriculum development and implementation are the realization of the second objective. The first has been advanced through the actions taken to meet the second and third goals as well as through the establishment of the Illinois Staff and Curriculum Developers Association.

Founded by faculty development and multicultural education advocates, the ISCDA is an organization that reaches beyond WIU and the HECA cooperating institutions to continue and expand the work begun through the HECA grant. With that in mind it approved an organizational structure, adopted a constitution, elected officers and an advisory board, and sponsored three state conferences and six Dealing with Difference Summer Institutes with

467

a threefold emphasis: curriculum, instruction, and campus climate. In addition to the workshops and keynote addresses by nationally respected leaders in multicultural education, the conferences and institutes facilitate networking among individuals and institutions committed to positive multicultural communication and interaction.

The institutes are actually a fusion of WIU's Cultural Diversity Cadre retreats and the ISCDA conferences and, co-sponsored by the Faculty Development Office, take place annually in late May at WIU. The level of commitment and interest among participants coupled with the caliber of the presenters and workshop facilitators—including James B. Boyer, Nancy "Rusty" Barceló, Carlos E. Cortés, Brenda M. Rodriguez, Derald Wing Sue, Beverly Daniel Tatum, Peggy McIntosh, Joyce E. King, Johnnella Butler, William Ayers, Christine E. Sleeter, and Sut Jhally—have sparked extraordinarily dynamic and penetrating analyses of multicultural issues during the institute and have led to greater integration of multicultural scholarship and insight into the participants' own teaching or into their inter-cultural communication and interaction.

Other aspects of the Expanding Cultural Diversity project and of the ISCDA are a Multi-cultural Resource Development and Advising Center, providing consultants as well as print, electronic, and audiovisual material on specific cultural diversity issues to pre-K-12 and college and university educators, and a web site (www.iscda.org), developed to foster ongoing exchanges of ideas and information among ISCDA members and others interested in multicultural education. Cooperating institutions for these initiatives have varied slightly since 1991 but now include Eastern Illinois University, Elmhurst College, Illinois State University, Illinois Valley Community College, and McHenry County College in addition to Western Illinois University.

As indicated above, Expanding Cultural Diversity began with a statewide, rather than a WIU focus. One CDC initiative that was started specifically with the WIU curriculum in mind but that grew to include campus and systemwide components was the Group Diversity course members developed (see above). Work on Group Diversity led to a proposal for Dealing with Diversity, a teleclass variation of the course taught by J. Q. Adams, a CDC member, produced through Governors State University, and distributed nationally by the Adult Satellite Service of PBS. Dealing with Diversity is a wonderful example of how the efforts of a few individuals can grow in unexpected, but rich and rewarding, ways. Effec-tively weaving graphics, interviews, documentary footage, and discussions into dynamic class presentations, the course has extended the work of the CDC as few members envisioned. It has taken on a life of its own, its success prompting a new production that retains the basic structure of the first while incorporating insightful new material and deepening participants' understanding of the many dimensions of cultural diversity.

Some of the committees initially active within the CDC have ceased to be or have evolved in interesting ways. The Student Study Group no longer exists, but the Focus on Harmony Committee now serves to link faculty, staff, and students in annual campus-wide Focus on Harmony events that emphasize, through simulations and hands-on activities, the **experience** as well as the **analysis** of some aspect of cultural diversity. The committee that developed the Group Diversity course has transformed and expanded itself into the faculty who teach the course. They meet periodically to discuss its challenges and to share their experiences with the course texts, the class activities, and student responses to both.

This review of WIU's Faculty Development multicultural activities affirms the university's—administration, faculty, staff, and students—commitment to diversity, but it can be misleading since condensing a decade's work into this compact form and stressing action, events, and accomplishments erases or screens from view the hundreds of hours of work involved as well as the false starts, the frustrations, and the failures. The positive emphasis has been intentional, since the purpose has been to describe a multifaceted model that has been judged successful on many levels and that readers can develop, broaden, or adapt to their own circumstances. But to present a realistic model, unsolved problems and ongoing challenges must be acknowledged. One of the most constant is the disinterest or the resistance of many university personnel to multicultural education. While participation in the CDC has been significant, the programs have reached hundreds, and evaluations have been very positive, neither Faculty Development nor the Cadre has convinced the majority of individuals within the campus community that understanding and responding to our changing student population necessitates rethinking and broadening our intercultural communication skills, our course content, our instructional strategies, and our programming priorities.

Obviously, to be committed to multicultural education at WIU, one need not identify oneself to Faculty Development or the Cadre since other diversity initiatives are sponsored through WIU's student services offices and student residential programs; faculty and other personnel also have access to multicultural education via their own professional organizations and their own reading. Still, interaction between Cadre members and nonCadre members on both individual and committee levels indicates discomfort, disinterest, resistance, and even hostility do exist. Anecdotal evidence from students and colleagues support this assessment—as does the invariable question by one or more participants when evaluating a specific multicultural program: "How can we get colleagues who need to hear this to attend?"

Though we do have a tendency in our society to use numbers—attendance figures, scores, grades—to judge success even when they may not be the most appropriate measure, having more members of the university community signal their greater awareness of and commitment to multicultural education remains a goal. Even a small group of individuals may be able to effect substantial change, but relying on a limited number of active workers to meet continual, many-faceted challenges that require specific expenditures of time and energy risks fatigue and stress—burnout—for those supporters. Also at risk are programs. Without people to carry through, to plan the action, investigate the options and repercussions, make the phone calls, set up the meetings, write the proposals, programs do not get started, or if started, they are not sustained. The CDC interaction with the mathematics and writing programs and with graduate assistants, for example, diminished because the persons who initiated the contacts turned their attention to other programs. Relying on too few people can mean stretching those individuals beyond their ability to respond.

The stamina and impact of a small group of enthusiastic, committed persons, however, should not be underestimated. Whether in a classroom, an office, an auditorium, or a residence hall, whether discussing an issue of diversity or actually interacting across cultures, individuals can advance the understanding and respect necessary for positive communication and action. Hence the necessity to keep alive the enthusiasm of those who recognize and want to strengthen the values of diversity within our society. The Cadre has helped generate and sustain enthusiasm by 1) enlisting the help of newly hired faculty and staff who, in many cases, have a strong background in multicultural education as well as a clear commitment to CDC goals and the energy, ideas, and keen interest that comes with a new professional position; and 2) bringing together individuals from across the university who share, and by sharing, reinforce, for each other their commitment to diversity. Crossing the lines that often separate administrators, faculty, students, and academic, civil, and student services personnel has been a valued aspect of this exchange since it has introduced participants to different perspectives and increased awareness of each unit's contributions to the mission and goals of the university. Rather than adapting the Bidpai woodpecker's attitude of exclusion and elitism or following the owl's game-playing strategy, WIU's Cultural Diversity Cadre has chosen inclusion and continuing grass-roots work as it helps move the campus community toward greater justice, equity, and diversity.

Endnote

[1] I want to thank Hallie Lemon for sharing this fable with me.

References

Banks, J. A., & Banks, C. M. (Eds.). (1989). *Multicultural education: Issues and perspectives.* Boston: Allyn & Bacon.

Faculty Senate. (1988, October 25). Agenda. Western Illinois University.

Felder, N. L. (1992). Implementing multicultural education within a multi-campus university. In J. Q. Adams & J. R. Welsch (Eds.), *Multicultural Education: Strategies for implementation in colleges and universities, Vol. 2* (pp. 93-98). Macomb, IL: Illinois Staff and Curriculum Developers Association.

Floyd, C. E., & Batsche, C. N. (1992). The leadership role of the academic vice-president. In J. Q. Adams & J. R. Welsch (Eds.), *Multicultural Education: Strategies for implementation in colleges and universities, Vol. 2* (pp. 99-109). Macomb, IL: Illinois Staff and Curriculum Developers Association.

Floyd, C. E., & Thurman, A. (1991). Leadership of the governing board and central administration: Providing the policy and budgetary framework for incorporating multicultural elements into college and university curricula. In J. Q. Adams, J. F. Niss, & C. Suarez (Eds.), *Multicultural education: Strategies for implementation in colleges and universities* (pp. 115- 120). Macomb, IL: Western Illinois University Foundation.

FY 2000 Priorities Statement (1998). Western Illinois University.

Hosic, J. F. (Ed.). (1912, February 19). Editorial: A new fable of Bidpai. In *The English Journal, 1*(2), 122-123.

Kayes, P. E. (1992). Access, equity, and cultural diversity: Rediscovering the community college mission. In J. Q. Adams & J. R. Welsch (Eds.), *Multicultural education: Strategies for implementation in colleges and universities, Vol. 2* (pp. 85-92). Macomb, IL: Illinois Staff and Curriculum Developers Association.

Planning and Status Determination Committee. (1991). Multicultural education: Rationale for development and implementation. In J. Q. Adams, J. F. Niss, & C. Suarez (Eds.), *Multicultural Education: Strategies for implementation in colleges and universities,* (pp. 135-137). Macomb, IL: Western Illinois University Foundation.

Planning Statement, 1991-1992 through 1995-1996. (1990, August). Western Illinois University.

Schultz, J. A. (1988). Stick to the facts: Educational politics, academic freedom, and the MLA. *Profession 88,* 65-69.

Wadsworth, E. C. (1991). Faculty development in support of multicultural education. In J. Q. Adams, J. F. Niss, & C. Suarez (Eds.), *Multicultural education: Strategies for implementation in colleges and universities* (pp. 109-114). Macomb, IL: Western Illinois University Foundation. [See this volume, pp. 457-462]

Wagoner, R. H. (1989, September 29). President's fall 1989 report to the university. Western Illinois University.

PERMISSIONS

CONTRIBUTORS

J. Q. Adams

J. Q. Adams is a Professor in the Department of Educational and Interdisciplinary Studies at Western Illinois University. He has worked extensively in the area of multicultural education as a consultant, presenter, and curriculum development specialist. He is currently developing a second *Dealing with Diversity* teleclass which incorporates many of the interviews he has conducted with scholars, politicians, writers, and students. His first *Dealing with Diversity* teleclass is distributed nationally by PBS.

Linda S. Aguilar

Linda S. Aguilar (M.S. in Education, Curriculum and Instruction; M.S., Counseling, Illinois State University; Nationally Certified Counselor), a faculty member in the Counseling Department at Joliet Junior College, teaches courses on career planning and student success. She has worked extensively with at-risk students in multicultural settings and has a wide variety of teaching experience in elementary and secondary schools as well as in community colleges.

Bem P. Allen

Bem P. Allen (Ph.D., Experimental Psychology, University of Houston) is a Professor of Psychology at Western Illinois University and has studied and researched prejudice, racism, and sexism throughout his 31-year career. He has a number of journal publications on these topics and has written about them in his published books. His strong interest in multicultural issues is reflected in his teaching, publications, and conference attendance.

Alexander W. Astin

Alexander W. Astin is Professor of Higher Education and Director of the Higher Education Research Institute at the University of California, Los Angeles. A highly respected researcher and scholar in several areas of higher education, among his publications are *Assessment for Excellence: The Philosophy and Practice of Assessment and Evaluation in Higher Education*; *What Matters in College: Four Critical Years Revisited*; and "What Matters in General Education: Provocative Findings from a National Study of Student Outcomes."

R. Jovita Baber

R. Jovita Baber is currently pursuing a doctorate in Latin American History at the University of Chicago. Prior to this she spent five years in education and educational reform as a bilingual social studies teacher in Chicago public schools, a history teacher in Oak Park and River Forest schools, and a bilingual literacy coordinator at the University of Chicago Center for School Improvement.

Silvia Balzano

Silvia Balzano (Ph.D. Educational Anthropology, University of California at Los Angeles) taught at the University of LaPlata in Argentina before coming to the U.S.A. She has published in both national and international journals, with several of her papers focusing on South American Indians.

James A. Banks

James A. Banks is Professor of Education and Director of the Center for Multicultural Education at the University of Washington. His numerous articles and books as well as presentations and workshops on multicultural education attest to his knowledge and leadership in this area. His books, many in multiple editions and used widely as textbooks, include *Multicultural Education: Theory and Practice*; *Teaching Strategies for Ethnic Studies*; *Educating Citizens in a Multicultural Society*; and the *Handbook of Research on Multicultural Education*.

Brett Beemyn

Brett Beemyn is an assistant professor in African American Studies and the director of a multicultural program at Western Illinois University. He is the co-editor with Mickey Eliason of *Queer Studies: A Lesbian, Gay, Bisexual, and Transgender Anthology* and the editor of *Creating a Place for Ourselves: Lesbian, Gay, and Bisexual Community Histories*. Currently he is writing a history of LGBT life in Washington, DC and finishing an anthology about male bisexuality.

Samuel Betances

Samuel Betances is Professor Emeritus of Sociology at Northeastern Illinois University where he taught undergraduate and graduate students for twenty years. He is a well-known and frequent lecturer on topics of diversity, social change, gender and race relations, demographic changes, and the impact of the global economy on group relations in the U.S.A. He is committed to building positive synergy through ethnic diversity and is noted for the ease and effectiveness with which he weaves humor into his discussions of critical diversity issues.

Nancy A. Birk

Nancy A. Birk (M.A., Counseling with an emphasis in Student Affairs, Southeast Missouri State University) teaches Creative and Critical Thinking, the required freshman seminar course at Southeast Missouri State University. As the Graduate Assistant for First-Year Experience Programs in the Office of New Student Programs, she co-ordinated the First-year Learning Team (FLighT) Program. Her research interests include first-year transition issues and academic advising for undecided students.

James B. Boyer

James B. Boyer, Professor Emeritus of Curriculum and American Ethnic Studies at Kansas State University is a founding member of the National Association of Multicultural Education and has been active in multicultural education for many years. He recently co-authored *Transforming the Curriculum for Multicultural Understandings: A Practitioner's Handbook* and continues to direct training institutes in educational equity and cultural understanding.

Robert Caruso

Robert Caruso (Ph.D., Counseling and Personnel Services, University of Maryland) currently serves as Vice Chancellor for Student Affairs at Western Carolina University. He has held a variety of administrative positions in student affairs and enrollment management over the past 25 years and has a continuing interest in student development and academic affairs issues.

Carlos E. Cortés

Carlos E. Cortés is Professor Emeritus of History at the University of California, Riverside. His research encompasses multicultural education, ethnicity issues, and media as a force in society. He has published in all of these areas as well as in history. Among his books are *Three Perspectives on Ethnicity: Blacks, Chicanos, and Native Americans* and *A Filmic Approach to the Study of Historical Dilemmas*. He is writing *Backing into the Future: A Brief History of Multicultural 21st-Century America*.

Linda Dittmar

Linda Dittmar (Ph.D., English, Stanford University) is Professor of English at the University of Massachusetts-Boston, where she teaches literature and film for the Women's Studies and American Studies Programs as well as the English Department. Her teaching, publications, and work on a range of curriculum planning and faculty development projects stress feminist, anti-racist, and multicultural perspectives. She is a member of the *Radical Teacher* editorial group.

Nada Elia

Nada Elia (Ph.D., Comparative Literature, Purdue University) is a Scholar-in-Residence in Afro-American Studies at Brown University. Her areas of interest and research are counter-hegemonic, especially postcolonial and feminist, narratives. She contributed to *Food for Our Grandmothers: Writings for Arab-American and Arab-Canadian Feminists* and has just completed *Trances, Dances, and Vociferations: Agency and Resistance in Africana Women's Narratives*.

James V. Fenelon

James V. Fenelon (Ph.D., Northwestern University) recently joined the faculty of the Sociology Department at California State University, San Bernadino. He teaches courses on race and ethnic relations and on discrimination. One result of his research on the cultural domination of Native Nations is his book, *Culturicide, Resistance and Survival of the Lakota "Sioux" Nation.* He is an enrolled member of the Standing Rock (Sioux) Nation and comes from Dakota and Lakota Native peoples.

Patricia L. Francis

Patricia L. Francis (Ph.D., Developmental Psychology, University of Oklahoma, 1980) is Executive Assistant to the President at the State University of New York College, Cortland. Her primary work in multicultural education has been curriculum and program development. She chaired SUNY Cortland's Center for Multicultural and Gender Studies and contributed significantly to the development of a course requirement on prejudice and discrimination. As a full-time Professor of Psychology, she regularly taught a course on gender and racial/ethnic stereotypes.

Donald Freeman

Donald Freeman is a Professor of Learning and Instructional Technology in the Division of Psychology in Education at Arizona State University. Over the course of his career, he has logged more than 20 years of experience in the design and conduct of research and program evaluation studies. He has published extensively in scholarly journals in the areas of program evaluation, professional development schools, and classroom instruction. He has served as an evaluation consultant in school program evaluation.

Ronald Gallimore

Ronald Gallimore (Ph.D., Northwestern University) is a Professor at the University of California, Los Angeles in the Department of Psychiatry and Biobehavioral Sciences and the Graduate School of Education. He has co-authored several books, including *Rousing Minds to Life: Teaching, Learning and Schooling in Social Context,* a summary of the Kamehameha Early Education Project experience and data, for which he and his co-author received the Grawemeyer Award in Education for "a work of outstanding educational achievement with potential for worldwide impact."

Geneva Gay

Geneva Gay is Professor of Education and Associate with the Center of Multicultural Education at the University of Washington-Seattle. Known internationally for her scholarship in multicultural education, she received the 1990 Distinguished Scholar Award of the American Educational Research Association and the 1994 Multicultural Educator Award from the National Association of Multicultural Education. Her writings include over 90 articles and chapters as well as *At the Essence of Learning: Multicultural Education.*

Claude Goldenberg

Claude Goldenberg (Ph.D., University of California, Los Angeles), a native of Argentina, is a research psychologist in the Department of Psychiatry and Biobehavioral Sciences, UCLA and Associate Director of the Urban Education Studies Center in the UCLA Graduate School of Education. He has received the American Educational Research Association's Outstanding Dissertation Award in the Empirical/Qualitative category.

Howard L. Hansen

Howard L. Hansen (Ph.D. Candidate, University of Nebraska-Lincoln) teaches mathematics to seventh-through-twelfth grade students at Southeastern High School in Augusta, Illinois. He has been actively involved with in-service and pre-service preparation of both elementary and secondary teachers of mathematics. He is especially interested in assuring equal access to the use of technology in the mathematics curriculum.

Stafford Hood

Stafford Hood, an Associate Professor of Counseling/Counseling Psychology at Arizona State University, has published in major journals and anthologies on program evaluation, educational assessment, teacher education, and bias in testing. He is co-editor of *Beyond the Dream: Meaningful Program Evaluation and Assessment to Achieve Equal Opportunity at Predominantly White Universities* and a consultant in program evaluation and bias in testing for universities, educational laboratories, foundations, school districts, and departments of education, state court systems, and professional licensing agencies.

Nick Ippolito

Nick Ippolito is a recent graduate of the College Student Personnel program at Western Illinois University where he was a co-instructor of a cultural diversity course. He is currently a residence hall director at the University of Illinois-Urbana/Champaign.

Duane M. Jackson

Duane M. Jackson chairs the Department of Psychology at Morehouse College. A graduate of the University of Illinois' Comparative Psychology and Behavior-Genetics program, his research and publications focus on various aspects of animal behavior, including relationships between learning and memory. He is a member of the Board of Governors for the National Conference on Undergraduate Research. As a teacher and scientist he is interested in incorporating multicultural perspectives into the teaching of science and into scientific research.

Edward Johnson

Edward Johnson (M.A., Human Relations and Community Affairs, American International College, Springfield, Massachusetts) is the chair of the Counseling Department at Joliet Junior College. He has facilitated workshops, consulted, and lectured extensively on issues of race, gender, socialization, and reintegrative programs and processes for parent-teacher organizations, as well as students and juvenile and adult offenders.

Shin Kim

Shin Kim is a doctoral candidate and adjunct professor in the School of Social Service Administration at the University of Chicago. Before beginning her Ph.D. Program she taught economics at Chicago State University. She has published articles in the *Journal of Developing Areas* and the *International Journal of Aging and Human Development* and has edited *The Emerging Generation of Korean Americans*. Her areas of specialization are immigration policies, economics, and social work implications.

Hallie S. Lemon

Hallie S. Lemon (M.S., English, University of Illinois, Urbana) teaches writing at Western Illinois University. She is currently writing articles and presenting workshops on the use of portfolios to teach writing and to assess teaching and learning. She has also begun researching the gender distinctions in electronic discourse communities.

Ming-Gon John Lian

Ming-Gon John Lian (Ph.D. in Special Education, Texas Tech University) taught in Taiwan and Texas before joining the faculty at Illinois State University in 1983. He has served as the president of the Illinois Division for Culturally and Linguistically Diverse Exceptional Children and chair of the Multicultural Committee of the National Association for Persons with Severe Handicaps. He received an outstanding faculty award from the Office of Multicultural Affairs in 1998 and the Strand Diversity Achievement Award in 1999.

Reinhard W. Lindner

Reinhard W. Lindner (Ph.D., Cognition/Instruction, University of Connecticut, Storrs) is a Professor in the Department of Educational and Interdisciplinary Studies at Western Illinois University. Dr. Lindner is a member of a number of professional research organizations, including the American Educational Research Association. His primary area of research involves the study of self-regulated learning. He publishes and presents at professional conferences regularly on this and related topics.

Joan Livingston-Webber

Joan Livingston-Webber (Ph.D., English Language, Indiana University) is an Associate Professor in the Department of English and Journalism at Western Illinois University where she teaches undergraduate and graduate courses in rhetoric, writing, and linguistics. She also directs the university Writing Center. Her interest in discourse and its analysis has led to research on the rhetoric of institutional documents and on copyright and postmodernism as well as on narrative and its culturally specific forms and functions.

Bansrajh Mattai

Bansrajh Mattai (Ph.D., Social Philosophy and Education, University of Southhampton, England) teaches sociology and cultural diversity in the Department of Social Sciences at Joliet Junior College. He has been teaching and lecturing on the subjects of multicultural education, cultural diversity, population, and sociolinguistics since 1974. His research interests are in sociological theory and the sociological bases of affective education.

Randall W. Maus

Randall W. Maus is a recent graduate of the College Student Personnel program at Western Illinois University where he was a co-instructor of a cultural diversity course. He is currently a residence life coordinator at West Virginia Wesleyan University.

Luise Prior McCarty

Luise Prior McCarty teaches in Educational Leadership and Policy Studies at Indiana University. Her areas of specialization are philosophy of education and epistemological issues in teacher education. Professor McCarty's research centers on 20th-century German and American philosophy; Dewey, Wittgenstein, Heidegger and Gadamer are special concerns. She has written and given invited lectures on the Wittgensteinian notion of "language games" in the U.S. and abroad and has coauthored several articles linking philosophy and pedagogy.

Peggy McIntosh

Peggy McIntosh, Associate Director of the Wellesley Center for Research on Women, founded and co-directs the National S.E.E.D. (Seeking Educational Equity and Diversity) Project for Inclusive Curriculum. She travels worldwide as a consultant on creating gender-fair and multicultural curricula. She has written many articles on curriculum change, women's studies, and systems of unearned privilege, including the ground-breaking essay, "White Privilege and Male Privilege: A Personal Account of Coming to See Correspondences Through Work in Women's Studies."

Timothy R. McMahon

Timothy R. McMahon is currently the Director of Special Projects within the Division of Student Services at Western Illinois University and teaches undergraduate courses in cultural diversity and leadership development. Previously he taught in the master's program in College Student Personnel at Western. He is a co-author of *Exploring Leadership: For College Students Who Want to Make a Difference.*

Vera Mitrovich

Vera Mitrovich (M.S. Ed., Adult Education, Northern Illinois University; M.A., Counseling, Governors State University; Nationally Certified Counselor) is a licensed clinical counselor. She has a private counseling practice in which she specializes in individual, marriage, couple, and family counseling and divorce mediation. She has counseled clients from diverse cultural backgrounds within a community college as well as within her private practice.

Jeanne B. Morris

Jeanne B. Morris (Ed.D., Early Childhood Education, University of Illinois, Urbana-Champaign) is Professor Emeritus in the Department of Curriculum and Instruction at Illinois State University where she coordinated the Early Childhood Education program. She is a consultant to a variety of local, regional, and national school districts, programs, and agencies working in early education.

Savario Mungo

Savario Mungo (Ph.D., Curriculum and Instruction, New York University, New York) is a Professor of Education in the Department of Curriculum and Instruction at Illinois State University, Normal. He has worked extensively in the field of cross-cultural communication and education as a presenter, consultant, and curriculum development specialist. His current research includes the development of multicultural strategies for use in classroom settings.

Karen A. Myers

Karen A. Myers (Ph.D., Higher Education Administration, Illinois State University) is Director of New Student Programs at Southeast Missouri State University. Currently she is a facilitator for a campus-wide diversity program, co-coordinator of First-year Learning Teams (FLighT), and teaches in the Higher Education Masters program. She has extensive experience in the areas of interpersonal communication, disability services, and first-year transition, and she has authored and co-authored articles on disability issues.

Judith K. Olson

Judith K. Olson is a Professor of Mathematics at Western Illinois University. She teaches mathematics and mathematics education courses for pre-service and in-service teachers while actively promoting the importance of mathematics for all, especially women and members of traditionally underrepresented groups. She directs "Connecting the Past with the Future: Women in Mathematics and Science," a National Science Foundation project that encourages the participation of women in mathematics and science.

Melfried Olson

Melfried Olson is a Professor of Mathematics and Director of Faculty Development at Western Illinois University. He works with pre-service and in-service elementary, middle, and secondary teachers of mathematics. He has been successful in securing funding for staff development school-based in-service projects at the national, state, local, and school levels. He works to address equity issues through curriculum development that includes appropriate materials and teaching strategies.

Carlos J. Ovando

Carlos J. Ovando is Professor of Education at Indiana University, where he teaches courses in multicultural education and curriculum and instruction. Throughout his career, he has explored factors contributing to the academic prosperity of minority students and ethnically diverse groups. He has written extensively on culture, language, and curriculum issues pertaining to language minority student populations and is senior co-author of *Bilingual and ESL Classrooms: Teaching in Multicultural Contexts*, a leading textbook for training bilingual and ESL teachers.

Leslie Reese

Leslie Reese received her doctorate in Comparative Education from the University of California at Los Angeles and was recognized by the National Association of Bilingual Education with an Outstanding Dissertation Award. She served as the Project Director of a UCLA longitudinal research study on the connection between home and school for immigrant Latino students in the Los Angeles area.

Jacqueline C. Rickman

Jacqueline C. Rickman is an Associate Professor in the Department of Educational and Interdisciplinary Studies at Western Illinois University. She teaches courses in human development, emphasizing the integration of technology, multicultural perspectives, and the concepts of collaboration and multiple intelligences into teacher preparation. Her current research involves the relationships in higher education among curriculum and program development, counseling and advisement, and retention, ableism, prodigiousness, and equity.

Catherine A. Riordan

Catherine A. Riordan is Professor of Psychology and Director of Management Systems at the University of Missouri-Rolla, Missouri's technological university. Her current research is in the area of human-computer interaction; she is especially interested in how information technologies are most effectively used by people working and learning in groups. She has a continuing interest in traditionally underrepresented ethnic and gender groups in technical fields and has conducted research and training on diversity issues in technological education and careers.

Brenda M. Rodriguez

Brenda M. Rodriguez is the Director of the Center for School and Community Development at the North Central Regional Educational Laboratory. She has developed and conducted leadership training on a broad range of diversity and equity issues, including intercultural conflict resolution, the recognition and reduction of personal and institutional prejudice, cross-cultural counseling, the creation of inclusive communities, and multicultural curriculum transformation.

Gaetano B. Senese

Guy Senese is Associate Professor of Foundations and Educational Leadership in the Center for Excellence in Education at Northern Arizona University. He has taught on the Navajo reservation at the Rough Rock Demonstration School and, in Junea, Alaska, worked with Tlingit-Haida Native American students. His writing focuses on Native American educational policy and policy history, and on culture and education, ethnicity, and social class identity. He is currently working on the history and development of Little Singer Navajo community school in Birdsprings, Arizona.

Jack G. Shaheen

Jack G. Shaheen, Professor Emeritus of Mass Communications at Southern Illinois University, Edwardsville, has written and spoken often on portraits of Arabs and Muslims in U.S. popular culture. He is the author of two books, *Nuclear War Films* and *The TV Arabs*, as well as numerous monographs and essays. A consultant on Arab issues with CBS News and a Department of State Scholar Diplomat, his work reflects his conviction that stereotypes of any group narrow vision and blur reality.

Pearlie Strother-Adams

Pearlie Strother-Adams is an Assistant Professor in the Department of English and Journalism at Western Illinois University where she teaches courses in journalism, mass communications, and news reporting and writing. In recent years, she has focused her research on media depictions of traditionally marginalized groups in the United States, with a special emphasis on the representation of African American males in popular culture.

Derald Wing Sue

Derald Wing Sue is the founder and president of Cultural Diversity Training and Professor of Counseling at California State University, Hayward. He is the author of numerous journal articles and books on the psychology of personality and on counseling across cultures, most notably, *Counseling the Culturally Different: Theory and Practice* and *Counseling American Minorities: A Cross-Cultural Perspective*.

Martha E. Thompson

Martha E. Thompson, is a Professor of Sociology and Women's Studies at Northeastern Illinois University in Chicago. Her commitment to curriculum development and pedagogical strategies for women's studies courses is longstanding. In her publications she has focused on ways to structure a classroom to build a community among students who vary in age, ethnicity, gender, literacy skills, physical ability, sexual orientation, and social class. *Women and Social Action*, the teleclass she developed, provides an example of her approach.

Emily C. Wadsworth

Emily C. Wadsworth (Ph.D., Administration and Policy Studies, Northwestern University) is Executive Dean for Communications, Humanities, Adult Education, Math and Science at McHenry County College, Crystal Lake, Illinois. Her primary work has been in women's studies, international/intercultural studies, and faculty development. Prior to her MCC appointment, she taught women's studies courses and coordinated faculty development programs at Northeastern University in Chicago. She continues to lead faculty workshops on multicultural curriculum transformation.

Janice R. Welsch

Janice R. Welsch is a Professor in the Department of English and Journalism and a Faculty Development Associate at Western Illinois University. She teaches courses in film history and criticism, women's studies, and cultural diversity and has coordinated many multicultural initiatives for the Society for Cinema Studies as well as for Western. She has been interested in integrating multicultural scholarship and perspectives into her own film and women's studies courses and in sparking a similar interest in curriculum transformation among colleagues.

Claire G. Williams

Claire G. Williams is a recent graduate of the College Student Personnel program at Western Illinois University where she was a co-instructor of a cultural diversity course. She is currently a residence hall director at the University of Maryland-College Park.

Mario Yepes-Baraya

Mario Yepes-Baraya (Ph.D., Research and Evaluation in Instructional Communications, State University of New York, Buffalo) is Research Scientist at Educational Testing Service in Princeton, New Jersey. His fields of specialization include multicultural/international education and science education, assessment and evaluation. He has taught multicultural education courses and has written a number of successful grants for multicultural education initiatives.

ADDITIONAL INITIATIVES OF THE
EXPANDING CULTURAL DIVERSITY PROJECT

Dealing with Difference Summer Institute

The annual Dealing with Difference Summer Institute (DWDSI) brings together state and national leaders in mulicultural education for presentations, workshops and discussions on cultural diversity issues, particularly those related to curriculum transformation, instruction, and communication and interaction across cultures. Participants include K-12 and two- and four-year college and university faculty, administrators and professional support staff. Dates of future DWDSIs are May 21-24, 2000; May 20-23, 2001; and May 19-22, 2002.

Multicultural Prism: Diversity in the Curriculum

Multicultural Prism: Diversity in the Curriculum is a CD-ROM that offers articles, graphs, video clips, syllabi and a database of multicultural resources to help educators prepare for and teach various issues related to race/ethnicity, gender, class, sexual orientation, ability and age. The CD includes information on immigration patterns, population trends, socio-economic status, curriculum transformation, instructional frameworks, teaching for equity and justice, and classroom assessment.

The Illinois Staff and Curriculum Developers Association

The Illinois Staff and Curriculum Developers Association (ISCDA) encourages research and an exchange of ideas on the professional development of college and university faculty and staff, curriculum change, and teaching effectiveness. It provides a forum to discuss issues of immediate and critical concern to educators committed to meeting the needs of students in the 21st century. The annual members' meeting is scheduled during the DWDSI each year.

Multicultural Resource Development and Advising Center

The Multicultural Resource Development and Advising Center can provide consultants as well as print, electronic, and audio-visual materials on specific diversity issues to faculty, staff, and administrators in universities, two-and four-year colleges, and K-12 schools. Resource Center materials can help educators find ways to integrate multicultural perspectives into the curriculum, develop pedagogy sensitive to the learning strengths of culturally diverse students, and strengthen the support structure within their institutions to insure the success of all students.

For further information about the Expanding Cultural Diversity Project check the ISCDA website (www.iscda.com) or contact J. Q. Adams (J._Q._Adams @ccmail.wiu.edu/ 309-298-1183) or Janice R. Welsch (Jan_Welsch@ccmail.wiu.edu/ 309-298-1103).